FINAL REPORT

OF THE

CANADIAN PANEL

ON VIOLENCE

AGAINST WOMEN

© Minister of Supply and Services Canada–1993

Catalogue No. SW45-1/1993E

ISBN # 0-660-15144-8

Also available in French
Printed in Canada

TO THE MINISTER RESPONSIBLE FOR THE STATUS OF WOMEN

MINISTER

In accordance with the mandate given to the Canadian Panel on Violence
Against Women, we are pleased to submit the attached Final Report.

Respectfully submitted,

Pat Freeman Marshall
Co-chair

Marthe Asselin Vaillancourt
Co-chair

CANADIAN PANEL ON VIOLENCE AGAINST WOMEN

PANEL MEMBERS

Co-Chair
Pat Freeman Marshall

Co-Chair
Marthe Asselin Vaillancourt

Judy Hughes
Mobina Jaffer
Diane Lemieux
Eva McKay

Dr. Peter Jaffe
Ginette Larouche
Donna Lovelace

ABORIGINAL CIRCLE MEMBERS

Claudette Dumont-Smith
Winnifred Giesbrecht

Martha Flaherty
Jeanne McDonald

ADVISORY COMMITTEE MEMBERS

Sally Ballingall
Judge Douglas Campbell
Jurgen Dankwort
Edna Elias
Dr. Patricia Horsham
Jennifer Mercer
Dorothy Reso Hickman
Constable Jane Spaans
Esmeralda Thornhill

Hélène Cadrin
Colleen Croft-Cannuli
Dr. Michael Dixon
Ron Ghitter
Pearl McKenzie
Soeur Cécile Renault
Dr. Philip Smith
Christine Spénard-Godbout
Germaine Vaillancourt

SECRETARIAT STAFF

Executive Director
Abby Hoffman
(June 1992 - July 1993)

Linda Blackwell
(August 1991 - March 1992)

Senior Advisor — Administration
Eloise Ryckman

Senior Adviser — Communications
Nicole Bourget

Senior Advisor — Liaison
Hélène Dwyer-Renaud

Senior Advisor — Research
Bonnie Diamond

Azaletch Asfaw
Jacqueline Barney
Michelle Bougie
Kirsten Cowen
Louise Delisle
Sandra Fox
Edith Garneau
Louise Gingras-Papineau
Nupur Gogia
Murielle Goneau
Mara Indri
Marcelle Lapointe
Lise Leach
Nicole Loreto
Guy Marcoux
Mary McBride
Marika Morris
Lise Nadeau
Karen O'Reilly
Line Poirier
Martine Rochon
Patricia Saulis
Margaret Shisko
Michelle Simms
Jennifer Tiller
Paula Walters

Linda Babulic
Roger Bélanger
Dave Cooper
Robert D'Aoust
Nathalie Ethier
Fay Frankland
Debbie Gibson
Carol Ann Godo
Denise Gomes
Jackie Holt
Lorraine Lapierre
Danielle Larose
Briar Long
Suzanne Madère
Elaine McArdle
Laura McFarlane
Gail Myles
Tracey O'Hearn
Josée Parisien
Tanya Rhodes
Marie Saikaley
Keith Sero
Laura Simmermon
Jo-Anne Stovel
Mary Trafford
Jeanne d'Arc Woods

FINAL REPORT CONTRIBUTORS

Contributing Writers and Researchers

Shelly Bressette

Ellen Hamilton

Joan Jenkinson

Chantal Cholette

Sandra Harder

Barbara Ladouceur

Editor (English)

Penny Williams

PMF Editoral Services

Copy Editor (French)

Joëlle Rouette

Translation Services

Jean-Michel Gazet

Tradinter (English to French)

John March

(French to English)

Design and Layout

Hangar 13 Art & Design Inc.

Acknowledgement:

In addition to the individuals listed above, the Panel would like
to thank the many people and organizations whose contributions
of time, energy and enthusiasm in various voluntary and professional
capacities were vital to the work of the Panel. In particular, a special
debt of gratitude is owed to the consultation agents, communication
agents, local organizers and interpreters who provided invaluable
support during the Panel's cross-Canada consultation process.

TABLE OF CONTENTS

PART THREE

EXPERIENCING VIOLENCE ~ POPULATIONS

PART FOUR

EXPERIENCING VIOLENCE ~ INSTITUTIONS

PART FIVE

THE NATIONAL ACTION PLAN

APPENDICES

CO-CHAIRS' MESSAGE

The Canadian Panel on Violence Against Women has just completed a unique and sometimes haunting journey. It was arduous, not because of its physical dimensions, but because of it psychological and political implications. Our report documents, more comprehensively than ever before, the unacceptable reality which many women in Canada have endured for decades but whose existence most Canadians have chosen to deny.

Canada's image abroad is that of a country with a high standard of living — a country dedicated to promoting peace in the world; a country where women have access to post-secondary education, and freedom of expression; a country where women are free to pursue the occupation they choose and to move about without constraint.

But the Panel learned that Canadian women are all too familiar with inequality and violence which tether them to lives few in the world would choose to lead. Canadian women have not enjoyed freedom of expression; rather, their fear makes them reluctant to speak out about the violence they experience. Canadian institutions have contributed to this situation — by denying that such violence can exist, they have supported misogyny and abuse of power.

Women came to the Panel with great generosity of spirit, hoping that by telling their truths and their stories, the lives of other women may be freed from violence. The breadth and depth of suffering described by them and now etched in our minds and in this report is our most profound impression of the Canadian landscape. By resolving to take action to eliminate violence against women, we can honour those women and change the landscape for future generations.

Many times the Panel members wished others in Canada could have been present to hear the truth, to see and understand the reality of the violence, and to confront the tolerance of violence. Our report will bring some of these experiences to you.

The Canadian experience was revealed to the Panel through face-to-face testimonies with thousands of individuals in 139 communities, in the 800 submissions we received and in our research. In tour after tour, at hearing upon hearing, in each of the provinces and the territories, women's voices told us of the horrors they endured. Through descriptions of the violence they survived, including the inadequate, ineffective and inappropriate responses to that violence they so often received, the link between inequality and vulnerability to violence was inextricably forged. It is abundantly and indisputably clear that women will not be free from violence until there is equality, and equality cannot be achieved until the violence and the threat of violence is eliminated from women's lives. This link is the foundation of our report. We know that the acknowledgement of this relationship has made our work and the task of implementing the report all the more challenging.

The tolerance of violence, in both principle and practice, has cost Canadian women dearly. One of the most tragic conclusions from our journey is the recognition that much of the violence women have endured was preventable. Solutions must be based on the fact that there is a high level of tolerance of violence, and therefore, that a policy of zero tolerance must be adopted by all levels of government – as well as within each and every organization in society.

We believe that a society that adopts zero tolerance of violence is a society that supports the basic human rights of each individual. It is a society which recognizes the importance of the United Nations *Universal Declaration of Human Rights* and the *Canadian Charter of Rights and Freedoms*, and the commitments they make to the right to security of the person, full entitlement to the protection and benefit of the law and, of course, the right to life.

While the Panel was doing its work, we were very aware there was a great deal happening in the world around us. But while commissions and inquests were helping to identify the problems and solutions, and while new laws were being created, women continued to suffer from violence. The tentative responses of the international community to the systematic rapes of women in Bosnia-Hercegovina were constant reminders to us that tolerance of violence against women knows no geographic boudaries.

Along with very different types of expertise and experience, the Panel and Aboriginal Circle members brought to their work a common vision of a better, safer society for all women and for everyone. Each member's commitment to that vision helped us through many difficult days. The activities of the Panel and the Aboriginal Circle were sustained and enhanced by the dedication of the secretariat staff members who worked tirelessly to ensure completion of the work. We have all worked in a way that we hope is faithful to the experiences of the women from whom we heard.

We wish to send a message of hope to all Canadians. We want our country to take the necessary steps from denial to acknowledgement, from tolerance to commitment, from inequality to the sharing of power, from institutionalized violence to zero tolerance of violence.

No hesitation can be tolerated. Women have spoken; women have written; women have acted. What will be the response? Our ultimate goal is the year 2000.

Now it is your turn. We urge you to lend your strengths, your hearts, your talents and your energy to changing the landscape which has kept the violence in place for so long. We have a rare opportunity to work together to implement real change, to create a society where there will be safety and equality for women. We can and we must do it now for ourselves, for our sisters and for our daughters.

Pat Freeman Marshall   Marthe Asselin Vaillancourt
Co-chair   Co-chair

PART ONE

THE CONTEXT

CHAPTER 1

THE FEMINIST LENS

INTRODUCTION

Every day in this country women are maligned, humiliated, shunned, screamed at, pushed, kicked, punched, assaulted, beaten, raped, physically disfigured, tortured, threatened with weapons and murdered. Some women are indeed more vulnerable than others, but all women, simply by virtue of their gender, are potential victims of violence. Moreover, the violence is often directed at them by those whom they have been encouraged to trust, those whom they are taught to respect, those whom they love. Violence against women cuts across all racial, social, cultural, economic, political and religious spectrums. While there is no question that violence may be conditioned by these factors, the fact remains that all women are at risk.

The voices of women throughout this report are a sample of what we heard during our consultations across the country*. Their words — unadorned, unedited — tell the story more effectively than volumes of explanation, exhortation and interpretation. The message is direct and urgent, carried by quotes throughout this text — voices of women of all ages, faiths, colour and class who have been there, are still there.

We know that Canadians have a sense that violence against women exists and that many women live with violence on a daily basis. However, we also know that Canadians do not have a real perception of the enduring repercussions of violence and how the experience and fear of violence affect the daily existence of women. There is no better way for people to appreciate these conditions than through the words of the women who have survived them.

This chapter begins by defining violence and its various dimensions, both subjects of a great deal of debate. This report emphasizes that violence must be understood as a continuum that ranges from verbal insults through physical blows to murder. The voices we heard, the submissions we received and extensive research demonstrate the many dimensions of violence against women — physical, sexual, psychological, financial and spiritual. For many women, all these are part of their experience of violence.

This chapter also looks at the severe human costs of violence against women, the driving force for us as Panel members. Yet, we also know that there are monetary costs, practically impossible to calculate accurately, but nevertheless an issue for all Canadians.

Each individual experience of violence must be seen in a larger social context. An effective analysis of violence against women requires a framework, or a way of thinking about the issue which emphasizes that acts of violence are socially structured. Our approach rests on the premise that although individual men make individual choices to be, or not be, violent toward women, explanations that focus solely on individual characteristics and traits cannot account for the scope, proportion and dimensions of violence against women today and throughout history.

We call this focus a feminist lens through which violence against women is seen as the consequence of social, economic and political inequality built into the structure of society and reinforced through assumptions expressed in the language and ideologies of sexism, racism and class. We see this framework as an essential first step in working toward the goals of our National Action Plan.

* *Throughout this report, the voices of women who spoke to the Panel are highlighted in italicized purple print. Where the voices of several women appear together, the testimonies of particular women are separated by the symbol for women.*

* *As explained in chapter 15, there are an estimated one million people in Canada reporting Aboriginal origins – that is, individuals who identify themselves as having some North American Indian, Métis or Inuit ancestry. In this report, the word Aboriginal is used to include all three groups, but where we wish to refer specifically to particular populations - as in chapters 14 and 15, and in the National Action Plan, Aboriginal is used to refer to North American Indian (Status, Non-Status) and Métis peoples; Inuit people are identified separately.*

While an examination and critique of gender inequality are often seen as the hallmarks of feminist thinking, a feminist approach also emphasizes the importance of recognizing women, not only as women, but as women of a particular class and race. These realities condition the lives of women in important and complex ways. A feminist analysis, if it is to be truly successful, must take the variations and the similarities among women into account. Our framework rests on the belief that violence is linked not only to the sexist nature of society, but also to the racism and class inequality upon which our society is based.

These social inequalities foster an atmosphere that tends to legitimize additional bases for social inequality, such as those linked to ability, age and sexual orientation. Any analysis of violence against women must include recognition of the complex ways in which inequality and power imbalances structure the lives of Canadian women. Only such an understanding can lead to ways of ending violence against women.

The feminist lens provides this report with a particular focus on the social contexts in which Canadian women live — "taken for granted" places, settings and activities, families, schools, workplaces, political organizations and parties, religious institutions, community organizations, sports teams and expressions of popular culture including television, advertisements and magazines. Later chapters provide a more detailed examination of the impact of inequality in key social institutions.

Women live in a social milieu textured by inequality, a reality that leaves them vulnerable to violence. As long as women have unequal access to choice and freedom, as long as women live with the fear of violence, their options will be restricted, their movements curtailed and their lives vitally affected.

Discussing violence against women is a balancing act. While we want to portray a sense of the truly horrific nature of violence against women and its implications, we do not want to portray women as the passive victims of violence or of male power. It has been women who have brought the issue of violence to the attention of the public,

and it is women who have developed the essential analysis of violence against women. It is also almost exclusively women who work in transition houses, sexual assault centres, women's health clinics and crisis centres. These women are in the forefront of dealing with violence against women. Women in all capacities have assisted, informed, advocated for and protected other women throughout history. Women have been tireless in their work on legal reform and in their fight for increased funding and expansion of social and support services. Women are indeed the survivors of violence, not the passive victims. We hope this report moves Canadians to comprehend both the stark reality of violence against women and women's extraordinary efforts to change the nature of Canadian society.

VIOLENCE AGAINST WOMEN

Myths and misinformation surround violence against women. One of the most pervasive is the myth that places responsibility for violence on the victim rather than on the perpetrator: women provoke, tease and taunt men, invite their sexual advances and then push them away. Women annoy, disobey and confront, thus leading or contributing to the violence they encounter. They were wearing the wrong clothing, drank too much alcohol, walked alone at night, etc.

We flatly reject any analyses that place any degree of responsibility for violence on the women themselves no matter what their actions, appearance, demeanour or behaviour. Such assumptions detract from useful work and from the formulation of solutions. When Canadians realize the staggering levels of violence against women across this country, they too will reject individualized or specious explanations.

[My husband] isn't making the support payments. On a few rare occasions, he takes [our son] for a visit. He tells [him] — he's only 4 years old — that if I don't go back with him, he'll never come and pick him up again. [Our son] cries, and I can't stand this situation. I'm trying to continue on with the father because of my child, but it's humanly impossible.

His fingers were digging into my arm, so I put my hand under his chin and pushed up hard. When I tried to get out of the car, he really blew up. "No fucking girl treats me like that!" Some nights I'd lie awake with crazy thoughts going around in my head: Maybe he has herpes or AIDS, and this was the only way he could get sex. Maybe I'm dying and I just don't know it.

♀ ♀ ♀

... he strangles me and takes me into the garage and tells me, "Now you're going to die." He has one hand on my throat and pulls back the other one to slap me in the face; with his fist in the air, he looks me straight in the eye and says, "You want to die?"

♀ ♀ ♀

The nightmare started right after the birth, which was very hard. He left me completely on my own and wouldn't let my mother help me. The fridge was completely empty most of the time, and he wouldn't let me ask my parents for help. My weight dropped to 83 pounds. When I asked my parents to give me some essential things for the baby, he kicked me in the coccyx, which had been injured by the particularly hard delivery. He took malicious pleasure in making a mess, in the bathroom, for example, where he spilt water all over the floor and told me I could wipe it up whenever I wanted. He ripped out the telephone line to cut me off from all assistance and potential help.

♀ ♀ ♀

My husband struck me on our honeymoon. He killed our first child by kicking the four-month child out of my uterus. My doctor asked me what did I do to make him so mad, our Anglican minister reminded me that I had married for better or worse, the lawyer wanted to know where I would get money to pay the fees, and my mother told my husband where I was hiding.

I called the police after my husband hit me. The officer arrived and said to me, "Would you mind shutting up and sitting down." He spoke to my husband even though I called him to help me.

♀ ♀ ♀

During the 27 years that I was married, I was continually abused both physically and emotionally. Twenty-two assault charges were laid against my husband, a few were dropped, but in most cases he was convicted. He never went to jail — he was merely sentenced to varying terms of probation. I left him many times and returned many times. I had no job and did not relish a welfare existence. To date, four years after I left him, there is still court action pending. My husband will probably win. He always has. Emotionally I am gaining strength although I am still afraid. Financially, I have nowhere to go but down. The money from the farm will not last long. I am too tired to fight anymore. Maybe some day I can go to sleep and never wake up.

DEFINING VIOLENCE

A shared definition of exactly what constitutes violence is crucial to the understanding of the sources and consequences of that violence. Although there has been a certain amount of debate on the subject, a proposed United Nations Declaration defines violence against women as

> ... any act of gender-based violence that results in, or is likely to result in, physical, sexual or psychological harm or suffering to women, including threats of such acts, coercion or arbitrary deprivation of liberty whether occurring in public or private life. [1]

The Declaration describes the persistence of violence against women as

> ... a manifestation of historically unequal power relations between men and women, which have led to domination over and discrimination against women by men and which have prevented women's full advancement. Violence against women is one of the crucial social mechanisms by which women are forced into a subordinate position compared to men. [2]

That violence against women is socially structured is the main tenet of this report. It is our belief that all social institutions, from the family through to the legal-judicial system, are characterized by unequal power relations between men and women. "Violence surpasses all other forms of abuse suffered by women. It occurs in private (families) and in public (pornography) and is the expression of the extreme limit of male dominance." [3] In the family, these power imbalances may express themselves in various ways, from an unequal division of household work or child care, to violent verbal, psychological, physical or sexual attacks. In the legal-judicial system, gender inequality is written into laws and manifests itself in charging policies and sentencing practices that fail to hold men accountable for their violent actions toward women.

While we recognize the extent to which violence against women is the outcome of inequality we also believe that individual acts of violence against women are individually willed.

> A man who exhibits violence verbally, psychologically, physically, sexually or financially toward his partner is not losing self-control; on the contrary, he is affirming his power, which he wants to preserve at all costs and which makes him neither monstrous nor sick. If he abuses his wife, it is because he has the privilege and the means to do so. [4]

Men who are violent bear sole responsibility for their violent actions by systematically using power and control to override the will of their victims, they make conscious choices including their choice of victim, the places and circumstances of their violence and the degree of force they use. Abusive behaviour cannot be explained away by loss of control or unfavourable circumstances. Problems within relationships, stress, alcohol, anxiety, depression and unemployment may contribute to violence against women, but they are neither acceptable excuses nor root causes. Other people under the same circumstances choose not to harm women. Removing these conditions alone will not end male violence against women.

In a society whose very structure condones male violence, all men, whether or not they are violent, derive substantial benefit from its institutionalization. The advantage may be as meagre as receiving preferential treatment in a group discussion, or as grand as avoiding competition with women for a job. The threat of violence also keeps women in unwanted relationships with men, defines the social situations and locations that women frequent, restricts women's activities in the workplace and undermines their potential for self-expression and self-confidence. All women pay the price of male violence: while not every woman has directly experienced violence, there are few who do not fear it and whose lives are not in some way affected and restricted by its pervasive presence in our society. [5]

NAMING VIOLENCE AGAINST WOMEN

All forms of male violence against women we refer to as woman abuse. The term "family violence" was widely used in both research literature and service delivery in the 1970s and 1980s to describe what actually constitutes abuse of women — not family. Although the home may be the most dangerous place for girls and women, the term is misleading and inaccurate.

> *The term "family violence" is a euphemism for violence against women and children, and it works to protect men .... Men's abuse is a social problem — they don't change because they don't have to.*

Like many of the people from whom we heard, we choose to name the violence accurately. Using the term family violence to describe what is overwhelmingly violence against women obscures the facts. Further, we feel that the term "family violence" masks the huge spectrum of violence that women encounter outside their intimate relationships or families. We focus on the damage violence does to women and not its effects on the family institution.

IDENTIFYING DIMENSIONS OF VIOLENCE

For the purposes of analysis, we have divided violence against women into five dimensions, all discussed in detail later in this report: physical, sexual, psychological, financial and spiritual. In an intimate relationship, these dimensions may be experienced as a progression. In other cases, the experience may be of a single dimension of violence, or a combination of several. For these reasons, when enumerating the different dimensions, we have chosen to illustrate both the random and the escalating nature of violence.

Physical violence, the most obvious, can range from pushing and shoving, to hitting, beating, torture and murder. Sexual violence — i.e., any form of non-consensual sexual activity ranging from unwanted sexual touching to rape — must be clearly distinguished from intimate sexual contact which is mutual and consensual in nature. Because sexual violence often takes place within socially sanctioned relationships — marriage, dating, live-in partnerships as well as familial, parental and work relationships — its identification and disclosure are more difficult.

Psychological violence encompasses various tactics to undermine a woman's self-confidence, such as taunts, jeers, insults, abusive language, threats of physical violence or isolation. The deliberate withholding of various forms of emotional support may also be used. In relationships where children are present, men may also taunt women regarding their suitability as mothers or feed lies to the children to undermine their love and attachment to their mothers. The Panel heard many instances of men spreading lies about their partners at their places of work, in the community and in social groups or denying them the

use of the car and telephone and monitoring their mail. Some men use various emotional and psychological tactics to ensure that a woman cuts ties with her nuclear and extended families. Such actions erode and eventually destroy a woman's social relationships, leaving her isolated and vulnerable.

Women are also the victims of financial violence. Male partners and/or family members may deny women access to employment opportunities outside the home or to other avenues for gaining some financial independence, such as part-time work or taking care of children in their own homes. Men may withhold or maintain control over all or substantial amounts of money. Women are sometimes cheated out of their inheritance, employment or other income. This may involve denying women access to financial records and knowledge about investments, income or debt. Senior women are often the victims of financial abuse.

Spiritual abuse erodes or destroys an individual's cultural or religious beliefs through ridicule or punishment. Perhaps one of the most heinous examples of such abuse was the establishment of the residential school system which resulted in the uprooting of Aboriginal children to be "educated" in the white educational system. Such education was founded upon the destruction of Aboriginal languages, traditions and beliefs in favour of the dominant culture. Residential schools provide a striking example of the interrelationships between racism, sexism and violence. Another example of spiritual violence is the exclusion of women from key positions in some religious institutions.

Categorizing dimensions of violence is helpful for discussion purposes and to underscore the breadth and depth of brutality women have endured and continue to endure. It is not so cut-and-dried in real life. The reality is that in many instances the violence women suffer entails a combination of all these dimensions. A woman who has been battered by her partner may have been raped by him, verbally maligned, psychologically scarred and financially deprived as well.

PREVALENCE OF VIOLENCE AGAINST WOMEN IN CANADA

Almost daily, newspapers, and radio and television broadcasts carry chilling reports of women harassed, women terrorized, women raped, women shot, women bludgeoned, women killed — almost always by men. So prevalent are these events that they have been described by one parliamentary committee as a "war against women." [6] And the accounts that reach the media are only a fraction of the events that never get reported, that remain invisible.

Despite a wealth of research in the area, we have only educated estimates of the prevalence of violence against women in Canada today. No matter what methodology is used, the figures are consistently alarming and, most researchers point out, underestimate the incidence of violence.

This is not likely to change because, for many women, there are good reasons not to disclose their experiences of violence. Fear of reprisal is the principal one: they keep silent often knowing from past experience that they will pay a painful price if they speak out. Another reason for silence is shame. Many women feel degraded by the abuse and cannot bear to talk about the violence they survive with family, friends or even strangers.

Some women have come to believe that they are somehow responsible for the violence. Their self-esteem has been so eroded that they consider themselves failures for not achieving the "domestic bliss" for which women are held responsible. The risk of being judged by those around them is often intolerable. Other women fear having to leave the relationship if they disclose its violent nature. Some are still hoping for change in the man they love; others know they cannot manage to support themselves and their children if they do leave.

Another major reason some women will not tell is that they know they will not be believed. Too often this has been reinforced by denial among friends and family members who have seen the signs of abuse and have done nothing to help. And tragically, some women cannot tell because they cannot remember. To survive they have blocked out memories too painful to recall. The best and most scientific methods of data collection cannot overcome these enforced silences.

Current research is also limited by its exclusion of many Canadian women. In particular, very little has specifically focused on the experiences of Inuit and Aboriginal women, women of colour, immigrant and refugee women, rural, poor or homeless women, women with disabilities, women with low literacy skills and lesbians. Also, much research is carried out in French and/or English, thereby excluding women who do not understand or speak these languages.

WOMEN'S SAFETY PROJECT

In the absence of nationally tabulated statistics on the full scope of violence against women, the Panel partially funded a community-based study in Toronto, the Women's Safety Project.[7] This work, already in progress when the Panel was appointed, was designed to overcome many of the usual limitations of studies on violence against women: subjects were randomly selected, the study took place in a centre with a diverse population and the large sample of 420 women meant more accurate statistics. In-depth interviews were conducted on a one-to-one basis by trained interviewers, and safety plans for the women interviewed were put in place. In addition, the project authors, Melanie Randall and Lori Haskell, brought with them an extensive knowledge of the topic. A detailed summary of the findings of the Women's Safety Project report to the Panel is found in Appendix A. The following highlights of the project's findings underscore what many women's groups have known for years: the statistics of violence against women in Canada have been thoroughly skewed by silence.

HIGHLIGHTS OF THE FINDINGS OF THE WOMEN'S SAFETY PROJECT

The following information is based on 420 in-depth interviews with women between the ages of 18 and 64.

SEXUAL ABUSE OF GIRLS (AGE 16 AND UNDER)

- **More than one half (54 percent) of the women** had experienced some form of unwanted or intrusive sexual experience before reaching the age of 16.

- **24 percent of the cases** of sexual abuse were at the level of forced or attempted forced sexual intercourse.

- **17 percent of women** reported at least one experience of incest before age 16.

- **34 percent of women** had been sexually abused by a non-relative before age 16.

- **43 percent of women** reported at least one experience of incest and/or extrafamilial sexual abuse before age 16.

- **96 percent of perpetrators** of child sexual abuse were men.

SEXUAL ABUSE OF WOMEN (AGE 16 AND OVER)

- **51 percent of women** have been the victim of rape or attempted rape.

- **40 percent of women** reported at least one experience of rape.

- **31 percent of women** reported at least one experience of attempted rape.

- Using the Canadian Criminal Code definition of sexual assault (this includes sexual touching): **two out of three women**, have experienced what is legally recognized to be sexual assault.

- **81 percent of sexual assault cases** at the level of rape or attempted rape reported by women were perpetrated by men who were known to the women.

PHYSICAL ASSAULT IN INTIMATE RELATIONSHIPS

- **27 percent of women** have experienced a physical assault in an intimate relationship.

- **In 25 percent of the cases,** women who were physically assaulted reported that their partners explicitly threatened to kill them.

- **In 36 percent of the cases,** women reporting physical assault also reported that they feared they would be killed by their male intimate. Typically, women reported that the fury and violence exhibited during attacks made them fear for their lives.

- **50 percent of the women** reporting physical assault also experienced sexual assault in the context of the same relationship.

- **All of the physical assaults on women** were perpetrated by male intimates.

In the Safety Project interviews, women were asked about a wide range of abuse in a variety of contexts and relationships, from being followed or chased on the street, to receiving an obscene phone call, being sexually harassed at work, being sexually assaulted and/or raped as a child or adult or being physically assaulted and/or beaten in an intimate relationship.

When all kinds of sexual violation and intrusion are considered, 98 percent of women reported that they personally experienced some form of sexual violation. This finding, in particular, clearly supports our assertion that violence against women affects virtually all women's lives. Such violence is the product of a society where men's violence is often presented as a form of entertainment, either as a sensation in the media or glorified in movies and on television. Awareness of the possibility of sexual violence exists in the consciousness of most women. In a 1993 Maclean's -CTV poll, 55 percent of women in Canada reported that they are afraid to walk the streets of their community alone at night. [8]

No one knows the absolute number of women in Canada who experience male violence. We do know, however, in a 1991-92 survey of residential shelters that 78,429 residents were admitted to 273 shelters in 1992. Sixty-nine percent of the 273 shelters had between 100 and 500 admissions for the year. On a given day, March 31, 1992, the majority of adult women residents of transition houses were between the ages of 25 and 34; children under the age of 5 represented 48 percent of all dependent residents. On that day, 25 percent of the residents had requested police intervention for the most recent violent incident and, in 51 percent of these cases, charges were not laid against the abuser. [9] We do know with certainty that in 1991, 270 women were murdered. Two hundred and twenty-five of these murders are solved. Of the solved cases, 210 women died at the hands of men. One hundred and twenty-one were killed by intimate partners. [10]

HUMAN, SOCIAL AND FINANCIAL COSTS OF VIOLENCE AGAINST WOMEN

The statistics of the preceding section indicate the extent of the violence against women but not the costs. The human costs — the central concern of the Panel — are impossible to quantify. We heard from women whose lives have been totally disrupted by violence, from women who had to move away from friends, family, jobs, educational opportunities just to survive, from women whose lives have been wrenched asunder by exposure to a host of violent men — fathers, grandfathers, brothers, boyfriends, uncles, husbands, lovers, acquaintances and strangers.

The enormous emotional toll of these relationships defies any accounting mechanism. Some women are unable to sustain relationships over the long term, and some are afraid to leave their homes, paralyzed by an experience of violence which keeps them hostage. Some must witness the legacy of a violent relationship as it affects their own children; some cannot support themselves because they are unable to keep a job due to stress and the psychological toll of their experiences. A Quebec study [11] compared the health of a sample group of women and children who had left a violent environment with women and children of a comparable group who had not experienced violence. It concluded that:

> The health of these women and their children was distinctly different from that of the general population, and they were affected first of all by problems of mental health ... women who have escaped violence for good are in better mental health, but this separation is above all beneficial for the children. These findings [of the study] suggest that the improved health of abused women, and especially that of their children, is conditional on their breaking away from the violent spouse. [12]

Women from violent relationships were five times more likely to exhibit psychological problems than women from the control group. The problems included severe anxiety and irritability (41.8% compared with 6.7% of the control group); depression (14.5% and 3.7% respectively); and periods of confusion or memory loss (5.5% and 0.4% respectively). In total, 45.5 percent of women from violent relationships exhibited such problems compared with only 9.4 percent of the women from the control group. [13]

Years of abuse or a single incident can cause nightmares for years and make physical contact or a healthy sexual relationship impossible. These costs are personal, substantial and potentially overwhelming. For some women, killing their abusive husbands was the final outcome in the cycle of violence. In Montreal, between 1982 and 1986, only three percent of all male homicides were committed by their female partners. In almost every case, the woman was in immediate or imminent danger of physical violence and was living in an abusive situation.

In at least half the killings of women, the men committed the murders because they could not accept the women leaving them; in other cases they committed the murder as revenge for having "lost control" over their wives' lives; in at least one case out of four, the men had previously used violence against their female partners. [14]

The physical costs are also tremendous. Broken limbs, scars, lacerations, cuts, bruises, internal damage, brain damage, reproductive damage including the inability to bear children, these are but a few of the physical costs that women endure. Some women pay with their lives. A Quebec study shows that approximately 20 percent of women admitted for emergency surgery are victims of violence. [15] Battering accounts for one in every four suicide attempts by women. Compared with women who have not been abused, 40 percent more battered women report that they use drugs to sleep; 74 percent more use drugs to relieve anxiety. [16]

The monetary costs of violence against women are hard to calculate. An experience of violence puts a woman in touch with a variety of institutions. The lack of co-ordination among these institutions means it is difficult, if not impossible, to follow someone through the process or to make an accurate accounting of the human and financial costs of violence against women. However, some very obvious conclusions are possible. Some research provides an indication of the costs, but there is an urgent requirement for clear and consistent documentation of the links between violence, health and health care costs.

Every misdiagnosis or missed diagnosis adds significant costs to the health care system. There are thousands of women in Canada who have received inappropriate medical care after an episode of violence. We heard of terrible hardship and suffering resulting from often-inappropriate treatment and tortuous incarcerations in hospitals. In many instances, these were the result of a misdiagnosis that led to dangerously inappropriate medications, use of straitjackets and other questionable medical treatments.

One Canadian study revealed the startling consequences of misdiagnosis and missed diagnosis of childhood abuse. Even though the correlation between multiple personality disorder and childhood abuse was recognized, the average length of treatment before an accurate diagnosis was made was 6.8 years. Of the 185 subjects in the study, 89 percent had had psychiatric care before receiving treatment based on recognition of their childhood abuse. Among those who had been misdiagnosed, there was an average of three previous diagnoses, the most common of which were depression, borderline personality disorder and schizophrenia. [17]

Another Canadian study tabulated the lifetime psychiatric health care costs for 15 women with multiple personality disorder as $4,144,115. This figure includes an average of 98.8 months in the health care system before the diagnosis of multiple personality disorder was made. The study projected a potential saving of $10 million if the abuse had been stopped and the 15 women had been diagnosed correctly before 10 years of age. The treatment of one woman in the study cost $870,000 over the 227 months she spent in the health care system before diagnosis of multiple personality disorder. The total cost of her 18 months of treatment after correct diagnosis has been $21,903. [18]

Other costs to the Canadian medical system, correct diagnosis or not, include the cost of prescription drugs such as anti-depressants, sleeping pills and painkillers; the cost of appointments with physicians, emergency treatment, hospital stays, ambulance services; and the cost of rehabilitative services such as physiotherapy or occupational therapy. The fact is the financial toll of violence against women is entirely preventable, an important recognition for a health care system already severely overburdened.

For women survivors of violence, work-related costs include time off without pay due to the results of injury and psychological trauma. They may also include the cost of using employment-based counselling services or sick leave, and in some instances it may even be necessary to leave a job altogether. Victims of violence may not be able to concentrate on work and may exhibit decreased productivity. Such costs accrue, not only to the women involved, but also to their employers, insurance companies, all levels of government, disability pension programs, workers, criminal compensation programs, etc.

The financial costs of violence against women are not restricted to health care and work-related costs; they also reverberate through the criminal justice system. Additional police resources, victims' treatment costs, insurance claims and court costs all add up. In cases where convictions and sentencing take place, the correctional system bears the costs of detention, incarceration, probation and parole. In some instances both defendants and plaintiffs use legal aid, a further cost to the system.

The cost benefits of violence prevention and effective programs for offenders have not been clear to many because such costs have never been realistically or comprehensively tabulated in Canada. Even a rough estimate of the cost associated with one crime of violence against a woman provides some appreciation of the need to prevent violence from happening in the first place. The costs of one sexual offence, where the offender serves three years in prison, can be very conservatively estimated at more than $200,000. The prison custodial cost alone would be approximately $50,000 per year for three years. Added to this would be the costs of police investigation, pre-trial and court processes, assessment, parole hearings, offender programs and after-prison care as well as some services to the victim.

One recent British Columbia study on multiple victims of child sexual abuse provides another useful starting place in calculating costs of crimes against women and children. This study found that 30 sex offenders had victimized at least 2,099 children. Perpetrators had sexually abused between three and 495 children each with the average being 70 victims per perpetrator. [19] The savings in both human pain and financial terms are apparent if each perpetrator had been apprehended and effectively deterred after the first occurrence, thereby preventing 69 crimes, sparing 69 victims.

And then there are the social costs of violence against women, which include an expensive range of social services and supports which must be maintained on an ongoing and emergency basis. Services for children need to factor in the costs of foster homes and additional child care workers. The educational system has to provide child welfare services over and above those of education, such as school crisis counsellors, tragic events teams, special education classes for children with learning disabilities resulting from violence, as well as special programs and educational initiatives on violence. Communities, municipalities, provincial and federal governments must bear the costs of transition houses, second-stage housing, mental health clinics, shelter programs, educational campaigns, special services for victims of violence, sexual assault centres and programs for violent men.

While we have not been able to attach monetary sums to all the costs outlined above, we know they are profound. Instead of devoting such a large percentage of already limited monetary resources to activities in *response* to the consequences of violence against women, would it not be much wiser to direct the funds to programs aimed at preventing the perpetuation of violence and to social change?

LOOKING THROUGH A FEMINIST LENS

The analysis in this report draws on a specific way of thinking about violence against women. Rather than focusing on the violent actions of individual men, our approach looks at the problem in a much broader social context. We are asking: What is it about our present and past social organization that fosters and supports violent actions on the part of men toward women?

Our approach is not new. We have taken a feminist approach reflecting work already done at the grass-roots level. In the pages which follow we will demonstrate how looking through a feminist lens enables us to see how gender, race and class oppress women and how these forms of oppression are interrelated and interconnected.

Two central tenets of feminism are the socially structured nature of gender inequality and the requirement for political action to overturn the power imbalance between men and women. Feminism redefined politics and placed issues previously defined as personal squarely on the political agenda. These include child care, birth control, sexual assault, housework, women's unequal wage levels and safe living environments. No longer, feminists asserted, was it acceptable to ignore women's inequality. Neither was it acceptable to attribute women's inequality to "bad choices" or "mistakes" made by women, their biology or a host of individual actions or decisions.

THE STORY OF THE PINK COAT

Every girl is given a pink coat at birth (boys get a blue one). It is a tightly woven garment made of meekness, passivity, self-abnegation and maternal instinct. The child grows up wearing this coat, which magically adjusts to fit her. If she wants to take it off, those around her advise against it: she could catch a cold and, in any case, she will be punished if she ignores their advice. She is also so pretty and feminine in her coat.

Some women become so used to the coat that [they] no longer know whether it's the coat or their skin that is pink. And their skin and the coat in fact become one and the same thing. In the end, they believe they are meek by nature and are only fulfilled when those around them are happy. These feminine characteristics then become their personality and not merely a social standard set for all women.

Women have to fight to make alterations to the pink coat. Those who try are judged severely (rejected by those around them, become lonely, etc.).

It is important to realize that society requires all women to wear pink coats. Women first learn what the coat is made of. Then they decide whether they will wear it all the time, sometimes or not at all. But the important thing for them is to choose what they really want, not what society expects of them. They must feel free to keep the coat or throw it away. The purpose of feminist action is to enable women to become aware of their "pink coat" heritage. [20]

It is interesting to note that the 1970 *Report of the Royal Commission on the Status of Women* did not mention the issue of violence against women. We can only surmise that its omission was not because it did not exist, but because of the long history of silence among women about their abuse. In less than 25 years, the silence has not only been broken, it has been shattered.

PATRIARCHY AND VIOLENCE

Violence against women, both now and in the past, is the outcome of social, economic, political and cultural inequality. This inequality takes many forms, but its most familiar form is economic. [21]

Day-to-day economic inequality, unequal political power, unequal protection under the law and unequal access to justice for women are all supported and perpetuated at the level of ideas. Language, myths, symbols, notions and beliefs about the superiority of men over women bolster the existing social structure and maintain women's inequality.

Understanding the concept of patriarchy is essential to our analysis of the nature of gender inequality and its impact on the vulnerability of women to violence, and of our society's tolerance of male violence against women.

THE PATRIARCHAL SOCIETY

Patriarchy in its wider meaning is:

> The manifestation and institutionalization of male dominance over women and children in the family and the extension of male dominance over women in society in general. It implies that men hold power in all the important institutions in society and that women are deprived of access to such power. It does not imply that women are either totally powerless or totally deprived of rights, influence and resources, but certainly women as a group have less power, less influence and fewer resources than men. [22]

In the social structures and dynamics of society, women and men have gender-specific roles in the power structure which, among other things, legitimize men's authority to be violent toward women. [23] Some men consider domination and control of women as their right; using violence when they see fit is not challenged. This in turn leads to widespread tolerance of male violence at both the individual and institutional levels.

The treatment of women, their labour, their reproductive capacity and their sexuality as commodities is certainly not just a product of modern industrial and capitalist society; it has been that way since long before the creation of Western civilization. Over time, women became a resource and a form of property acquired and controlled by men.

Today, the modern state and its supporting bureaucracy have broadened the locus of power from the patriarch in the family to a patriarchal state that reflects and sustains gender inequality in a variety of ways and locations in the social structure. [24] In concert, the patriarchal family model and the patriarchal state help to sustain inequality among women and men. This major enduring theme does not deny that most women have established greater relative equality over time, but they have done so within the context of a patriarchal society. The nature of gender relations and inequality in society can be better understood through an elaboration of the concept of heterosexism, a set of ideas about men and women and the relationship between them.

DIMENSIONS OF INEQUALITY

Canada ranks second among nations (to Japan) on the Human Development Index compiled by the United Nations. [25] However, when the Index is adjusted for gender disparities, Canada drops to 11th place overall. While the statistical basis upon which the UN compiles its Human Development Index is open to debate the following statistics illustrate the objective realities of gender inequality Canadian women face every day.

1. The average annual wage of women full-time workers in 1991 was $ 26,842. For men it was $38,567. [26]

2. The average wage of women increased by 14 % in the decade of the 1980s, while that of men remained constant. However by 1990, despite a decade of employment equity and increased educational attainment and work experience among women, women's earnings were still just 60.3 % those of men. [27]

3. Three out of four earners in the 10 lowest paying occupations are women. Eight out of ten earners in the highest paying occupations are men. [28]

4. The lowest average employment income in 1990 was for child care occupations at $ 13,518. [29]

5. The average income for female lone parent families in 1990 was $ 26,500. For male lone parent families it was $ 40,792. There were 165,245 male lone parent families and 788,400 female lone parent families in 1990. [30]

6. In 1989, only 7 % of all full professors at Canadian universities were women. In engineering and applied sciences women accounted for only 15 % of lecturers and instructors and just 1 % of full professors. Even in education faculties, only 15 % of full professors were women. [31]

7. 11 % of women in 2 parent families with pre-school children missed work in 1991 for family reasons. Only 2 % of men in these families had absences from work for family reasons. [32]

8. On average, women who work outside the home for pay spend almost an hour and a half more per day on unpaid household work, including domestic work, primary child care and shopping, than do men — 3.2 hours per day on average over a 7-day week compared with 1.8 hours per day for men. [33]

9. Four times as many women as men reported that 4 out of 5 domestic responsibilitites were mostly theirs. Women said they had the main responsibility for household shopping, cleaning inside the home, looking after ill children and taking children to activities. Men said they had primary responsibility only for "cleaning outside the home". [34]

10. 42 % of women household maintainers (i.e. the person responsible for mortgage, rent, taxes and upkeep) own their dwelling, compared with 70 % of male household maintainers. [35]

11. Elderly unattached women are among the poorest Canadians. But, while the percentage of these women living in poverty has gone down since 1980, an increasing proportion of all low income elderly people are women. [36]

12. In 1991-92, all levels of government expended $ 1.876 billion on adult correctional services. On an average day, there were 25,712 prisoners serving a custodial sentence. Women accounted for just 1,254 or 9 % of all provincial prisoners, and only 354 or 3 % of all federal inmates. [37]

13. Women account for 10 % of all persons charged with violent crimes and 20 % of those charged with property crimes. [38]

14. Breast cancer is the leading cause of death for Canadian women aged 35-54 and the leading cause of death from cancer for women aged 30-74. Less than 1 % of health care research funds are spent on breast cancer. [39]

HETEROSEXISM

Heterosexism is the assumption that a woman's life will be organized around and defined in relation to a man. It falsely presumes that all women will marry and have children, and that all worthy paths for women lead to marriage and motherhood. Opposition to heterosexism is often unfairly cast as an attack on the institutions of marriage and motherhood. In reality, opposition to heterosexism supports women's equality. It upholds a woman's right to be defined as an autonomous, independent person rather than being defined only in relation to men and children. It recognizes the diverse roles a woman plays in life and frees her to attach priorities to these roles as she sees fit. It supports a woman's right to choose her love partner with freedom, and it calls for a transformation of societal structures that support all freely chosen relationships.

Canadian society is organized around compulsory heterosexuality. Our culture and societal institutions function as if the primary role for women is that of wife and mother caring for her husband and bearing and nurturing children. In the ideal, she is the archetypal madonna: demure, slight, beautiful, chaste, deferential, passive, co-operative, alluring and servile. These feminine attributes prepare her to marry and be relegated to the private domain of the family. Her greatest assigned values are her reproductive capacity and her commitment to her family. Her domestic labour remains unpaid; her paid work remains underpaid.

In antithesis to the ideal woman, the ideal man is the protector and the breadwinner. He is seen to be best equipped for that role if he is bold, strong, powerful, active, competitive, virile and in command. These masculine characteristics have high value in the private realm of the family where he is seen to be the head of the household, and in the public spheres of commerce, law and politics. He is presumed to be a careerist first and a husband second. His masculine qualities are valued highly and are well rewarded in the marketplace. He carries these qualities with him into the public world where they become the core philosophy and where structures are crafted to suit the male experience.

We continue to live with the legacy of these archetypes. Despite modern reality, our institutions and social conventions are all constructed in a manner that limits choices for women in an effort to force them to conform to the role of wife and mother. Families, religion, politics, media and education are all organized around the concept of heterosexism and consistently reinforce and re-create the ideal by rewarding those who most closely conform to it and by punishing those who dare to be different. Hence the tomboy is tamed, the outspoken woman is silenced, the prostitute is cast out. Heterosexism is evident in worries about appearance, eating disorders, reluctance to participate in sports and hiding academic achievements to avoid appearing too smart or too successful.

The quest is supported in educational institutions that schedule dances instead of group social events, in religious institutions that perpetuate the ideology of male superiority and female inferiority, in workplaces that undervalue and underpay women, and in popular culture that sustains sexist assumptions about women.

The imbalance of power inherent in the masculine and feminine sex roles takes on greater significance when we look at the dynamics of male violence against women. Generally men are in control and women are controlled by them. Men are independent; women are dependent on them. When men choose violence as a means to control women, women have little power to withstand the violence. Even men who do not actively use violence against women often tolerate it by other men.

The mechanisms through which male violence can be challenged are also infused with the belief in the male right to rule women. Heterosexism is imbedded in all state institutions that women are likely to call upon — the police, the justice system and religious institutions. In these structures, women, particularly if they do not fit the idealized image of wife and mother, have little influence and power. They are often not believed, they are blamed for their own suffering and are urged to try harder.

If women attempt to gain economic independence to lessen their vulnerability, they come up against structural obstacles. The labour force remains organized around the heterosexist ideal, presuming women to be married, to maintain primary responsibility for the home and to care for children, despite their labour force participation. They are usually paid less than men, primarily found in lower status and more "servile" jobs, and frequently relegated to part-time positions with fewer benefits and pension rights. For women who are participating in the labour force or want to participate, inadequate child care can be a major problem.

Love relationships between men and women are celebrated and sanctified while same sex relationships are denied and reviled. Pension plans, health care schemes and insurance policies discriminate against them. Less apparent, but real nonetheless, are the difficulties faced by women who choose to remain unmarried or who choose not to have or cannot have children. They are consistently asked why not and are looked upon as unfortunate or somehow deviant. Lone parents, most of whom are women, lack societal supports.

On the surface, women who live within heterosexist boundaries seem better off. Many, without doubt, garner privileges, such as access to male resources, a husband's protection from other men and legitimacy for children born of the relationship. But these are all derivative benefits. The man continues to be the primary source of support, defines the terms of protection and gives the children his name. Power is his to wield as he wishes. In this arrangement the woman remains in a state of dependency on the man, vulnerable to his will.

If women choose to speak out against heterosexism and its inherent inequality, to resist it, to expose the male violence it supports, they are considered "shrill" and unwomanly and often face violence for doing so. Heterosexism is one of patriarchy's strongest and most insidious tools. It allows society to cast aside women's experience and construct a society on models of what patriarchy wants her to be, not who she really is or could be.

Sexism and sexist assumptions are also expressed in laws; in religious rituals; in economic practices; in myths and stories; in children's games, toys and reading materials; and in scores of additional places in society.

Patriarchy is not just a central concept in feminist analysis. For many women it is also a daily reality — the most violent and profound expression of patriarchal power sits at their dinner tables every evening and sleeps in their beds at night. Women who have experienced violence at the hands of their husbands and intimate partners, or their fathers, brothers, uncles or grandfathers, can speak all too clearly about male power; they have self-images, bruises, cuts, lacerations and broken bones that speak of their understanding of the patriarchal family. Although we recognize that positive aspects of family life can and do exist, for some women the reality is in stark contrast to the mythical images most Canadians hold dear.

It is ironic that, while separate and distinct from the public world of work and politics, the family is a private realm where men still dominate and exercise the same control they wield in the public arena. Traditional family relations also confer certain "conjugal rights" upon men. Exclusive and unlimited sexual access to women by men has been a cornerstone of the family, a right often interpreted by some men to extend to their daughters, nieces and granddaughters. It was not until 1983 that a woman could charge her husband with rape in Canada. Until then, men had the legal right to rape their wives without fear of reprisal. [40]

Even after marriages break down, some men continue to exercise what they believe to be their proprietory rights to their wives and children. The best evidence we have of this belief in ownership is the incidence of "intimate femicide," murder of a woman by someone close to her. It is estimated that women who are separated from their spouses are five times more likely to be killed by their intimate partners than are other women. [41] Male anger and rage over the loss of their wives/ property apparently have no obvious counterpart in killings of men by female intimate partners. "If I can't have her, no one will have her" is the ultimate expression of the patriarchal family ideology.

Beliefs about privacy and the separation of "home" from the "other" world increase women's vulnerability. They permeate law and politics where violence in the home continues to be perceived as being beyond public reproach. Police officers shy away from "domestics," and implicitly or explicitly the message goes out that what happens in the family is not the business of the public.

We are taught, encouraged, moulded by and lulled into accepting a range of false notions about the family. As the source of some of our most profound experiences, it continues to be such an integral part of our emotional lives that it appears beyond criticism. Yet hiding from the truth of family life leaves women and children vulnerable. Many of us, including policy makers, legislators, law enforcement personnel, judicial officials, doctors and religious leaders, are afraid to examine the reality of power relations within the home. Many are quick to dismiss disclosures of psychological, physical or sexual abuse because such events depart so profoundly from our idealized images of family life. For many it is difficult to reconcile the conflicting images of father/husband as protector and father/husband as perpetrator of violence. As difficult as this process is, it is important that we confront the potential dangers of family life for women and children.

Patriarchy also finds expression in religious institutions that have a long history of domination, control and the exercise of absolute power. The theological domination of women by men omnipresent in religious teachings extends into the day-to-day practice of religious institutions. Women are excluded from many important religious ceremonies, segregated from some settings and forbidden to hold certain positions of power. Acceptable relationships between the sexes are governed by outdated notions about men, women and families. Some religions enslave women to procreation by prohibiting birth control and abortion. Some clergy have sexually abused women and children or advised women to stay in dangerous family situations.

Many religious institutions have, through both philosophy and practice, contributed to conditions that support violence against women in the home and in society.

Ultimately, patriarchal society is synonymous with the political, social, cultural and economic inequality of women. Unequal political power is exemplified by the current representation of women in political office and by the predominance of a male political culture that operates along lines of male privilege. Unequal sexual freedom sees women as objects of consumption in pornographic magazines and sees females taking almost total responsibility for birth control and being denied access to full choice around issues of childbearing. Unequal legal power is manifested in laws that do not adequately protect women and children as survivors of abuse and in regulations that discriminate against women in the determination of their immigrant and refugee status. Unequal social power keeps women silent, even in the midst of abusive treatment by partners, employers, doctors, social workers and clergy.

The action plan proposed by this Panel stresses the importance of eliminating the conditions that support patriarchy by emphasizing that gender equality and freedom from violence are equal and concurrent goals. However, we recognize that the experiences and the degree of violence are different for women of colour, for women of different races and different cultural and ethnic backgrounds, for poor and elderly women, for lesbians and for disabled women. Their particular experiences of inequality and of violence are the outcome of a society which devalues, marginalizes and discriminates against them. It is not the race, ethnicity, colour, age, physical ability or sexual orientation which make the lives of these women so different; it is how individuals and various sectors in the social structure react to the reality of these women that compounds their experiences of violence and inequality.

OTHER BASES OF INEQUALITY

This report is about violence against women — violence women suffer because of their gender. But understanding the experience of violence requires understanding the combined impact of gender, race and class.

CLASS

In our discussion of patriarchy, we examined how laws, policies and social institutions are developed according to the interests and experiences of men; that the resulting social structures, referred to as patriarchal relations, are based on power, the dominance of men and the submission of women. Social inequality is indeed the outcome of the interrelationship between the structures of economic power and the organization of male power in our society. This blending of power relations pervades all institutions. To truly understand women's inequality is to recognize how patriarchy and capitalism operate in separate ways but also combine forces to diminish their interests and realities further.

To see this interrelationship in action, one only has to examine women's low economic status and participation in the labour force as secondary workers. Society relies on women to provide a whole range of caring services to men, to children, to the sick and old, most often for free or for little money. This sexual division of labour repeats itself in the workplace with women continuing to be concentrated in only three occupational groups: clerical, service, and managerial and administrative. [42] Most of the positions in these groups offer low wages, limited benefits, low career mobility and very little union protection. [43]

Patriarchal-capitalistic relations also divide women themselves into groups with different levels of choice, power and control over all things in life, from the basics of what we eat, where we live and sleep, our education and jobs, to our encounters with government and the healthcare and legal systems. A woman's exposure to and experience of violence will also be textured by her socio-economic position. Access to financial resources will determine the level and the type of support, counselling, legal advice and other survival strategies at a woman's disposal.

RACE

Patriarchy is not fully revealed solely in terms of gender and class power differentials. Race power relations are involved as well. Just as Canadian ideologies, policies and social practices are structured around male and elite values and experiences, they are also rooted in the belief that white people have the right to dominate. Canadians are generally presumed to be white and this is the central reference point of all social institutions. Therefore racism is structural in nature and cannot be explained as the product of bad communication among individuals.

> ... racism is [not] merely a misunderstanding among people, a question of interpersonal relations, or an unchanging part of human nature. Racism, like sexism, is an integral part of the political and economic system under which we live. This system uses racism and sexism to divide us and to exploit our labour for super-profits and gives some women privilege. [44]

In much the same way that men benefit from the inequality of women, both white men and white women benefit from the perpetuation of racism. For example, many white women and men in North America benefit from the conditions that drive women of colour out of their own countries in search of work alternatives in North America. White middle class families employ "nannies" from the Philippines, Malaysia and the Caribbean at lower wages than would be paid other workers in Canada.

For women of colour, race, gender and class issues intersect very clearly in the labour market. Women are already seen as a secondary source of labour. Added to this are racist ideologies that "justify" low wages for women of colour and racist hiring practices that force many women of colour into low status jobs with poor working conditions. It is easy to see how two oppressions, gender and race, interlock in a way that forces class oppression into play. This is not simply a layering of three separate oppressions but a complex interplay of oppressions that results in compounded social inequality.

When a woman of colour experiences violence she experiences it as a simultaneous attack on both her gender and her race. From experience she knows that anger and hatred directed at both these aspects of her identity are real. When she calls upon systems to respond she cannot trust the response because she knows that she is calling upon systems that do not understand, value or incorporate her experience either as a woman or as a person of colour.

The feminist lens reveals that while all women are at risk of male violence because of gender, their experiences of that violence are essentially informed by their race and class. So are the responses to their experiences. Building alliances across the issues that divide women will have to be given priority in the struggle to end violence against women. Patriarchy thrives on fragmentation and divisions. The existence of one oppression creates fertile conditions for the others. That is why all oppressions must be resisted together.

A strong coalition to end male violence against women is only possible if the differences among women are recognized, fully appreciated and equally applied to all endeavours to overcome patriarchy and end violence. The urgency and dimensions of that task will become clearer in the examination of forms of violence in the following section.

ENDNOTES

1   United Nations, *Declaration on the Elimination of Violence Against Women*, p. 6. The UN Commission on the Status of Women approved the draft in March 1993. The draft will go forward to the General Assembly in the fall of 1993. (Canada initiated the declaration.)

2   *Ibid.*

3   G. Larouche, *Agir contre la violence* (Montreal: Éditions La pleine lune, 1987), p. 32.

4   Dominique Bilodeau "L'approche féministe en maison d'hébergement : quand la pratique enrichit la théorie," *Nouvelles pratiques sociales*, Vol. 3, No. 2, (1990): 48

5   Barbara Hart, *Safety For Women: Monitoring Batterers' Programs* (Harrisburg: Pennsylvania Coalition Against Domestic Violence, 1988), p. 18.

6   Sub-Committee on the Status of Women, *The War Against Women: Report of the Standing Committee on Health and Welfare, Social Affairs, Seniors and the Status of Women* (Ottawa: House of Commons, June 1991).

7   Lori Haskell and Melanie Randall, *The Women's Safety Project: Summary of Key Statistical Findings* (Ottawa: Canadian Panel on Violence Against Women, 1993). The Canadian Panel on Violence Against Women has published the *Summary of Key Statistical Findings* resulting from the work of the Women's Safety Project as an appendix to this report. Unless otherwise indicated, all references to the Women's Safety Project in the body of the report can be found in detail in Appendix A.

8   Maclean's-CTV, "Anxieties Over Violence," *Maclean's*, Vol. 105, No. 01 (January 4, 1993), p. 25.

9   Canadian Centre for Health Information, *Transition Home Supplement, Residential Care Facilities Survey 1991-92* (Statistics Canada, 1993).

10 Canadian Centre for Justice Statistics, *Homicide Survey, 1991* (Ottawa: Statistics Canada, 1993).

11 L. Chénard, H. Cadrin and J. Loiselle, *État de santé des femmes et des enfants victimes de violence conjugale* (Rimouski, Que.: Département de santé communautaire, Centre hospitalier régional de Rimouski, Octobre, 1990), p. 71.

12 *Ibid.*

13 *Ibid.,* p. 41.

14 Andrée Côté, *La rage au coeur : rapport de recherche sur le traitement judiciaire de l'homicide conjugal au Québec* (Baie Comeau, Que.: Regroupement des femmes de la Côte-Nord, 1991), p. 139.

15 Jacqueline Dupuis, "L'urgence, le premier contact," *Nursing Québec*, Vol. 5, No. 5 (1985): 24.

16 J. Groeneveld and M. Shain, *Drug Abuse Among Victims of Physical and Sexual Abuse: A Preliminary Report* (Toronto: Addiction Research Foundation, 1989), p. 8.

17 Margo Riviera, *Multiple Personality: an outcome of child abuse* (Toronto: Education/Dissociation, 1991), p. 10.

18 Colin A. Ross and Vikram Dua, "Psychiatric Health Care Costs of Multiple Personality Disorder," *American Journal of Psychotherapy*, Vol. 47, No. 1: 103-112.

19 *Dimensions of Multiple Victim Child Sexual Abuse in British Columbia, 1985-1989* (British Columbia Ministry of Health, 1991).

20. G. Larouche, *Agir contre la violence* (Montreal: Éditions La pleine lune, 1987), pp. 36-37.

21 Louise Vandelac, Diane Bélisle, Anne Gauthier and Yolande Pinard, *Du travail et de l'amour* (Montreal Saint-Martin, 1986), *passim.*

22 G. Lerner, *The Creation of Patriarchy* (New York: Oxford University Press, 1986), p. 239.

23 Ginette Larouche, *Agir contre la violence* (Montreal: Editions La Pleine lune, 1987), p. 35.

24 Micheline de Sève, *Pour un féminisme libertaire* (Saint-Laurent: Boréal Express, 1985), p. 118.

25 United Nations Development Program, *Human Development Report 1992*, (New York: Oxford University Press, 1993).

26. Statistics Canada, "Earnings of Men and Women", in *The Daily*, January 14th, 1993, p.3.

27. Abdul Rashid, "Seven Decades of Wage Changes", in *Perspectives on Labour and Income*, Volume 5, No. 2, Summer 1993, pp. 13 & 18.

28. Statistics Canada, "1991 Census: Highlights", in *The Daily*, April 13th, 1993, p.1.

29. *Ibid*, p.1

30. *Ibid*, p.3

31 Statistics Canada, "Women in Academia — A Growing Minority", in *The Daily*, March 11th, 1993, p.3.

32 Nancy Zukewich Graham, "Women in the Workplace", in *Canadian Social Trends*, No. 28, Spring 1993, p.6.

33. *Ibid*, p.6.

34 Canada Health Monitor, "Highlights Report Survey # 6", January 1992, Price Waterhouse and Earl Berger, Toronto 1992, p.3.

35 Statistics Canada, Women in Canada — A Statistical Report, Minister of Supply and Services, Ottawa, 1990, p.27.

36 *Ibid*, pp. 108-109.

37   Canadian Centre for Justice Statistics, "Correctional
      Expenditures and Personnel in Canada", in *Juristat*,
      Vol. 12, No. 22, November 30th, 1992, p.1, and, Statistics
      Canada, *Adult Correctional Services in Canada* — 1991-92,
      Ottawa 1992.

38   Statistics Canada, *Women in Canada — A Statistical
      Report, op.cit.*, p.147.

39   National Action Committee on the Status of Women,
      "Review of the Situation of Women in Canada - 1992",
      Toronto, May 1992, p.12.

40   Department of Justice Canada, Research Section,
      *Sexual Assault Legislation in Canada: An Evaluation:
      Overview (Report No. 5)* (Ottawa, 1990), pp. 13-14.

41   Maria Crawford and Rosemary Gartner, *Woman Killing,
      Intimate Femicide in Ontario 1974-1990* (Toronto: The
      Women We Honour Action Committee, 1992), p. 52.

42   Statistics Canada, *The Daily,* March 2, 1993, p. 10.

43   Nancy Adamson, Linda Briskin and Margaret McPhail,
      *Feminist Organizing for Change: The Contemporary
      Women's Movement in Canada* (Toronto: Oxford
      University Press, 1988), p. 110.

44   C. Allen and J. Persad, "Fighting Racism and Sexism
      Together," as cited in N.L. Adamson et al., *ibid.*, p. 106.

PART TWO

EXPERIENCING VIOLENCE~

FORMS

INTRODUCTION

In Part I we referred to five dimensions of violence: sexual, physical, psychological, financial and spiritual. In this section we describe the different forms these dimensions of violence can take. Rape, incest, date rape and unwanted sexual touching are forms of sexual violence; slapping, shoving, hitting, stabbing and murder are forms of physical violence; shouting, swearing, taunting, threatening, degrading and demeaning are forms of psychological violence; withholding money, diverting or embezzling funds and controlling money are forms of financial violence; degrading a woman's spiritual beliefs or withholding or limiting the means for her to practise her spirituality are forms of spiritual violence.

It is not our intention to elevate one form or one dimension of violence above the others in terms of severity, impact or consequences. Rather, we intend to demonstrate that the definition of violence, its short and long-term consequences, and the legal, moral and cultural sanctions attached to it, are best appreciated in the context of the relationships and settings in which it takes place.

Statistics clearly indicate that in the majority of cases of violence against women, the victims and the perpetrators are known to each other and share some sort of relationship. [1] Women victims are more likely to be the daughters, sisters, intimate partners, dates, employees and acquaintances of the perpetrators — not strangers. This flies in the face of the classical rape myth of a chaste woman beseiged by a stranger who jumps out from behind a bush on a darkly lit street. Most people can identify the crime and injury to the woman in such a scenario although some still question the woman's right to be on the darkly lit street; debate whether her clothes were too provocative and want to know if she was truly chaste.

There is a significantly different reaction to the rape of a woman who is in a relationship with the man who rapes her — any relationship. It appears that once any relationship exists, regardless of how casual it might be, men have come to believe in their right to dictate the terms.

The closer the relationship the greater the burden of proof of injury required by the woman. This leaves women in intimate relationships with men extremely vulnerable. We know that the law against rape in marriage is seldom used. [2] This is not because women are not raped by husbands. On the contrary, the Women's Safety Project found that 25 percent of all rapes reported by women were committed by their husbands. Non-reporting confirms that women know, despite the current law, that reports of rape within marriage will fall on unwilling ears and reluctant justice. This is confirmed in all women's minds each time a woman is blamed for contributing to her own victimization by agreeing to have a drink with a man in his apartment, by inviting her date in for coffee, by agreeing to a midnight kiss. Such acts are deemed to signal agreement to a relationship, an agreement that nullifies a woman's right to say no to further physical intimacy.

In a relationship, society has given the man the power over a woman from the point of earliest acquaintance. Men exercise this power not only in intimate relationships and not only in sexual matters but in any social context where contact between women and men occurs.

The setting in which a relationship takes place can also amplify or diminish women's vulnerability to violence. Generally, the more private the setting the more vulnerable the woman. Again, while the peril of the street grips the attention of most people, it is the far less public venues that hold the greatest danger for women– the family home, the doctor's examining room, the boss's office. It is in these private spaces that men frequently exercise their power over women. Exposing the risks these settings present becomes the first step in reducing the danger.

Documenting the complex interplay among the dimensions of violence, the numerous forms violence can take and the relationships between victims and perpetrators in a full range of settings would fill many volumes. We have chosen several situations as examples to illustrate the infinite range of violence and to show how violent acts against women are influenced both by relationships and settings. The following chart is meant to assist in understanding these interrelationships.

FORMS OF VIOLENCE

Dimensions:	*Forms include:*
Psychological	*shouting, swearing, taunting, threatening, degrading, demeaning, inducing fear, gender harassment, witnessing*
Sexual	*rape, incest, unwanted sexual touching, date rape, harassment*
Physical	*slapping, shoving, hitting, mutilation, stabbing, assault, murder*
Financial	*witholding, diverting, embezzling or controlling funds*
Spiritual	*degrading one's beliefs, witholding means to practice, forcing adherence to a belief system*

* Almost all forms of violence have a psychological impact on the victim and hence the psychological dimension of violence against women is omnipresent.

* Ritual abuse, abuse of trust, pornography, stalking and misuse of reproductive technologies are forms of violence often experienced as a combination of psychological, physical, spiritual and sexual dimensions.

PERPETRATOR-VICTIM RELATIONSHIPS

- stranger
- spouse
- intimate partner
- acquaintance
- friend
- date
- family member/relative
- coworker/colleague
- person in a position of trust or authority
  - e.g.
    - employer/supervisor
    - custodial worker
    - service provider
    - teacher
    - volunteer leader
- business person
- state (e.g. police, public servant, elected official, military)

- stranger
- spouse
- intimate partner
- acquaintance
- friend
- date
- family member/relative
- coworker/colleague

- employee
- woman in an institution
- patient/client
- student
- participant
- consumer
- citizen, immigrant, refugee

*   *Sometimes the perpetrator and victim have no relationship whatsoever they are strangers to each other. However, in the majority of cases, the victim and perpetrator do know each other and have had some previous interaction. The nature of that interaction and the characteristics of the environment (interpersonal or institutional) within which it evolves help determine the nature of the abuse and its impact.*

SETTINGS

- house, apartment (one's own or someone else's)
- community: public space, street, park, transport system, restaurant, place of business, cultural, or recreation facility

- workplace
- institutions: school, hospital, place of worship, police station, residence

We purposely begin by looking at sexual violence enacted against women by strangers. While this is not the most common experience of sexual violence done to women, the past focus on family violence has often ignored sexual assault by strangers.

We then discuss violence where the perpetrators are known to their victims beginning with date rape and sexual violence in acquaintance or intimate relationships. We move on to discuss psychological violence in intimate relationships, an extremely common experience for women, less recognized in the literature and often not recognized at all in law. It is frequently the precursor to physical and sexual violence and has a devastating impact, sometimes undermining a woman's ability to escape other forms of violence. We then briefly look at physical violence in intimate relationships, forms that are more easily described and better recognized by society. This portion on violence in intimate relationships ends by addressing violence during pregnancy and examining women's fear of disclosing.

We go on to discuss child abuse. While our mandate did not call for such an examination, many women spoke of the damage done to them as girls and of the pain they still carry as a consequence of early victimization. We specifically focus on childhood sexual abuse, incest, female genital mutilation, the impact on girls and boys of witnessing abuse of their mothers and a preliminary investigation of the relationship between sexual abuse in childhood and revictimization in adulthood.

To illustrate the impact of the setting on the nature and response to violence, we then look at violence against women in the workplace — a setting that occupies much time and space in the lives of women and one that is so critical to a woman's ability to gain economic independence. We look at violence in the workplace generally and then at areas that pose unique and high risks to women, such as workplaces in nursing, education, domestic work and prostitution.

This section ends with a discussion of five forms of violence that are less easily categorized and, in our opinion, less well understood and acknowledged by society.

Ritual abuse is a heinous form of violence that is only now coming to light, particularly in Canada. We suspect that Canadians are largely unaware of its existence. The serious problems of stalking and criminal harassment have only recently been acknowledged through new legislation in Canada. Pornography, on the other hand, has been the subject of protracted debate in this country, and discussions on the issue continue to be heated. Abuse of trust by physicians against patients, lawyers against clients, religious leaders against congregants, teachers against pupils and coaches against athletes is far too common. An institution's failure to take steps to prevent violence where trust can be breached or to stop the violence or to help a survivor is abuse in itself.

Women's reproductive capacity, another area of vulnerability, has been controlled by others and imposes social roles and obligations that alter and may limit her life's choices and chances. The fundamental right of women to full choice and control over their bodies is currently being challenged with the advent of new reproductive technologies.

The voices of women speak for themselves. From the stark and painful images of these realities, Canadians will begin to understand the complex and vicious nature of women's experiences of violence. We caution that much of what follows is difficult to read; we can barely begin to appreciate how difficult it is to live.

CHAPTER 2

WOMAN ABUSE IN THE CONTEXT OF PERPETRATOR-VICTIM RELATIONSHIPS

VICTIMS AND PERPETRATORS AS STRANGERS

SEXUAL VIOLENCE

Violence of a sexual nature is extremely difficult for women to discuss because of the intrinsically private and personal nature of sex and sexuality. However, the feminist movement has continually emphasized that sex and sexuality are political issues that require social and political analysis. Sexual assault and violence of a sexual nature must be recognized as crimes of power and domination; they must be understood as crimes that reflect the power of patriarchy.

In this report, the term "sexual abuse" describes any sexual activity performed against the wishes and consent of the victim. It includes being forced to engage in unwanted sex and to participate in unpleasant, violent or frightening sexual acts. Other forms of sexual abuse can include being forced to have sex with others, being forced to watch the performance of others, or being criticized for sexual performance. In 1983, the sexual offence of "rape" was abolished and replaced in the *Criminal Code* with three increasingly more severe levels of sexual assault.

- Sexual assault is defined as unwanted sexual contact without physical signs of abuse. This charge carries a maximum sentence of 10 years.

- Sexual assault with a weapon or with threats to a third party, or sexual assault causing bodily harm, is subject to a maximum penalty of 14 years.

- Aggravated sexual assault is defined as sexual assault causing serious bodily injury or endangering life. The maximum sentence is life imprisonment. [3]

In the context of these changes other significant alterations were made. Rules of evidence were changed to allow restrictions on questions related to the past sexual history of the victim. This change was commonly known as the "rape shield" provision.

The "rape shield" provision was struck down by the Supreme Court in August 1991, because it was claimed that it violated the rights of the accused to a fair trial. [4] New legislation allows questioning about the past sexual history of the plaintiff but only in situations where a judge deems it to be relevant to the case. Relevancy is determined by the judge in an in camera hearing. The new legislation also makes an effort to clarify "consent" to sexual contact as a form of defence for the accused. The accused would have had to take all reasonable steps to ensure that consent to sexual contact had taken place. [5]

Unwanted sexual contact is a reality many women will face in their lifetime. The threat of rape, sexual assault and sexual abuse corrals the activities of all women worldwide. Women limit their actions, control their behaviour, monitor their social interactions and live each day of their lives with the ever-present threat of unwanted or forced sexual contact.

Over the past 20 years, women's groups have advocated for recognizing sexual assault as a serious crime. They have also established a number of sexual assault centres which provide 24-hour access to counselling and other support services for survivors. However, the tragic fact is that despite all the changes, women are still unlikely to report these crimes.

Findings from the Women's Safety Project indicate that for women aged 16 to 60, one out of two women has been the victim of rape or attempted rape, and one in three reported at least one experience of rape. Taking all kinds of sexual assault as defined in the *Criminal Code* into account (this includes sexual touching), two out of three women, well over half the female population, have experienced what is legally recognized as sexual assault. [6]

It is crucial to remember that the majority of sexual assaults are never reported to police. A Winnipeg study reported that approximately 90 percent of women did not report sexual assault;[7] a Canadian-wide survey indicates that 62 percent of female sexual assault victims did not report assaults to police. [8]

In the latter study, women gave the following reasons for non-reporting.

- 50 percent believed that police could not do anything about the assault.
- 44 percent were deterred by their concern about the attitude of both police and the courts to sexual assault.
- 33 percent feared another assault by the attacker. [9]

In another study, women indicated fear and shame in talking about the assault. [10]

The reality of sexual assault does not conform to the myth of rape or sexual abuse. Consequently, the description of a woman's abuse is often questioned by friends, family, doctors, police officers and the judicial system: You were there of your own free will weren't you? You should have expected something like this to happen. What did you think he wanted? The way you were dressed, the fact that you drank with him — those are all signs that you were asking for it! These are the messages women receive and they are often the messages they tell themselves.

The short and long-term effects of sexual assault include depression, anxiety, trouble with interpersonal relationships, reduced job effectiveness, diminished sexual satisfaction, sexual dysfunction, sleeplessness and sleep disorders, and increased use of sedatives and sleeping pills. The added fear of contracting AIDS as a result of sexual assault can also increase a survivor's trauma. One study found that "most rape victims report having feared for their lives during their attacks, and some women say they would *rather* die than be raped and live. For many women, to be raped is, in essence, to die. Some women have killed themselves after surviving rape attacks, and many other victims consider it." [11]

During consultations, a psychiatrist had this to say about the effect of sexual assault on women.

We all have a sense of invulnerability that allows us to get up in the morning and believe that bad things are not going to happen. That sense of invulnerability is destroyed after sexual assault; it's as though one is out in the world without a skin .... Loss of sense of safety, [and] increased fears are often misdiagnosed. Our basic assumption that if we do the right things in living, our lives will be OK is destroyed. Victims experience an absolute loss of trust in others and loss of sense of justice. Women's sense of self and sense of attachment are fractured. With that comes a profound loss of self-esteem and self-worth. Sexual violence violates the basic tenets of our being.

VICTIMS AND PERPETRATORS AS ACQUAINTANCES

ASSAULT IN DATING RELATIONSHIPS

All of this is hard for me to speak of because I was raped by my boyfriend when I was in first year [university]. Even now, knowing it was not my fault, it is more intellectual than believing it for sure. I found the Women's Centre a really safe place to talk about it. It really affected my school work. I had to drop some of my courses, ones his friends were in. He is still on campus and when I see him, he looks at me to intimidate me, and I am a wreck for a week ....

♀♀♀

I was raped by two of my drinking buddies in a small town up north, while my other three buddies watched. I did not do everything I could have to fight them, I did not bite the penises they stuck in my mouth ....

What we now know about the incidence of violence in dating relationships paints a shocking picture. In a research study that involved 304 Toronto high school students, one fifth of the young women interviewed stated that they had experienced at least one form of assault in a dating relationship. Sixty percent of the students said they had been exposed to violence in dating relationships, either directly as a victim or as an offender, indirectly as a witness or through hearing of violent acts in other relationships. [12] A recent study done with 246 university students revealed that 42.6 percent of the participants had physically abused a female partner, such as slapping her in the face. [13] A study of 308 male undergraduates in four Canadian universities found that 70 percent reported having engaged in at least one of 11 abusive acts during the calendar year preceding the study. [14]

PERPETRATORS AND VICTIMS AS INTIMATES

SEXUAL VIOLENCE

There are few statistics available on the incidence of sexual assault in marital or live-in relationships in Canada. Findings from the Women's Safety Project [15] reveal that the overwhelming majority of sexual assaults were perpetrated against women by men who were known to them.

- 81 percent of the sexual assaults at the level of forced or attempted forced sexual intercourse were perpetrated by men who were known to the women:

- 38 percent husband, common law partners or boyfriends;

- 31 percent dates and acquaintances; and

- 12 percent other relationships such as friends, authority figures, etc.

While forced sexual relations within such relationships have been illegal in Canada since 1983, few cases of marital sexual assault are reported to police. [16]

Both moral obligations and dependency in marriages and families are systemic barriers to women disclosing their experiences of sexual violence. At the same time, sexual violence in intimate relationships is clouded by the implicit and explicit assumption that women have a "duty" to perform any sexual act their partners desire, whenever they so desire. Some women spoke of being forced to have sex with others or forced to watch sexual performances. Other women relayed their experiences of being prostituted by their male partners or having their own sexual relations videotaped and recorded.

Sex became less like lovemaking and more like the expression of anger, it seemed to centre more around humiliation (mine) and power (his). I was sodomized on numerous occasions and forced to perform sexual acts which I considered degrading and disgusting, I have been "offered" sexually to other men, some of whom have been complete strangers, and pestered for eight solid years for swapping and all combinations of three and more way sex.

♀ ♀ ♀

He threatened me if I wouldn't have sex with him; physically assaulted me during sex; made me feel so uncomfortable or threatened that I felt I had to have sex; forced/intimidated me to participate in sexual acts that I felt were degrading; compared me unfavourably to other sexual partners; brought up my sexual past to hurt me; called me hurtful sexual names; accused me of seeing other men; insisted that I have sex with him after he had abused me; flaunted his affairs with other women; purposely neglected my sexual needs to hurt me; withheld sex/intimacy from me as a form of punishment; forced me to participate in sexual acts that caused me physical pain; threatened me with weapons during sex; accused me of having sex with someone else when I wouldn't have it with him; controlled whether or not I used contraception without regard to how I felt; used sex as a way to get me back or keep me in the relationship.

Media and myth continue to influence our perceptions and our understandings of sexual assault. Every day we are exposed through the media to violent portrayals of women as victims of sexual assault in all its forms. More often than not, the perpetrators are presented as strangers. The reality, however, is a different story. Sexual assault very often occurs in situations where women are presumed to be, and often presume themselves to be, risk free.

If we can accomplish one thing in our discussion of sexual assault, it is to impress upon women and upon the public that sexual assault is often perpetrated by someone with whom a woman has an ongoing relationship: a friend, a neighbour, the friend of a parent, a date, a co-worker. Such relationships must, in no way, detract from defining these acts of power and dominance as sexual assault.

Violence in intimate relationships between adult women and men may include one, all or a combination of the various dimensions of violence.

I looked for help since 1979. I didn't get help. I stayed because I needed money. I was never good enough for my husband. He said I wasn't a good mother. When I was ill he denied me care. I threatened suicide he didn't care, he turned over and went to sleep .... Mental violence is as bad as physical violence. Before I was married I used to laugh and smile but my husband told me to stop. He tells me I can't have friends. He won't take me out. He keeps all the money. He tells me I'm stupid, ugly. He told me not to go to my daughter's graduation. When I told him he never liked her, he just turned up the volume on the TV .... He kicked my oldest daughter. He strapped my son. His behind was black and blue .... He expected to use me sexually but not to be a lover. He was rough. He tried to rape me. I told him that. He said he could do what he wanted because I was his wife .... I went to work but you lose control, you have to give the money to your husband, do all the housework and care for the kids ... and get physically and emotionally abused ....

PSYCHOLOGICAL VIOLENCE

Violence in an intimate relationship often begins with verbal abuse. Such abuse may well start in a dating relationship and escalate long before the couple move in together or get married. It can entail derogatory remarks about the woman's intelligence, abilities, social skills, appearance, education, job, income, child-rearing practices or house-maintenance abilities. Any topic is fair game. The tone of verbal abuse is patronizing, loud, demeaning, degrading, insulting, vulgar and often threatening. Verbal abuse need not be delivered in a loud voice. It is understood. It can be said in a smooth tone: "If you leave, I'll have you locked up." Or sarcastically: "You'll never see the kids again." Verbal abuse is in fact a form of blackmail, its purpose being to scare and to ensure that the female victim fulfils the man's wishes so that he does not act on this threats. [17]

He would either force me to sit on a chair at the kitchen table or trap me in the office at work while he would scream at my face for hours while he would explain in vivid detail all the things he would do to hurt or disfigure me .... My very drunk and stoned husband sat my 12 year-old daughter down with the threat of a gun and explained to her that he hated me because I was a woman and all women were trash so he would have to kill me.

♀ ♀ ♀

I had to endure physical beatings, verbal abuse using strong, profane language and name calling on my street which all the neighbours could hear, phone calls at 2 in the morning, making death threats, having his friends call me up and threaten me, his business partner phoning and threatening to kidnap my son ....

In most instances verbal abuse does not happen in isolation, rather it accompanies one or a combination of other forms of violence. Its impact may not be immediately apparent but when prolonged and persistent it will eventually erode, and may even destroy the self-image and self-confidence of a woman. One woman related a chain of events set off by verbal abuse that eventually completely silenced her physically. She spoke of the long road back to conversation.

About six months after we were married, he told me never to talk unless it was important. I had no way of knowing what he considered important. So, I didn't say anything at all. After seven years of isolation, physical and emotional abuse, I became almost mute .... I gradually lost control of my vocal cords. After leaving [my husband], I decided to try to learn to speak again. I went to a full year of weekly speech therapy lessons.

The impact and often the intent of verbal abuse is extreme psychological torment and is a large part of the strategy of men to control women.

I guess I could best describe my husband as a control freak. He literally controlled every aspect of my existence such as what time we got up, the brand of shampoo we used, what time we went to bed, the food that was bought and not bought, where we went, what movies, plays and programs we watched or did not watch, who came into our house and who didn't, where I went, who I saw, talked to, didn't talk to ....

♀♀♀

He was hypercritical of everything I did, said or thought. Although this man would be hard pressed to put a meal on the table without assistance, he breathed down my neck as I cooked, questioning my every move, doubting me, continually eroding my self-confidence. The only time I drove our car was when I was alone; he was on me every second he was with me. I couldn't do anything right and the more he criticized me the clumsier and more inept I became ....

Such abuse has great power to induce fear in women because it is accompanied or followed by some form or threat of physical abuse. The abuse includes threats of harm to the woman, her parents or siblings, her children, friends, even pets. Some women spoke of being watched and monitored by their partners, having their mail read, having telephone conversations supervised and long-distance phone bills examined. Conversations with service people such as gas station attendants, delivery persons, maintenance people were often scrutinized and questioned. Generally the tone was accusatory.

It started on our honeymoon and it became obvious that my husband was an out-of-control violent alcoholic with drug problems. He was uncontrollably jealous. I was allowed no contact with my friends either in person or on the phone except my immediate family. Neither my daughter nor I was allowed any physical contact with anyone for any reason.

♀♀♀

He monitored my time and made me account for my whereabouts, would not give me enough money to meet needs, acted irresponsibly with family finances, denied me medical care, was jealous or suspicious of my friends, accused me of having affairs, kept me from seeing or talking to family/friends, restricted my use of the car, restricted use of the telephone, monitored mail/telephone calls, refused to respect my privacy, refused to allow me to work outside the home, accused me of being crazy, threatened to hurt my family, threatened to hurt me physically, did things on purpose to frighten me, deprived me of sleep, forced me to eat, harassed me while I was at work, threatened to destroy articles that are important to me, and did so.

PHYSICAL VIOLENCE

As indicated above, the power of the psychological dimension of abuse is compounded by its connection to both the threat and fact of physical violence.

I was chased through the home with a kettle of boiling water, I was hit squarely in the back of the head with a porcelain mug filled with freshly poured, scalding hot coffee, and by countless other flying objects. I have been cornered naked in a bathtub full of water and had my husband turn on the vacuum cleaner and "jokingly" threaten to throw the metal nozzle at me.

Physical abuse can begin at any point in the relationship, it can come completely out of the blue and can appear to be a totally isolated incident. The shock of the attack is overwhelming.

In the second month of our relationship, the first of a long string of assaults began. In the midst of an argument, my husband suddenly lost control and pushed me onto our bed. In a rage, he ripped the closet door off its moorings and literally flung it down on top of me. Then he jumped with all his weight on top of the closet door. I was immobilized and had difficulty breathing. He bit me very hard on the cheek just under my left eye. I was completely stunned by the incident. My first mistake was not putting on my coat immediately afterward and walking out at that very moment. What kind of person goes around biting people in the face? I just didn't know what to make of it. In a way I was embarrassed for him, to have seen him so apparently out of control ....

The devastating reality of physical violence is that it often begins with "minor" assaults such as a slap that likely would not result in any long-term physical injury or any signs that the abuse took place. But the tragic fact is that these incidents may be the precursor of increasingly violent actions that leave some women permanently paralyzed or with permanent or long-term impairments such as loss of vision, hearing and other motor skills. Some women survive murder attempts.

My ex-husband shot me through the head as I slept and left me for dead. I managed to walk downstairs where my daughter was calling for help .... My husband proceeded to stab me with such force that the knife-tip broke off in my intestines. He robbed me of my eyesight, my sense of taste and smell ... he robbed me of my family and my stepchildren ....

Other women do not survive.

Our daughter was killed in a sex murder .... He should have been stopped 10 years ago, when he wrote a letter threatening to kill his second wife. He was a volleyball coach. He preyed on young women, 16, 17 years old. He was 33 years old, and allowed back into the school system. His pattern of violence was getting worse, but no one stopped him. Our daughter was separated from him when she was killed. She decided she wanted out. She finally came to the realization of what a jerk he was, a liar, a thief, a conniver. She made arrangements for her sister to meet her at the airport — he showed up instead. He threatened suicide on many occasions. She had supported him. He quit his job. He raped her before he killed her, stabbed her to death. He says they made love. The truth will never come out in court.

Statistics indicate that on average two women were killed by their intimate partners every week in 1991. [18]

VIOLENCE AND PREGNANCY

The biological ability to bear children can leave women vulnerable to specific kinds of violence. During pregnancy and child rearing, the violence women encounter from their intimate partners differs from other more systemic forms of violence. Although the horror of violent attacks against women is not gradable, there is no question that physical attacks on pregnant women are particularly heinous. Studies reveal that most of the injuries sustained by pregnant women are to the face, breasts and abdomen. In one American study of 501 women, pregnant battered women experienced twice as many abdominal injuries as non-pregnant battered women. [19] Women with a history of abdominal injuries were more likely to experience pregnancy complications than other women. [20] For instance, women who are abused are twice as likely to have miscarriages as women who are not abused. [21]

As disturbing as such cases are, our consultations and existing research suggest that they are fairly frequent. In one Canadian study involving 200 battered women, 30 percent of the women were pregnant when assaulted and 40 percent of the women revealed an increase in the severity of the violence. [22] In another study by the London Family Court Clinic, approximately half of 90 women were pregnant when assaulted. [23]

Sometimes men's violence is linked to a profound jealousy of women's ability to give birth and of the presence of an interloper — a newborn baby — in a relationship. If violence against women is an expression of male power, intensified violence against pregnant women can be perceived as an attempt to exercise additional control in the face of the overt expression of female power that pregnancy provides.

Doctors need to be able to recognize the signs of abuse in pregnant women and know how to ask the right questions and how to respond to cases of abuse. Abuse of women continues to be misdiagnosed and under-reported because physicians fail to ask women appropriate questions. Many women are also reluctant to reveal the abuse.

THE FEAR OF DISCLOSING

Most women who face abuse in any of its forms, particularly in the context of intimate relationships, are afraid to speak about the violence. They are afraid to leave and they are afraid to stay. They are terrorized in the situation they face daily, but the terror of a life outside may be more overpowering. One woman described the apparent inevitability of her life.

While on my knees before him as he swung the poker down again and again so close to my head I could feel the wind from it on my face and hearing him say over and over "I could kill you, I could kill you," I envisioned my brains splashing forward onto the carpet. I willed him to do it, to end it all quickly, I waited on my knees for the blow that would set me free once and for all. I believed at that moment that this was my destiny, that the reason I had been placed on this Earth was to die at his hands and that his destiny was to kill me, that all roads led to here, to this particular moment.

To comprehend this notion of "destiny" and "inevitability," it is important to recognize the cumulative effects of abuse. The first incident appears as one isolated flare-up. Perhaps the second and third attacks might be attributed to stress or excessive alcohol consumption. Subsequent attacks might also be, in the eyes of the woman, explainable, understandable. Large gaps of time may pass between abusive incidents. The patterns that outsiders see as completely discernable, even predictable, easily escape the woman who lives with her tormentor on a daily basis. Once the pattern is in place, women feel ashamed to admit that a particular attack, perhaps one which is severe, is not the first episode they have faced. They are embarrassed to admit that this has happened before; that they have remained in a situation where they and their children are at risk.

It is probable too, that the abuse has included prolonged psychological attacks and threats that, undermine a woman's self-confidence, courage, self-esteem and volition. Very often the threats are acted upon. Over time a woman has been told, perhaps, that she is stupid, useless, incompetent, worthless. She has been threatened that if she discloses her experiences, no one will believe her; they will think she has lost her mind; they will always believe him over her. She has been told that she could not possibly support herself and her children; that her job skills are non-existent; that she is a terrible mother; that her children hate her; that people see her as worthless and hopeless. Her family and friends have been the subject of threats; he will get to them first and tell them that she is crazy; that she is addicted to pills and booze. She has been warned that he will hurt someone she loves and cares about; her mother, her sister, her best friend. She has been told that he will fight for, and be granted, custody of their children; that he will kidnap the children and she will never see them again; that he will hurt the children, if he has not already done so. She has been threatened with being committed to a mental institution; being deported; being cut off from her family and friends. She has been told that she will be financially strapped for the rest of her life; that he will not have to support her or their children; he will declare personal bankruptcy to avoid giving her any money; he can afford a better and more skilful lawyer who will ensure that he gets the best financial settlement. When we ask why women stay in violent situations we need to remember these realities. As one woman told us:

> *The real damage is to your understanding of yourself as a human being. I believed there was something fundamentally flawed, that I was missing something that other women who weren't being abused had.*

Unfortunately, some women who live with violence in their intimate relationships have a legacy of such experiences from their childhood.

It is tragic that much of the violence women encounter takes place within the context of what should be an intimate, caring and trusting relationship. Partner abuse, rape and date rape, incest and child abuse are all forms of violence perpetrated by an individual with whom the victim is connected intimately, either by marriage, through blood ties or through dating or live-in relationships. In situations where women expect trust, support, respect, compassion and love, some women experience violence, sometimes and indeed often, in all its various forms and dimensions.

The scope of woman abuse in intimate relationships is profound. A single abusive encounter or years of abuse takes a tremendous physical, emotional and psychological toll on a woman. Some recover through counselling and supportive intervention in their lives. Some do not. Some women die a violent death at the hands of their intimate partners.

CHILD ABUSE

Child abuse is slowly gaining recognition in Canada as the serious phenomenon that it is. It affects children from every economic, racial, cultural, religious and educational background, yet there is still resistance to addressing violence against children as a fundamental abuse of power and trust. Although not specifically included in the Panel's mandate, any discussion of violence against women must include an awareness of the amount of violence committed against girls, and the effects violence against women has on children. Similarly, child abuse cannot be discussed or understood without being placed in the context of a patriarchal system which promotes violence against women, children, people of colour, the elderly and all those without equal social power. Childhood sexual abuse affects the impact of violence experienced by adult women. Sexual violation as young girls can become the first link in a lifelong chain of violence for many women.

A 1990 report, *Reaching for Solutions* from the Special Advisor to the Minister of National Health and Welfare, listed 74 recommendations to the federal government for eliminating child sexual abuse in Canada. The report deals with the role the federal government must take in the recognition and prevention of child sexual abuse and acknowledges that "... social attitudes and values related to male and female sexuality ... condition males to be sexual predators and females to be sexual victims ... patriarchal society has set the conditions for sexual assaults and harassment, including the sexual abuse of children." [24]

Women who met with the Panel recounted their experiences of childhood victimization and emphasized childhood sexual abuse, incest, female genital mutilation and the impact of children witnessing violence against their mother, often committed by their own fathers. Further, the Panel felt it was vital to acknowledge and investigate the relationship between sexual abuse in childhood and the likelihood of revictimization as adult women, a link documented both statistically and in women's personal accounts.

SEXUAL ABUSE

The Women's Safety Project defines extrafamilial sexual abuse as:

... unwanted sexual experiences with persons unrelated by blood or marriage, ranging from attempted sexual touching (touching of breasts or genitals or attempts at touching) to sexual assault and rape or attempted sexual assault and rape, before the victim turned 16 years of age. [25]

Sexual abuse can also include other "sexually threatening" experiences, such as sexual propositions, being followed or chased, and having the abuser expose his genitals (flashing). [26] The prevalence of extrafamilial abuse is high. When the narrow definition is used, eliminating non-contact abuse such as "flashing" and sexual propositions, over one third (34%) of women in the Women's Safety Project survey reported at least one experience. [27] This finding is consistent with the results of other studies. [28] As over one

out of three women in the survey has experienced some form of sexual violation from a non-relative before the age of 16, the impact on women's lives cannot be ignored.

Extrafamilial sexual abuse is committed by strangers, but more frequently the perpetrator is known to the young girl. [29] The abuse of trust by caregivers, teachers, clergy, coaches and others with authority over children is unfortunately often aided by the very institutions in which they work. Schools and religious groups often encourage and demand awe, respect and obedience on the part of children toward those in authority. Until children are able to question and resist those with power over them, child sexual abuse by men in positions of trust will continue.

The effects of child sexual abuse on the victim can be long lasting and severe. Although trauma can vary depending on the experiences of the individual woman, every woman experiencing childhood sexual abuse is negatively affected in some way. [30]

We heard from many adult survivors who underscored the devastating impact of their childhood experiences.

A lack of trust holds me back from letting go of my emotions in a relationship. I can't seem to let my hair down and have fun. I never put myself in any situation where men may be. I don't really go out much. Because of these things I am looked upon as a snob, man-hater and boring person.

The Metropolitan Toronto Special Committee on Child Abuse indicated in its 1991 annual report that survivors are at increased risk for certain self-destructive behaviours and personality disorders. A survivor of child abuse is seven times more likely to become dependent on alcohol or drugs and 10 times more likely to attempt suicide than people who were not abused as children. The Committee also reported that 60 to 70 percent of runaways and 98 percent of child prostitutes have a history of child abuse. Eating disorders, such as bulimia and anorexia, are also associated with sexual abuse in childhood. [31]

INCEST

The Women's Safety Project defines incestuous abuse as "any kind of exploitative sexual contact or attempted sexual contact that occurred between relatives, no matter how distant the relationship, before the girl turned 16 years old." [32] The Women's Safety Project survey found that 17 percent of women in the study had had at least one experience of incestuous abuse before the age of 16. Most were abused by fathers, stepfathers and uncles. These men are also most likely to commit very intrusive abuse such as rape and attempted rape. [33]

Recognizing the prevalence of sexual abuse by family members means accepting that families are not sacred havens of safety for children, but places where the abusive power dynamics of the larger society are played out. Patriarchal social patterns and roles which define the family as inviolate private space and insist on the unquestioning obedience of children encourage incestuous abuse and make it difficult for abused children to be believed, let alone protected.

I believed in the greatest con of violence — the smile, the promise of love and trust and belonging ... the manipulation so that you accept the distorted view of reality ....

Traumatic results of incest include low self-esteem, feeling isolated or cut off from emotion, feeling powerless, obsessed with order or chaos, self-mutilation and suicide or suicide attempts. Incest survivors also report other effects shared with survivors of extrafamilial abuse, such as repressed memories of the abuse, drug and alcohol addictions, eating disorders, difficulties around sexuality and dissociating — leaving their bodies during moments that trigger the trauma of the original abuse. [34]

I was in and out of the hospital for depression, and no one asked me the right questions and I had blocked it. I was sexually abused by my father from age 4 until he killed himself when I was 16 .... Everyone thinks that professional families are cosy, and no one will say anything about what is really happening.

An association in the United States known as the "False Memory Syndrome Foundation," acting as an advocacy group for families of survivors, alleges that therapists "plant" stories of incest, sexual abuse and ritual abuse in their clients. [35] Once the far reaching after-effects of incest, such as suppressed memories, are understood, it becomes clear that the complicated arguments about false memory act as a smoke screen which protects those who don't want to believe what seems too horrible to be true — that fathers, stepfathers, brothers, uncles and grandfathers can and do rape little girls.

Denial of sexual abuse is not a new phenomenon. From the time of Freud, the issue of false memory has been raised to discredit the reality of the experiences women reported. Although Freud at first believed the experiences of sexual abuse his clients reported, under pressure from colleagues and his own denial, he later categorized their testimonies as "fantasy." It is clear now that Freud was working with sexual abuse survivors and not "delusional women."

The many courageous survivors who came to speak to the Panel expressed an urgent need for help and justice. The energy survivors are now using to make themselves believed is energy which should be used in their healing.

Current research indicates that multiple personality disorder (MPD), [36] a state where the personality becomes fractured into a range of personalities as a mechanism for coping with abuse, is almost always associated with severe childhood abuse trauma, particularly sexual abuse. Signs of the disorder include gaps in short-term memory, headaches, rapid mood, speech and behaviour changes, and hearing voices inside the head. MPD allows the survivor to cope with childhood trauma by blocking it from memory, but the repercussions of the disorder can cause confusion and fear when survivors find themselves in situations without knowing how they got there. Survivors with MPD are often accused of lying because they cannot remember previous events. Healing involves the painful process of recovering, exploring memories and feelings held by the distinct personalities and integrating these experiences. Women told us of their challenges around multiple personality disorder.

I am an incest survivor. I was 18 months old when my father and two grandfathers started abusing me. I have multiple personalities and split memories. No one identified me as being an abuse victim or even as ill until a few years ago. Yet I had chronic pain and mental depression for years .... The hospitals and the church knew I was an incest victim. A hospital which knew of his sexual abuse of me sent him back to our family and left us with him ....

Survivors also develop coping mechanisms. Although they grow out of the negative experience of sexual violation, these coping mechanisms can become positive sources of strength, such as using humour and developing a sensitivity to hypocrisy and insincerity. [37]

FEMALE GENITAL MUTILATION

One form of child sexual abuse often mentioned in the Panel consultations was female genital mutilation. A "traditional" practice performed on young girls between the ages of 8 weeks and 14 years, it is widely practised in many African countries, in Oman, South Yemen, the United Arab Emirates and in some parts of Indonesia, Malaysia and India. [38] Some forms of genital mutilation are practised in Europe, Australia, the United States and Canada among people who have migrated from countries where the practice continues.

The term "female circumcision," widely used to describe genital mutilation, is misleading since it suggests similarity between male circumcision and female genital mutilation. There are no similarities. The term "mutilation" more accurately describes the three procedures involved.

- Clitoridectomy/Circumcision: the removal of the prepuce of the clitoris, or the clitoral hood, preserving the clitoris itself and the posterior larger parts of the labia minora.

- Excision (reduction): the removal of the prepuce and the glans of the clitoris together with adjacent parts of the labia majora and without the closure of the vulva.

- Infibulation: the cutting of the clitoris, labia minora and much of the labia majora. This is followed by stitching together the two remaining sides of the vulva to close up the vagina, leaving only a minuscule opening to allow urinary and menstrual flow. Slivers of wood are used to prevent the vagina from sealing fully.

Genital mutilation creates immediate and long-term health risks for women. Immediate effects include shock, infection, failure to heal, septicemia (blood poisoning), tetanus, injury to adjoining organs, hemorrhage and urine retention. Long-term consequences include scarring, vulva dermoid cysts and abscesses, acute and chronic pelvic inflammatory disease, infertility, urinary tract infections, difficulty with urination and difficulty in expelling menstrual flow.

The World Health Organization has consistently and unequivocally advised that such practices should be banned and that no health care workers should perform such practices in any setting and under any circumstances. In Canada, female genital mutilation is recognized as a form of child sexual abuse. In 1992, the Department of Justice declared that a person who performed such practices could be charged with assault causing bodily harm. Parents can be charged with being parties to the offence and if they fail to seek medical treatment for the child, they can be charged with criminal negligence causing bodily harm.

Female genital mutilation is a brutal expression of patriarchy and patriarchal power. The practice of genital mutilation is designed to ensure the chastity and "purity" of young women and ultimately, this practice identifies women as property: property to be exchanged and protected so that its market value is not impaired. Apart from the severe and life-threatening side effects, genital mutilation also denies women access to their own sexuality and to the enjoyment of sexual expression by robbing them of the physiological means to do so.

CHILD WITNESSING OF WOMAN ABUSE

When children witness their mothers being abused they often experience profound psychological effects. Child witnessing is common: in one Quebec study of abused women, three quarters of the women's children were present for episodes of battering. Many of them experienced verbal abuse during the violence against their mothers. [39]

One of the earliest experiences I remember is sleeping with my mother, and being thrown out of the bed against the wall while my mother was raped. That's how she had every one of us. I felt that the abuse was my fault, if I only did things better...

Children react to witnessing the abuse of their mothers in a variety of ways. Low self-esteem, anxiety, poor performance in school, running away, guilt and feeling responsible are all common reactions. Some children, especially boys, begin to take part in the physical and psychological abuse of their mothers. [40] By internalizing and normalizing the experience of violence, especially male violence against women, these children may be far more likely to engage in violent behaviour themselves and to accept violence as a way of dealing with conflict. They are more likely to subscribe to dominating systems of gender relations, confining sex roles and to view men as powerful and violent, and women as passive victims. [41] An automatic correlation between viewing violence as a young child and becoming violent as an adult does not exist. While patriarchal social roles and support for male exploitation of power results in some boys becoming abusers as adults, [42] girls seldom if ever become abusers, regardless of their childhood experiences. [43] As always, it is important to recognize that the individual and social factors which precipitate violence are not excuses. Every abusive man must take personal responsibility for his violence. The violent man who tries to keep his spouse in the relationship by playing on her sympathy for his own abusive childhood is an all too common story. By no means does every boy growing up in a violent home become an abuser. [44] Clearly, the witnessing of woman abuse by children is a powerful tool in reinforcing already overwhelming patriarchal norms of male dominance, female submission and the use of violence.

REVICTIMIZATION

Revictimization is a term used to describe the statistical finding that women who have been sexually abused as children are more likely to experience victimization again as adults. The Woman's Safety Project shows that a link does exist between childhood and adult experiences of sexual violence. [45]

Multiple abuse in childhood results in women being more severely revictimized as adult women than women who were abused only once as children. There is also a relationship between the "severity" or level of intrusiveness of the childhood abuse and the risk of revictimization. These findings are consistent with results from other studies. [46]

The Women's Safety Project found that regardless of a woman's abuse history, she is at risk of a rape or attempted rape, simply because of the high prevalence rates.

- 50 percent of women have experienced sexual assault at the level of rape or attempted rape. [47]

However, the statistics which look at the relationship between an experience of childhood rape and of adult rape — excluding all rape attempts that were successfully resisted — show that an experience of child sexual abuse at the level of rape affects a woman's chances of being raped again as an adult woman.

- 69 percent of the women who were raped in childhood were also sexually assaulted at the level of rape after the age of 16 years compared with 46 percent of the women in the sample survey who were never raped in childhood. [48]

Children who are sexually violated use various methods of coping and resisting. Mental resistance includes dissociating — leaving the body, going numb or blacking out. Survivors who have been violated at the level of rape as children may use these same strategies during an adult experience of rape. These survival skills are testimonies to their incredible strength of will and courage. However, they are methods of protection which will not stop a rapist from carrying out his intention.

It is impossible to explain all the links between childhood sexual abuse and revictimization as adult women. While we can categorically reject any analysis that attempts to lay blame on women victims and survivors, and casts them as "abuse magnets" or as seeking out abusive relationships, we cannot readily provide alternatives based solely on statistics. Only the experiences of women who have lived these violent cycles can say what they really mean.

In light of the increased awareness of sexual abuse against boys, theories are being expounded which attempt to link male sexual abuse of children to their own abuse histories. While it is possible to see how experience of sexual abuse in childhood would reinforce male social conditioning, a strict cause and effect relationship cannot be established, either statistically or theoretically. All men who abuse children are directly and personally responsible for their actions.

We say that men who abuse must have been abused. If that were the case, [women] would all be rapists.

Revictimization, is a phenomenon brought about by male sexual violence against women. It is important to keep this in perspective at all times. Women who were sexually violated as girls must be helped to protect themselves from revictimization. However, ultimately women should not have the responsibility of having to "protect" themselves, responsibility must fall to men to stop their violence. The way to end revictimization is to end sexual violence.

CHAPTER 3

VIOLENCE IN THE CONTEXT OF SETTINGS

To understand the complexity of violence against women, it is important to look at the setting in which it occurs. Many of the forms of violence described in the previous section occur in settings such as schools, hospitals, parks, stores, construction sites, restaurants, etc. Characteristics of a setting shape and reinforce power relationships. These processes in turn, have the potential to foster abuse. The following section focuses on one such setting: the workplace.

WORKPLACE

In a society where work plays a fundamental role in human interaction and where work occupies the largest portion of our waking hours, unsatisfactory, unsafe and threatening work situations have a critical impact on individuals.

In the span of human history, women's presence in the paid labour force is relatively short. In recent years, however, there has been a veritable revolution, and by January 1991, 60 percent of women over 15 years of age were involved in paid employment in Canada. These figures translate into a paid labour force that is approximately 45 percent female. [49]

While women are increasing their representation in the labour force, the workplace environment is still the outcome of a historical process from which women have been largely excluded. Consequently, policies and practices have been established both independent of women's input and ignorant of women's experiences. These conditions breed an atmosphere which is ripe for abuse of women.

Because workplaces vary — women work in their own homes, in the homes of others, in offices, shops, factories, etc. — some women are more vulnerable to violence at work. Women told us of workplaces where they were the targets of direct and personal violence including verbal, physical and sexual harassment, assault and psychological abuse.

... a friend in Winnipeg, an apprentice machinist ... worked night shift with a lead hand who regularly gave her assignments like the one she told me about "to machine a chrome diameter." She spent hours trying — and failing — to do what he asked. She only discovered what was going on in this case when a friend (male) overheard the lead hand laughing over what he had done. You can't machine a chrome diameter, you can only grind it. But she didn't know that. After three years of such treatment, she quit the trade. She is now a self-taught carpenter.

In a variety of incidents, women told us of being forced to behave in ways which stereotyped them as "stupid" or which objectified and demeaned them.

A woman working in a Prince Albert card shop who had to wear a promotional button saying "I Guarantee It" was dismissed when she refused to continue wearing the button because it invited sexual comments from male customers. By forcing the woman to wear the button, her employer was asking her to tolerate sexual harassment as a term and condition of her employment.

In traditionally male-dominated occupations, women work in a male culture as foreign as any overseas country, that has a different language, a different set of values and a different measure of success and failure. [50]

Among the most important facets of workplace violence is the fear of reprisal and loss of job if the abuse is challenged either informally or through institutionalized reporting mechanisms where these exist.

HARASSMENT

Sexual Harassment and Poisoned Atmosphere: Although sexual harassment is a relatively new field of study, it is the form of workplace violence with which most Canadians are familiar. One difficulty with the concept is the many ways in which it may be defined. This leads to confusion and inconsistency in discussions of sexual harassment.

Regardless of the form it takes, sexual harassment sends out a clear message: women are tolerated in the job market only because men are willing to do so, but men feel their real place is elsewhere. What is more, if they do not want to be excluded or cast out from that market, they must obey the implicit rules, the unwritten codes, that follow from historical practices. [51]

Consequently, all women at some point in their lives are likely to experience sexual harassment. In a recent review, complaints fell into two categories: quid pro quo scenarios where something is demanded in return for something else and hostile work environments or "a poisoned atmosphere," where the harassment is more insidious and may not necessarily be directed at an individual woman. [52] A hostile work environment is created by repeated, unwelcome, harassing behaviour. Examples include leering or suggestive looks, sexual remarks, teasing or insults and the posting of pin-up calendars or centrefolds.

A review of case law in Canada reveals that successful judgments have dealt primarily with cases of quid pro quo sexual harassment where a woman has been refused employment, had benefits withheld, been dismissed or forced to resign because she rejected sexual advances. [53]

A recent Supreme Court decision (*Janzen v Platy Enterprises*, 1989) expands the notion of quid pro quo harassment. In this particular case, two women who worked as waitresses complained that the restaurant cook was "continually pawing them and made lewd comments regarding them." In its ruling, the Court established that victims of this type of harassment do not have to prove that they were fired or denied benefits as a consequence of their failure to take part in sexual activities. The Court ruled that quid pro quo sexual harassment can also be understood as having taken place in situations where employees are subject to uncalled-for gestures and propositions or comments of a sexual nature, whether or not they are threatened with loss of economic or employment benefits. [54] However, a recent judgment of the court of Quebec could be decisive in the recognition of poisoned environment as quid pro quo. The facts of the case are fairly simple. A high school teacher filed a com-

plaint of sexual harassment against a colleague in the same school alleging that he displayed a sexist, vulgar and uncalled-for attitude when she was in the teachers' room at the same time as him. The colleague promptly responded by bringing an action for defamatory libel in the Court of Quebec. Rendering judgment in that matter, the judge recognized that there were enough facts and indications to find that the atmosphere that the man in question created in the staff room could constitute sexual harassment. [55]

For the most part, hostile atmosphere harassment, the more insidious of the two, is still addressed only incidently in cases where quid pro quo harassment is the major issue. Often women feel uncomfortable, maligned or alienated as a result of this atmosphere.

Other Forms of Harassment: There have been only very marginal adaptations of the workplace to ensure the physical and secure well-being of people with disabilities. Women with disabilities are at an increased risk of physical injury and overall, their life situation places them at greater risk for workplace violence. Women of colour and immigrant women are often positioned in the labour market under very difficult conditions which severely limit their financial security and expose them to racist and sexist harassment.

VIOLENCE IN DIFFERENT WORKPLACES

The concentration of women in service industries helps to explain their increased exposure to workplace violence. [56]

Nursing: In the summer of 1990 the British Columbia Nurses Union commissioned a telephone survey of 505 members randomly selected from its membership. Its findings indicated that during the five years before the survey, 72.3 percent of the nurses had been abused or threatened. Among the 365 who experienced violent episodes, the most common types of physical abuse were grabbing (83.3%), hitting (78.9%) and kicking (62.5%). Some nurses were verbally assaulted, threatened with violence, mentally or sexually harassed. [57]

I am a survivor of abuse, like many people in the helping professions. Violence against nurses is not recognized as a problem of workplace violence. The hospital said it couldn't put in safety features because of the cost. Nothing is available for the emotional health of workers. It's taken as part of the job if you want to work ....

In a study done by the New Brunswick Nurses Union in 1990, patients were found to be the primary perpetrators of abuse against nurses. [58]

In a more recent survey of Saskatchewan nurses, similar patterns emerged: 81 percent reported verbal abuse, 54 percent physical abuse and approximately 39 percent said they had been sexually harassed. Almost 75 percent reported abuse from patients, about 53 percent from physicians and 42 percent reported abuse from patients' families or friends. [59]

Education: Schools and universities are also experiencing increased levels of violence, teachers and students alike. Many schools in Canada are establishing policies around the issue of violence and the presence and use of weapons in schools. Women students in particular experience hostility, exclusion and sexist remarks and attitudes from male professors, students and administrators. They are also subject to certain "traditions," particularly in engineering faculties, that are based on sexist and misogynist beliefs about women. As more recent studies indicate, professors have interpreted challenges to sexism in education as infringements of their academic freedom, an attitude that silences women and perpetuates a poisoned atmosphere. [60]

Domestic Work: As discussed later, foreign domestic workers report that their workplaces, generally the homes of fairly well-to-do Canadian couples, can be violent. The legislation under which such women come to Canada places them in an extremely vulnerable situation. At times they may be virtual prisoners of their employers, held captive by threats of deportation or other legal actions.

Prostitution: Women working in the sex trade face forms of violence and degrees of risk that are specific to their own workplace and to the nature of working relationships with pimps or dance club owners.

While some might argue that there is an element of choice involved in the decision to enter prostitution, the choice is made within a limited set of options and often in the context of extreme pressure, threats of physical violence and lack of a support system. A woman does not simply wake up one day and decide to be a prostitute. An identifiable pattern in a chain of events leads her there. The social system has utterly failed many women.

I have met a woman who worked as a prostitute because she was trained in it from an early age. When she was 7, an old man next door molested her. When she was 10 her father came into her bedroom at night. By the time she was 15 her older brother and all of his friends had access to her bedroom too. And then we wonder why we have a problem in our culture with prostitution and we wonder what to do about it.

Almost all young women who end up in prostitution were attempting to escape abusive homes. Some may have been placed in foster-care situations where sexual abuse is considerably higher than in non-foster homes, an experience that simply compounds the abuse they have already endured. [61] Once on the street they are incredibly vulnerable to the attention they may receive from pimps or boyfriends who begin the "courtship" with support, gifts and attention. Once indebted, they are required to "pay back" their debts through prostitution.

Once the pattern is established, pimps control the young women by denying or restricting their access to money, monitoring their social contacts and physically, psychologically and sexually abusing them, thereby maintaining them in a completely dependent and susceptible relationship.

A girl was trying to buy out of her relationship with her pimp for $500. He picked her up in broad daylight and started smashing her face into his car but stopped because she was messing his car. He continued, using a pole. He brought her back to the shelter before 10:30 so she wouldn't miss curfew and so she could work the next night.

Women working as prostitutes are subject to extreme physical and sexual abuse by "johns" who feel that the monetary exchange actually buys them a body to do with what they will. Violent attacks may include theft, beatings, mutilation, strangling, the use of weapons, acting out dangerous sexual fantasies and murder. And the social perception of prostitutes as castoffs and throwaways often leaves them more vulnerable to abuse and lack of protection from police officers. In some cases, law enforcement officers expect and demand sexual favours in exchange for protection or leniency in charging procedures.

The fact that women enter prostitution as a means of economic survival speaks volumes about the nature of women's inequality in Canadian society. Prostitution thrives in a society that lacks real economic equality, and promotes the treatment of women as possessions or chattels. In the short term, women working in the sex trade need safe working conditions and arrangements. In the long term, the goals must be to provide the means to achieve equality and create real choices for women and to build a society in which men would find it unthinkable to buy a woman's body for sex.

CHAPTER 4

UNDER-ACKNOWLEDGED FORMS OF VIOLENCE

Some forms of violence merit special attention because so often women are not believed when they describe their experiences in these areas. They have nowhere to turn to for support and very few services exist to respond to their needs properly. Ritual abuse, stalking, pornography and abuse of power and misuse of reproductive technologies are forms of violence that almost defy understanding or solutions. As in all forms described in this report, the violence inherent in these activities is committed precisely because of women's gender and overall unequal status in society. It is about the desire to gain power and control over another human being. There is a particular urgency to address these problems.

RITUAL ABUSE

We do not know the full dimensions of ritual abuse in this country. We do not know all the dynamics involved, the international connections or relationships between different regions and different cults. The Panel did, however, hear from many women from all regions of Canada who named themselves as survivors of ritual abuse. Through their compelling testimony, a phenomenon of violence was detailed that urgently requires recognition in Canada.

Ritual abuse is defined as a combination of severe physical, sexual, psychological and spiritual abuse used systematically and in combination with symbols, ceremonies and/or group activities that have a religious, magical or supernatural connotation. Victims are terrorized into silence by repetitive abuse over time and indoctrinated into the beliefs and practices of the cult or group. [62]

There are no statistics on ritual abuse in Canada. There is an overwhelming inclination on the part of many people to deny the experiences of those who have survived ritual abuse. This is not surprising given the hideous nature of these crimes.

> Disbelief protects people from their own fears, disgust, horrors and often their own memories and realities. And it stops them from listening. When a violent, gruesome movie or television show attracts millions of viewers, this is considered normal behaviour, yet when survivors of ritual abuse speak out about having survived torture, ... repeated rapes, and of witnessing ritual murder, we are told it's not possible, that we must be either lying or crazy. [63]

It has taken 20 years of concerted effort by women's groups and by survivors of abuse, incest and rape to make people aware of the prevalence of violence against women. It appears that it will, unfortunately, take time to convince people of the reality of the atrocities committed by ritual abusers. There is a clear parallel between the long-standing disbelief of sexual abuse survivors and the present disbelief of ritual abuse survivors.

The costs of society's denial and tolerance of ritual abuse have been very high for its victims. Some have paid with their lives. Others are consumed by their struggle to survive, as they attempt to deal with flashbacks of the tortuous abuse they experienced and the very real fear of injury and death from dangerous perpetrators. Active cult members threaten and harm survivors in a multitude of ways, including triggering programming induced when the survivor was a child.

This was a generational cult that is linked and connected throughout the country. They use programming and brainwashing. I recently met a member from the past. She said two words to me and all I knew is that I felt like killing somebody. Cults are big business. They're involved with drugs, child porn, "snuff" movies and white slavery. It's hard to recall what happened and who is involved because you're fragmented into so many parts that you don't remember. I'm still trying to find out what they did to my head. It's different than other forms of sexual abuse, and nobody knows how to treat it. I live in fear. As long as I live dissociated, I live fine. But sometimes I'm frightened of the other parts of myself. Some of the people that did this to me are still alive and still in my life .... I'm dealing with great guilt because of some of the things I was made to do. It makes me so angry. A cousin warned me to stay away. He had changed his identity. You don't know how big it is. My real parents were murdered .... It makes me feel so helpless. I was involved in snuff movies and child porn.

The specifics may vary from group to group but usually there are four basic components to the indoctrination process of ritual abuse. Survivors told the Panel of intergenerational and extrafamilial cases where adults or older teenagers had regular and trusted access to young children. Initially the cult interferes with and eventually breaks the natural bond of a family and replaces it with a bonding to the cult or group through a range of techniques, often with the co-operation of the family.

My ritual abuse began when I was 7 or 8. I was told I would be physically harmed if I spoke of the abuse. I was not raised as human. I saw one girl being sacrificed, my age, and my mother was the one cutting up her insides. I was forced to sacrifice her and I felt I was torturing her just to save myself. I held parts of the body as it was being cut up. A cross was inserted into my vagina at these ceremonies, making me ready for a higher position. I have memories of unexplainable intense emotion, getting strong feelings of getting sick, psychosomatic bruises, pain, not being able to breathe, marks on my body. We moved 18 times by the time I was 16. I spent most of my time in and out of hospitals. Types of abuse that were done to me included molestation, forced intercourse, sodomy, group sex with adults, being photographed, breeding a child for later sacrifice, being forced to sacrifice a girl, cannibalism.

In the second stage, the victim is forced to take part in the abuse of others. Victims come to learn that their survival depends on their acceptance by the group and that acceptance depends on their participation in cult activities.

Survivors said they were required to take vows and oaths of secrecy, sometimes signing a commitment or some form of contract. Among small children, their signature may in fact be a bloodied handprint on a document.

The final step in the indoctrination process is the use of mind-control techniques such as hypnosis, mind-altering drugs or the implantation of messages triggered to prevent victims from disclosing their abuse. Other techniques establish dissociative behaviours which make it difficult for survivors to recall and subsequently talk about the abuse they endured. Mind control is accomplished through long-term and repeated use of torture, pain and deprivation of the young victim. [64] Perpetrators use threats and violence in attempts to ensure the silence of survivors.

As a result of ritual abuse, children have no ability to bond with those outside the cult or group; over time they learn that their safety lies in identifying completely with their abusers and distrusting all others. They grow up with very low self-esteem, frequently have difficulty with common social bonding and interaction skills, are withdrawn and have deep-seated feelings of guilt and shame. One of the most difficult things for survivors to do is come to terms with and disclose their abuse.

The profits from ritual abuse activities are reported to be extensive. Repeatedly the Panel heard of filming or videotaping of the abuse and of survivors recalling experiences of child prostitution. Other illegal activities frequently mentioned included drug trafficking.

The courage of the survivors of ritual abuse who came to meet with Panel members must be remarked upon. Most are threatened with death should they disclose their abuse, and many have seen those who threaten them murder others; the fear is real.

Women paid a high price for disclosing; one was clear she would have to go to bed for a few days to recover from the trauma of telling us her experiences. Some found they had to communicate with the Panel by tape or through a different personality to cope with the threats and to escape the intense programming that still holds them captive.

For others there has been ongoing harassment by cult members. Some have had to leave their homes and sever all ties with their communities to take up an unenviable existence living "underground."

Not only survivors of ritual abuse but their therapists as well have been the targets of organized efforts to discount the experiences of violence. Incredibly, there are those who assert that survivors' memories are false, and some go on to charge that therapists are deliberately planting false details into the psyche of patients. It was clear from the experiences related by survivors who came to speak with the Panel that they have been further injured by encountering disbelief and denial.

As with all survivors of abuse, the strength of the human spirit is remarkable. Ritual abuse survivors talked to the Panel about the flashbacks they lived with, as well as their coping mechanisms which often overpowered the most sophisticated of programming techniques used by the cult. Most used coping techniques to "ground" themselves or help themselves return to the present from flashbacks. Some described the ways in which they had to cope with the ignorance of medical staff if they were hospitalized and were refused whatever they needed in trying to cope with triggers or to ground themselves in the present — often with something like a cigarette or cup of tea that "was against the rules." Some were put at risk of self injury as a result.

Among the ritual abuse survivors the Panel met were women with many diverse experiences. Some said they were struggling with multiplicity; all had found it extremely difficult to find any useful therapeutic help. Many had painful stories of all the unhelpful therapy and medical treatment they had endured while trying to cope at the same time with the impacts of the knowledge of the abuse they had endured.

Therapeutic responses to survivors of ritual abuse have been limited in not only their effectiveness but in their very existence, because therapists are not taught about ritual abuse in their training. The treatment of multiplicity is necessarily long term. Only very recently has a preliminary Canadian study found that the most extreme forms of multiplicity can not only be distinguished from less complex forms but their treatment can be differentiated as taking longer, with a completion time of around six years. This is an important insight. Deprogramming techniques that are reported to be successful are being used with cult survivors in both Canada and the United States.

There is no specific recognition of the crimes associated with ritual abuse in the Criminal Code and very limited levels of understanding by law enforcement officers, legal practitioners and adjudicators. It is not surprising then, that prosecution of these crimes is also very limited and rarely successful. In the meantime, the safety of women and children from perpetrators of ritual abuse is dangerously limited, and survivors of ritual abuse do not, therefore, enjoy the equal benefit and protection of the law.

Doctors, counsellors and therapists working with ritual abuse survivors also must deal with discrediting, denial and disbelief from the medical profession and their own professional communities. This can affect their clients and patients in a number of ways. For example, one of the few therapists in this field might reluctantly stop working with survivors because of burnout, the impossible conditions of practice or the closure of a service.

Survivors of ritual abuse continue to pay a high price for the disbelief they encounter. Without recognition and support it will be impossible for many to come to terms with their experiences. Adding further pain to those who have already been so injured seems at odds with any notion of a just or a more equitable society.

STALKING/CRIMINAL HARASSMENT

Stalking is persistent, malicious, unwanted surveillance, and survivors believe that there is nothing they can do to stop it. Stalking is considered by many as the most potentially lethal of crimes in the area of woman abuse. [65]

If a woman feels her safety is in jeopardy, it should be recognized by the police as serious, that she be treated as deserving of protection, and that, where at all possible, charges be laid against the abuser. There must be a law against threatening.

♀ ♀ ♀

After a few weeks of rest at my parents' place with my child, I broke out of that hell and made the final decision not to go back and live with my torturer. Then he blew up against my parents, the child and me.

He started harassing me night and day over the telephone.

When I started my courses at the university and was in a very weak state again (I even had to have my books carried by someone else), he constantly followed me and harassed me: in the parking lot, where he waited for me, at the snack bar, in the library. One evening, he forced me into his car and took me somewhere, I don't know where. I was terrorized. In the early hours of the morning, when we were headed toward the [North Shore], I begged him to turn around and, in the end, he took me home. The next day, I had an exam and failed it. Then he stole the papers concerning the legal proceedings I had started to get custody of my child. I had to be accompanied by someone for a number of months when I went to or left the university.

My baby had to have physiotherapy sessions twice a week; my husband went with me. He stole my keys, my handbag, my personal papers, locked up the baby for long periods, and enjoyed seeing me worry about the screams of the child, who was exhausted after the physio session.

One day, when I went out for a walk to relax, he followed me, and I had to return home. He then threatened me, saying that, no matter what the court's verdict might be, he would make sure he got justice, that he would find a way to go on legal aid and would fight back until I died, that he would never leave me in peace.

In the winter of 1991, he tripped me on a ski hill, and I almost skied off into the woods. Then he fled. Shortly afterward, when I was talking to a ski patroller, he went into a terrible fit of jealousy and threatened to punch us both out if he saw us together again.

Throughout Canada, women are followed, battered and killed, often by men who stalk their victims like hunters stalk prey. Stalking is an invasion of a woman's personal security. A stalker may begin by phoning and harassing a woman; he may send her letters, call her place of work, call her friends and family, follow her to work, follow her home, taunt and torment her. In some instances, these "nuisance" behaviours end in the death of the woman.

Many women who spoke to the Panel described the fear they experienced as a result of continual harassment or being stalked. Their stalkers were usually known to them — ex-husbands or ex-boyfriends, but sometimes the perpetrator was a complete stranger.

Until very recently, stalking per se was not considered a crime in Canada. The Criminal Code prohibited certain types of harassment, including loitering and prowling near a person's home at night, indecent and harassing phone calls, persistently following someone, and "watching and besetting" any place the person happens to be. [66] But until something physically happened to a woman, she had little recourse to the law for protection. Survivors reported that both police and judges are reluctant to take them seriously.

In June 1993, in an effort to increase the protection offered to women, the federal government passed a law creating a new offence of criminal harassment to deal with stalking. Under the new legislation, criminal harassment will now be legally recognized to include:

- persistently following someone;
- spending extended periods of time watching someone's home or place of work;
- making harassing telephone calls to someone and/or to his or her friends;
- making contact with someone's neighbours or co-workers; and
- contacting and threatening someone's companion or spouse.

We are encouraged by this initiative. It sends a clear message that the behaviour of men who stalk women is criminal and will not be tolerated. It also recognizes women's rights to personal security and to the freedom of living their lives without fear. It must, however, be part of a more comprehensive and better co-ordinated response to meet the needs of survivors.

PORNOGRAPHY

The word pornography comes from two Greek words: "porne", meaning whore and "graphos", meaning writing about or drawing. Pornography's essential message is that all females are whores by nature and whores, by definition, exist for sexual use. Pornography's version of reality is that women love to be raped, deserve to be beaten and exist only to serve male sexual desires — indeed, that women are inferior and naturally subordinate to men. Pornography says that women enjoy humiliation and pain. [67]

Much debate surrounds both the definition of pornography and its relationship to violence against women. Since the 1960s, there has been a steady increase in the availability of pornography in Canada. Material once available only in the form of photographs or magazines bought under the counter at a few outlets in the sleazier districts of major cities is now found in corner stores and video rental shops virtually every

where in the country. The mildly explicit adult magazines such as *Esquire* and *Playboy* of the early years have been overcome by a flood of imitators whose content has become more sexually overt and violent as competition increases.

Satellite dishes and computer modems bring porn movies and "compusex" into homes that are otherwise accessible only by plane and boat. [68]

Adult videos have become more and more widely distributed and are currently responsible for a substantial share of business sales. "In Quebec, the pornography industry generates nearly $300 million in declared income alone, much of which goes to the government. In 12 years, the profits of this industry in North America have risen from $5 million to $5 billion. Pornography, prostitution, the drug trade and organized crime together make up the largest industry in the world in monetary terms. The issue is more one of freedom of trade than freedom of expression." [69]

Telephone sex services are also available to a wide audience. All these technologies know no financial or national boundaries, can be reached from almost anywhere and are available to viewers of all ages. [70]

Since the late 1970s, Canadian feminists have been working toward recognition of this strong link between pornography and violence, harm and degradation of women and children. On the other hand, civil libertarians and some arts groups view anti-pornography arguments as censorship and defend the existence of pornography on the basis of freedom of speech. In the words of one researcher:

We are also suspected of violating freedom of expression when we denounce the exploitation of women in pornography. But whose freedom of expression are we talking about? Are we violating freedom of expression when we denounce sexism in advertising and educational materials? Do I have the right to express freely my contempt and anger toward a person by abusing that person? [71]

Despite the ongoing, and at times lively debates, there is general agreement among feminists that pornographic materials can be distinguished from erotica by examining the issue of power. The intent of both is the sexual arousal of the consumer or reader. Erotica portrays or describes people in situations of mutual respect and pleasure to achieve this effect; pornography relies on the depiction of domination and unequal power relationships through the degradation and humiliation of human beings, generally women and children.

Strict causal relationships between pornography and violence against women may be difficult to determine, but there is growing evidence that makes the link. In a study of 30 residents of a shelter for assaulted women, 17 described pornography used by their partners and 37 percent reported some kind of abuse experience with pornography. The abuses described by these women ranged from being verbally abused for not performing the way women performed in the pictures, to being forced, sometimes tied up, so that their spouses could engage in sexual activity the pornography advertised. The pornography depicted the full range of sexually explicit materials, from Playboy to violent pornography. [72] An Alberta study included two groups, a control group of 38 women in non-abusive relationships and a group of 27 women currently or previously involved in abusive relationships. Of the control group only five of the respondents' partners were heavy users (several or more times a month) of pornographic magazines and none were heavy users of videos. Of the other group, 13 were heavy users of written pornography and 10 were heavy users of both written and pornographic videos. [73]

All heavy users of both written and video porn in the Alberta study were also abusers of their female partners. Of the heavy users of pornography, 14 asked their female partners to replicate acts seen in pornography; 12 pressured their

female partners to replicate acts; seven threatened female partners to compel them to replicate acts seen in pornography; six were physically forced to perform them; 21 pressured their female partners to have sex when they did not want to; 21 physically forced their female partners to have sex when they did not want to; 22 expected their partners to be sexually available at all times; and 10 compared their female partners to pornography models. [74]

In our own consultations we heard of instances where pornography played a significant role in the abuse women encountered.

My husband is also a great consumer and proponent of pornography. As a psychology professor he teaches students that there is no correlation between the consumption of pornography and the commission of violent or sexually degrading acts. Outside the classroom, however, and in the privacy of our home, I saw again and again how my husband mimicked with me what he saw in pornographic magazines and films. I believe in retrospect that the early beatings I received were sexual in nature and because they were committed in the so-called throes of passion or under the guise of uncontrollable male arousal, I did not even recognize the fact that I had been beaten.

♀♀♀

Pornography was involved in sex. I was tied up, handcuffed, blindfolded and gagged as my husband looked at porn .... I was numb ....

♀♀♀

When women tell you stories of their abuse, they very frequently mention being compelled to go to "adult" movies, being forced to perform sex acts described in pornographic magazines or being verbally and physically abused because they were "fat cows" who didn't look as sexy as the porn models, or didn't perform the acts in as fantastic a way.

A male abuser told us that pornography had a direct impact on his perceptions of women and subsequently, on his actions.

My exposure to and use of pornography both in my growing-up years and later while spending years in prison definitely promoted an attitude of dehumanizing opinions toward women. Women were seen as a sub-human vehicle to use in promoting sexual gratification. Pornography use became both compulsive and addictive especially in an institutional setting. Upon release from prison [where I was] for a crime of a non-sexual nature, I committed sexual crimes for which I was rearrested and re-incarcerated back in a prison setting. Pornography for me helped promote and reinforce selfish sexist attitudes and experiences against women.

In a study suggesting that the majority of consumers of pornography are young males between the ages of 12 and 17 years, 35 percent of the young people surveyed said they liked watching sexually violent scenes such as rape, torture and bondage. [75] For many young people, pornography is sex education.

There is very little published material on the role of racism in pornography, or on the links between pornography and racism. Yet in magazines and videos, women of colour are often featured as "exotic." Mainstream men's magazines such as Playboy and Penthouse frequently publish photo features which degrade women of colour and feed and build upon ideas perhaps already existing in the mind of the viewer. [76]

However, we are somewhat encouraged by the results of a recent Canadian poll on the sale of sex magazines: a total of 55 percent of respondents felt such magazines discriminate against women, and 56 percent oppose the sales of such magazines. [77]

Debates about the casual relationship between pornography and violence against women will likely rage on for years. In our research we have found information that both refutes and confirms the relationship. However, in many ways we see these debates as missing the point. Whether pornography leads directly to acts of real violence, it still degrades women, atomizes them into pieces of a sexual puzzle and depicts them in subservient and demeaning poses and positions.

In the recent Butler decision, the Supreme Court of Canada recognized the harm done to women by pornography. This decision is referred to in our discussion of the legal system.

Pornography can be seen as a product of a certain kind of society — one where it is considered acceptable to portray women and children as sexual objects for the mass consumption of men. Such images encourage men to perceive women and children as less than whole human beings.

ABUSE OF TRUST

Abuse of power or breach of trust is a form of sexual violence and exploitation which involves the abuser's profound betrayal of trust placed in him by those who come to him for assistance. It is a very misunderstood form of violence, as many people are not aware of the power imbalances inherent in most professional/client relationships. The formal structure of most "helping" institutions supports unequal power distribution. Those who do not recognize and work to eliminate the incredible power professionals hold over those using their services, are tolerating and encouraging violence. Perpetrators of breach of trust can be anyone who holds a position of responsibility and expertise, often protected and encouraged by a hierarchical institutional structure. A person is in a position of trust, or a trust relationship exists, when that person has a special role, status or knowledge, which confers elevated levels of power or authority on him. Common individual perpetrators are psychiatrists and therapists, doctors, teachers and coaches, spiritual leaders, lawyers and police officers. The institutions which support the professions most commonly involved in abuse of trust cases, breach the contract of trust which they have made with the public both before and after an offence is committed. By not carefully screening their members, not working to prevent abuses before they occur and not adequately addressing cases of abuse after they've happened, churches, bar associations, hospitals and police forces fail to provide the adequate and respectful service which is their responsibility. Although boys and men can be sexually violated and exploited by those in trust positions as with every other form of sexual violence, the vast majority of offenders are men and those at risk of violence are women.

I was staff counsellor for... During that time the leader of the organization was having sex with almost every female client that came to us for counselling. The six women with whom I worked, including myself, would also work with these women after they had seen the "Boss." It was a very damaging situation. These women would have to work on the fact that this man was not really interested in them as a lover, or in even having a long- or short-term affair...they were simply being used by him... They came to him for help and they ended up with more problems.

Doctors, psychiatrists, lawyers, are all individuals to whom we turn when we are in a crisis, and feel unable to manage a situation on our own. A hierarchical relationship is established from the outset, with the abuser being in the position of powerful "expert" and the victim in the position of dependent "laywoman." In a case of armed robbery, the gun plainly in sight, the power of the robber and the lack of power of the victim to resist handing over her valuables is evident. In a case of abuse of trust, the "gun" is just as present. However, it is hidden behind a badge, a diploma or a title. The power imbalance at the core of many of our day-to-day relationships with professionals is hidden. This means that abuse of trust offences are sometimes mistakenly seen as consensual. However, the presence of the "hidden gun" of knowledge, power and authority, combined with the usually vulnerable state of the victim, means that the victim is not in a position

where she can freely give her consent. Because there is no clear overpowering with force, women who become victims in abuse of trust cases often feel guilty, for "allowing" the abuse to happen. The actual form of the assault may vary: "seduction," one-time abuse, progressive abuse or role-reversal where the abuser places his client in a position where she must support him through personal problems. Abusers may also try to perpetuate this illusion of a mutually consensual love affair, often framed in such a way to ensure the guilt and silence of the woman: "If you talk about it, people will not understand the true love that unites us," or "I may lose my license to practice medicine and we will no longer be able to see each other." The importance of secrecy is enormous and places increased pressure on the victim. A typical scenario might entail the physician, religious advisor, therapist, lawyer, etc., offering comfort to the client, followed by increasingly greater intimacy, followed by sexual contact.

He chose to hurt me at a time when I was particularly vulnerable. I stopped seeing that psychiatrist, and I didn't see another for about 10 years. Then I started consulting a woman psychiatrist, who asked me, "Aren't you, by any chance, imagining these things?" [78]

There is little sense of public accountability in many professional institutions. Most are self-regulated, and investigations are conducted within the body of the institution. It is not a comforting thought for a young victim of a teacher's molestation to realize that in order to bring her abuser to justice, she must convince his co-workers and colleagues, who all hold the same authority over her as her abuser, that he is guilty. A victim is similarly discouraged from bringing forward a complaint against a police officer, when she knows the investigation will be carried out by fellow officers.

There are several recognized cases in Canada where institutions allowed repeated and brutal abuse by professionals to continue unchecked. The survivors of residential schools, the young women of Grandview, the men of Mount Cashel orphanage for boys, and hundreds of other lesser known cases are all examples of breach of trust through tolerance of violence by Canadian regulatory institutions.

Abuse of power and breach of trust are difficult concepts to grasp. The entire structure of society, and of the institutions which hold our trust, protects and fosters the sexual exploitation of women by men in positions of power. The culturally defined image of men such as priests, teachers, coaches, police and doctors — seen as the ultimate "good guys," makes it difficult for a woman to realize that what is happening to her is not a "tragic love affair" or "her imagination," but a brutal betrayal of faith she placed in someone she was taught to believe would help her. When the regulatory bodies do not try to prevent abuse and are uncaring, disrespectful or hostile to women making complaints, they compound an already traumatic experience and show their lack of concern for the public served. There is no excuse for an authority/expert figure to cross the line by turning a helping relationship into a sexual one. It is not an attempt at closeness. It is not an "accident." It is not a form of "therapy." It is sexual exploitation and abuse, and must not be tolerated.

REPRODUCTIVE TECHNOLOGIES

There is growing debate from the feminist perspective on the range of issues concerning reproductive technologies. Where once women's health and interests were subordinated to and controlled by dominant male medical practitioners and practices, today reproductive technology presents new and perhaps even more pervasive threats to women and their autonomy; women now have even less control over procreation than in the past. [79] The fear is that the humiliation and pain that women have endured in relation to child bearing will increase with the advent of new and relatively untested reproductive technologies.

The federal government established a royal commission to study the benefits and risks associated with these technologies. It is our hope that careful consideration will be given to the human and social costs of reproductive technologies including the potential for further jeopardizing women's freedom of reproductive choice.

Endnotes

1   Maria Crawford and Rosemary Gartner, *Woman Killing: Intimate Femicide in Ontario 1974-1990* (Toronto: Women We Honour Action Committee), p. 27.

2   Lori Haskell and Melanie Randall, *The Women's Safety Project: A Community-Based Study of Sexual Violence in Women's Lives* (Toronto: self-published, 1993). See Appendix A.

3   Dianne Kinnon, *Sexual Assault* (fact sheet prepared for the Canadian Panel on Violence Against Women, Ottawa, 1993), p. 13.

4   Marilyn Pilon, *The "Rape Shield" Decision: Evidence in Sexual Assault Cases* (Ottawa, Library of Parliament Research Branch, September 20, 1991), pp. 1-5.

5   *Bill C-49: An Act to amend the Criminal Code (sexual assault)*, (Ottawa: Government of Canada, June 15, 1992).

6   Lori Haskell and Melanie Randall, *The Women's Safety Project, op. cit.*

7   Julie Brickman and John Briere, "Incidence of Rape and Sexual Assault in an Urban Canadian Population," *International Journal of Women's Studies*, 7:3 (May/June 1984), pp. 195-206.

8   Solicitor General Canada, *Canadian Urban Victimization Survey, Bulletin 4: Female Victims of Crime* (Ottawa, 1985), p. 3.

9   *Ibid.*, p. 4.

10   Jillian Ridington, *Beating the "Odds": Violence and Women with Disabilities* (DisAbled Women's Network Canada, March 1989), p. 14.

11   Margaret T. Gordon and Stephanie Riger, *The Female Fear* (New York: The Free Press, 1989), p. 9.

12   Shirley Litch Mercer, *Not A Pretty Picture: An Exploratory Study of Violence Against Women in High School Dating Relationships* (Toronto, 1987), pp. 6-7.

13   Line Robitaille and Francine Lavoie, "Les relations de couples des jeunes et de la violence: une étude exploratoire," *Les Cahiers de recherche de l'école de psychologie* (Montreal: Université Laval, January 1992), p. 3.

14   Walter S. DeKeseredy, "Woman Abuse in Dating Relationships: An Exploratory Study," *Atlantis*, 14:2 (Spring 1989): pp. 55-62.

15   Lori Haskell and Melanie Randall, *Women's Safety Project, op. cit.*

16   Department of Justice Canada, Research Section, *Sexual Assault Legislation in Canada: An Evaluation: Overview (report no. 5)* (Ottawa, 1990), pp. 44-45.

17   Diane Prud'Homme with the collaboratioan of l'équipe de la maison d'hébergement La Bouée régionale du Lac-Mégantic, *La violence conjugale ... C'est quoi au juste? C'est un moyen pour un homme de contrôler sa conjointe.* (Montreal: Regroupement provincial des maisons d'hébergement et de transition pour femmes victimes de violence conjugale, Spring 1990), p. 16.

18   Canadian Centre for Justice Statistics, *Homicide Survey, Policing Services Program* (Ottawa: October 1992), Table 17.

19   A. Berenson et al., "Drug Abuse and Other Risk Factors for Physical Abuse in Pregnancy Among White Non-Hispanic, Black and Hispanic Women," as cited in Barbara Lent, "Obstetrical issues in wife abuse," *The Canadian Journal of Obstetrics/Gynaecology & Women's Health Care*, 4:5 (1992), pp. 330-333.

20   T. Goodwin and M. Breen, "Pregnancy outcome and fetomaternal haemorrhage after noncatastrophic trauma," as cited in Barbara Lent, "Obstetrical issues in wife abuse," *ibid.*, pp. 330-333.

21   E. Stark, et al., "Wife abuse in the medical setting: an introduction for health personnel." *Domestic Violence Monograph* (April 1991), *ibid.*, pp. 330-333.

22   Battered Women's Advocacy Clinic, London, Ontario, as cited in Barbara Lent, "Obstetrical issues in wife abuse," *op. cit.*, pp. 330-333.

23   Peter Jaffe, *Wife Assault as a Crime: The Perspectives of Victims and Police Officers on a Charging Policy in London, Ontario from 1980-1990*, as cited in Barbara Lent, "Obstetrical issues in wife abuse," *ibid.*, pp. 330-333.

24   Rix Rogers, *Reaching for Solutions: the Summary Report of the Special Advisor to the Minister of National Health and Welfare on Child Sexual Abuse in Canada* (Ottawa: Minister of Supply and Services, 1990), p. 9.

25   Lori Haskell and Melanie Randall, *The Women's Safety Project, op. cit.*

26   *Ibid.*

27   *Ibid.*

28   Robin F. Badgley, *Sexual Offences Against Children*, vol. 1 and 2 (Ottawa: Minister of Supply and Services Canada, 1984) and Diana Russell, *The Secret Trauma: Incest in the Lives of Girls and Women* (New York: Basic Books, 1986).

29   Lori Haskell and Melanie Randall, Women's Safety Project, *op. cit.*, Table 3.5.2 "Relationship of Extrafamilial Perpetrators by What Kind of Sexual Abuse."

30   Lori Haskell and Melanie Randall, *The Women's Safety Project, op. cit.* and Ellen Bass and Laura Davis, *The Courage to Heal: A Guide for Women Survivors of Child Sexual Abuse* (New York: Harper & Row, 1988).

31 The Metropolitan Toronto Special Committee on Child Abuse, *1991 Annual Report* (Toronto: The Metropolitan Toronto Special Committee on Child Abuse, 1991), p. 2.

32 Lori Haskell and Melanie Randall, *The Women's Safety Project, op. cit.*

33 *Ibid.*, Table 3.5.1 "Relationship of Incestuous Perpetrators by What Kind of Sexual Abuse."

34 Ellen Bass and Laura Davis, *The Courage to Heal, op. cit.*, pp. 33, 36-38, 42-45, 48-54.

35 Leslie Bennets, "Nightmares on Main Street," *Vanity Fair*, June 1993, p. 48.

36 Some survivors prefer the term multiple personality adaptation or multiplexity to better recognize that it is a testimonial to their survival of the abuse.

37 Ellen Bass and Laura Davis, *The Courage to Heal, op. cit.*, pp. 46-47.

38 First Workshop on Female Genital Mutilation, Women's Health in Women's Hands, October 1992, Toronto.

39 S. Kerouac, M.E. Taggart and J. Lescop, *Portrait de la santé des femmes violentées et de leurs enfants* (Montreal: Université de Montréal, Faculté des sciences infirmières, 1986).

40 Peter Jaffe, D.A. Wolfe and S.K. Wilson, *Children of Battered Women* (Newbury Park, California: Sage Publications, 1990), pp. 21-25.

41 Ginette Larouche, *Agir contre la violence* (Montreal: La pleine lune, 1987).

42 Peter Jaffe, D.A. Wolfe and S.K. Wilson, *Children of Battered Women, op. cit.*, p. 22.

43 For example, more than 93 percent of charges related to conjugal violence in Ontario are brought against men. Most of those laid against women are counter-charges brought about by their abusive spouses, or are the result of action taken in self-defence. Solicitor General of Ontario, *Law Enforcement Activity in Relation to Spousal Assault in Ontario for the years 1986 and 1987,* as cited in Ontario Women's Directorate, *Wife Assault: Dispelling the Myths.*

44 Statistics on boys from homes where male violence was witnessed who grow up to be abusers are inconsistent. They range as high as 60 percent of boys becoming abusers in adult life (Education Wife Assault, *Fact Sheet on Wife Assault in Canada* [Toronto: Education Wife Assault, 1985], to only 12 percent (Deborah Sinclair, *Understanding Wife Assault: A Training Manual for Counsellors and Advocates* [Toronto: 1985].

45 Lori Haskell and Melanie Randall, *The Women's Safety Project, op. ci.*

46 Diana Russell, *The Secret Trauma, op. cit.*

47 Lori Haskell and Melanie Randall, *The Women's Safety Project, op. cit.*, Table 4.2.2, "Prevalence of Sexual Assault, Definitions Compared."

48 *Ibid .*

49 Statistics Canada, *The Daily,* March 2, 1993, p. 2.

50 K. Braid, Director of Labour Programs at Simon Fraser University, British Columbia (Submission to the Canadian Panel on Violence Against Women, Ottawa, 1992).

51 L'intersyndicale des femmes, "La violence faite aux femmes dans les milieux de travail" (Paper presented to the Panel on Violence Against Women, Quebec, 1992), p. 18.

52 Monique Gauvin and Ann Robinson, "Sexual Harassment" (Paper prepared for the Canadian Panel on Violence Against Women, 1993), pp. 4-5.

53 M. Drapeau, as cited in M. Gauvin and A. Robinson, *ibid.*, p. 5.

54 *Ibid.*, p. 4.

55 *Ibid.*, p. 5.

56 L'intersyndicale des femmes, "La violence faite aux femmes," *op.cit.*, p. 20.

57 British Columbia Nurses' Union, *Survey On Violence* (British Columbia, February 1991), p. 13.

58 New Brunswick Nurses Union (Presentation to the Panel on Violence Against Women, March 4, 1992).

59 Saskatchewan Nurses survey: Perkul, Lynda Kushnir, "Nurse Abuse in Saskatchewan: Sticks and Stones May Break My Bones, But Names Can Never Hurt Me," as cited in Marg Ommanney, "Nurses Often Abused, Study Shows," *The Star Phoenix* [Saskatoon], April 15, 1993, p. A3.

60 Huguette Dagenais, "Au-delà du principe, la réalité : Problèmes spécifiques rencontrés par les femmes dans l'exercice de la liberté universitaire," as cited in Monique Gauvin and Ann Robinson, "Sexual Harassment," p. 19.

61 Dawson, as cited in Anna Pellat, *Juvenile Prostitution: A Consideration of the Child Welfare Response* (Edmonton - Legislative Planning, 1988), p. 5.

62 Daniela Coates, "Ritual Abuse," (Research paper prepared for the Canadian Panel on Violence Against Women, July 1992).

63 Gail Fisher-Taylor, "Ritual Abuse: Towards A Feminist Understanding" (No journal or other reference cited), p. 36.

64 Daniela Coates, "Ritual Abuse and Multiplexity," (Unpublished manuscript, 1992).

65 Paula Todd, "Victims of Love," *Homemaker's*, Jan/Feb 1993, pp. 19-21.

66 *Ibid.*, p. 16.

67 Resources Against Pornography (Submission prepared for the Canadian Panel on Violence Against Women, Toronto, March 24, 1992), p. 1.

68 Jillian Ridington, "Pornography" (Research paper prepared for the Canadian Panel on Violence Against Women, 1993).

69 Micheline Carrier, *La Pornographie: base idéologique de l'oppression des femmes* (Sillery, Québec: Apostrophe 1, 1983), p. 63.

70 Jillian Ridington, *op. cit.*

71 Micheline Carrier, *La Danse Macabre: violence et pornographie* (Sillery, Quebec, Apostrophe 3, 1984), p. 55.

72 Susan Cole, "Pornography and Harm" (Prepared for the Metro Action Committee on Public Violence Against Women and Children, November 1987), p. 41.

73 Alberta Coalition Against Pornography, *Pornography: Links to Violence Against Women* (Submission to the Canadian Panel on Violence Against Women, February 18, 1992), p. 4.

74 *Ibid.*, pp. 4-5.

75 J. Check, *Curriculum Development Research Needs Assessment: Attitudes and Behaviour Regarding Pornography and Sexual Coercion in Metropolitan Toronto High School Students,* as cited in Ontario Women's Directorate, *Sexual Assault: Pornography: The Links* (Toronto, November 1990), p. 1.

76 Jillian Ridington, "Pornography," *op. cit.*, p. 23.

77 "Majority Oppose Adult Magazines Gallup Poll Shows" *Toronto Star*, April 25, 1993, p. A13.

78 Independent Task Force commissioned by the College of Physicians and Surgeons of Ontario, *The Final Report of the Task Force on the Sexual Abuse of Patients* (Toronto: November 25, 1991), p. 21.

79 Monique Bégin and Lise Martin, "Espoirs et dangers: les femmes contemplent l'avenir de la reproduction: Institut Canadien de Recherches sur les Femmes, *Femmes et technologies de procréation: outils de recherches* (Ottawa: Institut Canadien de Recherches sur les Femmes, October 1989), p. 2, 66.

PART THREE

EXPERIENCING VIOLENCE ~

POPULATIONS

INTRODUCTION

The discussions of the prevalence and the forms of violence in this report detail the breadth, complexity and intensity of women's experiences of violence. All women are vulnerable to male violence; all women fear it at some level, are potential victims and suffer pain when struck or when verbally and psychologically tortured; all women look for ways to explain or understand what is happening to them; and all women want to be safe. Surely it is their right.

But some women are more vulnerable than others. The degree of their exposure to violence is dictated not only by their individual circumstances but by broader factors including their class, culture, race, colour of skin, sexual orientation, physical and mental abilities, education, age, where they live, language and literacy levels. However, although such characteristics affect the intensity and degree of a woman's vulnerability to violence, they do not alter the conditions common to all women. It is not the "human" condition, rather it is the "woman" condition.

There are three factors underlying women's specific vulnerability:

- the widespread acceptance in our society of the subordination of women to men and the subordination of some women to other women;

- women's dependence on men and male systems; and

- isolation (physical, psychological and social) from the mainstream.

Within the hierarchy of a patriarchal society, the subordination of women renders them susceptible to violence everywhere: the home, the workplace, the streets and all public places, cities, rural areas and at the hands of family, institutions and service providers.

Women's dependence on men and male systems is economic, either through individual control, through inequities in the workplace, or through a controlling and dead-end social service system; psychological, through societal pressure to link up with a man, any man; and physical, such as the dependence of women with disabilities on their caregivers or women from another culture and language who must rely on their husbands to communicate with the outside.

The third common factor, isolation, sets the scene for abuse of all forms. The isolation can be physical, social or psychological.

The following discussion focuses on how these three major issues, which influence the vulnerability of all women, are intensified by the circumstances of individual populations. It would be false to assume that all women are equally at risk. A subset of a patriarchy is a further hierarchy among women. Although few women have complete access to power within Canadian society, some women face more barriers than others. For example, the relatively stronger social position of a well-educated, white, affluent daughter or mother may not protect her from male violence but it will certainly increase her chances of being believed if she seeks help. A police officer may be more likely to urge her to press charges if he believes that, as the victim, she will make an articulate, credible witness in court. On the flip side, an immigrant domestic worker who speaks little English or French is less likely to be believed by police or judges. This is not an assumption; unfortunately, this is a reality.

For the purposes of discussion, we have grouped the specific populations as follows: older women, women living in poverty including women with low literacy skills, women with disabilities, rural women, lesbians, women of official language minorities, women of colour, young women and immigrant and refugee women and domestic workers.

The grouping of certain categories of women together does not suggest that they are homogenous, with exactly the same characteristics, problems and needs, but they do share certain barriers to equality and particular vulnerabilities to violence. Although the focus of this chapter is on violence and its relationship to individual populations, the discussion is relevant to all women. Their diversities are subsumed in the commonality of all women's experiences.

CHAPTER 5

OLDER WOMEN

Society has a disdain for older women, thinks we are parasites ... listens to us "with a grain of salt."

INTRODUCTION

In 1991 there were approximately 1.84 million women over the age of 65 and 1.22 million women between the ages of 55 and 64 living in Canada. [1] It is a population prone to abuse. Elder abuse is not gender neutral; older women are the main victims of violence. As many as one in 10 elderly people experience abuse [2] and, according to the Ontario Advisory Council on Senior Citizens, at least two out of three victims are women. [3] Other anecdotal sources give a higher estimate. Family members constitute the most significant source of abuse, accounting for 79 percent of cases. Approximately 34 percent of the perpetrators are the children of the women being abused, and approximately 23 percent are the spouses; 22 percent are other family members including in-laws, grandchildren, etc. Landlords (predominantly owners of private senior citizens' homes) and professionals (mostly those working in private residences or institutions) are the next most prevalent source of abuse of elderly women. [4]

BIAS STEMMING FROM WOMEN'S SUBORDINATION IN SOCIETY

"Ageism," the discrimination against and the devaluating of older people, especially women, is inherent in our society and culture. The media's message is that old is ugly, young is beautiful and that women's value is based largely on their beauty. Discrimination against older women in the workplace goes unchecked in a society that does little to empower or integrate them. Forty seven percent of women over the age of 65 who live alone live in poverty, despite government benefits. [5] And those women living with husbands or partners generally are dependent on the man's income or pension.

Divorced or separated women 55 to 65 years of age are particularly vulnerable to poverty. This in turn makes them vulnerable to abuse. Their age places them in limbo. If they are not working in the paid labour force, they are considered too old to find work and, because they are too young for the Canada Pension or Old Age Security, many end up on welfare. A society that has perpetuated images of women as family supporters rather than income earners has severely limited the economic alternatives of this group of women. While their home skills are indeed valuable, they are not perceived as such in the paid labour market.

DEPENDENCE

Abuse of older women has been called "wife battering grown old," by some researchers.

The survivor was married for 50 years to a verbally abusive man who expressed controlling behaviour toward the family and had sole control of the finances. He attempted to hit her on many occasions, and did strike her when she was older. The husband developed dementia in his later years, and all his negative characteristics came to the fore. He couldn't control his temper. On one occasion, he pushed her to the floor, resulting in permanent injury to a weak hip. She now has a pin in her hip and arthritis. He would not help her get up and denied pushing her. He would also deny his verbal abuse .... The husband went away on business trips and left no money behind .... She never knew where she stood with him; he could adopt a "pleasing attitude" so the abuse was not obvious to others. He treated his son and daughter differently: his son could do no wrong, his daughter no right. There is intense pressure on women to give care. "You resent it, but you do it ...." The attitude professionals took to the survivor's situation was, "How could she abandon him, when she's put up with it for so long?"

Senior women are particularly vulnerable to physical and psychological abuse, active neglect [6] and financial exploitation. Physical abuse may include the unnecessary use of restraints, forced feeding and overmedication in addition to the more "traditional" forms of physical abuse. Psychological abuse involves inappropriate control of activities, the removal of the right to make decisions when the woman is still able to do so, isolation and confinement.

Abuse of older women in institutions can include all forms of violence. Owners of institutions sometimes take their money, providing little in return. Women are verbally abused by attendants and physicians, they are overmedicated, actively neglected and under-stimulated intellectually and socially. Moreover, their almost complete powerlessness in institutional settings leaves them highly vulnerable to sexual and physical abuse.

Major barriers to overcoming abuse of elderly women are poverty and the fear of it. Lack of money equals lack of control over their own lives. Financial abuse can entail withholding money or possessions through fraud, trickery or force. Sometimes elderly women are persuaded that they are no longer capable of managing their own affairs, and are intimidated into turning over control of their finances to the abuser. Caregivers and family members may coerce older women into signing over property and other material wealth in "exchange" for caregiving, perhaps by threatening to place them in an institution if they don't. In essence, these women are robbed and then cast aside.

Those women who are both physically and financially dependent on their caregivers — whether in homes of relatives or friends or in institutions — are particularly vulnerable. The very dependence of one person on another for such basic human needs as food and personal hygiene can create a breeding ground for abuse. And for a woman who is poor or if her finances are controlled by someone else, there is no escape.

ISOLATION

The social and economic isolation of older women leaves them highly vulnerable to all forms of violence, an isolation that also cloaks the abuse in secrecy. Older women do not tell of their experience for many reasons. They may be physically, financially or emotionally dependent on their caregivers; they may be afraid of retaliation; they may hope the person will change; and, in the case of abusive children, they may keep silent out of a feeling of responsibility for the child or a sense of shame over their child's actions.

Certain groups of older women, such as immigrant women who are often linguistically, culturally and socially isolated, are especially vulnerable. These women are blocked from seeking help from outside by the language barrier and by their cultural norms.

Depression among immigrant seniors is high .... [They] are afraid or unable to go out, don't speak the language; unlike at home, they have nothing to do once the grandchildren are grown; the role of the family changes so they are no longer respected.

CONCLUSION

The unequal status of older women in our society must be addressed. Our culture must integrate elderly people into our communities in a way that respects their input and roles, eliminates poverty and discrimination and does not exploit women, the traditional caretakers of elderly people.

CHAPTER 6

WOMEN LIVING IN POVERTY

Poverty is bound up with violence. This means that social programs must be top budget priorities, especially ones that meet the most fundamental needs — food, housing, health care, local economic development ....

♀♀♀

I am a single mother with four children. My husband made only two support payments. One of my children is allergic to milk. On social assistance, I couldn't afford formula but I bought it at the expense of my other children.

INTRODUCTION

Violence thrives on, but is not unique to, poverty. The ferocious impact of violence on poor women is intensified because of the extra level of suffering; poverty is abusive in itself. It is also a condition that recognizes few population boundaries. Poverty can imperil all women — women of colour, immigrant and refugee women, domestic workers, young, middle-aged and old women, women with disabilities, able women, women of all linguistic minorities, rural and urban women, lesbians and heterosexual women.

Systemic discrimination against poor people can also lead to unfair treatment. This is apparent in the legal system.

- Legal aid funding, which has always been low, is being cut back.

- Lawyers who accept legal aid cases are overworked and underpaid. This affects the quality of their work.

- Complaints about violence which originate from public-housing complexes are answered much more slowly than those originating from middle-class neighbourhoods.

- In determining child custody, the judiciary equates the best interests of children with income, and women's economic status is usually lower than men's following separation. [7]

I'm a small-town girl who married someone and was with him for 11 years. I left him three times. You're fighting at every step of the way. I have nothing good to say about the legal system. Nothing is explained to you, nothing is shown to you, nothing is given to you at all. I don't like the term "domestic violence" because it takes away from exactly what happens to you. It's assault. I left with three children, a suitcase, $20 and a box of Tide. It took a long time to get financial support. The process you have to go through is humiliating: welfare, the legal system.

BIAS STEMMING FROM WOMEN'S SUBORDINATION IN SOCIETY

Women are more likely to be poorer than are men by virtue of their gender. Between 1971 and 1986, the number of women living in poverty increased by 110 percent compared with a 24 percent increase during the same period in the number of men living in poverty. [8] By 1989, 60 percent of the 2.5 million Canadians living in poverty were women. [9]

The percentages from the labour force are as dismal: 67 percent of all minimum wage earners are women, and 72 percent of the part-time labour force, where the average hourly wage is less than $7.00 with no benefits, are women. Women with the same education and skills as men performing similar work are paid anywhere from $6,000 to $10,000 less per year than men. [10]

This trend of increasing numbers of poor women in Canada has been described as the feminization of poverty. "Poverty among women is the result of a number of injustices directed towards women, including discrimination and inequalities which persist in our society. These inequalities are often accentuated, especially during tough economic times ...." [11]

Single women account for approximately 40 percent of all poor women. Lone parent women are in the very worst economic position. [12] Those between 16 and 24 years of age have almost no chance of being financially secure. A full 81 percent of these young women had income below the poverty line in 1987. [13]

> *After enduring 27 years of abuse, I am forced to live on $10,000 annually, I have severe health problems caused by the abuse and the four years of the court process, and I am often depressed and sometimes suicidal. When I tried to get a divorce, 21 court dates were set and my ex-husband hired and fired four lawyers in a four-year period. The divorce was finally granted in 1990 but the division of assets is still pending. The equity in the farm property has decreased due to the length of the litigation, and employment opportunities are limited for women over 50 years of age .... My husband has a high paying job, lives in a home of his own while I reside in a small apartment and may need to apply for social assistance.*

Homeless women are among the poorest of the poor, and there are many in Canada although exact numbers are difficult to estimate. We do know that in 1991, in one Toronto district alone, there were about 20,000 people living on the streets, in parks and hostels, many of whom were women. [14] According to workers in shelters for homeless women, the majority of these women have been victims of incest, sexual or physical abuse. "Shelters and the street can sometimes be a welcome alternative to the fear they feel at home." [15] On the streets, they are easy targets for further assault. [16]

> *Mental health facilities have dumped ex-residents into the downtown areas without adequate housing and support leaving them easy victims to attack and without resources to tell their stories, never mind to avoid the next assault.*

Rural women, many of whom rely on agriculture, fishing, tourism and part-time employment, are subject to poverty. The recession, the new unemployment insurance guidelines and a crisis in the fishing industry are "resulting in skyrocketing rates of poverty." [17]

Despite government assistance, older women are vulnerable to poverty because, having spent less time in the paid work force, these women receive far less assistance than their male counterparts.

In 1986, 74 percent of women with disabilities reported an annual income below the poverty line of $11,000. [18] This holds despite the fact that disabled women need more money than able-bodied women to maintain a similar standard of living.

Because they are subject to employment and educational discrimination based on racism, women of colour are more vulnerable to poverty. The rate of unemployment among Black women is more than 20 percent, [19] and living conditions for these women have not improved in many years.

Seventy percent of immigrant women who do not know English or French work in low-paying jobs such as domestic work, piecework, assembly work and janitorial work. [20]

Aboriginal women are among the lowest income earners in Canadian society earning less than Aboriginal men, non-Aboriginal women and non-Aboriginal men. In 1985, 25 percent of Aboriginal women had no income at all. Those women with incomes averaged $9,828 that year. [21]

Already at the extreme margins of the job market, illiterate women will be even worse off in the coming years. Between 1986 and the year 2000, it is predicted that 64 percent of all jobs created will require 12 years of education, and almost half these jobs will require 17 years, in other words, a university or college education. [22]

DEPENDENCE

Although financial independence does not always mean that a woman will decide to leave, it helps. Without it, the only option is to endure. The decision to leave a violent relationship is complex; poverty makes it more so. Nor does social assistance provide enough financial security for a woman to leave, particularly if she has children to support. If a woman is abused, poverty even limits her ability to seek legal or medical redress.

> The roof over the head of many Canadian women may be a dangerous one, but it seems warmer than a Canadian winter street. Knowing her financial situation, a woman may deny the danger she is in. Even in non-abusive relationships, economic dependency wears hard on a woman's mental and emotional health. [23]

Illiteracy blocks most avenues of choice in life. Their lack of access to decent jobs, to programs and to information that would help them break away from abusive situations is such that economic independence is next to impossible. Campaigns about woman abuse and support services, so often advertised in print, are inaccessible to them. Phone numbers flashed across a television screen, printed inserts delivered with child benefit cheques and newspaper articles never reach this population. Literacy programs do exist, but their accessibility is restricted by a lack of child care facilities and limited funding for child care and transportation.

ISOLATION

Poverty creates its own ghetto, isolating those in its grip from the mainstream. Poor families encounter systemic barriers which place their children at a disadvantage within the system.

> Poor children generally have lower standards of living and nutrition, health care, and adequate shelter than do other children .... Poor children are more likely to get into trouble with the law, become pregnant and abuse alcohol and drugs. Poor children are less likely to finish high school. With few skills and an inadequate education, they will be unable to find skilled jobs with decent salaries .... And so the cycle of poverty continues. [24]

CONCLUSION

Poverty pushes women to the very margins of society where they are ignored on the very issues that shape their lives. They have neither the societal, political or financial clout nor the energy and time to lobby for change, especially if they are single mothers working full time outside the home. Working to end poverty is integral to ending systemic inequality and violence against all women.

CHAPTER 7

WOMEN WITH DISABILITIES

The police were ignorant about the reality for disabled women .... My husband came home, very drunk, one morning at 2:00 a.m. .... He beat me and went to bed, threatening to come out and shoot me if I made any noise. As soon as he fell asleep, I got out of the front door. I couldn't get any aids or get dressed, so I crawled across the street to a friend's house in my nightgown. It was snowing, the police said that they would take me, but not the kids, to a transition house. One of them said: a man has a right to enjoy the company of his children in his own house. Finally, they said if I wished to "kidnap" my children they would look the other way but they wouldn't help.

♀ ♀ ♀

After suffering daily abuse behind closed doors [at the office] and in public for two years from [him and two other colleagues], involving comments on my private body parts, my disability, my personal appearance, my slowness, my competence, public and private ridicule and threats regarding my cognitive, sexual and manual ability, my performance, one afternoon [he] called me into his office and slammed the door. [He] ordered me to sign a waiver saying I would never take him to the Human Rights Commission .... He turned the lock in the door and leered and said, "I have come to bring a little joy into your pathetic life," as he came toward me. [I] was able to fight him off and get away ... [W]hen [I] told him [I] was trying to get a transfer, he told [me] that [I] was old and crippled and no one would want [me].

Perpetrators know that disabled women are vulnerable and are given no credibility before police, lawyers, judiciary. Judges do not believe any woman, let alone disabled women. A disabled woman who actually gets [her] case to court does not know what court is and [the] lawyer does not walk her through it ....

INTRODUCTION

Eighteen percent of all women in Canada have a disability. [25] They face both the threat and the reality of all the forms of violence confronting non-disabled women, but their disability compounds, alters and increases their vulnerability.

As a group, women with disabilities share a range of common issues, but it is important to recognize the major differences within this group.

Disability is defined as any disturbance of normal sensory, motor, perceptual, cognitive, emotional or behavioural function that results in special needs or in being perceived by others as handicapped in some way. There are four major categories of disabilities. Their descriptions have been adapted from the book *Courage Above All.* [26]

Mobility Impairment: This category includes many conditions which result in individuals requiring the aid of wheelchairs, crutches, canes or walkers to achieve mobility. The wide range of disorders which can make moving painfully slow or unco-ordinated include cerebral palsy, juvenile arthritis and multiple sclerosis.

Hard of Hearing and Deaf: Deaf refers to a hearing impairment which is so severe that the individual is impaired in processing linguistic information through hearing, with or without amplification. Hard of hearing is a hearing impairment, permanent or fluctuating, which adversely affects processing linguistic information, but which is not included under the definition of deaf.

Blind and Visually Impaired: This category applies to individuals who are either wholly or partially without sight. Some vision losses are more serious during nighttime darkness, and other conditions affect peripheral vision.

Developmental Disability, Intellectual Impairment, Psychiatric Disability and Learning Disability: These terms refer to a range of impairments which include mental or physical illness, brain injury, dementia, senility and Alzheimer's disease, and developmental or intellectual disabilities.

Then there are the "invisible" disabilities, such as epilepsy and AIDS, and "multiple" disabilities that include a combination of the above.

There is certainly no question that women with disabilities are more vulnerable to violence. According to one source, approximately 83 percent of women with a disability will be sexually assaulted during their lifetime. [27] "Close to 40% of women with developmental disabilities (including those with learning disabilities and intellectual impairments) will be victims of sexual abuse before the age of 18." [28] Of the 245 women with disabilities who responded to a 1988 survey, 40 percent had been raped, abused or assaulted, and 64 percent had been verbally abused. Women with multiple disabilities suffered multiple forms of violence. [29]

Women with disabilities are often subjected to psychological violence which takes the form of messages to demean women with disabilities, that they are less valued, more of a burden and less socially significant than other women. These messages come from all corners of society. The burden of proof is difficult for a non-disabled woman claiming that she has been abused; for a disabled woman it is nearly impossible.

A deaf woman was raped and the judge asked her why she didn't say no. The judge let the rapist off because he said he couldn't understand her testimony ....

BIAS STEMMING FROM WOMEN'S SUBORDINATION IN SOCIETY

While women are generally socialized and conditioned to be nice, polite and submissive, women with disabilities are further socialized to be compliant, passive and grateful for any help they receive — a condition that increases the risk of abuse.

The current lack of accessible employment also compounds the problem. Most women with disabilities are underemployed and restricted to low-paying jobs. A 1988 survey found that 58 percent of women with disabilities were living below the poverty line in Canada. Only 45 percent of the respondents were in the paid labour force, and almost half the unemployed women who were mothers reported a yearly income of less than $10,000. [30] Poverty and its direct impact on a woman's ability to control her life enhances her vulnerability to violence.

DEPENDENCE

Women with disabilities point to a wide range of barriers which prevent them from achieving an independent lifestyle. Lack of access to appropriate caregivers and to community support services, social attitudes, barriers to adequate education and the ensuing economic inequality all place them in dependent and vulnerable positions.

Since many women with disabilities require personal care of varying degrees, their physical dependency together with their lack of consumer control over personal care arrangements place them at a great risk of abuse. Sometimes they are able to arrange for personal attendants to assist them at home but often they must live in a medical or care facility.

Family, relatives, friends, caregivers or institutions sometimes deliberately or thoughtlessly disregard the needs of women with a disability to control or punish them. They are left without food, medication, physical supports needed for mobility, or the social and emotional supports needed by everyone. Part of the impact of such neglect is its constant reminder of the disability. Their dependency on caregivers intensifies their experience of violence and reduces their access to support, information and assistance. The refusal to acknowledge a woman with a disability as a sexual being, combined with the responsibility for intimate body care, can result in a callous disregard for personal distance on the part of a caregiver and a level of control that is conducive to abuse, particularly sexual abuse. An Alberta study found that 88 percent of the victims with disabilities knew their sexual abusers, but less than 10 percent of the offenders were convicted and 80 percent were never charged. [31]

Many women with disabilities are unable to move beyond a state of learned helplessness. They internalize the attitudes of their caregivers and their families that they cannot look after themselves. Since emotional dependency is often combined with economic and physical dependency, threats of withdrawing support can become a prime means of controlling a woman with a disability. It may prevent her from revealing abuse and leaving a situation where physical or sexual abuse may also be happening.

Financial violence is often experienced by women with disabilities who may have to beg for money because they have been stripped of the dignity to control their own financial world. We heard of instances where women with disabilities lost their support or pay cheques to controlling family members, partners and "friends." We also were told of situations where women with disabilities were coerced into signing over control of their funds, sometimes in "exchange" for care.

ISOLATION

Women with disabilities often cannot get adequate education, not because they are not accepted into mainstream educational programs, but because they are hampered by lack of accessible transportation, wheelchair-accessible buildings, study materials available in alternate formats, such as braille, or alternate forms of communication such as signing interpreters. If they had the opportunity to acquire the knowledge, skills and means to establish an independent lifestyle, their isolation and vulnerability to violence would decrease.

The lack of accessible women's shelters, and the inability of many shelters and support services to provide sensitive service to women with disabilities, are largely a consequence of inadequate funding. Most women's shelters and support services are aware of the specific needs of women with disabilities but cannot afford to make the facilities physically accessible or to train staff to respond appropriately to those special needs. As a result, women with disabilities who are suffering the aftermath of sexual, physical or psychological violence have nowhere to turn, especially in rural areas.

Women with disabilities have the same reasons as non-disabled women for deciding not to report abuse: fear, dependency, shame, self-blame, fear of retaliation, lack of confidence in the legal system and a lack of support. But they have the added burden of proving that they are "normal" before they are perceived as credible. The credibility of women with disabilities is systematically questioned when they report abuse, particularly in the case of women with developmental, psychiatric and learning disabilities who may be unable to communicate independently. Women who are deaf are unable to report their abuse when there are no signing interpreters or special technologies. There are few resource materials available in braille or "talking book" format for women who are blind. Women who are dysfunctional due to substance abuse or psychiatric illnesses are turned away from shelters because they are "too disruptive."

Most courts are not accessible — usually computers for the hard of hearing are not allowed in courts; people with speech impediments cannot communicate. Disabled people are asked in court if we know the difference between lies and truth; it is an insult to most of us, being treated like children.

CONCLUSION

Women with disabilities must contend with the false assumptions of a society that views them as helpless and dependent. These assumptions increase the risk of manipulation and abuse by family members and caregivers and create barriers to independent living. These barriers find expression in educational institutions, the labour market and workplace, and health care and legal systems. Women with disabilities continually receive the message that they are merely tolerated in society; their experiences and their needs are consistently placed at the margins of social debate and social change.

CHAPTER 8

RURAL WOMEN

To date we have had over 700 families housed here and handled over 6,000 distress calls. Approximately half of these calls were from the rural and remote areas. That means, in effect, there are at least 3,000 women out there who have, at one time or another, cried out for help and support in abusive situations. This may only represent the tip of the iceberg, since it only encompasses those women who have actually sought out the services of a transition house. It is logical to assume that many more exist who have cried out to family and friends, or worse yet, who continue to suffer in silence .... Isolation adds to the hardship these women already endure.

♀♀♀

I hope that the hell is over. I live in a rural area with my two young children. The Ontario Provincial Police have told me that the fastest they can get to my house in an emergency is one hour. Between 2 a.m. and 6 a.m. there is no one available at all.

INTRODUCTION

Some women spend their entire life in the same rural community, and their attachment to the land, friends, family and a way of life are strong magnets that anchor them in place.

Just as there is no typical rural area in Canada, there is no typical picture of a rural woman and her experience of violence. She may be English, French, Acadian or Aboriginal. She might live in a farming community, a mining town or a village that depends on fishing, trapping or tourism. She might work outside the home, have children, look after the children of her neighbours, commute to

a nearby urban centre, or work on a farm or in a fish processing plant. [32] Whatever the particular situation, there are 3.1 million women living in rural Canada according to the 1991 Census. [33]

BIAS STEMMING FROM WOMEN'S SUBORDINATION IN SOCIETY

Violence is a secret; [it is] never discussed because it threatens the webs of relationships which hold rural communities together.

♀♀♀

In rural communities, everyone thinks you are the perfect little family, so you are too ashamed to reach out.

The ingredients for a conspiracy of silence are omnipresent in rural communities. Myths about the privacy and sanctity of family life abound. If anything is amiss, close-knit family networks and a high degree of community interdependency close ranks to deny it. Entrenched networks that confer power on high-profile community leaders who may themselves be abusers, or be friends or business acquaintances of an abuser, circumscribe community action and isolate abused women from other community members and resources.

A study conducted in Manitoba showed that many people simply don't believe that wife assault occurs in rural communities. [34] An Ontario study determined that in rural communities the victim of violence was often blamed for her own victimization. [35] Identified beliefs in the duty of women to obey their husbands, combined with sexist assumptions about the role of women, create psychological as well as physical prisons for victims of violence.

DEPENDENCE

In one town, the mine owns all the land and housing. If you're abused, you can't even rent accommodation, you have to uproot your kids and leave town.

There is no question that economic downturns, industrial layoffs, farm crises, fish plant closings, etc. have an impact on the incidence of violence against rural women, particularly within households. The additional stress, financial concerns, feelings of frustration and inadequacy can all compound a woman's vulnerability. In addition, financial concerns have a tremendous impact on a woman's decision to leave a violent relationship. She may feel guilty about leaving a family in a difficult situation, and she may be unable to scrape together enough money to get herself and/or her children to an alternative living situation.

ISOLATION

The same geographical limitations that make it difficult for a woman to leave a violent situation also reduce her access to outside help. Police or family and friends who are called upon for aid can be hampered by distance, weather and driving conditions.

Rural communities in financial trouble may cut spending on the very services that residents need most desperately. This results in a decline in the provision of social services, closed transition houses and dormant community centres. There may be a transition house or a sexual assault centre in another area but access may be complicated by a lack of transportation, no private phone lines to call for help or no space at the facility. In some locations, a boat or plane may be the only way for a woman to get to health, legal and shelter services. Such modes of transportation are usually expensive and not readily accessible to either women or the service providers.

Immigrant women or linguistic minority women are doubly isolated in rural communities because of the lack of support through their culture or through culturally appropriate services to respond to their needs.

For immigrant women who live on farms or in rural communities, the problem of violence is even worse since they are extremely isolated from the rest of the community culturally, and in situations of violence they tend to keep to themselves.

CONCLUSION

Women living in rural and isolated communities are especially vulnerable to violence because of their geographical isolation, the current economic crisis in many rural communities, the shortage of resources and services in their regions or the great distance between themselves and available resources. They may also experience community denial or a lack of confidentiality. No woman in Canada should be expected to leave her home in search of safety or access to adequate services.

CHAPTER 9

LESBIANS

INTRODUCTION

Violence is a daily reality faced by lesbians, at home, on the streets, at school and in the workplace. Until Canadian society overcomes its hatred of lesbians, they will continue to be harassed and abused. More services are not the only answer. Traditional patriarchal thinking values women primarily in relation to men, fears the love which women have for each other and elevates the conventional nuclear family beyond all other realities. This thinking will have to change to enable all people in Canada to live free of the fear of violence.

BIAS STEMMING FROM WOMEN'S SUBORDINATION IN SOCIETY

Women who have emotional and sexual relationships with women have been ostracized and marginalized historically; little has changed. Lesbian relationships are perceived as a direct affront to the cornerstone of a patriarchal society.

Consequently, lesbians are subjected to heterosexism and violence not only by individuals but also by institutions. In Canadian society all institutions, either directly or indirectly, work to enforce heterosexuality as the only acceptable relationship between consenting adults. Heterosexuality is supported in films, magazines, music, popular culture, advertising, schools, churches and family life. This inhibits the ability of lesbians to realize alternative expressions of sexuality, friendship, childbearing, parenting and spirituality, and indeed, also jeopardizes their safety. Many fear that the open expression of their affections will make them vulnerable to being beaten, ostracized, evicted, sexually harassed, fired, prevented from adopting children and losing custody of their children. In many cases their fears are well-founded.

A Quebec study of 1,000 lesbians found that 10 percent were victims of socio-economic, psychological and professional abuse because of their sexual orientation. [36] Although the media have recently begun to acknowledge "gay bashing," relatively little is known about "lesbian bashing," which appears to be as prevalent. Statistics are not kept by police.

Lesbians are often targets of sexual assault or rape, based on the assumption that "all they need is a good lay."

I am a lesbian and have been "out" for 12 years. Ten years ago I was sexually assaulted at knifepoint in my apartment by a man who had been watching my partner and I from the fire escape. We were playfully washing dishes after dinner, just before she left for home. After she had gone and my roommate had gone for a walk, I took a bath in the empty apartment. At that point the rapist broke into my home. During the assault he asked me if I was a lesbian. I answered no, fearing his rage and his knife ....

Lesbians are also harassed verbally and sexually in their workplace, fired or forced to quit.

Two women I know who were partners taught riding at the same riding school. They came out to their truck one day and found the word "lesbians" spray-painted on it in large letters. Soon after, one of the woman was brought before a meeting of the entire board of directors and publicly accused of being a lesbian. She was then fired. The second woman was fired shortly thereafter.

Lesbian relationships are not immune to acts of violence and aggression. Like battering of women by men in intimate relationships, violence within a lesbian relationship disempowers a partner and attempts to regulate her conduct and thought. Lesbians seldom raise this issue for fear of reinforcing stereotypical images of lesbians as "sick" or "perverse." Although research into the incidence and prevalence of such violence is virtually non-existent in Canada, women who spoke to the Panel contend that it is the result of institutionalized heterosexism which isolates lesbians and adds pressure to their relationships.

Just as sexism and misogyny ... [are] at the root of violence within heterosexual relationships, internalized homophobia and sexism are central to abuse within lesbian relationships. Thus anger, fear and rage can be misdirected at partners who can come to represent the things we have learned to hate in ourselves and who may symbolize all that we have been taught to fear in our hetero-sexist and misogynist culture.

In the context of a society in which hetero-sexuality is compulsory, lesbians must constantly confront a range of social, economic and political obstacles. Many continue to lobby for the inclusion of sexual orientation as a fundamental right in the Constitution, the *Canadian Charter of Rights and Freedoms* and in all provincial human rights legislation. [37]

ISOLATION

Lesbians live outside the protection enjoyed by other people in Canada. They are isolated from mainstream privileges and from services for abused women. Lesbians are often reluctant to turn to the police because law enforcement officers have a long history of treating lesbians abusively. Social service personnel can also make it difficult for lesbians who often need lesbian-specific information and assistance on legal, health and criminal justice issues. Service delivery people may shun, ostracize or ignore lesbians, blocking access to services and information.

CONCLUSION

Lesbians must not be subjected to violent attacks, harassment, verbal abuse and discrimination in society on the basis of sexual orientation. Lesbians must have the right to live in an envi-ronment free from discrimination and violence, with full human rights protection and equal access to services.

CHAPTER 10

WOMEN OF THE OFFICIAL LANGUAGE MINORITIES

A woman living in a rural Francophone community is isolated on two levels, and she has to live with violence since there is nothing available in rural communities.

♀♀♀

The closest centre is 60 miles away, and the services that are offered are in English.

INTRODUCTION

For Francophone women living outside their own linguistic and cultural boundaries, the situation is exacerbated by isolation from the mainstream. The 1991 Census indicates that the use of French is declining rapidly everywhere in Canada except Quebec and New Brunswick. [38] Francophones living in minority-language communities are located principally in Acadia, where they represent 12 percent of the total population, and in Ontario, where they constitute five percent of the population. In the west and northwest of the country, Francophones make up only two percent of the population. [39] Francophones outside Quebec are fighting for their linguistic and cultural survival. This continuing decrease in numbers accentuates their minority and in turn the isolation that can foster violence.

BIAS STEMMING FROM WOMEN'S SUBORDINATION IN SOCIETY

Generally, the French-Canadian community does not recognize the existence of violence against women. For [it], this is just an issue for women's groups. It is a problem which our communities continue to ignore. As a result of traditional values prevailing in isolated communities, female victims of violence are confined behind a wall of absolute silence and required to accept their lot. [40]

History provides clues to the source of this denial. In the legacy of Francophone populations, the Catholic Church has had considerable influence on values and behaviour. While this is still true, the degree of influence has declined. The church taught women that their devotion and obedience to the church and to their husbands were essential to the survival of the community. Francophone women who experienced violence asked their parish priest for help, he tried to deal with the problem by urging them to show patience, tolerance, forgiveness and greater self-control in the future. The priest often told them to return home and offer their suffering as a sacrifice to God. [41]

Women absorbed a great deal of responsibility for preserving the Catholic faith, the Francophone language and the Francophone culture. The welfare and survival of the community depended not only on their unstinting devotion but on their willingness to deny their own needs and interests.

Francophone women quickly learned that by speaking out about violence, they would undermine religious, family and community values. But their silence has and is undermining their rights as women.

Any emancipation is seen as a danger [by the spouse and/or community,] because in small Francophone communities, that would also imply the break-up of a patriarchal structure. If the wife does not remain at home, if she is not the sole guardian of the faith and culture, if because of her independence and the new ideas she is trying to convey, she is no longer the property of her spouse ... then of whom would he be master? [42]

DEPENDENCE

Given this history, women living in Francophone minority-language communities face great challenges in their decisions to seek help. They stand to be condemned by both their community and their family, losing the support of both.

This perceived responsibility, reinforced by teachings, to preserve their marriages at any cost has created a ghetto of dependence for many women. The combined might of their society, their religion and their economic situation lock them into stasis. Their choice is no choice.

ISOLATION

Statistics from 1986 indicate that approximately 60 percent of Francophones outside Quebec reside in urban areas. [43] The urbanization of Francophones is a major factor in their assimilation since they become routinely exposed to English in the workplace, with friends and at home. In major urban centres outside Quebec, the Francophone minority may seem very small since it is supplanted by other much larger linguistic and cultural groups.

Most shelters for battered women or centres to help the survivors of sexual abuse are not readily accessible to Francophone women in minority-language communities mainly because of language barriers. Consequently, women cannot easily resolve, escape and heal from violence with services that are culturally and linguistically inadequate for them. Thus a woman's decision to seek shelter means not only leaving her community, friends and relations, often her only sources of support, but also taking her children out of French school. [44] This adds to the guilt she already suffers for bringing about such a rupture in her own and her children's lives.

In light of such circumstances women often "choose" to keep quiet.

The Franco-Manitoban woman prefers to remain silent rather than seek shelter somewhere she feels she will not be fully understood.

Alternatively, women can break the silence in English.

A Francophone woman in a crisis situation who needs immediate help will use the language spoken by "everybody" so as to be sure of being understood. It takes all the courage she has to seek help. She has no energy left to start debating language issues.

Even though most Francophone women from minority-language communities have learned to function in English, they are often misunderstood when they express themselves.

There are really no French services at the Centre. The Anglophone employees feel that they [Francophone survivors] can get by in English. But the Francophone victim needs not only to relate her story but also [to share] her feelings. For example, there has already been a case of considerable confusion at the Centre between a Francophone victim and employees. Because the survivor said she had not been beaten by her husband, she was told that she could not stay at the Centre. However, what the survivor was trying unsuccessfully to explain was that her husband had bitten her.

Services in Quebec for English-speaking minorities are comparatively better than services for French-speaking minorities in other parts of Canada, but there are still problems for women fleeing from violent situations. According to the *Quebec Act Respecting Health and Social Services*, social services must be provided in French and English throughout Quebec. Certain local community service centres (CLSCs) and hospital centres are predominantly English-speaking, while others provide service in both languages. In regions that are almost exclusively

French-speaking, nursing and counselling services are also provided in English to the Anglophone population. Interpretation services may also be available in the courts, and some community services show consideration for the needs of Anglophones. For example, each regional health and social services board must present the Minister of Health with an action plan that outlines its human, physical and financial resources in a program that reaches out to the Anglophone minority. [45]

The Quebec model for the provision of services is not perfect, but it does provide some balance between the services it makes available in English and French. However, in some regions, survivors of violence have expressed dissatisfaction with the lack of services for English-speaking citizens of Quebec.

CONCLUSION

Communicating in one's own language is a fundamental right of all women who seek services to deal with their experiences of violence. Communication is determined not only by one's knowledge of a language but also by an appreciation of cultural concepts, traditions and linguistic nuances. In the midst of crises, women living in minority-language settings are in no position to struggle with language barriers. Their ability to survive their experiences will be conditioned by their access to services and support in their own language.

CHAPTER 11

WOMEN OF COLOUR

My three year old daughter, born in Canada, comes home from school with tear stains on her glowing brown cheeks. I, happy to have her back, assume she had a fight with another child about her blue shoes again ("blue is for boys," another toddler insists to her dismay).

"Are you hurt, baby?"

"Yes."

"Where?"

"I don't know," and she sobs throwing my heart in my own clenched fist again.

"What is it baby?"

"Vanessa called me "Paki" again. I am not a "Paki"."

I feel enraged. And helpless. What do I tell her. That yes, baby, you are called a Paki because you are brown or because your parents were born brown in Pakistan? "But Paki is a bad word, Amma, like asshole. I am not an asshole."

As an immigrant woman of colour, I have experienced the violence of sexist, classist and racist ideologies. In my own country, it was sexism and classism. In Canada it's all three together.

As a mother of three children (16, 12, 3) I have seen my children facing senseless violence of all three factors combined, almost on [an] everyday basis.

I see my lesbian friends and single mothers of colour from our ethnic communities... [cast out] facing homophobia combined with racism, sexism and classism.

Our experiences vary according to gender, age, the nature of our work and our sexual orientation. Few instances of violence experienced by us are actually directly physical.

If we were to decide to fight each instance of violence suffered by us each day, we will need ten more lives and only one thing to do in each of them.

I wonder if we will reach anywhere still. [46]

INTRODUCTION

As Canadians, women of colour are often left standing outside. A prevalent myth in Canada is that Canadians are white. Regardless of how long women of colour have been Canadian, whether their families have been here for generations, whether they were born in Canada or whether they have immigrated, they are asked the questions: "Where are you from?" "What is your nationality?" It is assumed that to be a non-white is to be a non-Canadian — forever.

"Women of colour" refers to all women in Canada who do not identify themselves as white, whether they are from Asia, Africa, the South Pacific, the Caribbean, the Middle East, South or Central America; whether they are immigrant and refugee women of colour; or women of colour who were born in Canada and whose families have been here for generations. Although Black women are included in the definition of women of colour, many prefer simply to be referred to as Black women.

Women of colour are a group of women with diverse cultural, linguistic, economic, social and sexual orientations. The use of the term is not meant to lump together women of all racial and ethnic groups, as their experiences differ in many ways. For example, South Asian women alone can be from six different countries, with 22 different languages, with five different religions, from various socio-economic classes, different castes and different racial groups. [47]

Racism is deeply embedded within Canadian institutions and structured into the social, economic, political and cultural life of the country. The systemic nature of racism is the product of the historical development of Canadian society and is reinforced on a daily basis. Racist "jokes," innuendos, assumptions, stereotypes and discriminatory remarks are the unfortunate hallmarks of contemporary Canadian society.

Since racism and sexism are root causes of violence, women of colour in Canada are obviously extremely vulnerable as they are subjected daily to both forms of harassment on an individual and systemic level. They hold little societal power to protect themselves and their children or to shape structural responses to the violence they experience.

The weight of racism combined with the one generated by sexism crushes our spirits and makes our pain invisible.

♀ ♀ ♀

Racism has the same effects among Black people — loss of dignity, respect, control, inability to protect self and family, and the loss of respect of the Black community for their family — as does wife battering to family members. Black women have already been burdened, humiliated and ravaged by those factors from birth.

♀ ♀ ♀

Racism hurts. It might be more painful than physical abuse.

♀ ♀ ♀

Racism is violence. It is a hopelessness and a disempowerment used against us by all people of both sexes.

♀ ♀ ♀

Black women being beaten by young white males has become quite a phenomenon in —, violence and racism side by side.

Although all women of colour are alike in terms of facing sexist, racist, homophobic and class-based abuse, a woman who has recently come to Canada from Africa faces different barriers than does a woman of African descent whose family has been here for several generations.
Various cultures are often used as an excuse to accept or perpetuate violence. Racism, cloaked in the more respectable mantle of "cultural considerations," results in stereotypes about violence being part of the "culture" of a people. This can be an excuse for non-intervention within the legal system and other services based on the misinformed fear of interfering with the practices of another culture. However, no cultural practices or norms can be used to justify violence.

BIAS STEMMING FROM WOMEN'S SUBORDINATION IN SOCIETY

Women of colour are faced with violence based on their gender within their own communities and on their gender and race in the rest of society.

Though men of colour do not have the same power as white males in the dominant system, they still can and do exert power over women.[48] But women of colour also are abused by white men and by white society. Trying to determine if she is hurt in relation to her colour or to her gender creates a fragmented identity based on gender and race, a situation that compounds the experience of violence for women of colour.

The women of colour who spoke to us during our consultations suggested that the problem of violence is worse for Black women because of white-skinned privilege in all levels of society. When a woman of colour is abused by a white male, the racist and sexist motives cannot be separated. In pornography, often the most degrading depictions are of women of colour who are targets on the basis of race as well as gender.

Women of colour can also experience racism at the hands of white women: "For women of colour, the concept of violence also includes the active participation of [white] women, being controlled by women, being oppressed and exploited by women ...." [49]

Racism is a strategic factor in violence against women because it affects the roles and actions of both the women survivors and their abusive partners. Women of colour understand the racism against men of colour since they themselves also experience it. When these partners behave violently against them, it is difficult for women of colour to seek assistance from existing services which they identify as part of the racist power structure.

> Black women and other racial minorities have long perceived elements in police forces and social service agencies as dangerous to their communities. They know, that by calling the police, they risk getting their men maimed, psychologically humiliated and often times killed. Systemic racism in Canadian society and in the institutions of justice place racial minority women between a rock and a hard place — we have forced them to choose between their loyalty to community and their personal safety. These women will continue to choose silence until our social and justice institutions deal with racism and sexism. [50]

The women themselves are also directly subject to violence and racism on the part of the legal system. Black women spoke of their experiences.

Lots of prejudiced things here, I talk sometimes about it, but I always say that I don't want to make it a black-white issue. But the staff are not fair to black people. We black inmates are together as one, we talk about our different opinions but we don't fight. The guards say we are always fighting, but they provoke [us] a lot. Our background is to talk, to be happy — it provokes them. I think it hurts them to see us as one, being happy, they don't expect this from black people.

... When I used to teach drawing, one of the models I knew from the lesbian community had a number of large bruises on her ribs and back. A couple of evenings earlier she had been dancing in a gay bar. The police were called when a scuffle broke out on the dance floor. She was standing at the side of the dance floor trying to calm some people down. The police grabbed her and without pausing to clarify whether she had been involved, they took her away in the police van. The police officers drove her to a back street where they beat her. As they assaulted her she heard them call her names like "lesbian" and "nigger." Although I encouraged the woman to make a formal complaint, she was afraid. She said that being Black and lesbian would mean that she would not have a chance against the police.

As in all groups, there is denial of violence against women, a lack of awareness and an unwillingness of some individuals in the community to acknowledge the importance of these issues. Women of colour also indicated that awareness of violence against women needs to be heightened among themselves. Some Black women state that they must stop protecting Black men. The men must take responsibility for their own actions and Black women must start calling the police. However, this awareness is contingent upon the elimination of systemic racism.

We can bring the violence of the police down on our men's heads or we can suffer silently.

♀ ♀ ♀

It is deadly the way police react in communities of colour.

DEPENDENCE

Our capitalist society is classist, sexist and racist, so Black women are at the bottom. It's harder to get work and money. Loss of a spouse's income is even more devastating. Also our credentials from the Caribbean aren't recognized so trained nurses work as cleaners.

Many women of colour find themselves near the bottom of the economic hierarchy. Regardless of qualifications held from inside or outside of Canada, they often end up in subservient jobs, unable to change occupations. Their position within the labour market is defined by the nature of their racial and/or ethnic identity which allows them only to exist in relation to the labour performed, that is, labour with social and political overtones of subservience. [51] Clearly, if a woman is unable to support herself and/or her children, escaping violence is even harder.

ISOLATION

... we are falling through the cracks. Our violence, like us, remains invisible ....

Although organizations working in the area of violence are required to be accessible and open to the needs of all community members in crises, women of colour report insensitivity, lack of awareness and a general indifference to their realities.

Many services and organizations which work with women survivors of violence are not accessible to the women from our communities because of attitudinal and systemic barriers including lack of appropriate language and cultural context, insensitivity to social class, political and religious realities and racism. [52]

Women of colour often face three major impediments to appropriate services: racism from those involved in service delivery; a lack of services specifically focused on their needs, even when the demographics of the community would demand such availability; and the peripheral role women of colour play in the structuring and delivery of mainstream services. If they had services specifically designed and staffed for, and by, women of colour, they feel this isolation would be reduced, and they would receive real help in a crisis. A lack of specialized services leaves women of colour isolated and more likely to return to the violent situations from which they were seeking escape.

CONCLUSION

We are tired, as victims, of having to prove that racism exists ... tired of saying the same things over and over again with no results.

The combined oppressions of racism and sexism are not adequately recognized in the context of violence against women. Until this gap is closed, there remains a pervasive threat to eliminating violence against women — all women. Women of colour have expressed the need to address systemic racism in all institutions of society including justice, community, health and social services, education and government. They want their inherent equality to men and to white women to be acknowledged and validated, and they need relevant services and programs.

CHAPTER 12

YOUNG WOMEN

It seems like it's part of everyday life to just be afraid all the time.

♀♀♀

Abuse in your family is even more difficult, sometimes when you disclose — your family will abandon you, disown you and it can happen that some family members will physically come after you to kill you.

♀♀♀

One young woman described her experience on the bus .... Young men on the bus threatened them. The young women reported it and one male got a two-week suspension [from school] — those involved were all 12 and 13 years old. She also described an experience her sister had when they were at a summer camp; boys tried to rape her sister while she was sleeping in her tent — those involved were 7 years old.

INTRODUCTION

More than 10 percent of young high school women are treated violently in their relationships. [53] Of 1,550 young women studied in Quebec CEGEP's, 68.3 percent experienced unwanted touching, 44.1 percent received unwanted sexual propositions and 9.8 percent received propositions with threats. [54]

Approximately 51 percent of all sexual assaults happen to women between the ages of 16 and 21. [55] As with all types of violence against women, most of the violence is perpetrated by men known to the victim. These numbers are probably low because most teenage and youth violence goes unreported. Adolescents are unwilling to talk about it to anyone other than their peers, and 25 percent will not disclose their experiences to anyone. [56]

BIAS STEMMING FROM WOMEN'S SUBORDINATION IN SOCIETY

Young women are particularly vulnerable to violence because they are subject to the power and rules of adults and have few avenues to affect change. Young women spoke of feeling powerless — at home, in educational institutions, in the media and in politics. They are especially vulnerable because violence appears to thrive in schools and on campuses, in dating relationships and in families. The often sexist and misogynist voices of adult men — fathers, teachers, employers and other males in authority — overpower young women.

A teacher mocked me for suggesting he replace the word "men" with "humans." He said "Oooohh Humans ... she thinks it should be Huuuumaaans." The class laughed, but I didn't. I told him it wasn't a joke afterwards and he just said "oh." Does he or doesn't he know how it makes me/women feel?

Young people feel that violence is the outcome of jealousy, power and control seeking by young men, the consumption of drugs and alcohol, a familial history of violence, communication problems, peer pressure and the use of pornography. Other sources point out that violence in intimate relationships is the result of "the adherence of society to standards of inequality between the sexes." [57] This is played out in relationships and occasionally reinforced by familial histories of abuse and peer pressure. A Canadian researcher found that abusive male students support other abusers and therefore increase the likelihood of further violence and recurrent abuse. They actually encourage their peers to feel good about using power and control in their relationships with women. [58] Young women are impeded in their struggle to achieve equality and to end violence by such attitudes and by men's fear of losing the power they have always taken for granted.

My boyfriend wants me to himself 24 hours a day. I feel like I'm in a glass tank with water filling up the sides. I've even had to get my family to lie for me so that he'll back off a bit.

Young women also experience systemic abuse: the education system fails to incorporate the issue of equality between women and men into the curriculum. The media play a powerful and subversive role in supporting violence, not only overtly in depictions of abuse and misogynist images but through more subtle presentations of men in positions of power and young women as sex objects. Rarely are young women provided with positive and diverse role models on television, in music, videos or films.

Women experience sexual harassment everywhere. Guys in cars honk at you, bosses, colleagues, fellow students, professors ... there's sexist jokes, comments, movies, commercials. It's everywhere and people seem to think it's just a normal part of the way things work.

This abusive social context inhibits a young woman's ability to develop positive images of herself, her body, her future career and personal potential. In a study involving about 1,000 adolescent women, the respondents expressed fairly positive interests and concerns about many other issues, but worried a great deal about their looks, reflecting society's own emphasis on the physical image of women. [59] Researchers have linked anorexia and bulimia to young women's overwhelming desire to conform to the images of female beauty that surround them.

DEPENDENCE

Young women reported feeling vulnerable to the men around them they were supposed to be able to trust the most — their fathers, uncles, brothers, teachers, doctors, school coaches and fellow male students. Because of that vulnerability and lack of trust, young women are reluctant about reporting abuse. Many told the Panel that when

they had reported to the school administration that they had been abused by a teacher, nothing was done about it. School counsellors, even when aware of sexism and violence, often do not have the power to initiate structural change. Certainly, young women cannot affect change themselves in such situations.

One of our teachers [highschool] said .... "She wears that again ... I'll fuck her." Lots of problems with teachers .... One of our teachers [high school] said "Men have to tame their women."

The issue is complicated by society's tendency to blame the victim. For instance, despite the fact that young women are encouraged by the media and pressured by peers to wear certain clothes, they are also told, when they are abused, that by wearing these clothes, they asked for men's sexual attention, slander or sexual assault. This tendency to blame the victim is especially prevalent in cases of acquaintance and date rape in which myths about female and male roles and sexuality come into play. As a result, young women are often afraid and ashamed to report abuse.

ISOLATION

Some young women are more vulnerable to violence than others. There are often great pressures to conform to dominant middle class, heterosexual, white, able-bodied society in high school and among peers. Young women who don't conform — those from poor or immigrant families, women with a disability, lesbians or young women of colour — are often targeted for abuse in the form of harassment, isolation, exclusion or physical and sexual violence.

CONCLUSION

We cannot afford to be naive about the life of young women today. They are hurt daily by abuse and violence in ways that take advantage of the vulnerability of their youth. Young women are aware and are capable of working to end violence. All they need are the power and the means to effect change. They have the right to live and work in a safe environment.

CHAPTER 13

IMMIGRANT AND REFUGEE WOMEN AND FOREIGN DOMESTIC WORKERS

Systems don't work for immigrant women. These women have even less power than other women and are faced with discrimination, racism, language disability ....

♀♀♀

[I]f it is difficult for a French or English-speaking mother to survive the legal system; for an immigrant, non-Canadian woman, it is impossible. The lower our status on the social ladder, the more we are abused by the system.

♀♀♀

The long-lasting consequences of torture are not recognized by most health providers. Many refugees are reluctant to access the few existing services due to linguistic and cultural barriers, coupled with intense feelings of shame.

♀♀♀

Some women refugees escaping war often marry the wrong man in order to stay in Canada and find themselves in an abusive relationship.

♀♀♀

Domestic workers come hoping to be protected by their employers but instead are abused by their employers.

♀♀♀

... all the violence you can imagine is there [in the foreign domestic program] in a one-to-one relationship with [a foreign woman's] employer ....

INTRODUCTION

Under the *Immigration Act*, immigrant applicants fall into four categories: independents, family class, assisted relatives and refugees.

Independent immigrants are selected based on a point system which judges the potential labour market skills and contributions applicants can make to Canada's economy and society. They are generally people whose education, skills and background make it highly likely that they will become self-sufficient contributors to Canada within a short period of time.

Canadian citizens, over 19 years of age, may sponsor close relatives as family class applicants. This category is limited to immediate family members or certain other dependent relatives under the age of 19. They are not assessed under the point system. A Canadian who sponsors his or her relatives can be obliged to provide assistance if necessary for up to 10 years.

Assisted relatives are family members who do not qualify under family class, but who have relatives in Canada willing to help them get established. The assisting relative accepts responsibility to help them, if necessary, for up to five years. They are assessed under the point system used for independent immigrants.

A refugee is defined by the 1951 United Nations Convention and Protocol Relating to the Status of Refugees as a person who:

> ... owing to well-founded fear of being perse-cuted for reasons of race, religion, nation-ality, membership of a particular social group or political opinion, is outside the country of his nationality and is unable or, owing to such fear, is unwilling to avail himself of the protection of that country; or who, not hav-ing a nationality and being outside the coun-try of his former habitual residence as a result of such events, is unable or, owing to such fear, is unwilling to return to it. [60]

Canada's *Immigration Act* and Regulations have adopted the same definition. People claiming refugee status are classified as principal applicants — the individuals making the claim — and dependants — the applicants' spouses and/or children. Most advocates now argue that existing legislation and its definition of a refugee discriminates against women.

For refugee women the situation is further compounded. They have immigrated not as a matter of choice but as one of survival.

Refugee women flee their countries for several reasons.

- They fear persecution in the form of imprisonment, torture or death for their political or religious beliefs or their race or nationality.

- They have been physically and sexually harassed, abused and tortured by government officials, police and military officers for the activities of their spouses, children or other family members.

- They have been abused because of their gender.

  The common element experienced by a female political prisoner is violent sexual attacks upon her body and psyche, which are consciously designated to violate her sense of herself, her female human dignity. [61]

Because refugees are forced to flee the country of residence,

> the acculturation process may be quite different in nature since migration did not occur as a matter of choice. Many refugee women may have been exposed to physical and emotional torture and may bring with them emotional scars. They may worry about the well-being of loved ones left behind in the turmoil of their country. [62]

A fifth avenue of entry into Canada for foreign women is on a temporary work permit issued through the Live-in Caregiver Program (LICG) which came into effect in April 1992 and replaces the 1981 Foreign Domestic Movement (FDM) Program. Employment and Immigration Canada records indicate that in the last decade, more than 80,000 people, 97 percent of whom are women, [63] have entered Canada as foreign domestic workers. Most are from Asia (particularly the Philippines), the Caribbean (particularly Jamaica), Latin America, Africa and the United Kingdom. Most are women of colour.

The LICG brings workers to Canada to do live-in work as caregivers when there are not enough Canadians to fill the available positions. Their temporary work permits dictate that, during the first year of their stay in Canada, they must continue to work for the employer named in their authorization. The permit may be renewed for a second year but it is only applicable to the employer named on the employment authorization. If it is a new employer, the woman must apply for a new employment authorization. The LICG Program makes additional stipulations: live-in caregivers must have the equivalent of a Canadian Grade 12 education and six months full-time training in the field or occupation related to their work (child care, gerontology, etc.) or equivalent practical job experience. [64] As the name implies, live-in caregivers are also required to reside in the homes of their employers for the full two years.

BIAS STEMMING FROM WOMEN'S SUBORDINATION IN SOCIETY

Fear, lack of knowledge and intolerance shape Canadian attitudes toward immigrants, refugees and foreign domestic workers. Some Canadians blame them for causing increased unemployment and the recession. And while the Canadian government encourages immigration, not all immigrants are given the tools they need to integrate successfully into all aspects of Canadian life. They are often viewed as not quite Canadian and frequently treated as second-class citizens. Cumulatively, these factors make integration and adjustment difficult and intensify the risks for women already in violent situations who must face a double layer of male dominance — that of their own situation and that of the society to which they have come.

As in virtually all cultures, immigrant women bear a disproportionate responsibility for ensuring that the needs of the family are met. Relationships that are not "working" properly are a source of personal shame and guilt for many. In their eyes, seeking outside assistance would only bring shame and disgrace to the extended family. "Immigrant women play the role of family guardians and educators and immediately feel responsible for problems encountered within the family unit." [65] Discussion of violence within the family is still taboo in many cultures. Violence can be viewed as an "illness," and marriage vows keep women in situations of violence "in sickness and in health."

Immigrant and refugee women frequently face strong patriarchal networks of extended kin. Husbands, particularly when faced with the different equality standards of women in Canada, may try to exert power to keep women in traditional subservient roles to compensate for their own loss of social standing. When the women begin to adjust to life in Canada and start to change their perceptions of marital relationships,

> "The husband loses or is afraid of losing his influence over his wife. Problems may then rise in the form of violence against the woman. In many cases the instigator is not only the husband, but also the brother, a cousin, a friend of the family and so on. All men have a right of control over women; this is the cult of masculinity." [66]

In this context, an immigrant woman may have her whereabouts, activities and her friends constantly monitored. Women can become confined to their communities.

Statistics tell us that about 70 percent of immigrant women who do not know either official language are slotted in low-paying job ghettos. [67] Such jobs offer poor working conditions, low rates of pay and scant union protection, making women highly vulnerable to potential abuse by management and to economic change. Immigrant women can be targets for abuse in the workplace based on their gender, race, manner of dress and language.

For women with educational credentials and skills gained outside of Canada, prospects for employment relevant to their training and experience are dim. Many immigrants must augment their education with Canadian equivalents, a sometimes lengthy process. Another barrier to employment is the lack of Canadian experience and women are often forced to take positions that do not match their skills or education to obtain this experience. They then find themselves unable to progress beyond these levels. As a result, highly educated and skilled immigrant women are often relegated to domestic work, piecework in garment or other light industries, assembly and janitorial work. In such situations, immigrant and refugee women may be unwitting targets of sexual harassment and exploitation if they are not yet aware of cultural norms and legislation governing conduct in the workplace. Having a fragile attachment to the employment market, they may endure this abuse rather than risk losing their jobs.

A key to control is that refugee women lack knowledge of the laws. They remain silent in their communities for fear of a cultural stigma and labelling against them. They are also revictimized in the hearing process.

When women do decide to flee their countries, they continue to be at risk throughout their entire ordeal. Border crossing guards, guides and immigration officials have all been known to demand sex in "exchange for safe passage," protection or immigration "leniency." In refugee camps and settlements, women are vulnerable to violence from state officials whose role it is to protect refugees and from members of their own refugee male population. While both women and men refugees are disempowered, the male refugees can still exercise control over women's bodies and lives.

The irony of the term "refugee" is that it signifies powerlessness and subjection while ostensibly conveying protection. Refugees have no rights. It is the prerogative of states to grant them asylum, refugee or immigrant status, or to deport them. The vulnerability of women refugees is compounded by the very fact that they are women.

Since the 1951 UN Convention and its protocols did not adequately protect women refugees, the Women at Risk Programme was established by the United Nations High Commissioner for Refugees (UNHCR) in response to the need for special protection and resettlement for women at risk. Canada has participated in the program since 1988. Changes in 1990 to procedures and guidelines spelled out two categories for eligibility under the program. The first is for women who "will be in precarious situations where the local authorities cannot ensure safety;" the second defines women at risk as "applicants who are not under immediate peril but who are existing in permanently unstable circumstances which allow for no other remedy." The program also helps resettlement efforts through work with government and non-government sponsoring agencies. In 1991, 61 women were admitted to Canada under this program.[68] Some revisions are being made to speed up overseas procedures.

However, the refugee determination system is still inadequate since it is based primarily on men's experiences. Neither legislation nor the definition of refugee acknowledges that women are subject to violence specifically because of their gender, either by individual men or by the state. Recent media reports of the "rape camps" in Bosnia underscore the horrors that women and girls face by virtue of their gender.

> ... [The] testimony ... of scores of ... former female inmates from 10 Serbian brothels (rape camps) has begun to expose the widespread practice of sexual abuse over the past eight months in Bosnia where Serbian forces are estimated to have raped at least 14,000 and as many as 30,000 Muslim and Croat women, some of them held for months as forced prostitutes.[69]

Bosnian human rights investigators claimed in December 1992 that the practice was widespread and systematic, with 53 documented cases of rape victims who are pregnant and estimates of many more too afraid or ashamed to come forward.[70]

In some cultures, such as those of Turkey, parts of Lebanon, Egypt, Syria and Algeria, death is the punishment for loss of virginity before marriage and is accepted as essential in preserving family honour. In some parts of the world — in Egypt and West Jordan, for example — if an unmarried woman becomes pregnant she is encouraged by her family to kill herself. If she will not, she may be murdered and her death reported as suicide.

The numbers are believed to be far greater than official death records indicate. Other examples include women in Iran who can be whipped, raped and disfigured for failing to adhere to the dress code, such as wearing the *chador*.[71] Sexual torture can also be inflicted upon women as a punishment for not conforming to the cultural norms imposed on them solely on the basis of their gender. In some countries, individual violence against women is condoned by the state and sometimes it is the woman who is punished.

> Some governments maintain legislation making it possible for the victims of rape to be charged with criminal offences. Under Pakistan's Hudood Ordinance, women convicted of extramarital sexual relations — including rape and adultery — can be sentenced to be publicly whipped, imprisoned or stoned to death .... Many governments clearly regard rape and sexual assault as less serious offences than other human rights violations. This is a particularly frightening prospect when the perpetrators of these rapes are those same policemen and military personnel charged with the protection of the public.[72]

Women in those countries from which most refugees come, are traditionally excluded from politics and publicly active religious, racial or nationalistic groups. Members of such groups are often persecuted and receive protection as refugees because of their membership or beliefs.

There is some movement to recognize women's persecution based on gender in both the legislation and the definition of refugee women. In 1984, the European Parliament called upon states to recognize women who are facing inhumane treatment for reasons related to their sex as "members of a particular social group." This move would broaden the interpretation within the present Convention. [73]

In 1985, the UNHCR Executive Committee supported a recommendation to include gender as an explicit criterion for refugee status, but implementation was left to the discretion of individual states. Canada has not amended its definition to specify gender as a criterion but has produced guidelines on interpreting gender as being part of a particular social group.

The Guidelines Issued by the Chairperson Pursuant to section 65(3) of the *Immigration Act for Women Refugee Claimants Fearing Gender-Related Persecution*, released by the Immigration and Refugee Board on March 9, 1993, outline a new process for using gender-based persecution as grounds for refugee status. The guidelines state that "as a developing area of the law, it has been more widely recognized that gender-related persecution is a form of persecution which can and should be assessed by the Refugee Division panel hearing the claim." [74] However, these guidelines do not go far enough since they are not mandated and therefore cannot be enforced under laws or legislation.

In July 1991, the UNHCR Executive Committee released *Guidelines on the Protection of Refugee Women* which address the issue that women "fearing persecution or severe discrimination on the basis of their gender should be considered a member of a social group for the purposes of determining refugee status. Others may be seen as having made a religious or political statement in transgressing the social norms of their society." [75] For a woman to establish grounds, by membership in a gender-defined particular social group, she must show that she has received harsher treatment than the general population or other women. This is an unfair requirement since it amounts to her having to pass two tests; men only must pass one.

Before the new guidelines were introduced, the Refugee Division, on February 19, 1993, found that a woman had a well-founded fear of persecution if she belonged to a particular social group of women. "[U]nprotected ... women or girls [are] subject to wife abuse ...[and] ... women or girls [are] forced to marry according to customary laws." [76]

Judgments with regards to refugee women's gender-based claims are, far from uniform. On November 18, 1992, a claim was dismissed because the Refugee Division panel rejected the argument that "battered women who do not receive state protection" [77] constitute a particular social group. The difficulty in establishing claims of gender-related persecution lies in the Refugee Division panel's determination of whether the various forms of violence and fear of violence experienced by women are considered "persecution." The circumstances giving rise to women's fear of violence are often unique to women. In hearing claims, decision makers often fail to consider, and are not required by legislation to consider, evidence that the state offers no protection to women, either by condoning violence against women or by failing to prevent it. Unfortunately, where violence by the authorities or private citizens not under state control is concerned, a woman has difficulty supporting her claim if she lacks statistical information on the incidence of violence against women in her country of origin. The disparity of these two cases reveals the weakness of guidelines which fail to define gender as a ground for persecution, along with race, religion, nationality, political opinion and membership in a particular social group.

There is also a stereotype that violence is more prevalent and/or accepted in non-Western immigrant communities. We are aware of no statistics that support this notion. However, this myth poses a barrier to disclosure of violence for immigrant and refugee women. Lack of cultural sensitivity also aggravates the problem as Canadian mainstream ways of dealing with wife abuse may be ineffective and culturally offensive. An example is the case of a policeman asking a Somali woman to show him the physical marks on her body as proof of the beating her husband allegedly inflicted on her. Such a request revealed a total disrespect for her religious beliefs, and her inability to comply with the police officer's request because of those beliefs places her under continued threat of abuse. [78]

Cultural misunderstandings and lack of knowledge about other cultures may lead officials and service providers to believe these myths which are further reinforced by low numbers of immigrant women reporting violence to mainstream services. Officials and service providers may be reluctant to intervene on behalf of an immigrant woman, believing that to do so would violate cultural boundaries. It must be clearly under stood that culture cannot be used as an excuse to support violence against women.

For foreign domestic workers, the situation in Canada can also be a difficult one. Advocacy groups have roundly criticized the new Live-in Caregiver Program (LCGP). They argue that its educational requirements are inherently sexist and racist. In most of the countries from which the women come to Canada, they have limited access to any educational opportunities because they are poor and because they are women.

The program leads to exploitive working conditions such as long hours, minimum wages, no pay for extended hours and breach of employer-employee contracts. As a result domestic workers are vulnerable to economic, psychological, sexual and physical abuse and exploitation. The female employer often sets the boundaries between herself as mistress and the domestic worker as employee. This can result in psychological abuse through threats, insults, curses, intimidation and even false accusations. Many workers have also been physically abused, sexually harassed, sexually assaulted and raped by their male employers.

I remember the first time I think something was funny was one night, I was sleeping and I feel someone in my clothing, feeling up my private parts. This happened after I was here for a month. I jumped up because I was frighten and when I look it was him — the man I was working for. He hold my mouth and tell me to be quiet. He smell of alcohol and I did not know where his wife was, but it was late at night. He kept pushing his finger down in my private parts and blowing hard. When I told him it hurt he asked me if I didn't birth to one baby already. He tried to push me down on the bed but I wouldn't let him. After he finished, he jumped off me, spit on the floor, and tell me if I tell his wife or anybody he would send me back to — or that I go to jail. I was really frightened. I really believed that I could get locked up. For what, I don't know, it happened seven or eight times. I was scared to tell anybody, further I didn't know where to turn to. I didn't know anybody here.

The abuse that domestic workers are vulnerable to extends beyond the employers to their children and even friends.

Another worker was asked by her employer to stay in their home while they were on holidays. One day her employer's son came home with his friends. She was asked to serve them coffee. Later she was asked to join them not knowing they had put something in her drink. She was raped not only by her employer's son but his friends as well. She was hospitalized for awhile and is now staying in a shelter in —.

The employer exercises control over virtually every sphere of their lives, and their access to support and assistance can be completely circumscribed by their legal obligation to live in their workplace. While the Government of Canada establishes the parameters, it fails to take responsibility for ensuring that employers keep the women safe or treat them fairly.

To qualify for permanent residence, foreign domestic workers must hold a good work record for the two-year period and must also be able to meet additional criteria which include upgrading of skills, volunteer work in the community, financial management, personal suitability, etc. In addition, evidence of "potential for self-sufficiency" must be proven which includes not only their ability to find suitable work in a chosen field but also to support any dependent family members they wish to sponsor to come to Canada. In assessing whether domestic workers meet these criteria, immigration officers have great discretionary powers. Their assessment of "community involvement" may influence substantially their decision to grant or deny landed immigrant status, a criterion especially difficult to meet, if the woman is working 15 hours a day in her employer's home.

Domestic workers who want to change their place of employment must first convince Employment and Immigration Canada that they have a valid reason for leaving and that they have not violated any of the requirements of the Live-in Caregiver Program. While this process would appear relatively simple, for many domestic workers it is an extremely intimidating process which they hesitate to pursue for the following reasons.

- Most domestic workers are supporting family and dependants in their home countries. Initiating any grievance process, they fear, will jeopardize their own livelihood as well as that of their families.

- Many live-in caregivers, such as refugee and immigrant women, come from countries with a well-founded mistrust of authority and state officials. Any process which could bring them into contact with these people is often avoided at all costs.

- Women believe that immigration officials are more likely to take the word of a Canadian employer over the word of a foreign domestic worker.

- At the time of the woman's assessment for landed immigrant status, a satisfactory employment record is required. Live-in caregivers fear that any grievance may jeopardize their chances of obtaining landed immigrant status.

- Employment and Immigration Canada takes no action against employers who breach their contracts, and nothing guarantees a domestic worker that her next employer will be any better than her current employer. Domestic workers fear that they will be blamed for the transgressions of their employers.

These fears are compounded by the dread of losing their temporary work status, their jobs and their right to stay in Canada. Foreign domestic workers are often left with little choice other than to endure their situations.

As domestic workers across Canada have pointed out, the new program is regressive and will not alleviate the exploitive conditions that make domestic workers vulnerable to violence. It has been consistently argued that domestic workers should be granted permanent landed immigrant status upon entry to Canada rather than temporary work permits, that the educational experience and skills levels of foreign domestic workers be assessed equitably and fairly and that the live-in requirement not be mandatory. In effect, the Live-in Caregiver Program should be eliminated.

DEPENDENCE

The majority of immigrant women enter Canada under either the assisted relative or family class categories which legally connect them to a sponsor. This legal relationship is hierarchical and, while practical in facilitating immigration of women, gives state sanction to the notion of family in which the man is the breadwinner and the woman is dependent for financial support.

Some immigrant women come to Canada as "mail-order brides," and other women may have temporary status as visitors or students, factors that make their position even more tenuous. Women, as newly arrived "applicants" sponsored by male relatives, can be virtually dependent. This exacerbates their vulnerability to violence.

Abusive men who have sponsored their wives or other female family members may use the threat of deportation to control them and keep them in situations of violence. This threat is not based in law. "Your status is your own. This is of particular importance to women. Neither your spouse, nor your employer nor your sponsor can have you deported. Specifically, your Record of Landing is your own document." [79] Unfortunately, this basic information is not given directly to women in their own language when they arrive in Canada. Many immigrant women are led to believe they can and will be deported if they end their relationship with their sponsor. This gives abusive men tremendous control, and many women lack the language skills or support networks to obtain information or assistance to escape violence. Abusive husbands can prevent their wives from obtaining information about their legal rights because lines of communication are often between the male sponsor and officials.

It's such a disgrace among immigrant men to go to jail in some communities, that the woman is less safe from the husband in the long run if he is jailed for abusing her.

Deportation orders can only be issued after an adjudicated hearing to determine whether a person has violated immigration law. Such violations include false passports and convictions under the *Criminal Code* with a sentence of more than six months imprisonment. Leaving a spouse is not sufficient grounds in and of itself to deport anyone, nor is the withdrawal of sponsorship grounds for denying continued residency to adults already residing in Canada.

The fact is that it [immigration law] is giving an extreme weight to the sponsoring partner in the immigration process, and this [means that], when violence against the woman happens she is doubly punished. My three friends were very clear that the power gap between them and their husbands made them stay in their relationships. They were helpless, fearing an extra humiliation: to go back to their country when there was little left there.

A woman may be kept in a violent situation because she believes that if her sponsor withdraws financial support, she will lack the means to survive. In fact, if a sponsor defaults on his obligation to provide financial support, a woman does have options. Like other residents of Canada, she may qualify for social benefits in accordance with stipulated eligibility requirements, up to a maximum allowable limit. She may likely, however, be unaware of the availability of social assistance or not know how to apply.

Immigrant women told us what would have made a difference for them. Information given by immigration officials is generally given to the man who may deliberately withhold it from the woman. By controlling the information about immigration he can exercise power by choosing what information, such as legal reasons for deportation, to disclose based on his own self-interest.

For refugee women, the ordeal does not necessarily end with their arrival in Canada. Once they are considered eligible for resettlement here, refugee women must meet the immigration admissibility criteria which gauge their ability to establish themselves in Canadian society. This is particularly difficult because these criteria are based on skills generally held by men; skills and strengths of women are not credited as employment assets. The stereotypical view of refugee women as passive and dependent, coupled with their vulnerability, may lead to the perception that they cannot achieve economic independence in the expected time. A major change in perception must be brought about: women refugees must be seen as victimized rather than as victims, as individuals rather than as appendages of others.

Once settled in Canada, refugee women face a myriad of other issues. Like immigrant women, their lack of independence leaves them highly vulnerable to violence within relationships and families as well as to violence based on racism and discrimination. For instance, the stress that surrounds family reunification is significant. Before claimants can apply for family reunification (i.e., sponsoring other family members to come to Canada) they must have landed immigrant status, a process that generally takes at least three years. A woman waiting in her own country is at greater risk during this time, and a woman who is in Canada, separated from family and support systems, will be vulnerable due to her isolation. She will also have to become autonomous and self-sufficient to survive. Her spouse may be threatened by her independence when he does join her in Canada, and he may react to his loss of control with violence. Such violence can trigger the trauma of pre-migration and migration experiences of violence. Current support and counselling services do not take this into account.

Sexual assault can have a particularly severe impact on a woman whose culture places a high value on virginity, chastity and fidelity. [80] She may no longer feel worthy to continue in her role of wife or mother, especially if the assault becomes known. Immigrant and refugee women can be more vulnerable to sexual assault by strangers as an expression of racism and by spouses due to their financial and social dependence. [81]

Shelters may also not present a viable option for some refugee women. Moving out of their homes reflects the homelessness and poverty they have already endured as refugees. Confinement and sharing limited space can be a reminder of a prison or a refugee camp. Leaving the family home can result in ostracism and judgment from relatives in Canada, from the ethnic community and from family back in the country of origin. Refugee women indicate that they would prefer to live with friends. They also question the justice of having to leave their homes rather than have the abusive partner leave. [82]

Abused immigrant and refugee women coming to me for counselling tell me over and over again to please help my husband as he is the only family that I have in this country.

♀♀♀

In ... [refugee women's] former lands police, soldiers, prison guards and other authorities were either the ones actually carrying out the abuse or were affirming and legitimizing the suffering.

♀♀♀

Rape was to be expected when troops were conducting counter-insurgency operations. [Refugee] women from these countries find that it takes a long time to develop trust in police and other authorities.

♀♀♀

You must understand that in a year and a half of our program, we have reached only seven refugee women who are able and willing to speak of sexual assault, — it takes a long time ....

Some groups have suggested that the real solution lies in giving immigration status to immigrant and refugee women upon entry to Canada independent of their fathers, husbands or brothers. However, under the current point system many women would not qualify for "independent" entry.

For foreign domestic workers, the dependence and vulnerability of their situation is exacerbated by the live-in requirement of their stay in Canada.

... living-in [with your employer] means that you lose the ability to make decisions, to have independence, a sense of adulthood; implicitly you are not allowed to live your own life ....

Because their admission into Canada requires them to live in a private household and to wait for two years before being eligible to apply for permanent residence, domestic workers are highly vulnerable to sexual harassment and violence. Furthermore, Employment and Immigration Canada has no authority to intervene in the employer-employee relationship or to enforce the terms and conditions of employment.

The live-in requirement restricts the personal, recreational and social life of caregivers. Without a place of their own, it is difficult for them to make friends, entertain, have any kind of sexual relationship and be part of a larger social circle in the community. For many women the lack of transportation and irregular hours make it impossible to pursue leisure or educational opportunities. At best, the live-in arrangement reduces live-in caregivers to the status of a dependent child; at worst, an indentured slave.

ISOLATION

It is difficult for many of us to imagine the world facing a newly arrived immigrant or refugee woman or a foreign domestic worker coming from a very different culture. She may have been separated from her spouse or other family members for a long period of time. She may not speak either English or French, and may have little information about her new country. She must struggle to find a balance between her traditional disciplines and experiences and those of her new world. She may not know how to handle some situations, such as dating or other social activities. She may have never experienced racism. Many of the factors that make these women vulnerable to violence also act as barriers to disclosure and prevent them from seeking or obtaining assistance. They may not be able to understand even the first steps they need to achieve independence.

As their children integrate into Canadian society through school and their husbands assimilate through employment, training or other social interactions, immigrant women who do not work outside the home may find themselves very isolated. An immigrant woman may have little or no knowledge of the Canadian educational system or not know how to deal with school authorities.[83] Already dependent on her husband, she may also feel she is losing her children to a foreign culture.

Immigrant women lack well-established networks of social and family support. Being away from parents, siblings and close friends intensifies the pressure. She may be blocked from the one traditional escape route she was comfortable with, that of returning to her own family. Taken together, both social isolation and cultural pressures are formidable barriers to immigrant or refugee women reporting abuse and trying to leave violent situations.

Experiences in the labour force can be equally isolating for immigrant and refugee women. Many must adjust to unaccustomed poverty in an affluent society during their early years in Canada. They might find themselves in low-paying jobs to provide financial support for their families if their husbands are unable to find employment. The immediate need for income may supersede language training opportunities. They may find themselves working a double or triple day, expected to assume full domestic responsibilities and provide emotional support to family members.

The lack of language skills has a high impact on employability and a direct link to safety and equality. The 1986 Census indicated that the labour force participation of immigrant women unable to speak English or French was 45.6 percent compared to 65.4 percent for women able to speak an official language.[84] Women comprised two thirds of the immigrant population unable to speak either of Canada's official languages.[85] Women may also be unable to take full-time language training programs because they have no one to take care of their children.

The inability to communicate effectively in the English or French language keeps women powerless and isolated, often at the lowest political, social and economic levels of Canadian society. It affects their social and family relations, employment opportunities and access to social service resources. In a crisis situation, women may not know where to go or even that assistance is available to them. They may not have the language skills to communicate with social service workers. [86]

Many women spoke to us about language training. Canada provides language training for new immigrants, but since it is not universally accessible, women often do not have adequate access to these programs. Until recently, the Canada Employment and Immigration Commission provided language training for those who were assessed under the point system and therefore expected to enter the labour market. Because the majority of women who immigrate to Canada come as dependents under the family class or assisted relatives category, they were not eligible for language training and the accompanying basic living allowances, which would allow some financial independence. Women also face significant obstacles in trying to determine their eligibility for language training. They may not be aware of the availability of low or no-cost language training programs, or of their sponsor's responsibility to pay for this training.

In late 1990-91, new language programs were introduced through the new Immigrant Language Training Policy. This should improve immigrant women's access to language training and subsequently give immigrant women increased control over their own lives.

While a lack of language training certainly aggravates the problem of violence against immigrant and refugee women, the lack of services for all women and particularly immigrant and refugee women who are the victims of violence compounds the issue. Few legal, health, social services, shelters or transition houses are relevant to their cultures. Cultural interpreters are not readily available and there is great variance from

province to province. Interpreters often lack knowledge about the issue of violence. In worst-case scenarios, a family member — the abuser himself — is asked to do the cultural interpreting.

As mainstream services do not fully respond to the needs of immigrant or refugee women, many women turn to community and immigrant women's associations. The chronic underfunding of these organizations precludes co-ordinated and consolidated work in creating real changes regarding sexism, racism and poverty. Provincial and territorial policies seem to be based on the belief that the federal government has exclusive responsibility for funding services. At the federal government level, government departments often believe that Employment and Immigration Canada will fund the total range of services. These jurisdictional confusions leave immigrant and refugee women "falling through the cracks." Governments have a responsibility to initiate and participate in co-ordinating efforts to ensure that funding to immigrant women's organizations is sufficient to provide not only responses to violence but also preventive outreach services.

Information on services in the languages of immigrant communities is also lacking, as are effective means of distribution. Women told the Panel of the lack of outreach, both in disseminating information and in providing access to services.

Refugee women have further insensitivities inflicted on them. The detention centres used to hold individuals pending execution of deportation or exclusion orders or to hold those who have failed to comply with departure orders are not gender sensitive. Conditions in detention centres have been singled out for criticism in some regions of the country. In Toronto, for instance, the Toronto Refugee Affairs Council (TRAC) Sub-Committee on Detention noted that women were being held in the same areas as men to whom they were not related and that they were often under the observation of male guards. The TRAC Sub-Committee also reported that inadequate facilities for the proper care of young children can lead to splitting of families, thus causing further hardship for the women. Detention facilities are overcrowded and lack privacy. Detainees have limited access to day-to-day necessities.

For the domestic worker, the isolation of a new country is enforced by the live-in requirements. One domestic worker describes her particular circumstances.

... worked for a family from seven in the morning until midnight. The employer paid the airfare and when I arrived I was treated like a slave. I did not get any money for my seven months work and was given four hours off twice a month. I did not have access to the phone and was threatened by my employer with deportation. This is mental abuse.

Conclusion

Lack of services, lack of language skills and access to language training, poor employability, lack of recognition of foreign credentials, and immigration laws which make their entry into the country contingent upon their dependent status to their husbands all combine to marginalize many immigrant women and intensify their social, economic, cultural and political isolation and their vulnerability to violence.

Until guidelines specifically articulating gender as a ground for persecution are legislated, Immigrant and Refugee Board officials are free to respond on a case-by-case basis. To leave women's safety and lives in the hands of individuals who may have little understanding of women's circumstances in other countries, is an intolerable violation of women's human rights.

The safety of foreign domestic workers cannot be assured when they are dependent upon an employer who has the benefit of citizenship, higher credibility and greater knowledge of the system, and when they must live in the home of that employer without any scrutiny from the system.

A country that prides itself on its multicultural policies should interpret the failure to address the experiences and needs of immigrant women as a fundamental breach of its commitments.

ENDNOTES

1   Statistics Canada, *Age, Sex and Marital Status: The Nation* (Ottawa: Minister of Industry, Science and Technology, 1992), p. 141.

2   K.A. Pillemer and D. Finkelhor, "The Prevalence of Elder Abuse: A random sample survey," *The Gerontologist*, as cited in *Elder Women Speak Out on Abuse* (Winnipeg: Senior Women Against Abuse Collective, 1988), p. 28.

3   Donna Shell, *Protection of the Elderly: A Study of Elder Abuse* (Winnipeg: Manitoba Council on Aging, 1982), p. 32.

4   Aline Grandmaison, *Protection des personnes agées : Étude exploratoire de la violence à l'égard de la clientèle des personnes agées du CSSMM* (Montreal : Centre de services sociaux du Montréal Métropolitain, Direction des services professionnels, 1988), p. 23.

5   National Council of Welfare, *Poverty Profile, 1980-1990* (Canada: Minister of Supply and Services, 1992), p. 69.

6   Jean-Luc Hetu, *Psychologie du Viellissement* (Quebec : Méridien, 1988), p. 258.

7   Lise Corbeil *"The Impact of Poverty on Fairness in Judicial Processes"* (Paper presented in Geneva) (Ottawa: National Anti-poverty Organization, February 5, 1992), pp. 5-6, 8 and 10-11.

8   Morley Gunderson and Leon Muszynski with Jennifer Keck, *Women and Labour Market Poverty* (Ottawa: The Canadian Advisory Council on the Status of Women, June 1992), pp. 7-8.

9   Alberta Status of Women, *Women Against Poverty: A Report of the Alberta Status of Women Action Committee* (Alberta: Alberta Status of Women Action Committee, 1989), p. 2.

10 *Ibid.*, pp. 5, 7.

11 Martine Carle, "Violence Against Women: The Feminization of Poverty," *Communiqu'elles*, Vol. 18, No. 3 (May 1991): 15-22.

12 National Council of Welfare, *Women and Poverty Revisited/La femme et la pauvreté, dix ans plus tard* (Ottawa: Minister of Supplies and Services Canada, 1990), p. 7.

13 *Ibid.*, p. 58.

14 Olga Lechky, "Health and the Homeless," *The Lion's Tale*, Vol. 9, No. 2 (Spring 1991): 1-12.

15 *Ibid.*, pp. 1-12.

16 Eileen Ambrosia, Dilin Baker, Cathy Crowe, Kathy Hardill, *The Street Health Report: A study of the health status and barriers to health care of homeless women and men in the City of Toronto* (Toronto: Street Health, May 1992), p. 51.

17 Martine Carle, "Violence Against Women: The Feminization of Poverty," *op. cit.*, pp. 15-22.

18 Joanne Doucette, *Violent Acts Against Disabled Women*, DisAbled Women's Network (Toronto: DisAbled Women's Network, 1987), p. vii.

19 Marjorie Villefranche, "La pauvreté des femmes," as cited in Martine Carle, "Violence Against Women: The Feminization of Poverty," *op. cit.*, pp. 15-22.

20 Joan Jenkinson, *Let Me Tell You: Language Rights for Immigrant Women* (Toronto: Community Legal Education Ontario), p. 7.

21 National Council of Welfare, *Women and Poverty Revisited, op.cit.*, p. 112.

22 Joan McFarland and Aisla Thomson, *Education for Women and Girls: Recommendations for Achieving Equality - Brief to the Liaison Committee of the Council of Ministers of Education, Canada - CCLOW Brief No. 89.1* (Toronto: Canadian Congress for Learning Opportunities for Women, August 21, 1989), pp. 13-14.

23 Alberta Status of Women, *Women Against Poverty: A Report of the Alberta Status of Women Action Committee, op. cit.*, p. 65.

24 *Ibid.*, p. 3.

25 Cathy McPherson "Out of Sight, Out of Mind: Violence Against Women with Disabilities," *Canadian Women's Studies Journal*, Vol. 11, No. 4 (Summer 1991): 49.

26 Liz Stimpson and Margaret C. Best, *Courage Above All: Sexual Assault Against Women with Disabilities* (Toronto: DisAbled Women's Network - Toronto, Autumn 1991), pp. 6-7.

27 L. Stimpson and M. Best, *Courage Above All, op.cit.*, p. 1.

28 Hélène Morin and Josée Boisvert with L'Association de Montréal pour la déficience intellectuelle (Submission to the Canadian Panel on Violence Against Women, Ottawa, 1992), p. 5.

29 Jillian Ridington, *Beating the Odds: Violence and Women with Disabilities* (Toronto: DisAbled Women's Network, March 1989), p. 1.

30 Jillian Ridington, *Different Therefore Unequal: Employment and Women with Disabilities* (Toronto: DisAbled Women's Action Network - Canada, April 1989), pp. 27-28.

31 Dick Sobsey, "Sexual Offenses and Disabled Victims: Research and Practical Implications," *Vis-a-vis*, Vol. 6, No. 4 (Winter 1988): 1.

32 Wendy Milne (Research paper prepared for the Canadian Panel on Violence Against Women, Ottawa, 1993).

33   Statistics Canada, *Profile of Urban and Rural Areas - Part A: Canada, Provinces and Territories, 1991 Census* (Ottawa: Minister of Industry, Science and Technology, 1993), p. 6.

34   Maureen Schwanke, as cited in Wendy Milne, *op. cit.*

35   Molly McGee, *Women in Rural Life: The Changing Scene*, as cited in Wendy Milne, *op. cit.*

36   Luce Bertrand, *Le rapport Bertrand sur le vécu de 1000 femmes lesbiennes*, as cited in Andrée Côté, "Lieux de travail et homosexualités; la répression du lesbianisme au travail, en continuité avec l'hétérosexisme de l'État canadien," in *Homosexualités et tolérance sociale*, eds. Louis Richard and Marie-Thérèse Seguin (Quebec: Groupe de recherche interuniversitaire et interdisciplinaire sur la gestion sociale, 1988), p. 52.

37   Mary Eaton, "Theorizing Sexual Orientation" (LLM thesis), pp. 149, 177.

38   Chantal Hébert, "Québec français, Canada anglais," *Le Devoir [Montreal]*, January 13, 1993, pp. A-1, A-4.

39   Secretary of State of Canada, *L'État des communautés minoritaires de langue officielle: indicateurs de développement*, as cited in Chantal Cholette (Unpublished paper).

40   Fédération nationale des femmes canadiennes-françaises (Submission to the Canadian Panel on Violence Against Women, Ottawa, March 1992).

41   Réseau, Winnipeg (Submission to the Canadian Panel on Violence Against Women, Ottawa, April 1992), pp. 2, 8.

42   *Ibid.*, p. 2.

43   Secretary of State of Canada, *L'État des communautés minoritaires de langue officielle: indicateurs de développement, op. cit.*

44   L'Association des Acadiennes de la Nouvelle-Écosse (Submission to the Canadian Panel on Violence Against Women, Ottawa, March 1992), p. 5.

45   Quebec National Assembly, *Act Respecting Health Services and Social Services and Amending Various Legislation* (Quebec: Quebec Official Publisher, 1991), p. 11.

46   Fauzia Rafiq, *Violence Against Immigrant Women of Colour* (Research paper prepared for the Canadian Panel on Violence Against Women, Ottawa, 1993).

47   *Ibid.*

48   Rozena Maart, *Violence Against Women of Colour* (Research paper prepared for the Canadian Panel on Violence Against Women, Ottawa, 1993).

49   *Ibid.*

50   Glenda Simms, "Double Jeopardy: Minority Women and Violence" (Keynote Address at Alternatives: Directions in the Nineties to End the Abuse of Women, Winnipeg, June 6, 1991).

51   Rozena Maart, *Violence Against Women of Colour, op. cit.*, p. 4.

52   Maria Shin and Michele Kerisit, *Violence Against Immigrant and Racial Minority Women: Speaking with our Voice, Organizing from our Experience* (National Organization of Immigrant and Visible Minority Women, 1992), p. 1.

53   Shirley Litch Mercer, *Not a Pretty Picture: An Exploratory Study of Violence Against Women in High School Dating Relationships* (Toronto: Education Wife Assault, 1988), p. 7.

54   Centrale de l'enseignement du Québec, *Harcèlement sexiste, harcèlement sexuel, agression sexuelle à l'endroit des étudiantes du primaire et du secondaire* (Quebec: Centrale de l'enseignement du Québec, 1985), p. 9.

55   Lorie Haskell and Melanie Randall, *Women's Safety Project, op. cit.*

56   June Henton, Rodney Cate *et al.*, "Romance and Violence in Dating Relationships," as cited in Eileen Morrow, "Dating Violence," in *A Handbook for the Prevention of Family Violence*, ed. Suzanne Mulligan, Hons. B.S.W. *et al.* (Hamilton, Ontario: The Community Child Abuse Council of Hamilton-Wentworth, 1990), p. 26.

57   Francine Lavoie, Lucie Vézina, Annie Gosselin and Line Robitaille, *VIRAJ: Programme de prévention de la violence dans les relations amoureuses des jeunes* (Laval, Quebec: Cahiers de Recherche de l'École de Psychologie, 1992), pp. 4-9.

58   Walter DeKeseredy, "Male Peer Support and Woman Abuse in University Dating Relationships: An Exploratory Study," as cited in Eileen Morrow, "Dating Violence," *op. cit.*, p. 2.6.

59   Canadian Teacher's Federation, *A Cappella: A Report on the Realities, Concerns, Expectations and Barriers Experienced by Adolescent Women in Canada* (Canadian Teacher's Federation, 1990), p. 11.

60 United Nations, *Convention and Protocol Relating To The Status of Refugees*, Article 1(A)(2). Adopted on July 28, 1951, by the United Nations Conference of Plenipotentiaries on the Status of Refugees and Stateless Persons convened under General Assembly resolution 429 (V) of December 14, 1950.

61 Ximena Bunster, "The Torture of Women Political Prisoners," as cited in Maria Rosa Pinedo and Ana Maria Santinoli, "Immigrant Women and Wife Assault," in *Towards Equal Access: A Handbook for Service Providers Working with Survivors of Wife Assault,* ed. Fauzia Rafiq (Ottawa: Immigrant and Visible Minority Women Against Abuse, August 1991), p. 68.

62 *Ibid.*, p. 48.

63 Employment and Immigration Canada, *Statistical Profiles and Forecasts of the Foreign Domestic Movement,* as cited in Judith Nicholson (Research paper prepared for the Canadian Panel on Violence Against Women, Ottawa, 1993).

64 "Ottawa Revises Foreign Nanny Rules," *Toronto Star*, June 11, 1993, p. A16.

65 Maison d'hébergement pour femmes immigrantes de Québec, *Femmes immigrantes violentées ... une réalité,* (Ste-Foy, Quebec: June 1989), p. 4.

66 *Ibid.*, p. 4.

67 Joan Jenkinson, *Let Me Tell You: Language Rights for Immigrant Women* (Toronto: Committee on Language Equity and Community Legal Education Ontario, 1989-90), p. 7.

68 Employment and Immigration Canada, Matching Centre, Settlement Branch, *Women At Risk: Arrivals by Province (1988-1991),* as cited in Helene Moussa (Research paper prepared for the Canadian Panel on Violence Against Women, 1993).

69 Richard Beeston, *"A Hateful Burden," The Times*, December 17, 1992.

70 *Ibid.*

71 Ninette Kelley, *Refugee Women and Protection: Criteria and Practices for Determining Refugee Status* (Summary of comments made at the CRDD Working Group on Women Refugee Claimants: Training Workshop for Members, RHOs and Legal Services, Toronto, April 4, 1990).

72 *Rape and Sexual Abuse: Torture and Ill-treatment of Women in Detention* (London, England: International Secretariat, Amnesty International, 1991), p. 7.

73 Ninette Kelley*, Refugee women and Protection: Criteria and Procedures for Determining Refugee Status, op. cit.,* p. 2.

74 Guidelines issued by the Chairperson Persuant to section 65(3) of the *Immigration Act*, Women Refugee Claimants Fearing Gender-Related Persecution (Ottawa: Immigration and Refugee Board, March 9, 1993), p. 12.

75 *Ibid.*, p. 12.

76 *Ibid.*, p. 14.

77 *Ibid.*, p. 14.

78 Helena Moussa, *Violence Against Refugee Women, op. cit.*

79 Employment and Immigration Canada, *A Newcomer's Guide to Canada* (Ottawa: Department of Supply and Services, 1991), p. 33.

80 Kathy Wiebe, *Violence Against Immigrant Women and Children: An Overview for Community Workers*, 2nd ed. (Vancouver, B.C.: Women Against Violence Against Women/Rape Crisis Centre, 1991), p. 41.

81 *Ibid*, p. 41.

82 Helena Moussa, *Violence Against Refugee Women, op. cit.*

83 Kathy Wiebe, *Violence Against Immigrant Women and Children: An Overview for Community Workers, op. cit.,* p. 3.

84 Ravi Pendakur and Michel Ledoux, *Immigrants Unable to Speak English or French: A Graphic Overview* (Multiculturalism and Citizenship, Policy and Research, Multiculturalism Sector, February 1991), p. 40.

85 *Ibid*, p. 1.

86 Kathy Wiebe, *Violence Against Immigrant Women and Children: An Overview of Community Workers, op. cit.,* p. 2.

CHAPTER 14

INUIT WOMEN

THE LEGEND OF THUNDER AND LIGHTNING

An important part of Inuit culture are the legends that teach right from wrong and determine what is acceptable within the culture. Storytelling is an essential means of educating, and legends and myths preserve the laws of life from one generation to another. Many Inuit legends illustrate the unacceptability of violence against women and children, legends which have remarkable similarity from Alaska, across the Canadian Arctic and into Greenland. These include the legends of Kaujjajjuk, an abused child who grows up to destroy his abusers and become a hero, and the legend of the great sea goddess, known by many names including Sedna or Talilajuk, who after being abused by her family transforms into a woman/sea creature, thereafter rewarding good people with food and punishing those who disobey her by holding back animals and stirring up the sea. Another well-known legend explains the origins of thunder and lightning:

There were two sisters and they were tired of being abused. They wanted to get away from their father and husbands so they walked northwards. They walked a long way towards the mountains. They killed a caribou by drowning it in a lake. They found a dead whale on a beach and were able to eat it and use the fat for their lamps. They built fox traps out of stones .... They were able to survive very well but they kept on walking further away. The younger sister kept asking her older sister, "Sister, sister, what should we become? Should we become caribou?"

"No," said the older sister. "We would still be scared if we were caribou."

"Sister, sister, should we become seals?"

"No. A seal is afraid of people too."

"Sister, sister, should we become walrus?"

"No. We would be hunted and we would be scared again."

"Sister, sister, should we become polar bears?"

"No. Polar bears are killed too."

The sisters continued to talk in this way until there was a terrible storm, and then the younger sister asked, "Sister, sister, can we become thunder and lightning?"

"Yes!" said the sister. "Thunder and lightning are not afraid of people."

And so the older sister dragged a dried sealskin over the ground and made the sound of rumbling thunder. She struck two flint stones together and made lights. The spirits of the sisters rose and joined the thunder and lightning in the sky. Everywhere Inuit go they are in fear of thunder and lightning.[1]

INTRODUCTION

Few groups in Canada have undergone as dramatic a change to their condition as Inuit during the last 40 years, change which has rocked the very structures which gave families strength and kept societies healthy. Nowhere is this upheaval more tragic than in the manifestation of violence against Inuit women, which by all accounts increased when Inuit were plunged suddenly into a world where there was little or no respect paid to their culture and laws. Traditionally, women had a balanced, decision-making role in Inuit society, but today that heritage is blurred by a history of colonization and social turmoil, and a debate has emerged as to whether violence against women and children is acceptable in Inuit culture.

While women and children of every society are vulnerable to abuse of power and control, far greater is their danger when the structures which protect them and affirm their value are ripped away. The means to eliminate violence against Inuit women must come from within their society, from the wisdom of a culture which has survived great odds and from the dynamic ideas and strengths of Inuit women and men who are building a better future. In the words of one Inuit leader, *"Because of our culture, we require different solutions to our problems. Because of our isolation and the smallness of our population, we require local and culturally appropriate remedies. Women need to be recognized as one of the most important pillars of our communities."* [2]

POPULATION

There are approximately 36,000 Inuit in Canada, [3] living in small communities across the Arctic, including the northern coasts of Labrador, the Ungava and Hudson Bay coasts of northern Quebec and the northernmost regions of the Northwest Territories. Small pockets of Inuit reside in urban and regional centres, many drawn to jobs provided by government and other organizations in Yellowknife, Ottawa, Winnipeg, Goose Bay and Montreal. By far the majority of Inuit live in isolated communities, connected only by telecommunications, air transportation and annual summer sea-lifts.

The political bodies that govern and represent Inuit are varied. Locally, Inuit have limited municipal powers on hamlet and town councils. In the federal government, only one riding, Nunatsiaq, represents a majority of Inuit and, in provincial and territorial governments, only the Northwest Territories allows for truly Inuit jurisdictions to be represented in its legislature. Aside from federal and provincial/territorial governments, land claims settlements have resulted in Inuit decision-making bodies among the western Arctic Inuit, or Inuvialuit, of the Northwest Territories and the northern Quebec, or Nunavik, Inuit. Inuit have moved closer to establishing Nunavut in the central and eastern Northwest Territories, which in 1999 will become a new territory of Canada with province-like powers and an Inuit majority.

National Inuit organizations made up of representatives of all Inuit regions include the Inuit Tapirisat of Canada (ITC) and Pauktuutit, the Inuit Women's Association. Internationally, Inuit are represented by the Inuit Circumpolar Conference (ICC) which meets every three years with delegates from Alaska, Canada and Greenland. The 1992 Inuit Circumpolar Conference, held in Inuvik, was the first conference in which Inuit representatives from the former Soviet Republic of Chukotka participated.

HISTORICAL ANALYSIS

Modern Inuit communities face a myriad of challenges exacerbated by chronic high unemployment and extreme cost of living. Escalating social problems including family violence, housing shortages, youth suicide, child abuse and substance abuse tear at the changing fabric of modern Inuit communities. Violence against Inuit women must be understood within the context of modern-day turmoil and a history of cultural upheaval.

Educate [people] that working to end violence against women and children will not cause cultural genocide ... the real question is how will the culture take on the problem, make it its own and find ways of solving it that keeps the culture alive and evolving.

Traditionally, Inuit women's skills were essential to the daily existence of their families in one of the world's most challenging environments. Inuit women were decision makers, providers of shelter, clothing and food, experts in health and social issues, spiritual leaders and primary educators of children and youth.

The Inuit woman was the head of the household and made all decisions on the running of the home. This included the training of her daughters and daughters-in-law. Traditionally, the sense of community was family and extended family, so Inuit women extended their role as head of the household into the community. [4]

The underpinning of Inuit justice was the respect and authority given elders. This basic law of respect was taught from early childhood, the key to its success being the intensive training children received from parents, grandparents and other relatives. Elders describe how important discipline was in their own childhood in learning to be productive people, knowledgeable in the laws that preserved the community. These laws included the protection of people within the community from violence.

I did not know of anyone beating up someone weaker. If a young person was bad, he was disciplined strictly and always made to understand the reasons for the discipline. Everyone respected their parents and elders, there was no talking back. I didn't know of any people who broke this law. Everyone respected one another, and I never saw any terrible fights. [5]

Justice was always handed out by elders. The Inuit Cultural Institute describes the Inuit equivalent to the courts as a tribunal made up of elders who were asked to intervene when there was trouble. The elders would give advice and positive support to a troublemaker or, if the crime was severe, they would embarrass, shun, banish or, in very extreme cases, order the killing of an offender.

Traditional Inuit society was similar to other cultures in the practice of arranging marriages, which ensured all adults found partners during the childbearing years and bloodlines were protected against intermarriage. Strict laws surrounded marriages, discouraging promiscuity, incest and early pregnancy. To many young women, however, marriage was a frightening event, and there are many stories of women being carried off kicking and screaming by their potential husbands.

My mother told me I was going to marry this man and I said, "No. I am not! He is so ugly .... I will get germs" .... I cried and I ran away and I did not want to marry him. But it didn't matter what I wanted. I had to do it, it was the law and I had no choice. [6]

Once a young woman was married it was common practice for her to live with her spouse's family. Her mother-in-law became her counsellor and teacher. Inuit elders describe how successful arranged marriages were and say that there was little spousal abuse in comparison to today. Part of this success was because of the respect all members of the society gave the rules, which preserved unity within the family and the community.

Spousal assault was very shameful, and it was the most embarrassing thing for a person if the elders would get together to discuss you. Women were told not to talk back or nag our husbands, to be good and not make our husbands angry. Women were respected, and they were working all the time, as was the husband. [7]

While lessons can be learned from the ideas behind their traditions, modern Inuit women do not advocate returning to a world where they were limited in choices or confined by roles which have little relevance today. In fact, many young women are questioning some traditional practices and are asking, "Are arranged marriages not a form of violence against women?"

I was forced to marry someone that I had never seen before, someone I did not want to have as my husband. Right from the start, my life was shattered. Right from the start, he battered me .... He automatically started hitting me because he knew that I was supposed to be his wife.

In the words of Northwest Territories government leader Nellie Cournoyea, *"When someone says, "I want to practice my culture," it doesn't mean going back to freezing in igloos and hunting with bows and arrows. It means regaining the control we had over our lives before."* [8] Any discussion of abuse of women in traditional times must consider the historical context. While it is clear that traditional Inuit society protected women from violence, the roles of men and women and the definition of crimes differed from what they are today.

Traditionally, husbands and wives had distinct and well-defined roles, which were essential to life in small hunting camps where the possibility of starvation was a daily reality.

In my time people did not play games about who did what to who, survival was everything. If you weren't doing your job well, you would be poor. As a woman you had a great deal of work to do, you must be an expert at making warm, dry clothing or your husband and children might freeze. A husband must be serious about his hunting or his family would starve to death. [9]

At the same time there were remarkable exceptions to gender stereotypes if one compares Inuit and European societies. While Inuit men were usually the hunters, some women did hunt regularly, and in some families where there were no older boys, girls were trained as hunters by their fathers. Women as well as men were spiritual leaders, or shamans. Female figures were as powerful as any in Inuit myths, and male and female babies were named for departed souls, regardless of gender.

An important difference between traditional and modern attitudes toward violence against women is the definition of abuse. Elders today report confusion about the *Canadian Criminal Code* because the definition of assault in traditional Inuit law was quite different. Today's definition of sexual assault would have been too broad for the days of arranged marriages.

Men used to fight with women to have sex. That is the way it used to be. As long as the parents agreed, then the man could have the daughter, even if she didn't want to. When we took a wife she had to be taught for a long time before she would agree to sex [willingly]. That is because she had been taught all her life not to be with men .... Today if we did the things we used to, all the men would be in jail. [10]

While perceptions of abuse differ from today, traditional Inuit society did not condone what was defined as a crime, including excessive violence against women.

People did not abuse women in the old days, we were told that men would starve if they did .... If they were abusive they did it secretly so no one would know, and if people found out they would be very angry at such hypocrites. Abusers would be counselled, and if they didn't listen and wouldn't obey the rules, then they would be treated very strictly by elders and made to feel embarrassed and ashamed. This was the worst thing that could happen to an Inuk, to be made to feel ashamed. [11]

When abuse threatened lives or disrupted family unity, elders were quick to intervene with counselling and, if necessary, tribunals. When these initiatives didn't work, couples could be separated.

Very abusive people who hurt their partners secretly were despised .... Sometimes the abusive husband was separated from the wife if people were worried about the wife. Separation is more common today, but it did exist before too .... Inuit ways were to survive. [12]

Traditionally, Inuit lived in small hunting camps, and it was possible to know how everyone else was feeling by the subtle ways people communicated. Victims of abuse were easily identified by changes in their behaviour, such as sudden quietness or depression. As elders and older relatives felt it was their responsibility to care for the community, intervention was a matter of course.

If people noticed something bothering someone they would try and find out what it was. They would go for long walks with the person and, after asking many questions, the person would finally say what was bothering them .... Sometimes the elders would be asked to come and help the person deal with the problem. Nowadays people see that someone has a problem, but they don't do anything. [13]

CULTURAL TRANSITION

Inuit came into contact with western society sporadically at first, beginning with the early explorers of the 16th century, and then more frequently during the 19th century, as whalers, traders and missionaries moved into the Arctic. There are many stories of the changes brought by these early non-Inuit "visitors" to the Arctic including the whalers who hunted off Arctic shores for three centuries, eventually wintering there and setting up temporary camps among Inuit who were fascinated by their relative material and technological wealth. The history books seldom mention women's roles during these transition years, nor do they discuss the insidious changes to how men viewed Inuit women. That Inuit women were abused there can be no doubt.

When I say "way back," I mean before my time, and I am pretty old. The descriptions and stories that I heard are of funny boats that used to be seen travelling around at a distance. Because it was not known who they really were and where they came from, Inuit called them "arnasiutiit" or Women Kidnappers .... However old they are, those **arnasiutiit** *[had] a tendency to kidnap women.* [14]

A common activity was the trading of women for the "riches" of the outside world. Elders remember tales of abuse against Inuit women throughout modern history, dating from the days of the *sikatsi* (Scottish) whalers through to the RCMP and military camps of the 1950s and 1960s, when food and supplies were traded for Inuit women.

There were many abuses of Inuit women by **qallunaat** *[non-Inuit]; sometimes they would get jealous and beat women up. I used to hear about* **qallunaat** *going after Inuit wives. I once heard that people were starving at one place and so a wife had sex with the* **qallunaat** *there in exchange for tea and sugar .... I have heard about Inuit selling their wives. They didn't want to at first, but the* **qallunaat** *traded things like bullets and tobacco for sex. The Inuit got paid for sharing their wives .... That's how it began.* [15]

The destructive effect on Inuit family unity and laws was immediate. Inuit women sometimes lived with non-Inuit men for years until the men returned to their southern homes without their newly acquired families.

If you see an elder who looks a little white, then you know that his mother was sold to a white man. Some qallunaat *are like ducks. They come up here like birds in the spring. They mate and they lay their eggs. Then the male goes away. They give their eggs to the Inuk woman, and they go away. Even if that woman loves him, he can just leave. [16]*

Soon after the explorers and whalers came the missionaries. The first missions were established by the Moravians along the Labrador coast in the mid- to late-18th century to teach Christianity and "how to read and write the Labrador dialect in a Moravian orthography." [17] By 1862, most Inuit in Labrador belonged to the Moravian Church and had been taught to read the Bible. Anglican and Catholic missions were established throughout the western and eastern Arctic during the mid-1800s, with missionaries quickly learning the language, translating the Bible into dialects and asserting control over their "flock."

While missionaries are credited for introducing a writing system to Inuit, they also founded the first schools in the Arctic and were responsible for thousands of Inuit children being taken from their traditional camp homes to residential schools, including those in Inuvik, Chesterfield Inlet and Goose Bay. Charges of abuse against missionaries and teachers at these schools have led to an internal inquiry by the Catholic Church, and graduates of the Chesterfield Inlet residential school are planning a reunion to discuss the experiences they underwent as children. The power of the missionaries was immense.

The first arrivals of missionaries were quite scary to some Inuit. They effected a lot of fears and even killings. First of all, missionaries considered Inuit primitive .... I went to their schools and lived with them 10 months out of the year. But they did not allow me to speak my own language in their schools so that I began to think that there was something wrong with my language. At that time, I used to feel that I was in two hells — one while I was in school, the second when I went home. [18]

Our traditional values have broken down; [they are] still there, but weak. We are trying to take on the values of the dominant culture. Children were sent to boarding schools because our parents were afraid they would lose the family allowance if they refused to send us. Organized religion was shoved down our throats .... I remember being in school and being slapped if I spoke my own language. That was a heavy situation. No one else in the world would allow themselves to be treated like that .... The white man came along and said that he knew who made the sun that shines down on us. I am not picking on the culture that came from across the water, but a genocide happened. [It] needs to be recognized that it is a violent past — tuberculosis, smallpox, genocide.

For hundreds of years, contact with the outside world was marked by the desire of non-Inuit people to exploit the Arctic's physical and human resources, but it wasn't until the period between World War II and the Cold War years of the 1950s that the most audacious moves were made to impose Euro-Canadian society on Inuit. The Canadian government sped up a massive resettlement program to bring Inuit families from small hunting camps to permanent settlements, creating new, larger communities dependent on social welfare programs. Distant Early Warning, or DEW, Line stations were constructed across the Arctic, and military bases, with bars serving alcohol, were established.

In one of the most extreme demonstrations of paternalism and exploitation of Inuit, during the 1950s the federal government uprooted families from Inukjuaq (formerly Port Harrison) in northern Quebec and Pond Inlet and Arctic Bay, Northwest Territories. These families were moved to the High Arctic to create the new communities of Grise Fiord and Resolute Bay. The federal government stated the move was because of diminishing game stocks, but the Inuit Tapirisat of Canada (ITC) has charged that the move was made to establish Canada's sovereignty in the High Arctic during the height of the Cold War.

Inuit had never before lived in the harsh environments of these places.

It was like landing on the moon .... There was no vegetation, no sign of animals and, of course, no stores. There was no wood for housing ... and no fresh water nearby except salt water or icebergs .... I remember one particular time with my mother [who was] carrying a baby on her back. She and I fetched food from the RCMP's garbage a few miles away because we had no food. We came home only with empty cans and a little bit of leftovers. [19]

Allegations have also been made that women were sexually abused in return for food and that Inuit were used for physical labour for which they received no compensation.

The ITC has also brought this issue to the attention of the United Nations Working Group on Indigenous Peoples, urging that the wording of the UN Declaration on Indigenous Rights must emphasize that governments provide redress for groups subjected to "forced exile or relocation." The ITC contends that fundamental human rights were violated by this relocation, including the right to life, liberty and security of the person, the right to be free from cruel, inhuman or degrading treatment and the right not to be subjected to arbitrary detention.

During the course of this upheaval, Inuit systems of justice, education, health, government, social services and spirituality were completely replaced by non-Inuit institutions. The tribunals of elders were replaced by a European-based criminal justice system, and responsibility for education

was taken away from parents and grandparents and given to government-hired teachers from the South. Written language was introduced, and attempts were made to standardize regional dialects and create a common Inuktitut language. The midwives and traditional healers were told not to practise, and transient nurses were brought in to provide medical services. Shamanism was replaced by Christianity. And ironically, social services were introduced to "correct" the problems that were the direct result of external control over Inuit affairs.

Today, the appalling failure rate of non-Inuit systems of justice and social services to deal with the challenges facing Inuit communities has fuelled the movement to self-government at all levels. As the government officials throw up their hands in despair, Inuit communities look inward to what has given them strength.

It may be true that the physical part of our culture has been eroded to the point where it can never return to its full potential. But the non-physical part of our culture — our attitude towards life, our respect for nature, our realization that others will follow who deserve the respect and concern of the present generation — are deeply entrenched within ourselves. The presence of our ancestors within ourselves is very strong. The will to survive is there.

If we are to survive as a race, we must have the understanding and patience of the dominant cultures of this country. We do not need the pity, the welfare, the paternalism and the colonialism which has been heaped upon us over the years .... The Inuit were once strong, independent and proud people. That is why we have survived. That strength, that independence and that pride must surface again. We must prove to Canada that the original citizens of this country will not lie down and play dead. After all, the Inuit have been described by the United Nations as a people who refuse to disappear. [20]

Crucial to the development of new systems to improve Inuit society will be legitimizing Inuit women's experiences and ending violence against them.

FORMS OF ABUSE

Although most incidents of abuse against women go unreported, reports from police, hospitals and social services indicate an extremely high rate of violence against women and children in Inuit communities. There are no studies on the actual number of Inuit women who have been victimized, but it is clear from the limited information available that the situation is alarming. Inuit women are abused physically, sexually, emotionally, mentally and financially as well as politically and systemically. Inuit women are punched, kicked and slapped. Their hair is pulled, they are scratched and bitten, berated and made to give up their pay cheques. Inuit women are threatened and isolated from friends and family. They are slashed with knives and razor blades. They are raped, they are impaled, they are beaten in front of their children. Inuit women are killed.

At the same time there are few community safe homes or shelters, rape crisis centres or women's advocates in the Arctic, and the limited resources available to victims are overburdened. As Inuit communities become more aware of the degree of violence against women, there is an increasing outcry not just for more services, but for more-effective and relevant services that meet the needs of Inuit women.

Inuit women experience the same types of violence that all women in Canada experience. This section addresses those issues most discussed by Inuit women today.

WIFE ABUSE

Statistics never show the whole picture, nor can they begin to describe the fear and oppression so many Inuit women live with in their homes on a daily basis.

It was already bad when we got together, I got beaten, but it got worse when alcohol came .... We had no food to eat because he spent it on booze. He would be especially mean in the middle of the night when he had been drinking and the rest of the community was asleep. Many times he would wake up all the kids in the middle of the night and tell them to get out.

The types of violence most commonly inflicted on women by their intimate partners include, but are not limited to, physical violence or abuse, psychological or emotional abuse, financial abuse and sexual abuse.

My husband is a layman in the church, he was from the beginning and still is. It has been four years since he has stopped drinking in the community, and now he only drinks when he is away on meetings .... It has been four years since he was physically abusive .... I know for a fact that [there] is another woman .... I am amazed that I am still alive today from all the beatings I got in the past ... part of my head has been pulled apart because of my hair being pulled.

Physical violence or abuse includes slapping, punching, shoving, biting, pulling hair, choking, kicking, burning, burning the body with a cigarette, throwing things at the victim or using an object to inflict injury. Domestic violence and wife battering are other terms used to describe violence or other abusive acts within an intimate relationship. Abuse can begin on the first date, on the wedding night, during pregnancy or while a woman is in labour or breast-feeding.

Psychological or emotional abuse is a means to control women. It can include threatening the woman, her children, her family, friends or pets; controlling or disrupting a woman's personal routine such as eating or sleeping; or monitoring her movements outside the home. A woman is often kept in a state of terror through constant verbal assaults which embarrass, insult or otherwise inflict hurt, shame or fear.

Not long ago in our community, a man got angry at his brother-in-law. So he went home and got his wife out of bed and made her come with him to the brother-in-law's place. He got out his gun and fired at the house. He fired 40 bullets in half an hour. For me that's terrorism. Can you imagine, your violent husband who has beaten you so many times makes you watch him with a loaded gun. She knew that he could have just turned and fired at her at any time. And the kids! She needs help. He needs help. He terrorizes the whole family.

Financial abuse is used to threaten and/or control women. Financial abuse ranges from threatening to withhold money to controlling all family finances. It includes taking money from a woman who may be the sole financial provider for the family. Women may be forced to beg or perform other degrading acts for money to buy food or other necessities.

All these years and he has never put one dollar in my hands, even though I get family allowance and disability cheques. He takes it all .... When my husband goes shopping he buys gifts for [another] woman, and I am the one who has to take ... [them] to her.

Sexual abuse can and does happen in intimate relationships. It is a crime of power and control. Sexual abuse includes any sexual activity against the wishes or without the consent of the victim, including being forced to engage in unwanted sex; being forced to participate in unpleasant, violent or frightening sexual acts, which may include group sex, anal sex or the use of objects; being forced to have sex with others or being made to watch the performance of others. Sexual abuse also includes being criticized for sexual performance, being denied sex and being subject to excessive jealousy.

I knew of a guy who prostituted his girlfriend, and they were an established family with several children.

Not all abusive men are abusive all the time. There can be long periods between violent episodes. The abuser may blame his behaviour on factors such as work or financial pressures. Once a pattern of violence has been established, it rarely ends without outside intervention, usually police and the courts.

Nearly half of all women who are abused in the Arctic are victimized in their own homes. [21] Resources for victims and treatment for batterers are non-existent in most Inuit communities, and the number of battered women is increasing at an alarming rate. Wife abuse complaints to the RCMP rose by 30 percent in the Northwest Territories between 1989 and 1990,[22] and Iqaluit's women's shelter has tripled its occupancy rate over the last five years. Inuit women use safe shelters more than any other group in the Northwest Territories, though they represent less than half of the female population. [23] These statistics can be partially explained by increased reporting of violence by women as a result of the growing awareness generated by northern women's organizations and government that violence against women is not acceptable. However, Inuit elders testify that wife abuse is far more common today than it was in the past.

SEXUAL ASSAULT

Sexual assault is any sexual activity against the wishes and without the consent of the victim. It can include, but is not limited to, rape by a stranger, rape by an acquaintance, domestic sexual abuse, sexual harassment, sexual abuse of children, incest and gang rape.

All indications suggest that the number of sexual assaults of Inuit women is high. In the Northwest Territories, sexual assault reports have doubled over the last decade and are four to five times higher than in the rest of Canada.[24] A study on sexual assaults in the North released in 1991 found that almost all of the assaults were committed by someone known to the victim. [25] Those at highest risk for being sexually assaulted were young women between the ages of 13 and 18; girls aged 7 to 12 were at the next highest risk. [26] From these statistics, it is clear that the home can be a very dangerous place for Inuit girls and women.

A male elder from Pangnirtung called a radio phone-in show and said that rape is just part of a woman's life and they should just learn to live with it.

♀ ♀ ♀

We need a rape crisis centre here in Iqaluit. If there had been someone qualified here I would have stayed. They have a crisis line but it is a hot-line only.

That most men who sexually abuse women are known to the victim indicates that many sexual assaults probably go unreported, particularly in Arctic communities where there are few services for victims. At the same time, sexual assault reports are increasing, though services to meet the needs of victims are not. According to the 1992 report on gender equality in the Northwest Territories, *The Justice House*, "It is clear from the court dockets that sexual assault occupies a great deal of the court's time," [27] but in most Inuit communities there are no victim advocates or legal services, and in most of the sexual assault cases appearing before court, the victim has never received any preparation, let alone referral, counselling, support or follow-up.

A concern raised by women's groups, including Pauktuutit, is that sexual assaults in which the victim or the abuser was intoxicated seem to be viewed as less serious crimes by the court. Pauktuutit is currently involved in challenging court decisions they feel do not reflect the enormity of the crime. The attitudes of people within the justice system toward Inuit women have come under scrutiny. A widely publicized controversy arose when *The Edmonton Journal* published the following comments by a Northwest Territories judge, Michael Bourassa: "The majority of rapes in the Northwest Territories occur when a woman is drunk and passed out. A man sees a pair of hips and helps himself." [28] Women's groups took issue with the comments because they seemed to reflect a dehumanizing attitude that the sexual assault of a drunk Inuit woman is somehow more understandable and less harmful to the victim.

An Inuit RCMP [officer] in Rankin Inlet broke into two women's houses while drunk, got into their beds, ... fondled them and tried to talk them into sex. He was convicted, got time and served it, and then transferred to Inuvik.

In Labrador, Inuit women have suggested that the racist attitude of the police discourages victims from reporting sexual assaults.

Sexual abuse of intoxicated women has been discussed around kitchen tables. Because there is no reporting system, victims of violence continue in deteriorating lifestyles which often end up in suicide attempts and other serious social problems. This type of suppression is prevalent in all Labrador coastal communities. Due to the attitudes of some RCMP officers on the coast, allegations of racism are discussed [by Inuit] .... Frustrations grow with no knowledge of where to report incidents. Inuit are hesitant to speak out for fear of future repercussions when dealing with these services. [29]

CHILD SEXUAL ABUSE

Child sexual abuse is any sexual contact with a child by an adult or teenager. Child sexual abuse is usually committed by someone in a position of power or authority and can be committed either by a stranger or by a family member. The term child sexual abuse as used by Inuit encompasses both abuse by strangers and by family members; Inuit generally do not use the word incest. Child sexual abuse both inside and outside the family is seen as extremely serious and harmful.

[M]y oldest son ... is in jail waiting for his trial on assault charges on my sister's young daughter. But he saw what ... his father did for years, so it's a cycle. He watched all this and is very angry ....

The impact of child sexual abuse on victims is severe, and the effects can last a lifetime. When a child is sexually abused by a family member, the emotional relationship between the child and the abuser is seen as having a more serious effect on child sexual abuse victims. Many adult survivors of child sexual abuse may develop drug, alcohol or substance abuse problems or eating disorders. Others may intentionally injure themselves with razor blades or other sharp objects. Some adults turn to prostitution or may have difficulty sustaining healthy personal relationships. Some may commit offences. Professionals are beginning to question the relationship between the high rate of suicide in Arctic communities and the high rate of unresolved child sexual abuse.

A recent study determined that the average age of victims of child sexual abuse in the North was 9.7 years and the average age of the abuser was 29 years. [30] Since many victims of abuse go on to abuse others, there is an increase in the proportion of young child sexual abusers from age 10 through the teenage years. [31]

Arctic communities have begun to come to terms with the enormity of the problem of child sexual abuse but statistics are not readily available, primarily because so many cases of abuse are not reported. In Pauktuutit's ground-breaking study, *No More Secrets: Acknowledging the Problem of Child Sexual Abuse in Inuit Communities*, it was reported that 85 percent of the health care professionals, police and social workers contacted said that they knew of a child who had been sexually abused or a case of abuse that had not been reported. [32]

In addition to the lack of services available to victims of abuse, community attitudes can further isolate women and children. Community awareness is being raised by individuals and by local and national Inuit women's groups, but many victims still report that they felt ashamed when they came forward with their abuse. In small communities where there are many interrelationships and confusion over the laws and the criminal justice system, some victims are pressured to keep quiet about abuse.

Some do not want the perpetrator to go to jail, to lose a father or [provider]. Sometimes a mother denies that child sexual abuse is happening in her family because of her need to remain married. The cycle of abuse may be reoccurring in the family, from one generation to the next, and if the adults have not come to terms with their own experiences of abuse, they may have great difficulty with their child's current problem.

It is very difficult for people to disclose in a small, isolated community, or even a larger centre, for fear of everyone in the community finding out about it. There is much concern about embarrassment, shame, guilt and repercussions from family members, friends and the community. Along with many of the possible social factors, the victim may fear ostracism. In addition, it is not easy for the local people [Inuit in the community] to trust transient professionals in the medical, social [work] or law enforcement fields who often stay around for only a year or two. That is not to say there have not been long-term residents from the South who have made a contribution to the treatment of victims and offenders. [33]

One of the most disturbing findings of the *No More Secrets* research is that myths that child sexual abuse was, or is, acceptable still exist, though Inuit organizations and leaders have made many statements recently to deny this. [34] Pauktuutit has been active in dispelling the myths and confusion over the acceptability of violence against women and children in Inuit culture. Pauktuutit has stated the following concerns:

It is hard to help a child in a small town like this. If you do something, you pay the consequences. If you do nothing, the child pays the consequences. The community must become aware.

[T]he justice system has made statements which could lead people to believe that child sexual abuse is commonplace in Inuit culture. In recent years, some Inuit child sexual offenders have been given very light sentences in court rulings. The courts have, at times, accepted interpretations of traditional Inuit values and attitudes that perpetuate the myth. The three common themes that have been presented are: child sexual abuse is normal in Inuit society; when an Inuk girl starts her period, she's ready for sex; Inuit do not believe that it is wrong to have sex with young girls. [35]

Lots of kids are coming forward about childhood sexual assault. In the last two weeks, six people have been accused of sexual assault or childhood sexual assault.

Leonie Barry, a victim of child sexual abuse from the age of 7, tried to keep silent because she feared a backlash from her community. Only as an adult, when she realized that other girls — including children in her own family — were being assaulted by the same men, did she come forward and give evidence which helped convict the abusers. But she still remembers her pain and her isolation:

What happens to us young people when we don't trust the elders? Who counsels us? ... They told me to shut up and they tried to make me keep quiet .... But how can I keep quiet when it's my own [family] .... I know how hard it was for me and I'm a grown woman. I can't even imagine how hard it was for that little girl. [36]

When I was being sexually abused as a child, I did not trust anyone, especially elders. Where do kids go when they don't trust elders? I have had to fight for any help I got. Kids should have help immediately. I only knew my daughter was abused because she had chlamydia.

Treatment and education, including programs for adult survivors of child sexual abuse, are essential in Inuit communities if the cycles of abuse are to be stopped. Social workers currently have the mandate to investigate and intervene in child welfare concerns, but they are unable to deal with the long-term counselling and support needs of victims and offenders. Research in Labrador revealed the following:

Adults who are past victims of child abuse themselves have not been counselled to deal with their problems. Often this becomes a way of life, creating a cycle which if undetected by professionals continues. Healing needs to begin with the family.

When abuse is reported, efforts are made to remove the offender and not the victim, but often when there is not enough evidence to lay a charge, the victim is removed. When victims are removed they are flown to Goose Bay, away from family and friends, increasing the effects of victimization and revictimization. On average, offenders are jailed two or three months and given probation with no therapy or counselling. [37]

ELDER ABUSE

Many elders live in extreme poverty. Since many worked outside the wage economy, their pensions are inadequate to meet their needs, and allowances are not made for the extremely high cost of living. In traditional communities, food and other staples would be provided by younger family and community members. Nowadays, elders often find themselves expected to assume responsibility for raising their grandchildren with no additional financial support. Elders have been robbed of money and possessions by children with addictions, and have been victims of violence perpetrated by family members.

I know of older women who ended up in hospital because they were given so much work by their families. I know of one woman who has been raising children since 1930.

♀♀♀

It's also hard for families — like mine — which depend on pension cheques. The pension cheques are very small, ... and the amount of pension you receive depends on the amount you paid into the pension plan through your work ... pension cheques don't go very far in the North.

SUICIDE

The most distressing problem facing Inuit families is suicide among their youth. It is 10 times higher among Inuit between the ages of 16 and 30 than among any other group in Canada. [38] In some small communities, suicide is the number one cause of death. In one Nunavik community, nine people committed suicide during a 24-month period, and six others died as a result of substance abuse. [39] The Statistics Division of RCMP Headquarters in St. John's, Newfoundland, reports that from January to October of 1992, there were 27 cases of attempted suicide in Nain, which has a population of 1,140. Of those, 24 were alcohol-related and 10 involved youth under the age of 18. Some of these were repeat attempts. [40] In the Baffin region of the Northwest Territories, which has a population of under 11,000, there were 10 suicides and 37 recorded attempted suicides between 1981 and 1988. [41] Deaths by suicide are likely under-reported, since "coroners sometimes list suicides as accidental deaths to help keep the prestige of the victim's family in these small communities." [42]

The way things are now, instead of coming up with solutions, we are watching young people commit suicide. Young people are choosing death rather than living.

Family breakdown has been noted by researchers as a cause of youth suicide, particularly in homes where "problems such as alcohol abuse, depression, hopelessness, idleness and feelings of uselessness among the parents ... translate into feelings of hostility and acts of violence between mother and father and subsequently the emotional deprivation, neglect and abuse of children." [43]

Rosemary Kuptana, president of the Inuit Tapirisat of Canada (ITC), describes suicide as a cry for help from Inuit young people who are suffering from the effects of "intergenerational tension, intra-family violence, altered and destructive relationships between husbands and wives, family break-up and generally an increase in disruptive domestic life in Inuit communities." [44]

Usually youth between 17 and 20 [attempt suicide]. When we ask the ones who survive an attempt why they did it, they usually say it is because their girlfriend left them. When we ask why she left, they say it was because they were beating her. Fifteen- to 16-year-olds are beating their girlfriends.

Women in the North also link long delays caused by the circuit court system and suicides and attempted suicides by both victims and offenders forced to endure long waits between court appearances. [45]

Inuit who attempt suicide are usually sent to hospital outside their community, and there are no permanently based psychologists in Inuit regions to provide treatment and therapy for suicidal youth.

People leave and they come back to things being exactly the same as they were.

In Iqaluit, volunteers have organized a crisis line for people to receive crisis intervention counselling and referrals. This toll-free line is available to residents of Baffin, Nunavik and parts of Keewatin. Recently, Inuit organizations and mental health groups have held meetings and conferences to discuss youth suicide. Community mental health and alternative healing methods are beginning to grow in many Inuit communities.

The youngest child I have seen was a 5-year-old girl who was suicidal.

This epidemic can be stemmed. One community in northern Quebec which used the media to publicize the crisis in their community and to ask for help has begun to see positive results from a concerted effort to reach their youth. The provincial government has begun to provide some funding for prevention initiatives and some grants to create employment. The mayor of this community strongly believes that using the media can be effective in reaching both those suffering and those in a position to help, and is encouraged by preliminary results.

ABUSE OF TRUST BY PROFESSIONALS

We had a teacher years ago in Igloolik who was abusing young boys. We tried to get rid of him but it was really hard because of the teachers' union. He was just sent to another community. I personally went to the principal about one teacher, as did parents. The principal said it was out of his hands, we had to talk to the board, but we could not get past him to talk to the board. When the teacher found out what was happening, he went to another community. He was arrested, charged and convicted in that community.

♀ ♀ ♀

We know of two or three prominent abusers, and we can go see their victims in the correctional institute. They go from community to community devastating a generation of victims.

♀ ♀ ♀

I was abused by a doctor when I was a teenager. The doctor is still here. I am afraid to go public or get it in the news because I won't get any support.
A doctor working here was accused of assault. He moved to Quebec and continues to practise, and the professional body has no power to call him back here to face the charges.

♀ ♀ ♀

A lot of sexual abuse by teachers is coming out. When they are convicted, it comes out that their former colleagues knew and sent them to new communities. People either are not believing or they minimize the damage people do. Other professionals support the abuser. They have no idea how many abusers there are out there. One man who got six years had been sent to 20 communities in 22 years. Nobody said they did not want the abusers in their community because nobody tells them what they are doing.

A major societal problem now being discussed is that of professionals who abuse. Anecdotal evidence suggests a not insignificant number of doctors, teachers, clergy and social workers who have been "kicked up North" to avoid prosecution in southern Canada continue to abuse women and children. The pattern appears to be that these professionals often move to a new community when on the verge of being discovered and/or prosecuted, leaving countless victims and untold suffering in their wake. Southern Canadians are just beginning to come to terms with abuse by physicians, clergy and other professionals. When the remoteness of

Inuit settlements and the difficulty victims face when reporting abuse by professionals to non-Inuit authorities are taken into account, it becomes a huge problem that few have been willing or able to confront.

SOCIAL INSTITUTIONS

The failure of modern institutions and organizations to prevent violence against women has implications in the Arctic for Inuit women who are part of a culture which has undergone a deep and devastating transition.

... for no other segment of society do we require, need and publicly support refugee camps, otherwise known as women's shelters. While recognizing the necessity of safe places for women, we continue to tolerate the conduct which gives rise to the existence of shelters. Violence is not a "family" issue, it is not a "domestic" issue, it is not a "women's" issue. It is an issue for all of society to address. [46]

In the words of John Amagoalik, a prominent and well-respected leader, "The invasion of southern society into our homelands has created turmoil among our people. Chronic unemployment, high drop-out rates in our schools, substance abuse, family violence, the highest suicide rate in Canada, overcrowded housing and rising crime has turned our world upside down." [47] The needs of all individuals in Inuit society must be addressed by institutions and organizations to create a climate of zero tolerance for violence.

Systemic racism must also be acknowledged as a significant barrier to equality for Inuit women. In one report, 72 percent of respondents indicated they believe there is racism against Inuit in Canada, and 64 percent said they have personally experienced racism. [48]

White people push away from whites who go with Inuk, because if you get to understand and respect Inuk then you won't put them down."

THE FAMILY

Many traditional support services in Inuit culture were provided by the family. The mother, father and grandparents were the child's main educators, and the family remained a cohesive unit through all its members' lives. This role changed suddenly when children were ordered by southern authorities to attend regional schools which separated them from their family for most of the year. Later, community schools forced families to move off the land and settle in larger communities to be near their children. Inuit elder Ipellie Kanguk points to the destruction of the family structure as one of the most important reasons for today's problems:

When we were small we were like clay being moulded into a human being .... The mother was the main teacher .... Now our culture has been changed by non-Native culture. The government makes the rules in our community and you have to live by those rules. The reason why Inuit do not assert themselves is because we have given away our children to the teachers and to the government. We damaged our culture by giving away our children.

Today when children become teenagers they don't listen to their parents any more. They are adopted ... [by] their teachers instead. They have to listen to their teachers. They believe their teachers. I know it's good to be educated and learn, but teenagers only respect their teachers, not their parents. This is very different from the old days. [49]

The role of women within the family and the community has undergone many changes. While women had fewer choices during traditional times, elders say there was less violence and the recognition and value of women's work contributed to their self-esteem.

You are number one an Inuk, and number two a woman. It's hard to stand up for yourself.

It is clear that women were important decision makers in traditional times.

The women used to stay in the camp and look after everything while the men were hunting. They were the planners. They looked after the future for their children and their grandchildren. The men, all they did was bring the food, most of the time. Decisions by either [women or men] were made with respect for their partner's skills and needs. Because of the harsh arctic climate and terrain, the woman's skills at seamstressing were critical to survival, as was her ability to store and prepare food. Thus the traditional gender roles were relatively balanced. [50]

In the 1960s and 1970s, we sent our young people to foreign schools and they came back, like me, and found it very difficult to fit in. Parents still had the values of keeping the family together, close connections with relatives. When we came back, we broke ties to that circle. We didn't learn the traditional values of being a man or a woman.

Nowadays that balance is lost. While increasing numbers of Inuit women are joining the paid work force — in some communities more frequently than Inuit men — they are also expected to keep up their family responsibilities. Such attitudes can be very frustrating. Mary Sillett, former president of Pauktuutit and currently a commissioner with the Royal Commission on Aboriginal Peoples, expresses the needs of working Inuit women:

Looking at my grandmother's life and my life, she had the elements to deal with, but her responsibilities were well defined. She worked hard ... and so did my grandfather. They worked equally hard. Today, women have many more stresses to deal with. They are expected to develop the skills to go out and make money ... and then they have to take care of the kids and the home. On top of this, many women are involved in community activities, improving the well-being of their communities. Women today live in an increasingly complex world and have to meet incredible challenges. [51]

CUSTOMARY ADOPTION

Adoption has traditionally been handled informally by Inuit, "without the expense, psychological trauma or isolation from their natural parents that is common in other contemporary cultures." [52] The goal of customary adoption is to ensure that families who want children are able to adopt and that mothers who are unable to care for their children can find a welcoming home. "Teachers confirm that girls in high school are more likely to have and adopt out their babies than turn to abortion..." [53]

One of the most distinctive and positive aspects of Inuit customary adoption is that many children continue to have contact with their natural parents. In small communities or out on the land, such information would be difficult, if not impossible, to keep from the children, and some children who have been adopted out report close relationships with their birth families.

In Nunavik and the Northwest Territories, Inuit customary adoption is legally recognized. While women continue to support and practise customary adoption, many also suggest the need for safeguards to ensure that children are well cared for. However, any regulations or safeguards to guide the practice of customary adoption must be controlled by Inuit.

There is also concern that some non-Inuit may be taking advantage of government recognition of Inuit customary adoption in the Northwest Territories. Inuit children may be adopted by non-Inuit and removed from their heritage, their natural relatives and their community ... "Inuit customary adoption should be limited to Inuit and those recognized by Inuit communities as Inuit or who are related to Inuit." In this case as well, the solution lies in Inuit control of the processes surrounding customary adoption. [54]

Inuit in Labrador continue to experience obstacles to customary adoption. Cases of deliberate misrepresentation of intention and process by social workers persist. Inuit children intended for customary adoption have been taken away from their families and given to adoptive parents who are unknown to the birth mother/family, and efforts to locate these children have been unsuccessful. [55]

RELIGIOUS INSTITUTIONS/CHURCHES

Clergy have been part of the problem and must become part of the solution. The access they have to people is incredible. Address the problem from the pulpit, and espouse zero tolerance for violence.

♀♀♀

"Born Again" is like a passing thing. You hear that someone is "Born Again" and then that is over. Our children are seeing them one day praying over everything and the next day drinking and abusing maybe even 10 times worse than before. We see our own Inuit priests committing adultery and who knows what else. We see on the news every night that Catholic priests are being charged with abuse. So why should we suffer for foreign beliefs that don't work for us?

♀♀♀

The Pentecostals say "I hit my wife ... it's an act of God."

♀♀♀

Christianity has not helped. [It] offers instant solutions and paradise and all that, and doesn't deal with the problems they don't want to touch.

♀♀♀

... we extinguished our rights by converting to Christianity. Our rights were run over by accepting a new faith but, at the same time, not taking on the faith properly.

♀♀♀

A woman ... told me that she saw the Devil sitting on her knee telling her to kill her parents because they had done bad things to her. Where do you think she got these ideas?

♀♀♀

I had a talk with the social services, and I was told that I would only get better by praying to God.

Many Inuit hold deep religious convictions. As Inuit are striving to find a balance between traditional and *qallunaaq* ways, Inuit women spoke of their need for the church to value Inuit culture and address the safety of women as well as provide spiritual guidance. The women's voices speak for themselves.

SOCIAL SERVICES

Support services that deal with violence against women are almost non-existent in most Inuit communities. Social workers are overburdened with generic case loads. Often only one worker handles all the community's social assistance administration, child welfare investigations, foster home placements, adoptions, probation orders and counselling. There is seldom the time to provide the long-term counselling victims of violence need, and the lack of other support services in the community to inform victims about their options further isolates women caught in cycles of violence.

What can you do about wife assault? You call out, the transition house is in Goose Bay, it causes major upheaval and they don't have the culture there. People get to Goose Bay, and they miss their family, friends and Nain. There are no Inuit workers there, it is culturally inappropriate, and it does not work.

Many social workers are non-Inuit and may not be sensitive to the culture of the community.

The system of territorial government follows the southern model. This means that human and financial resources are not applied in a way that meets human needs in the North. There are about 3,500 to 3,600 bureaucrats working in the territorial government. About 800 of those are social workers. 99.9 percent are white and have been trained in the South and don't understand Native culture.

Inuit women who have been traumatized find it difficult to confide in someone who does not speak their language or share their culture. Moreover, it is intimidating to seek recourse in a system dominated by non-Inuit professionals.

There are a whole bunch of reasons why it is less scary to get punched up once a week than to leave.

Many young social service graduates seek short-term employment in the North to gain experience to qualify for southern jobs. Novice social service providers, however well-intentioned, often do not have the expertise needed to deal with the tremendous social problems that have developed in the North.

A number of women looked for help from social services but they didn't get it because no one in the department had experience.

The wrong kind of services or lack of services can cause as much harm in the community as the incidence of violence. These problems are compounded by a high turnover of non-Inuit staff, which prevents a community from establishing a relationship of trust with counsellors and other professionals.

If you send a young white person here who has no experience, they will just crack up within a month.

Maintaining confidentiality is a problem in small communities. Inexperienced staff may not have sufficient training or a satisfactory understanding of the importance of maintaining confidentiality in effective treatment or of the devastating results of breaches of confidentiality. The lack of physical locations that provide a measure of privacy can stigmatize those seeking treatment, since the entire community will know who is seeing the social worker. In some communities, services are provided in conjunction with

recreational programs such as crafts, or health services such as pre- or postnatal classes. While more Inuit social workers are being hired, on-the-job training is a problem because of the isolation in which they work, and separate departmental mandates have resulted in limited progress in addressing issues. With limited funding, health and social service agencies work independently of each other. Currently, there are family violence prevention programs in every Inuit region, but the resources allocated for these programs are not sufficient to meet the specific needs of each community. Local social services committees are being encouraged to take more control over program delivery in their communities, and the Government of the Northwest Territories is currently negotiating the transfer of control of social services to several communities including Cape Dorset and Cambridge Bay.

Use both Inuk and white ways of social services. Look at pros and cons of both in each situation.

♀ ♀ ♀

Let's face it, how many people with master's degrees also speak Inuktitut? Maybe we need local people to [provide] ... the healing process that will work best here.

While women's shelters are a recent development in the North, they are few and far between, and all are operating above full occupancy on a regular basis. [56] In 1992, the Baffin Regional Agvvik Society doubled the size of its safe shelter, which offers haven to battered women and their children from many Arctic communities, and yet it is still reporting close to 110 percent occupancy rates. Apart from overcrowding, this situation breeds the constant fear that desperate women will be turned away. As well, when shelters operate at and above full capacity, staff are kept busy dealing with crises and the logistics of feeding and organizing the women and children in the shelter. Little time is available for long-term counselling and advocacy.

Recently, a community group in Coppermine got tired of waiting for government funding and opened up a safe home on their own. In Pangnirtung, a women's group asked the Anglican Church to donate one of their buildings for use as a shelter. Volunteers co-ordinate counselling and the operation of the building and a safe-home network.

> *Baffin Regional Council gave a woman social worker hell for providing assistance to a woman to get to [a] shelter in Iqaluit. They said it was providing a holiday for her and that really it was the man who needed a holiday because she was probably nagging him.*

However, a debate has emerged in the Arctic about shelters or safe homes. One of the most common criticisms of safe homes in the Arctic is that victims must be flown out of their communities to regional centres where shelters are established. The disruption to women's and children's lives is immense. Employment and school are discontinued, precious housing is jeopardized and women are cut off from all their usual support systems of family and friends. While women's groups throughout the Arctic are requesting that shelters be available in their community, funding is difficult to locate. At this time, only a handful of shelters exist in Inuit regions.

Shelters in the Arctic are often criticized by those who insist they are not culturally relevant to Inuit. Elders are concerned that families are unable to heal when women and children must go so far away for safety. The concept of the extended family, which characterizes Inuit family structure, has further prevented women from speaking out. Family problems have traditionally been resolved within the family; however, some people prefer the confidentiality of social services. In confronting the issue of family violence, Inuit women may suffer ostracism and discrimination by members of the community. The interrelationships of families in one community are complex, and there may be many repercussions for victims who assert themselves, including the loss of employment or housing opportunities.

In Holman, a local community health representative is providing information on the dynamics of family violence and holding healing workshops in the western Arctic. Julia Ogina says that communities must first be aware that there is a problem and recognize the dynamics that influence violence; then they have to organize a healing process.

> *There's a lot of pain in the communities, a lot of anger and a lot of grief about all the abuse they have had. The violence hurts the victims ... it hurts the children ... but it also hurts the whole community, everybody becomes a victim of it.*

Ms. Ogina describes the need to help women who have been abused learn how to take care of themselves and each other:

> *The healing involves self-care as well. The women must ask, "How would I be different if I wasn't carrying this load around all the time?" By talking with each other they can put that load off and deal with the pain. The woman has to look at her life and say, "How can I get the rest I need? How can I get away from the person who is abusing me? How can I learn to say no when relatives and others always dump their problems on me. How can I learn to rely on others who can help me feel better?"* [57]

> *Some women are relocated only after begging. It is policy to offer women the option of relocating, but the woman has to find out about the policy. Some social workers say they only relocate a woman if "she presses charges" .... Some social workers refer women to the shelters, some don't.*

♀♀♀

> *A child may tell a social worker, but there will be a relative in the department, and so the report will be stopped.*

The challenge to find more culturally appropriate means to meet the immediate needs of victims is currently under discussion at local, regional and national forums. Inuit elders advocate for family-healing services where couples are counselled and individuals are advised on traditional Inuit rules by elders. Many young Inuit women, however, are concerned about the danger they face when traditional counselling is not effective in eliminating the violence against them. In the meantime, the number of battered Inuit women is increasing faster than means to protect them are being instituted.

JUSTICE

In the past, Inuit traditional law was well known to everyone in the community, justice was handed out according to a consensus of opinion by elders, and matters were dealt with expediently. Nowadays, few people other than some legal experts seem to feel comfortable with the current complicated justice system in the North. The majority of victims of family violence in the Arctic are Inuit women, and yet there are few legal services and very little understanding of the court process and the criminal justice system. Gender bias within the justice system has been identified by women's groups and government inquiries as having a significant impact on the lives of Inuit women.

The justice system comes up with policies and laws, and not one Inuk has studied them. The only time we get to be part of it is at the court hearings. Lots of young people see at these court hearings that big and little crimes are treated the same way. [The] justice system doesn't come for a long time so those who committed the crime worry for a long time.

In 1991, Pauktuutit received funding from the now-defunct Court Challenges Program to prepare legal arguments based on the premise that consistent leniency in sentencing in sexual assault cases where the victim and offender are Inuit interferes with the constitutional rights of Inuit women to security of the person and equal protection and benefit of the law. [58]

In 1984, three Inuit men were given light sentences for having sexual intercourse with a mentally impaired 13-year-old girl. In sentencing, the judge said "the morality or values of the people here are that when a girl begins to menstruate she is considered ready to engage in sexual relations."

In another case, the same judge sentenced to six months in jail a father who had sexually abused his daughter; the short sentence was justified on the grounds that the man was a good hunter and a competent provider for his family. The lenient nature of these sentences indicates a tolerance of such crimes within the legal system. This practice of sentencing inhibits women from coming forward because they are further victimized by a system that can't represent their needs and concerns. [59]

Lots of rules and regulations protect the abuser. You can rape someone over and over again because you are never helped to get out of the cycle. The community is not given ways to work with the abuser. The system does not give ways to help anyone.

In June 1992, a report on gender equality was released after a 16-month study of the justice system in the Northwest Territories. The report contains 90 recommendations on how the justice system can be made more sensitive to women's experiences. It also deals with the absence of services to inform, support and counsel victims and their families, the need for interagency co-operation, the need to raise public awareness about violence and the necessity of training professionals in gender equality. [60]

The justice system has been accused of further vicimizing women and children. *"For victims of violence to make use of the courts and the legal system itself, it is imperative that they be aware of these structures and how they operate. The majority of residents at Nutaraq's Place have little knowledge of court procedures or the justice system in general."* [61]

The case of Kitty Nowdluk-Reynolds clearly demonstrates that Inuit women do not always receive fair treatment from the justice system. After being brutally raped and beaten in her home community of Iqaluit, Ms. Nowdluk-Reynolds moved to British Columbia. When she did not respond to a subpoena compelling her to appear in court as a witness, she was arrested, handcuffed and escorted over 8,000 miles, spending five days in jail along the way. Ms. Nowdluk-Reynolds was strip-searched, given a delousing bath and transported to the courthouse in the back of a van with her rapist. The Royal Canadian Mounted Police Public Complaints Commission concluded, *"The Commission ... may be pardoned for wondering which victimizing incident had the greater effect, the sexual attack on June 7, 1990, or the treatment accorded to her by the criminal justice system."* [62]

It's a zoo at court here, we should sell tickets.

♀ ♀ ♀

What about my rights? I felt like I had been raped all over again. It was not worth it. I got no justice. There was absolutely nothing.

The circuit court system also serves to deny women in the North the right to timely disposition of sexual assault, wife assault and child sexual abuse cases. In the Baffin region of the eastern Arctic, for example, one judge serves 13 communities, resulting in large backlogs and long periods between court appearances. Many abusers have learned to use the circuit court system to their advantage by obtaining frequent delays.

Although there are justices of the peace in each community, the positions are becoming difficult to fill with Inuit. Inuit are sometimes reluctant to assume these positions because judging others — who are often family members — is contrary to Inuit culture, and those who do are often subject to retribution. Justices of the peace can only hear certain offences, and defendants who plead not guilty are automatically referred to circuit court.

Owing to the small population of northern communities, there is competition between defendants and prosecutors for available legal services. As a result, lawyers and court workers are placed in a conflict-of-interest situation since they represent the batterers who have peace bonds against them and also represent the victims in court when necessary.

A woman was abused and suffered attempted murder, and her daughter was murdered. Her boyfriend who did it gets full-time legal assistance from a team of lawyers. She gets the occasional call from a Yellowknife lawyer who will turn the case over to someone else for the trial. She probably will only get to meet her lawyer 15 minutes before the trial.

Between 1989 and 1992 there were approximately 11 provincial and federal inquiries, task forces and commissions dealing with some aspect of Aboriginal justice. [63] More and more justices of the peace are Inuit, although Inuit women are still not well represented in court. Justice Canada has hired an Inuit victim/witness assistant who can help prepare women and children for court, but so far she has only been able to focus on the town of Iqaluit. As well, communities in the North are beginning to discuss Aboriginal justice alternatives, including diversion committees.

Using the criminal justice system is like trying to fine tune something with a crowbar when it is inherently broken.

In 1992, Pauktuutit received funding from Justice Canada to undertake a study on Inuit women and the administration of justice in Inuit communities in Canada. The project is a direct result of Pauktuutit's work on family violence, sexual assault and the treatment of women by the justice system.

OFFENDERS

While there is a debate in the larger Inuit community on the best ways of dealing with offenders, Inuit are clear that current means of treating offenders are definitely not working. The judiciary often minimizes the severity of sentences for domestic violence and child sexual abuse, and revictimizes women and children through cultural misinterpretation and ignorance. Young Inuit women have expressed their concern that justice dispensed by community committees and/or tribunals of elders cannot adequately ensure their safety or provide effective counselling. Young women want offenders to serve their sentences in the mainstream system and be provided with counselling while incarcerated. Along with changing the legal system, effective, holistic, rehabilitative and cultural approaches to the treatment of male offenders must be adopted. At present, there is no counselling or other follow-up in the communities. The entire family must receive treatment to heal.

We hear of people who have been to jail and enjoyed the experience, who want to do it again. Others hear [this] and want to commit the crime so they can go down there too.

♀♀♀

There is no young offenders' facility in the Northwest Territories: is that not against the law?

♀♀♀

I have never seen anyone come out of jail okay.

A problem posed by the lack of facilities is that young child sexual offenders are housed in the same group home as their victims because of a lack of treatment facilities. [64] Appropriately trained staff experienced in handling cases of child sexual abuse are not always available to deal with these situations.

Jail is a system created by white middle-class men, because the loss of freedom and the stigma attached to it have a significant impact on that social group. Those deterrents don't work here.

Jail, with food, recreation facilities and educational opportunities, is preferred by some Inuit to living in overcrowded conditions. It is not uncommon for youth to commit a crime with the hope of being sent to jail.

The kids here are mostly the ones doing break and enter. Family violence means they walk the streets, [are] bored, [they] act out. Several kids have done b and e's in order to get out of the home. Some kids have said to the RCMP, "How many more b and e's do I have to do to get into the group home?" They want to get out of the home with drunken parents and see this [group home] as a nice home — three meals a day, nice bed. They don't know about the structure we impose though. We have kids here with 15 and 16 charges of b and e's.

♀♀♀

If you fix half the problem, you have not fixed it at all.

POLICE

Inuit communities are policed by the RCMP or the Quebec Provincial Police. Many Inuit women have complained that the RCMP is unwilling to respond to domestic violence calls, and the lack of response results in injury and death. There are communities in which convicted abusers serve on the force, and naturally women are reluctant to report incidents of violence. There are communities without an RCMP detachment, and others must rely on answering machines with messages recorded in English only. There are communities with no police services. Court orders such as restraining orders and peace bonds are not enforced and are therefore meaningless.

Lack of cultural understanding, inappropriate attitudes, negative experiences and an intimidating judicial process are common reasons for victims of violence to stay silent and live in fear. Another obstacle is lack of commitment to the communities by officers who are often on a two-year tour of duty; however, officers are now being encouraged to complete longer tours.

There is only one person to police the whole town. Anytime I call the police they don't bother to come.

♀♀♀

Right now with the situation, it seems that we would need five police officers, instead of just one.

♀♀♀

Often you just get a recording, and the cops only answer it if they get bored.

♀♀♀

The police are too bizarre to even start on. They definitely need policies regarding treatment of victims. If there is nothing in the manual, they can't think for themselves. Any policy at all would be great.

♀♀♀

How do you get the RCMP to respond to domestic violence? Call and tell them "Help, help, my husband is beating me with a gram of hash."

♀♀♀

I talked to a woman here who is living in the same house but separate from the man, which is common here. Her husband had held a knife to her throat. She called the police, and they did not come. She called back and got an officer on the phone who had been convicted of assaulting his wife. She just hung up. What's the point?

There is a belief that male, non-Inuit police have allowed violence against women to continue and escalate because they lack an understanding of the dynamics of family violence. This is often compounded by cultural misunderstandings and the acceptance by police officers of deliberate misrepresentation of cultural defences by perpetrators. Many Inuit women are reluctant to report assault by a partner to a non-Inuit officer, and many detachments have very slow response times. Many officers choose not to respond to domestic assault calls, especially if there have been previous calls to the same address. Women in communities that are served by an answering machine often receive no response to their calls for help. Some officers assume women reporting by phone have been drinking, and they do not respond. If an officer does not respond, no report is made and documentation will be missing which is crucial to the collection of evidence for future prosecutions.

HOUSING

The housing crisis in the North is a major obstacle preventing women from leaving violent situations. All communities have long waiting lists for housing. As well, women often have little or no protection in rental agreements where leases are in their partner's name. In cases where housing is provided by the spouse's employer, abused women may be afraid to call the police in case their husband loses his job and the family is left homeless. In spousal assault cases before the court, the threat of losing housing has been a factor in giving offenders shorter or no jail sentences. [65]

The housing crisis is considered one of the most significant causes of stress in Inuit communities today. It is not uncommon for three different families to share one small house. In 1992, the Honourable Don Morin, Minister of Housing in the Northwest Territories, told the Standing Committee on Aboriginal Affairs, *"we don't enjoy the luxury of having an old stock of houses we can repair. We're talking about getting people out of snow banks and tents and into some sort of housing. It's a basic, basic need."* [66]

Many of the North's social and health problems are exacerbated by the overcrowded housing conditions. ITC representative Kayrene Nookiguak told the Standing Committee on Aboriginal Affairs:

Overcrowded housing doesn't by itself cause spousal assault, but no one can deny the family pressure that builds up over time as a result of overcrowding and lack of privacy is a [contributing factor] of spouse assault. Overcrowded housing is not by itself the reason why so few young Inuit are graduating from high school, but the pressures of overcrowding, the lack of quiet places to study, etc. surely don't help. Overcrowding housing did not by itself cause the TB outbreaks in Repulse Bay and Rae-Edzo, or the E.Coli 0157 outbreak in Arviat that claimed several lives last year, but the overcrowded and rundown housing definitely contributed to their spread. [67]

In Labrador, where housing conditions are believed to be the worst, 100 percent of respondents in a Pauktuutit study said housing is a serious problem. [68] The population of Nain is 1,140, with an average of 50 babies being born each year. The housing allocation over the last three or four years has been one house per community per year. There are up to 14 people living in houses that have no plumbing or sewer lines, and people are put on waiting lists for 13 to 14 years. [69]

Growing up as a child in Labrador, I recall my mother and I living with different families because we did not have our own home. For single mothers, it was a way of life to move from house to house in order to have shelter. I recall waking up in the morning with my blankets frozen to the wall with no heat, and any water, which was usually kept in buckets, was frozen. Thirty years later, the problem still exists but to a larger degree considering the population growth. [70]

The Government of the Northwest Territories has recently proposed policies to eliminate housing subsidies to government employees and to establish a user-pay program for heat and utilities. Unsubsidized rent for a 100-square-metre, unfurnished detached house ranges from $1,080 per month in Yellowknife to $1,922 per month in Rankin Inlet or Cambridge Bay, [71] and utilities alone can exceed $1,000 per month.

In the Arctic, the real costs of housing are enormous, and Inuit organizations are concerned that the elimination of subsidies, which in some communities will increase housing costs by 500 percent, will discourage Inuit from entering the largely government work force. Oolootie Kunilusie, a high school counsellor, describes the hardship such rent increases will mean to her and her student husband who moved to Iqaluit from Pond Inlet to train and find work:

I am a young Inuit mother with one child and another on the way. I have a job which I really enjoy and feel is benefiting young people .... We have been struggling to make ends meet. My daughter who is now 5 was staying at day care but isn't staying there any more because we just can't afford it. We are proud of trying to better our lives for our family. That's why we were devastated to hear of the rent increases.

I don't know what I'm going to do when my baby arrives ... I basically won't be able to afford to work with the new rent increases and utility bills and pay[ing] my sitter. I even thought of putting my baby up for adoption ... I will probably have to move back to my home community because, without relatives to depend on for country food, food in Iqaluit is too much. [72]

The Status of Women Council of the Northwest Territories has expressed alarm at the proposed housing policy, in spite of "hardship allowances" to be provided by the Government of the Northwest Territories. [73] This policy will disproportionately affect Inuit women, especially single mothers, who are often employed in lower-wage entry-level positions, and will discourage young Inuit women from furthering their education and pursuing careers in their home communities because of prohibitive housing costs. [74]

Drastic cuts to federal funding for new social housing construction will have a severe impact in Inuit communities, since the Northwest Territories Housing Corporation will only receive funding to build half as many houses as it did two years ago. The proportion of households in core need [75] of housing in the Baffin, Keewatin, Kitikmeot and western Arctic regions ranges from 28.7 percent to 43.7 percent. The *Housing Needs Survey 1992* identified a need for 3,584 affordable, adequate and suitable housing units across the Northwest Territories. Considering the rapidly increasing population, these cutbacks have dire implications for Inuit in the North. [76]

Teachers have stated that the proposed housing policy will force them to leave Igloolik, and teachers from other regions would not relocate there when faced with $2,000 monthly housing costs. In some cases, housing costs would exceed a teacher's net salary. As a result, the high school would likely close, and students would be once again forced to leave their home community to continue past Grade 9. [77]

POVERTY

While Canadians in general enjoy a high standard of living, Inuit and other Aboriginal communities live in conditions comparable to those of Third World economies. The transition from a subsistence economy to the paid work force has created generations of Inuit who depend on social assistance and live below the poverty line in the most expensive communities in Canada. Many small Inuit communities have very high unemployment rates. One study reported that unemployment was rated as a problem or a serious problem by all the communities surveyed. [78]

Women are generally poorer than men, and this is particularly true since the breakdown in family structures has left many Inuit women to support their children by themselves.

Men fathering children in common-law relationships with one or more women and not assuming financial or parenting responsibility is a problem in many Inuit communities, and without child support provisions, [it] causes major financial difficulty for women and their children. Women can be reluctant to pursue legal action for support for fear of losing custody of their children in retaliation. [79]

Poverty is a major issue for Inuit. Children in Inuit communities sometimes go to school without food or proper clothing for the harsh weather. In Baker Lake, where unemployment is around 80 percent, [80] Susan Toolooktook started a food bank and a group of volunteers continually raise funds. Ms. Toolooktook began her project by walking over 50 kilometres in -40° weather to generate publicity. Irene Tiktaalaaq describes Ms. Toolooktook's quest:

She was very frustrated with hearing people ask for someone to give them a cup of flour or a cup of milk to help them make it until their next pension cheque, frustrated with people dropping by her house and asking for something small like that and not having anything to give them. Susan wanted to help people — because she knew they really needed the food items they were asking for — but she was out of food herself. [81]

The seal hunt protests begun by southern environmental groups have had a serious impact on what was a major source of income. Inuit still rely on seals for food and clothing but no longer generate income from selling sealskins, and therefore can no longer pay for hunting supplies.

Many Inuit families still try to spend time out on the land, hunting and fishing, clam digging or berry picking, as the seasons dictate. This is out of necessity, for few families can afford to feed themselves solely through wage employment and buying from the northern stores. [82]

The lack of employment and the inability to support one's family by traditional means contribute directly to increased stress and tension, and without coping skills, this tension may erupt as misdirected anger and violent acts committed against family members. Without the ability to generate income, women can be forced to remain with abusive partners.

EDUCATION

While the Northwest Territories and Nunavik education systems have fared better by including Inuit languages, a high drop-out rate among Inuit students is prevalent throughout the Arctic. As of 1986, 53 percent of Inuit had less than a Grade 9 education. Less than one percent held a university degree. [83] High unemployment and no perceived opportunities for success discourage youth from completing high school, and post-secondary education entails leaving one's community, which can be very traumatic. As well, family problems and tension between generations who have different views on education can lead to young people dropping out of a school system they find irrelevant to their lives.

Youth here have no hope. They are told they have to go to school, but when they ask what comes after and they learn they will have to go South for further education, they quit.

A major reason for dropping out is the violence youth live with in their homes. Many of them are or have been victims of child sexual assault or regularly witness their mothers being physically and verbally abused at home. Many live in poverty or with a parent or sibling with addictions. In an overcrowded house, they may not get enough sleep nor have a place to study. They may also suffer from nutritional deficiencies because of poverty or neglect.

When youth do leave their communities to pursue post-secondary education, they face major obstacles in urban centres.

You have to remember this is not like coming off a farm to come to a city; it is coming from a completely different area ... where the only mode of transportation to go any other place is by air .... You have to understand that these students go through an awful lot, just moving from, say, Broughton Island to Ottawa. Broughton Island is a small community of about 450 people. The only school they have [known] is the little school there. They may have had an exchange trip once or twice in that 15 or 20 years, but to go to a city like Ottawa is a total change. All of a sudden you are inundated with being able to go to a McDonald's or whatever else, all these attractions a city has, some not so bad, some not so good .... There is getting on and off [a bus]; it is ... something they have never experienced. [84]

[When some young people arrive in cities, they] ... feel as alienated and isolated as if they were in jail. [85]

There is an incredible amount of violence that happens to our students. I don't know how some of them keep coming to school.

Some young people who have gone to larger centres to continue their education have fallen victim to foul play or have died from exposure or other accidental causes. Young people from small communities can be overwhelmed by cities, and living away from family and other support networks, they are often vulnerable to the dangers of urban environments.

Twenty years ago, Inuit languages were at risk of being lost completely, but they are now thriving in many regions. This is in part because of changes to education policy which led to the formation of locally controlled education committees, Inuit language instruction and training programs for Inuit teachers. Unfortunately, not all Inuit regions have been as fortunate as others. On the Labrador coast, Inuktitut is mainly spoken by elders. Although efforts are being made by educational facilities to return to the language, youth feel that they will be ridiculed if they are heard speaking Inuktitut.

All our lives while growing up we were told to speak English, not Inuktitut ... [those who spoke their language] were scorned ... and as a result an attitude of shame developed. Ten to 12 years ago, Inuktitut immersion began in schools for the children of these parents who were told to speak English and not Inuktitut. It is very important for these parents to speak to their children in Inuktitut at home and take pride in Inuit culture and being Inuit. [86]

EMPLOYMENT

While women traditionally have had few opportunities to develop skills for paid employment through education and training, increasing numbers of women are seeking work outside the home. Inuit women are now more likely to finish school than Inuit men, and adult education centres are unable to accommodate all those seeking training. However, major obstacles continue to prevent women from entering and succeeding in the work force, including lack of child care, poverty, few local employment opportunities and societal attitudes that expect women to run the household as well as work at a job. Violence in the home has a direct impact on a woman's ability to maintain employment, and women who are abused can be prevented from working outside the home by abusive partners.

Even in the workplace, men sexually abuse. It happened to me with a personnel officer at a hospital seven or eight years ago. I thought I would lose my job. He made me pose for a picture.

Training programs and facilities, while increasing in numbers, fail to meet modern needs. Local employment is scarce or of a short-term, make-work nature, and many businesses continue to "import" non-Inuit staff from the South.

Inuit women in the workplace face the same harassment and violence in the workplace as all women, but their experiences are often compounded by racism and paternalism.

There are power issues here — around race, class, competence — that are not present in other areas. People here are disempowered in so many ways.

♀ ♀ ♀

I have concerns about psychological abuse in the workplace. I am a single mother. What do I do when I don't have the power to address someone who is abusing me at work? How do I make a complaint about someone without actual evidence? How do you know what is and isn't abuse?

Bilingual Inuit staff, who are often paid less than their white, better-educated co-workers, take on extra responsibilities by virtue of their ability to communicate in their mother tongue. Being able to communicate in an Inuit language is generally not recognized or valued by increased compensation.

A project for working with child [abuse] survivors could not find professionals who were willing to work in the regions, even though they advertised for a full year. Really, this was lucky because now they will have to train the community.

Arts and crafts produced by Inuit are recognized internationally as representative of the grace and beauty of the Canadian Arctic and of Canada as a nation. Inuit art is often proudly presented as official gifts to heads of state and other visiting dignitaries. Income generated by wearable arts and crafts such as mukluks, *kamiks* (boots), parkas and slippers — which are largely produced by women — in addition to weavings, appliquéd wall-hangings, baskets and porcupine and moosehair tufting contributed $9.7 million in the Baffin region alone in 1986, representing 11 percent of the region's total income. [87] The industry is an important source of income for women.

I would have liked to have given you statistics about what violence the hospitals are seeing all along the coast, but that would have taken too much time and involved too many people. So I will talk generally about what we see in this hospital, involving people just in[side] these walls, all of them hospital employees. Ninety of 140 hospital employees are Inuit. Fifty-nine of that 90 are women. Forty-six of that 59 are living with some kind of violence in their own life. Twenty-eight of these women have been visibly physically abused. You know just by looking at them that they have been abused. Showing up with bruises, scratches, bite marks. Of these 90 Inuit, 31 are men. Twenty-three of them have been physically or mentally abusive to their partners. Of 12 interracial couples, 10 have shown abusive behaviours. Children of three women employees have committed suicide. Children of 10 other women employees have attempted suicide.

There are, however, industry-related difficulties including the availability and cost of raw materials and tools, inadequate marketing and low prices. Problems also result from women having to work a double or triple day, often juggling child-care and household responsibilities and seasonal tasks associated with hunting and fishing. [88] There is also the very real possibility that these arts and crafts will not be available much longer because not enough young women are learning traditional arts and crafts skills. "Craft work is associated with low pay, exploitation and a past way of life." [89]

One of the needs of modern Inuit women and their families is quality, affordable child care, which is often completely inaccessible in most Inuit communities. The traditional support networks of elders and relatives are severely taxed by the sheer number of children in communities and by an increased need for child care because of the switch to wage economies. Organized child care has been identified as a need by women's groups, employers and adult educators. In some Inuit communities, women have asked for training in early childhood education and have tried to establish their own child-care services. In Pond Inlet, a community-organized day-care centre operated successfully with experienced, Inuktitut-speaking women from the community until the bureaucracy of applying for child-care funding became too overwhelming and frustrating.

Since 1986, two of the three Inuit women in top management have resigned due to harassment/violence by their husband. In May [1992], two women have resigned from their jobs due directly to violence/harassment by the husband. Also in May, [we] got one request for a change of job due directly to violence. So altogether we will have to train three new people because of violence in May. The effect of this violence against women has a big toll on the functioning of our workplace.

Self-government in Nunavut will result in increased opportunities for professional and semi-professional jobs in local communities and will encourage more people to get an education.

HEALTH

With the introduction of government health care, power was stripped from the traditional healers, entrenching a non-Inuit approach to health care. While, traditionally, Inuit women were the major providers of health care in communities, they have now been replaced by federal government nurses, most of whom are transient and spend only a few years working at community nursing stations before moving on. General practitioners visit communities every month or two, but often they are only able to administer "assembly line" medical attention. Travelling clinics, such as dental, ophthalmological or ear-nose-throat, are set up for a day or so in each community, and all those requiring specialized treatment must be seen before the clinic is moved to the next community. Only Goose Bay, Iqaluit, Povungnituk and Kujjuaq provide limited, regionally based hospital services, though a hospital is being planned in the Keewatin region.

[There is] only one point of medical access here. If the doctor does not agree with your choice of care, there is nobody else. You have to pay $2,500 for air fare and expenses to get a second opinion.

In regions without hospital services, Inuit must go to larger centres such as Yellowknife, Churchill, Winnipeg, Montreal and St. John's for treatment, and the frequent travel of patients from small Inuit hamlets to cities has become the norm. This is particularly difficult for pregnant women, who must leave their community several weeks before their due date. For many patients who may have never left their home community, medical treatment in large urban centres can be a terrifying experience, and there are often insufficient numbers of trained medical interpreters. Transportation costs keep family members from visiting patients requiring lengthy hospital stays, and home care programs, if available, are extremely limited. HIV and AIDS patients are also expressing their need to live and be cared for in their home communities with their families. [90]

Major health concerns facing Inuit include an increase in diseases such as lung cancer, sexually transmitted diseases and HIV/AIDS, epidemics of hepatitis A and B, the suspected health risks associated with PCB contaminants at abandoned DEW Line stations and the recent discovery of radioactive cesium levels in everything from tundra moss to Inuit mothers' breast milk. Health boards and Inuit organizations are demanding more control over health research and disease prevention.

My second child is 24 and in a Montreal hospital. He has been there [for] four months because of problems with his lungs and heart because of the beatings I got when I was pregnant. He was born at only four pounds. He may have to go through heart surgery again. I was sent to see him, but he was unconscious for two days after surgery so he won't remember.

People with disabilities are an invisible minority in the Arctic. Women with disabilities can be virtually housebound, particularly during the winter months. Communities do not have public transportation or vehicles equipped to transport people with disabilities. Government codes to ensure accessibility apply only to buildings of three or more stories, which are a rarity in most Inuit communities. *"For the roughly one in 10 people in the eastern Arctic with some kind of physical disability ... this is probably the most difficult place to live in North America."* [91] Many parents of children with disabilities are forced to relocate to a larger community such as Iqaluit, Yellowknife or a southern urban city to have access to health care and other programs, services and facilities.

Nurses in northern communities are under a great deal of stress, since they are the only health care workers providing on-call 24-hour service. *"It is of great concern to the Labrador Inuit that in some communities there is just one nurse ... [who] must work five days a week and be on call 24 hours a day, seven days a week, 365 days a year."* [92] The frustrations and loneliness of the cross-cultural situation in which they find themselves, in addition to the lack of resources, make burnout and turnover rates high.

> *People who come from down south get a couple of days of videos to teach [them] about [the] life of Inuit but it's not enough. The Quebec system forces new doctors to come north after graduating, so the resentment doesn't help.*

There have been numerous complaints against health care providers in northern communities. Many residents of Inuit communities feel that they are denied appropriate medical care because of bias, racism or misconceptions and that preferential treatment is often given to non-Inuit and prominent Inuit residents. Nurses, who generally have a vehicle at their disposal, have been accused of being reluctant to make home visits, forcing families to transport very ill patients to the nursing station, usually by snowmobile, in all weather conditions.

> *One woman comes in each week [to the health centre] with a beating [being] the primary reason for her visit. Two women each day come in with depression, abdominal pain or fractures. They don't identify the problem as family abuse, but it is often the case.*

There is jurisdictional confusion in Labrador about who is responsible for providing health care services to Inuit. Four different groups define health policy for Labrador Inuit: the federal government through Indian and Inuit Health Services of Health and Welfare Canada, the Department of Health of the Government of Newfoundland, Regional Health Services and the Labrador Inuit Health Commission.

> These groups do not work well together, despite efforts on everyone's part. All groups have different priorities and different understandings of the needs and how they should be met .... We do not feel that regional and national MSB [Medical Services Branch] personnel are sensitive to the differences between Inuit and Indian. We are constantly sent documents that refer only to status Indians, to chief and council, to tribal councils, etc. At meetings we always have to remind people that we do not live on reserves, that our circumstances are different ... One document written by the MSB presented to us at a national meeting actually said that there were no isolated communities in the Atlantic region. [93]

> *It goes from bad to worse. A young man from Pond Inlet was sent to the Clarke Institute in Toronto. He was sent with no money; [he] wandered around Toronto and somehow got to the Institute. The staff was angry because he would not speak English, but he couldn't.*

Due to the transience of health care professionals in Inuit communities, identification of abuse, referral and long-term support are often forgotten aspects of northern health care. Recently, however, a program of community health representatives (CHRs), who are usually Inuit from the community, has been developed in regions including Labrador and throughout the Northwest Territories. The CHRs receive on-the-job training to provide public health promotion and increase awareness, which includes providing information about family violence and sexually transmitted diseases.

ALCOHOL/SUBSTANCE/ SOLVENT ABUSE

Substance and solvent abuse has been identified as a major social and health problem in Inuit communities. While the availability of solvents and aerosols is controllable, gasoline is easily accessible in remote Inuit communities. The Northwest Territories ranks second in Canada in alcohol consumption per capita.[94] Children have been found outside during the winter, unconscious and near death from sniffing solvents. Children growing up in homes in which substance and solvent abuse is a daily reality are at grave risk of repeating the same behaviour without early intervention.

The high incidence of solvent abuse by youth has been attributed to a lack of identity and a sense of confusion resulting from the conflict between Inuit and white cultures. Traditional activities have no relevance to today's youth, and there are few recreational facilities or activities to fill the long hours in isolated communities. Unemployment, poverty, hopelessness, neglect, peer pressure and the media have been identified as contributing factors.

The community of Inukjuak in northern Quebec (Nunavik) has targeted solvent and substance abuse as its number one priority. The youngest sniffer known to the school principal in Inukjuak is 8 years old. The community is taking active steps to combat solvent abuse by combining "internal exile" in a group home and detoxification with relearning traditional survival skills out on the land.[95] The community identified 44 known substance abusers.[96] Meetings are held with all known substance abusers and their parents to educate them about the dangers of solvent and substance abuse and to deal with the problem as a family and a community. Elders are advised of prevention activities and guide the prevention group in establishing a youth camp. The mandate of the prevention group is to find ways to deal with the high rate of substance abuse, but their activities have expanded to include all other areas of prevention and education. These activities include hiring a community health representative; holding training and information sessions for individuals and community groups; contacting alcohol and drug treatment centres to establish local

follow-up and aftercare for clients returning from treatment programs in larger communities; and working with local school authorities to plan prevention programs for students which promote cultural and traditional values.[97]

Five years ago, sniffing was very secret. But now there is so much, so many doing it, that everyone knows.

♀♀♀

I have one son who sniffs ... who is addicted .... He says he is not sniffing, even when I catch him ... he has said it is because he is depressed by his brother being shot. But he started on drugs even before his brother was shot. Lots of times my belongings have been destroyed by him. My house is practically empty now. Lots of times I don't bother buying things that I would like to have because I know it will be destroyed anyway ... I have spoken to the police force and social services but they have done nothing. I wonder if the police have even bothered to write down what I have told them.

♀♀♀

Here almost every household has gas stored outside their house.

♀♀♀

[One] woman talks to her alcohol and drug counsellor by telephone every two weeks because the counsellor is in Toronto.

♀♀♀

People get on Canadian Airlines to go to the rehab centre, and the first thing they do is order a drink.

While some communities have declared themselves dry, illegal alcohol consumption is a growing concern.

They make alcohol out of ketchup here sometimes. You aren't supposed to drink it before 48 hours. One guy drank a whole bunch of it before it was ready and he died of alcohol poisoning. In the autopsy, his [blood] ... was 45 percent alcohol.

Women who live in dry communities may be reluctant to report assaults for fear of being charged with alcohol offences themselves. Children born with fetal alcohol syndrome suffer a range of physical ailments and psychological effects including learning disabilities. This preventable syndrome is causing increasing concern among health care and other professionals because of significant rates of substance abuse by women. Public education and further research are urgently needed to help people fully understand the effects of substance abuse on their unborn children.

MIDWIFERY

Inuit have the highest birth rate of any population in Canada, but the ability of Inuit women in the North to control the way in which they choose to deliver their children lags far behind southern Canada. Before the establishment of communities, women were in control of their own birthing. During the early days of settlement life midwifery was an accepted practice until government health care professionals insisted that all expectant mothers fly out to regional hospitals well before their due date and deliver their babies there. The emotional and mental stress of this relocation on a pregnant woman can be severe and puts added strain on the family left at home to cope without her.

The whole process of being pregnant and giving birth has not changed since time began.

The goal of the Inuulitsivik Health Centre in Povungnituk, Quebec, is the takeover of services by Inuit. The facility began by offering a culturally integrated maternity and midwifery program which has as an objective that Inuit midwives will train other Inuit women in their communities. While women in Nunavik are still moved from their communities to give birth, the Povungnituk Maternity Centre is preferable to the hospital in Moose Factory, Ontario, where women had been sent previously — a three-hour flight away and no interpreter available.

Women's groups in the North are asking for more community-based health services and for the re-establishment of traditional midwifery practices so women can have the choice of delivering children in their home community or at a larger medical facility. Before the resettlement of Inuit, midwives were an integral part of Inuit culture and were greatly respected. The current practice of separating the pregnant woman from her community imposes severe hardships on the whole family and often turns what should be a joyous event for women into a lonely trauma.

REPRODUCTIVE HEALTH

In 1991, a scandal broke out surrounding abortions at Yellowknife's Stanton Hospital when a Baffin resident reported to the media that she had undergone the procedure without anesthetic. A tribunal was appointed to investigate complaints of inadequate medical procedures. It was determined that procedures performed at the Stanton Hospital were not in accordance with those detailed by the Society of Obstetricians and Gynaecologists of Canada, which includes administering oral and/or intravenous analgesic. Of 28 patient files pulled at random, none received local or general anesthetic.

Some physicians acknowledged that a few patients were in sufficient pain that they required physical restraint by nursing staff to ... complete the procedure [safely]. Patients also reported, and physicians acknowledged, they had screamed, cried and yelled for the physician to stop the procedure. [98]

In addition to medical procedures being performed with no pain relief, the review committee reported on other issues that were presented, such as the lack of information, the imposition of physicians' religious beliefs or personal values, poor attitudes of physicians and differing perceptions of complaints. *"One woman said the doctor asked her, When's your next birthday? ... Oh, you'll be back here before then. Your kind always are."* [99]

A supplementary, or dissenting, opinion prepared by one member of the tribunal speaks of the power imbalance between physicians and patients, and states a concern about complaints being made but not heard.

It is interesting to note that some patients reported complaining to a particular physician, but the same physician subsequently stated that they had not received any complaints. It appears that the analogy of "not being heard" extended beyond the operating room. [100]

Whenever you do a big story, like the abortion story, there is a backlash ... and I felt very alone. But I would think of the women on the tables, and it would keep me going.

The supplementary opinion stated that

[p]ain is pain. Women can and do bear considerable pain in the course of their lives. Within modern medicine we anticipate that, as much as is possible, we will be spared unnecessary pain. Where that doesn't occur we are right to seek an answer. Where the system doesn't hear the complaint, we are right to speak more loudly. If we keep saying what has happened, in a way that doesn't require second guessing or reading between the lines, then we may have started toward solving the problem. [101]

... By knowing how something happened we can use that information to identify ... other situations and generally to improve our lot as women and as a society. [102]

Youth in some communities are reluctant to approach the nursing station or other medical facility for contraceptives because of the likelihood of receiving a lecture instead of sound information. In such instances, an important opportunity to educate youth on the need to practise safe sex and on sexually transmitted diseases is lost.

The *Report of the Abortion Services Committee* includes a recommendation that

[a] policy should be developed by the Department of Health to provide guidelines for physicians and nurse practitioners in the employ of the Department or regional health boards to deal with a variety of reproductive health issues, including the provision of appropriate contraceptives to youth, and the responsibility for support, counselling and referral for abortion and sterilization procedures. The policy should include an affirmation that reproductive health decisions are made by clients in consultation with medical professionals and that the objective of such procedures is to support individual choice. The Department of Health should have an advisory body representing all regions which would advise on traditional aboriginal values and teachings. [103]

While abortion is a controversial issue and is not a choice made by many Inuit women, women who choose to terminate a pregnancy must have access to safe medical procedures without having medical personnel impose their personal or religious values on these women.

An inquiry into abortion procedures at the Yellowknife hospital resulted in over 30 recommendations including having more information available to women on health care and instituting an independent ombudsperson who could receive complaints about health professionals and investigate them. [104] Pauktuutit supports these recommendations.

COMMUNITY INITIATIVES

Pauktuutit has started a dialogue on family violence by holding public meetings and publishing documents that help women tell the story of their abuse.

Recently, Pauktuutit has begun to address the need for women of different generations to work together. Support groups made up of survivors of child sexual abuse have sprung up in many Inuit communities including Pond Inlet, Goose Bay, Inuvik and Pangnirtung. They offer counselling and court preparation to child victims.

Treatment programs for abusers do not exist in most Inuit communities or regions; at this time, jail is the only institution dealing with abusers. In some Inuit communities, men's support groups have been formed recently and are helping men come to terms with their experiences.

The Inuit Broadcasting Corporation (IBC), which broadcasts across the Canadian Arctic on the Television Northern Canada (TVNC) network, aired a phone-in television show in Inuktitut and English to address the needs of child sexual abuse survivors. Individuals phoned in with questions which were answered by Inuit counsellors, and a network of counsellors stood by their telephones in many Inuit communities. IBC also produced and broadcast a video about the formation of the Pangnirtung women's support group.

An Iqaluit group concerned with the lack of information and advocacy for women who are victims of violence pooled their resources and produced a video in English and Inuktitut which helps prepare victims who testify in court. TVNC broadcast the video, and three weeks of call-in shows and panel discussions were also produced which dealt with violence and the justice system.

MEDIA

The media are powerful tools that have great potential for educating the public on issues of violence and abuse. TVNC, which is widely watched in the North, provides programming in Aboriginal languages. It celebrated its first anniversary in January 1993. TVNC covers cultural events, tackles tough issues such as family violence, child sexual abuse and substance and solvent abuse, and links Inuit communities that are spread over thousands of miles. Ethel Blondin, Member of Parliament for the Western Arctic, states *"... funds for Native broadcasting are among the best-spent public dollars in the country."* [105]

Mass media and the desire for instant gratification leads to great frustration.

Cutbacks to Inuit and Aboriginal communications total more than 40 percent in less than three years. There was a 25 percent budget cut in 1990, and budget cuts announced in early 1993 by the federal government, which provides funding through the Northern Native Broadcast Access Program, are expected to be crippling.

TVNC will be a powerful tool to spread the word.

This cutback will undoubtedly mean the loss of jobs, possibly the closing of production centres and the elimination of [assistance for] small communities to maintain their basic communication services .... Young people have very few opportunities to hear their own language spoken and to see contemporary life reflected in the media. It is ironic that in this, the International Year of the World's Indigenous People, Canada is in apparent violation of United Nations' agreements on supporting and promoting indigenous culture and language. [106]

These cutbacks will detrimentally affect current family violence public education initiatives in the North.

While additional research is needed, Inuit women are extremely concerned about the link between violence in mainstream television programming, movies and heavy metal music videos and violent behaviour, unacceptable attitudes and sexual behaviour in children. Most communities receiving television transmissions by satellite do not have adequate control over programming, and decisions on which channels to broadcast are usually made by town or hamlet councils.

The only way to solve problems is to reach people through the media.

In February 1993, at the ninth Pauktuutit Annual General Meeting, held in Happy Valley-Goose Bay, Labrador, a resolution was passed calling for Pauktuutit to "lobby and call upon governments and politicians at all levels to inform people about the harmful effects of violence on television and [in] videos on children," and further, that "Pauktuutit support the development of regulations controlling the exposure of violence on television and in videos." [107]

The media portray us as awful, as women wanting to put men away.

Today's Inuit youth are the first generation to grow up in the settlements, and many suffer from a lack of identity and a sense of confusion caused in large part by the invasion of southern culture, which usually bears little resemblance to life in the communities and has no relevance to traditional Inuit culture or values.

[The media say] "Aw, here is another bunch of women bitching."

The media have significant roles to play in exposing violence against women, and as active partners in bringing about zero tolerance of violence.

LEADERS/ROLE MODELS

In recent years, a number of Inuit leaders and politicians have been convicted of acts of violence against women. Inuit women have expressed serious concerns about leaders' and politicians' lack of understanding concerning issues of violence, their inability to protect and promote women and women's issues, and their influence as perceived role models.

Big name persons, leaders, councillors, teachers, are abusing their wives and kids. No one will talk; they think that the big name person is more important than the victims, and they are afraid. It needs to come out publicly if big name people are abusing their wives and kids. And it needs to stop.

Inuit women have identified fairness, high moral standards, commitment, honesty and being respected by their communities as desirable characteristics for leaders. Inuit leaders are also expected to understand their culture and history, and speak their mother tongue. Unacceptable characteristics or behaviours include dishonesty, insensitivity, wife battering, child abuse and alcohol or drug abuse.

The RCMP refused to charge the Minister for Social Services for holding his wife at gunpoint. This kind of thing blows communities apart, leads to more suicides, because people cannot handle it.

Inuit women are exercising greater control over their quality of life through the development of policies and programs, and they have demonstrated their commitment to achieving social change. Social issues are moving higher up on the agendas of national organizations such as the Inuit Tapirisat of Canada, which recently held a three-day round table on health, housing and justice issues in Happy Valley-Goose Bay, Labrador.

There are some extremely powerful women, some incredible women in the smaller communities, who have worked so hard to put together women's support groups and be a resource in their community .... They try to keep alive qualities of love, caring, sharing and the good traditional ways. [108]

If I call myself Inuk, but if I am not speaking Inuktitut and living the Inuit way, then I am not making myself a role model.

Oftentimes, community leaders have been themselves victims and perpetrators of family violence. Community, regional and national representatives of Aboriginal peoples who abuse their authority are often dealt with lightly because aside from their abusive behaviour they are good political representatives.

A lack of acknowledgment and motivation to act against leaders who abuse is a problem in Labrador because of possible future repercussions. Leaders at the community level are highly regarded, even by family members of victims, as good political leaders. Because Labrador is limited in strong leadership representatives at the community and provincial levels, leadership qualities often overshadow incidents of spousal or sexual assaults. In small coastal communities, there is no recourse for victims of leaders apart from the criminal justice system. When charges are dropped because of lack of evidence, usually when alcohol is involved, there is nowhere for the victim to go for support. The repercussions on the victim and members of the family, who may be employees of the abuser, can be severe and acts of speaking out are often met with reprisals. In the past, elders in the community dealt with abusive situations of any type and their advice was adhered to, but over the past 10 to 15 years they have lost their perceived authority due to the implementation of various community representative groups, i.e., social services, community councils, etc.

This type of dictatorship undermines issues of concern which are the very mandate of a representative body and as a result, social problems continue at the community level if these concerns are not addressed by overseeing national bodies. [109]

Our pain and daily abuse is not talked about. Women have to be designated to organizations, departments, boards, etc. They can't ignore you when you're right there.

Pauktuutit is currently developing a code of conduct for Inuit leaders, both men and women.

SELF-GOVERNMENT

Inuit are currently progressing toward increased self-government in many areas, anxious to assume control over how communities will determine their future. While at the local level, Inuit women hold fewer decision-making positions than men, there is a growing number of Inuit women in regional, national and even international positions.

Six thousand Inuit live in 14 communities in the Nunavik region of northern Quebec, along the coasts of Ungava Bay and Hudson Bay. The region has achieved a substantial degree of self-government. The 1975 James Bay and Northern Quebec Agreement transferred administrative responsibility for areas including education, health and social services from the provincial government to local and regional institutions in the Nunavik region. [110]

Inuit in other regions have not had the same success in their quest for self-government. Land claims negotiations with Inuit in Labrador have been delayed for more than a decade as provincial and federal governments have alternately refused to come to the negotiating table. The Labrador Inuit Association has again presented a proposal on Inuit self-government to the Premier of Newfoundland and is persisting in its efforts.

While the challenges ahead are immense, self-government has the potential to help Inuit women assert themselves as an important force in making the decisions that govern their lives. Martha Flaherty, president of Pauktuutit, writes of the need for Inuit women to begin the process:

We are deeply committed to the preservation and enhancement of the language, culture, values and traditions of our society, and we are searching for ways of incorporating these into the laws which govern us .... We want to ensure that Inuit women are in a position to contribute fully and effectively ... in regional self-government initiatives, land claims and the national aboriginal justice scene, and we want to see these discussions lead to action. [111]

Inuit self-determination is essential in determining community needs and the services to meet those needs. Inuit women must be involved as active and equal partners in all self-government initiatives to ensure women's priorities are reflected.

CONCLUSION

The Arctic is set for change once again. Inuit communities are recognizing their legitimate right to control their own destinies and are on the brink of developing new systems of Aboriginal justice and government. Self-government will provide Inuit with the power to bring about positive change, heal their communities and determine the rules by which they will develop meaningful and culturally appropriate ways of preventing abuse of women.

This generation today is going on to tomorrow. I would like to tell people who are bringing up children to bring them up right. Do something good for your children, and if you love them, teach them what you want them to learn, teach them what you want them to be. Your children will grow up and go away from you, they will have to know how to live, and the world will not be the same as it is now. Try to help your child as much as you can by teaching them to respect others and to think not just of themselves but of everyone else. We have to help our children to be thinkers. We have to bring up children who will be kind. Don't teach your children to be cruel. [112]

While all victims of violence are isolated in their fear, guilt and pain, Inuit women living in small communities with few services are particularly vulnerable. Often government services are provided by non-Inuit staff who neither understand Inuit culture nor have an accurate perspective of the problems facing victims. A long history of abuse throughout the colonialist past affects the attitudes brought to the issues of today. Rigid stereotypes of male and female roles encourage men to assert control over women and children in their families, but at the same time, changes to Inuit culture have confused these roles. Many of the values which were the foundation of traditional communities need to be adapted to meet the realities of modern Inuit life. The attitudes that accept, minimize and contribute to violence against Inuit women need to be re-examined and changed, and in the Arctic, the dialogue needed to achieve this must be relevant to the Aboriginal cultures.

In 1992, the Inuit Tapirisat of Canada
unanimously passed a resolution stating:

*Inuit are increasingly conscious of how these
acts [of violence] form a cycle of violence which
is passed on from one generation to the next, and
are the root cause of much of the alcohol abuse,
substance abuse and suicide in our communities
.... Few resources are available to people at the
community level who wish to help both the
abused and the abusers, and so ... break the cycle
of violence .... The Inuit Tapirisat of Canada
recognizes the urgency of these problems and
commits itself to working closely with
Pauktuutit to address them .... All reports of the
Panel on Violence Against Women must reflect
the needs of Inuit women, especially with regard
to the desperate need for culturally appropriate
treatment programs and permanently funded,
culturally appropriate treatment facilities — for
both the abused and the abusers — designed and
implemented by Inuit for Inuit .... The ITC
should aggressively lobby the federal, provincial
and territorial governments for longer sentences
and greatly improved counselling services for
persons convicted of family violence and/or
child sexual abuse.* [113]

Throughout the Arctic, individuals, local support
groups, counsellors, government and Inuit
organizations are sending out the message that
violence against women is unacceptable.
However, the support services to enforce the
message are tragically lacking. The North has a
long history of oppression and intergenerational
abuse and is experiencing the effects of
tumultuous changes. Inuit communities need
help to meet the overwhelming challenges facing
them, but past interventions from outside have
proven short-lived, transient and ineffective.
Future solutions must come from the
communities and be inherently Inuit.

1   As told by Ipellie Kanguk, Pond Inlet, Northwest Territories and adapted by Oleepaka Anaviapik.

2   John Amagoalik (Background paper prepared for the Canadian Panel on Violence Against Women, Ottawa, 1993).

3   Statistics Canada, *The Daily*, March 30, 1993, p. 12.

4   Pauktuutit, *Arnait: The Views of Inuit Women on Contemporary Issues* (Ottawa, 1991), p. 10.

5   Rachael Uyarasuk, Igloolik, Northwest Territories, personal interview, 1993; translated by Oleepaka Anaviapik.

6   Naki Echo, Iqaluit, Northwest Territories, personal interview, 1993; translated by Oleepaka Anaviapik.

7   Rhoda Karetak, Rankin Inlet, Northwest Territories, personal interview, 1993; translated by Oleepaka Anaviapik.

8   Nellie Cournoyea, "Everybody Likes the Inuit," in *Northern Voices: Inuit Writings in English,* ed. Penny Petrone, (Toronto: University of Toronto Press, 1988), p. 286.

9   Rhoda Karetak, Rankin Inlet, Northwest Territories, personal interview, 1993; translated by Oleepaka, Anaviapik.

10 Simeonie Akpik, Lake Harbour, Northwest Territories, personal interview, 1993; translated by Oleepaka Anaviapik.

11 Teporah Qapik Attagutsiaq, Arctic Bay, Northwest Territories, personal interview, 1993; translated by Oleepaka Anaviapik.

12 Simeonie Akpik, Lake Harbour, Northwest Territories, personal interview, 1993; translated by Oleepaka Anaviapik.

13 Ipellie Kanguk, Pond Inlet, Northwest Territories, personal interview, 1993; translated by Oleepaka Anaviapik.

14 Minnie Audla Freeman, "Living in Two Hells," in *Northern Voices: Inuit Writings in English* (Toronto: University of Toronto Press, 1988), pp. 235-236.

15 Rachael Uyarasuk, Igloolik, Northwest Territories, 1993; translated by Oleepaka Anaviapik.

16 Simeonie Akpik, Lake Harbour, Northwest Territories, personal interview, 1993; translated by Oleepaka Anaviapik.

17 *Northern Voices: Inuit Writings in English*, ed. Penny Petrone (Toronto: University of Toronto Press, 1988), p. xii.

18 Minnie Audla Freeman, "Living in Two Hells," in *Northern Voices: Inuit Writings in English,* ed. Penny Petrone (Toronto: University of Toronto Press, 1988), p. 239.

19 Martha Flaherty, "I Fought to Keep my Hair," in *Northern Voices: Inuit Writings in English,* ed. Penny Petrone (Toronto: University of Toronto Press, 1988), p. 276.

20 John Amagoalik, "Will the Inuit Disappear from the Face of this Earth?" in *Northern Voices: Inuit Writings in English,* ed. Penny Petrone (Toronto: University of Toronto Press, 1988), pp. 209-211.

21 Arctic Public Legal Education and Information Society, *NWT Survey of Sexual Assaults and Sentencing,* as cited in Katherine Peterson, *The Justice House: Report of the Special Advisor on Gender Equality* (Yellowknife: Department of Justice 1992), p. 33.

22 Katherine Peterson, *The Justice House: Report of the Special Advisor on Gender Equality* (Yellowknife: Department of Justice 1992), p. 32.

23 Department of Social Services, Government of the Northwest Territories, *Family Violence Prevention Programs Statistical Analysis,* as cited in E. Hamilton (Research paper prepared for the Canadian Panel on Violence Against Women, Ottawa, 1993).

24 Julian Roberts, *Sexual Assault Legislation in Canada: An Evaluation,* as cited in Katherine Peterson, *The Justice House: Report of the Special Advisor on Gender Equality* (Yellowknife: Department of Justice, 1992), p. 33.

25 Arctic Public Legal Education and Information Society, *NWT Survey of Sexual Assaults and Sentencing,* as cited in Katherine Peterson, *The Justice House: Report of the Special Advisor on Gender Equality* (Yellowknife: Department of Justice, 1992), p. 33.

26 Northwest Territories Teachers's Association, Status of Women Committee, *Are Women and Children Treated Fairly by the Justice System?* (Yellowknife, 1991), p. 23.

27 Katherine Peterson, *The Justice House: Report of the Special Advisor on Gender Equality* (Yellowknife: Department of Justice 1992), p. 33.

28 S. Tom (Research paper prepared for the Canadian Panel on Violence Against Women, Ottawa, 1993).

29 N. Jarrett (Research prepared for the Canadian Panel on Violence Against Women, Ottawa, 1993).

30 Pauktuutit, *No More Secrets: Acknowledging the Problem of Child Sexual Abuse in Inuit Communities* (Ottawa, 1991), p. 5.

31 Pauktuutit, *No More Secrets: Acknowledging the Problem of Child Sexual Abuse in Inuit Communities* (Ottawa, 1991), p. 9.

32 Pauktuutit *No More Secrets: Acknowledging the Problem of Child Sexual Abuse in Inuit Communities* (Ottawa, 1991), p. 7.

33 Pauktuutit, *No More Secrets: Acknowledging the Problem of Child Sexual Abuse in Inuit Communities* (Ottawa, 1991), p. 7.

34 Mary Sillett, "Treatment of Inuit Women in the Law" (Speech to the conference Aboriginal Alternatives to the Canadian Justice System, sponsored by the National Association of Friendship Centres, Ontario: nd); Joyce MacPhee "Flaherty: Inuit women must have say in justice," *Nunatsiaq News* [Iqaluit], December 11, 1992, np; Northern News Services, "Violence against women a major problem in North," *News/North* [Yellowknife], September 7, 1992, p. 10; Mary Sillett, "Child Sexual Abuse in Inuit Communities: Acknowledging the Problem is the First Step Towards Healing" (Speech to Naomi's Family Resource Centre, Winchester, Ontario, November 7, 1991); Martha Flaherty (Speech to the Conference "Achieving Justice: Today and Tomorrow," sponsored by the Honourable Kim Campbell, Minister of Justice, Canada and the Honourable Margaret Joe, Minister of Justice, Yukon, September 3-7, 1991, Whitehorse, Yukon); many others.

35 Pauktuutit, *No More Secrets: Acknowledging the Problem of Child Sexual Abuse in Inuit Communities* (Ottawa, 1991), p. 10.

36 Leonie Barry, youth delegate, Pauktuutit Annual General Meeting, Happy Valley-Goose Bay, Labrador, February 23-25, 1993.

37 N. Jarrett (Research paper prepared for the Canadian Panel on Violence Against Women, Ottawa, 1993).

38 Department of Social Services, Government of the Northwest Territories, *Annual Report from the Director of Family and Children's Services*, as cited in E. Hamilton (Research paper prepared for the Canadian Panel on Violence Against Women, Ottawa, 1993).

39 Noah-Adamie Qummaaluk, Mayor of Povungnituk, telephone interview, March 22, 1993.

40 N. Jarrett (Research paper prepared for the Canadian Panel on Violence Against Women, Ottawa, 1993).

41 Joshie Teemotee, "Report on Eastern Arctic Suicides for the period from 1981 to 1988" (Paper presented at Inuit Tapirisat of Canada Round Table on Social Issues, Happy Valley-Goose Bay, Labrador, February 26-28, 1993).

42 Joshie Teemotee, "Report on Eastern Arctic Suicides for the period from 1981 to 1988" (Paper presented at Inuit Tapirisat of Canada Round Table on Social Issues, Happy Valley-Goose Bay, Labrador, February 26-28, 1993).

43 Pauktuutit, *The Problem of Suicide Among Inuit Youth*, as cited in E. Hamilton (Research paper prepared for the Canadian Panel on Violence Against Women, Ottawa, 1993).

44 Pauktuutit, *The Problem of Suicide Among Inuit Youth*, as cited in E. Hamilton (Research paper prepared for the Canadian Panel on Violence Against Women, Ottawa, 1993).

45 Inuit Tapirisat of Canada Round Table on Social Issues, Happy Valley-Goose Bay, Labrador, February 26-28, 1993.

46 Katherine Peterson, *The Justice House: Report of the Special Advisor on Gender Equality* (Yellowknife: Department of Justice, 1992), p. 18.

47 John Amagoalik (Background paper contracted by the Canadian Panel on Violence Against Women, 1993).

48 Pauktuutit, *Arnait: The Views of Inuit Women on Contemporary Issues* (Ottawa, 1991) p. 36.

49 Ipellie Kanguk, Pond Inlet, Northwest Territories, personal interview, 1993; translated by Oleepaka Anaviapik.

50 Janet Mancini Billson, "New Choices for a New Era," in *"Gossip": A Spoken History of Women in the North*, ed. Mary Crnkovich (Ottawa: Canadian Arctic Resources Committee, 1989), p. 46.

51 Pauktuutit, *Arnait: The Views of Inuit Women on Contemporary Issues* (Ottawa, 1991), p. 12.

52 Janet Mancini Billson, "New Choices for a New Era," in *"Gossip": A Spoken History of Women in the North*, ed. Mary Crnkovich (Ottawa: Canadian Arctic Resources Committee, 1989), pp. 53-54.

53 Janet Mancini Billson, "New Choices for a New Era," in *"Gossip": A Spoken History of Women in the North*, ed. Mary Crnkovich (Ottawa: Canadian Arctic Resources Committee, 1989), pp. 53-54.

54 Pauktuutit, *Arnait: The Views of Inuit Women on Contemporary Issues* (Ottawa, 1991), pp. 20-21.

55 Inuit Tapirisat of Canada Round Table on Social Issues, Happy Valley-Goose Bay, Labrador, February 26-28, 1993.

56 Katherine Peterson, *The Justice House: Report of the Special Advisor on Gender Equality* (Yellowknife: Department of Justice, 1992), p. 78.

57 Inuit Tapirisat of Canada Round Table on Social Issues, Happy Valley-Goose Bay, Labrador, February 26-28, 1993.

58 Pauktuutit, "Pauktuutit's Court Challenge: An Update," *Suvaguuq: Special Issue on Justice*, Volume VIII, Number 1: p. 11.

59 Mary Sillett, "Child Sexual Abuse in Inuit Communities: Acknowledging the Problem is the First Step Towards Healing" (Notes for a speech to Naomi's Family Resource Centre, Winchester, Ontario, November 7, 1991)

60 Katherine Peterson, *The Justice House: Report of the Special Advisor on Gender Equality* (Yellowknife: Department of Justice, 1992).

61 Susan Sammons, "Band-aid Solutions for Family Violence," in *"Gossip": A Spoken History of Women in the North*, ed. Mary Crnkovich (Ottawa: Canadian Arctic Resources Committee, 1989), p. 122.

62 Royal Canadian Mounted Police Public Complaints Commission, *Public Hearing into the Complaints of Kitty Nowdluk-Reynolds: Commission Report* (Ottawa, 1992), p. 47.

63 Pauktuutit, "Aboriginal Justice Issues - Task Forces, Commissions and Inquiries in Canada," *Suvaguuq: Special Issue on Justice*, Volume VIII, Number 1: p. 4.

64 Pauktuutit, *No More Secrets: Acknowledging the Problem of Child Sexual Abuse in Inuit Communities*, (Ottawa, 1991), p. 10.

65 Inuit Tapirisat of Canada Round Table on Social Issues, Happy Valley-Goose Bay, Labrador, February 26-28, 1993.

66 House of Commons, *Minutes of Proceedings and Evidence of the Standing Committee on Aboriginal Affairs*, Issue 26, p. 26:27.

67 House of Commons, *Minutes of Proceedings and Evidence of the Standing Committee on Aboriginal Affairs*, Issue 13, p. 11.

68 Pauktuutit, *A Community Perspective on Health Promotion and Substance Abuse* (Ottawa, 1990), p. 4.

69 N. Jarrett (Research paper prepared for the Canadian Panel on Violence Against Women, Ottawa, 1993).

70 N. Jarrett (Research paper prepared for the Canadian Panel on Violence Against Women, Ottawa, 1993).

71 Government of the Northwest Territories, "A few words about the Territorial Government's new Staff Housing Strategy," *Nunatsiaq News* [Iqaluit], February 5, 1993, pp. 14-15.

72 Inuit Tapirisat of Canada Round Table on Social Issues, Happy Valley-Goose Bay, Labrador, February 26-28, 1993.

73 Todd Phillips, "Critics charge housing policy threatens everyone," *Nunatsiaq News* [Iqaluit], January 8, 1993, pp. 1-2.

74 Kenn Harper, "Housing policy punishes Nunavut," *Nunatsiaq News* [Iqaluit], January 29, 1993, p. 9.

75 "Core housing" need is defined as: (any household paying 30% or more of its income for shelter or occupying a dwelling which is too small for the size and composition of the household or a dwelling which is in need of major repairs - structural, electrical, plumbing, heating, fire safety - and which does not have sufficient income to obtain an adequate or suitable dwelling on the housing market without paying 30% or more of its income for shelter." Standing Committee on Aboriginal Affairs, *A Time for Action: Aboriginal and Northern Housing* (Ottawa, 1992), p. 58.

76 Inuit Tapirisat of Canada, "Open Letter to the Legislative Assembly of the Northwest Territories from the NWT participants in the Inuit Round-Table on Social Issues, Happy Valley-Goose Bay, Labrador, February 26-28, 1993."

77 "Housing policy would close Igloolik school," *Nunatsiaq News* [Iqaluit], January 22, 1993, p. 7.

78 Pauktuutit, *A Community Perspective on Health Promotion and Substance Abuse: A report on community needs in the Northwest Territories, Nunavik, Quebec and Northern Labrador* (Ottawa, 1990), Table 1(A).

79 E. Elias, Coppermine, Northwest Territories, telephone interview, 1992.

80 Irene Tiktaalaaq (Submission to the Inuit Tapirisat of Canada Round Table on Social Issues, Happy Valley-Goose Bay, Labrador, February 26-28, 1993).

81 Irene Tiktaalaaq (Submission to the Inuit Tapirisat of Canada Round Table on Social Issues, Happy Valley-Goose Bay, Labrador, February 26-28, 1993).

82 Janet Mancini Billson, "New Choices for a New Era," in *"Gossip": A Spoken History of Women in the North*, ed. Mary Crnkovich (Ottawa: Canadian Arctic Resources Committee, 1989), p. 43.

83 Statistics Canada, *Highlights of the Statistics Canada Presentation to the Royal Commission on Aboriginal Peoples* (Ottawa, 1991) np.

84 House of Commons, *Minutes of Proceedings and Evidence of the Standing Committee on Aboriginal Affairs*, Issue 24, p. 24:13.

85 House of Commons, *Minutes of Proceedings and Evidence of the Standing Committee on Aboriginal Affairs*, Issue 24, p. 24:14.

86 N. Jarrett (Research paper prepared for the Canadian Panel on Violence Against Women, Ottawa, 1993).

87 Northwest Territories Advisory Council on the Status of Women, "Summary of Arts and Crafts: Women and their Work," in *"Gossip": A Spoken History of Women in the North*, ed. Mary Crnkovich (Ottawa: Canadian Arctic Resources Committee, 1989), p. 214.

88 Northwest Territories Advisory Council on the Status of Women, "Summary of Arts and Crafts: Women and their Work," in *"Gossip": A Spoken History of Women in the North*, ed. Mary Crnkovich (Ottawa: Canadian Arctic Resources Committee, 1989), p. 215.

89 Northwest Territories Advisory Council on the Status of Women, "Summary of Arts and Crafts: Women and their Work," in *"Gossip": A Spoken History of Women in the North*, ed. Mary Crnkovich (Ottawa: Canadian Arctic Resources Committee, 1989), p. 217.

90 Inuit Tapirisat of Canada Round Table on Social Issues, Happy Valley-Goose Bay, Labrador, February 26-28, 1993.

91 Greg Coleman, "The inaccessible north," *Nunatsiaq News* [Iqaluit], July 10, 1992, p. 11.

92 Labrador Inuit Health Commission (Brief presented to Inuit Tapirisat of Canada Round Table on Social Issues, Happy Valley-Goose Bay, Labrador, February 26-28, 1993).

93 Labrador Inuit Health Commission (Brief presented to Inuit Tapirisat of Canada Round Table on Social Issues, Happy Valley-Goose Bay, Labrador, February 26-28, 1993).

94 Alcoholism and Drug Addiction Research Foundation, *Canadian Profile: Alcohol and other drugs 1992* (Toronto, 1992), p. 48.

95 Canadian Broadcasting Corporation, "Addiction in Inukjuaq," *Prime Time News*, March 23, 1993.

96 Inuit Tapirisat of Canada Round Table on Social Issues, Happy Valley-Goose Bay, Labrador, February 26-28, 1993.

97 Johnny Inuppaq Naktiraluk, The Municipal Corporation, Inukjuak, Quebec, letter to Board of Directors, Pauktuutit, September 17, 1992.

98 Anne Crawford, *Supplementary Opinion to the Report of the Abortion Services Review Committee* (Yellowknife, 1992), pp. 2-3.

99 S. Tom (Research paper prepared for the Canadian Panel on Violence Against Women, Ottawa, 1993).

100 Anne Crawford, *Supplementary Opinion to the Report of the Abortion Services Review Committee* (Yellowknife, 1992), p. 4.

101 Anne Crawford, *Supplementary Opinion to the Report of the Abortion Services Review Committee* (Yellowknife, 1992), p. 16.

102 Anne Crawford, *Supplementary Opinion to the Report of the Abortion Services Review Committee* (Yellowknife, 1992), pp. i-ii.

103 Government of the Northwest Territories, *Report of the Abortion Services Review Committee* (Yellowknife, 1992), pp. 17-18.

104 Government of the Northwest Territories, *Report of the Abortion Services Review Committee* (Yellowknife, 1992).

105 National Aboriginal Communications Society, "Native Broadcasters Await Stay of Execution," press release, Yellowknife, January 15, 1993.

106 Taqramiut Nipingat Incorporated, "Cutbacks to Native Communications threaten Inuit language and culture," press release, Salluit, Quebec, March 5, 1993.

107 Pauktuutit, *Resolutions* (Happy Valley-Goose Bay, Labrador, 1993).

108 Lynn Brooks, "Guided by Our Bellies," in *"Gossip": A Spoken History of Women in the North*, ed. Mary Crnkovich (Ottawa: Canadian Arctic Resources Committee, 1990), pp. 39-40.

109 N. Jarrett (Research paper prepared for the Canadian Panel on Violence Against Women, Ottawa, 1993).

110 Pauktuutit, *Arnait: The Views of Inuit Women on Contemporary Issues* (Ottawa, 1991), p. 36.

111 Martha Flaherty, "Seeing the Unseen: Inuit Women and Justice," *Suvaguuq*, Volume VIII, Number 1: pp. 2-3.

112 Simeonie Akpik, Lake Harbour, Northwest Territories, personal interview; translated by Oleepaka Anaviapik.

113 Inuit Tapirisat of Canada, *Resolutions* (Ottawa, 1992).

CHAPTER 15

ABORIGINAL WOMEN

THE ABORIGINAL CIRCLE —
THE PROCESS

Several events led to the formation of the Aboriginal Circle and to its participation on the Canadian Panel on Violence Against Women. The groundwork was laid by individual Aboriginal women and groups such as the Ontario Native Women's Association which published a report, *Breaking Free*, to bring national recognition to the Aboriginal woman's struggle against violence. Studies were also conducted by national Aboriginal women's groups such as Pauktuutit (Inuit Women's Association of Canada), the Native Women's Association of Canada (NWAC) and the Indian and Inuit Nurses of Canada, now the Aboriginal Nurses Association of Canada.

In June 1991, a report entitled *The War Against Women* was presented to Parliament. The report recommended "that the federal government, in consultation with the Native Women's Association of Canada and other Aboriginal women's organizations, establish a task force on family violence in [A]boriginal communities." [1]

In August, the Honourable Mary Collins, Minister Responsible for the Status of Women, introduced a national process, the Canadian Panel on Violence Against Women, to consult with the people of Canada in their communities about violence against women and find solutions based on those discussions.

The Minister also announced the formation of the Aboriginal Circle; its members were "to act as advisors" to the Panel. However, no appointments were made, and no terms of reference for the Aboriginal Circle were defined. NWAC, not satisfied with the limited mandate of the Circle, initiated a series of negotiations between the Minister and Aboriginal women's groups including Pauktuutit and the Aboriginal Nurses Association of Canada.

The outcome of those initial meetings proved both timely and positive; four Aboriginal delegates joined the Panel, which was already in progress, in mid-November. The Circle enhanced Aboriginal representation on the Panel, which already included among its original nine members Elder Eva Mackay, appointed by the Assembly of First Nations.

The mandate of the Aboriginal Circle was expanded to ensure that Aboriginal women's interests were adequately represented in the Panel's proposed process. The Circle's specific tasks were to identify the concerns of Aboriginal women relating to violence; to organize consultations to reach Aboriginal communities; and to evaluate research and develop recommendations relating to violence against Aboriginal women.

From the outset it became clear that the status of the Aboriginal Circle members was distinct from that of other Panel members. The authority and responsibility of the Circle became a point of contention for both the Aboriginal Circle and Panel members.

The Aboriginal Circle members believed that their appointments were integral to the process and that as members they should have the same authority and responsibility as other members of the Panel. They presented these concerns to other Panel members. A meeting was convened and the issue was finally resolved. It was agreed, by Panel and Circle members, that the Aboriginal Circle would have equal status throughout the process.

Members of the Aboriginal Circle became full partners in the first federal process to engage the participation and representation of Canada's Aboriginal women. For the first time in history, the voices of Aboriginal women from remote and isolated regions, from cities and penitentiaries, would be heard at a national level.

Phase One of the process involved conducting over 400 consultations in 139 communities from January to June 1992. Panel and Circle members met with Aboriginal women in almost every community they visited. The Aboriginal women who participated in the community consultations spoke with courage and dignity, often in the face of adversity from their own people.

Phase Two of the process involved the development of a separate document to provide a historical perspective on Aboriginal women and to provide a context for the unique issues identified during consultations. Recommendations based on the collective voices of Aboriginal women are incorporated in the National Action Plans.

The Aboriginal Circle members shared in the ongoing work of the Panel. The presence of Elder Eva Mackay and the commitment of the Aboriginal Circle strengthened the Panel process and its mandate.

OUR STORY

Aboriginal women held a position of authority in the family, clan and nation. Traditional societies universally recognized the power of women to bear life. It was believed that women shared the same spirit as Mother Earth, the bearer of all life, and she was revered as such.

By virtue of her unique status, the Aboriginal woman had an equal share of power in all spheres. In some traditional societies, such as the Six Nations of the Iroquois Confederacy, the clan mother held the esteemed position of appointing and deposing the chiefs or heads of clans. In other societies, such as the Montagnais, decision making was shared equally between women and men.

One common misconception held by Europeans, and perpetuated by their general ignorance of traditional Aboriginal societies and their own patriarchal structures, is that Aboriginal women were subservient to men. In fact, early European explorers and fur traders depended heavily on the innate abilities and survival skills of Aboriginal women for their survival in the "New World."

The early years of French and British colonization in Canada brought extensive change for the Aboriginal people of this land. Their economic infrastructures, sustained by vast natural resources, were perceived as uncivilized by early colonists who were unacquainted with the Aboriginal people's non-materialistic culture.

During the fur trade, colonists used Aboriginal people for their hunting and trapping abilities to exploit Canada's natural resources for commercial gain. Early land exploration and subsequent treaty making — the foundation of the colonization process — were largely dependent on the survival skills and communication abilities of Aboriginal guides and interpreters. Aboriginal nations were also sought as military allies during the colonial wars between the French and the British and between the British and the Americans as well as during the American Civil War.

It was also during the fur trade, when Aboriginal women first came into contact with Europeans, that the Métis nation was born. Métis women walked in two worlds. Their language was a blend of European and Aboriginal languages. Their way of life embraced both Aboriginal and white customs, enriched by the bringing together of two cultures and passed on to their children. The Métis nation was born from the strength of Aboriginal women, and their nation's survival depended on them.

With the coming of European colonists, the long and systematic devolution of the Aboriginal woman's inherent rights, her equality and her unique status began. It eventually eroded and undermined her valued position among her people. The Aboriginal woman was denied any formal leadership role during the treaty-making process between the European and Aboriginal nations. Her role as a wife, mother and grandmother diminished as European attitudes and values toward women were gradually adopted by Aboriginal society.

Pre-Confederation policy involved the converting of Aboriginal people to European religions and the reform of existing Aboriginal social, economic and political structures to reflect the European institutions of the day. Family-oriented social structures were gradually replaced with the European class system; communal economies in which Aboriginal women enjoyed economic and social equality were exchanged for the barter-and-trade economy dominated by Aboriginal and European men; and Aboriginal women lost their status when the traditional matriarchal societies were displaced by the European patriarchy which considered women and children to be men's property.

Following Confederation, the *Indian Act* was legislated in 1876 to "govern Indians in Canada." This Act was to become the government's most effective tool in the abolition of Aboriginal women's rights, status and identity, and it left in its wake a path of cultural and social destruction. The lines that separated Aboriginal women — Status from non-Status and Métis — were clearly drawn. The law separated Aboriginal people through classification and created a new social order that would eventually divide nations, clans and families.

The *Indian Act* was to "continue until there is not a single Indian in Canada that has not been absorbed into the body politic, and there is no Indian question and no Indian Department." [2] This goal was pursued by outlawing spiritual practices, severing Aboriginal peoples' connection with the land, destroying traditional Aboriginal economies, indoctrinating Aboriginal people into the dominant culture by force through church or state-run residential schools and through legally denying Status to all women who married non-Status or non-Aboriginal men and their children.

Aboriginal peoples who wished to acquire a university or professional education, leave the reserve for extended periods or send their children to public rather than residential schools, in addition to women who married non-Status men, were forced to give up their rights under the *Indian Act* and join white society.

I was married for 42 years. You work together, have joint goals and talk about our work and live peacefully. Kids today who form relationships through alcohol have nothing to talk about. In the past, drum dances and tea dances were held to celebrate the end of hard work. Now when elders see the younger people carry on these ceremonies, they are happy. But for some reason, the women don't dance any more.

The *Indian Act* prohibited three or more Indians from taking organized action against civil servants. A pass system was introduced in 1885 to prevent organized political activities and to keep parents from visiting their children in residential schools. Spiritual practices and gatherings such as the Sun Dance, the Thirst Dance and the potlatch were outlawed, as were wearing traditional dress and dancing of any form, to sever spiritual connections. The pass system fell into disuse in the early 20th century, despite aggressive attempts at enforcement by the Department of Indian Affairs.

Local political structures comprised male chiefs and councils, as set out in the *Indian Act*, but they were administered and controlled by Indian agents. Also, local by-laws had to be approved by the federal government. Indian agents had full control over daily life, and as the justices of the peace, they had authority over the administration of "justice."

Local economies were destroyed by preventing the sale of produce off reserve, and reserve lands could not be mortgaged to finance the purchase of farm implements which were needed to develop an agricultural economic base. Aboriginal peoples were restricted to cultivating an area of land that could be maintained by personal labour and were restricted to using "simple implements as he would likely be able to command if entirely thrown upon his own resources, rather than to encourage farming on a scale to necessitate the employment of expensive labour-saving machinery." [3] Converting Aboriginal peoples from nomadic hunters and gatherers to sedentary farmers was seen as the most economical and humanitarian approach. As one historical source stated: "they had to make up their mind to one of three policies ... to help the Indians to farm and raise stock, to feed them or to fight them." [4]

At home, on land "reserved" by treaty, Aboriginal women faced new challenges. In most southern regions, the traditional economy of hunting, fishing and gathering was displaced by agriculture. Aboriginal women worked along with their mates, learning new skills, but they also maintained traditional economic activities, wherever resources allowed, to supplement their meagre existence. They continued to practise midwifery, herbalism and ceremonies long after these activities were outlawed by the *Indian Act*.

In spite of the daily hardships, Aboriginal peoples endured, often by faith and prayer alone. Many converted to Christianity, surrendering traditional beliefs in favour of the white man's religion, while others clung fiercely to their traditional ceremonies, forced underground by Canadian law.

The *Indian Act* determined who was entitled to be registered as an "Indian" under Canadian law. Section 12 (1)(b) of the *Indian Act* stripped Aboriginal women of their Status rights upon marriage to a non-Status Aboriginal or non-Aboriginal man. Over the next century, many Aboriginal women, their children and grandchildren were dispossessed of their inherent rights. It was illegal for them to own, reside on or be buried on "Indian" lands, and they were denied any monetary benefits resulting from treaties. These laws were in direct contravention of the existing unwritten laws of the traditional Aboriginal societies.

The human rights violations suffered by Aboriginal women were second only to the multiple horrors and abuse that their children were subject to throughout the residential school era. The residential school system cut to the very soul of Aboriginal women by stealing their most valued and vital roles of mother and grandmother, along with their children.

The children returned from the residential schools to their homes and communities, unfamiliar with the language and culture of their people. Traditionally, elders, grandmothers and grandfathers were the first teachers of Aboriginal children; they passed on their knowledge, values and skills to the children by way of stories and legends. This oral tradition was dependent on trust, which was nurtured over time, between children and grandparents. In many cases, the residential school experience permanently severed this tie between child and elder, altering the values and identity of the child and traditional Aboriginal society forever.

The residential school era marked a turning point for Aboriginal women in Canada. Their rights, status and identity were now fading into near obscurity. Once fiercely proud and independent, Aboriginal women now struggled daily for survival, amid the turmoil of violence and abuse that had become a new reality.

For Aboriginal women, living in post-Confederation Canada meant living in two worlds — the white world and the Aboriginal world. Many were forced to give up their Status rights upon marrying a non-Status or non-Aboriginal man. Without the support of family and community, the cities became new homelands for these women. Here, Aboriginal women were domestic labourers, cleaners, cooks, factory workers. For Aboriginal women, higher education was not likely. Despite social and economic inequities, Aboriginal women worked diligently and survived.

Poverty became a way of life. Substandard housing, social welfare and lack of medical care were the Aboriginal woman's lot in the post-World War II era. While the country flourished with new-found vigour and resolve, her fragile world was crumbling beneath her feet.

Social conditions worsened with the introduction of the welfare system to the Aboriginal community. Traditional systems of family and communal support crumbled, and in time they were replaced by a growing dependency on "relief." Many Aboriginal families became second-, third- or fourth-generation "welfare families."

Historically, alcohol had been present in Aboriginal communities since contact was established with European colonists. Status Indians, however, were prohibited by law to purchase or consume alcohol, so alcohol consumption was limited to bootleg or homebrew. In 1954, the law was amended to permit alcohol consumption by Aboriginal people, and within four decades alcohol had made an indelible mark on the lives of Aboriginal men, women and children.

The strain began to take its toll on Aboriginal women, partially because of their loss of power and weakened status under the *Indian Act*. Aboriginal women fell victim to multiple abuses, which were inflicted on them as children, wives, mothers and elders, often at the hands of those most trusted. The abuse was kept hidden. Untreated, it spread to epidemic proportions. Most cases of abuse could be traced to the residential school, from where victims often carried the abuse back to their homes and communities.

After extensive hearings, the *Indian Act* was amended in 1951, but Indian agents retained their control over daily life and continued to serve as justices of the peace. In addition to the provisions of the *Indian Act*, provincial laws were applied to reserves "to involve provincial governments more actively in daily life and to reduce the unique legal status that reserves had enjoyed previously." [5]

One of the most significant consequences of the imposition of provincial laws was the enforcement of child welfare legislation and the accompanying imposition of urban middle-class standards. Thousands of Aboriginal children were deemed to be in need of protection and were removed from their homes in "the Sixties Scoop." [6] "Combined with the residential school system, it meant that generations of children were not raised within their families or communities, thereby never learning their traditional culture or patterns of parenting." [7]

In 1969, a white paper proposed the abandonment of treaties and treaty rights and the transformation of reserves in to communities in the interest of equality. [8] Aboriginal leaders and activists entered the battle for Aboriginal rights, and Aboriginal peoples, united as nations,

defeated the policy. After the "disastrous failure" [9] of the paper, the federal government was forced to abandon previous blatant paternalistic policies and attitudes and to seek the opinion of Aboriginal peoples. The federal government provided funding for regional and national Aboriginal organizations and transfered some administrative functions from the Department of Indian Affairs to local, predominantly male chiefs and councils. Women's cries for justice and equality, however, went unheard, and Aboriginal women's rights were rejected by their own Aboriginal leaders.

After a long and courageous campaign, Bill C-31 was passed in 1985 to amend the *Indian Act* "with the explicit objective of bringing it into line with the equality provision of the *Charter of Rights and Freedoms*." [10] Bill C-31 amended section 12(1)(b) of the *Indian Act*, which forced enfranchisement on Aboriginal women, and introduced legislation to restore Status rights to women who had married non-Status or non-Aboriginal men and to their children. The Bill also contained limited self-government provisions giving bands authority to develop their own membership codes.

Under the provisions of Bill C-31, by 1990, the Status population increased by 115,000. [11] Fifty-eight percent of those individuals reinstated under Bill C-31 were Aboriginal women. [12] It is significant to note that the majority of those seeking reinstatement (86 percent) cited as the reason for their application: personal identity, culture or a sense of belonging, correction of injustice or Aboriginal rights. [13]

Although separate funds for housing, education and other rights were designated by the federal government for the women and their families reinstated under Bill C-31, the funds were inadequate. A false perception exists that women and their children who were reinstated under Bill C-31 receive preferential treatment in the allocation of band resources. Families who had long been on waiting lists for housing, for example, saw families returning under the provisions of the Bill receive houses, built with those specially allocated funds, while they were forced to continue to live in often overcrowded and substandard housing.

Under Bill C-31, bands can determine their own membership. Since many chiefs and councils are opposed to the provisions of the legislation, Aboriginal women continue to be effectively denied their rights under Bill C-31.

Bill C-31 has been interpreted by some as a means of cultural genocide that will lead to the eventual extinction of Aboriginal peoples in Canada. This "ethnic cleansing" aspect of the Bill is clearly explained in the *Report of the Aboriginal Justice Inquiry of Manitoba*:

> The continuing discrimination enters the picture in terms of the differential treatment between the sexes regarding the children of Status Indians. This is an extremely convoluted registration scheme in which the discrimination is not readily apparent on the surface. It requires an examination of how the Act treats people to detect the fundamental unfairness. Examples are necessary to make this more obvious.
>
> Joan and John, a brother and sister, were both registered Indians. Joan married a Métis man before 1985 so she lost her Indian status under section 12(1)(b) of the former Act. John married a white woman before 1985 and she automatically became a Status Indian. Both John and Joan have had children over the years. Joan is now eligible to regain her Status under section 6(1)(c) and her children will qualify under section 6(2). They are treated as having only one eligible parent, their mother, although both parents are Aboriginal. John's children gained Status at birth as both parents were Indians legally, even though only one was an Aboriginal person.
>
> Joan's children can pass on status to their offspring only if they also marry registered Indians. If they marry unregistered Aboriginal people or non-Aboriginal people, then no Status will pass to their grandchildren. All John's grandchildren will be Status Indians regardless of who his children marry.

> Thus, entitlement to registration for the second generation has nothing to do with racial or cultural characteristics. The Act has eliminated the discrimination faced by those who lost Status, but has passed it on to the next generation .... Not only does the *Indian Act* maintain improper and probably illegal forms of sexual discrimination, but it also threatens the long-term survival of Indians.
>
> The current regime has a de facto form of a "one-quarter blood" rule. As shown in the previous example, intermarriage between registered Indians and others over two successive generations results in descendants who are not entitled at law to be status Indians. This may threaten the very existence of First Nations in the not too distant future, especially small communities who have considerable interaction with neighbouring Métis or non-Aboriginal communities.
>
> In our view, discriminating against Indian people by virtue of such provisions imposed by Parliament should cease. [14]

Bill C-31 will cause more Aboriginal people to lose or not qualify for Status rights than the *Indian Act*. Although on the surface Bill C-31 appeared to eliminate sex discrimination against Aboriginal women, it has created a new social order among Aboriginal peoples which continues to have a far-reaching impact on the lives of those reinstated under the legislation. [15]

While Aboriginal leaders have mounted political campaigns for self-government and constitutional reform, Aboriginal women have been at the forefront of a social revolution, demanding better housing, child welfare, education and health care.

The colonization process and the *Indian Act* have dispossessed Aboriginal women of their inherent role as leaders in their own nation and have created a serious imbalance in Aboriginal society that accords Aboriginal men greater political, social and economic influence and opportunity than Aboriginal women.

This balance must be restored, with Aboriginal women assuming their rightful position as full and equal partners in the shaping of their own destinies.

THE ABORIGINAL PEOPLES OF CANADA

Despite years of forced assimilation imposed by Euro-Canadian institutions, Aboriginal people have retained a strong sense of nationhood based on their ancestral tribal affiliations. There are 53 distinct Aboriginal nations in Canada today.

With the imposition of government policies like the *Indian Act*, these historical relationships have given way to a relatively new social and political order. The attempts of Aboriginal nations to restructure through political alliances to battle collectively for Aboriginal rights has resulted in the formation of separate and distinct identifications, often based on their legal status and subsequent relationship with the federal government.

Today there are five national Aboriginal organizations in Canada, representing an estimated one million Aboriginal people. [16] In their bid for separate and distinct identities as Aboriginal peoples, they have rejected the use of terms such as "Indian," "Eskimo," "Half-breed" and "non-status Indian," which have been imposed on them by government agents for generic classification.

There are approximately 511,791 Aboriginal people with "Status" rights as defined by the *Indian Act*, of whom approximately 300,000 live on reserves. [17] The 1991 Census indicates that approximately 135,265 people identify themselves as Métis; people who identify as Métis are most likely to live in Manitoba, Saskatchewan and Alberta; and, seven out of ten Aboriginal people live west of Ontario, compared with 29 percent of the total population. The 1991 Statistics Canada Aboriginal Peoples Survey found that almost three-quarters of the Aboriginal population of Canada is under the age of 35.

In 1981, Aboriginal peoples in Canada fought for and won the entrenchment of their rights within the Canadian Constitution. Section 35 of the 1982 *Canada Act* confirms that the Aboriginal people of Canada include those individuals with Status resulting from the *Indian Act*, the Métis and Inuit.

In this document, Aboriginal is intended to be inclusive of all Aboriginal peoples except Inuit, who are covered separately.

MÉTIS

The Métis emerged as a distinct people in Rupert's Land toward the end of the 18th century, where they developed a unique culture and identity based on their heritage as both Aboriginal and European peoples. Since 1869, the Métis have struggled for the recognition of their rights as a distinct nation. In 1870, Parliament passed the *Manitoba Act* bringing Manitoba into Confederation. Within 10 years, the Métis were dispossessed of their lands and their rights. The Métis were forced further west and north in search of lands and a viable resource base. The Métis were formally recognized as a distinct Aboriginal people in 1982.

STATUS

Aboriginal peoples have been identified and defined as "Indian" by virtue of the *Indian Act*. The "Status Indian" population is defined in section 12(1)(b) of the *Indian Act*. Many of these people are also referred to as "Treaty Indians," that is, Aboriginal people whose ancestors signed treaties with the British Crown.

Approximately 60 percent of this population resides on federal reserves, or lands "reserved" for them and held in trust on their behalf by the Minister of Indian Affairs and Northern Development. Nearly 20 percent of reserves are in "special access zones" with no year-round road access. [18]

NON-STATUS

Many non-Status Aboriginal people are descendants of those who lost their entitlement through voluntary or involuntary enfranchisement under section 12(1)(b) of the *Indian Act*.

Many Aboriginal people are forced to live in urban areas to pursue educational or employment opportunities or to receive health or other services not available on reserves. Individuals with Status rights who do not reside on a reserve are not accorded the same rights as Status people residing on a reserve since many Status rights are not "transportable." Women who are not permitted by chiefs and councils to live on their home reserve are forced to move to urban areas where they lack access to services and non-insured health, educational and other benefits. In general, Status people residing in urban areas have higher levels of education and employment than those living on reserves. However, they have lower levels of education, higher unemployment rates and lower average incomes than Canadians in general.

ABORIGINAL WOMEN'S VIEW OF VIOLENCE

Violence against Aboriginal women must be seen through the eyes of Aboriginal women. Aboriginal women do not share the same world as their non-Aboriginal sisters. Aboriginal women must engage in two simultaneous struggles — to restore equality with Aboriginal men and to strive to attain equality with non-Aboriginal women. It has been said that violence in Aboriginal families and communities is a "reaction against systems of domination, disrespect and bureaucratic control." [19]

Before the arrival of the European civilization, women were powerful. Since then, the western [non-Native] civilization has come and told men that they must take control. From here on in, we must, as women, reopen the eyes of our men, by claiming our positions as leaders and healers.

These differences must be acknowledged and respected. In Aboriginal society, the family is the heart of the community, an entity made powerful by human spirit. Families are linked to one another through kinship on the mother's or father's side, or on both. These extended families are representative of the traditional clan system of their ancestors. Many of them are matriarchal, with elderly women presiding as the head. Aboriginal communities are devoid of the non-Aboriginal "class" structure, and individual family standing is not measured by material possessions or accumulated wealth. Instead, a family is often valued by the contribution of its extended family to the community, its ability to get along with others and the strength and character of its members.

The ties that bind the Aboriginal family have been held sacred for many generations. Often this dependency on one's family has been the only means of social and economic survival, and Aboriginal women have been taught to uphold the tradition of family, sometimes at the expense of their own safety.

The extended family tradition in Aboriginal communities has been called both "a blessing and a curse," for the tradition that provides nurturing, love and protection to children and women can also cause the destruction of the family affected by violence. For a victim of violence in an Aboriginal community, disclosing her abuse would publicly shame her family and could result in being ostracized by the family, her only means of support.

Women stay in violent relationships through fear, threats, intimidation, pressure from the community leadership, the destruction of self-esteem and the imposed belief that survival outside the relationship or family is impossible. Also, these women may feel that no one would believe and/or help them.

One of Aboriginal women's greatest fears in disclosing violence in the home is that their children may be taken from them by provincial, or white authorities or by Aboriginal child welfare workers who may report to chiefs and councils. This fear is largely based on the historical relationship between child welfare agencies and the Aboriginal community. Many Aboriginal women will stay in an abusive relationship to keep the family together, and the perceived threat of losing their children keeps them silent. These women carry the pain of their abuse alone and in silence, sometimes for a lifetime.

The dignity and safety of Aboriginal women and their families must be preserved and protected when disclosing violence. Violence against Aboriginal women must be viewed from the perspective of Aboriginal women living within their culture and must be considered in terms of the reality of their situation. Some Aboriginal women may be prevented from reporting violence because of cultural values of kindness, reconciliation and family cohesiveness. [20]

Generally, Aboriginal women do not view themselves and their needs as separate from the needs of their children and families. Their roles as mothers, grandmothers and caregivers of their nation are still widely recognized and honoured by Aboriginal women today.

Some Aboriginal women do not relate to non-Aboriginal feminist philosophy and terminology because historically and culturally Aboriginal women were not subject to the European social structures that oppressed non-Aboriginal women. Aboriginal women have been subjected to extreme sexism and racism since contact was made with European colonists.

Violence in the home and in the community has severe consequences for Aboriginal women. In a study on federally imprisoned Aboriginal women, [21] the women prisoners reported victimization throughout their life. The violence they experienced was generally at the hands of men.

The Canadian Panel on Violence Against Women must be aware that the approach to the problem of violence is perceived differently in Native communities. Please do not change our perspective and ideas and solutions. Respect what people tell you. The problem is being dealt with through a holistic approach; we look at all aspects at the same time — sexual abuse, battered women, drug and alcohol abuse. We also involve men, we identify the problem as a family [problem].

For many Aboriginal women seeking to resolve their experiences of abuse, traditional methods of healing have gained widespread acceptance and respect. Women's healing circles and informal support groups have begun in many Aboriginal communities. These initiatives, which operate with little or no outside funding, reflect the commitment of Aboriginal women to restore the balance and well-being of their communities.

Aboriginal women have become leaders in the struggle against violence in their communities. A grass-roots movement by Aboriginal women who are seeking personal healing and healing for their families has increased awareness of the issue of abuse in the Aboriginal community.

Aboriginal leaders, however, have been slow to react. Most regional and national political organizations, grappling with self-government issues, have made little more than a verbal commitment to healing the violence in Aboriginal communities. Local Aboriginal governments, struggling for economic survival, are reluctant to commit their already meagre resources to concrete initiatives.

Both Aboriginal and non-Aboriginal governments must be active participants in this healing process. Governmental support must entail more than verbal commitments. The goals of "zero violence" for Aboriginal communities and the safety of Aboriginal women and children must be reflected in the actions of government at all levels — local, regional and national. These actions must include developing immediate and long-term initiatives to match the diverse needs and aspirations of Aboriginal women and the communities to help the healing process continue.

As Aboriginal women assume greater leadership roles, the priorities of national Aboriginal agendas are beginning to shift. National Aboriginal women's advocacy groups, such as the Native Women's Association of Canada, Aboriginal Nurses Association of Canada and Pauktuutit, the Inuit Women's Association, have become Aboriginal women's strongest allies in their struggle against violence.

There are many social, economic and political factors that have contributed to the oppressions that victimize Aboriginal women, and no single solution can meet all their needs. However, to guarantee that these needs are addressed with expediency and efficiency, Aboriginal women must regain their rightful place as full and equal partners within their families, their communities and their nations. The involvement of Aboriginal women is vital, and their participation must be an integral component in all healing initiatives.

For Aboriginal women, the Zero Tolerance Policy must be implemented in a culturally relevant manner. It must encompass individual, family and community healing, restore community standards which place equal value on women and men, and provide adequate public and private enforcement and response to end all violence against women in the home, the community and society as a whole.

NAMING THE VIOLENCE

Violence within the family is cyclical. For many victims, the abuse begins at birth and follows them throughout childhood and adolescence into their adult lives.

Abuse is often a learned behaviour. Many cases of violence in the Aboriginal community involve multi-generational offenders. In childhood, an offender may abuse siblings, and later in life, abuse his spouse. The abuse may also be perpetrated on a son or daughter, and in some cases, on grandchildren or even great-grandchildren.

The cycle of violence reinforces violence in the home. Current studies have found that many children who grow up in violent homes are more likely than other children to continue the cycle of violence and abuse into their adult lives. Boys who see their father beating their mother may grow up thinking this is the way men should behave. Girls growing up in violent homes often end up in abusive relationships as adults. Victims or survivors of abuse may have no concept of what a "safe," or non-violent, home is because they have never known physical safety during their lifetime. Violence may be perceived by the victim of abuse or by the offender as simply "a part of life," "a part of womanhood" or "a part of being Indian." To many Aboriginal people, abuse is perceived only as physical violence. Abuse may be physical, sexual, psychological, financial or spiritual. In many instances, a victim may experience a combination of two or more types of abuse.

An understanding of the cyclical nature of violence and of the social, political and economic factors that create a sense of hopelessness and despair helps to explain the behaviour but does not excuse it. The Ontario Native Women's Association states,

The respondents to our survey stressed that family abuse is wrong and they want it stopped now. Our Elders tell us that personal responsibility, self-control and respect for all people is a tenet of Aboriginal culture. It is the belief of the Ontario Native Women's Association that all Aboriginal men, women and children have a right to live in a violence-free environment. [22]

Aboriginal women must speak out about the violence on behalf of themselves and their children before they can realize their own personal healing or recovery and initiate lasting measures that will restore the well-being of their families and their communities. "How far healers go in their own healing is exactly how far they can take their people." [23]

In naming the violence, Aboriginal women must be afforded a greater role in the deterrence and sentencing of violent crimes against women. Their role in the development of all Aboriginal justice systems in the future must likewise be guaranteed and protected.

There are many types of violence in the Aboriginal community. Some of these forms of violence or abuse are shared by the larger, non-Aboriginal society, while others have a "cultural" dimension that is distinctive to violence in the Aboriginal community.

The following types of violence were identified during the Aboriginal Circle's consultations with Aboriginal women. These acts of violence, almost without exception, are perpetrated against individuals who are seen as less powerful than the abuser and therefore more vulnerable. These victims include Aboriginal women, children, elderly women, women with disabilities and lesbians (who are known in the Aboriginal community as two-spirited women). The abusers are most often men who are related to or associated with the victim.

PHYSICAL VIOLENCE

Physical violence is any physical act intended to harm, injure or inflict pain on the victim including slapping, hitting, burning, kicking, biting, pushing, hair pulling, choking, shoving, hitting with an object, threatening with an object, such as a knife or gun, and any action that causes physical harm to another.

My ex-husband was violent. When I married him I had to leave my home reserve. I felt so isolated. He intercepted my mail for seven years. My family didn't even know where I was. It was like someone took a gigantic eraser and wiped me from the face of the map. He nearly destroyed me.

Finally, one time he ploughed me over the balcony. I went through some boards and fell into a pile of wood. I was three months pregnant. I lost consciousness and I lost my baby. After that I knew I had to do something. He had a gun pointed at my head. I said, "This is our last meal together. You have a choice to kill me now, but I am leaving." He said, "No you're not — you belong to me." I told him "I'm not anyone's piece of merchandise and I won't stay here another day." I was never so scared in my life. I had to leave the reserve without my children because I had no child support. Everyone told me I was crazy and that the devil would take me because I broke my marriage vow. It took me five years to trust a man again.

♀ ♀ ♀

My father used to beat my mother all the time. When we were young I would hear them coming down the path toward the house after being out drinking. I could hear him yelling and him hitting her. The next day we would go to school and the blood of my mother could be seen on the snowbank and her hair on the road.

PSYCHOLOGICAL VIOLENCE

Psychological violence involves the abuse of power and control by the abuser toward his victim. It includes intimidating, terrorizing, threatening, humiliating, insulting, pressuring, destroying property, controlling the movements of one's partner, inducing fear, isolating the victim from friends and family and withholding emotions of love, caring, understanding.

Violence is really bad up North. It is really hard for me to visit my community. Women are walking around bruised; children are running around afraid. I have to rescue someone's children every time I am up there. No one recognizes psychological abuse.

My daughter suffered the most. He said she wasn't his because she wasn't like his family. She carries those scars. She asks me, "Do I look different, Mom?" I drew her a family tree for her to recognize her ancestry and so she could see that she had her grandmother's Scottish looks.

♀ ♀ ♀

I have been asked to speak for a survivor who was afraid to be here today. She was mentally abused by her husband for years. It wasn't until two of her daughters were suicidal that she was able to find the courage to leave.

♀ ♀ ♀

He phoned me one night and told me to read the papers the next morning. My friend was coming to stay with me that night. He didn't show up. The next morning I read the papers; my friend had been found dead in his car. They said it was due to carbon monoxide poisoning and no foul play was involved. [He] called me and said, "You got any more friends coming to stay, bitch?"

SEXUAL ABUSE

Sexual abuse includes all acts of unwanted sexual attention or exploitation including inappropriate touching, exposing the victim to pornographic materials, molesting, sexual assault with an object, forced bondage, date rape, gang rape, rape within an intimate relationship and harassment.

I was abused by my parents who were alcoholics. I was sexually abused. I was abused in foster care. I went back to the reserve to be sexually abused by siblings. My daughter was gang-raped at a party when she was 16. It is almost normal in this area. She hasn't named them because she is afraid that I would take legal action. The other people who were there were afraid of these guys. I never heard about it until two years later. My daughter doesn't have respect for the courts. She says she would just get victimized again.

INCEST

Incest is any form of sexual contact or attempted sexual contact between relatives, no matter how distant the relationship.

Gang rapes happen, on and off reserve, white men and Aboriginal men, young women and old women. A young girl was at a party, her stepfather and her uncle raped her in front of a friend and some young boys. They stuffed her mouth with pills to try and kill her to prevent her from telling. The friend and the young boys tried to stop it from happening. When the friend told the community social services worker what had happened, the community told the girl it was her fault that she got raped because she went to the party. She pressed charges and the judge asked her if she wanted to continue. The stepfather killed himself, and then it came out that there was incest all through the family over generations.

♀ ♀ ♀

A friend of mine had foster daughters. She found out her husband had been raping them for years. He was sentenced to 90 days. There was no appeal from the Crown attorney.

CHILD SEXUAL ABUSE

Child sexual abuse is any sexual contact inflicted on a child. It includes molesting, including fondling of the victim's genitals; inappropriate holding, touching or kissing; enticing a child to engage in sexual activities; exposing the child's genitals or exposing the abuser's genitals to a child; coercing the victim to touch the abuser's genitals; urging or forcing the child to engage in or witness sexual acts, including masturbation, oral sex, sodomy and sexual intercourse, with the abuser and/or another party; and exposing a child to pornographic materials or movies.

I feel scared to go out at night. A lot of drinking goes on there weekends. I have two boys and a girl and I'm scared for them. I was raped when I was 12 and I experienced child sexual abuse. It was a long time ago but I can never forget what happened. It's like it was yesterday. I told my mom but not my dad or the cops. My mom said my dad would kick me out. The man kept doing it to girls after that. I was beaten by my parents. My mother and two sisters were killed in a fire. I have problems drinking and finding a place to stay.

ϙ ϙ ϙ

By the time I was 10 years old I was raped four times. Nothing was done for me. Since then he abused at least 20 children and was put away three times .... My hope is that I ... will never have a little girl because she'll never have the right to say or do anything .... No one will ever understand how much energy it takes to get up and shake a man's hand .... If I had a broken leg, I would get a cast. Children need good counselling.

ϙ ϙ ϙ

I was gang-raped at 2 1/2 years of age by a grown man, his brothers and friends. My brother assaulted me until the police intervened, and then my grandfather started. I remember them raping me and putting a diaper on me and the diaper filling with blood. They broke my feet, and I remember being put in a room and them coming in to give me suckers. Why did my family do this to me?

FINANCIAL ABUSE

Financial abuse is any act which involves the deceitful use of a person's money or belongings, the misappropriation of resources or using money or resources to exert power and control. It includes taking pension money or other forms of family support, forcing parents to provide free child care, denying one's family of money for food or shelter.

Recently a man and a woman were fighting, people just watched. The woman was covered in blood. I tried to help and she struck out at me. I understood. A few days later she [told me] she was scared that if she had accepted my help, it would have been a threatening situation for her. Over the weekend, her husband left her to go on a drinking binge, he left her with no groceries. She said, "Oh well, maybe it's the best thing for me to have a good sleep, and the kids will be safe."

SPIRITUAL ABUSE

Spiritual abuse is the erosion or breaking down of one's cultural or religious belief systems. Perhaps one of the most pervasive examples of spiritual abuse is the establishment of the residential school system.

Child abuse in residential schools and by cultural destruction invoked by imperialist/colonial powers has lead to not just family disintegration but [to] the disintegration of individual Aboriginal people. This spiritual violence, the loss of sense of self, was related to alcohol abuse and the inability to form bonds with others.

ϙ ϙ ϙ

An interdenominational group of churches has offered to loan us the money to buy the house for healing. We are excited but afraid they may still be trying to force Christianity on us. And any kind of Christian affiliation may mean that Aboriginal people won't come.

ϙ ϙ ϙ

Some religions have taken advantage of the lack of Aboriginal education [by providing] [Aboriginal people] with the religious teachings of their own sects, and often these groups have satanic tendencies.

155

In some Aboriginal communities, abuse is perpetrated by church representatives who impose Christianity or by self-proclaimed elders who prey upon women and children in Aboriginal communities and submit them to sexual, physical, emotional and psychological abuse. Self-proclaimed elders sometimes use their powers to abuse third parties on the request of others.

PREVALENCE OF VIOLENCE

The chances for an Aboriginal child to grow into adulthood without a single first-hand experience of abuse, alcoholism or violence are small ... the tragic reality is that many Aboriginal people have been victimized, and the non-Aboriginal community has largely ignored their suffering. [24]

The following sample of statistics conveys the pervasiveness of violence against Aboriginal women and children and the urgent need for solutions.

- There is a serious lack of research on Aboriginal women, particularly Métis, Status and non-Status women not residing on reserves and elderly women, who are victims of violence and abuse.

- A study by the Ontario Native Women's Association found that eight out of 10 Aboriginal women had personally experienced violence. Of those women, 87 percent had been injured physically and 57 percent had been sexually abused. [25]

- According to a London, Ontario area study, 71 percent of the urban sample and 48 percent of the reserve sample of Oneida women had experienced assault at the hands of current or past partners. [26]

- It is estimated that between 75 and 90 percent of the women in some northern Aboriginal communities are battered. [27]

- In a 1991 study conducted by the Indian and Inuit Nurses of Canada, the three leading contributing factors to family violence were found to be alcohol and substance abuse, economic problems and second- or third-generation abusers. [28]

- A Northwest Territories survey found that 80 percent of girls and 50 percent of boys under 8 years old were sexually abused. [29]

- There are no available statistics on racially motivated attacks on Aboriginal women. However, in "the largest child exploitation case in Winnipeg's history," a 52-year-old man pleaded guilty to 16 charges of sexual assault involving 16 victims. Police discovered more than 100 videotapes containing approximately 700 hours of footage of the man sexually assaulting "drugged, unconscious or dazed young girls. The girls were between 11 and 15 years old, and as many as 50 different children had been assaulted and videotaped. Only half were positively identified; the majority of those were Aboriginal." [30]

- During consultations at the Big Cove reserve in New Brunswick, which has an on-reserve population of approximately 1,600, [31] the Aboriginal Circle was told: "Between January of 1991 and December of 1991, my staff made a record of the following cases: 36 cases of child abuse, 14 cases of other violence in the home, 13 cases of sex abuse, seven attempted suicides, three rapes, 10 custody cases resulting from neglect."

- There are many reports that Aboriginal women are harassed on city streets more often than non-Aboriginal women both by the public and by police.

RESEARCH — EXISTING AND EMERGING NEEDS

While much work has been done to determine the status and condition of Aboriginal women in Canada, much remains to be done. Part of the mandate of the Canadian Panel on Violence Against Women and the Aboriginal Circle was to identify gaps in research and services. To determine the needs, and the services required to meet those needs, research must be funded and undertaken by Aboriginal women in the following areas:

- The *Indian Act* needs to be analyzed from the perspective of Aboriginal women especially its continuing discrimination and the lessons to be learned from its current application and applied to future self-government negotiations.

- The Canadian justice system clearly fails Aboriginal women, and many Aboriginal women have serious concerns about current community justice initiatives. Aboriginal women must receive funding to undertake relevant research and be fully engaged by all government departments working on pilot projects on justice in Aboriginal communities. Policing, by both Aboriginal and non-Aboriginal officers or forces, must be included and immediately addressed.

- The education system does not meet the needs of Aboriginal students. Research and consultation must be undertaken with the Aboriginal community to determine the needs of students and ensure that those needs are met.

- Métis women are underrepresented and rarely consulted. Métis women's associations must be given the resources to determine the needs of their communities and the services which will meet those needs.

- The links between childhood sexual or physical abuse and solvent abuse, suicide, homelessness in urban areas and prostitution must be examined.

- The needs and safety issues of elderly women must be addressed and researched to determine what services are required.

- The effects of residential schools on women and their particular requirements for healing must be examined.

SHARED ISSUES

Regardless of distinctions made by the government — on or off reserve, in a Métis community, Status or non-Status — the problems Aboriginal women encounter are remarkably similar. However, Aboriginal women living in remote communities experience additional difficulties because of geographical distance.

This section discusses different groups of Aboriginal women, the services they may contact for assistance, larger systems such as police and the justice system, and institutions that have a significant impact on shaping the current reality of Aboriginal peoples.

CHILDREN

Many Aboriginal children grow up with a sense of hopelessness and despair. Their self-esteem is eroded by institutionalized racism, an educational system that does not reflect or value their culture and historical contributions, and a legacy of poverty, violence, substance abuse and premature death.

A national study by the Aboriginal Nurses Association of Canada indicates that Aboriginal women and children under 15 years of age are most frequently physically abused. [32]

When you are a child living in it, it is normal. You need to be taught that it is not the only way.

With epidemic numbers of children being physically and sexually abused, youth grow up thinking incestuous assaults are a normal part of life. Nearly nine percent of Aboriginal mothers are under the age of 18, compared with 1.2 percent of the larger population. [33] Because of chronic housing shortages, existing units are overcrowded, sometimes housing two or three families together. It has been suggested that this situation has aggravated the problem of physical and sexual abuse.

Aboriginal children who witness violent acts against their mothers or other family members often experience long-term emotional and behavioural problems that may be acted out at school, at play and in the home. Children who abuse other children emotionally, sexually or physically have often witnessed or have been victims of these same types of violence either at home or in their community.

> *Abuse works as a cycle. I know of a 10-year-old foster child who told me that her mother deserved to be beaten.*

Children whose parents are addicted to alcohol, drugs or solvents grow up with minimal supervision or direction and engage in adult behaviours well before maturity. Alcohol and drug use by parents contributes to a child's lack of medical care, developmental delays, behaviour problems, substance abuse, school failure and neglect. On some reserves, 100 percent of all Aboriginal children have been taken into temporary or permanent care at some time. [34]

In 1993, the attempted suicides of six children from Davis Inlet raised the issue of solvent abuse among Aboriginal children, especially in northern and remote communities. The practice of "sniffing" solvents such as gasoline, glue, nail polish and other household chemicals by Aboriginal children has been public knowledge in Canada for many years, yet there are no treatment programs for Aboriginal children and youth that are available in their communities.

Substance abuse by children requires serious examination. Urgent comprehensive treatments must be implemented for child substance abusers, and immediate research is needed to ascertain the relationship between child substance abuse, especially glue and gasoline sniffing, and child sexual abuse in the home and the community.

The removal of Aboriginal children from their family and community by child welfare authorities has also contributed to the breakdown of the Aboriginal family. During the last several decades, child welfare agencies indiscriminately removed Aboriginal children from their families and communities, primarily for reasons related to poverty, and placed them in foster care institutions or had them put up for adoption by non-Aboriginal families.

Many Aboriginal children were adopted by families living outside Canada and have never returned. Aboriginal children who were adopted into non-Aboriginal homes have been subjected to racism and other forms of violence including sexual and physical abuse while they were wards of the court. Most Aboriginal children adopted by non-Aboriginal families lose all contact with their Aboriginal family and community, and consequently, they lose their own cultural identity as an Aboriginal person.

> *We still have residential schools, and there is still abuse. It is different than before, but it is still there. A boy said to me, "All they care about there is for me to get the bed made and sit still. I just got a call from my little sister who told me she can't go to school because she has a black eye and hair pulled out by Dad. How can I concentrate when I am thinking about this?"*

Extended families can also further victimize children and adult survivors. Sometimes child welfare agencies place abused children with members of the extended family without adequate investigations to assess the child's safety from abuse.

There have been cases of political interference with child custody. In a deliberate misinterpretation of traditional cultural practices, one band cited "custom adoption" as the reason for its refusal to honour a court order to return two minors to their mother. The woman had been forced to leave her home reserve to escape her violent partner; the children were sent to the reserve to visit their father's parents. During the visit, custody was awarded to their paternal grandparents by the band council. A band spokesman was quoted as saying "Our recommendation is that [the mother] reconcile with her husband. The [abuse] can be worked out through family mediation." [35]

YOUTH

Along with normal adolescent difficulties, Aboriginal youth face additional stresses. Many Aboriginal children grow into troubled adolescents because of physical and/or sexual abuse. Many move to cities either to continue high school or go to college or university or to seek employment, since there is chronic and extremely high unemployment on reserves.

There have been gang rapes of teenagers. They're afraid to mention it. One was reported, but charges were withdrawn because the victim was scared. There were two gang rapes last year, in a house in which drinking goes on. One girl refused to go back to her foster home. The three guys that did it, nothing happened to them. They get the girls drunk and use them, have sex with them. They use drinking as an excuse.

Most youth from reserves or small communities are not prepared for city life. Many of those who are able to find employment earn only minimum wage, and without job skills or training, are frequently unable to maintain employment. Many are not aware of community resources or how to gain access to cultural supports. There is a very high attrition rate among those in educational programs.

Children who flee abusive situations at home often end up in large urban areas without the education, skills or experience they need to survive. In 1986, 45 percent of the on-reserve and 24 percent of the off-reserve Aboriginal population aged 15 and over had less than a Grade 9 education. [36] Many Aboriginal adolescents are left with few options; they may be forced into prostitution or other criminal activities to live. Even though a pervasive sense of hopelessness is common on many reserves, many youth end up even worse off in the city but do not want to return home as a "failure."

Young men brag about "scoring" and don't understand the concept of date rape. They don't want to be forced to wear condoms, and if girls carry them, they are considered sluts.

Youth who come into conflict with the law end up in detention centres or group homes. Without counselling and early intervention to help them make positive life choices, upgrade their education or obtain job skills or training, they repeatedly come into conflict with the law.

The percentage of Aboriginal women in prostitution is unknown. The Aboriginal Circle is aware that prostitution is a reality for many Aboriginal women in large urban centres.

Many young people congregate in inner-city areas, where they find companionship and a sense of belonging with other Aboriginal people who engage in the behaviour and activities they are most familiar with at home: alcohol and/or drug abuse and violence. Urban lifestyles are misrepresented by the media and reality bears little resemblance to the images transmitted to reserves or small communities. The city lights quickly grow dim.

Young women spoke to the Aboriginal Circle about Aboriginal street kids who they see as looking for self-identity. One of them said the cities are very attractive to young women from small communities.

"These women get caught very easily in street life because no one knows you or where you are."

Young Aboriginal women are not safe either in the Aboriginal community or within society at large. Frequently they are the targets of assault and rape by Aboriginal and non-Aboriginal men alike. During Panel consultations, Aboriginal women reported that in some communities Aboriginal men play a game called "pass-out," in which young women who are "passed out," or unconscious from alcohol consumption, are gang-raped. In some Aboriginal communities, it is considered a challenge to have sex with a virgin. Incest and child sexual abuse have been linked to an increase in teenage pregnancies and sexually transmitted diseases.

The 1991 *Report of the Aboriginal Justice Inquiry of Manitoba*, in examining the death of Helen Betty Osborne, states, "[A]boriginal women and their children suffer tremendously as victims in contemporary society. They are victims of racism, of sexism and of unconscionable levels of domestic violence. The justice system has done little to protect them from any of these assaults." [37] Many Aboriginal women feel that the system does not adequately investigate the deaths of women forced to live on the margins of society — prostitutes, drug addicts or those without homes. Nor are there enough convictions of offenders. [38]

Young Aboriginal women spoke to the Aboriginal Circle about the cultural confusion they feel. One young woman reported *"my mother lost her cultural ways and never went back to the reserve ... I was never taught to feel proud of my heritage .... There is a perception that 'white reality' is the absolute reality, and this is part of the balance of power .... Aboriginal cultures need to be revitalized, and women elders need to come out and be recognized for the strong leaders they are."*

Young people go through culture shock when they are sent out. No one shows them through the system. They should take us for two weeks before we go. Two out of five of us who went to high school there made it.

The Kahnawake Shakotiia'takehnhas Resource Centre in Kahnawake, Quebec, runs the very successful National Native Role Model Program, which began after Alwyn Morris won gold and bronze medals at the 1984 Summer Olympics. Seven Aboriginal role models now participate in the program. The goal of the program is to "promote and encourage among the Native people of Canada the adoption of healthy life-styles based upon the traditions of wisdom, love, respect, bravery, honesty, humility and truth." This is accomplished by "encouraging individual, family and community participation and responsibility in defining and pursuing their own vision of health by making role models available from Native communities. We will encourage our people directly in the adoption of healthy lifestyles as well as indirectly by supporting and reinforcing those individuals, families and organizations who serve their community in the pursuit of health and well-being." [39]

WOMEN WITH DISABILITIES

Aboriginal women with disabilities may see themselves as having three strikes against them; they are scorned as women, as Aboriginal people and as persons with disabilities. Many Aboriginal women with disabilities live in poverty because they are dependent on income security and face significant barriers to employment, especially in their home communities. There has been little research concerning their specific needs, and as a result they have been tragically neglected and misunderstood. Women with disabilities face the same oppressions as all Aboriginal women, but they are far more vulnerable to abuse and violence because of their disabilities.

In traditional Aboriginal societies, individuals with disabilities were believed to be gifted by the Creator and were held in special regard by family and the community. Families shared the responsibility for providing care and honoured their individuality. In modern society, Aboriginal women with disabilities are abused and assaulted by family members and by service providers and medical professionals in positions of trust. And for individuals with disabilities, all these people are in positions of trust. Women without speech or vision are more vulnerable to abuse, and their complaints generally lack credibility, especially with persons in authority.

In Aboriginal communities, public buildings and community services are not accessible by wheel-chair, and most remote and isolated communities lack video-display telephones for hearing impaired individuals, technological advances such as video fire alarms for the hearingimpaired and information in accessible language and non-print media. Standard on-reserve housing does not meet wheelchair accessibility requirements for washrooms, kitchens, etc., and the costs of renovating are prohibitive. Also, most shelters cannot accommodate women with disabilities. Most Aboriginal communities do not accom-modate wheelchairs or other means of personal transportation for people with disabilities.

Roads are generally unpaved, making wheelchair use hazardous. Dogs generally roam free on reserves and can be dangerous to those using wheelchairs. Without transportation, Aboriginal women with disabilities can be completely dependent on others to attend to their needs.

Living in a rural area means that disabled people have to leave their home for rehabilitation. They feel more alienated in the city and are more vulnerable.

In rural areas especially, Aboriginal women with disabilities can live as virtual shut-ins. Many are not eligible for provincially funded home care services (which could be an effective means of detection and intervention in cases of violence and abuse) because they live on reserve lands under federal jurisdiction. Aboriginal women with disabilities, and parents of children with disabilities, can be forced to move to urban areas, often into institutions, because essential services are not available on reserves.

The exclusion of Métis and non-Status women from federal non-insured health benefits and other forms of assistance available to Status women has created differences in treatment for Aboriginal women with disabilities and has created unfair and undue social and economic hardships for many.

There are few community-based services specifically geared to the needs of women with disabilities; many services in urban centres are not culturally appropriate, and most shelters are inaccessible to wheelchairs. Treatment for women with disabilities is generally restricted to a non-Aboriginal medical model and is not culturally appropriate to the needs of Aboriginal women.

WOMEN IN CONFLICT WITH THE LAW

It is more likely that an Aboriginal woman will go to prison than graduate from university. While representing less than four percent of Canadian women, 15 percent of federally sentenced women are Aboriginal. [40] In some provincial jails, they make up 80 percent of the population. Less than five percent of the entire Aboriginal population of Canada holds a university degree. [41]

We have lots of Aboriginal women in prisons, but they did not get there just because they stole but because they were violently abused. There is nothing out there when they get out, so they go back to crime trying to survive.

For Aboriginal women in conflict with the law, a prison sentence is the final act of violence imposed on them by a society that has oppressed them since birth. Of the federally sentenced Aboriginal women interviewed by the Task Force on Federally Sentenced Women, 61 percent indicated they had been sexually abused; 90 percent reported being physically abused. [42]

Until recently, the reasons for high numbers of Aboriginal women coming into conflict with the law have been largely misunderstood or ignored. Sexism and racism have been identified as two primary factors, along with poverty, violence, victimization and abuse. Many Aboriginal women are in prison for minor offences and fine defaults. Increasingly, Aboriginal women are imprisoned for violent crimes against the person including physical assault and occasionally manslaughter.

The present justice system is perceived by Aboriginal women as foreign and complex and unrepresentative of their needs. It is a dehumanizing process, based on punishment rather than healing and contravenes traditional Aboriginal principles of justice. Present-day systems strip Aboriginal women of their cultural identity and deprive them of contact with their people. Aboriginal women released from prison often have no place to go in or near their home community. Because there is a lack of half-way houses for women, women often serve a longer period of their sentence in prison than do men.

Incarceration is not the answer for Aboriginal women; for many it is a death sentence. In one 18-month period, five Aboriginal women committed suicide while incarcerated at the only prison for federally sentenced women, located in Kingston, Ontario. Another Aboriginal woman hanged herself across the street from the prison upon being released on parole. [43] Incidents of "slashing" and suicides by federally sentenced Aboriginal women have brought public recognition to the circumstances of imprisoned Aboriginal women. A healing lodge for federally sentenced Aboriginal women is under way in Saskatchewan. Recently, Aboriginal elders have been involved in traditional healing circles for Aboriginal prisoners; however, as noted during Panel consultations, these services are provided at the discretion of Correctional Services, and Aboriginal women have been denied access to traditional healing services for extended lengths of time as a means of punishment. Aboriginal women prisoners also reported that they are subject to "group punishment" whereby they are collectively disciplined for the actions of one or two of the Aboriginal inmates.

Alternative justice systems must be developed based on holistic models for healing that enable Aboriginal women to accept responsibility and accountability for their offences, within the context of their own culture and society. Aboriginal women must be involved in all levels of existing justice structures and must be equally represented in the development of proposed Aboriginal justice systems if these systems are to be truly reflective of their needs. Upon release from prison, Aboriginal women must have access to aftercare programs, parole supervision and halfway houses that are culturally appropriate if they are to acquire the necessary skills to succeed outside the institution and make the transition back to their own communities.

The philosophy of the new correctional facility for women in Fort Smith is in line with the federal government document called Creating Choices. *The move is away from a "secure" facility to a "safe" facility. No doors are locked, no windows are barred. The women are responding very well to this approach. So far, no one has escaped or re-offended. The centre is run on the premise that what the women need most is a place of safety to do their healing. When they arrive, the women are angry, upset and emotionally ill. They push the rules and then they calm down once they realize the place is safe. They have opportunities to talk about the violence with counsellors contracted for that purpose. They also have an AA program. The entire program is a training module in which job and life skills are taught. The women are placed in jobs in the community or go to school while at the centre. One woman plans to attend Arctic College in the fall. This is a first.*

♀♀♀

We all tend to be lumped together — if one Aboriginal inmate does something, we all get punished. A couple of years ago, if one Native inmate had music on, all Native inmates got the[ir] power turned off. Now, the racism is less overt, they show it by treating us differently. Last July, all of us were moved to the special needs unit, which is really just a special handling unit. We were all put there because two Native women got locked outside and the prison called it an attempted escape. Because of the disturbances, the suicides and breaking of windows, we lost everything, all our visits from elders and ceremonies and sweats, the treatment programs for drug and alcohol abuse and sexual abuse. The Native Sisterhood was only allowed to start meeting again this week, and our elders [are] coming in only occasionally.

LESBIANS

Aboriginal lesbians are oppressed on three counts: as Aboriginal people, women and lesbians by a society that does not honour women or indigenous peoples and in which lesbian sexuality is considered a threat. Aboriginal lesbians and gays identify themselves as "two-spirited people." There is little statistical data on Aboriginal lesbians. An informal survey by the Two-Spirited People of the First Nations, a Toronto-based organization representing 200 Aboriginal lesbian and gay members, indicated that 90 percent of its members have experienced either physical or verbal abuse as a result of their sexual orientation. Many have also encountered abuse because of racism.

Lesbians and gay men find themselves in cities built on racism and fed on the oppression of everyone who is not heterosexual, white and male. "... dyke!" is shouted at you from across the street. A white man comes up to you and mutters "squaw." Your friend is beaten up and you don't know if it's because the attacker didn't like Indians or fags.

Today, Aboriginal lesbians and gays are often not accepted in their home community and are ostracized by heterosexual Aboriginal people. A counsellor for two-spirited people reported a pervasive homophobia in the Aboriginal community which is manifested through violence toward two-spirited people and through ostracism by family and the community.

"... Two-Spirited People of the First Nations demand that our Aboriginal leaders be role models in their universal acceptance of all First Nations people in all of their complexity with all of their issues."

Two-Spirited People is developing its own strategies to combat violence toward lesbians and gays. It operates with limited resources and can only provide programs and services on an ad hoc basis. The Toronto-based group provides outreach, advocacy, education and prevention for HIV/AIDS, substance abuse, racism and homophobia, and it hosts community social and cultural events. Attempts to secure long-term funding to sustain its programs and services, however, have been unsuccessful. Because of its limited resources, the needs of two-spirited people for personal healing from racial violence and homophobia have largely gone unanswered. [44]

ELDERLY WOMEN

Exposure to outside society has eroded the natural, inherent respect that Aboriginal people have for their elders. Years of change and the adoption of modern lifestyles have also exposed Aboriginal elders to abuse by their families and Aboriginal communities.

Women elders in the elder housing centre live in fear of their family and the community. They are beaten by family members and other elders. Their money is stolen. Their peacefulness is stolen by others who engage in drunkenness, partying and break-ins. They don't report it because they are revictimized by their family ....

Abuse of the elderly contradicts traditional Aboriginal cultural values. "Indian elders are the keepers of our culture, tradition and language. Traditionally they had a very important role in the Aboriginal family and community. They were consulted on all matters, whether political, familial or social. They were respected by all community members and were cared for by their families or by the community." [45] Elders had power in the community. Like non-Aboriginal older people, they are now more vulnerable to injury, restraint, confinement, financial exploitation, insult or humiliation and sexual assault.

Many elderly Aboriginal people worked outside the wage economy and now, because of inadequate pensions, suffer from poor health, substandard housing, improper diets and have limited access to health care facilities. As with all elderly people in Canada, many are overprescribed medication or are susceptible to misuse or abuse of prescription drugs.

> *The majority of people who work with elders are women, and when they intervene to stop the abuse, they are abused at the time or on the street later. They fear for their children as well.*

Older Aboriginal persons have become targets for financial abuse by family members who show up on pension day and take money away from pensioners. Many reside with other family members in overcrowded living conditions. Family members with drug and alcohol addictions may leave toddlers and older children with family elders for extended periods of time. It is common practice to see elders assume full responsibility for raising young children. This increases their financial difficulties and causes physical and emotional stress. Elders may be the sole supporter of the extended family because there are no other sources of income; in 1985, 24 percent of persons living on reserves and 18 percent living off reserves had no income. [46]

Elderly people rarely report abuse because there may be nowhere to go in their community, and they dread having to go to a seniors' residence, which is usually in a larger centre and rarely has Aboriginal service providers or other cultural supports.

Aboriginal women recognize the valuable role that elders have in breaking the cycle of violence in their community. Their contribution to the development of Aboriginal self-government is critical. Elderly women must be restored to their valued place in Aboriginal families and play a significant role in the healing process.

COMMUNITY-BASED SERVICES

Aboriginal women do not have the same access to services and programs as other women in Canada. Many Aboriginal women, especially those who are dependent on fixed incomes and in remote communities, do not have access to transportation or telephone service. Transportation to and from many isolated and remote communities is by air or rail only, and many women do not have the financial resources to leave their community to avoid assault or abuse.

In Ontario, for example, on-reserve Status women must have transportation costs to go to a shelter pre-approved by the welfare officer assigned to the band. Some chiefs are reluctant to let women leave the community to go to a shelter in a larger centre because often the women do not return. [47]

> *When Aboriginal people talk to social service workers, we don't need to see the reaction of horror on their faces. It is what we live with.*

There is a profound lack of information in many Aboriginal communities regarding women's human and legal rights, family violence and existing services within and outside their community. In fact, lack of knowledge about legal and other rights is the single most frequent reason why women do not call the police or other access points of the criminal justice system. [48] There is also a lack of co-ordination of services, since social workers, teachers, health care professionals and other service providers work in isolation, resulting in fragmented care and prohibiting early detection and prevention of abuse.

If or when Aboriginal women do gain access to community services, they often find them inadequate or inappropriate. In remote and rural Aboriginal communities, receiving service from a shelter usually involves relocating entire families to an unfamiliar urban environment. Often there are no Aboriginal counsellors to counsel, help or give support to the victim. Facilities are often overcrowded and may have waiting lists. Women who seek assistance from shelters often find there is a limit to the length of time they can stay, which is not long enough to deal with their immediate needs let alone long enough to make long-term plans. Aboriginal women have also experienced racism from non-Aboriginal women staying in shelters and from non-Aboriginal workers. [49]

I worked at a transition house as the only Native worker, with mostly white women coming in. The staff tried to kick out one Native woman because they thought she was smoking marijuana in her room. Really she was burning sweet grass.

Many Aboriginal women find themselves trapped in violent situations, forced to return home because of lack of support or resources, or forced into exile in cities or towns where they face a system that is often unaware, uninformed and unconcerned about their culture and lifestyle. They miss the support of family members and friends, lack financial support and have limited job opportunities. They are frequently revictimized by the bureaucratic process of social services, medical or legal professionals, police and the justice system. Services are not co-ordinated, and women may have to retell the graphic details of their abuse to each service agency or government department. It is a dehumanizing process which occurs when victims most need to recuperate and restore their physical, spiritual, mental and emotional well-being.

Non-Aboriginal agencies are not equipped or set up to respond effectively to the needs of Aboriginal women and their families in a crisis, and Aboriginal people have criticized them as being inaccessible, inadequate and insensitive to Aboriginal concerns. Government-sponsored programs are described as "alien" and "know-it-all" and are seen as undermining Aboriginal values and as addressing only the symptoms. The result is frustration for both the non-Aboriginal worker and the Aboriginal women seeking help.

There is a high turnover among non-Aboriginal service providers in Aboriginal communities. Many are young people who have come to remote or isolated communities to gain enough experience to qualify for urban positions in the South. Often they lack sufficient expertise to deal appropriately or effectively with the complex social conditions in Aboriginal communities or do not have an understanding of the consequences of inappropriate interventions or actions. Many women at the Panel consultations spoke of breaches of confidentiality, with consequences ranging from women being reluctant to seek assistance to endangering women's safety. Cross-cultural training that is short and superficial, provided by those not living in the culture or community, can do more harm than good. The high turnover of service providers prevents the development of a body of specialized knowledge about the community and its residents.

When Native women come into the shelter, the workers check their heads for lice. They don't do that with white women.

With very limited resources, Aboriginal women have been forced to develop underground systems and makeshift safe houses to provide sanctuary and support to battered Aboriginal women and their children.

For Aboriginal women in isolated and northern communities, there are almost no services. Services outside the community are structured around the needs of non-Aboriginal women and gravely misrepresent the needs of Aboriginal women in the North.

Aboriginal women need the financial resources to address the root causes of violence in their homes and communities and to develop their own solutions for themselves, their families and their communities.

ABORIGINAL SERVICE PROVIDERS

There is a shortage of Aboriginal service providers in Aboriginal communities, and many lack sufficient training to deal effectively with the issues of violence and abuse. Many training institutes do not acknowledge the Aboriginal service provider's experience and authentic knowledge of the community. Service providers with a working knowledge of their traditional language and culture are invaluable, especially when working with the elders and in more remote communities.

Small communities where everyone knows each other tend to deny privacy and respect for those who speak critically of the need for change in the community, particularly in relation to family violence. So there is a denial of the problems.

Aboriginal service providers often work under tremendous stress, are overburdened by enormous responsibility and are seriously restricted by the lack of other professional services. Some service providers are torn between accountability to their people and to their employer. They are often underpaid and undervalued, resulting in a high rate of burnout.

At the nursing station we feel powerless. We have tried to start healing circles but people don't trust each other. Women are too scared to talk.

There is a need for trained crisis response teams and protocols to provide effective intervention and ongoing support to victims of violence and their families in Aboriginal communities.

Because of family relationships in most Aboriginal communities, many women are not comfortable disclosing their abuse, fearful of a breach of confidentiality. Aboriginal women need to feel secure about disclosing abuse and be assured that their privacy, dignity and safety will be respected and protected.

The participation of Aboriginal women must be integral to the development and delivery of all new services that affect them and their community. Aboriginal service providers play a key role in responding to violence against women, in raising awareness of the issues in communities and in co-ordinating the few services that exist.

GOVERNMENT PROGRAMS AND FUNDING

The federal government, by virtue of its unique relationship with Aboriginal peoples, is both morally and legally bound to represent the interests of all Aboriginal peoples. However, during the last two decades the federal government has begun deferring much of its fiscal responsibility for Aboriginal programs and services to the provinces. Some Aboriginal people view this as an attempt to convert Aboriginal communities from federal to municipal status. The recent "down-sizing and devolution process" by the Department of Indian Affairs and Northern Development and the development of tribal council affiliations to administer programs and services to Aboriginal communities have also contributed to administrative and jurisdictional confusion.

The new Legislative Assembly building would make a wonderful healing lodge for us, though maybe it would be better outside an urban area.

Government project funds are not equally distributed. Regardless of need, the communities or organizations that can best handle the bureaucratic process are those which receive funding. Most funding goes to Status populations because they are officially recognized by government, which is disadvantageous to all other Aboriginal people.

More federal initiatives are being administered by local Aboriginal governments to enable them to assume a greater role in the delivery of programs and services. These initiatives are often underfunded and therefore force communities to compete with each other. Sometimes the funds are not used for the greater good of the community. Aboriginal women's needs are not a priority in Aboriginal communities, and there is no accountability mechanism in place to ensure that all needs are met. Aboriginal women are grossly under-represented in local Aboriginal government and in regional and national Aboriginal organizations. As a result, Aboriginal women are not in a position to determine local priorities.

How can they put up a new $2.3 billion federal building and celebrate it when there is not enough money to keep women safe and help women in crisis?

♀ ♀ ♀

The federal government allotted so many funds to groups. Forty-six Native communities are expected to share $25,000 for family violence. These 46 communities speak 25 different languages.

For Aboriginal women, particularly Métis, non-Status and those living in urban areas, there is jurisdictional confusion over who is responsible for funding Aboriginal women's programs and services.

THE JUSTICE SYSTEM

There is a common belief among Aboriginal people that there are two kinds of "justice" in Canada: one for whites and one for "Indians." This has been well documented by the Royal Commission on the Donald Marshall, Jr., Prosecution and by the Aboriginal Justice Inquiry of Manitoba which also conducted comprehensive examinations of the circumstances surrounding the deaths of Helen Betty Osborne and J.J. Harper.

I fought the justice system for years. There was no one to help me. I was victimized in court. I was told I asked for it. Stitches weren't enough evidence. My children and I moved in with a friend ... I didn't have a job and I didn't want to be a burden. I went back to my husband. It didn't stop until I picked up a knife to defend myself. It was a long battle to overcome and I did it all on my own. We all have to work together to change the court system.

Aboriginal people are subject to two legal systems, neither of which serve Aboriginal women well. While Aboriginal people are governed by the same laws as other Canadians, they are also keenly aware that these laws have been applied differently to the Aboriginal population. The overwhelming number of Aboriginal people in Canadian jails and penitentiaries is a testimony to this fact.

In addition to the Canadian justice system, Aboriginal people are also subject to the law prescribed by the *Indian Act* from birth to death. For example, inherent fishing and hunting rights can only be exercised within reserve boundaries. Off reserve, Aboriginal people are subject to provincial laws on hunting and fishing. For an Aboriginal person to come into conflict with the law in Canada, she or he needs only to exercise their inherent Aboriginal rights.

Generally, Aboriginal people's perception of law is different from that of other Canadians. Canadian justice is a foreign and complex system rooted in concepts of crime and punishment. Aboriginal concepts of crime, punishment and justice focus on the "resolution of disputes, the healing of wounds and the restoration of social harmony." [50] Further, the Aboriginal perception of law focuses on atonement to the individual who was wronged, not on punishment of the offender to "pay a debt to society." There is little consideration of the victim in the Canadian justice system. Other Aboriginal philosophies in conflict with the Canadian justice system are those of non-interference, non-competitiveness, emotional restraint and sharing.

Aboriginal peoples also have difficulty with interpretations of guilt and innocence. There are no such concepts in Aboriginal culture and so there are no words in their vocabulary for "guilty" or "not guilty." This example comes from the Royal Commission on the Donald Marshall, Jr., Prosecution in Nova Scotia.

> There really is no such word as "guilty" in the Micmac language. There is a word for "blame." So an Indian person who's not as knowledgeable let's say in the English language if he were asked if he were guilty or not, he would take that to mean, "Are you being blamed or not?" and that's one of the reasons I found that Native people were pleading guilty is because they suspect that the question was "Is it true you're being blamed?" and the person would of course say "Yes," in other words, but the real question being, "Are you guilty or not guilty?" and the answer of course would be "Yes, I plead guilty," thinking that's blame. What they neglected to say was, "Yes, I'm guilty that I'm being blamed but I didn't do it." [51]

The legal system has long ignored women's realities in all its legislation and practices. It has not applied the law equally for victims and those accused; rather, it has become a process of revictimization. For an Aboriginal woman who must seek protection from violence, the justice system may pose a greater threat to her sense of security than the actual crime. Under Canadian laws, her children can be apprehended, and under the *Indian Act*, her rights to family property can be denied.

> *There is a strong push in the territories to bring justice down to [the] community level. Some of these attempts have had a negative impact on women. Justice is brought down to another male-dominated organization such as a band council. There are a few cases in which community leaders were approached to determine the sanction for the crimes and the offender got off quite easily. If we are seriously looking at community approaches to justice, we have to make sure that protecting women and children is built right in.*

Aboriginal women's understanding of law, courts, police and the judicial process is often defined by a lifetime of sexism and racism. Racism includes not only direct, overt experiences, although most Aboriginal people have known racism first-hand — most have been called "dirty Indians" in schools or foster homes or by police or prison guards. Aboriginal people have also experienced subtle differences in treatment and know it is no accident. [52] These experiences have instilled a deep-rooted fear and a mistrust of the Canadian justice system that are often compounded by a lack of knowledge of legal and constitutional rights. Aboriginal people have no respect for a justice system that does not respect them.

Aboriginal women in isolated or rural communities are further victimized by the circuit court system. "Aboriginal people ... are left with the unfortunately correct assumption that they are on the short end of a cut-rate justice system." [53] Most communities are served by the circuit court 10 to 12 times a year, but it is not uncommon for the hearings to take place over 100 kilometres away from the community it claims to serve. Many communities can only be reached by air, and cancellations because of inclement weather are not uncommon. As a result, either people travel long distances in dangerous weather conditions to find their court appearance has been cancelled, or people are charged with failure to appear when in reality they have been prevented from appearing because of weather conditions. Travelling circuit court parties of predominantly non-Aboriginal people rarely stay overnight in communities, and there is tremendous pressure to clear dockets in one day. Women have extremely limited access to civil justice and suffer from "unavoidable" delays.

> *Many offenders treat jail like a holiday. They live like kings. They get paid for being there. Many young men commit crimes so they can go to jail and play softball. Others commit crimes just before winter so they have a warm place to live. There are many repeat offenders. Taxpayers spend megabucks for them to be there while the woman is uprooted and left out in the cold. In fact, the jail in Hay River is nicer than the shelter.*

People have little time to consult with defence or prosecution attorneys, and plea bargains — which may or may not be in the accused's best interest — are commonplace. "We believe that defence counsel, in fact, do press their clients to accept 'deals' in situations that are not fair to them. Poor communication between non-Aboriginal defence counsel and Aboriginal accused and systemic pressures on counsel to 'cooperate' contribute to this practice." [54]

Many Aboriginal women do not perceive the Canadian justice system as a means of protecting themselves, their children or their rights; rather, they see the process as a revictimization. Aboriginal women report that the batterer is often better protected and defended in the courtroom than the victim.

Cultural "sensitivity" programs for judges and law enforcers that provide short and superficial training may do more harm than good by creating a false impression that violence is acceptable in Aboriginal culture. Aboriginal culture should not be considered in determining whether or not to lay criminal charges. Nor should it be used by law enforcers to decide whether or not to act on a complaint of spousal abuse. This is systemic racism because different standards of treatment are applied to Aboriginal people than to non-Aboriginal people.

Aboriginal offenders who have been charged and convicted of abuse do not have access to culturally appropriate rehabilitation services either while incarcerated or following their return home. Many return to their homes and communities without having resolved the personal issues that led to the offence; this leads to repeat offences by the abuser and to the further victimization of women and children.

Aboriginal communities in the Yukon are working in collaboration with territorial justice officials in justice circles, in which the communities are actively involved in the administration of justice. In domestic assault cases, the needs of both victim and offender are considered equally. Ideally, restoring individual dignity and safety, as well as appropriate sanctions for the offender, are the goals, and the entire community provides support to both the victim and the offender to achieve healing and end violence. Community alternatives are seen as preferable to incarceration; however, if alternative measures are not respected or deemed effective, the mainstream justice system is used. Any community justice initiative must involve women at all stages, from development to delivery.

While the Canadian justice system is ineffective at ending violence and achieving equality, many Aboriginal women are equally suspicious of a separate Aboriginal justice system.

I was charged with aggravated assault and sentenced to three months in jail. It was the fourth time my husband beat me up and the first time I fought back. I hit him with a beer bottle in the face .... Previously, I charged him with bodily harm when I ended up with a head injury after he beat me up. Tribal justice believed him and let him go. He has a history of violence; he pulled a gun on his ex-wife and her baby and almost shot a neighbour. I was charged because I was blamed for getting a chief removed. I'm angry. I wasn't given a fair deal.

Without equal participation, consultation and funding, Aboriginal women's organizations today would reject the establishment of an Aboriginal parallel justice system. There are three driving forces for this premise. First, women are enraged with the [Department of] Justice pilot projects which allow Aboriginal male sex offenders to roam free of punishment in Aboriginal communities after conviction for violent offences against Aboriginal women and children. Second, Aboriginal women oppose lenient sentencing for Aboriginal male sex offenders whose victims are women and children. Third, Aboriginal women and their organizations have hailed as a victory the unanimous ruling by the Federal Court of Appeal on August 20, 1992, which declared that it was a violation of freedom of expression to consult mainly men on Aboriginal policies affecting all Aboriginal peoples. [55]

Neither the Canadian justice system nor current Aboriginal justice initiatives entrench women's and children's rights to security of the person and to live without violence.

POLICING

Policing in Aboriginal communities, whether on or off reserve, urban or rural, is often inadequate and does not respond to the needs of Aboriginal women and children who require police protection. Some isolated communities are without police services, and it can take from two hours to two weeks for police to arrive. There is no standard application of police policies or protocols in intervention and law enforcement. Mandatory charging protocols are not applied consistently and court orders are meaningless without effective enforcement. One study found that 76 percent of those surveyed did not believe police would do anything. [56] The same study found that, of the women who had ever called for police assistance, 56 percent were dissatisfied or very dissatisfied with the performance of police. [57] "One transition house member ... reported that a police officer suggested that if she herself were being beaten, ... she tell police someone was trying to break into her house if she wanted a speedy response." [58] The failure of police to respond, or to respond appropriately, also affects future prosecutions. Statements may not be taken, injuries are not documented and evidence may be lost or destroyed.

The RCMP is an accomplice to the crime when they ignore my call for help. They say they can't do anything until the crime is committed. That is too late.

A number of Aboriginal women reported abuse by Aboriginal and non-Aboriginal police, including sexual harassment and assault. Many Aboriginal women are reluctant to report spousal and sexual abuse to police for fear of being abused again, because police do not provide adequate protection. Aboriginal women may also be afraid their partners may be "victimized or brutalized" by police. [59] Given the over-representation of Aboriginal people in Canadian jails, police are not seen as an effective means of seeking safety from violence in their home or community. Racist actions or child apprehension by "over-zealous" social workers [60] called in by police when such actions are unwarranted are only two reasons why Aboriginal people believe that police are not necessarily concerned with protecting their rights or safety.

They have tried to hire police officers, but no Native person wants to be one.

Aboriginal people are generally more comfortable dealing with Aboriginal police; however, these relations are not without difficulties. Aboriginal officers from the same community may be related to or socialize with abusers and can be very reluctant to charge family or friends. Aboriginal officers may also be more susceptible to political pressure or interference because of the immense control held by chiefs and councils, to whom the officer may report. Friction may also result from Aboriginal officers being perceived by the community as "flaunting their authority." [61] Provincial governments can also create problems. Recently, the Government of Newfoundland and Labrador refused to acknowledge two special constables in an Innu community who had completed a police training program for Aboriginal people in British Columbia. [62]

I went to the police ... for help. Instead of helping me they tried to have sex with me. I went to the RCMP who told me the only way they could help me was if he beat me up outside of the house. When I said, "But I'm the provider, can't you do something?" they said, "No, he's the head of the house."

Aboriginal and non-Aboriginal police in both rural and urban communities lack awareness of violence in Aboriginal families, and officers' failure to adhere to charging directives may most often result from the personal attitudes of officers. [63] Aboriginal women have also reported that police officers have refused to bring charges against an abusive spouse if they feel the woman will not make a good witness. There are few women on police forces in Aboriginal areas and no specialized domestic violence response teams.

Despite efforts to provide cross-cultural training by some forces, racism against Aboriginal people is prevalent on many police forces. Aboriginal officers also bear the brunt of racist actions and attitudes from co-workers and the public. This issue has received much public attention.

It's a great injustice to make a woman and her children stand on a highway in the cold weather at two a.m. waiting for a bus to Fort Smith. Men should be taken out of the home, not women.

♀ ♀ ♀

As my partner and I were patrolling, we saw a man beating up a Native woman. When I wanted to intervene, my partner said, "No, he'll take care of it." The man dragged the woman by the hair into an apartment building, and my partner said, "See, he took care of it."

HOUSING

Substandard housing and overcrowding in Aboriginal communities have reached crisis levels. For many years, report after report has detailed the insufficient number and substandard condition of housing units on reserves. Many communities do not have hydro, running water or sewage facilities. Only half of on-reserve housing units (35,000) are adequate and suitable; 31 percent have neither piped nor well water; 31 percent have neither piped sewage service nor septic fields. [64] Adequate housing is defined as that which "does not require major repairs and/or lack basic facilities. Major repairs include, but are

not limited to, defective plumbing, defective electrical wiring, structural repairs to walls, floors or ceilings. Basic facilities include hot and cold running water, an indoor toilet and a bathtub or shower." [65] The Canada Mortgage and Housing Corporation estimates that 24,070 Aboriginal households (35 percent of the Aboriginal population) living off reserves are in core need of housing. [66] Housing conditions have been identified as a primary factor in the high rate of violence, disease and accidental death in Aboriginal communities in Canada.

While the on-reserve population has more than doubled in the last 25 years, the annual number of new or renovated on-reserve housing units has decreased from 7,897 in 1983-1984 to 6,569 in 1991-1992. [67]

People are staying at the Salvation Army, they can only stay seven days, are given little or no breakfast and kicked out from seven a.m. until the night. He walks around all day looking for work and she walks around with the children. In the winter, they spend the day just trying to stay warm. People are afraid to complain about it for fear their children will be taken away. And these people are preaching Christianity.

Overcrowded housing is defined as more than one person per room per dwelling. The rate of overcrowded dwellings on reserves is significantly higher than the Canadian figure and is rapidly increasing; in 1986, the rate of overcrowding on reserves was 16 times higher than the Canadian rate. Funding has not increased since 1983. The Assembly of First Nations estimates that $3.3 billion is required to meet existing needs, that is, for new and replacement units, major and minor renovations and infrastructures. [68]

Overcrowded and substandard housing exacerbate family tensions and literally keep women in violent situations. There is often nowhere to go in isolated and remote communities, even for a short time, to escape violence. It is not uncommon for grandparents, parents and children to live in a standard-design three-bedroom house; staying with family or friends is not an option.

In February 1992, six Innu children in Davis Inlet died in a fire while trying to warm themselves with a hot plate in -34° weather (-64° with the wind chill). The community was helpless to save the children because Davis Inlet has no fire protection equipment. This tragedy focused attention on the overcrowded housing conditions and the lack of infrastructures and fire protection services in many Aboriginal communities, but to date no meaningful action has been taken to address the conditions in which many Aboriginal people are forced to live.

Aboriginal people are forced to live in houses with large cracks in the walls and plastic covering the windows since glass is too expensive to replace. Elders "must live in poorly heated homes without running water or toilet facilities. In winter it is not unusual for a person to be sleeping next to a wall that is covered with frost on the inside."[69]

> Lack of facilities creates undue hardship for the elderly and the infirm. Illnesses that are infrequent ... in other communities are annual events. The effects of dilapidated housing on the morale of our people is of great concern to our leaders. It is difficult to live with dignity and pride when such clear, visible evidence of poverty and inequity confronts you every day.[70]

Northern and isolated communities are greatly disadvantaged because of the high cost of materials, transportation and labour. Government departments and agencies establish inappropriate and inadequate policies that cause real suffering and harm to Aboriginal peoples. Indian Affairs and Northern Development housing allocations do not match the real costs of housing units and do not provide for additional costs such as site preparation.

Métis and non-Status families on fixed or moderate incomes do not have access to Indian Affairs funding and cannot afford Canada Mortgage and Housing Corporation (CMHC) mortgage rates and provincial property taxes. Ironically, in some Métis communities, dwellings financed by CMHC stand vacant, while substandard and overcrowded dwellings remain occupied.

As indicated earlier, approximately 115,000 Aboriginal people were reinstated to "Indian Status" under Bill C-31. Although the federal government allocated funds for housing specifically for these approximately 28,000 families,[71] the amount was insufficient to meet the demand, and as a result, current on-reserve housing shortages have escalated. There is a lack of consistency in the administration and delivery of Indian Affairs and Northern Development housing programs. Many Aboriginal people complain of unfair selection procedures for housing allocations and favouritism by band administrations and leaders. Women have no property rights on reserve lands, which makes women extremely vulnerable to violence.

Landlords are like vultures. They put people in holes, but for many it is the first time they have running water so they don't complain.

The termination of the Indian Affairs and Northern Development off-reserve housing program has left a serious void in housing for Aboriginal people living in urban settings. In response, many groups have formed Aboriginal housing co-operatives under CMHC initiatives. These units are collectively owned and offer subsidized rents for low-income families. In one southern Ontario city with an Aboriginal population of approximately 10,000, a non-profit housing organization for Aboriginal people presently houses 400 people. This agency has 477 applications for housing on file, representing 1,300 individuals.[72] Some co-ops have experienced a racial backlash from neighbours who fear their properties will be devalued.

The Native Council of Canada has expressed grave concerns about cuts to housing budgets. "What we have been told is to expect a 21 percent across-the-board cut this year ... and an anticipated 30 percent cut next year. So we're already looking at [a] 51 percent or better cut in an already inadequately funded program which is supposed to reach people who are most in need."[73]

Government housing policies for Aboriginal communities are inadequate. Building construction and standards often do not meet the requirements dictated by the northern climate and rural locations; housing units last an average of five years before prohibitively expensive major repairs are needed. The units are also small. Complicated policies prohibit the use of local resources, both human and natural. This eliminates on-the-job training programs which would generate income in local economies and would considerably shorten the current lengthy and cumbersome process.

The issue of homelessness of Aboriginal people in urban settings needs immediate action. There are many complex factors that can affect an Aboriginal person's ability to obtain employment and maintain housing. Holistic supports must be made available to help people escape life on the street.

POVERTY

The impact of poverty on the Aboriginal family and the community is immeasurable. Poverty, in its severest form, is a fact of life for many Aboriginal people, depriving them of their basic human rights and dignity. The absence of a sound economic base and extremely high levels of unemployment force Aboriginal people to live in overcrowded and substandard housing, which in turn directly contributes to poor health. But it is the daily stress, financial hardship and chronic despair inflicted by poverty that contribute to the widespread abuse of Aboriginal women and children.

Federal and provincial governments have not done enough to eradicate poverty from the Aboriginal community; they have, in fact, contributed to the poverty of Aboriginal people across the nation. Paternalistic laws and bureaucratic policies of the federal and provincial governments towards Aboriginal peoples have undermined traditional economies and have transformed self-sufficient Aboriginal nations into little more than "welfare states." Aboriginal people have not shared equally in the wealth from Canada's vast natural resources and maintain that the trust between their nations and the Canadian government, based on treaty and inherent Aboriginal rights, has been grossly violated.

When you live in poverty, you don't know there are places you can go for help. People focus on you more if you experience violence and come from a high-income group.

♀ ♀ ♀

There's less hope when you're poor. You're overlooked.

Aboriginal communities sustain the economies of nearby non-Aboriginal communities by purchasing food, clothing, recreational items, vehicles, etc., in these centres. Despite this investment, few if any Aboriginal people are employed in these businesses or in government offices located in these towns.

There are very few long-term, highly paid employment opportunities in Aboriginal communities. Aboriginal leaders have control over the few that do exist, and they usually fill the positions with their political supporters, friends and family members. In 1986, less than 35 percent of status women over the age of 15 living on reserve were in the labour force. [74] Education and experience are often not taken into account by employers. This leaves little hope for those who are not in special favour.

Aboriginal people in Canada have been kept in a state of abject poverty, many living in conditions similar to those of underdeveloped countries. Economic initiatives developed by provincial and federal governments do not fulfil the needs of a rapidly increasing Aboriginal population. Aboriginal peoples have been denied any meaningful role in the social and economic development of their communities.

There's lots of unemployment here. Last year I only got six weeks' work. When there's no money, you don't feel good about the way things are going. In the summer I fish from five o'clock in the morning until night time. It gives me something to do.

Recently, the United Nations named Canada the best place in the world to live; when the disparities between non-Aboriginal women and men are considered, Canada slips to eighth place. [75] One can only speculate how Canada would rate if the social and economic conditions of Aboriginal peoples in Canada were taken into account.

There are many single mothers, and even though the law orders men to give some money to their wives, men are often tempted to leave their jobs and go on unemployment insurance or welfare simply so they will not be required to give money to their wives.

Canadian governments fail to ensure that Aboriginal people share equally in Canada's prosperity.

EDUCATION

The Canadian educational system is facing two significant challenges to meet the needs of Aboriginal students. First, schools must take an active role in the detection and prevention of violence, and second, they must include Aboriginal culture in curricula.

At school they should not only address the problem of violence by strangers but also family violence and the psychological and emotional abuse, not just the physical abuse. Teachers should realize the importance of the issue. That issue needs to be as important as geography and mathematics.

Schools and day-care centres can become primary points for the detection and early treatment of child abuse. Teachers, counsellors and education workers, especially those in daily contact with Aboriginal children, do not always recognize the signs of child abuse and violence in the children. When symptoms are apparent, the school does not necessarily contact community services. There are no standard protocols established that direct schools if violence in the school or violence in the home is suspected or detected.

Canadian schools do not accurately represent Aboriginal peoples. Schools continue to teach children that Christopher Columbus "discovered" America. Modern history omits or distorts significant facts that have had a great impact on Aboriginal peoples and have helped shape the Canadian reality. Canadian curricula do not include such important information as treaties and residential schools, and only minimally allude to the *Indian Act*. Events of significance to the Aboriginal community are presented from a historical perspective with no link to contemporary society, and they are usually presented from a non-Aboriginal viewpoint.

The omission of Aboriginal peoples' authentic history and rich, diverse culture perpetuates ignorance and racism by non-Aboriginal people who must rely on equally misinformed media for information about Aboriginal people. This omission alienates Aboriginal students from the "white" educational system and contributes to a lack of self-esteem, cultural confusion and high drop-out rates. Sandra Ward of the Yukon Indian Women's Association explains:

> ... public schools separate us from our culture in many ways. We are alienated for our values and beliefs in the school community unless we fit into an "accepted pattern of life" or "way of thinking." Many native values and beliefs are very different from this "pattern" so, consequently, many of us either go through the school system suffering from an inferiority complex or drop out and retreat to our families where we are better understood and accepted. [76]

Education should be decentralized and reflect an understanding of the needs of various Canadian cultures.

Many Aboriginal parents don't make their children's education a priority, largely because of their own negative experiences, and fail to take the initiative to send their children to school.

I have been in education since 1969 as a teacher, vice principal, principal; I have been responsible for thousands of students with the abuse syndrome I experienced myself. I started working as director of education in my home community and asked to be involved in suicide prevention and intervention. Eight of 58 people in one year succeeded in shooting, hanging, etc., themselves. As an educator I see kids without their faces washed, no breakfast, late for school — no care in the home, or maybe their parents are passed out.

The 1986 Census revealed that only 17 percent of the Canadian population has no high school education. The following are percentages of Aboriginal people over 15 years old with no high school education: [77]

Status, on reserve	45%
Status, off reserve	24%
Métis	35%

While every effort must be made to provide sufficient support and motivation for Aboriginal students to finish high school and pursue higher education, youth must also be taught the skills and information necessary to succeed in urban areas.

Our children witness violence, sexual abuse. It's not dealt with properly. My daughter's friend came to school with two black eyes. The way they dealt with it was to phone the parents who did it. Children disclose to children, not adults, but they have no power to help. They are afraid of what the adults will do. They fear going to foster homes where they'll be abused more.

Education is the key element in breaking the cycle of poverty, violence and hopelessness currently afflicting Aboriginal communities in Canada. Self-government will provide many opportunities for involvement and success, and Aboriginal women and men must be given every opportunity to acquire the tools to maximize their potential and realize their goals. Both traditional and modern skills must be valued equally if the transition to a more self-determined social, political and economic life is to succeed.

Early detection of abuse means early intervention. Teachers and other education professionals play a vital role in breaking the cycle of violence in Aboriginal communities and in providing support for Aboriginal children in crisis.

Natives must be given back their right to their mother tongue; teaching should be done in this language.

TRAINING

Government training programs are a primary source of income and employment in most Aboriginal communities. Training programs are short term, usually 20 to 40 weeks, and are generally not accredited by a post-secondary institution. Job opportunities outside Aboriginal communities are limited and highly competitive, and government training initiatives do not provide the level of work-related experience demanded by public and private sector employers.

Because of the lack of an economic base to support long-term employment, Aboriginal communities depend on government training initiatives. Training initiatives in the Aboriginal community for Aboriginal women are scarce. Most training programs are aimed at Aboriginal men because they are seen as the providers for the family. Aboriginal women can pursue post-secondary education or vocational training only if they leave their community.

Métis and non-status women are often restricted from pursuing higher education because they are not eligible for educational assistance from Indian Affairs and Northern Development. The lack of day care or adequate child care, especially in northern and Métis communities, seriously impedes Aboriginal women's ability to work.

RESIDENTIAL SCHOOLS/CHURCHES

The residential school has been the Canadian government's most destructive and blatant tool of cultural genocide perpetrated against Aboriginal people in Canada's 125-year history. The residential school era has been described as a nuclear explosion "with the blast damaging some more directly than others, but with fall-out and nuclear winter affecting everyone." [78]

I was taken to residential school at age seven, and I did not go home until I was 16. We were forbidden to talk our own language. I know some older girls were sexually abused, but in my years the superintendent changed so I was fortunate. There was lots of mental abuse though. I can still experience sitting there with the whole dormitory crying. Some would not know their parents had died unless people came in on dogsled to tell them. If a child wet the bed, they would throw the child into a tub of ice water. We drank potato water, ate beans and leftovers, and the nuns and priest would eat gourmet meals .... When I came out of the residential school I did not know who I was. I did not know I was a Dene girl.

The internment and forced assimilation of Aboriginal children during the residential school era, from 1867 to 1967, severed the relationship between Aboriginal children and their families and communities. Residential schools forbade students to speak their Aboriginal language and forced them to abandon their culture. When they returned home, the young people could not communicate with family and elders, who were the cultural teachers. They had been forced to adopt white beliefs and values which were often in conflict with traditional teachings.

Raised in a cold, institutional atmosphere, Aboriginal children were deprived of parental contact, which left them with little knowledge of traditional child-rearing skills that had been passed from generation to generation. Furthermore, the traditional roles of women and men were dramatically changed. Many victims of abuse at residential schools in turn became the abusers, inflicting on their own children what they had been forced to endure at the residential school.

When the treaties were signed it was the beginning of betrayal and lies. Law we didn't understand was imposed on us. We were put in residential schools. We were denied our livelihoods and a place in white society. Since then we have been a source of cheap labour to industrialize Canada. We want compensation. You can't deal with the hurts of today unless you deal with the hurts of the past.

There is a need for further study of abuse at residential schools and its link to the high incidence of sexual abuse in Aboriginal communities today. Since 1987 when investigations began, many survivors have come forward to share their personal experiences of abuse.

Churches and governments have not fully acknowledged their part in inflicting abuse. They call for documented legal proof. Some churches have undertaken their own research to refute or minimize the seriousness of the abuse, particularly the sexual abuse committed by church officials.

One 1992 church report states, "had native people not been educated in the ways of the white majority, their chances of survival would have been quite tenuous." [79] In a similar vein, a recent report rejects "the conventional ... treatment of the Indian as victim" [80] based on written testimonies extracted from government and church archives which indicate Aboriginal support of and participation in residential schooling. In reality, parents who refused to send their children to residential schools faced legal action.

This type of abstract analysis succeeds only in diverting public attention from the critical issues concerning residential schools and their long-term impact on Aboriginal society, that is, the genocidal nature of the residential school system, the immorality of forced religious indoctrination and the arrogance and paternalism that permeated the system. [81]

There is both a moral and a legal obligation for the Canadian government and the churches of Canada, who jointly participated in the victimization of Aboriginal children, to share equally the responsibility of providing financial assistance to help heal residential school victims and their families and of compensating for their pain and suffering all living victims of abuse committed by staff at the schools.

One child lost is too many.

Recently, the Ontario government established a $23-million compensation fund for victims who were abused while wards of the Ontario School for Boys some 40 years ago. Meanwhile, victims of abuse at residential schools have been left to heal themselves, with no financial or other assistance for treatment. The refusal of church and state to compensate Aboriginal victims of abuse is nothing less than systemic racism.

The imposition of European religions on Aboriginal peoples has displaced their traditional belief systems and the role of women in Aboriginal societies. Many Aboriginal women remain in abusive relationships because their Christian marriage vows dictate forgiveness and tolerance of abuse. Religion has become a source of division and disharmony within contemporary Aboriginal society.

EMPLOYMENT

Aboriginal women have steadily been achieving higher levels of education and entering the work force in increasing numbers. Aboriginal women face the same obstacles in the workplace as all women, but their experiences are compounded by overt and covert racism.

Governments have instituted employment equity programs that target Aboriginal people, among others. Such programs assist a few, primarily urban Aboriginal people, and the jobs are usually clerical and secretarial positions with low wages. Few Aboriginal women can realistically aspire to middle and senior management positions, despite equality efforts.

National Aboriginal political organizations also reflect the gender imbalance found in local leadership and the workplace. Management is primarily male and support staff is predominantly female. However, while support positions are generally filled by women, not all are filled by Aboriginal women. National Aboriginal political organizations often deny positions or promotions to Aboriginal women in favour of non-Aboriginal women, even though there are many Aboriginal women with all the requisite education, skills and abilities. National Aboriginal political organizations are not unionized and support staff cannot express their concerns without fear of losing their jobs. Often jobs are not well defined, hours of work are not set and working conditions are poor. In addition, women are expected to perform additional duties. Many Aboriginal political organizations employ non-Aboriginal consultants without requiring the sharing of skills with an Aboriginal employee as a condition of the contract.

National Aboriginal political organizations have a moral and ethical responsibility to act as models for other employers, especially with regard to empowering Aboriginal women, by valuing lived experience and by hiring and promoting Aboriginal employees. All employees must have freedom of speech without fear of job loss and must be treated with dignity and respect at all times. Since national Aboriginal political organizations have moved the issues of poverty and unemployment to the top of their agendas, they must set the example by implementing pro-Aboriginal hiring and promotion policies.

HEALTH

The health of Aboriginal people in Canada is much poorer than that of the non-Aboriginal population: Aboriginal men and women live approximately 10 years less than non-Aboriginal Canadians. Death by suicide is almost three times higher for Aboriginal people than for other Canadians. Proportionally, more Aboriginal people die from violence and accidents or "preventable" circumstances than other Canadians. The leading causes of death among Aboriginal people are injuries and poisoning. [82] Injuries sustained through violence against women are included in this category.

There are several primary factors that influence the health of Aboriginal people. As a group, Aboriginal people live under the worst socio-economic conditions in Canada. The education and employment rates of Aboriginal people are significantly lower than the national average, while drug, alcohol and solvent abuse and violence, including sexual and physical abuse, are disproportionately higher. The health of the Aboriginal community and the physical, mental, emotional and spiritual well-being of its members cannot be isolated from other primary social and economic factors.

Health care in the Aboriginal community does not meet the demands of its growing population. The recent transfer of medical service delivery from federal to local control has not provided additional funds to develop new programs to satisfy existing and emerging needs. Aboriginal people have the right to a full range of medical services of the same quality as those in non-Aboriginal communities.

There are no provisions for non-insured health benefits for Métis and non-status Aboriginal people. There is considerable inconsistency in the provision of non-insured health benefits because status rights are non-transportable. Often individuals without non-insured health benefits will forego dental care and eye care and may not purchase prescribed drugs because of the cost.

Many Aboriginal women encounter discrimination and racism from medical professionals, most of which goes unreported. In the *Report of the Abortion Services Review Committee*, [83] of 28 randomly reviewed medical files of patients who received abortions at the Stanton Hospital in Yellowknife, none received any form of anesthetic. The absence of analgesics was seen by some as a deterrent to repeat procedures. Although cases involving Aboriginal patients were not identified, demographics of the Northwest Territories suggest that race was likely a contributing factor in the decision not to use anesthetic. [84]

Today more than half of Aboriginal mothers living on reserve are under 25 years of age, compared with 28 percent of the non-Aboriginal community. [85] It is common procedure in remote communities to bring pregnant Aboriginal women to hospitals in large urban centres two to eight weeks before their delivery date. This places undue hardship on expectant mothers, isolating them from home and community when they greatly need support. Language barriers, unfamiliar surroundings and changes to diet often compound an already stressful event.

In remote areas, Aboriginal patients needing hospitalization or specialized treatment must be moved to hospitals or other medical facilities in larger centres. As with maternity patients, culture shock, language barriers and the lack of medical interpreters pose major difficulties for those patients. Patients may be separated from family and other supports for long periods of time and the cost of transportation prohibits any regular contact. Since attitude and mental health are major factors in recovery and rehabilitation, these separations have a detrimental effect on patients and families. It is even more difficult for children who must undergo medical treatment away from home.

Status women living on reserves often have no choice of physician, since the Medical Services Branch (MSB) of Health and Welfare Canada contracts medical professionals to provide services. Medical appointments for women who need care or treatment in larger facilities are prearranged with physicians who have contracts with MSB to provide services. Medical coverage can be denied if patients choose not to see a MSB physician. In the case of doctors who abuse, women may have no choice but to continue to be abused in order to receive "health" care.

Remote communities are served by nursing stations, staffed by federally employed nurses and community health representatives, and physicians visit communities on a rotational basis. Because there is no continuum of care in most Aboriginal communities, abuse is not addressed as a cause of seeking medical assistance. Women are frequently overmedicated or misdiagnosed.

Right now the money spent on prescription drugs on a reserve is enough to run a small city.

Many women are also reluctant to seek medical assistance for injuries resulting from family violence because of fear or shame. [86]

The suicide rate among Aboriginal women is more than double the national average for other Canadian women. [87] Rates are highest among young Aboriginal women and decline slowly throughout adult years. Almost one fifth of the "violent" deaths among Aboriginal women are suicides. [88]

Because of the remoteness and small size of many Aboriginal communities, the potentially devastating impact of HIV/AIDS needs urgent examination. "There are several communities that are beginning to report high levels of HIV positive" and recent studies indicate that

Aboriginal people in Canada may already suffer a higher rate of infection than the mainstream Canadian population. [89] AIDS/HIV must be treated as a serious health issue, and there must be no jurisdictional confusion or refusal to pay for testing and/or treatment. Information must be widely disseminated, in Aboriginal languages and in a variety of media.

Lack of access to services, insufficient numbers of Aboriginal health professionals and service providers and poverty have direct, detrimental effects on the health of Aboriginal women.

Substance Abuse

Alcohol, drug and solvent abuse are rampant in Aboriginal communities in Canada. Substance abuse has had a devastating and far-reaching effect on Aboriginal people, and its victims have become increasingly younger with each successive generation. Alcohol, drug and solvent abuse have been linked to high rates of suicide, accidental and violent deaths, disease, child abuse and child neglect among Aboriginal people. More recently, the presence of Fetal Alcohol Syndrome (FAS) in Aboriginal children has been added to a growing list of problems caused by substance abuse.

The more my husband drank the worse it got. My children would hide in the room and not make a sound. I could feel when he was going to get mad. Anything you can think of, it happened to me. I nearly killed myself many times, but I would picture my children crying and I knew that I could not let my kids be put away in an institution. I left him several times, but he would promise to change [and] to get help. Well, I have not seen help yet.

Although substance abuse has been linked to sexual and physical violence, it is no excuse for violence against Aboriginal women and children. Substance abuse should not be a consideration when laying criminal charges related to physical or sexual violence against women and children.

Documentation on violence, produced by the Anishinabek in Ontario, states that alcohol and drug abuse does not cause violence but that the two are often present together because they both have the same root causes: low self-esteem, racism by the general population, social and economic conditions and the loss of Aboriginal social structures which were respectful of women, children and elders. [90]

Alcohol, drug and solvent abuse have a profound impact on the social and economic development of Aboriginal communities and are perceived as both causes and effects of the larger cycle of poverty and welfare dependency. Drug and alcohol treatment centres for Aboriginal people have indicated that the vast majority of addicts have suffered from violence as children and adults.

There is a lot of drinking on welfare days and festival days. At those times I feel like I'm in a war zone there is so much violence. There is so much blood our emergency unit looks like it's from the MASH unit.

♀♀♀

Alcohol is a surface problem. My first husband was violent and he didn't drink at all. My second husband was an alcoholic and he was also violent. Both men had the same attitude toward women.

♀♀♀

"It took me eight months after I left him to become an alcoholic. It made me sleep, it gave me courage to be in the company of other men and ... [it gave me] that 'I don't give a shit' attitude."

The waiting lists at these treatment centres are extremely long, and few support services are available in the Aboriginal community for recovering addicts when they return home after treatment. We must ask what chance for success do the children of Davis Inlet, who were sent to a treatment program in Alberta, have? Although the case received wide public attention, after

completing the program, the children will return to the same conditions and underlying factors that contributed to their substance abuse with no long-term plan of care. [91] These children are at grave risk for continuing a range of self-destructive behaviours, ranging from solvent abuse to suicide.

TRADITIONAL HEALING

The term healing is frequently used by Aboriginal care givers, and Aboriginal people in general, to describe the recovery process of victims of violence, abuse or addictions. The healing movement has gained momentum among Aboriginal individuals, most of whom are women, as a process of recovery to restore the natural balance and well-being of Aboriginal families and communities after suffering generations of violence.

Native spiritual articles which are still used in ceremonies are kept in museums. People think we [belong] ... in a museum. In those pieces of grass and trees are the spirits of our grandmothers and grandfathers. They are desecrated by others. There has been violence against Native men also through residential schools. They grew up not knowing how to be brothers, fathers, care-givers. If you have never seen a grand-mother be a grandmother, you don't know how to be one. How we are on downtown streets is not how we are meant to be.

A return to traditional Aboriginal practices, including pipe ceremonies, sweat lodges and healing circles, and to traditional Aboriginal spirituality have become widely accepted methods for healing Aboriginal victims of violence and abuse. Healing is generally viewed as a holistic and natural approach to recovery that includes self, family, community and nation. This holistic approach also embodies the emotional, spiritual, physical and mental needs of the victim.

Healing does not have any religious or spiritual connotation unless adopted by the individual as a matter of choice. All individuals who have suffered from violence or abuse must be free to realize their own form of healing, whether it be conventional treatments or traditional Aboriginal healing methods. Freedom of choice is critical in the healing and recovery process.

The healing lodge is a concept that has grown from the need for specialized treatment for Aboriginal victims of violence. It is a symbol that represents a place of healing or an environment that is conducive to individual, family and community healing. A healing lodge can provide both traditional Aboriginal healing practices and conventional, non-Aboriginal therapy or treatment for Aboriginal victims of violence and their families.

ABUSE BY SELF-PROCLAIMED ELDERS/ HEALERS

Some self-proclaimed elders/healers prey on Aboriginal children and women and subject them to sexual, physical, emotional and psychological abuse under the guise of healing. The problem is increasing as the healing movement grows. True Aboriginal elders, who are identified by the community for their experience and knowledge, are reluctant to denounce self-proclaimed elders/healers since it is contrary to the way they treat others. People are fearful of exposing self-proclaimed elders/healers lest they diminish respect for true elders/healers. As painful as this is to reveal, it must be made known. Many Aboriginal women in all parts of Canada spoke of the anguish they had suffered at the hands of these pretenders. We must have the courage to identify these people and take strong action to end their abuse.

There is bad medicine and good medicine on the reserve. The bad medicine is used against women if they try to disclose to the police or social workers or to leave the violence. Even some elders use bad medicine.

In addition to inflicting physical, sexual and psychological abuse on Aboriginal women and children, these people may also destroy their victims' spirituality.

RACISM

Racism is a major contributing factor in the continuing violence, oppression and systemic abuse that confronts Aboriginal women in Canada today. "Discrimination against Aboriginal people has been a central policy of Canadian governments since Confederation." [92]

I was assaulted because I was Native. I still have scars on my forehead. My children were attacked in the schoolyard by white boys. I intervened. The father came out and attacked me. The police told me to drop the charges or they would charge me, my daughter and my husband with assault. I had to repeatedly demand they take me to the hospital. And after, they censored my statement of the [insults] this man said to me. I went to court without a lawyer. He had a high-powered lawyer. The case was dismissed. I was broken. I haven't been able to work since....

There are no available statistics on racially motivated assaults on Aboriginal women; however, several recent cases demonstrate the magnitude of this problem. In Winnipeg, a man was convicted of drugging, raping and videotaping 50 young Aboriginal women ranging in age from 11 to 17 years. The brutal slaying of Helen Betty Osborne in The Pas, Manitoba, and the failure of Manitoba's justice system to bring the offenders to trial for 16 years, even though the identities of those responsible for her death were relatively well known in the community, is the most blatant example. However, it was not until 1988, one month after the death of J.J. Harper, an Aboriginal man who was killed by a Winnipeg police officer, that Manitoba created the Public Inquiry into the Administration of Justice and Aboriginal People, also referred to as the "Manitoba Aboriginal Justice Inquiry," in response to public demand. One must note the prompt action that resulted from the killing of an Aboriginal man but which was denied Helen Betty Osborne for 16 years.

On January 1, 1989, an Aboriginal woman named Minnie Sutherland was struck by a car in Hull, Quebec, after spending a night out with her cousin on New Year's Eve. The police officer who arrived at the scene did not believe witnesses who said she had been injured and, after depositing her in a snowbank, offered no assistance other than to call a taxi. When friends took her to a nearby restaurant to escape the bitter cold, the officer radioed to "cancel the taxi now, the squaw has decided otherwise." [93] Ms. Sutherland encountered another police officer in Ottawa, across the Ottawa River from Hull, when the friends who were driving her home stopped the car because she was unconscious. An ambulance was summoned, an attendant pronounced Ms. Sutherland to be intoxicated and instructed the police officer to take her to the detoxification centre. The detoxification centre adhered to its policy of not admitting anyone who is unconscious. The officer then took Ms. Sutherland to the Ottawa police station; when efforts to revive her failed, she was finally taken to hospital two hours after being injured. The hospital was not advised that Ms. Sutherland had been struck by a car. Ms. Sutherland died in hospital 10 days later from a blood clot caused by a skull fracture. During the inquest to examine the circumstances surrounding her death, an attending physician stated that had he known of the injury, Ms. Sutherland may have survived.

> *Last week in social services, a white woman was offered a cup of tea and an older Aboriginal woman was offered nothing. All should be treated equally.*

Sharon McIvor, who represented Ms. Sutherland for the Native Women's Association of Canada, said, "Minnie Sutherland is a high-profile case that shows what happens to us all the time." The then mayor of Ottawa supported the actions of the Ottawa police officer, stating, "it was New Year's Eve. [The officer] assumed she was drunk, which was a pretty safe assumption at any time." [94]

Aboriginal women are at a disadvantage in Canadian society by reason of their race and sex and in Aboriginal societies by reason of sex. Discrimination against Aboriginal women in government programs and services not only violates their Charter rights, it also perpetuates the systemic abuse of all Aboriginal women. The oppression of Aboriginal women resulting from patriarchal policies that exclude their full and equal participation in Canadian society cannot be eradicated without clear initiatives by both Aboriginal and non-Aboriginal governments to restore the cultural, social, economic and political position of Aboriginal women in their societies.

> *Violence that is one-on-one we can deal with. Institutionalized violence against Native people we cannot deal with. Native people are treated like badly kept sheep. The government has capped funding for Native education. [The] Children's Aid Society continues to remove our children from our homes.*

Racism in Canada creates and reinforces the invisible barriers that divide Aboriginal and non-Aboriginal society. These barriers, while unseen and often unspoken, are apparent by the lack of Aboriginal representatives in mainstream Canada's public and private sector institutions. Racism is perpetuated by ignorance and fear of another's culture and identity. Racism impedes open communication between Aboriginal and non-Aboriginal peoples and inhibits the development of any serious resolution to end social, economic and political inequality in Canada.

Racism is a reality in the daily lives of Aboriginal people in Canada. Aboriginal women fear exposing the violence in their communities because white society could misinterpret this information. The Ontario Native Women's Association debated for a year whether to release its report on wife battering, *Breaking Free*, for fear that it would be perceived by white society as a validation of the cultural stereotype of Aboriginal people as violent and hostile.

MEDIA

The Canadian media, past and present, have contributed to the general lack of understanding that exists between Aboriginal and non-Aboriginal people in Canada today. The non-Aboriginal media's representation of Aboriginal issues is often distorted by the media's own ignorance of Aboriginal peoples, and tainted by thinly disguised racist attitudes. As a result, Aboriginal peoples' issues are often minimized, trivialized or ignored by the mainstream media. The Canadian media are ethnocentric, particularly in their interpretation of Aboriginal people and their rights.

I want violence to no longer be accepted as a form of entertainment. Research has revealed the links between videos, television, films and alcohol and violence.

Attempts by Aboriginal groups to develop their own communications systems have been severely handicapped. There is no economic base to support independent community newspapers in smaller Aboriginal communities. Some local Aboriginal governments provide a weekly or biweekly newsletter to its members; however, the content is subject to censorship and production is dependent on discretionary funding from government agencies.

We see children act out and repeat what they saw on television last night.

In 1988, the Canadian Broadcasting Corporation cancelled "Our Native Land," a national radio show that featured Aboriginal content and linked Aboriginal peoples and groups and the Canadian public. *Native Perspective*, a national magazine published by the National Association of Friendship Centres, was also terminated because of a lack of funding. In 1990, the Secretary of State slashed the budgets for Aboriginal communications groups, and several of Canada's oldest and largest Aboriginal newspapers were forced into bankruptcy.

These and other cutbacks by the federal government have systematically undermined efforts to develop a national communications service on behalf of Aboriginal peoples in Canada. As a result, Aboriginal people today are still dependent on informal communications systems that are not necessarily dependable or accurate.

I don't think you can underplay the impact of the larger society .... It's not very easy to teach your children good values when there's another intruder in your house that's teaching them negative values every waking hour [television]. I'm not in favour of censorship but I am in favour of a balance of values in our media. This is where the free market fails us. The decline in values over the last few years is the government's responsibility. We must be vigilant to maintain [control over] ... part [of] our media and maintain it as a forum for our own values.

♀ ♀ ♀

We need a societal change so that people are not acting out the behaviour they see in videos. Children don't know where the pretending stops and the reality begins.

With no adequate regional or national communications system to inform Aboriginal peoples of their rights and issues, both Aboriginal and non-Aboriginal governments have maintained their oppressive authority over Aboriginal people's lives and future. Critical grass-roots issues such as violence and corruption in the Aboriginal community go unexposed and remain cloaked in secrecy, exempting those responsible from public scrutiny and accountability.

Mainstream media have a responsibility to present a balance of values and to acknowledge the effects of violent programming on children. Non-print communications in Aboriginal languages must also be used to maximize prevention and education in Aboriginal communities.

Mainstream media serve as powerful social critics. As the media regularly expose wrong-doing by political leaders and other prominent figures, they are also powerful instruments of public accountability. As public broadcasters, all media have a responsibility to reflect both positive and negative current affairs in Aboriginal communities. Freedom to speak to the press must prevail in Aboriginal communities as in mainstream Canadian society.

Television plays a large part in perpetuating violence against women by illustrating how men abuse women.

♀ ♀ ♀

Radio is the best means of communication here. It must be used for information programs on the subject.

PORNOGRAPHY

The advent of satellite television to even the most remote Aboriginal communities in Canada has made pornography an issue of growing concern for Aboriginal women. The lack of parental monitoring and control over these activities has heightened the impact of pornography on Aboriginal children and youth.

Porn makes me angry, even soft porn. It's easily accessible to 14-, 15- and 16-year-old kids. That's the way they learn to see women. If this is what we teach our young, what can we expect?

♀ ♀ ♀

My husband works in Labrador and buys a lot of pornography. One night I got so angry I nearly broke his neck. He touched me in a way that made me feel so sleazy. At work he has girlie pictures everywhere. When he comes back from there he has the same attitude. I loathe it.

The lack of social and recreational activities in Aboriginal communities has also been identified as a factor in the growing consumption of pornography, especially among Aboriginal youth. However, there is little statistical data linking the use of pornographic material to sexual abuse and violence in the Aboriginal community.

ABORIGINAL LEADERSHIP

Aboriginal men, and more specifically Aboriginal leaders, have recently come under scrutiny for their complacency and lack of commitment in initiating effective programs and policies to help stop abuse in Aboriginal communities. The 1990 *Report of the Aboriginal Justice Inquiry of Manitoba* stated,

> The unwillingness of chiefs and councils to address the plight of women and children suffering abuse at the hands of husbands and fathers is quite alarming. We are concerned enough about it to state that we believe that the failure of Aboriginal government leaders to deal at all with the problem of domestic abuse is unconscionable. We believe that there is a heavy responsibility on Aboriginal leaders to recognize the significance of the problem within their own communities. They must begin to recognize, as well, how much their silence and failure to act actually contribute to the problem. [95]

The reported quote of one band councillor was "Are you crazy? Me support a building that my wife can run to anytime she wants"?

At present, all Aboriginal political structures — band councils, Métis town councils, tribal council governments, regional and national Aboriginal organizations — are based on patriarchal European models. Like the non-Aboriginal government they are based on, Aboriginal governments do not give priority to women's needs, experiences and perspectives. In these organizations, most of the power rests with a small number of usually male Aboriginal leaders with little or no accountability to their members at the grass-roots level.

Aboriginal political organizations focus on popular issues such as land claims and self-government and give lower priority to health and social issues. Regional and national organizations do not have direct power but have influence with the federal government which does enact policies. Because these organizations are headed primarily by men, "women's issues" are not moved forward.

[We] need to change the minds of our leaders. They are often the worst hurt and the worst offenders, and they need to be healed first. If a leader is sick in the soul then the community is sick.

In 1992, the Supreme Court of Canada ruled that none of the existing national Aboriginal groups adequately represent Aboriginal women. Justice Mahoney stated, "NWAC [the Native Women's Association of Canada] is a recognized national voice of and for Aboriginal women" [96] and "the Court rightly found that none of the intervenants —Assembly of First Nations, Native Council of Canada and Inuit Tapirisat of Canada — represents the interest of Aboriginal women." [97]

There would be a major difference if the band council chief was a woman.

While Aboriginal women represent half of the total on-reserve population, less than 10 percent of chiefs are women. [98] This imbalance in leadership roles, although perceived by some Aboriginal leaders as a "cultural" phenomenon, may be attributed to the legal, social and economic inequality between men and women set forth in the *Indian Act*. Political reform is needed before further developments toward Aboriginal self-government are undertaken, and all current self-government initiatives must be thoroughly evaluated by Aboriginal women.

National and regional organizations have no power at the community level. Chiefs and councils have extraordinary power over the lives of every member of the community. They effectively control opportunities for employment, housing and education; have an influence over police, health and child welfare matters; have the power to enact by-laws; and in some communities decide their membership. Mismanagement, nepotism, favouritism or corruption within local governments cannot be redressed by community members. Provincial and/or federal authorities are reluctant to intervene in some Aboriginal communities to avoid conflict and political backlash.

Our male leaders hardly ever consult Aboriginal women's organizations ... we don't need to be taken care of, we have to make sure our rights are being respected and that our best interests are being served.

Aboriginal leaders must be held accountable for their personal acts of violence and abuse. It has been reported that there are elected Aboriginal leaders who physically and sexually abuse Aboriginal women and children. There are also reports that Aboriginal men have abused their authority as leaders and the public trust to exonerate friends and relatives of charges of wife assault, sexual assault and child sexual assault. Further, allegations have been made that attempts to seek disciplinary action against these leaders have resulted in complainants having their personal property damaged and receiving threats of physical violence.

This power dynamic is extremely dangerous for women who are abused and can make it very difficult for them to report violence. Women who report abuse may also experience retaliation such as the withholding of housing or employment, which directly affects them and their family. Aboriginal women in these circumstances are virtually helpless, hopeless and eternally silenced. In some instances, women have been forced to leave the community without their children and have been unable to get help from outside authorities who are afraid to challenge the local political power.

If women's rights are violated by Aboriginal leaders, there is no higher disciplinary organization or legal entity to which the leadership is accountable. Therefore, the rights of Aboriginal women and children are left to the discretion of Aboriginal leaders who have provided little or no protection for their private and public safety. Aboriginal leaders' failure to denounce openly violence against Aboriginal women and children and to provide adequate measures of protection are violations of their traditional roles as men and leaders.

SELF-GOVERNMENT

Many Aboriginal women oppose self-government; they fear that their rights will once again be denied, only this time it will be at the hands of their own leaders. They also oppose self-government because today's structures do not reflect the true spirit of traditional Aboriginal government in which women participated as full and equal partners.

I get a lot of resistance from the Chief and Council. Many [of them] have alcohol and family problems too. The whole community is dysfunctional. That is why I am afraid of self-government.

♀♀♀

Leaders must heal themselves and realize the importance of healing in society. Chiefs and councils need to start putting money into healing and begin to participate in these workshops and conferences themselves. Most leaders are carrying a lot of garbage. What comes from the mouth and the heart are two different things. Until we work from the bottom of our hearts, nothing will happen.

♀♀♀

The woman is the foundation on which Nations are built. [99]

Aboriginal leaders maintain that the *Indian Act* has displaced traditional forms of government and that reformed self-government structures will protect the rights of Aboriginal women. However, in the last two decades, Aboriginal leaders have not supported Aboriginal women in their struggle for equality, and it is unlikely that these same leaders would place the rights of Aboriginal women and children before their own political interests now.

Self-government has become a vague term that has to date eluded any meaningful definition or open debate by Aboriginal peoples. If and when Aboriginal government is to be reformed, Aboriginal women must be guaranteed both equal and full representation in the process. No true self-government can take place without the full participation of Aboriginal women.

THE CRISIS — A DEFINITION

An act of violence is:

- when one Aboriginal child is forcefully taken from home, family and community;
  - it has been estimated that 100,000 Aboriginal children were forced to go to residential schools;

- when one life is lost to suicide;
  - the suicide rate among Aboriginal women is more than twice the national average for women; [100]

- when there is one death related to substance abuse or an accident;
  - death by injury and poisoning is the number-one cause of death among Aboriginal people; [101]

- when one Aboriginal woman dies a violent death;
  - injuries sustained through violence are included in the number-one cause of death;

- when Aboriginal women and men are grossly overrepresented in jails and prisons;
  - Aboriginal women represent 15 percent of federally sentenced women while representing less than four percent of women in Canada; [102]

- when one child fails to grow up healthy;
  - Aboriginal children suffer from a range of violent acts, from neglect to sexual assault.

These acts are everyday tragedies in many of the hundreds of communities in which Aboriginal people live. These acts are occurring across the nation. The situation is critical. We must help these communities and individuals, but how?

HEALING

Healing is a word used by Aboriginal people to describe the recovery process of victims of violence, abuse and addiction. Healing begins at a personal level and is based on individual freedom of choice. Traditional healing takes a holistic approach based on the four directions of the Wheel of Life and treats the self as part of the whole. Healing is viewed as a purification of the complete being, that is, the physical, mental, emotional and spiritual selves. Holistic healing is a unified process of recovery encompassing self-healing, family healing, community healing and nation healing.

I am a survivor of five residential schools, and if it had not been for healing circles, I would have blown up by now.

The Medicine Wheel is an important symbol in Aboriginal culture. It teaches many cultural beliefs. One of these is that the four peoples of the earth are equal. The colours of the four directions represent each race as they contribute their gifts to the development of our life together. Within the four directions of the Medicine Wheel are the four seasons, the four times of day (morning, noon, dusk and dark) and the principles of honesty, sharing, kindness and strength. All of life is contained within these phases that continue to infinity.

In today's world, at the end of a century, we have become inured to a violent world. Our generation has never known peace. The effects of destructive practices are all around.

In the first part of the Circle we see and evaluate where we are; we all need to recognize the extent of the violence we live with and have come to know as a way of life. Each time a life is lost to suicide, tragedy or accident, each time an Aboriginal woman is imprisoned or murdered, each time we face corruption, destitution and despair, we must see through the confusion and, with the gift of our ancestors' vision, prepare the way to the future.

In the second part of the Circle, we must feel our relationships with each other, as people, and to the Earth, as caretakers of life. We must grieve for our culture, our children, our elders, ourselves. We need to be in touch with our pain and allow ourselves to feel and acknowledge life. Once we have that understanding, we can put hope into our lives, and with hope we can set our goals for healing.

In the third part of the Circle, we think about our realities and plan ways to bring changes into our communities and to inform and educate governments about this cause.

The fourth part of the Circle is action, which represents completion. It is a rare time where people on parallel paths meet. It is important to our grandchildren and the generations ahead that we are honest, that we accept the truth, that we acknowledge our true history, that we respect each other as equals, that we learn the best of each other's cultures, that we are willing to change and that we take action to end violence together.

The term "lodge" to Aboriginal people means the body, which is a resting place for the spirit and where the gifts of Gizhe Manitou are housed. A mother has been the lodge for her children, male and female. In healing, the individual must search for the original lodge and find healing within the family context. The Earth is the original mother of nations; nations must go back to the Earth to find their healing. Nature is the great healer and teaching provided by the Earth is one of our many gifts. All have their purpose and meaning.

A healing lodge can be a structure that an individual enters to find healing. It can be the beginning of healing from the effects of alcohol or drugs, incarceration, physical, sexual, emotional or ritual abuse, institutional and systemic abuse and generational oppression through residential schools, racism and the loss of culture. A healing lodge can be a maternal support, sweat lodge, safe home or teaching circle for anyone who is searching for healing.

The healing movement has gained momentum among many individuals, most of whom are women, as a way to restore the natural balance and well-being of Aboriginal families and communities after generations of violence. Traditional practices including pipe ceremonies, sweat lodges and healing circles and a return to traditional Aboriginal spirituality have become widely accepted methods of healing for Aboriginal victims of violence and abuse.

A network is needed between recognized and approved drug and alcohol treatment centres, Aboriginal women's shelters, community health centres and other related programs to engage the community in education and awareness of child sexual abuse, incest and other issues related to violence against women.

In adopting the objectives of healing, communities are obligated to offer healing and teaching to their own people. The well-being of the community is entrusted to the healing lodge. The vision of healing is far-reaching in that the future of seven generations are forever in the minds of the planners.

The main objective is to begin the healing. Healing lodges are intended to respond to a desperate need for change, for action. To prepare the way, it is necessary to take the first steps with care and understanding. We have spent many years studying, and examining a multitude of problems facing Aboriginal people in this country, and out of tragedy and violence we have reached the conclusion that healing must begin and the time is now.

Reality can change when we know our responsibilities and our spiritual beliefs and when we respect life and each other. The sacred knowledge of our ancestors will guide us through these troubled times and will help us heal ourselves. By knowing who we are and by caring about our families who are suffering, we will eliminate all that is negative and again become healthy in mind, body and spirit.

The recovery process can use conventional non-Aboriginal methods of counselling and therapy, including peer counselling, self-help groups and consultations with psychologists or other mental health professionals in conjunction with traditional means of healing for individuals and communities. While these forms of healing can have a positive outcome, it is essential that healing initiatives be researched and examined carefully to determine the impact on individual mental health and to protect the community from exploitation.

The Road to Healing, a gathering of Aboriginal spiritual advisors, elders and traditional healers from different nations across Canada was held in October 1992. The following recommendation was made.

A permanent, national council must be formed as soon as possible, to meet in different parts of the country, several times a year to focus its attention on the violence facing Aboriginal people. Some of the issues are spiritual abuse, the new generation of self-proclaimed elders, ritual and cult abuse and incest. The council will offer spiritual advice and indicate directions to be taken for survival. These gatherings will include the youth of our nations. This council will be directed solely by the elders of different nations.

The present band council system as determined by the *Indian Act* must be replaced with a system of self-government that is truly representative of the people. Until an Aboriginal Charter that safeguards Aboriginal women's rights is in place, the equality provisions of the *Canadian Charter of Rights and Freedoms* must be maintained as a minimum protection. Aboriginal systems of justice must hold all people accountable for their acts and treat them equally. Elders' councils must be involved in all aspects of community life and have the right to speak on any issue. A national council of Elders and youth is needed. An Aboriginal Human Rights Tribunal must be set up to provide redress for violations of human rights, to expose corruption and violations and provide remedies. A strong Aboriginal media must be supported to link nations and to educate all Canadian society about the dramatic changes in the Aboriginal world.

Because of many misunderstandings about religion, beliefs and practices concerning the term "healing," we recommend that a directory is created to evaluate workshops, programs and methods of healing and to outline problems associated with spiritual exploitation.

By virtue of our Aboriginal rights, derived from treaties and our inherent rights as the Aboriginal peoples of Canada and, sanctioned by the *Constitution Act of Canada*, the federal government must assume all fiduciary responsibility to engage appropriate measures to assist in the healing of all Aboriginal communities in Canada.

The sacred ceremonies, sweat lodges, medicines, healing plants and knowledge of healing that have been a part of our nations for thousands of years will again restore strength to our people. With the guidance of elders, we will heal and live in harmony with the Earth, with Aboriginal women regaining their rightful role as leaders and keepers of the culture.

CONCLUSION

As members of the Aboriginal Circle, we challenge you to turn words into action. In this report, we identify not only the problems that contribute to violence against Aboriginal women but also solutions.

No single policy can meet the diverse and complex needs of Aboriginal people throughout this land. The Aboriginal Circle also recognizes that, in these times of economic restraint, resources are scarce, and many existing Aboriginal programs and services are threatened. The Canadian government must acknowledge its legal and moral responsibility to address the issue of violence in Aboriginal communities.

Aboriginal women told us that what they need and demand is action — action to end the violence that has grown to epidemic proportions in Aboriginal communities. Violence that is destroying the lives of Aboriginal children, women, men and elders.

1993 has been declared the International Year of Indigenous People. It is both tragic and ironic that this announcement was followed by the attempted suicides of six Innu children in Davis Inlet, Labrador; that in the span of nine months, seven Micmac youth committed suicide in Big Cove, Nova Scotia; that five Cree girls and boys in northern Ontario committed suicide in as many weeks.

As members of the Aboriginal Circle, we urge the Aboriginal people of this land to declare 1994 the Year of Healing for every child, woman and man who has suffered the pain of violence: healing for our families, so we may live in harmony with one another: healing for our nations, so that we may unite in sisterhood and brotherhood. And healing for our Mother Earth, so we may restore her beauty in return for the many gifts that she has given us.

ENDNOTES

1   House of Commons, *The War Against Women: Report of the Standing Committee on Health and Welfare, Social Affairs, Seniors and the Status of Women* (Ottawa, 1991), p. iv.

2   Province of Manitoba, *Report of the Aboriginal Justice Inquiry of Manitoba* (Winnipeg, 1991), p. 73.

3   *Ibid.*, p. 71.

4   J.R. Miller "Owen Glendower, Hotspur and Canadian Indian Policy," in *Sweet Promises: A Reader on Indian-White Relations in Canada,* ed. J.R. Miller, p. 326.

5   Province of Manitoba, *Aboriginal Justice Inquiry, op. cit.,* p. 79.

6   *Ibid.*, p. 79.

7   *Ibid.*, p. 79.

8   *Statement of the Government of Canada on Indian Policy,* cited in *Report of the Aboriginal Justice Inquiry,* Province of Manitoba (Winnipeg, 1991), p. 79.

9   Province of Manitoba, *Aboriginal Justice Inquiry, op. cit.,* p. 80.

10   *Ibid,*, p. 201.

11   House of Commons, *Minutes of Proceedings and Evidence of the Standing Committee on Aboriginal Affairs,* Issue 12, p. 12:8.

12   Department of Indian Affairs and Northern Development, *Impacts of the 1985 Amendments to the Indian Act (Bill C-31): Summary Report* (Ottawa, 1990), p. ii.

13   *Ibid.*, p. 15.

14   Province of Manitoba, *Aboriginal Justice Inquiry, op. cit.,* p. 204.

15   C. Saulis, National Association of Friendship Centres, telephone interview, April 20, 1993.

16   This figure represents an increase of over 40 percent from the 1986 Census. Statistics Canada explains that "Demographic factors, such as changes in fertility and mortality, cannot explain an increase of this size over a five year period. Clearly, significant numbers of people who had not previously reported an Aboriginal origin did so in 1991, most likely due to heightened awareness of Aboriginal issues arising from the extensive public discussion of these matters in the period leading up to the 1991 Census." Statistics Canada, *The Daily,* March 30, 1993, p. 2.

17   Department of Indian Affairs and Northern Development *Basic Departmental Data-1992* (Ottawa, 1992)

18   *Ibid.*, p. 14.

19   Ontario Native Women's Association, *Breaking Free: A Proposal for Change to Aboriginal Family Violence* (Thunder Bay, Ontario, 1989), p.8.

20   "Squamish Family Violence Prevention and Treatment Model Project." cited in *Violence Against Aboriginal Women,* by T. Nahanee (Research paper prepared for the Canadian Panel on Violence Against Women, Ottawa, 1993)

21   *Survey of Federally Sentenced Aboriginal Women in the Community,* cited in *Creating Choices: The Report of the Task Force on Federally Sentenced Women,* (Solicitor General of Canada: Ottawa, 1990), p. 16.

22   Ontario Native Women's Association, *Breaking Free, op. cit.,* p. 9.

23   Esther Supernault, "We're Walking the Same Way Anyway," *Vis à Vis,* Volume 10, Number 4 (Spring 1993), pp. 6-7.

24   Rix Rogers, *Reaching for Solutions: The Report of the Special Advisor to the Minister of National Health and Welfare on Child Sexual Abuse in Canada* (Ottawa, 1990), p. 105.

25   Ontario Native Women's Association, *Breaking Free, op. cit.,* p. 17.

26   *Native Women's Needs Assessment Survey,* cited in *National Family Violence Abuse Study/Evaluation,* by Claudette Dumont-Smith and Pauline Sioui Labelle (Aboriginal Nurses of Canada, 1991), p. 18.

27   "Dragging wife abuse out of the closet," cited in *National Family Violence Abuse Study/Evaluation,* by Claudette Dumont-Smith and Pauline Sioui Labelle (Aboriginal Nurses of Canada, 1991), p. 18.

28   Claudette Dumont-Smith and Pauline Sioui Labelle, *National Family Violence Abuse Study/Evaluation* (Aboriginal Nurses of Canada, 1991), p. 43.

29   Brenda Daley, *Windspeaker,* cited in *National Family Violence Abuse Study/Evaluation,* by Claudette Dumont-Smith and Pauline Sioui Labelle (Aboriginal Nurses of Canada, 1991), p. 25.

30   Rhonda Gordon, "Coalition combats racism, sexism and denial," *Vis à Vis,* Volume 10, Number 4 (Spring 1993), p. 12.

31   Department of Indian Affairs and Northern Development, *Indian Register Population by Sex and Residence 1991* (Ottawa, 1992), p. 4.

32   Dumont-Smith and Sioui Labelle, *op. cit.,* p. 33.

33   Catherine McBride and Ellen Bobet, Department of Indian Affairs and Northern Development, *Health of Indian Women* (Ottawa, 1990), p. 7.

34   ARA Consultants, *Wife Battering Among Rural, Native and Immigrant Women* (Toronto: Provincial Secretariat for Justice, 1985), p. V-19.

35   Ruth Teichroeb, "RCMP stall on custody order," *Winnipeg Free Press,* April 18, 1993, p. 1.

36 House of Commons, Standing Committee on Aboriginal Affairs, *You Took My Talk: Aboriginal Literacy and Empowerment* (Ottawa, 1990), p. 6.

37 Province of Manitoba, *Aboriginal Justice Inquiry, op. cit.*, p. 475.

38 Jack Aubry, "Thunder Bay end of the line for many natives," *The Ottawa Citizen*, May 8, 1993, p. B4.

39 Kahnawake Shakotiia'takehnhas Resource Centre, *Mission Statement* (Kahnawake, Quebec, nd).

40 P. Mayhew, Canadian Association of Elizabeth Fry Societies, telephone interview, May 10, 1993.

41 Pamela White, *Native Women: A Statistical Overview* (Ottawa: Department of the Secretary of State, 1985), p. 16.

42 Solicitor General of Canada, *Creating Choices, op. cit.*, p. 43.

43 P. Mayhew, Canadian Association of Elizabeth Fry Societies, telephone interview, May 10, 1993.

44 Two-Spirited People of the First Nations (Submission to the Canadian Panel on Violence Against Women, Ottawa, 1992).

45 Dumont-Smith and Sioui Labelle, *Family Violence, op. cit.*, p. 11.

46 Department of the Secretary of State, *Canada's Off-Reserve Population: A Statistical Overview* (Ottawa, 1991), pp. 20-21.

47 ARA Consultants, *Wife Battering, op. cit.*, p. V-15.

48 *Ibid.*, p. V-19.

49 Ontario Native Women's Association, *Breaking Free, op. cit.*, pp. 31-32.

50 Province of Manitoba, *Aboriginal Justice Inquiry, op. cit.*, p. 27.

51 Freda Ahenakew, Cecil King and Catherine H. Littlejohn, *Indigenous Languages in the Delivery of Justice in Manitoba,* cited in *Report of the Aboriginal Justice Inquiry of Manitoba*, Province of Manitoba (Winnipeg, 1991), p. 38.

52 *Survey of Federally Sentenced Aboriginal Women in the Community*, cited in *Creating Choices: The Report of the Task Force on Federally Sentenced Women*, Solicitor General of Canada (Ottawa, 1990), p. 16.

53 Province of Manitoba, *Aboriginal Justice Inquiry, op. cit.*, p. 237.

54 *Ibid.*, p. 232.

55 T. Nahanee "Dancing with a Gorilla: Aboriginal Women, Justice and the Charter" (Paper presented to the Royal Commission on Aboriginal Peoples, November 1992, Ottawa), pp. 4-5.

56 ARA Consultants, *Wife Battering, op. cit.*, p. V-7.

57 *Ibid.*, p. V-12.

58 *Ibid.*, p. V-11.

59 *Ibid.*, p. V-7.

60 Union of Ontario Indians, *Anishinabek Family Violence Initiative* (North Bay, Ontario, 1990), p. 12.

61 ARA Consultants, *Wife Battering, op. cit.*, p. V-18.

62 L. Rich, telephone interview, May 10, 1993.

63 ARA Consultants, *Wife Battering, op.cit.*, p. V-11.

64 House of Commons, Standing Committee on Aboriginal Affairs, *A Time for Action: Aboriginal and Northern Housing* (Ottawa, 1992), p. 11.

65 *Ibid.*, p. 58.

66 "Core housing need is defined as any household paying 30 percent or more of its income for shelter or occupying a dwelling which is too small for the size and composition of the household or a dwelling which is in need of major repairs - structural, electrical, plumbing, heating, fire safety - and which does not have sufficient income to obtain an adequate or suitable dwelling on the housing market without paying 30 percent or more of its income for shelter." *Ibid.*, p. 13.

67 The number of new or renovated housing units indicated in 1983-1984 was before the implementation of Bill C-31; the 1991-1992 figures include allocations both for families reinstated under Bill C-31 and to meet ongoing needs. Department of Indian Affairs and Northern Development, *Basic Departmental Data - 1992* (Ottawa, 1992), p. 4,61.

68 House of Commons, Standing Committee on Aboriginal Affairs, *A Time for Action, op.cit.*, p. 12.

69 House of Commons, *Minutes of Proceedings and Evidence of the Standing Committee on Aboriginal Affairs*, Issue 27, p. 27A:82.

70 *Ibid.*, p. 27A:31.

71 House of Commons, *Minutes of Proceedings and Evidence of the Standing Committee on Aboriginal Affairs*, Issue 12, p. 12:8.

72 *Ibid.*, p. 27:15.

73 Standing Committee on Aboriginal Affairs, *A Time for Action, op. cit.*, p. 14.

74 Department of Indian Affairs and Northern Development, *Basic Departmental Data - 1992, op. cit.*, p. 79.

75 National Action Committee on the Status of Women, *Review of the Situation of Women in Canada 1992* (Toronto, 1992).

76 Barb Adam-MacLellan, "Nindal Kwanindur," in *"Gossip": A Spoken History of Women in the North*, ed. Mary Crynkovich (Ottawa, Canadian Arctic Resources Committee, 1990), p. 184.

77 House of Commons, Standing Committee on Aboriginal Affairs, *You Took My Talk, op. cit.*, p. 6.

78 Cariboo Tribal Council, "Faith Misplaced: Lasting Effects of Abuse in a First Nations Community," *Canadian Journal of Native Education*, Volume 18, Number 2: pu.

79 Thomas A. Lascelles, OMI, "Indian Residential Schools," *The Canadian Catholic Review* (May 1992), p. 7.

80 J.R. Miller, "Owen Glendower," *op. cit.*, p. 324.

81 Cariboo Tribal Council, "Faith Misplaced," *op.cit.*, pu.

82 Using standardized mortality ratio, injury and poisoning rank as the leading cause of mortality of Aboriginal people from 1980-1984. Interdisciplinary Working Group on Injury Prevention, Department of National Health and Welfare, *Final Report: Prevention of Injuries among Canadian Aboriginal People* (Ottawa, 1990), pp. 7-8.

83 Government of the Northwest Territories, Department of Health, *Report of the Abortion Services Review Committee* (Yellowknife, 1992), p. 22.

84 In 1990, the total population of the Northwest Territories was 53,801. Of the total, 20,836 were Inuit, 9,323 were Dene and 4,033 were Métis, totalling 35,292. Total non-native population was 19,609. Department of Health, Government of the Northwest Territories *The Northwest Territories Health Report 1990* (Yellowknife, 1990) p. 17.

85 McBride and Bobet, *Health of Indian Women, op. cit.*, p. 7.

86 Ontario Native Women's Association, *Breaking Free, op. cit.*, p. 36.

87 McBride and Bobet, *Health of Indian Women, op. cit.*, p. 11.

88 *Ibid.*, p. 10.

89 Jack Aubry, "Aboriginals brace for AIDS tragedy," *The Ottawa Citizen*, May 10, 1993, p. 1.

90 Union of Ontario Indians, *Anishinabek Family Violence Initiative* (North Bay, Ontario, 1990), passim

91 L. Rich, telephone interview, May 10, 1993.

92 Province of Manitoba, *Aboriginal Justice Inquiry, op. cit.*, p. 96.

93 Ron Corbett, "The life and death of Minnie Sutherland," *Ottawa Magazine* (October 1989), p. 80.

94 *Ibid.*, p. 85.

95 Province of Manitoba, *Aboriginal Justice Inquiry, op. cit.*, p. 485.

96 Nahanee, "Dancing with a Gorilla," *op. cit.*, p. 25.

97 *Ibid.*, p. 26.

98 A. Chabot, Assembly of First Nations, telephone interview, June 3, 1992.

99 Ontario Native Women's Association, *Breaking Free, op. cit.*, p. i.

100 McBride and Bobet, *Health of Indian Women, op. cit.*, p. 11.

101 Using standardized mortality ratio, injury and poisoning rank as the leading cause of mortality of Aboriginal people from 1980-1984. Interdisciplinary Working Group on Injury Prevention, Department of National Health and Welfare, *Final Report: Prevention of Injuries among Canadian Aboriginal People* (Ottawa, 1990), pp. 7-8.

102 P. Mayhew, Canadian Association of Elizabeth Fry Societies, telephone interview, May 10, 1993.

PART FOUR

EXPERIENCING VIOLENCE~

INSTITUTIONS

INTRODUCTION

A central part of our mandate has been to develop a National Action Plan to address the issue of violence against women. Any plan that targets such a complex and multi-dimensional subject must have, as its cornerstone, the goal of social change. The prerequisites for such change are knowledge and understanding of the issue; a detailed strategy for effecting change; a broad-based commitment to implementing that strategy; and a mechanism for periodically reviewing the progress of implementation. In the review of institutions contained in this section we elaborate on the weaknesses and shortcomings of institutions in responding to the safety and security needs of women in Canada. This examination forms the basis, ultimately, for our National Action Plan.

In the first part of our report, we spoke about the need to develop a "way of thinking" about violence against women that places individual acts of violence in a larger sociological context. Such an approach is essential for understanding the breadth, depth and persistence of violence against women, not only today but throughout history.

We emphasized the link between some of the conditions that women face in Canada today and the violence they face. These conditions are the outcome of the current social, economic, political and cultural context which can only be changed by altering social institutions. These changes, we argue, will provide the groundwork for a society that is safe for women.

In this part of our report, we identify and examine those social institutions that are the most salient to our understanding and to changing current patterns of gender, race and class inequality. These institutions impinge on women's lives on a daily basis. The legal system, the media, the health care system, the workplace, various service delivery areas and other key government sectors figure prominently in women's experiences of violence. Any analysis of these is strengthened by the voices and experiences of the survivors of violence: their lives provide the filter for our framework and recommendations. It is from these women, along with a multitude of people working in all aspects of this issue, that we have taken our cue.

Institutions must not be perceived as neutral settings that treat and are experienced by everyone in a similar fashion. Women and men experience life differently because of their gender; for some women the gender difference is compounded by race, class, ability level, age and sexual orientation. There is a bias in which social institutions, settings or programs operate to the advantage of one gender, race or class and to the disadvantage of others.

Tolerance of violence against women is unquestionably present in the social institutions we examined. In the health care system, many professionals remain indifferent to the continuation of the violence. Institutional personnel who may not behave violently themselves witness violent acts committed against women clients and do not know how to stop it. The atmosphere within many schools whether at the primary, secondary or university level is hostile to young women. The legal system remains self-serving, perpetuating ineffective and inadequate laws, policies, practices — and indeed, practitioners — which only serve to continue the denial of violence against women. In the military, women are subjected to sexist behaviour, language and treatment that undermine their personal power and jeopardize their career aspirations. In the workplace, the absence of sexual and general harassment policies, and the protracted nature of pursuing charges, often mean that women have to tolerate a hostile, dangerous and poisoned work atmosphere or lose their jobs.

Even when attempts have been made to address the scope and dimension of violence against women, these attempts, taken together, have been partial, incomplete and ill-conceived.

CHAPTER 16

SERVICES DELIVERED IN THE COMMUNITY

INTRODUCTION

Services delivered in the community are often the first point of contact for survivors of violence seeking information, support and advice. While many of these services are thought of as "women's" services, the following discussion includes a range of services delivered at a local level by community service groups, including health, social, educational and criminal justice services.

In our hearings we heard of positive experiences with services at the community level, but four important issues emerged that require immediate attention: inadequate and unstable funding, lack of co-ordination, lack of a cohesive philosophy and approach in the delivery of services, and last, but most important, the gaps in service provision across the country.

FUNDING

We need stabilized funding. If we have low bed nights we can't have staff because most of our funding is based on per diems.

♀ ♀ ♀

We should not have to tear down other programs to get money, and we should not have to run bingos to run services.

Many social services spend inordinate amounts of time and energy looking for money, filling out applications, tracking down leads on grant or funding alternatives and negotiating with sources for their annual budget allocations.

Women who made presentations to the Panel gave credit to shelters, transition houses and rape crisis and sexual assault centres for nothing short of saving their lives. In light of the important work done at the community level, many women

also expressed anger about the lack of funding. We heard over and over again about the tragedy of survivors forced to return to abusive partners because of inadequate funding.

The impacts of recessionary times are often greatest for women's services and other community-based services. Furthermore, any funding cutbacks then significantly jeopardize the very existence of services whose limited funding makes them fragile in the first place.

There is a lack of support for survivors to heal. When I started out two and a half years ago there were women who dealt with sexual abuse but only after three or four disclosures. We need a place they feel safe enough to come to in the first place.

♀ ♀ ♀

A phenomenal number of the women coming through here are survivors, and it takes nearly a year to get into special services. Some of the women want to start dealing with it, but it is unfair to start it here when once they leave they will have nothing. Women are in so much pain, what can I say to them, hold on for six months, nine months?

Many women working in the anti-violence movement expressed concern over the lack of alternatives for women and children leaving transition houses such as second-stage housing. Because they so often end up on the streets or on welfare, their only alternative may be to return to abusive situations.

Funding practices of all levels of government do not reflect the valuable and valued role of support services for survivors. Community level services often act as educational and advocacy resources to support the well-being of women and to raise the level of awareness of all community members about the pervasiveness of violence against women in the community. Front-line workers also help develop community action plans and protocols for the delivery of services. In shelters, they assist women in the process of re-establishing their lives. They play an essential role as referral and resource persons, and offer moral support to women who must interact with doctors, lawyers, social workers and employment agencies. It is obvious that their crucial role is not adequately recognized since they remain poorly paid, have few or no employment benefits and have very little job security. Front-line providers in Quebec described the high turnover and level of burnout among workers as symptomatic of the frustration created by the lack of funding.

From 1985 to 1990, the shelter occupancy rate nearly doubled, while the number of front-line workers remained the same. [1]

The overwhelming message is that community services require dependable, stable and adequate funding in order to survive. The cost of not recognizing the essential work they do is the higher cost of women never healing from their abuse.

We need funding for long-term services. These people were abandoned in childhood. We can't abandon them again. It takes an average of a year to deal with most of the pain.

Counsellors in front-line services made the following observations about funding and support.

We aren't talking about cutbacks due to the recession. We were never properly funded in the first place.

♀♀♀

Shelters are forced to be band-aid solutions.

♀♀♀

Financial and human resource constraints mean that responding to crisis is all that we can do. We want to be more proactive, but we don't even have resources to meet immediate needs of women wanting support groups for sexual assault and childhood sexual assault.

When you start a dialogue in a community about sexual assault and child sexual assault, you encourage people to speak out, and there aren't the services needed. It is dangerous to tell people to get help when there isn't any.

DEVELOPING A CO-ORDINATED RESPONSE

We need the social welfare system and the judicial system to work together to assist women who are leaving abusive partners.

An overarching theme of much of what we heard from community services was the need for a collective and co-ordinated response to violence against women. Because so many services are not part of an integrated network with a common goal, a common orientation and a common approach, the message to men who commit violence against women and to the survivors is neither clear nor consistent.

This lack of co-ordination means that survivors often come into contact with individuals (police, health care workers, spiritual advisors, lawyers, etc.) who are not aware of existing community services. Service providers, often working in isolation or in competition with one another, become discouraged and burn out as a result of the endless demand for more services and support. These conditions impede efforts to pool resources and to offer a full range of services, such as shelter support, advocacy counselling, medical and legal advice. Most important, lack of co-ordination undercuts any efficient response based on the practical needs of women survivors.

Some co-ordinated efforts are demonstrated by groups such as the Interdisciplinary Project on Domestic Violence, co-sponsored by nine national associations representing the police, social workers, child health workers, nurses, psychologists, teachers, lawyers, doctors and the church. The project's goal is "to improve the capacity of professionals to respond to the real needs of domestic violence survivors and perpetrators and to effectively address the whole issue of violence within families within their service mandates." [2] In Quebec, there are co-ordinated, interdisciplinary groups, *tables de concertation,* unique to the province which unite all agencies working in the anti-violence against women movement. These groups work within a socio-judicial approach which combines sentencing and support for the offender as part of the survivor's healing process. "... feeling supported by a multidisciplinary team at the start and throughout the criminal law process, women victims of violence are less fearful about reporting their situation and can go through all the stages of the legal process in order to reach a solution." [3]

Clear and accessible information is key to working in a concerted and collaborative manner. Such information provides women with choices. Survivors of violence should be made aware of the names, addresses and telephone numbers of agencies, organizations and institutions from which they can receive help. Presently, this information is not always accessible to all women because language needs and ability levels are not always taken into account. Printed material and radio and television information must take the cultural and language profiles of different communities into account. In some communities, survivors receive conflicting information depending on whom they contact, a situation that undermines their confidence in the system.

LACK OF A COHESIVE PHILOSOPHY AND APPROACH

Many community-based services, but particularly those of the feminist movement, have gone beyond "band-aid" solutions. The eradication of violence against women requires more than a patchwork, ad hoc approach; it means making changes in the entire social, economic and political fabric of the lives of women in this country.

The complexities of the problem are not consistently reflected in the policies and practices of social service delivery. Our consultations certainly indicated that not all community services necessarily share a feminist analysis of violence against women. Traditional social services are among the most deficient. The problem is still viewed in an individualistic and fragmented way, and approached with little or no consideration of a survivor's social, economic, political, cultural and religious milieu. Women told us that the attitude of social service workers is often patronizing and paternalistic and that traditional counselling services reflect sexist attitudes and approaches. Counsellors fail to believe women's accounts of their own experiences, blame the victims, do not look for the root causes of women's experiences of violence and often give inappropriate advice and responses to women's questions about their social, legal and health needs.

Social welfare agencies are terribly abusive to women in need. They treat us like second-class citizens. Social workers can be abusive, disrespectful, dangerous.

Women also told us that traditional social services are not designed to accommodate the lengthy and complex process of recovery from the destructive effects of violence. Survivors are often expected to function again in a very short period of time, an assumption that places far too much pressure on them. In some instances it forces them to return to violent situations.

Part of the problem is that most of the services, apart from those delivered from a feminist perspective, have little understanding of the long-term psychological impacts of violence.

Social services must hold the independence and self-determination of women survivors as their paramount goals. At the present time, this is far from the case. Social assistance legislation and regulations perpetuate dependence and work against women's struggles to become independent. Regulations ensure that any substantial additional income women receive, such as support payments, is deducted from their assistance cheques. Women reported being reluctant to leave an abusive partner out of fear that once they are dependent on social assistance they will be locked into this dependency over time.

A co-ordinated response entails not only a shared knowledge about the provision of services but also a common approach to the issue. At present there are no uniform techniques for evaluating the strengths, weaknesses and appropriateness of existing services, including those for men. Community services proceed on a trial-and-error basis in designing and providing programs for survivors and/or education and prevention strategies. We believe that this is the wrong approach, that it is expensive and potentially dangerous. The experiences of some communities could help shed light on the obstacles and problems of others. Yet, at the present time there are few, if any, opportunities for sharing such information on a national, regional or local basis.

GAPS IN SERVICE DELIVERY

Even a cursory review of the statistics (reflecting how many women are victims of violence) will give Canadians some appreciation of the great gaps in services the Panel found in its travels across the country. For example, in Prince Edward Island there is only one transition house for the entire island.

Community services are doing their best to meet the needs of survivors of violence, but there are significant gaps that undermine the effectiveness of service delivery. Differences in experiences of violence translate into different needs, and for many women, these needs are not being met.

In rural, isolated and northern communities there is a serious lack of resources for victims. Few communities have shelters, rape crisis centres or women's centres. Transportation to larger communities, where these services might exist, is often non-existent thus endangering the lives of women and their children by forcing them to remain in abusive situations. Few support services are available after 5 p.m. and on weekends. As well, the total lack of support networks for women working in the area of violence against women increases the women's exposure to danger.

We need support groups for survivors of sexual abuse in rural areas. Most groups and treatment are so far away from home that women don't want to leave their community which stops their enthusiasm to heal.

♀ ♀ ♀

The closest shelter is in Thompson and the train only comes three days a week. Often when women need to leave an abusive situation they have to find a relative to stay with to wait for the train.

SERVICES FOR WOMEN WITH DISABILITIES

Women with disabilities who find themselves suffering the aftermath of sexual assault or abuse often have nowhere to turn.

I moved into the city because of the accident, because my family did not know how to take care of me. Even the nurses down there don't know how to work with people with disabilities, so I had to come to the city even though I didn't want to.

Indeed, emergency shelters, rape crisis centres, sexual assault centres and counselling programs that are physically accessible to women with disabilities and which are experienced with their needs are still rare. These inadequacies are a direct result of funding shortages and a failure to account for the needs of women with disabilities.

There are no services in this community for hearing-impaired women [i.e., counsellors, therapists, etc.]. Having a third party [i.e., the interpreter] present during sensitive encounters with counsellors is intimidating and discourages women from seeking help.

Most prevention and support services aimed at victims of violence do not address the issues of the physically disabled women .... Lack of physical accessibility in society means when a woman is assaulted, there is virtually nowhere for her to go. I think that some places have made a real effort to become accessible, but generally accessibility is treated as a fringe issue. As long as accessibility is seen as extra, violence will always be more of a problem for women with disabilities. The ensuing social powerlessness of these women — isolation, poverty, lack of accessibility — makes them vulnerable to victimization. [4]

It is important to acknowledge that some organizations have worked very hard to provide accessible services despite the lack of financial support from governments. Others are well aware of the specific issues of women with disabilities but are unable to do anything about them because of lack of funding.

SERVICES FOR SURVIVORS OF RITUAL ABUSE

In cases of ritual abuse, survivors do not have access to appropriately trained counsellors and specialized support systems. Part of the problem stems from a complete lack of public recognition of the existence of ritual abuse. This has been further compounded by the absence of useful information and material to address the needs of survivors.

People don't believe that ritual abuse happens ... professionals do not get the training required ... and so they give inappropriate counselling or treatment.

SERVICES FOR IMMIGRANT WOMEN

Few legal, health and social services, shelters, transition houses, rape crisis centres or sexual assault centres are culturally or linguistically sensitive to the needs of newly arrived immigrant women. To deal with their experiences of violence, they need services and support sensitive to their culture and in their own language.

Shelters are not appealing to immigrants. They are isolating. Also they don't want to confide in total strangers.

♀♀♀

Small communities mean that cultural interpreters are often people we know, so there's a lack of confidentiality.

SERVICES FOR ELDERLY WOMEN

Elderly women do not have easy access to services suited to their needs and often encounter service providers and community workers with whom they have little in common. This results in feelings of isolation. Community workers who provide home-based services are often not trained in issues of abuse and if the victim does not raise it, nothing will be done.

SERVICES FOR MALE PERPETRATORS

The lack of effective programs for male perpetrators of violence must not be overlooked. Women clearly told us that funding must be limited to those programs whose guiding principles are founded on the belief that there is no excuse for being abusive toward women and that violence is a learned behaviour that is used because it is often beneficial to the male perpetrator. "Violence against women and children is a manifestation of power and control over family members, not a loss of self-control as the majority of abusers claim." [5] The effectiveness of any program must be measured against the goal of eliminating all forms of violence against women.

Intervention programs for violent men should not be considered as "treatment." "Violence is not a sickness (pathology) in 96% of cases. It is a choice. The man chooses violence; he makes this choice from a number of other measures or options in order to control or dominate his spouse." [6] Psychological or mental instability should never be used as an excuse for men's behaviour. Programs must deal with the imbalance of power between the sexes and, women told us, must go beyond anger management, which is typically the focus of many existing programs. All intervention techniques must make abusers recognize and accept responsibility for their acts, help them deal with their underlying attitudes of blaming other people (i.e., women), help them understand that violence is unacceptable. They must be forced to confront their own violence and its repercussions.

We also heard how programs must not replace incarceration but be offered in conjunction with legal sanctions.

Without accompanying jail time, treatment for offenders is a token gesture and an ineffective remedy for a serious crime. Instead of causing men to confront their violence, it allows them to reinforce the societal bias that their actions do not constitute a crime.

If inappropriately administered, offender programs can work against the best interests of women. Women who came forward suggested that standards for practice, guidelines for funding and suggestions for program evaluation and staff training must be developed with survivors' advocates, women's organizations and others possessing a women-centred perspective.

Issues of language and cultural sensitivity are often missing in these programs. Programs for offenders are also rarely offered in rural and isolated areas, and if they do exist, resources are often inadequate and the counsellors are ill-trained to deal with male violence.

In some cases, sentences were not only replaced by orders for therapy but sometimes therapy was ordered when there was none available in the community.

We share the concern expressed by survivors about the overall effectiveness of offenders' programs. Overwhelmingly, we were informed that mandatory programs for male offenders don't work. What evaluation there is indicates that about 50 percent of men drop out of the programs, and of those who complete treatment, about a third remain physically violent and two thirds continue to be psychologically abusive. [7] The majority of service providers consider the short duration of most programs and incarceration as contributing factors to their ineffectiveness.

> We must never forget that every contact with an abused woman may be the last and that the male abuser is likely to increase the control he exercises over his partner to the point of no return: murder or suicide. [8]

CONCLUSION

While we clearly recognize the importance of services delivered in the community, their lack of co-ordination and uneven delivery result in varying levels of service for women of different populations and locations. Until this is addressed by all levels of government, women and children will continue to be at greater risk of remaining in or returning to violent situations.

CHAPTER 17

HEALTH CARE SYSTEM

INTRODUCTION

Most survivors of violence come into contact with the health care system at some point; contact may be immediately following a violent incident or it may come years later as a result of a delayed or long-term reaction to the ordeal. The following discussion includes health care professionals, and a number of settings, such as hospitals, mental health clinics, physicians' offices and women's organizations, in its broad definition of the health care system.

Despite an increasing awareness of the issue of violence against women and of the needs of women survivors, the health care system continues to use the needs of men as a basis for defining the needs of all clients. This affects all women and revictimizes women who have been abused. Such problems stem as much from the approach and philosophy that permeate the health care system as from the structure, organization and delivery of services to survivors.

TRADITIONAL HEALTH CARE

APPROACH AND PHILOSOPHY

Although violence is a primary health issue for women, those responsible for health policy, health promotion and health service delivery do not usually recognize the many important links. Further, in its response to violence, the health system frequently inappropriately pathologizes behaviour that is a direct consequence of a social problem.

The health care system in Canada, as in most Western countries, continues to focus on alleviating "sickness" as opposed to looking at the root causes of health and ill-health. In part, this is because of the continuing predominance of the "bio-medical" model of medicine.

According to this model, individuals and their social context function separately. Because health professionals are generally educated to deal with the problems of physical and sometimes psychosomatic causes of ill-health and not the social causes of the problem,[9] the health system tends to ignore the origins of violence and concentrate on the symptoms — women's physical injuries and psychological problems such as anxiety, depression and low self-esteem. Consequently, medical professionals fail to take measures to prevent further abuse from occurring.

Health professionals may also hold attitudes that prevent involvement. For instance, some may be indifferent to the problem of woman abuse[10] or may hold sexist biases.[11]

This failure to recognize the problem may lead to harmful medical treatment, and every inappropriate medical intervention adds significant cost to the health care system.

While there is no question that survivors often require specific medical attention, treatment usually stops after physicians have attended to cuts, bruises, lacerations and broken bones and have written a prescription for drugs. As one emergency care physician stated: "We basically stitch them up and send them out." Approximately 60 percent of the battered women in one study who sought medical assistance received a prescription drug, usually a tranquillizer.[12] The prescription of "psychoactive" drugs to abused women not only derails long-term solutions and true healing, it also places abused women in further danger by impairing their ability to protect themselves and their children from assault or their ability to act to change their domestic situation.[13]

The medical system reflects the unequal power relations between women and men that exist in the larger society. For instance, the system exhibits a clear division of labour based on gender; despite significantly increased female enrolment in medical schools, the majority of physicians are still men, and nurses remain predominantly female. Despite the fact that nurses frequently have more one-to-one contact with patients and do so on a more continuous basis, power rests almost totally in the hands of physicians. Patients are a distant third in the chain of command.

STRUCTURE AND ORGANIZATION

... Medicine is practised within an extremely authoritarian, hierarchical, impersonal and distant organization. In addition, modern medicine is over-specialized and hence very fragmented in its application and is most alienating for the patient. The structure of power is a vertical one with the [male] physician at the top, the [female] nurse as an obedient and respectful assistant, and the patient as a passive creature, an infant, at the bottom. We may assume that this mode of relationship is even more damaging for women than for men since our socialization and the prevalent ideologies and power structures favour the conventional hierarchy and reinforce the traditional model of medical care. [14]

According to a 1986 study by the Canadian Advisory Council on the Status of Women, most women feel they cannot ask for a second medical opinion. Their doctors talk down to them and provide incomprehensible medical explanations.[15] The Alberta Committee on Sexual Exploitation in Professional Relationships found that many women also experience rough or insensitive handling of their bodies by medical professionals without explanation and without their consent. While doctors may not intend abuse or disrespect, failure to understand the patient's basic need for gentle handling, to engage in clear and respectful communication and to provide information and reassurance contribute to the potential for devastating experiences. [16]

Sexual abuse by medical professionals is an extreme manifestation of sexism in health care. In just over six months, the Ontario Task Force on the Sexual Abuse of Patients heard 303 detailed reports of sexual abuse by physicians and others in positions of power and trust. [17] Of cases of abuse of trust in mental health settings, 88 percent of sexual contact occurred between male psychiatrists and female patients. [18]

Several years ago ... [the community] faced very high levels of violence [suicide, spousal abuse, etc.]. Over the next two years, the people of ... [the community] identified a group of committed volunteers and set up a series of workshops to help heal these people and enable them to become helpers for others in the community. The visits to the clinic and the emergency room ... for consequences of violence plummeted to zero. In spite of the fact that this made a real difference, including health care costs, the program funding was discontinued last fall.

♀ ♀ ♀

The help that I have been getting from the shelter is how to control my anger and how to deal with my children. They have also helped me through times when I wanted to kill myself. They helped me deal with all my feelings.

Women have emphasized that healing requires long-term and intense counselling and that delays because of long waiting lists for counselling services cause undue and additional suffering.

TRAINING/EDUCATION

Health care professionals often do not recognize the signs of abuse. They do not usually receive feminist and culturally sensitive training oriented to the health needs of women, nor are they informed or sensitized to woman abuse, to the specific situations and circumstances of abused women and to the characteristics and consequences of violence against women.

Frequently, they do not know about local services or where to refer women for additional help. Although no medical school presently provides adequate training on the issues of violence, in a study of 143 Canadian and American medical schools, 58 percent of the schools did not provide any instruction about "family violence." [19]

There are alternative methods of practising medicine that could alter traditional physician-patient interactions. However, despite some developments, health professionals are not well trained in these alternatives.

The Panel was told of rampant sexism within medical schools.

The professors and male students would make jokes. "It is just a joke," they would say, but I would look around and none of the women were laughing.

Research, curricula, reading material and teachers tend to reinforce male realities and demonstrate certain attitudes toward women. For instance, some medical textbooks present women as helpless creatures, as hysterical and neurotic individuals who depend on the help of strong male physicians and, because of their neuroses and other "feminine" mental problems, benefit from psychiatric care. [20] Research can also be sexist, applying information from studies of men to women and failing to research health issues specific to women, such as woman abuse.

MENTAL HEALTH

I sincerely believe we are including many ills as mental that are primarily sociological and that we mental health workers are presumptuous in attempting to "cure" persons who are suffering from the emotional results of conditions that require political change, not psychological treatment.

The bio-medical approach also overlooks the multiple and interrelated forms of abuse experienced by women. According to one survey, 93 percent of women who reported physical abuse were also severely psychologically abused. [21]

I see physically and emotionally abused women every day. Women's mental health is very seriously affected by violence. Women come into my office saying, "I want to die."

Many women told us how they were psychologically abused and how they were subjected to a mix of violence: financial, physical, sexual and psychological. A 1988 study of 85 women in five Toronto hospitals found that 83 percent had experienced severe physical or sexual abuse in childhood and/or adulthood. Over three fifths of the women had experienced multiple kinds of abuse. However, only 35 percent of the women in the study who reported abuse had been asked about their abuse by health workers in the wards. Ignoring a woman's history of abuse in a mental health environment risks misdiagnosing the trauma caused by the violence. It may also lead to ineffective or harmful interventions. [22]

As with the physical health procedures, mental health services under the bio-medical model often fail to make the link between women's mental health and inequality and abuse. "Epidemiological data link emotional disorder with alienation, powerlessness, and poverty; all conditions that characterize women's disadvantaged status." [23] Ignoring these links results in women being blamed for their mental health problems and for the abuse and violence they experience.

I went to a mental health unit for 14 days and the abuse was never talked about. Instead I was treated for hyperactiveness [Ritilan SR] which caused me to get very ill. I left the hospital and returned to the abusive relationship. I felt I was to blame for everything that happened to me. The relationship became much more abusive when I returned.

[My husband] was rough. He tried to rape me .... I gave my husband my baby bonus. He called it my fuck pay. When I went to see a psychiatrist, he said I was the problem and not my husband, and I was then hospitalized.

Within mental health services there is the tendency to treat a woman's health problems as though she is the problem, to make her mental ill-health somehow her own fault. The labels, such as "hysterical", "neurotic", "paranoid", often attached to women are indicative of the contempt which many physicians hold for their mental health problems.

... the staff there work at affixing new labels to fit their mould and their regime of drug therapy or behaviour modification rather than acknowledge the real problem. Not only does the patient become more confused, their symptoms increase and thus their stay in hospital is increased considerably. My personal view is that the institution breeds insanity rather than healing.

COUNSELLING

If we are truly serious about helping women who are victims [survivors] of violence, we must honour their right to choose how and by whom they are cared for.

While counselling clearly falls under the broad spectrum of mental health, such services are often quite different from the mental health care delivered by psychologists and psychiatrists. Counselling services are usually victim-directed and survivor-oriented, and are thus more flexible and responsive to the individual's needs. The venue may also be quite different — community centres and safe houses — as opposed to psychiatric hospitals and other more traditional settings.

I had six years of good counselling. I think that's the only thing that kept me from going crazy .... The best counsellor I had was the one who really cared about me. She was like a well-trained wise friend. I see a counsellor's job as clarifying issues and options more than giving advice. We all have wisdom inside; sometimes it's just more hidden from us.

Many women told us that the most effective counselling they received recognized the links between women's unequal status and their mental and physical health, and understood the links between their experiences of violence and their different realities — whether they were women of colour, immigrants, elderly, etc.

Counsellors ... who are required to keep their fees low, have an average fee in the range of $50 per hour, and it is virtually impossible to obtain a counsellor for less than $35 per hour. These fees are modest when compared to the rate [of] OHIP-covered psychiatrists and general practitioners ... who are reimbursed by government for counselling services. However, given the economic problems which most women experience, few are able to pay any fee at all. And those who are willing to sacrifice other basic needs in order to see a counsellor frequently terminate their counselling process prematurely .... Given that the healing process for women who experience violence is generally fairly long-term, private practitioners are not a realistic option for most women. [24]

Why should I, who was victimized as an infant and as a child, be made to forfeit thousands of dollars as an adult for a crime committed by my father.

Women also emphasized the importance of community-based and community-controlled workshops, social gatherings, support groups and other self-help and healing groups that allow individual communities to deal with issues in a regionally and culturally sensitive and supportive manner; any look at health care in Canada must recognize these grass-roots initiatives as among the most effective ways to help women become more self-empowered.

PROTOCOLS AROUND VIOLENCE AND ABUSE

The crisis point when an abused woman enters the hospital may be her first, and often only request for help, and the response she receives is, therefore, critical. [25]

Few medical professionals and fewer medical institutions have developed or implemented specific guidelines or protocols to detect or provide early intervention in woman abuse. [26] Yet, at a minimum, 20 percent of women admitted for emergency surgery are victims of violence. [27]

At the local hospital there are all kinds of specialists, but none specialize in sexual abuse.

Studies indicate that women often will not reveal the causes of their physical and/or psychological problems because of fear of retribution from the abusive partner, shame, embarrassment and a perception that health professionals do not care. [28]

We heard of cases in which physicians and nurses interviewed women they suspected had been assaulted, in the presence of their partners. One study of women at a shelter revealed that of the residents who sought medical services following their most recent abuse episode, over one third reported that the attending physician did not ask how they came to be injured. Only one in five reported that the physician asked specifically if she had been abused. [29]

New Brunswick has recently developed protocols for physicians' private practices and for hospital emergency departments, recommending that care for abused women be integrated and co-ordinated with other community-based services. The protocols include a description of the etiology (causes and origins of diseases) and epidemiology (incidence, distribution and control of diseases) of woman abuse and some of the more common symptoms, including psychological as well as physical ones. The protocols give guidelines for interviewing the victim, suggest a nurse remain with her at all times and suggest that abused women be referred to the hospital social worker or to other community-based groups for advice, counselling and support. [30]

Saskatchewan has created a successful inter-hospital "domestic violence" committee and workshops to co-ordinate continuing education and to provide educational material and protocols for helping victims of abuse. [31] The Ontario Ministry of Health recently provided funds to a battered women's advocacy centre to provide outreach to front-line staff at hospitals and to family medical centres on the issue of lesbian battering.

In British Columbia, the Vancouver General Hospital has implemented a three-part program to help abuse victims. It was initiated after studies showed that most emergency room staff did not want to become involved in problems of violence within intimate relationships. Every woman who uses the emergency service is asked whether she is in an abusive relationship. According to one physician at the hospital: "We are making it as normal a question as asking about allergies." If accompanied, the woman is separated from her partner. Polaroid photographs are taken of the abuse victim; one is kept by the hospital and the other given to the woman. Once the woman's safety is ensured within the hospital, a social worker gives her counselling and information on community services and suggests contacting the police. [32]

She wants you to believe her story, tell her she's not crazy, that no one deserves to be beaten, that wife abuse is a crime, that there's hope the cycle can be broken and that we can get her help. [33]

ACCOUNTABILITY

I worked in a psychiatric facility in another province. I saw punishment and ridicule of patients for being sick. I even saw physical violence .... We had a union rule which was too weak — it stated that a worker had to be caught physically abusing a patient three times before firing was permissible.

Existing self-regulating professions within the health care system have failed to ensure the safety of female clients from sexual assault and breach of trust. The lack of effective accountability mechanisms protects physicians rather than the public, particularly women survivors of violence.

Women talked to us about lengthy delays when they formally complained about health care professionals. And if the complaints were lodged with institutions, the response was even slower; in some cases there was no response at all.

My daughter is head-injured, is severely mentally and physically disabled and is in an institution. She had reported multiple rapes and acts of fellatio by an orderly. I complained and they promised safety plans but never got back to me .... I've been treated like a lunatic. Assaults continued to happen. The police haven't been able to do anything. They see the hospital as responsible .... The hospital has no complaint system and is not accountable to anyone.

Complaints that are not handled appropriately and quickly constitute an institutional breach of trust and contribute to further trauma for survivors and their families.

Ethical care of patients must be given a higher priority by Canada's health professionals. There is widespread support among both patients and physicians for placing patient's rights at the centre of the practice of medicine. Quebec's code of ethics for the medical profession includes patient's rights, and there is a move to include such rights in other provincial codes of ethics for physicians. [34] The Canadian Nurses Association recently revised its code of ethics and has placed strong emphasis on the nurse's role as "patient advocate." [35]

The College of Physicians and Surgeons of Ontario played a leadership role when it established the independent Task Force on Sexual Abuse of Patients to examine education for doctors and the public, legal changes and criteria for assessing the appropriateness and dangers of "romantic" involvement with patients. Other self-regulatory bodies in other provinces have subsequently begun to look at sexual abuse by their members. The Saskatchewan Medical Board and the College of Physicians and Surgeons of Saskatchewan have established the Joint Committee on Sexual Abuse of Patients by Physicians; the College of Physicians and Surgeons of Alberta has set up the Committee on Sexual Exploitation in Professional Relationships; the College of Physicians and Surgeons of British Columbia has commissioned the Committee on Physician Sexual Misconduct; the Nova Scotia Medical Board has issued a report on sexual abuse of patients; and the Newfoundland Medical Board has established a committee to investigate the process of reporting sexual misconduct of physicians toward patients. [36]

MEETING THE NEEDS OF WOMEN

The problems many women experience with the health care system arise from their gender; they are particularly vulnerable to systemic abuse or abuse by health professionals. For instance, women in psychiatric wards are open to abuse by their caregivers, and because their credibility is always questioned, their reports of abuse are more likely to be dismissed and ignored. In one study, almost one third of the women interviewed had been physically or sexually assaulted during their stay in a hospital psychiatric ward. [37]

I recently visited a young female friend who was sharing with me her humiliation at having had all of her clothing removed by two male orderlies before being secluded. (She is a survivor of childhood sexual abuse.)

Another case of a woman who was particularly vulnerable to abuse is quoted in *The Street Health Report:*

I was in the hospital for an overdose and I was being tied to the bed with restraints. They were trying to make me take all these drugs and sticking tubes down my throat and catheters. Because of the pain I was struggling and the orderly punched me in the face. I was crying and crying, they treated me so bad. [38]

Older women and young women also have particular problems with the health system. Research shows that the abuse rate of elderly women within institutions is high. [39] They are also more likely to receive excessive and inappropriate drug prescriptions [40] and are less likely to be taken seriously by health professionals.

My doctor told me it was too much of a hassle for him to write me a letter to support my application for my own old age pension and that it would be easier if I just went back.

In the case of younger women, physicians often have not been trained to recognize the symptoms of eating disorders nor to understand the social context of their problems.

The poverty in which many Aboriginal women live makes them particularly susceptible to health problems. [41] Health care on reserves (for treaty Aboriginal peoples) is a federal responsibility. This causes a conflict in the provision of services between provincial and federal levels and results in inadequate care. [42] Non-Aboriginal health care services are often insensitive to Aboriginal cultures, and some health care service providers are racist toward Aboriginal people. Furthermore, on reserves and in isolated regions, there is no continuum of health care; physicians come and go, and women often have to be evacuated in order to receive treatment.

For women and men seeking counselling there are essentially no mental health services in northwest Saskatchewan. One mental health nurse and mental health social worker cover 13 communities spread over about six hours' drive from one corner to the other. I know of men who tried repeatedly to get help out of fear of becoming a spousal abuser but could find no counselling at hand.

Rural women are concerned about the quality of rural health care, including inadequate physician and hospital services and lack of non-institutional support services and emergency transportation links to urban hospitals. They are also sceptical about the confidentiality of physicians' services. Home care is also difficult to obtain in rural areas. [43]

The health system tends to treat women with disabilities paternalistically and to make their decisions for them. Women with a disability often have to fight to prevent sterilization and abortion, just as other women have to struggle to get access to these procedures. [44] In a study conducted by the DisAbled Women's Network, 63 percent of disabled women indicated they had been "medically assaulted." This includes being sexually assaulted during a medical examination, as well as being given medication or being operated upon without their informed consent. [45] Refugee and immigrant women from diverse cultural and linguistic backgrounds require services that are culturally sensitive and delivered in or translated into their own language. Unfortunately, the lack of appropriate services discourages such women from seeking help and may lead to further victimization. Immigrant women use medical services less because of barriers in communication and cultural insensitivity; [46] because it interferes with cultural practices or appears to be an invasion of privacy; because hospitalization may create dietary problems; and because examination by a male doctor may offend religious mores. [47]

Female genital mutilation is an extremely sensitive subject for immigrant and refugee communities. It can cause serious physical and psychological harm, and girls who have experienced it are twice as likely to die during childbirth and more likely to have stillborn babies. [48] Physicians must recognize the seriousness of the effects of genital mutilation and deal with the issue sensitively.

Refugee women may also need more specialized health services because of hardships they may have experienced in their country of origin, including malnutrition and severe dental problems, as well as sexual assault and other torture experienced in internment camps. [49]

CONCLUSION

Women survivors told us that they wanted more from the medical system. According to a Toronto survey, about two thirds of women reported that therapy had not been useful for them. The reasons cited were: treatment was piecemeal, treatment attempted to deal with behaviours or symptoms without considering underlying trauma and treatment was insensitive to women's needs or issues. [50] The health care system must develop an approach to women's experiences of violence that recognizes its root causes. The focus must be on long-term intervention rather than on piecemeal and short-term solutions. Medical intervention must proceed not by making decisions for women, but by enhancing their ability to analyze alternatives and find their own course of action.

CHAPTER 18

THE LEGAL SYSTEM

Women survivors of violence are often left unprotected, under-served, marginalized, demeaned and further harmed in their dealings with the legal-judicial system. Women and women's experiences have been starkly absent in the development of both law and legal practice. These silences translate into a system that, more often than not, fails women. Further, racist and prejudiced attitudes and practices put some women at even higher risk. The experiences of women victims of violent crime need to be placed front and centre in the review of the justice system and in making the necessary systemic changes.

The Panel heard numerous complaints about the extent to which the system is out of balance which cannot be corrected by small changes made in isolation. For example, mandatory charging by police in instances of violence against a woman is a good policy; however, it has detrimental consequences in the context of a dysfunctional system.

Many people told us that although offenders' rights must be respected in a democratic society, they must not take precedence over both the rights of individual victims and society's right to public safety. Many women told us that the legal system must focus on the rights and needs of women, particularly survivors of violence. Many Canadians also expressed concern over the treatment of children and the poor recognition of their specific needs within the system.

People are scared of judges, lawyers. They're scared of them because they have a degree. You feel like they must know better. They're afraid of the justice system and the status of these people. It must be made public: we're human first, then we're male and female. We've got to know more about the legal system. The police show up, and there are two big males standing in front of you. The police I had were excellent, but still intimidating.

There is a need for greater public accountability in the legal-judicial system. The inordinate amount of power vested in the key players demands that they be held accountable for their actions or, indeed, their inactions. Survivors of violence were angry at their treatment within the judicial system, pointing at the gaps in service, discrimination and lack of response to their needs. They called for a fundamental overhaul of the administration of justice.

This first part of this section examines the roles of the police, Crown attorneys, defence lawyers, judges, justices of the peace and the courts themselves in relation to survivors' issues. The examination includes the question of parole, probation and release of offenders and concerns relating to women in conflict with the law.

The second part focuses specifically on the legal system and the family. We look at issues such as custody and access to children in marriage breakdown where violence and abuse have been the key issues; support and enforcement; matters that concern children's interaction with the legal judicial system; and young offenders.

The final part of this section looks at statutes and legislation and addresses some specific areas that have been identified for change, including such issues as stalking and threats of violence, high-risk offenders, the "rape-shield" provisions, prostitution, pornography, sexual abuse involving breach of trust, gun control and the *Canadian Charter of Rights and Freedoms*.

THE ADMINISTRATION OF JUSTICE

POLICE

Help, when it is available, often comes from those who do not understand wife abuse and have little or no training.

♀ ♀ ♀

Officers are assigned to investigate sexual assault complaints when they are clearly uncomfortable dealing with the subject. Investigators are inadequately trained.

Several themes in common with other institutional settings were clearly articulated with respect to the role of police officers in cases of violence against women. These include training and education; better representation of women on police forces; increased effectiveness; accountability; community liaison; and changes to the types of services offered by police.

KNOWLEDGE ABOUT THE ISSUES

Many women told the Panel that police officers know little about the dynamics of violence against women or take violence against women seriously. Police, mostly men working in a "tough" culture, do not relate easily to women's fear. Their overexposure to horror and violence has desensitized them to pain and suffering, and their training does not include anything to offset this. Police often do not know or understand the degree of control men have over women, nor do they recognize the degree of danger men pose to women. They often believe the myths.

- Some blame women for inciting the violence and lose patience when a woman cannot leave a violent situation.

- Some lack sensitivity when dealing with a woman who has been beaten, sexually assaulted or terrorized by psychological intimidation.

- Many hold stereotypical views of gender, race and class, and fail to understand the needs and circumstances of specific groups of women, such as young, women with disabilities, immigrant or poor women, women of colour or of visible minorities.

Laws and the criminal justice system are sexist and often victimize women a second time. Women of colour, lesbians and prostitutes fear making reports because they will not be taken seriously.

While some police forces have instituted sensitivity training to dispel myths, general knowledge of the concerns pertaining to violence against women varies greatly across country. For example, the Centres locaux de services communautaires (CLSC) in greater Montreal and the Montreal police set up a pilot project to provide better follow-up support for victims when the police intervene. The CLSCs undertook to make police officers more aware of the problem of violence against women and the factors that need to be considered when a woman calls for help.[51]

Local women's groups across the country have displayed a willingness to work with police to equip them better in responding to violence against women. Too often this offer is refused and, even when it is accepted, tensions arise over the reluctance of police to respect a feminist analysis of violence against women, the approach which has proven the most effective in creating the changes that bring access to justice for women.

More women on police forces and female forensic photographers to gather evidence for court would increase the empathy of police response. Women can often share details of abuse more freely with other women, a reality that is particularly true for women from cultures that prohibit discussions of sexual matters. Police departments do not reflect the diversity of their own communities,[52] a fact which diminishes communication and consultation.

Explore the idea of allowing only women police officers to deal with domestic matters. This would eliminate the possibility of having a police officer who is a wife batterer himself coming to your house "to protect you" after your husband beats you up.

COLLABORATION

Many women told us that the lines of communication between police and communities are weak. As in other initiatives in the area of crime prevention, police focus mainly on property crime. They do not recognize the urgent need to make women's and children's safety a priority of crime prevention activities. There is an overwhelming need for police and survivor services to collaborate and co-ordinate overall responses to violence against women. For instance, campaigns such as "Sexual Assault Prevention is Crime Prevention" (by Metro Action Committee on Public Violence Against Women and Children) have been initiated by the community, not by police. In the absence of co-ordination, people are injured or die. Of paramount concern is the monitoring of programs, the accuracy and completeness of records; the timely dissemination of information; and the assurance that a case has a central co-ordinator. Police must also represent the needs of all citizens in the community by reaching out to minority communities so they too can turn with confidence to the police.

Collaborative efforts have to be established with the police, the health care system, the criminal justice system and social agencies to deal with domestic violence. Often a perpetrator is known to several agencies but the information is not shared. A comprehensive, co-ordinated approach to address violence issues is needed.

COMPLAINT PROCEDURES

Every police department [must] have a clearly defined and publicized accountability process, explain why charges are not laid, allow for a review of these cases.

♀ ♀ ♀

Accountability of police is non-existent. Young offenders experience so much abuse by police that they come to think that it's just part of being a kid.

There was a great deal of criticism of the self-protective nature of internal policing procedures which prohibit "due process" and hamper full respect of the complainant's rights. Concerns were expressed about how officers suspected of wrongdoing were provided with a clear record in exchange for their resignation. [53] Police departments do not have a clearly defined, publicized process of accountability that explains incidents when charges against officers are not laid, nor are these cases subject to review. Such procedures must be replaced with external, independent monitoring agencies or boards whose members would recognize and support the difference between the appropriate use of power and its abuse.

PROTOCOLS

[She] has been assaulted many times by her ex-partner. He has been in jail for it once and has several charges pending. He broke into her apartment, struck her repeatedly in the head with a 2 x 4 board she used to secure her balcony door and dragged her across the room causing permanent hair loss. She required hospital care. The police had physical evidence of assault, medical corroboration and prior convictions and charges. Still they refused to lay charges.

They told her to think about it, and said that in "more serious cases" they would pursue it further .... It is not enough to remove the man from the scene to allow him to cool down. The woman may be in extreme danger when he returns. Police are making unnecessary judgments about a woman's life.

Policy alone does not effect change; it is but one important element of an overall shift in the system. The consistent message the Panel heard during consultations was that police need to establish and adhere to strict protocols concerning violence against women. They need to maintain these conventions internally among all police forces and externally among all agencies. Such uniformity would help women anticipate the different elements of the legal process and help offenders understand the consequences of their violence.

RESPONSE TIMES BY POLICE

Police services to women victims of violence must be improved. Current protocols are sadly lacking. For instance, when responding to a call, police often do not give the woman adequate information on available transition houses; on social and legal services; on the case itself, or even their own name, number and telephone number. Nor do current protocols require that all reports of crimes affecting personal safety be given the highest priority and be responded to urgently.

One pressing problem is the time it takes police to respond to emergency calls; response time for repeat calls to the same address is even slower. Rural women are often without a rapid response system under any circumstances because of their geographic distance from police stations.

In some locations, there are now units dedicated to responding to woman abuse. The officers in these units receive specialized training to investigate and process sexual assault and other abuse cases. Although funding in this area is unfortunately not a priority, some police services across Canada are beginning to recognize the importance of specialized training and skills in responding to victims of violence.

CHARGING POLICY

Another area of concern is that aggressive charging policies for woman assault are not applied consistently and without prejudice. In 1986, the RCMP adopted a national wife assault charging policy and other forces quickly followed suit. However, women told us that actual police charging is still inconsistent. Federal and provincial governments fail to enforce existing directives instructing police to lay charges in cases of woman assault and implied or threatened assault.

Some officers try to talk women out of charging: "You are just doing this out of revenge; come back tomorrow after you have had a chance to think this through."

♀♀♀

Police faithfully believe they are doing their job but say that domestic violence is a grey area. Everyone has to use their own judgment as to whether charges are warranted. This tells us that if individual police [officers] don't think a woman is worth protecting, the administration won't force it.

Police are often reluctant to lay charges in cases where they cannot see any injuries or where there are no witnesses. By using their discretionary power, police support or deny access to the justice system for women according to their narrow criterion of the "good witness," that is, white, middle class, able, heterosexual, etc. Anyone differing from this ideal is considered less credible. This perception works against women on both sides of the law. For example, violent behaviour from women in conflict with the law violates the popular image of the ideal woman and is dealt with harshly by the justice system. Similarly, women who are assaulted who do not correspond to the ideal are often blamed for their own victimization.

There are encouraging signs that established and consistently enforced protocols lead to an improved response. The importance of this is underscored by a recent London, Ontario, study which found that a strict policy for laying charges in cases of woman abuse led to reduced violence, more appropriate court responses and more progressive attitudes on the part of officers. [54]

LEAVING THE HOME

Absence of policy to assure women's safety whether they stay in the home or seek refuge elsewhere is a problem. When a woman is forced to leave her home to seek safety, she is suffering additional punishment.

A system which removed the offender would send a definite message that wife battering is unacceptable in Canada.

If she chooses to remain, she must be adequately protected and provided with support services such as those found in shelters. When the woman does leave her home, "safe passage" to retrieve her belongings is often requested through police services. Frequently, however, this service is not adequate, and women are repeatedly placed at risk. Many women are not aware of their rights to this escort.

The victim rather than the assailant seems to be treated as the problem, i.e., removing her from home rather than the husband.

♀♀♀

This is particularly a problem with a disabled woman whose home is set up for her needs. Often the home is owned by the abused [woman] and removing her from the home plays into the abuser's hands.

RESTRAINING ORDERS AND PEACE BONDS

These instruments are designed to curtail the abuser's access to his victim. However, they are not consistently granted or put in place immediately after charges are laid. Delays are too long. To treat a breached order with leniency is also extremely dangerous since the very existence of an order is often the signal to the man that she really does not want him back. It is a time when the woman is at her most vulnerable. Women who are separated from their spouses are at particularly high risk and are five times more likely to be killed by their intimate partners than are other women. [55]

Orders and the language they use may differ but it is imperative that no loopholes allow the offender to feign ignorance or confusion in his understanding of the order. For example, at the moment there is confusion about the definition of the terms "direct contact" and "indirect contact." Seemingly harmless subtle or persistent gestures from an estranged partner are often signs of danger and can be terrifying for a woman. In the context of past violent behaviour, unwelcome gestures, such as sending flowers or a fax, innocuous in themselves, are still acts of "indirect contact" and are often ways to assert control. No-contact orders must be enforced, otherwise women are both disillusioned and endangered. They lose faith in the system and stop reporting violence.

Restraining orders might be more effective if they were used in conjunction with an electronic system of monitoring the offenders. Some police forces have implemented electronic alarm systems for high-risk victims identified by community-based victim services. These devices allow women to signal police immediately when confronted with danger. Unfortunately, they are only available in a few communities at the present time.

I had a restraining order on my husband two years ago. I gave him permission to come over to the yard to get the trailer, and he pounded on the door trying to get in. I called the police, they said that I broke the restraining order by letting him come over so they would not help me.

♀ ♀ ♀

We treat the refusal to take a breathalyser more seriously than the refusal to respect a peace bond.

SEXUAL ASSAULT

Women across Canada impressed upon us that police do not understand the crime of sexual assault. They described inappropriate responses and weak and limited protocols for dealing with sexual crimes. They were concerned that police did not always publicize incidents of sexual assault, leaving women unaware of the presence of a rapist in their midst.

Repeatedly, sexual assault complaints are considered unfounded particularly when the accused is known to the complainant. As with other crimes, the discretionary power of the police does not always reflect the best interests of women – for example, when it is exercised without an understanding that consent to a social interaction does not deprive the woman of the right to refuse a sexual interaction. Investigating officers frequently use language that trivializes the rape or implies that the victim is to blame for the assault because of her conduct. Often a focus on the victim's character or other personal characteristics, and a bias in favour of the accused based on his job, status and community service, have distracted from the fair implementation of the laws regarding sexual assault. One result has been that sexual assault committed by persons in a position of trust have rarely been acknowledged as crimes.

Police are not always culturally sensitive to women who are assaulted by their partners. We heard of instances where police used the abusive spouse to interpret for a victim who did not speak English. On the other hand, many women find police and the system inherently racist; women of colour often will not report assaults because they do not believe their partners will be treated fairly because of their race.

Women victims of sexual assault are still often put through very invasive procedures to collect evidence, even though there is evidence that DNA identification, a much less intrusive process, is useful in identifying sexual offenders. Given the difficulty in obtaining evidence against the accused in sexual assault crimes, we cannot afford to ignore DNA identification as a valuable tool.

CENTRAL INFORMATION SYSTEM

In some cases, regionally and provincially, police forces may lack centralized information bases and methods of tracking those who run afoul of the law. In some areas, there are no means of instantaneous intercommunication for the sharing of vital information for law enforcement.

Many who spoke to the Panel felt that a central information system and a national registry of dangerous offenders could enhance police effectiveness. A comprehensive central registry would alert all law enforcement agencies of an offender's previous violent crimes and would identify men who have been violent in intimate relationships. Police officers need a system that can provide immediate information when responding to calls involving intimate violence, and it is important that police have complete access to a violent sexual predator's history to assist in investigation, apprehension or treatment of that person. [56] Women across the country have also called for police to screen applicants for jobs working with children or in other positions of trust.

Expanding the Canadian Police Information Centre (CPIC) data base to include complete criminal history of offenders involved in crimes against women, details of all offences and conditions and details of release, would provide greater protection to the public. Giving officers access to this information in their cars would better equip them to respond to community needs. Unfortunately, police do not always forward the particulars of all charges and convictions to the Canadian Police Information Centre or record them on their individual information systems (computer or manual file) within 24 hours of receiving such information. [57]

Consistent and standardized data collection on reported incidents of wife assault, chargings, peace bonds and sentences would also assist in both policing and the framing of policy and legislation.

CROWN ATTORNEYS AND LAWYERS

The rights of the victim are trampled to protect those of the defendant. The job of the prosecutor is not to defend the victim, but rather to protect the interests of the state. On the day of trial, the Crown prosecutor did not even introduce himself to her.

♀ ♀ ♀

She was repeatedly refused access to the medical report on her injuries, and although the arresting officer had informed her at the time of arrest that her attacker was known to the police, she was later unable to obtain verification of this statement from either the Crown prosecutor or the RCMP.

The importance of the role of Crown attorney was emphasized in supporting women's safety. Many women mentioned that survivors were not made aware of the process of laying charges and testifying in court and commented on the limited involvement of survivors of violence in the process. Survivors need as much information as possible about the court process and procedures, about what they should expect from the trial process and about their rights as survivors and witnesses.

We were told of a number of instances where survivors were not told that their assailants (former husbands or partners) had been granted bail. Crown attorneys and lawyers need to adjust their practices and object to bail applications, particularly when offenders have previously breached peace bond or non-communication order conditions. Public safety interests are not always upheld through the careful determination of who poses a risk and who does not.

In a similar vein, it is not uncommon for Crown attorneys and lawyers to enter into plea bargains concerning the sentencing and charging procedures without consulting the victim. Plea bargains often result in the offender's record labelling him as much less dangerous than he is. Guidelines or protocols are scarce, and there is no monitoring of plea bargains. [58]

The trial process and the conduct of Crown attorneys and lawyers often present problems for women survivors. The court experience is made more stressful when women have to deal with more than one Crown attorney. In addition, the length of time it takes to prepare a case can sometimes result in the acquittal of assailants in sexual and physical assault cases. Crown attorneys can often afford only limited pre-trial interviews, in stark contrast to defence lawyers who can spend more time in the preparation of a case. [59] Often, under the guise of "providing the best possible defence," harassing and humiliating cross-examination tactics are used by the defence council thus increasing the harm that victim-witnesses experience during the trial.

She feels her case was poorly handled by the Crown prosecutor. The attack occurred in her home. Although she gave a statement to the RCMP shortly thereafter, she prepared a more complete second statement which the prosecutor refused to read until one day before court proceedings against the accused were scheduled to begin. The prosecutor did not interview her at any time before the hearing to discuss the defendant's version of events.

If Crown attorneys and lawyers are more highly sensitized to the dynamics of the particular form of violence being addressed in the trial process (rape, sexual harassment or battering), their knowledge of the issues will help them handle the trial process with the best interests of the survivor in mind.

Law societies have an important role to play in increasing the accountability of the legal profession. Unfortunately, most societies have not yet made priorities of women's equality and safety.

THE COURTS — THE TRIAL PROCESS

If our system continues to victimize the victim, how many will go through the court procedures?

♀ ♀ ♀

Women who have been through the court process believed there had been very little accountability from the system for its treatment of women. Almost none felt they had been dealt with fairly.

Both Crowns and judges share in the wide application of discretionary power to interpret laws that are broadly crafted, vague and ambiguous. In the absence of specialized knowledge, conventional wisdom is used. Not surprisingly, the courts reflect certain widely held notions about women and violence. Prevailing gender bias results in the victims often being blamed for the offence. There is a myth that women fabricate stories about being assaulted, and there is a tendency to underestimate the seriousness of a violent attack if the survivor does not report it immediately. The attack on a victim's credibility is successful mainly because the practitioners deciding the case are part of a society which believes that men are not at fault for losing control or for confusing innocent gestures with sexual signals.

After the assault, I got promiscuous with guys because I had no self-worth. If I went to court, they'd dig all that up and use it against me. It doesn't matter what you were like before, just how many people you slept with. The system is victimizing. You feel so helpless.

♀ ♀ ♀

We are told the accused is innocent until proven guilty .... Sitting in court, I would rather say the victim is guilty until proven innocent. It seems they are the ones on trial, they are the ones that must fight for help, the ones that come out of it too often even more hurt.

The issue of delays in court proceedings and trials is particularly difficult for women survivors. Too much time between the actual crime and the trial date gives an offender more opportunity to intimidate the victim further. Extending court time to include nights or weekends, setting dates for trials as early as possible and opposing adjournments can help to protect victims.

When I left him finally, the first court appearance was scheduled for September. The thought of being in the same room with him scared me. He had been watching me, following me and shouting obscenities at me. At the last minute, the case was remanded to late October. I had to get ready all over again and psych myself [up] to follow through with it. Had I known then that my husband would be allowed to manipulate the court system for four years, I would have [just] gone back to him. It would have been easier.

Other concerns regarding the protection of survivors were also raised. Many Canadian women noted that instituting contempt of court charges against a battered woman who refuses to testify is an inappropriate response. There are very real reasons why women make this decision, including threats and intimidation. The courts need to recognize the lack of true options available to a woman. The stress of the court-room experience is doubled by the existence of preliminary hearings. The requirement of recalling details of the crime twice results in normal variations in repeated stories which become issues of credibility.

Some cases require highly sensitive treatment and alternative court proceedings. The trauma of reliving the crime in an adversarial setting that is foreign, and often hostile, is rarely acknowledged. The provision of a screen for children was one limited recognition of the terror caused by having to face the accused. The complainants should also have private space within the confines of the courthouse to spare them the stress of media scrutiny and to avoid any contact with the accused.

There are many victims who are currently denied access to the courts because their needs are not met. For example, translation and interpretation services for women whose first language is not English or French, for women with hearing or visual impairments or for those who use bliss boards are often lacking throughout the court process.

Some women urged that all policies and procedural guidelines should be reviewed by representatives of the area's communities of women of colour, women with disabilities and poor women. The review should look closely at monitoring procedures to safeguard against gender, race, class or sexual orientation biases in implementing policies.

Currently, a ban on the publication of information that could reveal the identity of the sexual assault victim is guaranteed only during the trial. Preliminary hearings, court-related orders or quasi-judicial tribunals are not subject to the ban, and as a result, women experience unnecessarily negative consequences from unwanted identification. Women were clear that this legislative failure must be addressed. Information about past sexual victimization or other personal information is often not kept confidential. People spoke to the Panel about unnecessary risks to women caused by judges ordering full disclosure to defence attorneys, thereby allowing the abuser

to gain access to suchpersonal information as medical records, diaries, a victim's current address and details of past sexual history or past sexual victimization. Judicial orders have included the issuing of subpoenas to victim's counsellors and supportive friends, and the seizing of all personal material including the content of hard disk drives.

Other trial procedures were also noted as requiring review.

- Decisions on the extent of injury, pain and suffering are not always based on the survivor's testimony, medical documentation and other objective evidence. Decisions are often influenced by the victim's emotional state or physical demeanour at the hearing process. [60]

- Sexual assault cases are emotionally taxing, and women are clear about the importance of trial by a jury that is representative of the female/male ratio of the population to ensure the utmost fairness.

- Victims are denied justice when they are not able to convince Crown attorneys to appeal the verdict because of a lack of access to unedited transcripts.

- There were grave concerns about the practice of allowing judges to edit their judgments.

Despite the fact that their value has been recognized by many, victim-impact statements are not always used properly by lawyers and judges. Unfortunately, not all lawyers make sure that these statements are prepared, submitted and considered by the court before sentencing. Nor do judges always take into consideration in their sentencing decisions, the complainant's statements about the impact of a crime. Until adjudicators better understand the effects of crimes involving violence against women, the use of victim-impact statements is an important interim measure.

Upon the filing of a complaint, victims should be provided with an advocate/counsellor whose role it is to accompany them from the time the police intervene through to the end of the court process. The courts and law enforcement agencies must work co-operatively with victim advocacy programs to ensure that both the advocacy/shelter program and victim have the broadest possible access to legal information.

The Panel did hear some suggestions that a separate system within the existing legal system is needed to deal with crimes against the person, as opposed to crimes against property. Others advocated a special court session or court system to deal solely with crimes of violence against women.

The Family Violence Court in Manitoba seems to be effective in its handling of cases of domestic violence. The time required to handle cases is generally cut in half, to three months. Sentences are tougher, reflecting the view that wife abuse is a crime. More cases reach the sentencing stage.

The Family Violence Court in Winnipeg began operations on September 17, 1990. It is the first of its kind in North America and handles first appearances, remands, guilty pleas and trials for cases of spouse, child and elder abuse. Such a system is expected to allow cases to be dealt with more expeditiously and facilitate continuity by having the same Crowns and judges throughout the entire process. In addition, the legal practitioners have specialized training that allows them to respond better to women's needs.

At the end of the first year there is evidence that the specialized court is meeting its objectives in a number of areas. Despite the increase in the number of cases, the court has been able to stay close to its goal of processing most cases within a three-month period. Further, not only are more cases going to court but more cases are staying in the court to the point of sentencing. Prior to Family Violence Court approximately 51 percent of wife abuse cases proceeded to sentencing; at year end, 66 percent of the 1,093 cases analyzed proceeded to sentencing. [61]

JUDGES AND JUSTICES OF THE PEACE

The judge thus questioned her sobriety, her level of resistance to the attack (suggesting that she could have left the company of her assailant at any point in the evening). The judge's comments reflected his lack of information about what happened the evening she was attacked. The victim left court feeling that her character had been attacked.

♀ ♀ ♀

I very often deal with extreme violence, and I worry about my own desensitization because I see so much. [A judge speaking in private conversation.]

Absolute judicial power has frequently meant the licence to exercise conventional wisdom and prejudice. This also includes gender bias which is extensive and well documented. [62]

At present, trials often take place in a framework which presumes the innocence of the accused and demonstrates a significant disbelief of the victim. Consequently, during trial procedures, women survivors are often caused further harm and suffering by judges.

When judges give defence council latitude to badger a witness, she is further harmed. While we heard accounts of a few women who felt very lucky to have had a sensitive judge who was able and willing to cut through the tactics of the defence attorney, judges often fail to intervene to protect the victim-witness from cross-examination designed primarily to embarrass and humiliate. Victim blaming (often called victim provocation) moves the focus from "did he do it" to "does she deserve it." While victim provocation is a useful concept in assessing responsibility for some crimes, it has been used inappropriately in crimes against women, resulting in the reduction of charges, of sentences, and sometimes in acquittal.

Judges have considerable discretionary power regarding the admission and treatment of evidence. In court, the accused is considered a valuable source of accurate and reliable testimony. The expertise provided by academic and medical practitioners is often not questioned despite the fact that their past evidence may not have reflected an understanding of the dynamics of violence. Conversely, the criteria for qualifying "expert" witnesses do not allow women who have worked with victims to testify. The testimony of women victim-witnesses about their knowledge of the impact of the assault and the dangerousness of the abuser is often not regarded as credible. The Supreme Court of Canada (*Seaboyer*) in a dissenting judgment by Madam Justice L'Heureux-Dubé states that "... the concept of relevance has been imbued with stereotypical notions of female complainants and sexual assault ...." This judgment is an important starting place for a guideline for the relevance and admissibility of evidence in sexual assault cases.

These issues can be addressed by having a knowledgeable judiciary. One important step in this direction is mandatory judicial training. The training must challenge all long-standing prejudices and ideologies around issues of gender, race and class inequality in Canada. Judges are often not aware of the actual costs of raising children, the discrimination women face in the workplace, the effect of inappropriate sentencing in criminal law areas and a host of other equality issues that work against the safety of women. Women's groups should be the key educators in providing this training.

The course content of Canadian law schools does not adequately reflect a critical awareness of gender, race and class issues and their impact on the administration of justice and sentencing practices. Since all judges begin their education as lawyers, it is imperative that law schools include material and instruction aimed at increasing understanding and promoting equality and women's safety.

Representation is an important aspect of the make-up of the judiciary. Many women who appeared before the Panel support the appointment of more judges who demonstrate an understanding of bias and a commitment to equality. Judicial appointments and appointments to legal services boards, law foundation boards or law reform commissions do not reflect the diversity of the population. [63]

The Panel heard from many who felt that there should be regular and systematic reviews by citizens and advocacy groups of all judicial appointments and sentencing decisions especially for crimes of violence against women and children. Judges are not often removed from the bench when they do not serve the public interest, including women's interests, and judicial councils do not take adequate responsibility for processes to monitor the accountability of the judiciary. Often details or the nature of complaints are not subject to public scrutiny. The proceedings of the council are conducted in private with very limited lay representation. Indeed, some judges themselves have supported more open council proceedings and greater lay representation. Governments must ultimately take responsibility for making more non-judicial appointments to these councils.

In spite of the massive inequalities in the legal system, there is no one body or initiative whose primary responsibility it is to effect the sizable changes necessary to achieve equality and justice for women.

SENTENCING

Most of the men get 18-month sentences and then parole. They may have a poor prognosis but still something should be done because they go back out and they're dangerous.

Sentencing practices reveal a high level of tolerance for crimes of violence against women. Physical and sexual assault of women must be treated with the same degree of seriousness as other assaults, and sentences must reflect the seriousness.

Her assailant received a token slap on the wrist for his violent behaviour — despite a previous record of violence toward women. He is to be incarcerated in a work camp only when not at work. The system failed the victim. The judge made some "disturbing and interesting points" at the time of sentencing. Because the prosecutor had failed to enter into evidence pictures of her injuries and of the disarray of her apartment, and because he did not consider the totality of her expanded statement, much of the evidence supporting the charges was not considered.

Often short sentences for men who abuse women are justified by practitioners on a number of grounds such as the lack of available jail space. Sentences are often mitigated by other factors including the accused's employment and reputation in the community.

SENTENCING REFORM

The Report of the Sentencing Commission (1987) recommended the establishment of a permanent sentencing commission and a judicial advisory council. These alone will not adequately address the issue. Women with expertise on the issues of violence against women must participate in the structuring and be appointed to such bodies to co-ordinate the overhaul of sentencing practices. [64] An important component is the elimination of gender, race and class biases in sentencing.

"There is a need for a more contextualized approach to sentencing in woman abuse in intimate relationships, one that recognizes the dynamics of the battering relationship and its effect on the victim. [65] When an assaulter is found guilty and there is clear evidence that a crime took place, there is still no guarantee that the judge understood either the nature of the crime or its impact on the victim. [66] Often a previous relationship with the accused is treated as a mitigating factor. In one study, in just over half the cases where there was a person in a position of trust perpetrating the sexual assault, the breach of trust was not recognized as an aggravating factor in sentencing.[67]

There was also wide-scale recognition by presenters during the Panel consultations that if a husband is jailed, the abused woman may be protected from physical harm, but she will also likely suffer the economic consequences of her husband's jail term. A harsh jail term may reinforce a batterer's hostility toward the victim (i.e., that it was her "fault") and lay the basis for his future justification of abuse and violence. Women frequently recommended that the sentences for assaulters of women include mandatory counselling and that there must be consequences for men who fail to co-operate with this counselling.[68]

CORRECTIONS: WOMEN IN CONFLICT WITH THE LAW

The women in conflict with the law are victims before they become offenders.

♀ ♀ ♀

Because they are among the few women for whom survival has involved acting out against society as an expression of their outrage as opposed to directing rage against oneself — the most usual expression by women — they are locked up.

Many women in prisons have a lengthy history of sexual and physical abuse, poverty and a range of problems that placed them at a disadvantage. The correctional system needs to recognize these circumstances and provide women-centred programs to help women heal from past abuse. Authoritarian correctional environments reinforce symptoms of past sexual abuse in women.

Women who have committed crimes need healing models identical to other women and correctional environments that allow them to regain power over their lives. They have more in common with other women than with male perpetrators of crime. In recognition of the number of prisoners who are Aboriginal and women of colour, culturally appropriate information, services and counselling must be made available.

Many Canadians told us that women who kill husbands after years of abuse should have the right to claim "self-preservation" as a defence and not be charged with murder. A recent Supreme Court decision (Lavalleé) recognized that the history of abuse of a woman is relevant in assessing her guilt or innocence and allowed testimony regarding past abuse to be entered into evidence. Some women scholars believe that while the Lavallée decision does move the defence for abused women forward, it still treats the history of abuse as an excuse for the woman's action rather than recognizing that she defended herself in the only way she could. It still does not fully recognize that when a woman is threatened with death by a man whose past actions have proved that he can and will act on the threat, she knows that she cannot afford to wait to defend herself when he actively launches the attack on her life. In Canada, there are women in prison for killing abusive spouses. These women have not had the benefit of any self-defence argument during their trials. In light of new knowledge of the battered women's syndrome and the *Lavallée* decision, there is growing support for a formal justice review of these cases.

I know of a woman who deliberately broke her parole so that she would be sent back to prison. It was the only way she could see to escape the beatings from her husband.

Many women, even those who have committed serious crimes, pose little risk to the community. Public safety is often not realistically gauged when determining periods of incarceration for women, which results in sentences far in excess of what would safeguard the public interest.

Although the behaviour which brings most women into conflict with the law is rarely a serious transgression of the law, as a consequence they enter the socially sanctioned system which allegedly metes out justice but in actuality creates the conditions in which they are particularly vulnerable to individual and systemic revictimization.

PROBATION AND PAROLE

My ex-partner did not get charged for talking openly and at length about killing me because, according to the police, he did not say it directly to me. His probation was apparently not breached, and the conditional discharge for the assault was not even reviewed. The message is clear: men can talk about killing women and scare the hell out of them without any consequence except a peace bond.

The probation system is not accountable to female victims of violence. It fails to give priority to the victims' needs for security, potentially increasing their danger; probation is often inadequately monitored by probation officers who fail to understand violence against women; probation terms are often too short to allow for effective and supervised terms of counselling; and failure to comply with probation conditions seldom results in incarceration.

He pleaded guilty and the judge gave him a one-year probation, and this is after two court judgments against him before .... Who's paying for the crime?

A woman's right to safety must be the first consideration in deliberations on parole. Many parole board members lack expertise in the area of violence against women, particularly expertise drawn from the grass roots of the women's community. Selection criteria are not stringent, and many past appointments have been based on patronage rather than expertise.

Across the country, women told us that parole board practices do not reflect the interests, needs and rights of victims, or the element of danger posed by the abuser. If not appropriately supervised, work release programs and day passes can pose security risks to women. Victims currently cannot participate in parole board hearings even if they want to. They are usually not informed of the date of the abuser's release, and adequate protection is rarely provided for them at that time. Parole conditions seldom, if ever, stipulate the requirement not to enact violence against women.

He is up for parole in four years and for a day pass in two years. I am writing letters asking to speak to the parole board. I sent a copy of the victim-impact statement and a picture of my children. The way I look at it, we have two years to be safe and then it all starts up again.

A pardon is rarely dependent on whether the applicant poses a risk or not. Release decisions are made on the basis of a range of reports from various sources but rarely do they serve the interests of women's safety. Frequently, critical pieces of information do not find their way into these reports, and inappropriate decisions are made. At present, there is no mechanism for co-ordinating release decisions within the Department of the Solicitor General. At a recent coroner's inquest, suggestions for the establishment of an office of the public advocate within Solicitor General Canada were made. This office would act as an independent council with a mandate to review all release decisions.

Correctional Service Canada should also take the management of high-risk offenders more seriously. One suggestion was to create the position of a national co-ordinator for the management of sex offenders. This co-ordinator would report directly to the Commissioner of Correctional Services Canada. To give victims greater protection, authorities would need to share information relevant to the assessment of risk that a particular individual poses to the community. [69]

Lack of faith in the justice system is a consequence of the lack of accountability by public officials regarding violent criminal offences. System reviews to identify problems and make recommendations rarely take place. Inquests are one of a number of sources demanding tighter control on offenders and more accountability by public officials. [70] Inquests are not always held when a woman dies a violent death. Even when they are held, inquests are ineffective because there is no one responsible for implementing their recommendations. They are meant to be "the voice of the dead for the benefit of the living." Much violence is preventable. However, without accountability, the potential benefits of inquest recommendations are lost.

VICTIM AND WITNESS ASSISTANCE

My case has been mishandled by the police, the Crown, the Victim-Witness Program, the hospital. I walked into court alone. I wonder who is accountable to whom, and who is accountable to me. When you stand alone, you cry alone.

At present, the victim is often frozen out of the justice system in Canada. This intensifies the need for victim assistance programs to help survivors deal with the nature of their experiences and avoid being further harmed by the system. Existing programs do not always carry literature and videos in a variety of languages to inform all women of the full extent of their rights, nor do they provide lists of community resource people for women to use for guidance and support. Indeed, some court-based programs only deal with facilitating the movement of the victim through the system and offer little real support. And because funding may go only to institutionalized services rather than to community-based specialized services for women, the knowledge of the issues and the experience held by women's groups is not used sufficiently in the development of advocacy and victim assistance programs.

Victim support must include a co-ordinated community approach among the police, Crowns, judiciary and women working in the front-line services. Although legislation that addresses the concerns of victims of crime exists in all provinces, there is a need for a national strategy similar to the provincial approach introduced in Quebec by the *Act Respecting Assistance for Victims of Crime in Quebec*. This Act enhances the justice system's response to victims' needs by outlining the means and a financial mechanism to co-ordinate assistance. [71]

Greater attention must be directed to the issue of victim compensation. Going through a crime victim's compensation board can be as stressful as going through another trial, since the board process is similar to court hearings. Victims often must forfeit their social assistance cheques when they are awarded compensation. Awards are meant to repair damages done to victims and must be kept apart from any other livelihood. Short and stressful deadlines for claims are inappropriate, as are compensation decisions based on the outcome of a criminal trial. Currently, criminal injury compensation is only awarded when women pursue justice through the criminal process. All victims should be eligible regardless of whether criminal charges are pressed.

Under the current system, compensation awarded to assaulted women for pain and suffering is in the form of hours of counselling. Access to counselling is not always assured, and women are not always able to choose their counsellor and method of counselling.

The court rarely orders the perpetrator to pay for the counselling services required by the victim and other family members. Restitution for costs should be recovered wherever possible. At present, revenue generated from the victim-fine surcharge is often channelled into the consolidated revenue funds of the province. While it should never be the sole funding source for victims' needs, it should be directed into a special fund for victims. For example, surcharges levied against men convicted of sexual assault could help support services for victims of sexual assault.

The time periods of eligibility for compensation for adult survivors of child sexual assault require special attention. In civil law, the Supreme Court has now recognized that existing statutes of limitations which govern the time within which civil actions can be initiated is prejudicial to incest survivors because they do not recognize that women may not be able to recall or report abuse while still under the control of the abuser. New legislation has been passed in Saskatchewan and introduced in Ontario that takes this reality into account. However, there is still discrimination under many provincial statutes and criminal compensation boards. The other provincial governments must re-examine policies to ensure fair and equitable treatment and to recognize the special impediments these victims face when seeking compensation. Often it is years later that the victim is able to define the harm done to her. A strict interpretation of statutes of limitation can therefore pose an insurmountable obstacle to compensation for harm related to childhood sexual abuse. [72]

SOCIO-JUDICIAL INTERVENTION (QUEBEC MODEL)

The socio-judicial approach to effective intervention consists of consideration and understanding of the victim's needs; efforts to ensure adequate, co-ordinated intervention; efforts to obtain an effective and appropriate sentence; and a focus on the rehabilitative aspect of legal intervention.

In Quebec, the concept of joint, multi-disciplinary intervention in cases of violence against women led to the formation of consultation committees to pursue solutions. It was based on the realization that it was not enough to arrest and jail the abuser but that counselling was necessary to get at the source of the problem.

This process gives abused women the support of a multi-disciplinary team at the beginning of and throughout the criminal process. Under these circumstances, women victims of violence are less afraid to talk about their situation and are able to go through the whole legal process. The advantage of socio-judicial intervention is that it encourages violent people to adopt non-violent behaviour. It also sends a message to potential offenders that society does not accept violence.[73]

ADVOCACY

An advocate/counsellor's role is to accompany a victim from the time the police are called through to the end of the court process. It is an essential support especially considering the inequitable support of women in the legal system. Individual advocacy deals directly with the dysfunctional system. Political advocacy works to improve the system by naming the problems and pressing for change. Advocacy at both ends is now carried out by women's organizations but is seldom recognized as a legitimate activity and rarely, if ever, funded.

Upon filing a complaint, victims are seldom provided with an advocate/counsellor. Particularly in rural areas, there are no women's groups to provide support or advocacy for women survivors of physical or sexual assault who attempt to prosecute abuser. In such circumstances, consideration should be given having the police officers work with a woman in the community who could sensitize them to the issues, and who could support the victims of assault.

The courts and law enforcement agencies do not always co-operate with victim advocacy programs to ensure that both the advocacy/shelter groups and the victims are fully informed of their legal rights and the legal processes and procedures.

In this context there is an important role for women's groups. Their knowledge of the issues and of the experiences of women must be used in the development of advocacy and victim assistance programs. At present, limited funding for victims' services and women's centres make it difficult for them to obtain training and carry out advocacy on anything but a part-time and voluntary basis.

LEGAL AID

Women are being revictimized by the system. They are not believed by police, not a priority at legal aid. Victims are made to do most of their legal work.

Gender inequality is an issue in the legal aid system. Because more women than men use the civil court system, the current structure and service delivery of legal aid must be changed to meet women's needs.

Often the legal system presents a formidable challenge to women; it is too big, too complex and insensitive to their needs. Many women are either intimidated or ashamed to approach lawyers for assistance. Legal aid offices and official guardian offices should be restructured so lawyers are not the managers of these services. Lawyers who do accept legal aid cases are often overworked and underpaid, and women suggested that their "total control" often works against the interests of women who seek assistance. [74]

Across the country, there were concerns about legal aid clinic training. Clinic workers, including lawyers and para-legals, need to be more sensitive to the specific dynamics of violence against women. Any increase in the use of para-legals should be matched by increased training and a structure for co-ordinating their activities with other community workers. Clinics must be aware that abused women are generally reluctant to disclose any information about the abuse, to make decisions or to take formal legal action. Women with disabilities or language barriers face even more obstacles when seeking legal aid.

[She] personally faced incredible challenges. Left with over $7,000 debts not including mortgage. Had to find money for divorce. Made too much for legal aid, not enough to pay debts and a lawyer.

Legal aid clinics and services need more funding, particularly in rural and isolated locations. In particular, funding must be expanded to community-based groups to assist elderly women, immigrant women, women with disabilities and poor women. For some women their family income is too high to qualify for legal assistance but they may not be able to gain access to that income or to jointly held assets now controlled by their husbands. Some women have been forced to commit "criminal" acts to protect their children from a violent man. Legal aid for these women as they appear before tribunals or hearings is crucial. All these women present special circumstances that require greater flexibility in decisions to support their applications for legal aid.

The Legal System and the Family

When women's and children's safety and well-being are at stake, "private" settings can become a very public issue. The notion of family privacy must not be used to mask violations of the rights of the individuals in that family. For far too long the notion that families are private and beyond reproach has given men licence to abuse their intimate partners, their children and their parents. Legally, there are ways of fighting such abuse and controlling those who use abuse to their own advantage. [75]

Custody and Access to Children

A man who is willing to physically abuse his wife relinquishes the inherent right to unlimited access and/or custody of the children, and the family courts' decisions must reflect this.

In most cases, courts take the position that it is best for children to keep as much contact as possible with both parents. It is highly unusual for the court to deny a father access to his children unless there is strong evidence that he has abused them. Often court decisions do not recognize that children who witness their mother's abuse are as much the victim of emotional and psychological abuse as if they had been directly assaulted themselves.

I fear for my children. They witnessed violence against women — one woman — their mother. They witnessed a crime that never paid its due. The cycle of violence has not been broken. Will they follow in the same footsteps? The apple does not fall far from the tree.

The Panel heard strong support for recognizing this violence as part of custody and access assessments and deliberations during court hearings about children's "best interests." However, a broader interpretation of "best interests" is needed to ensure that court deliberations go beyond the financial ability to provide.

In Canada, the judiciary equate the best interests of the child almost exclusively with income. As women's economic status is lower than men's, especially following separation, their fear of losing their children is real.

Violent men will use custody proceedings as a way to maintain power and control over their partner.

The legal system has failed my son and me, and helps my ex-husband continue his abuse via the system. He cannot get at me physically and so uses the courts to continue to keep my life in chaos. He's always trying to find something to haul me back into court. No one has ever said I'm a bad mother or a bad person or any such thing, but time after time I am forced to defend myself in court over nonsense issues that judges keep allowing to happen.

Access is often an entry point for ongoing threats, intimidation and harassment of estranged partners and their children. Courts need qualified child assessors who are knowledgeable about violence against women, and they need community services such as supervised centres that allow for some restrictions and provide safety during visitation or access exchange. There was broad support for a review of the *Divorce Act* and all provincial and territorial legislation dealing with custody and access. An amendment to this legislation should explicitly state that violence by one spouse against another is relevant in determining custody and access issues. [76]

DIVORCE AND MEDIATION

A recent federal study revealed that women lose tens of thousands of dollars in earning capacity when they leave work to raise children. This loss is reflected in the lower wages women face when they re-enter the labour force compared with the wages they might expect if they had remained in the work force. Divorce settlements must recognize and reflect the economic gains women have forfeited to raise children. [77] While many judges understand the financial needs of men, they are totally out of touch with the budgets of single mothers. Several studies have suggested that low support payments drive women and children into poverty. [78]

> *Economic stress has been my biggest problem since my divorce. I am always tempted to get married for the economic security.*

Women spoke to the Panel about the inherent dangers in mediation. Mediation should only be used when there is a breakdown in communications. It is not appropriate when there is a history of violence or when custody and access are pending in violent situations. Experience has taught women that their rights are not protected and men can abuse the system freely, either by not showing up for scheduled sessions or constantly holding up the proceedings. Mediators should not assume they are dealing with a normal, non-abusive situation but should determine the root causes of the marriage breakdown.

> *I was forced into legal aid mediation from 9 a.m. to 1 a.m. and forced into an agreement mandated by the director of legal aid. I was not allowed to take a break. The agreement was not in my interest or my son's interest. I was threatened that my legal aid would be taken away. There are tons of loopholes that my husband is using. My husband is using the court system to abuse me. He is raping me financially, physically, sexually.*

Many women's groups have reinforced the importance of training for mediators, lawyers and judges in this area. Informed practitioners have suggested very clear protocols to protect women from being placed in dangerous or compromising positions during mediation. These protocols include detailed information on abuse history before mediation; assured availability of male-female mediator teams; separate interviews to ensure safety and full disclosure; and careful scheduling of appointments to protect victims from chance encounters with an abusive partner and the possibility of further violence. [79]

Women across the country recommended the development of matrimonial property standards that would give women interim possession of the home. Under the Ontario *Family Law Act*, the court can use a history of violence as one criterion in considering an order for exclusive possession for the woman. Although some government documents support this notion,[80] judges rarely give exclusive possession in cases of woman abuse.

SUPPORT AND ENFORCEMENT

Across Canada, we heard suggestions to improve support and enforcement. Evidence indicates that women with children come out of divorce situations in much worse financial shape than do men. Consistency is important in the level of support payments throughout the country. There is also a need for flexibility around the issue of support and enforcement. At present, social services offices can insist that women automatically register for spousal/child support. But when a woman is in danger, her safety could be compromised by an application which would reveal her location to her husband or his lawyer. In these situations the safety of the woman and her children should be of utmost importance and arrangements should be made to make it possible for her to receive support payments without revealing her whereabouts.

The reciprocal enforcement of these orders, from province to province, is of paramount importance. The enforcement of counselling and of legal penalties for non-compliance with support payment orders has been suggested. We also heard support for linking the husband's access to his children directly to performance with maintenance payments.

Garnishee [biological] fathers' wages to support their children. Or, as in Iceland, if a father doesn't support a child at least financially, he is jailed.

We need a mechanism that ensures mandatory payment of child support and allows women to obtain support payments without fear of intimidation. There is an urgent need for a regulatory ethics body with enforcement powers to prevent lawyers from helping men by-pass legislation mandating child support. Women across Canada stated that the support and custody enforcement agencies must use their power to apply liens against property and to seize assets when men default on their support payments. Seizures should be done without notice to prevent offenders from hiding assets through third-party ownership. If the support and custody enforcement agencies are unable to fulfil their mandate, they should be investigated and appropriate changes made.

Maintenance enforcement: the legal system is not doing what they say they are doing, they are not making sure women and children receive their support payments.

CHILDREN

I would like to see young girls protected from molestation, taken out of the house. I would like to see families assessed.

Children and adolescents come to court as young offenders, victims of violence, witnesses to violence and fragile pawns in custody and access disputes. Many women and men across the country expressed concern about the limited knowledge that significant numbers of judges and Crown attorneys have about children. The Panel heard repeated testimony about how children are further harmed by the very system that is supposed to protect them.

The courts need to co-ordinate their responses to the needs of abused women and their children. These needs are best served when police response and court proceedings are well integrated into support services in the community. One important example of this co-ordination is the response to children who witness their mother's victimization. These children suffer some of the same emotional and behavioural adjustment problems as children who are direct victims of violence, yet this often goes unrecognized by child welfare officials who must cope with competing demands for limited resources and who lack knowledge about the issue. Often shelter staff are hesitant to report the impact this violence has on children for fear that the court may punish abused women by threatening to take away their children. There is some consensus that provincial legislation should be amended to ensure the safety of these children and provide adequate resources to help mothers in these circumstances rather than threaten them with dire consequences. [81]

CHILD WITNESSES IN CRIMINAL COURT

There is a need to revise the law to reflect the increasing importance of child testimony in criminal proceedings. Children's court appearances, particularly where children are expected to testify against their abusers, are far too intimidating and traumatic.

The laws regarding child testimony in sexual abuse cases were significantly altered in 1987 [82] to facilitate the prosecution of child sexual abuse in a wider range of cases and to make testifying easier for child complainants. Research sponsored by the Department of Justice, however, revealed that these protections are unevenly applied across the country and are rarely used, [83] often because of a lack of resources and inconsistent training of judges and Crown attorneys.

Under current law, child victims of sexual offences may testify from behind a screen or from another room via closed-circuit video. The intent is to elicit better testimony from the child by reducing or eliminating the trauma of facing the alleged abuser face to face. Amendments are awaiting proclamation which would extend these provisions to include sex offence complainants or anyone who may have difficulty testifying "by reason of mental or physical disability." [84] Extending provisions even further to include cases where witnesses will experience trauma from seeing their abuser was advocated. However, to be used, such provisions must be accompanied by directed funding to cover their costs.

The Panel was told that further revision of child witness procedures is necessary including the waiving of certain evidentiary requirements in the case of children. For example, contradictions in a child's testimony should be given greater latitude than those in an adult's testimony. Hearings on cases that involve child sexual abuse should take place in a special place, such as a judge's chambers or other atmosphere that minimizes the trauma of the child and family. There was strong support for victim advocates to assist mothers who are attempting to prosecute the abusers of their children, and the children themselves. Research suggests that preparing children for court can make the experience less stressful. [85]

YOUNG OFFENDERS

Most Canadians are outraged at the increasing levels of violent crimes by young adolescents. With less tolerance for young persons' criminal behaviour and a demand for "get tough" legislation and programs, the *Young Offenders Act* has become a focal point in the debate about how to hold young persons more accountable for their behaviour. The Panel heard a different kind of concern in its tour. Although there was no doubt that young people need to be responsible for their behaviour at an age-appropriate level, many presenters stressed a need for a better understanding of the roots of violence and for more accessible rehabilitation programs. Many survivors and service providers talked about the clear links between growing up with abuse or witnessing violence and violent behaviour in the community. Too many survivors spoke of intergenerational patterns of violence.

The Panel heard consistent criticism of the *Young Offenders Act*. In many respects, this legislation has come to symbolize the country's inability to come to terms with the cries for help from its young people. More emphasis has been given to providing an adequate number of custody facilities and legal representation than to providing programs for young persons once they have entered the juvenile justice system. The Panel heard severe criticism of the Act's lack of direction and commitment to rehabilitative services. For example, section 22 still allows young persons (including serious sex offenders) to refuse treatment even if it is recommended by a judge, Crown attorney, parents and independent medical or psychological assessment. [86]

When we deal with young offenders, we must recognize that we are often dealing with an offender and a victim at the same time. Many front-line professionals, judges, lawyers and probation officers have not clearly addressed the link between violence at home and youth violence in the community. This is compounded by a lack of rehabilitative services that are essential in preventing an adult life of abuse.

Specific programs are needed to help adolescents deal with drug and alcohol abuse, abusive relationships, violent and impulsive behaviour and sexual abuse. Many adolescent sex offenders will go on to a life that creates literally hundreds of new victims of sexual assault if they do not receive the help they need now.

Recent rehabilitation research has consistently underscored the importance of understanding and targeting the causes of crime through intervention in an effort to reduce crime in general and violent crime in particular. [87] A review of prediction and treatment literature on young offenders yields considerable information about the factors that underlie those young persons at risk for committing crime along with those responses by communities that can either prevent or intervene effectively to reduce crime. [88]

> ... that the delivery of clinically relevant treatment services is a promising route to reduced recidivism. Whatever the social role of punishment, there is simply no evidence that reliance on just desserts or deterrence-based sanctioning will result in substantial reductions in recidivism. Rather, the promise of reduced recidivism resides in delivering appropriate correctional rehabilitative services to young people at risk. This may be accomplished in ethical and humane ways under a variety of conditions of just processing by the courts. [89]

Although 80 to 85 percent of young offenders are male, many jurisdictions across Canada are seeing an increasing number of female young offenders. Data from the Centre for Justice Statistics indicate that violent crime by females is increasing along with the female crime rate. [90]

While there is considerable knowledge on the prediction and treatment of young offenders, the majority of studies are on males. Little is known of the conditions and contexts of crimes committed by young women. [91]

It is important that the whole issue of the growing female crime rate and young female offenders be examined from a feminist perspective. There is potential to get caught up in the fury expressed by Canadians for all crime, and the unique issues confronting young women in Canada will not be duly considered. This involves a re-examination of the *Young Offenders Act* and provincial policies.

STATUTES AND LEGISLATION

INTRODUCTION

The *Canadian Charter of Rights and Freedoms* is an important step toward the goal of equality in Canada, but it is not used vigorously enough to achieve its full potential. The Charter's equality provisions could be used by all legal practitioners and adjudicators to measure and evaluate the impact of their own work on women's safety and equality.

The equality provisions of the Charter were introduced into a backward looking system based on tradition and precedence. The challenge is to balance this framework with new jurisprudence that takes into account the enshrined rights to equal benefit and protection of the law and to security of the person for women as well as men. A number of women impressed upon us that the violence done to them was clearly a violation of the *Canadian Charter of Rights and Freedoms*. The failure of the legal process and practitioners did not live up to the Charter guarantees.

A number of women were also critical of the *Criminal Code*, citing its lack of recognition of the specific dynamics involved in cases of male violence against women in intimate relationships. The *Criminal Code* must reflect a recognition of the physical, sexual and psychological abuse resulting from the subordination of women and children in such relationships.

STALKING AND THREATS OF VIOLENCE

We know that the danger is real, that a battered woman cannot get protection if the batterer makes death threats. Only her death proves that the threats were real.

Stalking is any unwanted communication from persons who have been or who have the potential to be abusive; it is an unmerciful pattern of terrorism that has been inadequately recognized by Canadian law. In some instances, these apparently "nuisance behaviours" end in the death of women. Many women who spoke to the Panel described their frustration and fear as a result of being harassed either by people known to them or by complete strangers.

The major problem with past legislation was that until something physical happens, there [was] no recourse open to women. [92] Relevant provisions in the *Criminal Code* were rarely used. When they were, the charges were for minor offences, and the laws required very unattainable evidence. As many women told us, short of being attacked or raped, they would get little help from the police. Women were frequently told to call the police "when something happens." There have been instances when police have arrested the perpetrator on a charge of mischief or watch and beset, both minor offences that carry a penalty of only six months in prison or a $500 fine. [93]

In cases of abuse and violence, particularly between intimate partners, women have been encouraged to obtain a restraining order. The lack of enforcement of restraining orders and peace bonds severely undermines their strength and offers virtually no protection against stalkers.

My ex-husband is crawling my neighbourhood. He stalks me. They [the police] told me to get a big boyfriend.

The Panel heard from advocates for strong stalking laws that would deal severely with men who repeatedly harass women. While, as we have clearly stated, laws are not the sole solution to violence against women, they give police and the people who work with women a valuable tool to end harassment before it leads to further violence. Alternatives, such as surveillance or incarceration for men who threaten or harass estranged partners and automatic jail sentences for those who repeat this behaviour, were also supported. [94]

In June 1993, Parliament passed a law on criminal harassment to deal more explicitly with stalking. As with all other reforms, implementation must be monitored to gauge effectiveness of the new law.

HIGH-RISK OFFENDERS

Women across the country expressed their distress at the high incidence of recidivism of violent offenders and the failure of the criminal justice system to provide effective support of the public safety. They were adamant about securing greater co-ordination, effectiveness and accountability by public officials in their dealings with those convicted of violent acts.

My abuser had an 18-year record I didn't know about. A person I didn't know came into my life and threatened my life. He got probation for hurting me, hurting my life. I am mad at society for not protecting me. Women aren't even protected from hardened criminals and highly dangerous repeat offenders!

It is widely held that gradual release with supervision is preferable to having an offender leave the penitentiary without a supervised period of re-entry into the community. Generally, an inmate is eligible for day parole after serving one sixth of the sentence in detention, and for full parole after completing one third. If these applications for parole are denied by the Parole Board, most offenders have the opportunity to spend the last one third of their sentence in the community under "mandatory supervision". [95]

Currently, some offenders deemed to be violent may be jailed until the last day of their sentence if a sentencing judge designates them a dangerous offender (DO). According to the existing legislation, an individual must have been convicted of a "serious personal injury offence" prior to the application for DO status by the Crown. At present, an application for this status must be introduced between conviction and sentencing.

Recently proposed high-risk offender legislation moves towards a more realistic assessment of the danger. Proposed amendments would allow the Crown to go to court near the end of a habitual criminal's prison sentence to ask that he or she be designated a dangerous offender. Further, if an offender meets the criteria set out in the dangerous offender provisions, to facilitate intensive long-term supervision, the Court could impose either an additional indeterminate sentence (possibly for life) or a definite sentence.

The draft legislation also stipulates safeguards such as automatic reviews by the National Parole Board of the cases of offenders held after the end of their sentence. [96] In addition, sex offender treatment and community supervision programs would also be intensified and strengthened.

Women across the country highlighted particular concerns in cases of sex offenders. They requested a clear policy or law that would address the legal system's inconsistent handling of sex offenders, both with law enforcement and in court. Dangerous offender applications have been used unevenly in such cases; predictions of dangerousness are markedly inaccurate because they rely on the harms of physical assault much more readily than on the harms of sexual abuse.

Many judges do not understand treatment programs and their limited ability to rehabilitate offenders. Expert testimony on risks posed by the accused is often questionable at best. Many women have requested use of the maximum charges and maximum sentences for sex offenders and for disciplinary procedures against judges who repeatedly make rulings or comments that do not reflect the serious nature of sexual violence.

Sex offenders perpetrate acts of substantial harm which are often not reported; even when they are, the perpetrator frequently re-offends. Incarceration alone is not effective in rehabilitating these men. [97]

These men are not monsters. They are your partners, brothers, neighbours. Because men deny for a long time, this is encouraged in our culture ... we have to help men get in touch with their own pain.

Many programs for sexual offenders are developed without a clear understanding of the dynamics of violence. As a consequence, these programs focus on issues such as sex education and anger management. Issues of power and control dynamics and misogyny must be addressed as part of the programs for rapists and for child molesters just as they are for men who batter. Incarcerated sex offenders should receive programs early in their sentence when the motivation to change is the highest, and before their hope and ability to co-operate have dissolved into cynicism and despair. While often a program is centred on the therapist's ideology, the program itself must be feminist, must force the offender to take responsibility for his violence, and must cover a broad base of problems.

Since the effectiveness of programs is unpredictable, and there is often no clear evidence as to whether an offender is responsive to programs, it is crucial to keep sex offenders under some form of scrutiny for some time after treatment. However, we do know that good programs reduce the number of men who will re-offend. [98] Sex offender programs are in a very early stage of development and are underfunded by the government.

THE RAPE-SHIELD DECISION

On August 22, 1991, the Supreme Court of Canada struck down the provision contained in section 276 of the *Criminal Code*, commonly referred to as the "rape-shield" law. As a result, the complainant's sexual history could not be excluded automatically from evidence in sexual assault trials. The admission of evidence of consensual sexual activity was, once again, at the discretion of the trial judge. On appeal from the Ontario Court of Appeal, a 5-2 majority of the Supreme Court of Canada found that section 276 of the Criminal Code was inconsistent with the *Canadian Charter of Rights and Freedoms* since it could result in the exclusion of evidence necessary for a fair trial and interfere with the principles of fundamental justice. [99]

Amendments to the *Criminal Code* on sexual assault (Bill C-49) came into force August 15, 1992. From the outset, there were continual and extensive consultations with women's groups on the drafting of this legislation. Financial support from the Department of Justice Canada facilitated contact among women and enabled these groups to present a collective position. This new legislation is intended to fill the serious void created when the rape-shield provision was struck down. More than ever before, there was a real attempt to balance the rights of the victim and the accused.

The legislated changes provide judges with clear guidelines for determining whether a complainant's sexual history can be admitted as evidence in sexual assault cases. The legislation stipulates the procedure that must be followed if the accused wants to introduce evidence of the complainant's previous sexual activity, and it places strict limits on the publication of this information. For the first time the term "consent" is defined as "... the voluntary agreement of the complainant to engage in the sexual activity in question." The new law also defines instances where there cannot be "consent" including when "the accused induces the complainant to engage in the activity by abusing the position of power or authority" and when "mistaken belief in consent" is used in defence. [100]

Creating new laws is not enough. Changing legal practice necessitates going beyond legislative reform. If those enforcing and administering the laws do not receive training, they will not appreciate and understand the reasons for reform or the new legislation itself. It is crucial to ensure that they are sensitive to the extenuating circumstances and take into account past abuses and the violent nature of society.

PROSTITUTION

Prostitutes, particularly those working the streets, face overwhelming risks every day. Some researchers found that close to 96 percent of the prostitutes (mostly women) they had interviewed were runaways. Current sentencing practices reinforce the notion that prostitutes are less important than other women, an assumption which is an affront to all women. Sentencing practices and legislation must be linked to an appreciation of the social reality of violence against all women, including prostitutes. For example, legislation that dictates sanctions against women who solicit makes prostitutes even more vulnerable. They cannot call the police for help because they risk being charged. As a consequence, clients often use this vulnerability to their advantage, and women are forced to work in less public, and usually less safe, environments to avoid detection.

PORNOGRAPHY

Depicting women and children in vulnerable, pornographic positions encourages a belief that aggression is OK and that men can use it for their own ends.

♀ ♀ ♀

[There are] portrayals of women on television as the weaker sex, getting abused. Pornography shows women asking to be abused. Women are coerced or economically pushed into prostitution yet will be perceived as looking for abuse.

Women who came forward clearly see violent, degrading pornography and child pornography as forms of violence against women and children. Many had experienced abuse directly, involving the use of pornography in crimes of violence against them or had their abuse filmed to become "entertainment" for others. Pornography promotes and encourages acceptance of other violence and many of the decisions to date on obscenity do not adequately protect women's safety or promote equality. Women who work in support services for abused women told us that many who use their services talk about abusers using pornography.

Governments in Canada have failed to control the distribution of pornography even though Canadian law has proscribed the publication and distribution of obscene material since 1892. The current provisions, legislated in 1959, now are found in section 163 of the *Criminal Code*, under "Offences Tending to Corrupt Morals," which states that any publication, a dominant characteristic of which is the undue exploitation of sex, or sex combined with any one or more of the following subjects, namely, crime, horror, cruelty and violence, will be considered obscene. Unfortunately the law is vague and deals with pornography as an issue of the corruption of morals when the real issue is the harm it causes women.

One of the other shortcomings of the law is that it relies on community standards of tolerance, a situation unlike any other law that deals with harm inflicted. The vagueness of the law and the lack of training in dealing with the harmful aspects of pornography undermine the effectiveness of enforcement both in the legal system and by Canada Customs.

... degrading or dehumanizing material places women (and sometimes men) in positions of subordination, servile submission or humiliation. They run against the principles of equality and dignity of all human beings ...

♀ ♀ ♀

Pornography is the most graphic representation of the attitude toward women which makes rape, wife battering, incest, sexual harassment and women's economic inequality, among other things, possible.

Pornography books are the guerilla manuals for men who want to assault disabled women. There was an article in Hustler about how to hit on a Down's Syndrome girl. Disabled women want independence and self-esteem and we're going to get it!

A recent Supreme Court decision in *R. v. Butler*, did clearly recognize that violent and degrading pornography causes harm to women. In dealing with the constitutional validity of the definition of obscenity in section 163(8) of the *Criminal Code*, the Court found that this section seeks to prohibit certain types of expressive activity and thereby infringes section 2(b) of the *Canadian Charter of Rights and Freedoms*, which guarantees freedom of expression. However, it found the infringement justifiable under section 1 of the Charter which subjects the rights and freedoms set out in it "to such reasonable limits prescribed by law as can be demonstrably justified in a free and democratic society." The Supreme Court agreed that the harm to women that is caused by degrading and violent pornography is of sufficient concern to Canadian society that it constitutes a valid reason for limiting freedom of expression.

In its consideration of the *Charter* questions, the Supreme Court noted that the purpose of section 2(b) of the *Charter* is to ensure that thoughts and feelings may be conveyed freely in non-violent ways without fear of censure. It cited its own recent decision in *R. v. Keegstra*, where it unanimously accepted that the prevention of the influence of hate propaganda on society at large was a legitimate objective. In other words, in the *Keegstra* case the Supreme Court had recognized that:

The harm caused by the proliferation of materials which seriously offend the values fundamental to our society is a substantial concern which justifies restricting the otherwise full exercise of freedom of expression.

In the *Butler* decision, Justice Sopinka acknowledged the important role of education, but held that it should complement legislation, rather than replace it. Education, too, may offer a means of combating negative attitudes to women, just as it is currently used as a means of addressing other problems dealt with in the *Criminal Code*. However, serious social problems, such as violence against women, require multi-pronged, complementary approaches by government. There is nothing in the *Canadian Charter of Rights and Freedoms* that requires Parliament to choose between education and legislation.

Women who spoke to the Panel believe that the *Butler* decision paves the way for decisive government action on pornography. They underscore, however, that government must clearly formulate the law based on concerns about violence, harm and degradation; the law should be careful not to restrict material that depicts mutual sexuality. They insist that women who recognize pornography as harm, and not as a moral issue, must be involved in any undertaking for a new law. Judges, police and other key personnel, such as custom officials, have insufficient knowledge of the *Butler* decision. Women urged that the decision and its implications be more widely publicized and distributed to justice officials throughout Canada.

HATE LITERATURE

Pornography can clearly be seen as hate literature against women, and the distribution of literature which promotes hatred is illegal in Canada under section 281.1 of the *Criminal Code*. As noted above, the Supreme Court has found these provisions to be constitutionally valid. However, offences must be committed "wilfully" and the Attorney General's consent is required before charges can be laid. The Fraser Committee recommended that section 281.1(4) be broadened to include sex, age and mental or physical disability, and that the requirement for the Attorney General's consent and the word "wilfully" be removed from section 281.2(2). This would make prosecutions much easier, since proving that someone intended to promote hatred can be impossible. These recommendations have not been implemented to date.

THE PROVINCES

Under Canada's Constitution, provincial attorneys general enforce the *Criminal Code*, and have the right to make laws establishing provincial censor (or classification) boards. Some attorneys general, as in British Columbia, have attempted to interpret "undue exploitation" under section 163.8 through guidelines issued to Crown counsel. These list types of material which could be a violation of community standards and which are used in determining whether charges should be laid in obscenity cases. Often such guidelines are put into a moral context and prohibit sexually explicit material while allowing free circulation of material that is degrading to women.

The provinces may enact legislation such as human rights acts. However, no province currently has a human rights act which deals directly with pornography. Section 14(1) of the *Saskatchewan Code* prohibits "the publication or display of material which restricts a person's guaranteed rights, exposes him or her to hatred, or affronts the dignity of any person on the basis of sex, race, creed, religion, colour, marital status, physical disability, age, nationality, ancestry, or place of birth." It was used in the successful prosecution of the *Red Eye*, a newspaper published by the Engineering Students' Society at the University of Saskatchewan. [101]

British Columbia's *Civil Rights Protection Act* has provisions which could be amended to allow individual victims and groups of victims of pornography to sue. The Fraser Committee recommended enactment of this kind of legislation to provide stronger civil remedies. This was supported by women's groups but the recommendation has not been implemented.

MUNICIPAL LICENSING AND BY-LAWS

Under the municipalities Acts, provinces can give over some areas of provincial jurisdiction to the cities. Cities cannot prohibit the sale of "sexually oriented material," but they can regulate businesses, traffic, etc. within their boundaries. Some cities have passed by-laws prohibiting the display of sexually explicit material below a certain eye-level or specifying that it be behind an opaque barrier. However, a Montreal by-law which prohibits display signs outside businesses which distribute or present "erotic" material was found to be "unconstitutional" by a judge of the Quebec Superior Court. Because the province empowered the city to pass the by-law, city officials plan to appeal. Meanwhile, the by-law will stay in effect. [102]

CIVIL REMEDIES

The Panel heard from women who believe that women should have the right to sue for injuries that result from pornography. They also emphasized that a civil remedy might contribute to our knowledge of the issue. As experience in setting up shelters for battered women and rape crisis centres tells us, women come forward when they see a way out and when their experiences are given validity. By providing victims with civil recourse, more information about the relationship between pornography and abuse from the perspective of the victims can be obtained. As civil law recognizes other injuries, justice requires that injuries inflicted by pornography be addressed in civil codes.

SEXUAL ABUSE INVOLVING BREACH OF TRUST

I'm from a small community. I have been harassed by a doctor since I was 15; I'm 23 now. Since then, five more of his victims have come to light. I was raped twice at 16 and 18. I'm scared of all forms of control over me.

The Panel's hearings left little doubt that sexual abuse involving breach of trust is pervasive in Canada. Many of the perpetrators are members of self-regulatory professions such as medicine, dentistry and law.

Although judges seem to understand other forms of breach of trust, such as financial breach of trust, sexual abuse that involves a breach of trust is one of the least understood forms of violence. It is still confused by the courts with consensual sexual activity because physical force is rarely used. It is also farthest from male judges' experience of assault which usually includes some kind of force and possibly a weapon to overpower the victim. When trusted individuals use their power and authority to overwhelm and then sexually violate, victims suffer substantial harm, but their ability to report the abuse and to be believed are severely compromised.

The present Criminal Code provisions for sexual assault do not explicitly identify assault by a person in a position of power or authority as an assault or, more properly, as an aggravated assault. The most recent amendments do recognize, however, that there can be no consent if the person accused is in a position of power or authority. The *Criminal Code* now states: "No consent is obtained ..., where ... the accused induces the complainant to engage in the activity by abusing a position of trust, power or authority."

Later, I was sexually assaulted by a chiropractor and by a doctor. The doctor was charged, and the police took over 200 statements from witnesses but the courts determined that he was too valuable to go to jail.

Sexual abuse involving a breach of trust is regulated through civil law as well as criminal law. The burden of proof for civil cases is deliberately less onerous than in criminal law; the sanctions and the purposes are also different.

One of the functions of civil legislation is to regulate the use of power by those members of society who are granted extraordinary power to carry out their jobs. Members of self-regulating professions enjoy two sources of power. One is associated with the status of their individual professions and one results from the authority to self-regulate that has been granted by governments. Removal of abusers from positions of trust, authority or power is critical to the safety of women and children who are in contact with them or will likely have contact with them in the future.

A great deal of attention has focused recently on the sexual exploitation and abuse of patients and clients by health professionals. Task forces have documented the existence of the abuse in the medical profession, and in one province new legislation has been introduced with the different levels of sexual abuse and related sanctions clearly articulated to respond more effectively and specifically to problems.

There has been a recognition that a more stringent level of safeguard must be imposed on self-regulating professions for several reasons. First, the nature of the relationship with the professional, particularly a health care professional, is such that it is necessary to discard some of the conventional boundaries and safeguards we have in society. We undress, submit to intimate examinations and touching, and disclose highly personal information to someone who minutes before might have been a stranger to us. If it is a therapeutic relationship, the power of decision making and judgment handed over to the therapist is particularly great. This extra level of trust decreases the likelihood of disclosure by the victim and increases the possibility that such reports will not be believed. Detection measures must be sensitive to subtle indications of abuse, and since public behaviour is not a good indicator of the propensity to abuse or to repeated abuse, detection and deterrence measures must be sensitive and effective.

Civil law suits constitute another important legal area. Women have begun taking civil actions against their abusers, but recognition by the courts of harm to victims has been very uneven. Sometimes with cases involving sexual abuse by a person in a position of trust, the courts have not recognized the abuse at all [*Norberg v. Wynrib* (BCCA), December 7, 1989 (unreported)]. However upon appeal to the Supreme Court, the abuse was recognized and an award made.

GUN CONTROL

Forty-seven percent of women killed by their spouses are shot. [103] Many of the people who approached the Panel from across the country felt that legislated gun control is one element in a co-ordinated national prevention strategy that would reduce risk for women. They advocated the registration and sale limitations of all firearms. Regulation would forewarn police of the presence of firearms when called on the scene of a domestic dispute, encourage owners to respect safe storage requirements and support enforcement of prohibition orders in cases of wife assault.

While recent federal legislation is a step in the right direction, there are many shortcomings. This law fails to ban all military assault rifles and ignores the requirement to have a family member who knows the applicant to act as one of the two references required on the application. The lax new storage requirements, exemptions on illegal high-capacity magazines and failure to control ammunition sales continue to pose unnecessary risks to women and the general public.

EQUALITY AND THE CANADIAN CHARTER OF RIGHTS AND FREEDOMS

Gender inequality plays a major role in violence against women ... this is the 25th anniversary of women being able to sit in a jury. Why does the government identify women as a special interest group? This does not imply that women are equal.

Women are not a special interest group. To designate 52 percent of the population as a special interest group is based on sexist logic and the overwhelming patriarchy of the society in which women's equality is sought. The *Canadian Charter of Rights and Freedoms* establishes women's equal claim to all aspects of Canadian society not as an appendage but as an integral part of the whole.

The *Canadian Charter of Rights and Freedoms* is an important starting point for legal professionals in developing, implementing and reviewing their work in the context of equality and freedom from violence for all those in Canada. The struggle for equality and justice in the legal system has brought important reforms in the past decade. Judges are slowly beginning to acknowledge the need for understanding women's inequality and the specific nature and context of violence against women. Slowly, judges are also recognizing that violence enacted against women deprives them of the promised equal benefit and protection of the law. The need for education in these areas for all legal practitioners is pressing. Many who need the training most do not elect to take it.

Ironically, access to the Charter through the courts is limited for many women on one hand, while activist groups observe that on the other hand, the Charter equality provisions are being misused to protect those for whom it is not intended: powerful business interests and those in the community who are disadvantaged by equality. This distortion combined with a long history of prejudicial attitudes in the legal system and a jurisprudence that predates the Charter equality guarantees points to the long road ahead before the vision put forth in the *Canadian Charter of Rights and Freedoms* is a reality in Canada. The suspension of funding for the Court Challenges Program, which assisted groups using the Charter to fight for issues of equality, has been a dramatic blow against women's equality.

Violence is far less likely between equals ... therefore, equality and respect of all people is a crucial concept which must be realized ... women have not yet achieved equality and this must be redressed. Otherwise our equality is not guaranteed.

Women across the country called for a number of changes to existing legislation and statutes to ensure compliance with sections 7 and 15 and 28 of the *Canadian Charter of Rights and Freedoms:*

> Section 7: Everyone has the right to life, liberty and the security of the person and the right not to be deprived thereof except in accordance with the principles of fundamental justice.

> Section 15: Every individual is equal before and under the law and has the right to the equal protection and equal benefit of the law without discrimination and, in particular, without discrimination based on race, national or ethnic origin, colour, religion, sex, age, or mental or physical disability.

> Section 28: Notwithstanding anything in this Charter, the rights and freedoms referred to in it are guaranteed equally to male and female persons.

Interpretation of the Charter must be broad enough to ensure that women have the same degree of "security of the person" as do men. The rights to "equal protection and equal benefit of the law" are enshrined in the Charter: the challenge is to make those rights a reality.

We heard support for a victim-centred, Charter-informed review of the justice system. This would provide the government with an opportunity to assess the laws and the administration of those laws against Charter guarantees to women, for example to measure the ability of laws to provide protection, benefit and security of the person. This Charter review would include:

- all legislation including all related regulations, policies, procedures and guidelines in all provinces;

- current practices and policies for appointments, hiring and training of all criminal justice participants and all those involved in the quasi-judicial processes;

- all protocols for dealing with victims of crime in the system; and

- the government's execution of responsibility, in terms of security of the person under section 7 of the Charter, that creates certain rights for the victims and obligations for government. [104]

CONCLUSION

We are taught from an early age to believe that we have recourse to the legal system for justice and safety. "The police officer is your friend." "Justice will prevail." Unfortunately, as we heard many times over, this image does not fit the reality of women who have experienced male violence. No aspect of the legal system is innocent. Women across the country expressed frustration, anger and scepticism about both the law and its administration. The legal system reflects and enforces the sexist and racist structures of Canadian society, and serves those interests, not those of women.

The legal system in Canada, in every aspect, at every stage, has been built around elite white male concerns and needs. As a system designed to protect property and maintain the status quo, it functions well. As a safeguard for the safety of women, children and men and as an administrator of justice, it fails on almost every count. The separate aspects of the legal system — courts, parole boards, police departments, legislators, law schools and many others — cannot be viewed in isolation from each other. Unless the entire fundamental base of justice in Canada is changed, to make women's needs and realities a priority, reforms will continue to be unevenly applied and ultimately to be ineffective. All those involved in the legal system in Canada must decide, both as individuals and as practitioners within institutions, whether or not they support the fundamental goals of equality and safety for all. This is the commitment which must be made, if Canadian legal institutions are to be worthy of the term "justice system."

CHAPTER 19

THE WORKPLACE

INTRODUCTION

Working for pay has become an increasingly important component of the lives of women in Canada. An examination of the relationship between paid work and women's experiences of violence, both direct and indirect, makes it over-whelmingly clear that the workplace reinforces inequality and unequal power relations on the basis of gender, race and class. When women see their work undervalued and underpaid, they receive potent messages about themselves and their social and economic value.

CHANGING THE WORKPLACE ENVIRONMENT

Many women face threats of assault and job loss, as well as actual assault and harassment every day in their workplaces. For some women these messages and actions of violence are comp-ounded by racism, class prejudice and discri-mination based on sexuality, age and ability level. Such conditions intensify women's vulnerability to violence and make their experiences of paid work more difficult and more dangerous.

> The woman in question had suffered six years of sexual and racist harassment at her place of employment, and as a result suffered from a nervous breakdown that prevented her from returning to work for four years ... sexual and racial harassment on the job is injurious to women's health ... sexual harass-ment makes women of colour particularly vulnerable to workplace harassment. Often women of colour are forced to work in a destructive environment which severely limits their opportunities. [105]

When speaking of the workplace, a woman with disability says:

> *When you are disabled, you have to prove all the time that you can do it. People just don't believe in you.*

In male-dominated occupations women face both overt and subtle forms of violence. The more insidious might include lack of integration into work units, isolation and lack of adequate facilities and privacy. A "male-dominated" work culture brings with it different vocabularies, social norms and practices, inherent sexism and an atmosphere that denigrates women.

> *Of course there is the violence you would expect, sexual harassment that takes the form of pin-ups, comments, leering, touching and violent language, sometimes directed at the woman or at women in general, but even more often simply buried in the traditions of the job .... You are not only a woman, you are the exception, the freak. Everyone knows your name, you don't know theirs.*
>
> ♀ ♀ ♀
>
> *I was a businessperson selling computers. I was the only woman and put up with dirty jokes, pretending I didn't care, trying to be a man.*

Health care workers told the Panel of the high risk associated with their work and argued that employers must create policies to deal with unsafe work environments, working alone, abuse, violent situations when dealing with patients and lack of support systems for victims. Shift work presents particularly high risks, with women finding themselves in isolated environments late at night. In addition, more subtle forms of violence such as being isolated, being subject to intense verbal, emotional, physical and environ-mental harassment and abuse often go unnoticed.

[I] was assigned to [a] suicidal patient who was hallucinating; in the course of five minutes the course of my life was changed. I felt a crunch of my face. I suffered a serious assault that ended my career as a nurse. Although the assault was a crime, I was discouraged [from] laying charges by the administration. The violence I suffered was not acknowledged ....

In service industries, where women are overrepresented, they are vulnerable to violence from members of the public who vent their frustrations at "the system", at policies or at the employees. This is front-line violence, often motivated by the same unequal power relations which lead to violence against women in the broader societal context. The Public Service Alliance of Canada which, as of March 1993, represents 142,000 federal public servants, has documented several cases.

The Canadian Labour Congress, during its 19th Constitutional Convention, in June 1992, stated that:

> Placing workers in stressful and confrontational contact with the public, inmates or clients without the proper security backup is an invitation for the violent expression of sexist, racist or homophobic attitudes against those workers. In Ottawa, a female halfway-house worker was murdered by an inmate already convicted of crimes against women. The employer's response was not to improve security and increase staffing levels, but to bar women employees from night duty. The refusal by employers, in the name of efficiency, to take responsibility in this area, is nothing less than criminal negligence. [106]

To some extent, workplaces tend to value and reward qualities that are often antithetical to the ways in which women operate in the world. While we must be careful not to reduce the distinctions between men and women to biologically determined differences, we recognize that the ways in which women work and experience the world may support a completely different orientation to accomplishing tasks, based on the principles of co-operation, sharing and consensus building as opposed to tough competition and empire building.

Women want more employers to commit to employment and pay equity, to promote them to senior management and to hire them in non-traditional occupations. Since part-time work is precarious and unprotected, women have asked for changes to employment standards laws that would provide part-time workers with the same level of protection, wage rates, job security, benefits and prorated pensions that full-time workers receive. "Women have more difficulty entering the workplace in full-time jobs than do men. They more often have access to part-time work. In Quebec, some 22.4 percent of women work part-time, compared to 6.8 percent men. This rate may even exceed 50 percent in some employment ghettos. Women earn two thirds of what men earn. What is more, 66 percent of workers earning minimum wage are women. Most of the working women in unstable jobs are excluded from the social security programs available in a number of businesses (sick leave, insurance, pension funds, etc.)." [107]

Lack of affordable and flexible child care is also a structural barrier to women's economic equality. "Today's working world was designed for men whose wives stay home. As many as 64 percent of mothers of children under 6 years of age were in the labour force in 1991. However, whereas an increasing number of mothers of young children work and need high-quality child care services at a reasonable price, the government has slowed growth in the child care services sector to its lowest level in 10 years." [108] This impediment is compounded by women's unequal access to job and language training and other skills development courses. Integration of family and work site should also be studied. Policies on family-related leave time, flexible hours, work-at-home provisions and other creative work-related alternatives are needed to establish an environment which promotes equity-based relationships between men and women in and out of the workplace. Over and over, we were told that economic parity for women must be a fundamental part of the strategy to eliminate violence against women.

MANAGEMENT AND UNION RESPONSIBILITIES

A woman who sits on a committee with a man who, during his lunch hours, habitually plays a video game with the goal of raping a female figure, asks: "How can he treat me as a respected equal when he has just spent his lunch hour trying to rape a woman?" [109]

It is the responsibility of the employer to ensure that all employees are able to work in a harassment-free environment. At present, few workplaces have progressive policies and programs on sexual harassment, race and ethnic relations, employment and pay equity. Their actions, when they do take action, are usually ad hoc in response to individual incidents of violence or harassment, an approach that cannot possibly sustain the long-term changes required.

Employers must understand that they have a role to play in supporting women if they are being assaulted.

Since the Supreme Court precedent-setting ruling in *Robichaud v. Canada* (Treasury Board), [1987] 2SCR 84) on employer liability for acts of sexual harassment committed by its employees, employers have been formulating policies and regulations on sexual harassment. In some cases, sexual harassment training sessions intended for managers are being given. However, they usually focus on employer liability and how to avoid it rather than on the rights of the victims, complaint procedures, conducting investigations and disciplinary measures. [110]

Even where workplaces have established policies and programs, they are often written in cumbersome legal language. The Panel was told that, on the whole, unions and management have done a poor job in identifying and spelling out complaint, grievance and investigative procedures, sanctions and courses of action. Often employers do not understand that disciplinary action is a necessary part of the policy. More important, most employers have failed to educate their employees, no matter what level, on the impact and consequences of workplace violence and harassment.

Employers should react to violence against women the same as they would be quick to act if someone had broken a window!

Although it is estimated that 50 to 90 percent of women have been harassed in the workplace, [111] few incidents are reported because of the employer's failure to provide a safe environment for the lodging of complaints.

Employees must feel confident that the employer will handle complaints competently through an investigative procedure that will result in an appropriate resolution.

Other reasons for low rates of reporting include the fear of ridicule, embarrassment, reprisals and of not being believed.

All too often, survivors of workplace violence and harassment are penalized for the audacity to confront their abusers and to seek reparation from their employers. We heard of incidents where the offending man was still working with or supervising a woman who had lodged a complaint about him. Harassers are not routinely moved out of the work area after the first complaint or during investigational procedures. A woman's livelihood may be threatened if she is forced to continue working with the harasser who may continue his harassment and may now have retribution added to his motives. If anyone is transferred to another area, it is often the employee being harassed. She is thus being denied the right to work in the position for which she was originally hired. Generally the employee is transferred because she, and her skills, are less valued than her abuser's.

The workplace is a hierarchy, and confronting sexist and harassing behaviour in that context can often mean:

> ... seeking redress from others with power, who share the same prejudices and biases as the abuser .... And because of the deeply ingrained sexist attitudes and values which are part of our culture, a victim of harassment may receive little or no support from her co-workers and even, sadly, from her union. [112]

It's too easy for society to excuse men by saying that's just how they are. For example, when someone reported sexual harassment, the boss just said, "well, that's just how men are," and that's a typical reaction when women complain, then there is no discipline taken at all against the men.

♀ ♀ ♀

Although we may report cases of sexual harassment, it's difficult to speak up when the people in authority to whom you report these problems laugh and think it's funny or that the behaviour is harmless.

The ability to work well is directly related to a safe workplace; this is a message we heard across the country. Women want employers to recognize work-site hazards and provide adequate security to ensure their safety. Some women recommended that employers expand Employee Assistant Programs (EAP) in the workplace to create greater awareness of the problem; to inform employees of community resources; and to encourage women to acknowledge their victimization and break their silence by providing them with a safe atmosphere in which to do so.

Many unions have failed to make ending violence against women a priority. They have failed to bargain for strong action on employee harassment or to extend collective bargaining protection to groups of women who are at greater risk of violence because of discrimination. These include lesbians, women of colour, immigrant women, women with disabilities, poor women, elderly women, women from linguistic minorities and women with low literacy skills. All too oftenpolicies and actions around harassment are traded away at the bargaining table. Women want unions and employers to understand the impact of all forms of violence on women. Stress and fear (whether as a result of violence at home or work) may lead to frequent absences, decreased productivity, low morale and poor work performance. Potential victims must be made aware that the workplace is safe and that there are support options for them.

[Unions] must encourage distribution of information on self-help literature and access of services to all employees, contract workers, sponsor public information campaigns and awareness sessions. Programs should be given in the working day as a general workshop for all staff to allow for anonymity and access.

Many unions, particularly those in a predominantly male work force, continue to reflect patriarchal assumptions and have not chosen to acknowledge harassment within their own membership. Unions have not actively encouraged women to fill executive positions or to participate in policy formulation.

Often if union leaders are male, women don't talk about why they're leaving their job.

Even more damning is the reticence of unions to act against sexism, racism and violence in the workplace; in effect, their inaction is tantamount to tolerance of violence in the workplace. Many women told the Panel that one solution would be sensitivity training, education and information on these issues and on alternative work environments and working relationships, provided by both employers and unions with the assistance of local women's organizations.

In some unions, attitudes to equality and safety issues are improving. "Within the Public Service Alliance of Canada, 34 percent of the chairs of union locals are occupied by women, and, in overall terms, women occupy 48 percent of executive positions within locals." [113]

- In a policy statement dealing with violence against women, the Canadian Labour Congress identified the need for clear policies and procedures to be laid down to ensure members' rights with respect to harassment during all union events. [114] The CLC also called upon affiliates to make a priority of collective bargaining agreement provisions to ensure protection against gender-related violence in the workplace and to provide paid leave for women who are victims of violence wherever it occurs. [115]

- A labour group in Toronto has sponsored workplace seminars on violence against women based on a feminist analysis of gender, race and class. The focus is on sexual assault, sexual harassment and woman abuse. The seminars highlight how violence affects women's working lives and outlines what men can do to stop the violence.

- The Canadian Auto Workers union has introduced a policy on violence against women and an advertising campaign on how it affects their members.

HEALTH AND SAFETY ISSUES

Existing health and safety legislation fails to reflect the impact of violence on health and does not consider women's needs related to the violence they experience. Occupational health and safety legislation rarely, if ever, allows employees to refuse work when it is unsafe due to harassment or potential violence without loss of wages. Moreover, workers compensation boards do not recognize injury from sexual harassment or post-traumatic stress disorders (PTSD). Those who study PTSD have found that, after experiencing severe and unexpected trauma, or being repeatedly and unpredictably exposed to abuse, most people tend to develop certain psychological symptoms that continue to affect their ability to function long after the original trauma. They may believe that they are essentially helpless, lacking power to change their situation. There are significant behavioural, cognitive and affective symptoms that are recognizable to appropriately trained mental health professionals. These can include recurring nightmares, sleep disorders, daydreams, intrusive thoughts that the abuse is reoccurring, flashbacks, a sense of powerlessness, a loss of control, isolation, depression, loss of interest in other people and activities, generalized anxiety, panic attacks, fears, phobias, sexual dysfunctions (in case of sexual abuse), and irritability. [116]

However, steps to include these issues within occupational health and safety guidelines and legislation are taking place. In the past, employers have dismissed or failed to react to incidents; ministries of labour have refused to investigate incidents; workers' compensation boards have denied claims and joint health and safety committees have refused to consider the issue when defining violence as a threat to health and safety.

A unique initiative has come from the Saskatchewan Ministry of Labour which has proposed amendments to its *Occupational Health and Safety Act* to address the problems of workplace harassment and violence.
The proposed definition of harassment includes [Article 2(1)(1)(i)]:

> Any objectionable conduct, comment or display by a person, made on a one-time basis or a continuous basis that: (A) is directed at and is offensive to a worker ... (C) may result in ill health or physical injury to the worker, and (ii) includes harassment on the basis of age, ancestry, colour, disability, physical size or weight, marital status, nationality, place of origin, race, religion, sex or sexual orientation. [117]

The definition of occupational health and safety in this proposed amendment includes: "the promotion and maintenance of a working environment that is free of harassment." [Article 2(1)(p)(v), p. 3]. Furthermore, it also clearly defines employer responsibility: "[to] ensure, insofar as is reasonably practicable, that the employer's workers are not exposed to harassment at the place of employment ...." [Article 3(c), p.6], as well as defining duties of workers including the need to "refrain from causing or participating in the harassment of another worker." [Article 4(b), p. 6]. The legislation also looks at the issue of violence in Article 14: "An employer at a prescribed place of employment shall develop and implement a policy statement to deal with potentially violent situations at the place of employment ...." [Article 14(1), p. 11].

CONCLUSION

Violence in the workplace is experienced in both subtle and overt forms by women every day. Employers fail to recognize that women's job performance will be affected by violence against them in any context and provide inadequate support for women victims of violence. The economic inequality of women leaves them more vulnerable to workplace violence. Women's workplace safety and their economic advancement are shared responsibilities of government, management and organized labour, and these jurisdictions must act to make women's safety their business. Women must have safe workplaces.

CHAPTER 20

WOMEN AND THE MILITARY

INTRODUCTION

There are two very different but related issues addressed in our discussion of women and the military: the situation and treatment of spouses of military personnel and sexual harassment, sexism, sexual assault and homophobia in the treatment of female members of the Canadian Forces. While we know that the issues are separate and distinct, we also know that they are inextricably linked to the overall culture that is the essence of military life.

MILITARY LIFE AND CULTURE

There is little denying that in many ways, the military is a world of its own. There is an over-riding "maleness" to military life. Military values place highest emphasis on physical strength, obedience, aggression and unquestioning acceptance of authority. The military is textured by a steep hierarchy with strict rules and a chain of command to ensure that all occurrences in the military are monitored and regulated by those in control.

> The very maleness of the military — the brute power of weaponry exclusive to their hands, the spiritual bonding of men at arms, the manly discipline of orders given and orders obeyed, the simple logic of the hierarchical command — confirms for men what they long suspect, that women are peripheral, irrelevant to the world that counts, passive spectators. [118]

Women as workers and as dependants are still perceived as unwelcome subordinates in the military world. The Canadian Forces have, until recently, excluded women from many occupations and command positions with the result that there are few women in positions of power.

Their unequal status as employees is reflected in barriers to full participation and a high prevalence of sexual and other forms of workplace harassment. Lagging response times and the inefficient handling of harassment complaints intensify women's unequal status and increase their vulnerability to violence. Although formal policies are in place, their enforcement is weak.

The sometimes severe isolation, and the institutional expectations of loyal support on the part of military wives toward their husbands and their husbands' jobs, fuel the potential for male abuse of power and heighten the vulnerability of the wives. Taken together, the philosophy, culture and various organizational structures and features of the military contribute to an atmosphere where violence against women is tolerated and even fostered.

VIOLENCE AGAINST MILITARY WIVES

The military culture is compounded by the structure and organization of military life. Military personnel have limited input regarding when and where they move. Their spouses and families suffer the consequences, moving frequently with little advance notice. This mobility undermines the ability of military wives to develop and maintain secure roots, both on and off bases. Women's long-term friendships, support networks, family ties and careers are always subject to military rules and their husbands' careers which hinge on accepting whatever assignment they receive.

Military procedures often require husbands to be absent from their wives and families for extended periods of time. It is not unusual for men to be away for months or for shorter periods at regular intervals. For women these absences can translate into long periods of stress, strain and responsibility that leave them feeling isolated and lonely. Often women adjust to the role and when their partners return, the readjustment is difficult. Compounded by the lack of access to family and friends, military wives are extremely vulnerable physically, financially and psychologically.

As military family members, spouses are under strong pressure to conform to traditional roles that support a patriarchal family structure. As dependants, women and children are controlled by the military through their husbands and through policies, programs and procedures from within the military organization. As a result, the violence experienced by wives is often the result of a lack of respect and an undervaluing of their contributions to military life.

The nearly total exclusion of dependants from military benefits and policy making is disempowering, which in turn helps perpetuate the abuse. Certain policies within the military mean that spouses have no legitimate avenues for influencing their home and work environments. We heard a litany of concerns about the lack of support systems on bases for military spouses; about their exclusion from positions on bases; the scarcity and inappropriateness of resources; and, in light of recent budget cuts to the Canadian Forces, fears of reductions to existing social services. Funds for activities of military wives, particularly for organizations seeking to change the status quo, are limited, and some activities are explicitly banned. These features of military life undermine the control women have over their own lives and increase the likelihood that they will be subjected to sexism and a general insensitivity toward any violence they may suffer.

A woman who had been posted overseas with her violent husband described to us her attempts to obtain social support and legal help from the base. On inquiring about a counsellor she had heard about who was a five-and-half-hour drive from the base, she was informed by a military lawyer that only military members were entitled to counsel in marital matters. She was advised to return to Canada for immediate private legal advice, an impossible solution for her. When the violence became worse her husband "was hurriedly posted back to Canada." However, she was forced by the military to remain behind for the sake of her children's schooling. Once back in Canada, her husband had time to liquidate all their savings, real estate and insurance. When she finally returned to Canada "financially crippled," the military absolved itself by claiming that estranged families were not its responsibility.

There I was with two children and three suitcases representing 20 years of marriage — no home, and still hundreds of miles from family, no support, no medical coverage .... My self-esteem was non-existent and my self-confidence shattered. I did not deserve to be treated like landfill refuse and neither did my children. The Department of National Defence stood by my husband in the days following and allowed him to deny support for his family, forcing us to go on welfare. This proud soldier even denied food for his own children and still the military refused to help. Finally after a few weeks in slow legal processes, a garnishment was enacted and stopped us from becoming street people.

Such experiences are particularly unacceptable in light of the fact that the military simply could not operate without the support of spouses and families. Families are certainly regarded as cornerstones of a man's success within the military, and married men are more likely to get promotions than are men without families or men living with women outside marriage. There is a lot of pressure on wives to "be a part of the military husband-wife team, even though she is not paid for her partnership"; she must not embarrass her husband or jeopardize his career with inappropriate behaviour, such as complaining about abuse or filing for a divorce.

Our stories are not unique by any means, but many women are afraid to come forward with their stories, especially wives still married to military members, because if this knowledge was to become widespread it becomes harmful to their spouses' careers.

The existing chain of command also places pressure on commanders. Commanders do not want their superiors to know of violence within their units. They seek to resolve problems quietly, before the superior realizes there is a problem. "Family problems" hinder the smooth functioning of the military machine. Therefore, the emphasis is often on silencing the problem by ignoring the issue. This fact, as well as the total lack of privacy or confidentiality afforded to members of the military or to their families, enhances the difficulties of military wives who have suffered violence in their relationships. They are often less likely to seek help outside their family and when they do, their experiences will likely become grist for the public gossip mill.

Response to violence against women is further complicated by the lack of consistency in policy and its application across bases. Police response to incidents of violence against military wives living on bases has always been hampered by a shared responsibility between military and civilian police jurisdictions. Only recently has the military police been given the mandate to lay charges. However, it is at their discretion to decide whether to lay charges and whether the case is "serious" enough to hand over to civilian police. The lack of consistent policies among bases means that women are subjected to the discretionary power of individuals who may themselves be sexist or violent. A woman moving from one base to another must constantly relearn, often through bitter experience, the policies of each military base. These inconsistencies are compounded for women living in a foreign culture.

In May 1989, National Defence Headquarters presented its Study Report on Family Support which suggested the establishment of Family Support Centres on all bases. [119]

There are now over 30 such support centres across Canada, providing useful resources and meeting places for women who are victims of violence. Their effectiveness seems, however, to depend on how they are operated: whether they are run by an independent professional, whether they have the authority to operate without interference from the military chain of command, the nature of the services they provide and the availability of information in many languages. According to some women we talked to, their effectiveness is also impeded by the fact that their financing is controlled by base commanders, in effect allowing them to determine how and by whom the centres will be controlled and used.

VIOLENCE AGAINST WOMEN MILITARY PERSONNEL

The case of a corporal at a base in Comox, B.C. who recently filed a formal complaint regarding sexual harassment with the Canadian Human Rights Commission, and a number of other cases of sexual harassment on the same base, demonstrate the difficulty military women have with sexual harassment in the military environment. The corporal, a 10-year veteran, was threatened with discharge for insubordination and forced to undergo a psychological exam following her complaints of repeated verbal violence. As well, her supervisors were said to have stepped up the harassment after she lodged a complaint. [120]

In 1989, another woman complained about a supervisor at National Defence Headquarters who touched her inappropriately and called her at home and asked about her sex life. She was told she was too sensitive. Eventually, she filed a formal grievance, and DND responded by formally acknowledging her complaint and offering her $25,000 as compensation. However, the woman refused the money and now wants to know what disciplinary action was taken against her supervisor. She wants to know whether he was dealt with as severely as he deserved, or whether he merely received a slap on the wrist. The *Privacy Act* makes this information unavailable to her. [121]

These are two examples of the harassment and abuse to which women in the military are subjected on a daily basis. Women account for approximately 10.5 percent of the members of the Canadian Forces. [122] Yet according to a survey of 5,642 Canadian Forces members conducted in October 1992 by National Defence, more than one quarter of women reported that they have been sexually harassed in the last year, mostly by older, married men. Most of the women's complaints were about sexual teasing, sexual looks and body language, and dirty words creating "an offensive, hostile or intimidating environment." Only one in five women lodged a formal complaint, partly because they feared it would hurt their careers. [123] These findings were echoed in a report prepared by a civilian board, the Minister's Advisory Board on Women in the Canadian Forces (MABWCF) which said that harassment in its various forms is reported by women throughout the Canadian Forces.[124]

While the MABWCF believes that the Canadian Forces' zero tolerance system appears to work in most cases, "... it is the almost routine denigration of women's participation by some seniors and peers that undermines integration."[125]

Harassment ranges from irritating comments or insults to serious, sustained and collective verbal attacks intended to destroy confidence and commitment. Statements of rejection or non-acceptance, such as "you do not belong" or "women should not be here," gender-related epithets, obscene anatomical references, deroga-tory references to female physiological functions, blaming or scapegoating women for pregnancy, inequitable treatment of genders (the "double standard") and collusion among peers or juniors are all forms of violence that make life difficult for women.[126] The MABWCF emphasizes that such forms of harassment are symptomatic of larger problems.

> The complaints and sexist remarks in these units are, in fact symptoms of a larger problem — an inability or unwillingness to adapt, which in turn is fostered by the tolerance of an atmosphere in which male NCOs [Non-Commissioned Officers] and peers can blame and criticize the female members with impunity.[127]

Overt hostility is reported within some combat units. Women are explicitly blamed for most of the men's problems, from extra work to lack of freedom.[128] In one unit, male members believe that the women in their unit are on trial. If the men can prove that the women have failed, then they can ensure their removal. They freely admit to calling the women derisive names, uttering threats and making it known that they do not want them there.[129] Pornography was not only tolerated, it was "pervasive" within the training camps and schools.[130]

Confidentiality and impartiality in the obligatory reporting of sexual harassment to the superior officer within the chain of command are always undermined when there is collusion among men. According to one woman: "On any small base the details of a sexual harassment complaint would be discussed in every mess on the same day it was made."[131]

It is not surprising that women are reluctant to report cases of sexual harassment. In fact, women have told us that should a woman report the abuse, the violence is likely to increase rather than decrease. As such, it is widely accepted that cases of sexual harassment and sexual assault are under-reported within the military. One ex-military member investigating cases of sexual harassment and assault on military bases reported that three of her informal visits to three military units disclosed three cases of sexual assault.

Currently, cases of sexual harassment and sexual assault are dealt with internally, according to military standards and rules. As a result, women who experience violence by men within the military environment are forced to seek help from the very system that generated the abuse in the first place. We are, however, encouraged by the introduction of a new reporting and grievance procedure modelled on more stringent civilian guidelines, with the involvement of a "harassment advisor" in all investigations which will operate outside the chain of command.[132]

A woman who has been abused requires specific health services. Women explained that the Canadian Forces has its own medical system, and members of the military do not qualify for provincial medicare. A woman member who has been sexually assaulted or harassed is forced to seek medical help within the military health care system where physicians are generally male and work within the prescribed confines of a military medical system. They have not been trained to respond or be sensitive to sexual assault or harassment. Only after a referral from a military physician is a woman able to see a civilian doctor. This lack of access to services off base under-mines confidentiality and creates the potential for further trauma.

RACISM AND HETEROSEXISM IN THE MILITARY

Racism and heterosexism are features of the military institution and have a tremendous impact on the lives of women who interact with the military either as employees or as spouses of military employees.

The most recent National Defence report on harassment in the military suggested there was "an apparently high occurrence" of personal harassment which was defined as unwelcome and improper references to race, religion, sexual orientation and physical characteristics. This form of harassment was reported by 32.6 percent of women and 19.4 percent of men. [133]

CONCLUSION

Conditions that create an environment conducive to abuse, barriers to reporting and to ending abuse for both wives of military members and female military members, employment restrictions to and unequal treatment of all women, lack of awareness of women's health needs and lack of accommodation for family obligations,[134] all perpetuate abuse of women in the military. The irony: the military's mandate is to defend the country and ensure nation-wide peace; yet, women within its ambit — citizens of the very population the Canadian military is supposed to protect — are mistreated and abused.

CHAPTER 21

EDUCATION

INTRODUCTION

Most of the people who talked to us about education said that the established educational system had a crucial role to play in ending violence against women. Educational institutions not only teach cognitive skills but also strongly influence the attitudes, beliefs and behaviour of young people. "Like the family and the media, elementary school can reproduce the gender-related roles and social stereotypes and, through various mechanisms, teaches boys and girls to view the sexes as two fundamentally different entities, two opposite poles: power and dependence, reason and feeling, important and useless, strength and weakness, aggressor and victim." [136]

Schools, colleges and universities need to reflect a certain approach to the world. That approach must be founded on the principle of equality and sensitivity to issues of gender, race and class and how inequalities have a detrimental impact on all Canadians. As well, the education system must move from a strict hierarchical model that places educators in authority over students to one that better incorporates power sharing, mutual problem solving and non-violent conflict resolution. As the institutions educate, they must also reflect and emulate an alternative vision.

Schools just do not prepare us to be assertive, we get intimidated about standing up for ourselves.

♀♀♀

In school, girls are encouraged to be self-effacing and quiet and well-behaved. We need to be taught to be affirmative, we don't really lack the ability, we just need to learn how to express it.

Intimidation: the present hierarchical system encourages pressure (do what you're told), lack of freedom and lack of democracy. This is the system teachers are subject to. And how we treat our teachers is going to affect how they treat their students. Think about this.

While other important venues such as community groups, service clubs, sports activities, the family, religious institutions and workplaces fulfil a role in education, it is the formal educational system that engages all young people for long periods of time and at the most formative stages of their lives.

ELEMENTARY AND SECONDARY INSTITUTIONS

EDUCATING AND INFORMING

Violence in school is a growing concern. There are more and more reports of children behaving aggressively in the playground and in the classrooms; of sexual harassment and date rape; and of racially motivated violence.

I've seen a lot of girls "gotten" in the hallway — pushed up against the wall and called bitch, slut, ... [and they] have to deal with come-ons.

♀♀♀

There is concern with safety issues around schools. Young women's safety is very different than that of young men's. Girls are often "rated" as they walk down halls. Guys do this secretly ... sometimes loudly, as you walk by.

In Quebec, a youth theatre group about date rape was banned in schools by the administration because of swearing and because they thought it was too realistic. But the students are the ones that most need to see this kind of thing. People think taking drugs and drinking start in Grade 9, it's not true, now it starts in grades 5 and 6, in elementary schools. All these issues have to be brought into junior high schools to educate kids.

♀♀♀

Schools often don't recognize that little girls (3, 4, 5 years old) are facing sexism, violence, etc. from the boys; it is often not recognized or acknowledged until girls reach puberty.

Many institutions already have special "violence awareness" events or theme weeks. Topics include non-violent techniques of settling disputes for young children who are using violence and confrontation, and street-proofing kids for their own protection from abduction and molestation. We see these activities as extremely important, particularly when they are introduced in a gender-sensitive way.

Young people also felt that some of the education programs they now receive in some schools are not getting the message across.

Students really get the same lectures all the time, (condoms, etc.) and many of the films we are shown in health class are from the 1960s and lend little credibility to our experience in the 1990s. These films are not taken seriously and we can't relate to them. Schools have to come up with something that we will listen to.

♀♀♀

We want "realistic stuff," and not big words that we can't relate to. More appropriate language is the key. Presentations should use language and situations that we understand. Some date rape presentations that we've had in schools are too technical and academic and we can't relate to what they're saying.

We know from our consultations that unless awareness activities are reinforced by ongoing overall messages in other course material, reading material, films, pictures, posters and additional teaching aids, the impact will be eroded. Most materials in the education system do not contain sufficient content on the issue of violence against women, violence in general or on the links between inequality and violence.

As outlined in our earlier discussion of child abuse, symptoms often go unheeded because many teachers have not been trained to recognize the signs. When teachers do make the links they may lack the skills to intervene in ways that are appropriate for the age group they teach.

I quit teaching after four years. I was disillusioned. There's no training about violence of any sort. Why teachers don't even know about normal adolescent development! This causes teachers to be intolerant of adolescents. Add this to a teen who is a victim of violence. Absolutely no tolerance and so these kids leave school. I was not required to study adolescent development and what I took was an inappropriate psychoanalytic theory.

All evidence indicates that early intervention and healing provide the greatest hope for abused children. It is important that teachers detect symptoms of abuse as early as possible and intervene appropriately. Periodic upgrading of these skills and issues should be mandatory for all teachers. They should also: "...rely on analysis of the children's daily lives in order to make the connection with the more general circumstances surrounding the children." [137]

We heard from many women working within local transition houses, sexual assault centres and women's centres who expressed a tremendous interest in opening up and strengthening ties with educators. Many of these front-line workers see public education as one of their central mandates. Their practical experience and perspective would add a unique dimension to education. Students also expressed the need to have presentations from front-line workers.

Guidance counsellors are out of touch with reality and need to be trained in the issues.

♀♀♀

We need to break down denial, people are always telling us what we should do, [we] need survivors talking about their experiences, and how they managed to survive. The key is that education won't make you understand that these things can happen to you unless you hear it from someone that you can relate to, that helps to break down denial ... [we] need to give kids a safe place to get answers to the questions they most want to ask.

While most teachers are respectful of their positions of trust and authority with students, there are some who breach that trust and misuse their authority to sexually assault children. This is such a heinous crime that it is easier for others in the environment to deny that it is happening at all rather than to face its existence. Teachers are not sufficiently aware of the signs indicating the presence of sexual assault, and protocols are not always in place to deal with incidents of abuse of students by teachers. Students who have experienced previous abuse may not know they can seek recourse and often they are not aware of whom they can trust to tell what's happening. Teachers who are found to have assaulted students continue to work in the educational environment.

AN ALTERNATIVE VISION

School curriculum should have the 4 Rs — reading, writing, arithmetic — and relating.

Violence against women will only be eradicated when major changes are made in the contemporary social, economic, cultural and political position of women. The educational system is an essential player in this process. It is imperative that, as early as possible, children be exposed to atmospheres, institutions and ideas that reflect a sensitivity to the issues of gender, race and class.

Feminist research has played an important role in critically assessing material used in the educational system. In addition to identifying the presence and persistence of sexist and racist images and messages, feminists have also noted that women and their accomplishments are often not included in teaching materials. The historical and contemporary accomplishments of all women, for example, women of colour, working class women, women with disabilities and lesbians are seldom, if ever, found in the textbooks of history, mathematics, science and literature. Few students leave the elementary and secondary school system with a good knowledge of women's historical and contemporary status in Canada. Such a knowledge gap invites inaccurate assumptions. While some improvement has been made in the last decade to include material on women's role in society, it is still meagre in many fields of study. Often the content is not well integrated or is tacked on or represented in ways that undermine the equality messages. "The French language contains this sexual discrimination which exists to a lesser degree in English. Women's existence must be recognized even in what we read. We must therefore use a language which specifically names women and men because language is not something outside or beyond social issues. Our way of saying things changes our way of thinking." [138]

The educational material reinforces stereotypes. Children think it's the norm, like mathematics discourages girls from going into sciences ... one of our teachers told his students that maths and sciences were for boys. This incident was reported and nothing was done about it. Students think the teacher has got to be right, teachers know all, that's the danger.

♀♀♀

The educational material is both gender and racially biased. The written word is seen as the bible so it is not questioned. No one seems to want to change the curriculum.

257

[The term] white men is always referred to and used as "neutral," but history is the history of white men. There should be obligatory courses on the integration of women into the curriculum.

Educators must recognize the richness that a feminist perspective can add to their own teaching skills and environment. Some educators openly resist such an approach and are not aware of the sexist, racist and class-biased behaviour they themselves manifest in the classrooms.

There is no information on women's equality in school curriculums so there is a lack of knowledge about what women have accomplished throughout history — there is no women's history included in course material or subjects. This lack of acknowledgement of women's struggles does not encourage us to see that we are equal to men; we lack a perception of equality.

♀ ♀ ♀

One of our teachers wanted to present a talk on how to do a critical, feminist analysis of education material [as it related to racial and disabilities discrimination] to the — , but once they saw her speech they told her not to talk about that topic.

Courses that focus on developing interpersonal skills, parenting skills, tolerance for diversity and cultural distinctiveness, a critical approach to the media, peaceful conflict-resolution skills and a philosophy of equality between genders and among all classes and races must be at the heart of an "alternative vision." These "relating" skills are as critical to self-preservation as reading, writing and arithmetic.

The schools could include [the topic of] date rape for example in a human relations course for both sexes — when they do it now, it's for the girls only; the guys need to take these courses too.

♀ ♀ ♀

Objectification: in schools this shows up by concentrating upon subject matter over and above student's personal skills. We focus on product — not people.

Work on issues of violence against women is already under way among some teachers, within women's teachers federations, in select school districts and in the context of a number of provincial/territorial ministries of education. For example in Ontario, the Federation of Women Teachers' Associations of Ontario (FWTAO) has played a leadership role with a "No to Violence" campaign. The objectives are to bring individuals and organizations together to prevent violence in their communities; to help communities establish co-operative structures to deal with violence; and to encourage communities to work at prevention rather than punishment only. However, more co-ordination is needed among all of these educators across the entire country, as well as the will to place a priority on the funding of such endeavours. From what we heard, community services run by women survivors of violence are often not brought into these strategies. Community, regional and provincial partnerships will be invaluable steps to long-term change.

We believe that all of the best intentions and efforts will fall short unless educational institutions work toward presenting an organizational structure that is free from sexism, racism and class prejudice. At present the majority of principals, vice-principals, school superintendents and other high-ranking educational officials in elementary and secondary schools are male, white, able-bodied and middle-class. Students observe these patterns of inequality and power imbalances and come to believe that this is the natural order of things. How can we then expect students not to re-create what they have come to see as the "way things are"?

There are not a lot of great female role models who are in positions of power.

What students see is badly out of balance. According to 1989-90 Statistics Canada data, 64 percent of elementary and secondary school teachers were women. [139] Their representation levels declined sharply in post-secondary settings: in 1990-91, women represented 39 percent of teachers in community colleges and 8 percent of full professors at the university level. [140] Breaking these patterns will give both male and female students a different message that will counter the prevailing myths about women and men and gender relationships.

We need more involvement of women in administration and policy making, etc. Women need to be part of the critical process in education, not just learning about the process.

The atmosphere in many educational institutions is hostile to girls and women. As well, some young women in high school told us that their teachers express overt sexism, racism and hostility toward gays and lesbians.

A female students asks for help in computer class and the teachers tells her not to worry because everyone knows that "girls can't do things like computers."

♀♀♀

A male teacher took all the young women in the class out into the hall to "pre-apologize" in the event that he would offend them with sexist remarks.

♀♀♀

A male teacher told one of the young women that he wanted to read more "explicit and personal stuff" in her journal.

♀♀♀

Teachers tell homophobic jokes and faggot is a word used all the time.

A male teacher leading study groups in math said: "I hate these study groups - when girls do poorly in math, they always blame it on the system."

♀♀♀

A substitute teacher called a girl a "slut."

♀♀♀

One teacher put sexist remarks beside his students' names. Another teacher spoke about "primitive blacks" and how girls should thank men by making love to them. Our posters about feminism were vandalized, and left us wondering where these males get their attitudes from?

♀♀♀

At a high school located in a middle-class neighbourhood, a women's issues group put up a number of posters explaining the meaning of feminism ... what feminism is and isn't, what lesbians are .... The posters were torn down or had the words "Nazi" and "bitches" written all over them .... The group was told that by putting up the posters they were asking for trouble ....

Young women, particularly in high schools, recounted the following incidents that reflect the ways in which violence manifests itself in early dating relationships and in daily casual school encounters.

Guys come up and put their arms around you — a lot of girls accept it. They are not taught to say no. Guys don't take you seriously if you do say no. Also, you are so accustomed to it, you don't realize you can say no. The words they use — the way they put things ... like "what's wrong with you — I'm only joking ...."

♀♀♀

In our high school there is an attitude problem which seems as bad as physical violence, because the boys at our school continually verbally abuse us. The males describe their insults and abuse as "just a joke."

Once you're aware of the potential for violence every male is capable of, it becomes more difficult to be friends with any of them and you find yourself avoiding them.

♀ ♀ ♀

Lesbians are ostracized in schools if they come out — the environment is not as open as it should be. To come out would expose her to ridicule, people would call her names, beat her up. It's hard to imagine a lesbian coming out in school.

While there are policies in place in most schools to deal with general violence, often those policies do not address harassment based on gender. Even when harassment policies are in place, anything short of physical violence is often ignored. Whether or not there is a policy in place, it is very difficult for girls to report sexual harassment and intimidation, and even when they do, they are often not taken seriously by authorities. Girls soon learn that they are on their own and must often endure the sexist atmosphere rather than risk making waves.

There is a backlash though if you stand up, and it comes not only from teachers, but from other students too. Feminists are called "lesbo radical bitch ...." Labels are used as part of the backlash from others.

Clearly, the patterns are established early. For them to change, they must be challenged early. And those challenges must be directed not only at students but at teachers, administrators and at a system that still reflects rather than confronts inequality on a daily basis.

POST-SECONDARY INSTITUTIONS

- In September 1989, at Wilfrid Laurier University in Waterloo, Ontario, a group of first-year men raided the women's dorm and plastered women's underpants defaced with ketchup and food to represent blood and feces over the cafeteria walls. They then captioned each panty with obscene remarks.

- In November 1990, the annual "No Means No" campaign at Queen's University in Kingston, Ontario was undermined by obscene and violent messages displayed at a men's residence. "No Means Dyke" and "No Means Kick Her in the Teeth" were some of the messages displayed by male students mocking the anti-rape and violence campaign.

- In October 1990, at the University of British Columbia, 300 written threats of extreme sexual violence by at least 30 young men were distributed to women students as they slept in their dorm rooms. Threats included: "You're a fat cow, but I'll fuck you anyways;" "What's the best thing about fucking a 12-year old? Killing her afterward;" and "We'll crush your cervix to oblivion." [141]

- In April 1990, less than six months after the Montreal massacre of female engineering students, members of an audience at a skit at the University of Alberta shouted, "Shoot the bitch, shoot the bitch," referring to a female student who had spoken out against sexual harassment in her faculty.

- In December 1991, at Humber College in Toronto, a woman was sexually assaulted and beaten in broad daylight within sight of her campus while witnesses watched from a nearby dormitory. That same month, at the University of Toronto, a second-year female medical student was stabbed five times with a "butcher-type" knife by her ex-boyfriend in the medical building on campus.

These events illustrate that students need exposure to information on the relationship between inequality and violence, in order to play a role in positive social change by confronting sexist, racial and class prejudice rather than reproducing it. Female students who spoke with us or provided written submissions argued that awareness of violence against women on university and college campuses is severely lacking. Students and faculty both need to learn about the effects of violence, and services are needed to help survivors deal with their experiences. Furthermore, the physical environment of campuses must be made safer for women, and they need to be treated with respect in classes.

Women are frightened about having to walk across campus and about speaking up in class. Violence limits us in our study choices, that is, where we study and when and how we are received in class. There is graffiti on my desk where I usually sit that says that women are disgusting; the lighting is terrible on campus and we suffer a lot from jokes.

♀♀♀

If a woman speaks out in class, then the male students will snicker and make comments. I believe that systemic violence exists within the school [university] system. The prevalent attitude of most male colleagues is one of belittlement of females' views.

♀♀♀

At student federation meetings [university] sometimes women won't speak out because they don't feel somehow that they have the right. Often when they do speak, they are consistently interrupted by men even though men don't interrupt each other. It makes us feel that what we have to say is not as important as what the men have to say.

Policies generally do not spell out women's rights and protection, do not acknowledge the systemic nature of sexism and violence, and do not provide effective complaint procedures on sexual harassment. Policies on sexual harassment encounter resistance often based on the following arguments: "There is a denial that sexual and sexist harassment exists and that this harassment is directed mainly against women; every action against sexual and sexist harassment is considered as violating freedom of expression, harassment thus being associated with 'free communication' between individuals." [142] Women university students feel that: "...policies against sexual harassment should be developed by the main parties concerned, that is by women. Committees against sexual harassment exist in most post-secondary institutions. However, they are either inactive or ineffective... There must be a realization of the extent of this phenomenon which harms women, and women must no longer be abandoned to it. Some institutions of learning and social education deny its existence or doubt the personal histories of women abused in those very institutions, instead of trying to help them and correct the situation." [143]

It is very difficult to monitor and get an accurate reflection of the course content of universities and colleges. Historically, both have played an important role in the promotion and dissemination of "alternative" ideas, and the philosophy of "academic freedom" continues to flourish. We do not challenge these basic tenets of post-secondary education but we do see that the lack of gender, race and class-sensitive education has a profound impact on women's ability to complete their education in a positive and safe atmosphere.

The patriarchal model continues on into university — the curriculum and course work focuses predominantly on male writers, books by men, history by men, male professors get tenure.

Sometimes we think we're equal, until we enter university, or the work force – that's when it really hits.

In educational programs... we see that women are still excluded from the subjects or disciplines studied. For example, no woman is mentioned in the content of the course on Quebec's political history in the twentieth century. However, major political debates in history resulting in notable changes were originated by women. One need only think of the women who fought for the right to vote, or, an even more striking example, of Thérèse Casgrain, the first MNA. This is only one oversight among so many others... How, then, can women identify with female models, other than those that have already been conveyed for too long, if, in 1992, we still only hear about the "great men" of history? [144]

AN ALTERNATIVE VISION

Faculties of education and professional schools, such as law, medicine, and social work, do not adequately address gender and race inequality and violence either as general subjects or in relation to their specific disciplines, yet graduates of these schools play a very significant role in responding to victims/survivors when they go on to practice in their professions. This lack of awareness and sensitivity is demonstrated in the way many professionals deal with women who have suffered violence.

All university or college students should be required to take a course in their first year that provides a forum for discussion of gender, race and class relations. It should include historical, philosophical, theoretical and practical information about the dimensions of inequality and their impact on society and the lives of citizens. Course content should range from personal encounters and dating relationships to larger social issues such as the integration of work and family responsibilities, pay and employment equity, and the relationships among these issues.

Although such courses do exist on some campuses and some students seek such courses out, these courses do not currently touch all post-secondary students.

We also received a clear message that many post-secondary faculty and administrators would benefit from similar exposure. While some post-secondary faculty members have been active in the women's movement and in developing feminist education, their numbers are limited, and many of them face hostility from administrators and colleagues. This prevents the acceptance of challenging ideologies around issues of gender, race and class and ultimately results in abusive, belligerent and dangerous environments for women students and educators.

Our consultations also revealed concerns regarding the relationships between post-secondary institutions and the larger community in which they are located. Too often, we were told, universities are isolated from the day-to-day events of the community. Too often the expertise and knowledge of community resource people are disregarded and seen as unsuitable for inclusion in post-secondary education. As we encouraged elementary and secondary schools to rely on community resource people, particularly with respect to violence against women, we extend this recommendation to educators and administrators in post-secondary institutions. As we were told:

There is an urgent need to change the university system by making the institution more involved in the community so that "knowledge" is made applicable to the context in which it finds itself, that is day-to-day life within the community.

Health and Welfare Canada is supporting centres of excellence in some Canadian universities to work on issues of violence against women. These centres function on a partnership model with community organizations. This type of model may help raise the awareness of the education community and the public and may help ensure that academic research is grounded in the practical aspects as well as in the theory of issues of violence against women.

Apart from what goes on once women are inside post-secondary institutions, there are the problems of accessibility to post-secondary education for many women, women of colour, lone-parents, refugee and immigrant women, women with disabilities and poor women. There are more male than female students at both the undergraduate and graduate levels. [145]

There continues to be a concentration of women in some programs and faculties while they remain under-represented in others that are traditionally "male" such as engineering, sciences and computer sciences. These faculties are still bastions of male culture where blatant sexism and intimidation of women are rife. It is hard for a woman to survive, let alone thrive, in such an environment. Information from the April 1993 Statistics Canada Labour Force Survey shows that out of 476,000 people working in natural sciences, engineering and mathematics in Canada, only 86,000 (18 percent) are women. [146] Information from the Women's Bureau at Labour Canada shows that, in engineering and applied sciences, in 1988, 12.6 percent of the full-time Bachelors and first professional degrees granted, and 12 percent of the Masters degrees, went to women. In 1988, the percentage of doctoral degrees granted to women in engineering and applied sciences was 8.6 percent. [147] It is clear that strategies that concentrate on preparing Canada's labour force for international competition will have to incorporate ways to increase women's participation in these fields.

The hostile environment toward women which exists in some faculties is described in the Carleton University's Architecture Review Committee's Report of December 1992. It examined abuse of power and sexual or other forms of harassment.

One inquiry about admissions was recently answered by a faculty member saying that the potential applicant would be better off staying home to take care of her children, because there are so many unhappy children in the world. The committee received reports of some faculty members and students using graphically obscene and/or violent imagery in publicly denigrating the work or person of their colleagues.[p. 22] ... The report speculates that the breakdown in professional relationships in the School is, in part, responsible for the use of sexist and sexual language in the learning environment when this occurs. This breakdown of professionalism also may make room for some male professors to act out their beliefs that women are sexual objects for men and do not belong in schools of architecture .... Finally, while a few faculty members may have been actively harassing and discriminating and abusing their power, the Architecture Review Committee emphasizes again that all members of the faculty who did not challenge these behaviours, who in fact condoned them by their silence and inaction, also share some of the responsibility for what has ensued. [p. 24] [148]

There are systemic and financial barriers to post-secondary education for women. The costs of obtaining an education have soared in recent years, and access to Canada Student Loans as well as the amounts received by students (both federal and provincial portions) have not kept pace with these costs. Government assistance for Aboriginal post-secondary students has suffered serious reductions in the past two years. There is an obligation to attend to the conditions that have made Aboriginal women among the poorest and least educated groups in Canada. We know that many students are being forced out of post-secondary education because of rising costs. Women, because of their general economic inequality, are most affected by these conditions.

There are not enough finances, and women always suffer from lack of finances; women are made to stop before they complete their degrees.

CONCLUSION

Placing the educational system under the feminist lens reveals problems of program content, form and structure. Rectifying program content is probably an attainable short-term goal. Given the will and some redirecting of finances, educational systems can address issues around violence and make the links between gender, race and class inequality and violence. Some schools, universities and colleges have already begun. Their examples provide important models for others. We are also optimistic that gender-sensitive prevention strategies, if implemented with rigour, can stem a lot of the violence against girls and women in educational institutions.

The problems of form and structure are more systemic and not as solvable in the short run. We know that efforts to increase the proportion of women professors and women principals, vice-principals and other administrative officials take more time and require a consistent will to do so. Similarly, access to student loans, programs that help single mothers stay in school, and employment and pay equity programs will not necessarily come overnight; nor will their effects be apparent immediately. All the more reason to accelerate efforts now.

We can not stress enough the importance of working on both content and structure simultaneously. Women told us that the principle guiding an analysis of the educational system must be to ask, not what is wrong with female students but what is wrong with the system and structure of education.

> Instead of focusing on women to try to find out what is not working with them in school, it would be better to analyse the system within which they must operate — the school. Sexist stereotypes in educational material, the attitudes of teachers and current sexist practices in the classroom are important factors in the acceptance of sex roles in everyday life. Teachers must consider how women's experiences outside of the classroom make it impossible for them to receive an education equal to men.

CHAPTER 22

MEDIA AND CULTURE

INTRODUCTION

... the images that are conveyed through film and TV are never neutral; they reflect the subjective experiences of the creators. And images are powerful; ... they are absorbed as they are seen, below the level of critical thought. They are with us forever. [149]

Ideas play a significant part in maintaining, reinforcing and reproducing inequality, and they are key to sustaining the existing power relations in society.

The ideas presented by the media and other popular cultural expressions are key, although not the only, forces supporting sexism, racism and classism. Television, advertisements, movies, magazines, books, posters, video games, toys, music and music videos are powerful portrayers of ideas.

Popular culture surrounds us and affects every area of human activity. Its images, sounds, stories and stars speak to our feelings and senses, bypassing our rational minds. We absorb their messages and ideologies unconsciously, taking them in like the air we breathe: regularly, necessarily, without choice ... the messages transmitted influence our beliefs and attitudes. [150]

We believe that these venues often purvey distorted messages about women and men and about violence against women.

Freedom of expression is an important tenet of a free and democratic society. The idea of regulating the media naturally causes people unease because regulation implies the potential for people with authority and power to wield that power to suit their own purposes and match their own political, social, cultural and religious positions.

Many people argue that censorship is not the answer to violence in the media. However, maintaining gratuitous and glamorized violence on television and in other media is an issue of women's safety and child protection. It is our responsibility as a society to reach a more equitable balance between artistic freedom and the issues of women's equality and safety, and the raising of children committed to these goals.

We must recognize that the media censor points of view daily. For instance, in news coverage, choices are made as to what to cover, by whom and from what angle. In these decisions, some things are deemed as worthy of coverage and others are regarded as unworthy or not important enough to merit coverage. These decisions are most often taken by men wielding journalistic "objectivity." Gender informs all our experiences and decisions.

An example of how the media censor women was the coverage of the Women and Violence Conference sponsored by the Canadian Mental Health Association and held in Banff in 1991. Although the conference had 80 workshops dealing with substantive issues regarding violence against women, coverage by major Canadian newspapers and electronic media reduced the entire conference to a "fracas" among women. The disruption in proceedings referred to by the media was an important challenge by women of colour who felt their issues were not receiving due attention. To characterize an important debate about racism as a fight among women reflects patriarchal assumptions about women and their interrelationships and about the importance of gender, race and class inequality in Canadian society. It is sometimes easier to cast complex issues in controversy and emphasize points of disagreement than to analyse and present fresh points of view.

The media also censor women by controlling the images and roles of women. Women are generally treated as sexual objects and made to appear intellectually weaker than men and incapable of surviving without them. "Sexy" women are used to "spice up" films, television programs, music videos or magazine covers and, according to much of the media, there is only one sexy kind of woman. She is skinny with large breasts and long legs, white, young and passive. The prevalence of such an image, in effect, censors the realities of most women and promotes the dominance of men.

HOW THE MEDIA CONDITION US

The media teach many things: that the present hierarchy is the "natural" order of things, that some groups are better than others, that men are better than women, that whiter skin is better than darker skin .... The media teach a denial of the interdependence of humans as social beings and that the only relationship possible for people is a competitive one. [151] The media teach a denial of the consequences of human actions. "This belief allows the creation of sensational, extreme images, in which the visual impact of physical violence can be emphasized, dissociated from the pain it causes." [152] The media teach the inevitability of violence, that violence is "intrinsic to the human condition with no possible alternatives; that violence is the domain of the masculine. This leads both to its glorification and eroticization." [153] And last, women are portrayed by the media either as the passive and willing victims of this violence or as some kind of monster if they resist.

Ownership of Canadian mass media is overwhelmingly American: 93 percent of our movie and video business, 90 percent of the recording business and 92 percent of book publishing are American-controlled. [154] Canadians spend half their leisure time watching television — an average of 23 hours per week per person. Canadian children spend more time watching television than they spend in the classroom. [155]

The average child observes more than 1,000 dramatized murders on television each year; [156] more than 100,000 acts of violence are viewed by the average television watcher in a decade. This culture of violence holds a hidden tolerance of violence against women. [157]

Of equal concern is the ever escalating portrayals of violence against women, and the linking of sex with violence. From T.V. movies that show graphic, detailed depictions of violent, brutal acts against women, under the guise of public awareness/social advocacy, to sexist or violent rock videos and advertising, to the verbal misogyny of comedians ..., to slasher films, to the pornography in local stores, we are being inundated with images that glorify and justify violence against women and male dominance of women. [158]

In a discussion of the Canadian Radio-television Telecommunications Commission (CRTC) report on television violence, Keith Spicer, CRTC Chair, made the following remarks.

While our report indicates that there is a link, although not necessarily one of cause and effect, between television violence and violence in society, common sense also tells us that this must be true. Look at how television helps to set fashion trends, introduce new ideas and expressions into our everyday conversation, or change purchasing patterns throughout the marketplace. Why else do advertisers spend millions on television commercials, if there is no impact on our behaviour? [159]

Women know and have been saying for years that violence against women, both overt and implicit, is pervasive in the media and encourages a culture of violence against women. Mr. Spicer too, admits that violence is found "everywhere" — in television, films, magazines and many other forms of popular culture. [160] Overt violence against women, in particular, flourishes in television movies, films and videos. Studies show that "ultra-violence" has moved from the fringes of popular culture to the mainstream. [161] Recent, popular mainstream movies such as *Silence of the*

Lambs, Whispers in the Dark, Sleeping With the Enemy, Unlawful Entry and *Raising Cain* — chiefly produced, directed and written by men — are built around the brutalization and ritual torture of female victims. [162] The Hollywood trend is: "you mix up some sex and violence, throw in a psychokiller and you've got yourself a hit." [163] *Basic Instinct* director Paul Verhoeven's first comment upon viewing his film was, "How can we put more tits and cunt into this movie?" [164] *Basic Instinct* was worth $100 million in box office business. [165]

> One of the most profitable films in 1991 was *Silence of the Lambs*, a story of a psychopath who not only murders women but also skins them. And then we had Arnold Schwarzenegger who bellows: "Consider this a divorce" just before he shoots his wife at point blank range in *Total Recall*. On T.V., the hugely successful *Twin Peaks*, held viewers captive over many weeks with tales of terrorization and brutal murders of beautiful women. [166]

In the majority of movie blockbusters, women are killed on the screen simply because they are women. If men don't kill women, women kill each other — usually because they are competing for a man. [167] Young teens experience more women-victimizing fare than any other group, through video rentals and cable premium stations, generally produced and distributed by men. [168]

In mainstream comedy, comedians express sexist and misogynist "humour" harmful to women. Humour can be used as a means of hurting and undermining its subjects and, because it is called "humour," it cannot be held accountable for the damage. How often have women heard the words: "I was only kidding, can't you take a joke?" The well-known comedian Andrew Dice Clay, in his home video *The Diceman Cometh*, boasts that if a woman doesn't "screw" him with enough enthusiasm he will burn her with a cigarette. In *Harlem Nights*, Eddie Murphy punches a woman in the stomach and then shoots off her toe because "that's what a man would do." [169]

In music videos — many of which "border on the margins of pornography" [170] — the violent imagery is dominated by white males with women portrayed as sexual objects who are often passive, subordinate and submissive. When women are depicted as being in control, they are often portrayed as "cold-hearted bitches." [171]

Misogyny is also endemic in popular music. For instance, the popular heavy metal group Guns 'N Roses, sings "I used to love her, but I had to kill her .... And now I'm happier this way." In another song, they say that rape is a sure-fire way to cure boredom. [172]

These examples of violence against women in popular mainstream media are not atypical; rather, they are typical of our culture.

PORTRAYAL OF WOMEN IN THE MEDIA

The media, which, for the most part, deny women access to media expression and disseminate messages which deny women equality and dignity, are sexist. [173]

ENTERTAINMENT MEDIA

The technologies of cable, VCR and video have created the "home entertainment phenomenon." What this means is that there is a huge volume of visual material available to us in our living rooms at the press of a button and for a price that is often less than a magazine. Every second corner of most cities, towns and villages in this country now hosts a video rental outlet sometimes offering hundreds of titles.

In general, the Panel was told that the media lack positive, egalitarian and diverse images of women. For instance, the majority of relation-ships portrayed in the media are between men and women; lesbians and lesbian relationships are few and far between, especially those in which lesbian relationships are portrayed with honesty and dignity.

With some exceptions, media images of women continue to be stereotypical, sexist and demeaning. Women of colour, lesbians, women as experts and in positions of authority are still rare.

The media portrayal of women of colour is also incredibly warped and stereotypical. When not simply ignored, they are portrayed in one-dimensional stereotypical images that fall within certain proscribed limits.

Their images are the most exploited .... They are visible and invisible: visible only when they play the parts assigned to them and invisible when it comes to recognizing their contribution to the worlds in which they live. [174]

Older women are also ignored by the media. According to popular cultural wisdom, a woman's physical appearance is her major and perhaps her only asset. To be financially lucrative for the media, women must be portrayed as young, slim and successful. Older women don't meet all these criteria.

Still missing from the screen are older female characters whose lives and faces show the evidence of their experiences, whose portrayals are both positive and realistic. Their absence supports the clear if unspoken assumption that women whose power and personal attractiveness don't match the soap opera standard are somehow lacking. [175]

The lack of positive portrayals of older women in the media undermines the value of older women in our society, and conditions women to fear growing old, rather than accept and enjoy the process.

Music videos and televised music programming, which are watched predominantly by youth, contain almost twice as many violent acts as commercial television. [176] Certain media images contribute to a deeply rooted acceptance by young people, of abusive sexual relations. [177] A recent study examining the effect of music videos containing violent and sexist lyrics on 75 male college students, indicated increased negative sex-role stereotyping of women and more acceptance of violence against women. [178]

Society learns what it sees and hears in the media.

We accept that children learn their ABCs by passively watching Sesame Street. We know what a powerful teaching tool the media is – that is why we bring televisions into the classroom. We as a society have to accept that the mass media portrayal of women is teaching us some very damaging attitudes toward women. These attitudes are not only implicated in violence against women, but in the inequality of women in general.

What society learns in the media supports men's power over women and threatens women's sense of well-being.

It is a power relationship that exists simply because such use of women's bodies – from pin-up girls to Bud commercials to porn – exist and is allowed to thrive. In other words, the very fact that any of it is even around and for sale gives men a powerful or superior feeling — conscious or unconscious — and at the same time saps many women of self-esteem, happiness, inner strength, beauty and inner peace.

Not only do the media help to create a culture of violence against women, negative media portrayal of women also causes deep psychological harm.

It is well-documented that negative and sexist attitudes and beliefs, learned from the media, about women, help facilitate sexual abuse and other forms of violence against women. It is also clear that mass media portrayals of women have negative effects on women themselves.

"A woman is conditioned to view her face as a mask and her body as an object, as things separate from and more important than her real self, constantly in need of alteration, improvement, and disguise." [179]

Furthermore, girls and young women are conditioned to comply with the limited professional and social roles found in the media. "The constant repetition of these images [stereotypical portrayals] tends to reinforce their perceived reality, thus influencing the attitudes of women, men and children, and encourages both women and girls to limit their horizons both socially and professionally to those roles which they see portrayed." [180]

Even when the media do present reasonably positive and successful role models for women, how they achieved their success is rarely depicted.

Night after night, on over two dozen episodes a season, teenage viewers see their counterparts on the screen poised for professional careers and productive adulthoods, but viewers rarely catch a glimpse of the steps one must take to achieve those goals. The cumulative result of these skewed depictions is a distorted message about the realities of growing up. Such inaccurate messages are of consequence in a society where millions of real life teenage girls are ill-prepared for a lifetime of work and face greater economic risk than boys their age. [181]

Certainly lower-income women are underrepresented in the media, given how many Canadian women live below the poverty line. "The women represented in the media are also primarily middle class. Little attention is paid to working class people who make up a large majority of the population. Therefore, career choices which are non-traditional but viable options for young women are ignored." [182]

WOMEN AND NEWS

Freedom of the press is guaranteed only to those who own one. [183]

A study examining the portrayal of women in 15 daily Canadian newspapers found numerous examples of sexist language and language that excluded women. Articles emphasized irrelevant but stereotypical features about women or

focused on the gender of the person undertaking the activity rather than the activity itself. This study also found that women were used as references less than 20 percent of the time and women had less than 30 percent of the bylines. [184]

Another study by the Canadian Radio-television Telecommunications Commission found that the issue of violence against women was discussed three times in 378 hours of broadcasting in Canadian television programming in 1989, and only 1.5 percent of all news and public affairs items were presented explicitly as a women's issues. [185]

The daily newspaper is a central aspect of any society. The casual inclusion of women as a commodity to be taken with morning coffee and last night's baseball scores is clearly an "everyday feature of Canadian life" that promotes male dominance and female subordination.

These examples, along with the example cited earlier of media coverage of the Women and Violence Conference, illustrate the news media's pervasive male bias and how women and women's issues are either under-represented or distorted in the news.

CHILDREN AND MEDIA VIOLENCE

Evidence shows that consistent exposure to stories and scenes of violence and terror can mobilize aggressive tendencies, desensitize some and isolate others, intimidate many and trigger violent action in a few. [186]

By the fall of 1987, 80 percent of all children's television programming in the United States was produced by toy companies. [187] One study reported that "violence was intrinsic to the plot" of 44 percent of toy-linked shows. [188] Between 80 and 90 percent of English television programming watched by Canadian children is produced in the United States. By contrast, in Quebec, approximately 90 percent of television watched by children from 2 to 11 years of age is produced in Quebec. [189] Further, research suggests that most children begin watching adult programs by the age of 4 and watch from 20 to 35 hours per week. [190] These programs include horror movieswith women and children as the targets of violence, [191] comedy shows, music videos and pornography. [192] In war and adventure movies, people of colour, particularly Asians and Middle-Eastern people, are featured as the enemies. [193] These statistics are reminders of the extent to which children are exposed to messages that perpetuate gender, race and class inequality and that promote the use of violence.

The effect of non-educational television and videos on children in their formative years has been the subject of much research. Studies support the belief that children demonstrate an increase in aggressive behaviour and heightened gender stereotyping as a result of long-term and repeated exposure to such programs.[194] A major study of young children found that children who watched violent television had higher frequencies of antisocial and violent play behaviours.[195] Apart from the influence of these messages, researchers also point out that time spent watching television and videos displaces time that would be spent developing ideas, thoughts and opinions through talking, discussions and exploring one's environment through play. [196]

Studies also show that media play an important role in conditioning sex-role stereotypes in young children. A qualitative research project conducted by VIVA Associates revealed that the media heroes of most children are violent male characters. Rambo, The Predator, The Terminator, and the actors Arnold Schwarzenegger and Jean-Claude Van Damme were often mentioned. Noted is the fact that these characters demonstrate limited interpersonal skills and rely heavily on violence as a means of personal and interpersonal expression. [197]

At the very least, images of violence against women desensitize viewers to the horror of it; at worst they instruct viewers including young children in the tools and techniques of violence. We must never forget the nature of

Marc Lepine's horrendous act. He was a heavy viewer of action/adventure videos and he carried out his deed Rambo style.[198]

When questioned about their media heroes, girls mostly admired the same characters as did boys, with a few notable exceptions. Julia Roberts, famous for her portrayal of a prostitute who "fell in love" and changed her life in the Hollywood movie *Pretty Woman*, was identified as a heroine, along with Wonder Woman. In both cases, the girls identified these women because of their looks, not because of their actions or other strengths.

The study found that boys believe that media heroes reflect appropriate male behaviour. They demonstrated behaviour that imitated the invincible protagonists. Boys were eager to talk about the violence and act it out. They demonstrated an acceptance of violence and war, and of the notion that male behaviour involves destruction and obliteration. While girls watched the same amount of violence, they responded with silence. It is significant for them that most of the women who they see portrayed in violent programming are passive, helpless victims who have no control over their lives. [199]

NEW TECHNOLOGIES

We will soon have even more choice: developing technologies, such as DBS (direct broadcast satellite) and video compression, promise a mind-boggling proliferation of media possibilities. As programmers fight for audiences in an increasingly fragmented market, they will certainly seek attention through sensationalism. [200]

New technological developments in audio, film and video, as well as computer animation have significantly changed the experience of the images. These technological developments have fuelled the industry trend to ultra-realism. However, this ultra-realism has been applied to portray, in ever more explicit and horrifying ways, act of unspeakable violence and brutality. [201]

Certain technologies, such as video games, require more than the viewer's passive participation, they actually involve the viewer/player in the on-screen activities, much of which portray men as violent characters and women as the passive recipients of male "heroism" and violence. Virtual reality is another technology which has recently become available in shopping malls and will likely become available in private homes in the near future. Virtual reality has the ability to reconstruct sensory reality; instead of merely viewing reality on the screen, one can enter and become part of that reality. The implications for society and for women of a "manufactured reality," in which people become players, are both scary and daunting given the prevalence of sexism and misogyny in other media. There is a need to monitor the development of these new technologies, evaluate the consequences to women and society in general and implement creative ways to minimize harm. Any such work must be done in full partnership with feminist groups involved in the media and arts.

MEDIA LITERACY

There is a lack of media literacy education in Canadian society to equip us to evaluate the media's messages and effects on people. Media literacy courses could cover everything from newspapers to rock videos, and other forms of advertising, to films. Courses would instruct children on the economics of media, how images are constructed and construed and the messages that underlie them. Instruction could also include how the portrayal of women and sexuality effects children.

REGULATION

At present the Canadian government delivers a double message about violence against women by, on the one hand, funding emergency services and treatment programs for victims, and on the other, refusing to take action at a structural level to outlaw the production and distribution of material that perpetuates the subordination of women.

There have been some attempts to regulate the media industry through Canadian Radio-television Telecommunications Commission (CRTC) guidelines. [202] However, non-punitive measures have elicited little or no compliance from industries. For example, a 1989 survey of soft drink and beer advertisements — 60 percent of which portrayed women in provocative dress, and none of which had men in provocative dress — found consistent violations of CRTC guidelines. The CRTC has failed to analyse the links between violence against women and the broader social conditions of gender, race and class inequality in Canadian society. In academic research, most work on gender stereotyping in the media has been done in isolation from work on the effects of violence against women, although the effect of both is to diminish, degrade and control women. Regulations on Canadian media content have also treated both issues as separate; regulations about the portrayal of women have little to do with violence, while those governing violence do not deal with the specific portrayal of women and violence. During our consultations, women asked that the CRTC concede that self-regulation has failed and acknowledge that legislation is needed to bring about the compliance of broadcasters. They argued that regulations should ensure compliance by making it an enforced condition of licensing. They asked for a new process that would allow greater and easier public input and participation. Also, advertising regulations with meaningful penalties for non-compliance must be developed.

Women also suggested that all public and
Canadian television and film institutions adopt a
policy of zero tolerance of violence against
women and against violence in general. Zero
tolerance is the only philosophy and standard
consistent with protecting the public safety and
reducing violence against women. Other suggestions emphasized that regulation is not sufficient
and recommended that groups, such as Media
Watch, monitor printed and electronic media for
the use of violence in programming, advertising,
films and rock videos. Implementing a system of
ratings based on portrayals of gender, race and
class inequality, for both shows and commercials,
would facilitate the monitoring process. In addition, we heard suggestions that awards and
recognition for responsible programming be
implemented.

WOMEN BEHIND THE SCENES

*Changes in employment and funding prac-
tices mean that women's view and reality
are reflected in what is on screen .... Women
must be included as co-creators and co-
leaders of this change process. In the words
of our great Canadian film maker, Kathleen
Shannon, "It matters who makes it."*

Women told us that to change the portrayal of
women in the media and to highlight women's
issues and counter depictions of violence against
women, there must be equal representation of
women throughout the media industry.
Submissions to the Panel emphasized the need
for change in media practice and procedures to
ensure that women have an equal voice in
determining and informing all aspects of the
industry. We were told that employment equity
policies founded on parity in funding and contract compliance are important vehicles for
moving women toward equal participation in the
industry.

We still have a long way to go to establish
gender, race and class parity in the media.

* According to Toronto Women in Film and
  Television, women are in the minority in key
  decision making, policy making and key
  creative jobs in the Canadian media industry.
  Only 14 percent of upper management in the
  public sector are women and only 1 percent
  in the private sector.[203]

* Industry funding practices are such that in
  1987-88, Telefilm Canada awarded only
  9 percent of total funds to women
  producers. [204]

* In 1990, only 4 out of 15 people on the
  Canadian Radio-television and
  Telecommunications Commission were
  women. [205]

PROVIDING ALTERNATIVE MESSAGES ABOUT WOMEN IN THE MEDIA AND THE ARTS

MEDIA ORGANIZATIONS

As well as individuals there are several women's
media organizations working to alter images of
women, to balance images and messages, and to
eradicate male bias in the media. Such organizations include: Toronto Women in Film and
Television, Moitié/Moitié in Quebec, Vancouver
Women in Film and the Women's Programs at
the National Film Board. [206]

This industry has the capacity to develop and
distribute "redemptive images" which
celebrate everyday human experiences of
connection, community, of diversity and
difference, of human conflict without
destruction of the other. These "redemptive
images" could help to heal the wounds
caused by centuries of violence. And we
guarantee that there would be a huge market
for these images. [207]

THE ARTS AND WOMEN

During our consultations, women across Canada spoke of the ways in which art, as a form of healing and as a vehicle for positive portrayals of women, could help reduce violence against women. Women involved in all facets of the arts see themselves as having an important role in this regard. For example, 14 out of 20 women artists in a Celebration of Women in the Arts survey saw art therapy as a concrete way for women artists to help survivors of violence express themselves. Others felt that women artists should be actively involved in both direct service provision to women survivors of violence, and on higher profile advocacy boards/agencies to learn, teach and develop artistic work on issues. [208] In addition, popular theatre, plays, puppet shows and stories could be used as teaching tools to educate both children and adults about violence against women.

A group of men suggested the creation of a men's film festival which would include films that examine all aspects of male life including work, family, play, sports, sexuality, spirituality and traditional roles. As we were told:

> *Men must examine and challenge our own behaviour and those of the men around us, and work to eliminate our own patriarchal, misogynist and abusive, violent behaviours and attitudes. Men must come together with other men to work collectively and actively, to take responsibility not only for the violence but for ending it as well.*

CONCLUSION

There is no question that the media are all too often a misogynist force distorting women's realities in Canadian society. Violence against women and the misrepresentation and degradation of women in the media foster conditions in which violence against women thrives. The power of the media to create negative conditions for women could be transformed to counteract the harm done and to encourage countervailing stories and images that properly reflect and speak of women's varied realities. Media power could help end violence against women.

273

CONCLUSION

From our examination of these institutions, we have drawn the following conclusions which form the basis for the National Action Plan which appears as Part Five of this Report.

KNOWLEDGE AND UNDERSTANDING

Overall, what we heard convinced us that institutional practice is based on a lack of a systemic understanding of the issues: violent acts are perceived to be, and are often treated as, individual pathological responses by "sick" men. In some cases, women are blamed, as in cases of sexual assault by an intimate partner.

To a large extent we see the lack of understanding of violence against women as the outcome of a mistrust of, and bias against, feminist analysis and feminist therapeutic and political approaches to violence against women. The women's movement was largely responsible for placing the topics of battering, rape, sexual assault, child abuse and date rape on the political and social agenda of this country. As we move toward understanding and solutions, we feel Canadians owe a debt to a number of groups in the women's movement that have worked, and continue to work, on the issue of violence against women and to explain that violence in the larger social context of inequality.

We have seen how gender, race and class inequality structure the lives of women. Inequality and power imbalances take options away from them. Their social, economic, political and cultural choices are limited, their voices silenced, their actions curtailed, and their physical situations dangerous. Many people told the Panel that the link between equality and freedom from violence must be recognized.

BREAKING BARRIERS

Significant barriers prevent change to our social institutions. Women continue to be severely under-represented in many social institutions, particularly in places and positions with decision-making powers. Even in areas where there are larger numbers of women, such as teaching and health care, they are under-represented in management positions where they would be able to take a larger role in policy development and implementation. Finding women to fill jobs is not a guarantee that sexism, racism and class inequality will disappear, or even be addressed. Such goals are contingent upon ensuring that such groups as women of colour, refugee women, poor women, immigrant and disabled women, for example, have access to the tools that will help them reach positions of power: education, child care, language skills and training programs.

We see women's under-representation in social institutions as the outcome of a society that continues to foster the notion of patriarchal ideology founded upon an artificial separation of "home" and "work" and the myth that women should maintain primary responsibility for raising children and doing the work at home.

Apart from the under-representation of women working in institutions, there are also significant barriers preventing survivors of violence from getting access to services. Language barriers, location, lack of transportation, lack of knowledge about services available and regional differences in services all combine to inhibit women survivors from coming forward. And if women do overcome all these impediments, they then often face a lack of sensitivity to their experiences and a general lack of knowledge of the issues of violence against women. Such conditions create such a hostile atmosphere for women who are often in their most fragile state, it is no wonder that many are reluctant to seek support.

PUBLIC ACCOUNTABILITY

The institutions we examined tended to ignore their responsibility to uphold women's safety and security and to neglect their obligation to be publicly accountable.

Institutions often operate behind closed doors denying any scrutiny of their operations by members of the public. As a consequence, institutional and personal tolerance of violence against women and of inequality persist—unchecked and unchallenged.

ENDNOTES

1   Regroupement provincial des maisons d'hébergement et de transition pour femmes victimes de violence conjugale, *Étude Économique* (Montreal, Quebec: September 1990), p. XXIX.

2   Interdisciplinary Project on Domestic Violence, *The Other Side of the Mountain: Climbing, Still Climbing* Final Report, Phase II (Ottawa, January 1991), p. 4.

3   Yves Morier, Catherine Bluteau, Guy Bruneau, Claire Lessard, Pierre Beaudet, *Intervention sociojudiciaire en violence conjugale* (Montreal: Wilson & Lafleur Ltée, et Centre Éducatif et Culturel Inc., 1991), p. 74.

4   Joanne Doucette, "Disabled Women and Violence," *Breaking the Silence* (Winnipeg: Coalition of Provincial Organizations of the Handicapped (COPOH), 1988), pp. 36-37.

5   Rudolf Rausch "La femme et les enfants d'abord," *Quand l'amour fait mal* (under the direction of Jacques Broué and Clément Guèvremont) (Montreal: Saint-Martin, 1989), p. 112.

6   *Ibid.* (Annexe: L'homme violent: une approche globale), p. 184.

7   Nancy Burns, Colin Meridith and Chantal Paquette, *Treatment Programs For Men Who Batter: A Review of the Evidence of their Success* (Ottawa: Research Section, Department of Justice Canada, July 1991), p. 56.

8   Rudolf Raunch, *Quand l'amour fait mal, op. cit.*, p. 115.

9   R.E. Dobash and R.P. Dobash, *Violence against wives: a case against the patriarchy* (New York: Free Press, 1979). Linda MacLeod, *Wife battering in Canada: The vicious circle* (Ottawa: Canadian Advisory Council on the Status of Women, 1980). E. Stark et al., "Medicine and patriarchal violence: The social construction of a private event," as cited in Jean E. Innes et al., *Models and Strategies of Delivering Community Health Services Related to Woman Abuse* (Edmonton: University of Alberta, 1991), p. 9.

10   *Ibid.*, p. 9.

11   *Ibid.*, p. 9.

12   Tearmann Society for Battered Women, *Medical Services or Disservice?: An Exploratory Study of Wife Assault Victims' Experiences in Health Delivery Settings* (New Glasgow, Nova Scotia: Tearmann Society for Battered Women, 1988), pp. 16-17.

13   *Ibid.*, p.37.

14   Monique Bégin, "Re-designing Health Care for Women," *op. cit.*, pp. 21-22.

15   The Centre for Women Health Steering Committee, *Proposal to Establish a Community Health Centre for Women* (Toronto: The Centre for Women Health Steering Committee, December 1988), p. 11.

16   The Committee on Sexual Exploitation in Professional Relationships, *Beyond the Silence, Toward a Solution* (Province of Alberta: An Independent Committee of the College of Physicians and Surgeons, June 1992), p. 5.

17   *The Final Report of the Task Force on Sexual Abuse of Patients* (Ontario: An Independent Task Force Commissioned by the College of Physicians and Surgeons of Ontario, November 25, 1991), p. 83.

18   M. Carr and G.E. Robinson, "Fatal Attraction: The Ethical and Clinical Dilemma of Patient-Therapist Sex," as cited in Kathryn Morgan, Ph.D. (Department of Philosophy, Women's Studies Program, and Centre for Bioethics, University of Toronto), *Philosophical Analysis: Permissibility of Sexual Contact Between Physicians and Patients, Part 3: The Gender Lens* (Paper presented to the College of Physicians and Surgeons of Ontario, nd), p. 2.

19   H.A. Holtz et al., "Education about adult domestic violence in US and Canadian medical schools, 1987-1988," as cited in Jean E. Innes et al., *Models and Strategies of Delivering Services Related Women Abuse* (Edmonton: University of Alberta, 1991), p. 9.

20   Kay Weiss, "What Medical Students Learn About Women," as cited in Kathryn Morgan, Ph.D. (Department of Philosophy, Women's Studies Program and Centre for Bioethics, University of Toronto), *Philosophical Analysis: Permissibility of Sexual Contact Between Physicians and Patients, Part 3: The Gender Lens* (Paper presented to the College of Physicians and Surgeons of Ontario), pp. 14-15.

21   *Ibid.*, p. 3.

22   Temi Firsten, "Violence in the Lives of Women on Psych Wards," *Canadian Woman Studies*, 11:4 (Spring/Summer 1991), p. 47.

23   A.F. Heller, *Health and Home: Women as Health Guardians*, as cited in The Centre for Women's Health Steering Committee, *Proposal to Establish a Community Health Centre for Women* (Toronto: The Centre for Women's Health Steering Committee, 1988), p. 13.

24   Beverly Lepischak with the Coalition for Feminist Mental Health Services, *Missing the Mark: Women's Services Examine Mental Health Programs for Women in Toronto* (Toronto: Coalition for Feminist Mental Health Services, January 1992), p. 45.

25 Hospital Spousal Abuse Committee, *Spousal Abuse: Information and Protocol for Hospitals,* as cited in Jean E. Innes et al., *Models and Strategies of Delivering Services Related Women Abuse* (Edmonton: University of Alberta, 1991), p. 19.

26 *Ibid.,* p. 13.

27 Jacqueline Dupuis, "L'Urgence, le premier contact," *Nursing Québec,* vol. 5, no. 5 (1985), p. 21.

28 V.K. Drake, "Battered women: A health care problem in disguise," *Image,* Vol. 14, No. 2 (1982), pp. 40-47. W. Goldberg and A.L. Carey, "Domestic violence victims in the emergency setting," *Topics in Emergency Medicine,* Vol. 3 (1982): pp. 65-76. D. Kurz et al., *Identification and intervention with battered women in hospital emergency departments* (Ottawa: National Clearinghouse on Family Violence, Health and Welfare Canada, undated). V.P. Tilden and P. Shepherd, "Increasing the rate of identification of battered women in an emergency department: use of a nursing protocol," as cited in Jean E. Innes et al., *Models and Strategies of Delivering Community Health Services Related to Woman Abuse* (Edmonton: University of Alberta, Edmonton, 1991), p. 9.

29 Tearmann Society for Battered Women in Nova Scotia, *Medical Service or Disservice?, op. cit.,* p. 13.

30 Jean E. Innes et al., *Models and Strategies of Delivering Community Health Services, op. cit.,* p. 19.

31 *Ibid.,* p. 25.

32 Judith Lavoie, "Third of women in emergency wards may suffer domestic violence," *Times Colonist [Victoria],* April 22, 1992, p. A7.

33 *Ibid.,* p. A7.

34 The Committee on Sexual Exploitation in Professional Relationships, *Beyond the Silence, op. cit.,* Appendix A, pp. 1-3.

35 Canadian Nurses Association, *Code of Ethics for Nurses for Nursing* (Ottawa, November 1991), p. 21.

36 *Achieving Zero Tolerance in the Self-Regulating Professions* (Draft by Pat Marshall), pp. 9, 12-13.

37 *Ibid.,* p. 46.

38 Eileen Ambrosia et al., *The Street Health Report: A study of the health status and barriers to health care of homeless women and men in the City of Toronto* (Toronto, May 1992), p. 52.

39 Aline Grandmaison, *Protection des Personnes Agées: Étude exploratoire de la violence à l'égard de la clientèle des personnes âgées du CSSMM (Centre de Services Sociaux du Montréal Metropolitain)* (Montréal: Direction des Services Professionnels, October 1988), Annex B.

40 The Federal/Provincial/Territorial Working Group on Women's Health with assistance from Anne Rochon Ford, *Working Together for Women's Health: A Framework for the Development of Policies and Programs* (Federal/Provincial/Territorial Working Group on Women's Health, April 1990), p. 28.

41 Denise Avard and Louise Hanvey, *The Health of Canada's Children: A CICH Profile,* as cited in National Council of Welfare, *Health, Health Care and Medicare: A report by the National Council of Welfare* (Ottawa: National Council of Welfare, Autumn 1990), p. 16.

42 *Ibid.,* p. 17.

43 Alberta Status of Women Action Committee, *Women Against Poverty* (Alberta, public hearings held in June and September of 1989), p. 75.

44 National Anti-Poverty Organization,"Working Summary of Community-Based Literature on Health Inequities," *Selected Bibliography Compiled from Submissions to the Literature Review on Health Inequities* (Ottawa: National Anti-Poverty Organization, November 1987), p. 13.

45 Joanne Doucette, *Violence Against Disabled Women* (Toronto: The DisAbled Women's Network, based on a study conducted in 1986), p. xxi.

46 Susan Desel, "Women in Health," *Healthsharing: A Canadian Women's Health Quarterly,* Vol. 12, No. 3 (1991): p. 32.

47 Equal Opportunity Consultants, "Immigrant, Refugee and Racial Minority Women and Health Care Needs: Discussion Paper," (Toronto: Equal Opportunity Consultants, 1991), pp. 4, 7.

48 "Circumcision of girls slammed," *The Vancouver Province,* May 13, 1993, p. 5.

49 *Ibid.,* p. 2.

50 Women's Counselling Referral and Education Centre, *Missing the Mark: Women's Services Examine Mental Health Programs for Women in Toronto* (Toronto: Coalition for Feminist Mental Health Services, January 1992), p. 44.

51 Michelle Doyon and Renée Audy, *Mémoire déposé au sous-comité chargé de la condition féminine qui étudiera le problème de la violence contre les femmes* (Ottawa: Regroupement des CLSC du Montréal Métropolitain, 1991), pp. 4-6.

52 Nena Cervantes, *From Fright to Fight: Combatting the Battering of Filipino Women and Children with Community Support* (Toronto: Network of Filipino Women, October 1988), p. 21.

53 The Ontario Civilian Commission on Police Services, *Report of an Inquiry into administration of internal investigations by the Metropolitan Toronto Police Force* (Toronto: The Ontario Civilian Commission on Police Services, August 1992), p. 14-18.

54 Peter Jaffe, Deborah Reitzel, Elaine Hastings and Gary Austin, *Wife Assault as a Crime: The perspective of victims and police officers on a charging policy in London, Ontario from 1980-1990* (London: Department of Justice Canada, Solicitor General Canada, and Ontario Minister of the Solicitor General, 1991), pp. iii & iv.

55 Maria Crawford and Rosemary Gartner, *Woman Killing: Intimate Femicide in Ontario 1974-1990* (Toronto: Women We Honour Action Committee, 1992), p. 52.

56 Office of the Chief Coroner Ontario, *Inquest into the Death of Christopher Stevenson: Verdict of the Jury* (Toronto: Ministry of the Solicitor General of Ontario, September 8, 1992, to January 22, 1993), pp. 13, 22.

57 Dorothy Pedlar (Commissioner), *The Domestic Violence Review into the Administration of Justice in Manitoba* (Winnipeg: Manitoba Justice Department, August 1991), p. 26.

58 E.N. Hughes (chair), The Law Society of British Columbia Gender Bias Committee, *Equality in the Justice System,* Vol. 2 (Vancouver: The Law Society of British Columbia, 1992), pp. 7/41-42.

59 Patricia Marshall, "Sexual Assault, the Charter and Sentencing Reform," *Criminal Reports,* Vol. 63, No. 3 (September 1988): pp. 216-235.

60 Nova Scotia Advisory Council on the Status of Women, *Report of the Criminal Injuries Compensation Board,* submitted to the Honourable Thomas McInnis, Q.C. Attorney General (Halifax: Nova Scotia Advisory Council on the Status of Women, April 1990), p. 9.

61 E.J. Ursel, *Family Violence Court, Research Project, Preliminary Findings,* submitted to Court Implementation Committee (Winnipeg: Department of Sociology, University of Manitoba, December 1990), p. 18.

62 Mona G. Brown (ed.), *Gender Equality in the Courts* (Winnipeg: Manitoba Association of Women and the Law, March 1991), p. 1/34.

63 Federal-Provincial-Territorial Conference of the Ministers of Justice, *Federal Department of Justice Immediate Follow-up Actions to National Symposium on Women, Law and the Administration of Justice* (Yellowknife: Department of Justice Canada, September 1991), p. 2.

64 Patricia Marshall, "Sexual Assault, the Charter and Sentencing Reform," *Criminal Reports,* Vol. 63, No. 3 (September 1988): p. 225.

65 E.N. Hughes (chair), The Law Society of British Columbia Gender Bias Committee, *Equality in the Justice System,* Vol. 2 (Vancouver: The Law Society of British Columbia, 1992), p. 7/61.

66 Patricia Marshall, "Sexual Assault, the Charter and Sentencing Reform," *Criminal Reports,* Vol. 63, No. 3 (September 1988): p. 219.

67 Maryellen Symons and Pat Marshall, *Breach of Trust in Sexual Assault: Statement of the Problem, Part One: Review of Canadian Sentencing Decisions* (Toronto: Ontario Women's Directorate and METRAC, 1992), p. 10.

68 New Brunswick Advisory Council on the Status of Women, *Male Violence in Relationships and the Justice System* (New Brunswick: New Brunswick Advisory Council on the Status of Women, December 1989), p. 27.

69 Office of the Chief Coroner Ontario, *Inquest into the Death of Christopher Stevenson: Verdict of the Jury, op. cit.,* p. 13.

70 Office of the Chief Coroner Ontario, *Inquest into the Death of Jonathan Yeo, Verdict of the Jury* (Toronto: Ministry of the Solicitor General of Ontario, April 13, 1992, to August 17, 1992), p. 25.

71 *Bill 8* (1988, Chapter 20): *An Act respecting assistance for victims of crime,* National Assembly of Quebec, Second Session, Thirty-Third Legislature, 1988.

72 Beth Beattie, "The Inequity and Inappropriateness of Applying Statutes of Limitations to Civil Actions Arising from Childhood Sexual Abuse," *Family and Conciliation Courts Review,* Vol. 31, No. 1 (January 1993): pp. 65-89.

73 Yves Morier, Catherine Bluteau, Guy Bruneau, Claire Lessard and Pierre Beaudet, *Intervention sociojudiciaire en violence conjugale* (Montreal: Wilson & Lafleur Ltée and Centre Éducatif et Culturel Inc., 1991), pp. 37, 57, 70, 140, 144, 148, 149, 151, 174.

74 Lise Corbeil, *The Impact of Poverty on Fairness in Judicial Processes,* submitted in Geneva (Ottawa: National Anti-Poverty Organization, February 5, 1992), p. 6/13.

75 Yves Morier, Catherine Bluteau, Guy Bruneau, Claire Lessard and Pierre Beaudet, *Intervention sociojudiciaire en violence conjugale, op. cit.,* pp. 27-28.

76 National Symposium on Women, Law and the Administration of Justice, Vancouver, B.C, June 10-12, 1991, *Recommendations from the Symposium* (Ottawa: Communications and Consultation Branch, Department of Justice Canada, 1992), p. 141.

77 Ken MacQueen, "*Moge vs Moge:* Ordinary People and A Lesson in Social Reality," *Ottawa Citizen,* December 18, 1992, p. A1.

78 Cristin Schmitz, "Women, kids driven into poverty by low awards under Divorce Act," *The Lawyers Weekly,* Vol. 10, No. 16 (August 31,1990): p. 1.

79 Holly A. Magana and Nancy Taylor, "Child Custody and Mediation and Spouse Abuse: A descriptive study of a protocol," *Family and Conciliation Courts,* Vol. 31, No. 1 (January 1993): pp. 50-64.

80   Ontario Ministry of the Attorney General, *Marriage as an Equal Partnership: A Guide to the Family Law Act Booklet* (Toronto: Ministry of the Attorney General, 1987), pp. 12-13.

81   Peter Jaffe, Susan Wilson, Shiela Cameron, Rhonda Zajk and David Wolfe, "Are Children Who Witness Wife Battering in Need of Protection?", *The Ontario Association of Children's Aid Societies Journal,* Vol. 31, No. 7 (September 1987), pp. 3-7.

82   *An Act to Amend the Criminal Code and Canada Evidence Act,* (formerly Bill C-15, passed in the House of Commons on June 23, 1987), R.S.C. 1985, c. 19 (3rd Supp.).

83   V. Schmolka, *Is Bill C-15 Working? An Overview of the Research on the Effects of the 1988 Child Sexual Abuse Amendments* (Ottawa: Department of Justice, 1992).

84   *Criminal Code,* R.S.C. 1992, c. 21, s. 9.

85   Louise Sas (Principle Investigator) et al., *Reducing the System-Induced Trauma for Child Sexual Abuse Victims Through Court Preparation, Assessment and Follow-Up* (London: Child Witness Project, London Family Court Clinic, January 1991), p. 116.

86   Alan W. Leschied and Christopher W. Hyatt, "Perspective: Section 22(1), consent to treatment under the *Young Offenders Act," Canadian Journal of Criminology,* Vol. 28, No. 1 (January 1986): pp. 28-86.

87   D.A. Andrews, Ivan Zinger, Robert D. Hoge, James Bonta, Paul Gendreau and Frances T. Cullen, "Does correctional treatment work? A clinically relevant and psychologically informed meta-analysis," *Criminology,* Vol. 28, No. 3 (1990): pp. 369-404.

88   D.A. Andrews, Alan W. Leschied and Robert D. Hoge, *Review of the Profile, Classification and Treatment Literature with Young Offenders: A Social-Psychological Approach* (Toronto: Ministry of Community and Social Services, 1992), pp. 131-146.

89   Alan W. Leschied, Peter G. Jaffe, Don Andrews and Paul Gendreau, "Treatment issues and young offenders: An empirically derived vision of Canadian juvenile justice," in Raymond Corrado, Nicholas Bala, Rick Linden and Marc LeBlanc (eds.), *Juvenile Justice in Canada: A Theoretical and Analytical Assessment,* (Toronto: Butterworths, 1992), p. 364.

90   Jeffrey Frank, "Violent Youth Crime," in *Canadian Social Trends* (Ottawa: Statistics Canada, 1992), p. 6.

91   Marge Reitsma-Street, "A Review of Female Delinquency in Canada," in Alan W. Leschied, Peter G. Jaffe and Wayne Willis (eds.), *The Young Offender Act: A Revolution in Canadian Juvenile Justice* (Toronto: University of Toronto Press, 1991), pp. 248-287.

92   Janice Turner, "When women are stalked," *Toronto Star,* August 15, 1992, pp. F1/F2.

93   *Ibid.*

94   Maria Crawford and Rosemary Gartner, *Women Killing: Intimate Femicide in Ontario 1974-1990* (Ontario: Women We Honour Action Committee, April 1992), p. 166.

95   National Parole Board, *Detention: A Summary of the NPB Detention Policies* (Ottawa: Ministry of Supply and Services, October 1990).

96   *An act respecting corrections and the conditional release and detention of offenders and to establish the office of correctional investigator* (Bill C-36: Assented to 19th June, 1992), S. C. 1992, c. 20, pp. 63-64.

97   Dr. W.L. Marshall and Sylvia Barrett, "The Case for Treatment," in *Criminal Neglect: Why Sex Offenders Go Free* (Toronto: Doubleday Canada Ltd, 1990), p. 149.

98   Personal interview with Dr. William Marshall, professor at Queen's University.

99   Marilyn Pilon, *The "Rape Shield" Decision: Evidence in Sexual Assault Cases* (Ottawa: Library of Parliament Research Branch, September 20, 1991), pp. 1-2.

100   Bill C-49, *An Act to Amend the Criminal Code* (sexual assault) (Ottawa: Government of Canada, June 15, 1992).

101   *Saskatchewan Human Rights Commission vs The Engineering Student's Society et al.,* [1984] 5 CHRR 2074.

102   The information here was taken over the phone from the By-law Department at the City Solicitor's Office for the City of Montreal; the Montreal city by-law number is #8887 and it is currently in effect.

103   Heidi Rathjen, "Gun Control: An Analysis of Bill C-17," *Women's EDUCATION des femmes,* Vol. 10, No. 1 (Winter, 1992-1993): p. 48.

104   The Advisory Board on Victims' Issues, *Victim's of Crime in Ontario, A Vision for 1990s* (Ontario: The Advisory Board on Victim's Issues, June 1991), pp. 21-22.

105   Women's Legal Education and Action Fund (LEAF), *LEAF Lines,* 4:4, (Toronto, January 1992), p. 6.

106   Canadian Labour Congress (CLC), *Violence Against Women Policy Statement. We Can do it: End the Violence Against Women* (19th Constitutional Convention, June 8-12, 1992, Ottawa) articles 44 and 45, p. 7.

107   L'Intersyndicale des femmes, *La violence faite aux femmes dans les milieux de travail* (Study presented to the Canadian Panel on Violence Against Women, Quebec, December 6, 1992), p. 14.

108   The Public Service Alliance of Canada, *Superwoman Syndrome* (Ottawa: Working document, PSAC Regional Women's Conference, February 19-21, 1993), p. 1.

109   Jillian Ridington, *Pornography* (Research paper prepared for the Canadian Panel on Violence Against Women, Vancouver, 1993).

110 Monique Gauvin and Ann Robinson, *Violence Against Women and Sexual Harassment* (Research paper prepared for the Canadian Panel on Violence Against Women, Quebec, 1993).

111 Canadian Labour Congress (CLC), Violence Against Women Policy Statement, *We Can do it: End the Violence Against Women,* Article 38, p. 3.

112 *Ibid.,* Article 41, p. 6 and Article 42, p. 7.

113 Public Service Alliance of Canada, *Le complexe de la superfemme, op. cit.*, p. 2.

114 Canadian Labour Congress (CLC), *Violence Against Women Policy Statement, We Can do it, op. cit.,* Article 53, p. 8.

115 *Ibid.,* Article 62(a), p. 10.

116 Lenore E. Walker, *Terrifying Love: Why Battered Women Kill and How Society Responds* (New York: Harper & Row, 1987), pp. 48, 179-180.

117 Bill C-56, *Proposed Occupational Health and Safety Act,* 3rd Session, 22nd Legislature, 1993, article 2 (1)(1)(i). Further references will be cited parenthetically.

118 Susan Brownmiller, *Against Our Will*, as cited in Organization of Spouses of Military Members (OSOMM), *Brief Presented to the Senate Committee on National Defence* (June 1986), p. 9.

119 Director General Personnel Services/Family Support Program Project, *Study Report on Family Support* (National Defence Headquarters, May 1989), p. 5.

120 Status of Women Canada, *Wirestories,* July 4, 1992.

121 Status of Women Canada, *Wirestories,* July 17, 1992.

122 Minister's Advisory Board on Women in the Canadian Forces, *First Annual Report* (Ottawa, March 1991), p. 5.

123 *The Ottawa Citizen,* May 6, 1993, p. A-7.

124 Minister's Advisory Board on Women in the Canadian Forces, *Second Annual Report* (Ottawa, 1991-1992), p. 18.

125 *Ibid.,* p. 18.

126 *Ibid.,* p. 20.

127 *Ibid.,* p. 19.

128 *Ibid.*

129 *Ibid.,* p. 21.

130 *Ibid.,* p. 22.

131 *Ibid.,* p. 24.

132 *The Toronto Star,* May 6, 1993, p. A-10.

133 *The Ottawa Citizen,* May 6, 1993, p. A-7.

134 Minister's Advisory Board on Women in the Canadian Forces, *Second Annual Report, op. cit.*, pp. 27-34.

135 Madeleine Aubin et al., "Pratiques pédagogiques : construire une pédagogie féministe dans des classes du primaire," *Recherches féministes,* Vol. 1, No. 1 (1988): p. 93.

136 *Ibid.,* p. 93.

137 *Ibid.,* p. 95.

138 *Ibid.,* pp. 94-95.

139 "The Elementary-Secondary Teaching Force," *Education Statistics Bulletin,* Vol. 14, No. 8 (Ottawa, October 1992).

140 *Ibid.*

141 Megan Williams, "If Boys Will be Boys, Girls Will Now Take Action," *This Magazine,* Vol. 26, No. 4 (October/November, 1992), p. 19.

142 Monique Gauvin,"Le harcèlement sexuel et sexiste comme pratique d'appropriation des femmes: la situation dans les universités canadiennes," *Égalité* (printemps 1991), p. 210.

143 L'Organisation des femmes (ODFA) dans l'Association national des étudiants et étudiantes du Québec (ANEEQ), *Les conditions d'études et de vie des étudiantes* (Mémoire présenté à la Commission parlementaire sur l'enseignement collégial) (Montreal, November 1992), p. 12.

144 *Ibid.,* p. 13.

145 Statistics Canada, *1991 Census; Major Fields of Study Postsecondary Graduates: The Nation* (Ottawa, 1993), pp. 192-193.

146 Statistics Canada, *The Labour Force; Feature: Persons not in the Labour Force* (Ottawa, April 1993), p. B-29.

147 Women's Bureau, Labour Canada, *Women in the Labour Force,* 1990-91 edition (Ottawa, 1991), pp. 81, 84, 87.

148 Architecture Review Committee, *The Architecture Review Committee's Report* (Ottawa: Carleton University, December 21, 1992), pp. 22, 24.

149 Barbara Barde, with Toronto Women in Film and Television (Submission to the Canadian Panel on Violence Against Women, Toronto, March 1992), p. 1.

150 Sandra Campbell, "Aspects of Canadian Popular Culture: Messages About Violence and Gender Behaviour" (Submission to the Canadian Panel on Violence Against Women, Ottawa, August 1992), p. 1.

151 *Ibid.,* p. 5.

152 *Ibid.,* p. 11.

153 *Ibid.,* p. 5.

154 *Ibid.*, p. 4.

155 MediaWatch, "Images of Women Workshop," (Submission to the Canadian Panel on Violence Against Women, Ottawa, March 1992), p. 2.

156 Martin Lee and Norman Solomon, *Unreliable Sources, A Guide to Detecting Bias in the New Media,* as cited in Jan D'Arcy, *Trying to Change the Shape of a Brick that has Already been Built into the Wall* (Ottawa: National Film Board of Canada, January 1993), p. 5.

157 *Ibid.,* p. 5.

158 The Kingston Pornography Action Committee (Submission to the Canadian Panel on Violence Against Women, Ottawa, March 1992), p. 1.

159   Keith Spicer, "CRTC Takes Proactive Approach to Addressing Television Violence, "*News Release CRTC,* (Ottawa: CRTC, May 27, 1992), p. 1.

160   *Ibid.,* p. 1.

161   Sandra Campbell and Jo-Anne Corbeil with Viva Associates, "A brief summary of findings from a qualitative research project on the impact of television on children" (Submission to the Canadian Panel on Violence Against Women, Toronto, March 1992), p. 4.

162   Sandra Campbell, "Aspects of Canadian Popular Culture," *op. cit.,* p. 8.

163   *Ibid.,* p. 7.

164   *Ibid.,* p. 3.

165   *Ibid.,* p. 7.

166   Barbara Barde with Toronto Women in Film and Television, *op. cit.,* p. 2.

167   Sandra Campbell, "Aspects of Canadian Popular Culture," *op. cit.,* p. 8.

168   Kathy Maio, "Hooked on Hate," *Ms. Magazine,* Vol. 1, No. 2 (September/October 1990): p. 44.

169   Sandra Campbell and Jo-Anne Corbeil, "Media Violence and Children," in *A Handbook for the Prevention of Family Violence* (Hamilton: Community Child Abuse Council of Hamilton-Wentworth, December 1990), p. 8.8.

170   Jan D'Arcy, *Trying to Change the Shape of a Brick, op. cit.,* p. 16.

171   Sandra Campbell and Jo-Anne Corbeil, *A Handbook for the Prevention of Family Violence, op. cit.,* p. 8.8.

172   *Ibid.,* p. 8.9.

173   MediaWatch, "Images of Women Workshop," *op. cit.,* p. 1.

174   *Ibid.,* p. 3.

175   *Ibid.,* p. 4.

176   Jan D'Arcy, *Trying to Change the Shape of a Brick, op. cit.,* p. 16.

177   *Ibid.,* p. 24.

178   *Ibid.*

179   MediaWatch, "Images of Women Workshop," *op. cit.,* p. 2.

180   *Ibid.*

181   *Ibid.,* pp. 3-4.

182   *Ibid.,* p. 4.

183   Gaye Tuchman, *Making News: A Study in the Construction of Reality* (New York: The Free Press, 1978), p. 133.

184   MediaWatch, "Images of Women Workshops," *op. cit.,* p. 6.

185   Erin Research, commissioned by the CRTC, *The Portrayal of Sex Roles in Canadian Television Programming,* 1985 (Ottawa: Ministry of Supply and Services, 1986), p. 26.

186   Jan D'Arcy, *Trying to Change the Shape of a Brick, op. cit.,* p. 18.

187   *Ibid.,* pp. 11-12.

188   *Ibid.,* p. 12.

189   *Ibid.,* p. 13.

190   Sandra Campbell and Jo-Anne Corbeil, *A Handbook for the Prevention of Family Violence, op. cit.,* p. 8.10.

191   *Ibid.,* p. 8.5.

192   Jan D'Arcy, *Trying to Change the Shape of a Brick, op. cit.,* p. 15.

193   Sandra Campbell and Jo-Anne Corbeil, *A Handbook for the Prevention of Family Violence, op. cit.,* p. 8.5.

194   *Ibid.,* p. 8.13.

195   Sandra Campbell and Jo-Anne Corbeil, *A Handbook for the Prevention of Family Violence, op. cit.,* p. 8.14.

196   Sandra Campbell and Jo-anne Corbeil, *A Handbook for the Prevention of Family Violence, op. cit.,* p. 8.11.

197   *Ibid.*

198   Barbara Barde with Toronto Women in Film and Television, *op. cit.,* p. 4.

199   *Ibid.,* p. 6.

200   Sandra Campbell, "Aspects of Canadian Popular Culture," *op. cit.,* pp. 3-4.

201   Barbara Barde with Toronto Women in Film and Television, *op. cit.,* p. 3.

202   MediaWatch, *Brief on MediaWatch monitoring of beer and soft drink advertisements* (Toronto: MediaWatch, December 1, 1989).

203   Barbara Barde with Toronto Women in Film and Television, *op. cit.,* p. 6.

204   *Ibid.*

205   Chantal Maillé with Valentina Pollon, Simone de Beauvoir Institute, Concordia University, Montreal, *Primed for Power* (Ottawa: Canadian Advisory Council on the Status of Women, November 1990), p. 21.

206   Barbara Barde with Toronto Women in Film and Television, *op. cit.,* p. 7.

207   *Ibid.,* p. 8.

208   Celebration of Women in the Arts, *Results of Survey of CWA Members on Violence and Economic Issues* (Toronto, Summer 1991).

PART FIVE

THE NATIONAL

ACTION PLAN

THE NATIONAL ACTION PLAN

Introduction

This section of the report addresses the solutions to the problem of violence against women. The Panel believes that inequality increases women's vulnerability to violence and limits their choices in all aspects of their lives. In turn, women cannot achieve full equality while they are subjected to violence in their daily lives. The Panel is therefore committed to two goals: the achievement of women's equality and the elimination of violence against women. The National Action Plan (NAP) identifies concrete steps twoard the achievement of both goals. The proposed actions are neither simple nor easy to implement. They demand a sustained and co-ordinated response. They demand a new set of priorities and a new way of looking at the world. They also demand recognition of the differences among women and the diverse approaches required to address the concerns of all women.

The National Action Plan begins by calling on our goverments to fulfil their international commitments with respect to women's equality. When women have achieved legal, economic, social and political equality they will be able to make choices in their lives which truly reflect their interests. They will no longer have to suffer violence out of fear, poverty, shame or powerlessness. The Equality Action Plan deals with those aspects of formal equality that the Panel believes have the greatest bearing on the vulnerability of women to violence.

- Equality rights

- Equal access to the legal system

- Political and public service participation

- Mechanisms for women

- Women and the economy

- The Family

- Women and the tax/transfer system

The National Action Plan introduces the concept of zero tolerance and a policy framework for its implementation. Zero tolerance means that no level of violence is acceptable, and women's safety and equality are priorities. All organizations and institutions are strongly encouraged to review their programs, practices and products in light of the Zero Tolerance Policy which includes:

- an accountability framework;

- implementation steps; and

- a zero tolerance model for organizations and institutions to follow.

The policy is applied to key sectors in society — services (health and social), legal, workplace, military, education, media, religious institutions and the federal government — to illustrate the nature and magnitude of the changes required to ensure safety and equality for women in Canada.

Health and social services and the legal/justice system are crucial to women since these sectors often offer first response when violence happens. Women look to these sectors for protection, redress and healing.

The education system, the media and religious institutions shape attitudes and behaviours, and have a critical role to play in advancing equality and ending violence. The workplace, a site of much violence against women, is key to women gaining economic independence and thereby reducing their vulnerability to violence.

The military is dominated by men and male values. Newly admitted as workers in a full range of occupations, women face discrimination, harassment and violence. Spouses of military men are also deeply affected by military policy and culture.

Governments have a major role in protecting women's rights, promoting equality and providing leadership to the application of the Zero Tolerance Policy.

Application of the Zero Tolerance Policy in these eight sectors will provide a foundation for zero tolerance at every level in Canada. It is not just up to governments, institutions and organizations to ensure equality and safety for women: individuals and communities also have a role to play. Therefore, in the Action Plan for Individuals, we have provided examples of actions which individuals can take as intimate partners, parents, children, friends, co-workers and community members.

We conclude by proposing accountabilty and monitoring mechanisms to ensure that the National Action Plan is fully reviewed and responded to. The Zero Tolerance Policy underscores the importance of accountability at all levels and in all sectors. It is critical that the federal government, which must take the lead in implementing the National Action Plan through its various departments, be closely monitored to assess the adequacy of its activities both at the individual departmental level and collectively in accordance with a zero tolerance approach to violence against women.

---

*   *Although all of the actions enumerated in the National Action Plan are applicable to all women in Canada, actions which apply uniquely to Aboriginal and/or Inuit women are noted by use of the following symbols:*

 Aboriginal   *Inuit*

SECTION 1

EQUALITY ACTION PLAN

Introduction

Equality has been defined as,

> ... both a goal and a means whereby
> individuals are accorded equal treatment
> under the law and equal opportunities to
> enjoy their rights and to develop their
> potential talents and skills so that they can
> participate in national political, economic,
> social and cultural development and can
> benefit from its results. For women in
> particular, equality means the realization of
> rights that have been denied as a result of
> cultural, institutional, behavioural and
> attitudinal discrimination. [1]

Canada already has a strong, stated commitment to
gender equality and a legacy of statutory measures
aimed at achieving equality. The *Canadian Charter of
Rights and Freedoms*, employment equity and human
rights legislation at the federal, provincial and territorial levels are all manifestations of our commitment to equality. However, while Canadian law provides, in broad terms, for equality and non-
discrimination, true gender equality in which women
participate equally in all facets of society is not the
day-to-day reality. Statistical profiles of women in
Canada consistently describe the specific economic,
political, social or cultural forms women's inequality
can take. The experiences of Canadian girls and
women reflect these statistical measures every day.

In addition to its domestic measures, Canada has
made clear and unequivocal international commitments to achieving equality for women by signing a
number of international conventions and declara-
tions. These include the Universal Declaration of
Human Rights, [2] the United Nations Convention on
the Elimination of All Forms of Discrimination against
Women, [3] including General recommendation
No. 19 [4] which specifically addresses the issue of
violence against women, and the adoption in 1985 of
the Nairobi Forward-looking Strategies for the
Advancement of Women.

We believe that concrete, practical fulfilment of
these commitments along with significant change in
key areas of women's lives would make a critical
difference in achieving women's equality in our
society, thereby reducing women's vulnerability to
violence.

While women face systemic barriers and inequality
in all sectors of society, we have chosen to focus on
the following fundamental dimensions of women's
lives: formal legal equality, equal access to the legal
system, political and public service participation,
national mechanisms to promote women's equality,
participation in the economy, the family and the role
of women within it, and the tax system.

Although we have not been able to deal with all the
subjects that would comprise a comprehensive
equality agenda, we want to underscore that full
equality will only be achieved when biases and
discrimination no longer exist in any aspect of
women's lives.

Two underlying principles guided us in our selection
of recommendations. First, there is the need to
enhance women's economic independence — the
lack of which is inherently tied to women's
experience of violence and which limits their options
once violence has occurred. This can best be
achieved through measures such as equal access to
work opportunities, fair compensation for work
performed, the provision of support at key
transition points in the lives of women and sufficient
income in retirement. Second, women must be
recognized and treated as autonomous beings,
distinct from their familial relationships and from
their male partners in particular.

Unless otherwise specified, our recommendations are directed to the federal level of government. This is not to downplay the role that provincial and municipal governments, organizations, communities and individuals must play in achieving equality for women but rather to recognize the responsibility of the federal government to demonstrate leadership in the fulfilment of Canada's national and international commitments. We expect action to begin immediately. This is in keeping with Canada's commitment to the implementation of the Nairobi Forward-looking Strategies which aim at achieving equality for women by the year 2000.

Equality requires that no adverse distinctions be made on the basis of race, class, sexual orientation, linguistic, immigrant or visible minority status, age or ability. When we talk about the achievement of equality, we mean equality for all women. We recognize, however, that equality does not necessarily mean treating all women the same. There may need to be differential treatment for some women in order for all women to realize their full potential. In many cases, we have identified changes which must be made to our laws, to political and governmental practices, to our economy and culture to ensure the full participation of specific groups of women.

The recommendations are not in any order of priority. They are all important and in most cases, complementary.

I EQUALITY RIGHTS

In Canada, equality rights are fundamentally enshrined in the *Canadian Charter of Rights and Freedoms* and in federal, provincial and territorial human rights legislation.

Key Problems

*   The laws which specifically address equality do not refer expressly to certain women (for example, lesbians) nor do they offer adequate protection against discrimination (for example, in the case of Aboriginal people).

*   Human rights legislation is insufficient to help women achieve equality. There are major limitations with respect to the scope, application, remedies and enforcement of the legislation, and its individual, complaints-based processes.

*   The lives of certain Aboriginal women are governed by the *Indian Act*, which means that in some cases their equality rights are compromised.

*   Women refugees often face gender bias before coming to Canada and on their arrival in Canada. Their experiences are not adequately recognized by our laws.

Canada's Commitment:

To ensure a legal basis for the equal rights of women. [5]

Fulfilling Canada's commitment includes:

E.1   **Adding sexual orientation as one of the prohibited grounds of discrimination in the *Canadian Human Rights Act* and to provincial and territorial human rights legislation where it does not presently exist, without limitation with respect to the definition of family or marital status.**

E.2   **Ensuring that human rights legislation has the power to address systemic discrimination, as well as individual, complaint-driven cases of discrimination.**

E.3   **Guaranteeing that Aboriginal women are recognized and protected in the human rights legislation which applies in all provinces and territories regardless of treaty rights.**

E.4   **Eliminating the discrimination among different categories of Aboriginal women and their children in the *Indian Act*.**

E.5   **Realizing Aboriginal, including Métis, aspirations for self-government, guaranteeing the direct participation of Aboriginal women and protecting their rights under the *Canadian Charter of Rights and Freedoms* in the negotiation of any agreements, treaties or land claim settlements.**

E.6   **Changing, through legislation, the grounds for granting refugee status to recognize persecution on the basis of gender explicitly.**

II   EQUAL ACCESS TO THE LEGAL SYSTEM

Women's lives are governed by the general laws of Canadian society which are based on British Common Law and the French Civil Code. These laws embody the values, customs and traditions of societies which have been dominated and largely shaped by European males. As such, they do not reflect the unique experiences and circumstances of women, nor do they take into account the realities of different groups of women such as Aboriginal women, Inuit women, women of colour, immigrant women, refugee women, young women, older women, women with disabilities and lesbians.

The laws and the manner in which they are interpreted and applied have a direct bearing on the choices and experiences of women who are victims of violence.

Key Problems

•   Laws which appear to be gender neutral may have a differential and adverse impact on women.

•   Not all women have equal access to the legal system. Women are often unaware of their rights due to the absence of appropriate and accessible information. Many lack the resources, particularly financial, to exercise their rights.

•   Not all women are treated equally before the law. Women frequently face overt discrimination by those responsible for enforcing the law. If they are members of Aboriginal, Inuit or ethnic communities, or if they are immigrant or refugee women, they may encounter racist and ethnocentric attitudes in addition to the discrimination they face on the basis of gender. Lesbians and women with disabilities may also have to contend with heterosexist and stereotypical images of what constitutes a "normal" woman.

- For certain women — members of Aboriginal, Inuit, immigrant, refugee and minority language groups — language barriers restrict access to the justice system. Others, namely Aboriginal and Inuit women and women living in rural or isolated areas, encounter difficulties due to the absence of services. For women with disabilities or low literacy skills, the lack of services in alternative forms creates a barrier.

- Unlike criminal law, there are no national standards for the provision of legal aid in civil law cases. This can severely limit women's opportunities for redress or settlement, particularly in family law actions.

- Current Aboriginal justice system projects do not respond to the specific needs and concerns of Aboriginal women.

Canada's Commitment:

To establish legislative and administrative mechanisms to ensure that individual women and women as a group may, without obstruction or cost to themselves, obtain redress for both discriminatory actions and systemic discrimination.

Fulfilling Canada's commitment includes:

E.7 Reinstating and expanding the Court Challenges Program,[6] extending its application to provincial and territorial laws, and providing full and adequate funding for its application by the respective level of government.

E.8 Strengthening human rights legislation in consultation with equality-seeking groups, and adequately financing the Canadian Human Rights Commission and its provincial and territorial counterparts to pursue women's equality, investigate systemic discrimination and provide redress, and more efficiently and effectively resolve individual cases of discrimination.

Canada's Commitment:

To investigate the problems associated with the relationship between the law, and the role, status and material circumstances of women.

Fulfilling Canada's commitment includes:

E.9 Funding equality-seeking groups to build upon the gender equality work of the Canadian Bar Association and law societies across Canada by reviewing all legislation and common law principles to determine if they have a differential or negative impact on women, or particular groups of women, and amending them accordingly.

E.10 Establishing national standards and financing for the provision of legal aid for family law cases.

E.11 Working with provincial and territorial governments to implement mandatory gender and race sensitivity training for all law students, lawyers, judges and para-legal personnel.

E.12 Guaranteeing the equal participation of Aboriginal and Inuit women in the design and implementation of Aboriginal and Inuit justice systems.

III POLITICAL AND PUBLIC SERVICE PARTICIPATION

In general, women are under-represented in Canada's political institutions and the public service. As a result, laws, policies and programs do not reflect women's priorities, meet their needs or respond to their concerns. For example, there is insufficient funding for programs to promote equality or eliminate violence; the health care system does not respond adequately to female victims of violence and women's health issues in general; and economic policies do not recognize women's unpaid contributions, their work patterns or their poverty.

Key Problems

In Politics

- The dominant ethic in politics is neither receptive nor particularly attractive to women.

- Women, especially Aboriginal women, women of colour and women with disabilities, are under-represented in all political parties and in elected offices in Canada.

- Women are overrepresented in the volunteer ranks of political parties, but are often employed in menial tasks and are under-represented in decision-making positions.

- There are financial barriers to women's political participation at all levels.

- Women frequently face harassment and denigration when participating in politics.

- Aboriginal leaders in local, regional and national governments are not accountable to Aboriginal women and, therefore, do not adequately uphold their rights nor advance their issues.

In the Public Service

- Despite measures to rectify historical imbalances, women are under-represented at the higher levels of decision making in the public service. [7]

- The *Employment Equity Act* does not extend to Parliament, the federal public service or federal agencies, boards and commissions. [8] Treasury Board's Employment Equity Policy has only led to modest progress in the representation, recruitment, promotion and retention of target group members. [9]

Canada's Commitment:

To ensure equality of participation by women at all levels of government, to encourage women to exercise their political rights and to provide equal access to the ranks of political parties and other organizations.

Fulfilling Canada's commitment includes:

E.13 Implementing the recommendations regarding the full participation of women in the political process contained in the report of the Royal Commission on Electoral Reform and Party Financing, *Reforming Electoral Democracy*. [10] **Similar recommendations should be extended to provincial and municipal politics.**

E.14 Encouraging Aboriginal and Inuit women to assume leadership roles in all levels of government.

E.15 Developing and implementing a policy against harassment — including harassment on the basis of sex, race, religion, ethnic origin, age and sexual orientation or level of ability — for members of Parliament, their staff and federal political parties.

E.16 **Implementing the recommendations contained in the report of the Task Force on Barriers to Women in the Public Service,** *Beneath the Veneer.*

E.17 **Extending the application of the** *Employment Equity Act* **to Parliament, the federal public service and all federal agencies, boards and commissions. Furthermore, ensuring that all federal political parties report to Parliament, on an annual basis, on the composition of their staff and the staff of members of Parliament.**

IV MECHANISMS FOR WOMEN

Canada has established a variety of mechanisms to promote equality for women. At the federal level these include the Minister Responsible for the Status of Women and her department, Status of Women Canada (SWC), the Canadian Advisory Council on the Status of Women (CACSW), women's bureaus and programs or advisors in a variety of departments. In addition, the Women's Program of the Secretary of State provides funding to assist national, regional and local groups to pursue equality for women through a variety of activities.

These mechanisms, and in particular women's groups, have been essential in raising public awareness, taking action on issues of concern to women including violence against women, and in lobbying to put women's issues on the political agenda.

Key Problems

• No federal government department has the statutory authority to develop, oversee and co-ordinate the implementation of the government's agenda for women and to ensure that gender equality is promoted and achieved through all federal policies, programs and legislation.

• Policies, programs and legislative proposals are often developed without the involvement of the federal mechanisms for women. When these mechanisms are consulted, it is frequently after policy directions have been set.

• Within departments, women's bureaus or advisors are frequently bypassed, sidelined or ignored in the development of legislation, policies or programs.

• The diversity of Canadian women is not adequately reflected in the composition or substantive work of many government mechanisms for women.

• The contributions of non-governmental organizations in articulating women's views, monitoring and evaluating government products and advocating for change, are not adequately recognized, nor are such organizations adequately funded, consulted or involved in legislation, policy and program development.

Canada's Commitment:

To strengthen national mechanisms for monitoring and improving the status of women at all levels in the government and ensure adequate resources, commitment and authority to advise on the impact on women of all government policies, programs and legislation; to disseminate information to women regarding their rights and entitlements; and to cooperate with other government agencies and non-governmental organizations.

Fulfilling Canada's commitment includes:

E.18 Enacting a "Status of Women Act" to identify the specific obligations and responsibilities of the federal government to ensure that the rights to equality and safety of all Canadian women are supported and advanced.

The Act would:

- Designate the Minister Responsible for the Status of Women as a senior minister with the power and authority to enforce the Act, including the development and implementation of a multi-year plan with clear objectives and target dates aimed at achieving gender equality and implementing a policy of zero tolerance.

- Provide the Minister with the authority to participate, with the support of the Status of Women ministry, in the development and final review of all federal government policies, programs and legislative proposals for their impact on all women and to propose amendments as required.

- Enhance the capacity of the Status of Women ministry to support the Minister through the provision of adequate resources for consultation, research, policy development and analysis, and to monitor the government's progress on equality and women's safety.

- Develop a framework for equality and safety to guide departments in their policy analysis, program development and legislative drafting to increase sensitivity to gender and the differences among women as a result of age, ability, race, colour, sexual orientation or other characteristics.

- Ensure the full participation of national groups seeking equality for women in the implementation of the Act, through the creation of a permanent Advisory Board. Among its members, the Board would include Aboriginal and Inuit women, women of colour, immigrants, lesbians and women with disabilities. Board members would provide policy advice and guidance to the Status of Women ministry, particularly with respect to the government's multi-year gender-equality plan and the development of the equality and safety framework. The exact membership, role and responsibilities of the Advisory Board would be determined in consultation with relevant groups.

- Make the government accountable for its progress on women's equality and safety by requiring the Minister to report to Parliament, on an annual basis, on the gender impact and consequences of government policies, programs and legislation, including progress toward achieving the objectives and target dates established in the multi-year gender-equality plan.

E.19 Requiring the deputy ministers of federal departments to be accountable for the implementation of the equality and safety framework. They would be required to allocate resources sufficient for the task and provide their staff with appropriate training, developed in co-operation with the Status of Women ministry.

E.20 Elevating the Sub-Committee on the Status of Women of the Parliamentary Standing Committee on Health and Welfare, Social Affairs, Seniors and Status of Women to full committee status, and requiring its participation in the review of the estimates of all departments to ensure the resource allocations of government appropriately promote women's equality and safety.

Canada's Commitment:

To stimulate the formation and growth of women's organizations and to give financial and organizational support to their activities.

Fulfilling Canada's commitment includes:

E.21 Ensuring the full participation of organizations seeking equality for women, including those representing particularly vulnerable groups, in the formation of public policy by providing adequate, long-term, stable funding.

Canada's Commitment:

To ensure that statistics based on appropriate indicators of women's differential participation in the country's economic structures are available.

Fulfilling Canada's commitment includes:

E.22 Requiring all departments responsible for the compilation and dissemination of statistics to provide data based on gender and other significant demographic characteristics.

E.23 Providing gender-specific data on the impact of economic restructuring.

E.24 Ensuring that Statistics Canada regularly collects and includes data on both the remunerated and unremunerated contributions of women in national economic statistics and in Canada's Gross National Product, especially their contributions to child rearing, caregiving, household, voluntary and community activities. Public policies must be based on this fuller understanding of the social and economic life of the nation.

V WOMEN AND THE ECONOMY

Women contribute significantly to the Canadian economy through both their paid and unpaid labour. They do not, however, benefit equally from the fruits of their labour. The lower wages paid to women and their status as unpaid workers at home lead to their dependency on the wages and status of their male partners, or relatives. Often the female gender and poverty go together, particularly for older women, women with disabilities and female lone parents.

For Aboriginal women living on reserves or in isolated communities, the barriers to employment are severe. In many cases, these communities do not even have the economic base to provide employment. It will require a concerted effort on the part of the federal government and the Aboriginal leadership to create viable economies to support Aboriginal workers in their own communities. While it is beyond our mandate to resolve this matter, we challenge the federal government and the Aboriginal leadership to address this fundamental issue and to ensure that Aboriginal women are directly involved at every stage in the process.

Women who are financially autonomous in our society are those who are able to benefit from the widest range of options and opportunities. Our recommendations, therefore, work to support women's full participation in the work force and to facilitate their ability to make independent choices.

Key Problems

- Women earn an average of 60¢ for every $1.00 earned by men. [12]

- Underemployment is disproportionately high for women. In addition, there are particular groups of women which are chronically overrepresented among the unemployed and underemployed due to systemic barriers.

- Women are concentrated in a few occupational categories, where they are compressed in the lower levels. [13] Certain women, particularly immigrants, are also concentrated in piecework and domestic work which tend to be non-unionized and pay minimum or below minimum wages. Furthermore, the majority of part-time workers are women. [14]

- Women, particularly immigrants and refugees, often come to Canada as dependants. They enter low-paying jobs or do not work at all, do not have equal access to information about services and programs available to them and may have a cultural heritage which impedes their seeking employment. In addition, many face language barriers or have qualifications which are not recognized in Canada.

- The labour market is often unwilling to recognize the capabilities of women with disabilities or to make adjustments to facilitate their work.

- The labour force participation of women is limited by the fact that they are still the primary caregivers and carry an unfair burden with respect to other domestic duties. Generally, workplace policies and programs are not designed to help balance work and family responsibilities.

- The lack of state support for the costs of child-rearing is a significant barrier for female social assistance recipients who might otherwise enter the work force and reduce their dependency on the state.

- Women do not have the same training, employment and promotion opportunities as men.

- Women are disadvantaged in their old age by lower pensions and income [15] due to non-participation in the paid labour force. Domestic work is not compensated nor used in the calculation of pension credits. The fact that they may have disrupted their careers to have children and to care for family members is not adequately acknowledged or addressed.

- Farm women and other self-employed women operating businesses as independent principals, often face discrimination in their access to financial and other resources necessary for the success of their business ventures.

- Farm women and other women contributing to family-operated businesses are rarely co-owners of business assets or formal partners in the management of enterprises. They seldom have a legal agreement underpinning their business association and do not always receive economic returns (wages, profits, income) in their own right commensurate with their contributions.

- Even when there are employment possibilities in Aboriginal communities, nepotism or favouritism can restrict opportunities for women.

Canada's Commitment:

To provide a range of affordable, accessible and quality child care.

Fulfilling Canada's commitment includes:

E.25 **Implementing a national child care plan based on the principles of equity and flexibility and supported by regulations and standards governing child care workers, programs and facilities.**

E.26 **Ensuring co-ordination among all levels of government with respect to the funding, regulation, taxation and provision of child care.**

E.27 **Encouraging workplace child care services through incentives such as funding, space or tax relief.**

Canada's Commitment:

To ensure public consensus on the need and desirability for women, men and society as a whole to share the responsibilities of raising children and caring for other family members.

Fulfilling Canada's commitment includes:

E.28 **Changing the attitudes and regulations governing maternity and parental leave to ensure that maternity is not treated as an illness; to encourage either parent to take advantage of parental leave; to ensure women and men are treated equally with respect to wage and non-wage benefits or costs; and to remove disincentives such as the current two-week waiting period for receipt of unemployment insurance benefits or the absence of income top-ups above unemployment insurance.**

E.29 Amending provincial and territorial labour standards where necessary to ensure the right to maternity and parental leave for both public and private sector employees.

E.30 Encouraging employers, unions and professional bodies to recognize and support non-work responsibilities by exploring alternative work arrangements with respect to time worked, scheduling and location and developing and implementing workplace education programs to ensure that both women and men take advantage of such arrangements.

Canada's Commitment:

To ensure employment equity for women.

Fulfilling Canada's commitment includes:

E.31 Implementing the recommendations in the report of the Special Committee on the Review of the *Employment Equity Act*, entitled *A Matter of Fairness*.

E.32 Extending the *Employment Equity Act* to cover "more than just numbers." For example, adding measures which would ensure the retention and promotion of women and the fostering of positive work environments.

E.33 Mandating the hiring of a fair percentage of Aboriginal employees, including women, when providing economic assistance to stimulate growth in towns or cities which derive benefit from neighbouring Aboriginal communities.

E.34 Eliminating nepotism and favouritism within Aboriginal governments and programs and ensuring the adherence to fair, competitive recruitment and employment practices, based on merit.

Canada's Commitment:

To guarantee women equal pay for work of equal value.

Fulfilling Canada's commitment includes:

E.35 Developing and implementing pro-active legislation on pay equity including clear guidelines, time frames, scheduled rates of improvement and strong enforcement measures.

Canada's Commitment:

To strengthen training programs for women.

Fulfilling Canada's commitment includes:

E.36 Working with provincial governments to develop a strategy for training and employment to assist female school leavers and women re-entering the work force, to promote occupational desegregation, to help women in declining sectors, to recruit and retain women in high-growth, high-skill, non-traditional and traditional sectors, and to enhance their skills and promote diversification through the use of technology.

E.37 Providing training and skills upgrading, particularly for self-employed women in sectors undergoing rapid restructuring, to ensure that their businesses become or remain competitive.

E.38 Tailoring training to meet women's needs and accommodate their differences with respect to caregiving responsibilities, language abilities, life skills, training hours and location.

E.39 Increasing training funds available to designated groups (women, Aboriginal women, Inuit women, women with disabilities and visible minority women), through the Canadian Jobs Strategy, and, ensuring the equitable participation of designated groups in all labour market adjustment and training programs.

E.40 Reinstating all special needs counsellors and designated group co-ordinators in federal employment and training programs. Their elimination under policy changes has severely reduced access for designated groups to employment counselling and other assistance.

E.41 Ensuring that government-run training and employment programs provide women, young women and other vulnerable groups with access to training programs which promote higher skill levels, such as apprenticeships and workplace-based training, rather than the low-skill training programs which women currently dominate.

E.42 Providing additional resources for training programs and changing the eligibility criteria so they are not limited to those who are currently on unemployment insurance.

Canada's Commitment:

To introduce measures to avoid exploitation of part-time and piece workers, who predominately are women and reduce the trend toward the feminization of part-time, temporary and seasonal work.

Fulfilling Canada's commitment includes:

E.43 Reviewing federal, provincial and territorial labour standards, including an assessment of their application and enforcement. They should be updated, standardized and uniformly applied and enforced.

E.44 Designating home-based workers, including female farm employees, female migrant farm labourers and domestic workers, as employees under federal and provincial labour standards and ensuring, through effective monitoring and enforcement measures, they are covered under the same regulations concerning wages and working conditions as those performing similar work within the regulated workplace.

E.45 Including clauses in all labour legislation providing permanent part-time workers with prorated benefits and ensuring that casual employees are entitled to the same non-wage benefits, on a prorated basis, as permanent staff.

Canada's Commitment:

To introduce measures which recognize the importance of and provide support to women in business, including self-employed women, women traders, women in small industries and women in family enterprises, such as farming.

Fulfilling Canada's commitment includes:

E.46 Expanding and adequately funding the **Farm Women's Advancement Program** [16] with priority given to funding to improve farm women's economic security and autonomy. This would be done through support to farm women's groups for initiatives to analyze, advocate, consult and increase awareness of farm women's options and legal rights as business partners.

E.47 Providing incentives to encourage legally recognized co-ownership and co-management by women of family businesses, including farms.

E.48 Implementing a mentor program, similar to the **Step-Up Program.** [17] It would include an ongoing consultant/advisor to provide assistance to participants; selection of successful business women with whom participants would be paired; a training component designed in consultation with participants to develop the knowledge and skills required to start a business or encourage its growth; and a small business loan available upon successful completion of such a program.

E.49 Ensuring Aboriginal women have equal access to funds provided for economic development through such programs as the **Canadian Aboriginal Economic Development Strategy.** [18]

Canada's Commitment:

To direct special attention, in the provision of social assistance, social services, education, training and employment, to the needs of female victims of violence, female lone parents and women with a high vulnerability to poverty.

Fulfilling Canada's commitment includes:

E.50 Recognizing the trauma experienced by female victims of violence and developing pre-training programs with counselling to assist them in making the transition into the labour force. Working with women in the shelter or second-stage housing movement to provide employment counselling and assistance to occupants.

E.51 Implementing training and employment programs which take into account the full range of barriers to labour force participation facing female victims of violence and female lone parents. This includes the psychological impact of long absences from the labour force, the lack of financial resources, the need for child care, the requirement to have appropriate clothing and equipment and the need for sound advice on career options and progression.

E.52 Facilitating and encouraging the labour force participation of female social assistance recipients, particularly female lone parents, by providing a combination of social assistance and training or employment income which ensures a standard of living above the poverty line.

E.53 Supplementing the income of older women, who have limited employment prospects but are not yet eligible for retirement benefits, to ensure them a reasonable standard of living.

VI THE FAMILY

The family is one of the fundamental units of social organization in Canadian society. While family structure can take many forms — extended, nuclear, lone parent, couples of same or opposite sex, with or without children, with or without a formal contract of marriage, etc. — families are generally characterized by varying degrees of material and social interdependency among their members. The nature and degree of dependency can change with age, gender, relationship and status within the family. Roles and functions ascribed to or taken on by various members of the family also differ.

The family itself has been a venue for playing out social and economic inequality on the basis of gender. Historically, biology has been destiny with respect to roles within families. The reproductive function of women has generally been extended to include primary responsibilities for child care and child rearing.

Young children are socialized in the family environment for the gender-based roles they will assume as adolescents and adults. Although some intergenerational shifts in role responsibility occur, family role patterns, reinforced by other institutions such as school, work and the media tend to be repeated from one generation to the next, despite significant economic changes in favour of women and the advent of greater reproductive choice.

Key Problems

- Women assume the bulk of household work, child-rearing and child care responsibilities without monetary compensation.

- Women's discretionary and leisure time declines with marriage and children, particularly if they are employed outside the home, while that of male spouses increases.

- Family dissolution is increasing, and the number of female lone parents living in poverty or near poverty is increasing.

- Different standards for fathers and mothers appear to apply in custody and access decisions.

- Freedom of choice on reproductive matters is sometimes compromised by local limitations, particularly on the availability of abortion.

Canada's Commitment:

To ensure equality during marriage and at its dissolution.

Fulfilling Canada's commitment includes:

E.54 **Recognizing in all aspects of policy the diversity of family structures and composition, and eliminating discrimination arising from the characterization of the family as having a male head of household with a spouse and children in varying states of dependency on the male breadwinner.**

E.55 **Implementing educational programs for men, women, young boys and girls to create greater awareness of shared obligations within the family, particularly responsibilities for child rearing.**

E.56 **Providing child care and after-school care so women as well as men have access to leisure, educational and other personal development activities.**

E.57 **Signing and implementing the International Labour Organization Convention and Recommendation No. 165 regarding access to employment without discrimination arising from family responsibilities.** [19]

E.58 **Ensuring that criteria that are free of gender bias are developed and applied to decisions on custody and access.**

E.59 **Ensuring that child support orders are fairly determined and enforced. This would Include consideration of the adoption of an advance payment scheme until such time as universal compliance with spousal and child support orders is achieved.**

E.60 **Ensuring that the right to reproductive choice and abortion is not compromised.**

VII WOMEN AND THE TAX/TRANSFER SYSTEM

Although it does not intentionally set out to discriminate on the basis of gender, the Canadian taxation system reflects and sustains the economic and social structure and, as such, embodies some significant gender biases which work to the disadvantage of women.

As well, the increasing movement away from the corporate sector to income taxes collected from individuals as the major source of government revenues has had a substantial adverse impact on the real income of individuals and families. The regressive nature of some tax measures, such as the child care expense deduction, benefits higher income earners who are more likely to be men. Women, as the greater proportion of lower income earners, must spend more of their income on consumables, and are therefore more adversely affected by consumption taxes such as provincial sales taxes and the goods and services tax.

The direct and indirect costs of raising children and the fact that these costs are borne primarily by women is not adequately recognized in the Canadian tax and social benefits system. This factor, combined with lower wages for work traditionally performed by women, reinforces the assumption that children are the responsibility of the mother and tends, therefore, to justify her temporary absences from the labour market.

Under the Canadian system, married partners are treated as a unit for some tax purposes. The presumption that income is equally shared within families is false. Current policy can create disincentives for the higher income-earning spouse, usually male, to have his spouse in the paid labour force, even while strong economic incentives may exist for her to do so in order to achieve and maintain her economic autonomy.

Key Problems

- Female lone parents, who are among the lowest income earners, receive limited support through the tax system because the primary tax benefit available to them, the equivalent-to-married credit, is non-refundable.

- Child care is subsidized through deductions rather than benefits or credits. This increases the tax benefit for those most able to pay.

- The lack of full indexation of child benefit payments and child-related tax credits (such as the GST credit per child), erodes their value over time.

- Canadian tax policy does not take into account the impact of tax measures on individuals on the basis of gender.

- The taxation of child-support payments, while containing elements of fairness in theory, is complex and often inappropriately implemented. This reduces the financial resources allocated to the custodial parent (usually the mother) in the interests of the child.

- Tax benefits from contributions to RRSPs and private pension plans benefit higher income earners and long-term labour market participants. As a result, women are placed at a disadvantage.

Canada's Commitment:

To take all appropriate measures, including legislation, to modify or abolish existing laws, regulations, customs and practices which constitute discrimination against women. [20]

Fulfilling Canada's commitment includes:

E.61 Analyzing all proposed tax system changes for bias or adverse effects based on gender.

E.62 Acknowledging through the tax system the costs of raising children and the reduced capacity of families with children to pay taxes. This includes raising the income level threshold at which the child benefit is reduced, fully indexing all credits and benefits under the new federal child benefit program and increasing the maximum deductions under the child care expense deduction and making it convertible to a refundable credit.

E.63 Treating spouses as individuals for tax purposes by abolishing the married and equivalent-to-married credits, and replacing them with new measures which explicitly recognize the costs of raising children, including refundable tax credits for low earner parents, particularly lone parents.

E.64 Addressing the taxation and collection problems in the current child support order system by introducing a tax credit approach, and using the tax collection system as a means for enforcing child support payments.

E.65 Fully indexing income tax brackets.

E.66 Increasing and fully indexing the claw-back threshold for OAS benefits.

E.67 Making automatic the credit-splitting provisions of the CPP for ex-spouses.

ENDNOTES

1 *The Nairobi Forward-looking Strategies for the Advancement of Women*, (Ottawa, 19), p.7. Reprinted by Status of Women Canada from the *Report of the World Conference to Review and Appraise the acheivements of the United Nations Decade for Women: Equality, Development and Peace* (United Nations Document A/Conf.116/28)

2 *Universal Declaration of Human Rights* as reprinted by Multiculturalism and Citizenship Canada, Human Rights Directorate in *Observance of Human Rights Day December 10, 1988: The 40th Anniversary of the Universal Declaration of Human Rights 1948-1988:Report of Canada to the United Nations* (Ottawa, 1989)

3 *Convention on the Elimination of All Forms of Discrimination against Women* as reprinted by the Human Rights Directorate Multiculturalism and Citizenship Canada, with the permission of the Department of Public Information of the United Nations, (Ottawa, 1990)

4 General recommendation No. 19 (Eleventh session, 1992) as reprinted in Arvonne Fraser and Miranta Kazantsis, *International Women's Rights Action Watch:(IWRAW) CEDAW #11* (University of Minnesota, 1992), pp. 28-32.

5 Unless otherwise specified, the Panel has excerpted "Canada's Commitment" statements from the Status of Women publication entitled, *Fact Sheets: Nairobi Forward-looking Strategies for the Advancement of Women, Issues and the Canadian Situation*, (Ottawa: 1992). The Fact Sheets summarize the *Nairobi Forward-looking Strategies*, in point form, by issue, and offer current information on Canadian government action towards equality.

6 The Court Challenges Program was a federal initiative which provided financial assistance to selected individuals and groups to litigate equality rights cases relating to federal legislation, practices or policies under section 15 of the *Charter*. The program was designed to provide access to the courts for women and other minority groups. It was cut in the 1992 federal budget, despite the protests of equality rights advocates.

7 Minister of Supply and Sevices Canada, The Report of the Task Force on Barriers to Women in the Public Service, *Beneath the Veneer*, (Ottawa, 1990), pp. 37-38.

8 Minister of Supply and Sevices Canada, The Report of the Special Committee on the Review of the *Employment Equity Act, A Matter of Fairness*, (Ottawa, 1992), pp. 2-4.

9 *Ibid.*, p. 3.

10 Minister of Supply and Sevices Canada,The Report of the Royal Commission on Electoral Reform and Party Financing, *Reforming Electoral Democracy*, (Ottawa, 1991).

11 *Beneath the Veneer, op. cit.*, p. 9.

12 Abdul Rashid, "Seven decades of wage changes," in *Perspectives on Labour and Income*, Volume 5, No.2, Summer 1993, p.13.

13 Nancy Zukewich Graham, "Women in the Workplace," in *Canadian Social Trends*, No. 28, Spring 1993, pp. 4-5.

14 *Ibid.*, p. 3.

15 Statistics Canada, *Women in Canada - A Statistical Report* (Ministry of Supply and Services, 2nd edition, Ottawa, 1990), pp. 121-124.

16 The Farm Women's Advancement Program was developed in 1988, by the Farm Women's Bureau of Agriculture Canada. Its objectives are: to aid in the achievement of legal and economic equality for farm women; promote the participation of farm women in the agricultural industry's decision-making processes; and, encourage the recognition of the contribution of farm women to the well-being of the agricultural sector.

17 The Step-Up Program is a business expansion program for women in Ontario, sponsored by the Federal Business Development Bank and the Ontario Ministry of Industry, Trade and Technology. It provides the skills women need to expand their enterprises. It was piloted from April 1991 to April 1992 with 25 protegees and 25 mentors.

18 The Canadian Aboriginal Economic Development Strategy is a federal initiative designed to provide long-term employment and business opportunities to Canada's Aboriginal citizens, by giving them the means to effectively manage their own business enterprises, economic institutions, job training and skills development.

19 Recommendation No. 165 as found in *International Labour Organisation,* International Labour Conventions and Recommendations 1919-1991, Volume II (Geneva, 1992), pp. 1248-1254

20 *Convention on the Elimination of all Forms of Discrimination against Women, op. cit,* p. 6.

SECTION 2

ZERO TOLERANCE POLICY

The Context

1. Male violence against women is at a crisis level in Canada and must be urgently addressed.

2. Violence against women is a violation of a most basic human right to security of the person.

3. Violence against women is a manifestation of historically unequal power relations between men and women. This unequal relationship has led to domination over and discrimination against women by men, endangering women and preventing their full advancement in society.

4. Violence against women is one of the crucial social mechanisms by which women are forced into a position subordinate to men.

5. Violence against women is a product of a sexist, racist, heterosexist and class society and is perpetuated through all social institutions and the attitudes and behaviours of members of all Canadian communities.

6. Violence against women is an abuse of power and a betrayal of trust. It precludes the establishment of egalitarian relations and inhibits the mutual respect that women have a right to expect as individuals and as a social group.

7. Violence affects women's abilities to exercise freedom in their homes, workplaces, on the streets and in their communities.

8. Organizations, institutions and governments do not effectively detect and deter violence against women and thereby perpetuate the abuse of women and endanger their safety.

9. The statistical rate of repeat offences is very high for crimes of violence against women, and society puts women at risk by denying this fact.

10. Violence against women includes various types of abuse — psychological, financial, verbal, sexual and physical. It affects all women but with different consequences for Aboriginal and Inuit women, young women, elderly women, women of colour, immigrant women, refugee women, domestic workers, women with disabilities, women from different linguistic backgrounds, women living in rural, northern and isolated communities and lesbians.

11. Much of the violence against women is preventable, but society has not taken the appropriate measures to guarantee women's safety.

12. The severe and costly impact of violence on women, both physical and psychological, can also be measured in terms of lost potential and damage to children.

Declaration

The Canadian Panel on Violence Against Women declares:

- Equality and freedom from violence are rights of all women, and it is the responsibility of every individual, community, government and institution in Canada to work toward securing these rights.

- The elimination of violence will best be achieved through the adoption and rigorous application of a policy of zero tolerance.

- To this end we urge each person and every organization in Canada to commit to the equality and safety of women and implement the Zero Tolerance Policy.

Zero tolerance is based on the following principles.

1. No amount of violence is acceptable, and the elimination of violence against women must be an absolute priority.

2. Those with responsibility for public safety have an obligation to take the most comprehensive and effective action possible to prevent violence from happening and to limit the harms from violence when it has occurred.

3. Policies, practices, programs and products which do not support women's safety must be dismantled.

4. Sexist and racist practices and other forms of discrimination and bias which encourage or support acts of violence against women must be eliminated.

5. The rights of the victim in the legal system must at least be equal to the rights of the accused.

6. Victims must not be blamed for the violence committed against them.

7. Governments and institutions have a primary responsibility to demonstrate leadership and to provide resources to achieve equality and to end violence.

8. Individuals and all communities within Canadian society have a responsibility to work toward ending violence and achieving equality for all.

The Policy Framework of Zero Tolerance

Adoption of the Zero Tolerance Policy means making a firm commitment to the philosophy that no amount of violence is acceptable, and that adequate resources must be made available to eliminate violence and achieve equality.

The elimination of violence against women can only be achieved through recognition of the equality of women. Equality initiatives will enhance women's options and reduce their vulnerability to violence.

Ending Violence ⟷ Equality
Zero Tolerance Policy ⟷ Equality Plan

To this end, a separate equality action plan has been developed which includes mechanisms to assist government in ensuring that all policies, practices and programs embody the principles of equality for women. These initiatives will support groups, organizations and institutions in achieving their goal of equality for women.

The policy framework for zero tolerance outlined below complements the equality action plan. It includes:

- an accountability framework which identifies criteria for zero tolerance to help an organization change its operations by making the elimination of violence and support for women's safety integral to all its activities;

- an outline of steps to be taken in implementing the Zero Tolerance Policy;

- a model for organizations or institutions to use as a guide to implementing the zero tolerance criteria to change business practices.

Institutions can use the Zero Tolerance Policy to examine their operations for the degree to which they support women's safety, enhance or promote women's equality, and are sensitive to gender issues.

The Zero Tolerance Policy is generic and is equally relevant to support groups, non-government organizations, services, corporations and government institutions.

Accountability Framework

The following criteria are to be used to shape the work to be undertaken and to evaluate progress made in reaching zero tolerance. All criteria apply to any activity carried out and to evaluations of progress.

All activities must unequivocally support and promote women's safety and security through:

Eliminating gender, race and class bias

- by identifying and eliminating any element or underlying assumption that undermines women, for example, myths, stereotypes or roles, based on gender, race or class;

- by recognizing women's realities and experiences as different from those of men; and

- by introducing measures that further equality.

Ending violence

- by supporting victims and redressing harms when violence occurs;

- by implementing policies and practices that ensure women's safety; and

- by identifying and eliminating problem areas and situations, including at all work sites, that create danger or promote or tolerate violent actions or harassment for women within the organization.

Ensuring inclusion

- by recognizing the interconnections between the structures of economic power and the organization of elite white male power in society;

- by basing decision making on data and research that accurately reflect women's safety, different realities, experiences and perspectives; and

- by engaging, at each and every stage of all activities, the full participation of women who represent the diversity of Canada and who have direct experience, working knowledge and a demonstrated commitment to equality and ending violence.

Implementation Steps

To apply the Zero Tolerance Policy, a group, organization or institution has six major steps to take:

1. Commit

Formally adopt the Zero Tolerance Policy on violence. Communicate to every member and client/consumer of the organization that women's safety is a priority, and no amount of violence is acceptable.

2. Committee

Create a zero tolerance action committee to oversee implementation with membership that includes senior management and a majority of women drawn from all areas and all levels of the organization who represent employees/workers, management, unions and client/consumer groups.

3. Review

Undertake safety audits of work sites, physical plants as well as of policies, practices, procedures and programs, to detect and deal with situations and employees/workers posing a risk to women's safety.

4. Act

Develop an action plan to detect, deter and prevent violence against women and to ensure women's safety in all aspects of operations and products. Benchmarks and timetables should be built in, and all stakeholders should be directly involved in the plan's development and implementation.

5.   Resource

Ensure that the zero tolerance action committee has adequate human and financial resources to be effective. Allocate funds for implementation of the action plan.

6.   Evaluate

The zero tolerance action committee must oversee the adoption of and adherence to the Zero Tolerance Policy, must ensure ongoing monitoring and evaluation of the progress made and must report on achievements in their annual report.

Zero Tolerance Model

The following model focuses on the specific aspects of an organization's operations and work; it should be reviewed and realigned using the zero tolerance criteria. Actions are recommended to guide the evaluation and reformulation of operational activities.

A.   Priority Setting/Allocation of Resources

A.1   Statement of Commitment

A written commitment to the promotion of women's equality and safety must be included when developing goals, objectives or mission statements, undertaking strategic planning exercises and setting priorities.

The statement is the formal recognition of women's equal access to all resources, programs and information. It is based on women's experiences and realities including those of victims and survivors.

A.2   Funding

Women's equality and safety needs must be considered in the design of budgets, including core funding, subsidies and grants. The model requires institutions and organizations to account for funding as follows:

- Compensate the value of women's contributions adequately.

- Grant fiscal resources to institutions, agencies or organizations conditional on their adoption of the Zero Tolerance Policy. To facilitate compliance, human and/or financial resources should be provided, where possible, to support the development of action plans and the achievement of a zero tolerance commitment.

B.   Human Resource Management

B.1   Appointments and Hiring

The intensity of the screening process for appointments and hiring must increase in proportion to the degree of trust or power inherent in the position, especially if the position involves access to children or adults who are vulnerable. Priority must be given to the following hiring criteria to ensure women's safety.

- Through an in-depth check of references and background, confirm that there is no evidence that a prospective employee or appointee would pose a safety risk to co-workers or clients/consumers. The onus is on the candidate to disclose previous criminal convictions.

- Demonstrated understanding of equality issues and the dynamics of violence.

- Personal support of and commitment to women's equality and safety.

B.2   Performance Review and Promotions

Promotions should be based on several factors:

- There are no reasonable and probable grounds for concern that the individual would pose a safety risk or tolerate violence against women.

- The individual has not demonstrated sexist or other discriminatory attitudes, behaviours, or tolerance of violence against women.

- Training on issues of women's safety and equality has been completed, and understanding of that training has been demonstrated.

- Power, authority and trust have been used appropriately by the individual.

- The individual supports and is committed to women's safety and equality.

- The individual conforms to workplace policies on violence, including harassment.

B.3   Training

All employees/workers must receive proper training on woman abuse, sexism and racism. In-depth training must be given to all senior staff; to individuals specifically involved in any process to address complaints or solve problems related to women's safety and equality; to individuals who implement policies and procedures; and to individuals who make decisions on the allocation of resources or assess service/program delivery.

Curricula must be developed and delivered in partnership with individuals who have expertise in working with equality issues and violence against women.

Training on violence against women issues must be integrated into all existing courses and curricula, rather than given as a single course.

Basic training must cover the nature and harms of inequality and discrimination; the incidence of women abuse; the specific situations and circumstances of women survivors; the characteristics and consequences of violence against women; all forms of violence; sexism; racism; the needs of women with disabilities, elderly women and lesbians; the ways a victim may initiate disclosure or inquiry; barriers to disclosure and how to respond appropriately; violence prevention training, such as non-violent and non-discriminatory methods of resolving conflicts; and self-defence training given by women's organizations.

In-depth training must recognize the risk of harm posed by abusers, including those abusing through a breach of trust; difficulties in identifying and helping abusers; and the potential abuse of survivors' rights and safety in investigation and adjudication processes.

B.4   Personnel Policies

Develop and implement comprehensive personnel policies on issues related to women's equality, including employment equity and pay equity; women's safety, including sexual harassment, gender discrimination and violence prevention; and support for victims.

A policy on harassment must consider women's objective and subjective experiences and the intent of the harasser. The policy must identify complaint, grievance and investigative procedures, and redress responsibilities including disciplinary action to be taken to resolve the complaint.

•   Make it easy for victims to report.

•   Define sexual harassment and recognize that gender harassment, which can undermine the business or service delivery atmosphere, is as harmful a form of sexual harassment as the more commonly recognized forms.

•   Include a step-by-step strategy for recognizing, investigating and resolving incidents of sexual harassment.

•   Resolve complaints without delay and in a manner which protects the confidentiality of complainants.

•   Provide for facts to be accurately recorded, kept on file for a significant time period and held in strict confidence.

•   Ensure that remedial action is taken immediately (i.e., under three months) that satisfies and never penalizes the victim.

•   Provide measures for separating parties during the complaint procedure, if necessary, but never to the detriment of the victim.

•   Provide outside legal counsel who have an understanding and concern for women's safety issues.

•   Ensure that punishment/restitution reflects the severity of the crime.

•   Include dismissal in the policy as the most severe penalty for harassment.

•   Leave policies must be developed or amended to support victims of violence who are absent from work due to violence.

•   Grant leave for victims of abuse, and for parents of children who have been abused and who require time off for counselling, support, court appearances and other related activities.

•   Guarantee the positions of employees/ workers who have been victims of violence upon return from leave.

•   Employee assistance programs must support employees/workers who may be victims of violence and refer them to appropriate community support services.

•   Dismissal of staff or appointees who do not comply with behaviour or harassment policies and/or who commit acts of violence must be ensured.

C.   Legislation/Regulation/Policy

C.1   Acts, statutes, by-laws, registries, codes in development and the granting of licences must uphold and protect women's safety and security. This includes protection from further abuse by individuals or systems. They must also recognize women's different needs and realities.

D.   Programs/Services/Practices

D.1   Safety/prevention practices and programs that recognize and eliminate the opportunities for abuse and violence within an organization must be considered when drafting guidelines and directives supporting the organization's mandate.

- Develop protocols for workers/employees to use to recognize and confront violence by a colleague or in potentially violent situations.

- Inform workers/employees about available support which can be given to women experiencing violence.

- Post signs stating that acts of violence including sexual and gender harassment, racism and other forms of discrimination may result in the perpetrator being fired.

E.   Consultation

E.1   The following criteria must be considered when setting up committees, advisory bodies, councils or activities such as hearings.

- Invite a proportional number of women representing specific groups of the community to participate.

- Incorporate the expertise and experiences provided by participants in all planning, program/service activities and human resource practices.

F.   Co-ordination

F.1   All parties, processes, activities and projects on the same or related subject areas must co-operate and collaborate to make links among issues where the relationship to equality and violence is less apparent.

G.   Research and Evaluation

G.1   Research undertaken through pilot projects, experimentation and the resulting data collection and analysis must reflect the priorities of women. It must be measured against its contribution to women's equality and women's safety; give equal recognition of and support to feminist research methodology; and include specific gender and race breakdowns.

G.2   Self-evaluation is a requisite element in assessing the effectiveness and success of any policy, practice, program or service in reaching equality and promoting women's safety. At a minimum, self-evaluation must include the following activities.

- Gauge and take into account the different impact of each activity on women and men.

- Examine and evaluate how the specific needs of women are being addressed.

- Evaluate how existing resources can be redirected to respond to the identified needs.

H.   Education/Promotional Activities

H.1   Awareness campaigns, publications, advertising and other communications products must include the following activities.

- Adopt non-sexist/non-racist images and verbal communications which portray women in the full range of occupations and reflect all client groups.

- Give equal value to women's experiences and needs.

- Provide all materials in culturally relevant, plain language, in a range of media (including large print and braille) and where necessary, provide linguistic and sign language interpretation.

- Promote non-violent images and messages in support of women's safety and security.

I.   Physical Environment Management

I.1   Support for women's safety and security must be reflected in the physical design of facilities and maintenance of properties including public and semi-public spaces such as parks, shopping malls, public transit systems, workplaces, and public buildings.

- Provide for women's safety during any construction and renovation.

- Support women's safety through provisions in by-laws and other legislation regulating municipally operated spaces such as underground garages.

- Increase the safety and security of isolated working conditions through the use of regular patrols and communication devices.

- Ensure escape routes.

J.   Accountability

J.1   In working in or dealing with an organization, women workers/employees, women clients and consumers must be guaranteed that their safety and security will be upheld.

- Work in an open and transparent manner.

- Disclose information about processes and objectives freely.

- Invite public scrutiny of work.

- Keep the public and all stakeholders informed on progress.

- Adopt a code of behaviour which emphasizes non-sexist, non-racist and other non-discriminatory behaviour and which includes a sexual harassment policy as well as a complaints process. The complaints process must guarantee that all complaints are documented and investigated within a reasonable time period. Penalties and remedies that recognize the harms done to the victim must also be defined.

- Review policies, procedures, practices, programs, services or activities undertaken by the zero tolerance action committee annually to assess and publicly report on the organization's performance in reaching zero tolerance.

SECTION 3

ZERO TOLERANCE ACTION PLANS

In this section, we recommend specific actions to be undertaken in key sectors which complement the adoption and implementation of the Zero Tolerance Policy. The eight sectors are:

- Services (Health and Social)
- Legal
- Workplace
- Military
- Education
- Media
- Religious Institutions
- Government

Actions in each sector are stated as recommendations and may be aimed at several actors within the sector or at specific individuals, organizations or institutions. Given the complexity of some sectors and the scope of changes required to redress historical inequities, some recommendations may be accompanied by further details explaining the intent and nature of the action to be taken in the particular area.

For ease of reference, we have organized the recommended actions into two categories.

- New orientations are fundamental shifts to the individual sector. Once implemented they will support equality and create safety and security for women.

- Zero Tolerance Actions are addressed to all or to specific actors in individual sectors. These are presented according to the 10 activity areas highlighted in the Zero Tolerance Policy:

A.   **Priority Setting/Allocation of Resources**
B.   **Human Resource Management**
C.   **Legislation/Regulation/Policy**
D.   **Programs/Services/Practices**
E.   **Consultation**
F.   **Co-ordination**
G.   **Research and Evaluation**
H.   **Education/Promotional Activities**
I.   **Physical Environment Management**
J.   **Accountability**

Only those activity areas requiring attention by specific individuals, institutions or organizations have been included for each sector. For activity areas not specifically addressed, individuals, institutions and organizations should refer to the generic recommended actions under the same activity heading in the Zero Tolerance Policy.

The Panel proposes that all actions begin immediately, with results to be achieved by the year 2000. In some instances, more specific time frames are suggested.

SERVICES SECTOR

Introduction

Services are critical to the women and children victims and survivors of violence and are often the very first point of contact for women seeking information, support and advice. A broad definition of the services sector has been adopted for this action plan to reflect the results of the Panel's consultations. It includes settings and service providers from the social/community services and health care fields. Specifically, the following key participants have been identified:

- non-governmental services including shelters, sexual assault centres, rape crisis centres, women's centres, men's programs and other community groups;

- governmental services including social service agencies, hospitals and medical clinics;

- self-regulating bodies and professional associations;

- physicians, psychiatrists, other health practitioners such as nurses, psychologists, therapists and counsellors;

- ministries of social and/or community services;

- ministries of health; and

- federal government departments responsible for health, welfare, social services, Indian and Northern Affairs, and other relevant federal government departments.

Key Problems

Approaches to the needs of victims and survivors and subsequent interventions are changing. Nevertheless, key problems remain in both the delivery and the basic philosophy that underpin the services sector.

- The lack of stable and ongoing funding for non-governmental services has created gaps in the overall network of service delivery, particularly for shelters and second-stage housing. Women working in community-based organizations are poorly paid and have very little job security.

- The needs of certain populations of women, such as Aboriginal and Inuit women, women with disabilities, immigrant women, women of colour, refugee women, domestic workers, lesbians, rural women, young women, elderly women and women from linguistic minorities are not being adequately met.

- The needs of children including those who have witnessed violence are often neglected because of funding inadequacies and the lack of recognition that the witnessing of abuse is in itself a type of abuse.

- A wide range of programs, services and counselling techniques are currently employed in responding to victims and survivors. Many of these services work independently, and the lack of a common approach or orientation creates an uneven and unco-ordinated response, sending an unclear message to both the men who commit the violence and the women who survive it.

- The bio-medical approach practised in health care separates the human body from its social environment. For women survivors of violence this means that the issue of violence is isolated from its context, and, in effect, makes them responsible for their condition.

- Health care practice also tends to ignore the link between the mind and the body. Consequently, the multi-faceted nature of violence is not recognized. Violence is often considered an illness requiring a medical response. The symptoms of violence are the only focus; the underlying causes are ignored. Survivors are attended to with medication or considered mentally ill and referred for psychiatric treatment.

New Orientations

The federal government and provincial/ territorial ministries of social and/or community services.

S.1 **Provide ongoing funding to all services for short-, medium- and long-term planning. Core funding is recommended for community-based, non-governmental services such as women's shelters, sexual assault centres, rape crisis centres and women's centres. Sustained funding is recommended for government agencies and institutionally based services. Some experimentation through pilot projects should be employed to investigate ways of expanding both the community-based and government-based service networks.**

Details

Funding must be at a level which allows all services to be culturally relevant and to provide accessibility to all women in the community.

The allocation of funding must provide for fair and equitable compensation and benefits to workers in the community sector and for staff training and development needs.

Funding must provide for the expansion of services in both non-governmental and governmental service networks. For shelters, specifically, the following additional services should be accommodated:

- *minimum stay of 30 days followed by an evaluation of the client's needs for her future;*

- *counselling and support groups for children;*

- *temporary accommodation for victims of sexual assault;*

- *development and co-ordination of satellite houses and other services in remote and Isolated communities;*

- *second-stage housing; and*

- *educational/advocacy activities.*

The following additional services/programs are recommended for government service agencies:

- *multi-disciplinary teams in institutionalized settings;*

- *peer support counselling programs;*

- *self-help groups;*

- *family support services;*

- *short- and long-term counselling for children including children's groups;*

- *offenders groups; and*

- *services for adolescent offenders.*

Provincial/territorial, ministries of health, and the federal department responsible for health.

S.2 There must be a major reorientation of the philosophy underpinning health care delivery from that of piecemeal treatment to a comprehensive model of healing which considers the person as a whole and understands the multi-faceted nature of violence and the complex ways in which all its dimensions — physical, sexual, psychological and social — interact.

S.3 There must be a recognition of the essential contribution made to the healing process of survivors by services delivered at the community level which are not medically oriented and not attached to institutions such as hospitals or clinics. This includes contributions by self-help groups, immigrant health services and other culturally appropriate services. Such a recognition will require a significant re-allocation of financial resources to these community-based services.

Federal departments responsible for health, welfare and social services, provincial-teritorial ministries of social and/or community services, and health, professional associations, frontline workers, social workers, other service providers.

S.4 To ensure completeness, continuity, consistency and quality of service delivery, national standards must be developed and established for the provision of adequate services.

Details

Examples of such standards could include:

- *a crisis line in each community (a toll-free 1-800 number in remote and isolated communities);*

- *a counsellor in each community with knowledge of all forms of violence against women and of specialized services and community support services to respond to these needs;*

- *an emergency shelter or services within one hour commuting distance of each community;*

- *local, safe, pre-arranged transportation in each community to reach the shelter or other community services;*

- *integrated approaches to counselling to provide help to both the victim (including children) and the offender on a separate basis but within a global feminist intervention framework. Co-ordination would be ensured by the respective service providers; and*

- *protocols and procedures to assist in detecting physical, sexual and emotional abuse in victims of violence.*

S.5   All services dealing with Aboriginal and Inuit communities must acknowledge and work to alleviate the underlying social factors that directly contribute to alcohol, drug and solvent use. Additional supports, as identified by communities, must be made immediately available until such time as sufficient education, employment/economic base and adequate housing are in place to alleviate those underlying causes.

Communities across Canada.

S.6 Each community must establish a standing committee to co-ordinate services to survivors/victims of violence against women. Membership must include primary providers of service to women and children who have experienced violence – shelters, rape crisis centres, women's centres, social services, police and hospitals/nursing stations. There must be equal participation of community services, government agencies and institutionalized services.

Start-up costs and sufficient funds must be provided for administration and ongoing human resource requirements.

In Inuit and Aborigional communities, this committee would act as a liaison mechanism and pursue complaints pertaining to services.

Zero Tolerance Actions for all Organizations and Individuals in the Services Sector

Priority Setting/Allocation of Resources

S.7 Subscribe to a client-centred model of service delivery. This means that services exist to meet the needs of clients/survivors and not those of service providers. Such an approach strives to redress the power imbalance between the client/survivor and the service provider and enables clients to have input into and control over the development and delivery of services. This ensures that clients/survivors have access to information to assist them in making choices.

Accountability

S.8 Adopt a code of ethics based on the Zero Tolerance Policy that guarantees the rights to dignity, respect, confidentiality, safety and security.

Details

Adherence to the code must be ensured through:

- *the adoption of a comprehensive strategy for educating service providers and users about the philosophical underpinnings, the values and the principles inherent in the code;*

- *performance reviews;*

- *strong sanctions (warnings, missed opportunities for promotion, dismissal, suspension of licence) for violating the code; and*

- *effective complaint procedures.*

Local women's organizations that represent the diverse realities of women and have expertise in this area must be involved.

Zero Tolerance Actions for Specific Organizations

> All non-governmental services including shelters, sexual assault centres, rape crisis centres, women's centres, men's programs and other community groups and governmental services including social service agencies, hospitals, community health agencies and medical clinics.

Priority Setting/Allocation of Resources

S.9 **Re-direct existing resources to make services more culturally sensitive and more accessible.**

Details

- *providing linguistic and cultural interpretation;*

- *keeping service providers informed about changes in immigration and refugee laws and policies; and*

- *making traditional healing practices available to Aboriginal women.*

Services to facilitate accessibility could include:

- *making child care more available;*

- *providing physical accessibility and making available new technology, such as TDD phones and ASL interpreters, that enable people with sight and hearing loss to use the services;*

- *accommodating the special needs of women with psychiatric disabilities;*

- *making specialized counsellors/resource individuals available (whether on site or through referrals) to Aboriginal women, Inuit women, women of colour, immigrant women, refugee women, women with disabilities, elderly women and lesbians;*

- *providing counselling services in small Inuit communities in conjunction with services such as health, crafts or recreation to provide increased anonymity and confidentiality;*

- *responding to the needs of women involved in pornography and prostitution through crisis intervention services, referral services, support and counselling, and where possible, shelter;*

- *providing services that recognize the needs of lesbians; and*

- *responding to the needs of women in the military, as dependants and as personnel, through support and information about their rights and access to financial resources.*

Human Resource Management

S.10 **Recruit survivors who have previously used the services and who are healed.**

S.11 **Provide specialized training on the needs of women with disabilities, elderly women, Aboriginal women, Inuit women, immigrant women, women of colour and refugee women; on the power imbalance and trust inherent in any relationship between a service provider and a client; and on feminist intervention skills.**

Co-ordination

S.12 **Adopt a co-operative working partnership with legal and other services directly involved with survivors of violence. This partnership would be grounded in mutual respect and recognition of each other's value and expertise. To achieve this, procedures and protocols must be established to identify gaps, solve problems, avoid duplication and share expertise; and linkages must be maintained with all sectors of the community (schools, businesses, other community organizations, religious institutions and other agencies), so these sectors can remain current on resources and can draw on available expertise.**

Research and Evaluation

S.13 **Undertake the systematic collection of data to determine the needs and percentage of users by forms of violence and populations.**

All self-regulating bodies and professional associations.

Legislation/Regulation/Policy

S.14 **Improve access to formal complaints and discipline procedures for victims and survivors.**

Details

This can be accomplished by:

- *ensuring that a complainant's letter is not sent to the health practitioner or service provider without the complainant's explicit knowledge and consent;*

- *granting the complainant the right to intervene in a disciplinary hearing; and*

- *establishing criteria for expert testimony.*

Programs/Services/Practices

S.15 **Improve or develop standardized protocols and procedures to assist professionals in detecting physical, sexual and psychological abuse in survivors.**

Details

Examples include:

- *explaining how to create the opportunity for clients to disclose their abuse in private without the presence of a partner;*

- *demonstrating how to assess the extent, severity and duration of the violence by asking non-directed, non-threatening and non-judgmental questions;*

- *recommending, as normal follow-up procedure, the immediate referral of clients to appropriate community support services;*

- recommending that detailed records be kept of injuries and conditions of abused clients detected as a result of a thorough physical examination, including injuries that might be considered minor, such as scratches and bruises, which could be used as medical evidence in the event of subsequent legal proceedings;

- recommending the setting of appropriate boundaries between the practitioner and a client; and

- recommending trauma healing and counselling for sexual assault as a priority when seeing newly arrived refugee women, especially if torture is indicated or suspected.

Research and Evaluation

S.16 Undertake research to evaluate the effectiveness, efficiency and efficacy of the roles of professionals in addressing the needs of women who experience violence.

S.17 Review or encourage the development of new screening or diagnostic tools to assist professionals in making links between past or present problems of violence and various conditions suffered by women such as depression, anorexia and bulimia.

Education/Promotional Activities

S.18 Undertake a public education program which includes:

- the existence and the role of the self-regulating body, its complaints process and how to access the system; and

- examples of abusive behaviours, the warning signs that violence by a health practitioner or service provider may occur and how to get help after being abused, including the necessary procedures for reporting abuse perpetrated by health practitioners and service providers.

S.19 Provide all clients with accessible information in plain language on clients' rights, the necessary procedures for reporting abuse by professionals and service providers and the effects of prescribed drugs.

All health practitioners including physicians, psychiatrists, nurses, psychologists, therapists.

Programs/Services/Practices

S.20 Follow a feminist intervention approach with the appropriate use of medical and psychiatric services.

S.21 Make links between past or present experiences of violence and various conditions suffered by women such as depression, anorexia or bulimia.

Co-ordination

S.22 Liaise with community services, such as transition houses, police and social service agencies, through participation in interagency committees on violence against women or other co-ordinating mechanisms within the community.

All ministries of social and/or community services.

Priority Setting/Allocation of Resources

S.23 Continue to recognize and financially support the efforts undertaken by community organizations to pursue the development of services relevant to violence against women. These efforts could include educational programs and materials for such groups as Aboriginal women, immigrant women, refugee women, women from linguistic minorities and women with disabilities, and the translation of such materials.

S.24 Support only those programs for men which have adopted a policy of zero tolerance, whose clients have been sentenced and which have involved the participation of local women's groups working with women survivors.

S.25 Allocate resources equitably between services working with women survivors and those working with offenders.

S.26 Implement contract compliance in funding and granting powers to institutions and agencies such as social service agencies. Funds or grants would be conditional depending on adoption of a zero tolerance policy and a commitment to participate in a community-based and co-ordinated response to violence against women.

S.27 Ensure that funding for initiatives to prevent violence against women in Aboriginal and Inuit communities comprise a portion of all service delivery contracts and contribution agreements.

S.28 Simplify application, proposal and reporting procedures to allow greatest access to funds by community groups. Liaison personnel must be made available to provide training in proposal writing, access to information on government funding, etc.

Human Resource Management

S.29 Establish registries of professionals with expertise in various forms of violence including sexual abuse, elder abuse, ritual abuse and feminist intervention skills. These registries should be available to interdisciplinary teams and services working in the field of violence against women.

Legislation/Regulation/Policy

S.30 Develop policies to end violence against women from a zero tolerance and equality perspective and not from a family violence perspective.

S.31 Assist women victims of violence in regaining economic independence by:

- recognizing the time needed to heal;

- amending relevant legislation and regulation to ensure that welfare assistance not be reduced in cases where support payments are also received; and by

- providing comprehensive pre-employment training.

S.32 Establish registries to monitor service providers found guilty of breach of confidentiality, breach of trust or convicted of sexual assault, sexual harassment or woman abuse.

S.33 Recognize that a child who has witnessed the abuse of a mother is an abused child and requires appropriate support services.

S.34 Protect Aboriginal and Inuit children in a culturally appropriate way. To achieve this, efforts must be made to keep children in safe and healthy Inuit and Aboriginal settings that reflect their cultural identity.

Programs/Services/Practices

S.35 Amend all procedures and protocols used by social service providers in their work with women victims of violence to reflect a gender, race and class analysis.

S.36 Recognize, as a legitimate social work practice, the use of a feminist intervention approach by service providers working in government settings. Encourage its adoption as a standard approach.

S.37 Acknowledge the experience and analysis of front-line workers by using them as paid trainers, paid expert witnesses, paid educators and paid consultants to provide input in program development and implementation.

S.38 Give serious consideration to supporting services initiated by, developed by and tailored to the specific needs of immigrant women, refugee women and women of colour.

S.39 Disseminate information on availability of government programs to community service providers, in the language appropriate to the community.

Consultation

S.40 Establish a permanent advisory committee to collaborate with government in reviewing and approving funding proposals from community organizations and government institutions and agencies for projects concerning violence against women.

Details

The committee would also monitor and assist in integrating into the government policy-making process, the work accomplished by government-funded projects dealing with violence against women. Survivors, front-line workers and women of all groups would be represented.

Co-ordination

S.41 Recognize and encourage social service workers to network and co-operate with front-line workers, health practitioners, community service workers and to participate in interagency committees on violence against women or other community co-ordinating mechanisms.

S.42 Promote co-operation and collaboration among all parties, all processes and all activities and projects in government settings related to violence against women and to equality.

S.43 Ensure that co-ordinated crisis response teams in Inuit and Aboriginal communities are at least 50 percent Inuit or Aboriginal and include appropriate community members and professionals such as elders, social workers, teachers, nurses, community health representatives and victims' advocates.

Research and Evaluation

S.44 Conduct and/or sponsor qualitative, quantitative and evaluative research on violence against women in collaboration with front-line workers and other community groups directly linked with the delivery of support services to women survivors of violence.

Details

Specific topics would include:

- *the distinct forms of violence and its prevalence among different groups of women;*

- *factors identified by survivors in stopping violence in relationships;*

- *the outcome of various community practices and strategies employed to deal with woman abuse; and*

- *the effectiveness of support groups for men, including program and external factors which affect program outcomes.*

- *research findings must be made public.*

Education/Promotional Activities

S.45 Use a feminist perspective based on gender, race and class to describe the nature of all forms of violence against women in all materials and documentation related to violence against women.

S.46 Use non-print media such as audio tapes and broadcast through Aboriginal and Inuit radio and television to reach both Aboriginal and Inuit women.

Priority Setting/Allocation of Resources

S.47 Recognize institutional medical services, community-sponsored and governed services, self-help groups and health promotion programs including violence prevention programs as health care services.

S.48 Recognize and support traditional healing services as legitimate forms of healing for Aboriginal and Inuit women. This would include suicide support groups, holistic family healing, an enhanced role for elders and guidance and participation by Aboriginal and Inuit women's advocacy groups.

S.49 Implement contract compliance in funding of institutions and agencies such as hospitals and community health agencies.

Details

Conditions could include the adoption of a zero tolerance policy and a commitment to participate in a community-based and co-ordinated response to violence against women.

Human Resource Management

S.50 Use front-line workers and health care providers in the development of health service delivery protocols.

S.51 Ensure that Aboriginal peoples and Inuit have access to a full range of training opportunities to meet the self-identified needs for community-based healing and treatment programs for victims of violence.

Legislation/Regulation/Policy

S.52 Revise all health policies to recognize the complexity of violence against women and the fact that violence is not an illness.

Programs/Services/Practices

S.53 Recognize and promote the use of a feminist intervention approach with the appropriate use of medical and psychiatric services.

S.54 Establish "healing centres" on a pilot project basis to provide a safe and supportive environment for women who are in crisis as a result of violence.

Details

These centres could be long-term residential centres that provide alternative services such as crisis intervention and referral services to current medical and psychiatric models of service delivery.

S.55 Establish registries of feminist therapists from which women can choose their own therapist.

S.56 Provide client advocates in all health facilities.

S.57 Increase the level of services in Aboriginal and Inuit communities to treat alcohol, drug and solvent abuse.

Details

These services must have the appropriate professional expertise to deal with the underlying issues of violence and must promote an holistic approach.

S.58 Ensure that Aboriginal and Inuit women seeking or receiving treatment outside of their communities have access to follow-up counselling and other services once they return to their communities.

S.59 Ensure that long-term care for victims/survivors/offenders in Inuit and Aborigonal communities is designed and delivered by Inuit and Aboriginal people. It must address the root causes of violence in addition to symptomatic behaviours such as addictions. The community must be able to determine the service delivery models.

S.60 Disseminate information on the availability of government programs to community health service providers, in the language appropriate to the community.

S.61 Integrate the issue of violence prevention into health promotion programs.

Co-ordination

S.62 Recognize and encourage health practitioners to network and co-operate with front-line workers and community service workers and to participate in interagency committees on violence against women or other community co-ordinating mechanisms.

Research and Evaluation

S.63 Conduct and/or sponsor qualitative, quantitative and evaluative research on violence against women.

Details

Specific topics would include:

- *the costs of violence to the health care system including costs associated with misdiagnosis and missed diagnosis, and the total amount of human resources involved;*

- *the links between experiencing violence and various conditions suffered by women, such as depression, anorexia and bulimia;*

- *the identification of the psychological consequences of torture and the development of effective treatment programs for torture victims and their families; and*

- *the specific needs of Aboriginal women with disabilities and of Aboriginal elderly women.*

Education/Promotional Activities

S.64 Use a feminist perspective based on gender, race and class to describe the nature of all forms of violence against women in all materials and documentation related to violence against women.

S.65 Use non-print media, such as audio tapes and broadcast through Aboriginal and Inuit radio and television, to reach both Aboriginal and Inuit women.

Federal department responsible for health

Legislation/Regulation/Policy

S.66 Undertake, in co-operation with the provinces and territories, an assessment of the capabilities, the scope and the use of provisions of current funding mechanisms such as the *Canada Assistance Plan* and the *Canada Health Act*, in responding to the needs of women survivors of violence.

D. Programs/Services/Practices

S.67 Guarantee that all Aboriginal and Inuit women receive the same standard and quality of services as women in non-Aboriginal and non-Inuit communities.

Details

This can be achieved by having community members identify their community's needs and by ensuring that services are developed and delivered by Aboriginal people.

S.68 Increase the level of services in Aboriginal and Inuit communities to treat alcohol, drug and solvent abuse.

Details

These services must have the appropriate professional expertise to deal with the underlying issues of violence and must promote an holistic approach to violence in Aboriginal and Inuit communities.

S.69 Support the establishment of a network of healing centres to incorporate addictions and other services.

Legal Sector

Introduction

At present, the legal system does not bring much justice to women in Canada. Increasingly, it has become a series of formalized processes relying on technicalities and tactics where priority is given to following rules and precedent instead of attempting to assure that justice is achieved. As exercises in truth seeking, legal practices fall woefully short of any acceptable standard. In this action plan, solutions are put forward to be addressed by the following key participants:

- police forces

- boards and commissions

- courts and tribunals

- law schools

- voluntary legal associations

- law societies

- federal, provincial-territorial governments.

Key Problems

Justice for women in Canada has always been elusive. It was men who sat at the table writing the laws and then administering them, protecting their interests in property and safety in the process. All the rules and the evidentiary processes for determining guilt or innocence were determined from the male perspective. This exclusion from the formulation, administration, application and interpretation of the law diminished women's access to justice. It also resulted in their being harmed rather than helped by much of their contact with the system.

As the legal systems evolved, a series of safeguards were incorporated to try to balance power between the accused and the state. These safeguards have become known as the fair trial rights of the accused.

There was no obligation to consider the impact of these provisions or any other aspect of legal practice on the victims of the crime until the introduction in 1985 of the *Canadian Charter of Rights and Freedoms* equality section which supports the right to equal benefit and protection of the law for all victims as well as the accused. Even with that obligation in place, little has been done to bring a fair balance to the system. There has, however, been a clear articulation by the Supreme Court of Canada on the nature of the equality that must be achieved. In stressing the equality of outcome and therefore the importance of different treatment to reach that goal, the Supreme Court provides the framework for the large-scale initiatives and changes that are needed.

The limited criminalization of the violence committed against women is a great violation of their basic human rights to equal benefit and protection of the law, to security of the person and sometimes to life. Denial of the existence of violence is reinforced when acquittals result because of a technicality due to the process and not related to the guilt or innocence of the accused. It also comes with trivial sentences that in themselves deny the seriousness of what occurred. When crimes are inadequately defined or ignored in law, some men are given immunity from prosecution while their victims are either denied access to the courts altogether or are filtered out of the legal system in the early stages.

When the knowledge of judges is tainted by bias and myths and is marked by an absence of relevant and complete information on crimes of violence against women, the resulting adjudication cannot be fair. The rights to life and to security of the person have been severely jeopardized for women when judges have not understood the severity of the crimes of sexual assault, assault of women in intimate relationships, and threatening behaviours leading to the murder of women.

Women's lives are diminished and limited and their inequality reinforced by the violence perpetrated against them and by the fear of the next violence.

Children's safety in Canada has also been significantly jeopardized by a legal system that does not effectively deal with crimes of violence against children.

In the past, the lack of knowledge and understanding of crimes of violence against women and against children and the biases related to gender, race and class held by those administering the law were not recognized to exist at all and certainly were not deemed important enough to require remedial interventions. Legal practitioners and adjudicators were not held accountable for their behaviour and for their contributions to the violation of women's and children's equality and security. Only very recently has there been some recognition that specialized knowledge is necessary for the adjudication of these crimes. The civil process shares many of the same limitations. Although feminist legal theorists have been detailing the problems for a number of years, the legal community is now scrutinizing the legal system for bias for the first time.

The laws created, the determinations of innocence or guilt, the treatment of women victim witnesses, sentencing practices and release decisions for offenders are some of the practices which, imbued with bias, have had a negative impact on the basic human rights of women.

The legal system must undergo considerable systemic change. Some changes, such as the judicial education programs on gender equality, are being introduced but in a limited and leisurely fashion.

To the extent to which women do not receive equal benefit of the law, their basic human rights are being violated, and the equality provisions of the *Canadian Charter of Rights and Freedoms* have been offended. Laws and practices which contribute to the subordination of women are unconstitutional. There is, therefore, considerable urgency to change them.

New Orientations for the Legal Sector

L.1   In the legal system, the tolerance of violence as it exists in unfair laws, the bias of adjudicators, and other discriminatory practices related to the administration of justice have produced significant violations of women's basic human rights. Consequently, the adoption of zero tolerance is the major new orientation for this sector.

L.2   The change in the criteria for appointment of police commissioners, judges and other adjudicators to give priority to those with a demonstrated understanding of equality issues and the complex dynamics of violence against women would produce a fundamental shift in the legal system that is or will be necessary to achieve justice for women.

L.3   Implement the equality provisions of the *Canadian Charter of Rights and Freedoms* fully for women victims and women offenders.

L.4   Introduce a new fundamental principle of justice that protects the right of everyone to have a response from the legal system that is free of gender, race and class bias.

L.5   Account fully to women for their equality and safety. This should be done by all organizations in the legal sector.

Zero Tolerance Actions for All Organizations in the Legal Sector

Priority Setting/Allocation of Resources

L.6   Commit publicly to eradicating existing gender, race and class bias in the legal system and to fully supporting women's and children's Charter rights.

Human Resource Management

L.7   Provide training on the role of the legal system in promoting women's equality. Issues to be included in the training would deal with the unacceptable tolerance of violence in the legal system; how implementing women's rights to equality and security will change current legal practices; constitutional issues affecting women; strategies that promote the equality of women and children in the legal system; recognizing dangerous offenders; assessing the volatility of situations involving abuse and recognizing threats to women's safety; and recognizing racism including that which is directed at Aboriginal and Inuit peoples.

L.8   Evaluate the extent to which there has been an incorporation of cross cultural and gender specific knowledge provided in training, into policy formulation and practice.

Education/Promotional Activities

L.9   Initiate, with equality-seeking organizations, education programs that emphasize equality and access to justice and are designed for members to help highlight the current inequities within the legal system.

L.10   Create and disseminate to the public, in as many languages as possible, education materials that acknowledge and explain the problems of inequality and the lack of safety for women within the current legal system. Explain the changes that implementation of zero tolerance will bring.

Zero Tolerance Actions for Specific Organizations

All police forces, boards and commissions.

Human Resource Management

L.11   Recruit Aboriginal women, women of diverse cultures and those who demonstrate knowledge and an understanding of issues of sexism and racism.

L.12   Differentiate between the appropriate use and abuse of power in all policies affecting staffing practices and in the review of officers.

L.13   Provide training for all members of the force. It should teach force members how to determine the risk of further harm posed by offenders, according to research and prior patterns of abuse; explain evidentiary and safety issues related to stalking and criminal harassment, children who witness violence, disabled persons who are abused, ritual and cult abuse, date rape, sexual abuse involving breach of trust, and the use of pornography or other sexually violent media in the perpetration of abuse.

L.14 Provide cross-cultural information and training from members of Aboriginal and Inuit cultures and other cultures to improve police responses to women from different cultures and to underline the unacceptability of violence in any culture.

L.15 Provide counselling or employee assistance programs to help officers cope with the stress of their jobs in non-violent ways.

Legislation/Regulation/Policy

L.16 Create and enforce the implementation of policies to ensure that initial police response, decisions on arrest, detention and terms of any release support the safety of the victims and prevent their revictimization. For example, work to provide a maximum response time of 30 minutes in northern, remote and rural communities.

L.17 Ensure that police force policies clearly reflect the priority given to the safety of people over the protection of property.

L.18 Enforce policies dealing with officers who abuse women. They must be identified as unfit to serve in law enforcement and must experience the full consequences of the law.

Programs/Services/Practices

L.19 Create specialized units to deal with sexual assault by strangers and acquaintances, woman abuse and all crimes of harassment and assault against women and children.

L.20 Initiate programs to remove the abuser from the home whenever possible and use technology, such as alarms for women and electronic monitoring devices for the abuser, to support the woman's safety in her home. Strengthen the application of peace bonds and restraining orders through their quick implementation and by communicating the relevant information quickly to other law enforcement personnel. Confiscate firearms and other weapons from those charged with abuse.

L.21 Collect DNA evidence from all those accused of sex offences and create a DNA data bank to help identify serial offenders.

L.22 Review and evaluate the Rape Evidence Kit with an eye to reducing the level of intrusiveness while maintaining the standards required for collecting sound evidence.

L.23 Initiate, with women and women's organizations, safety audits of public and semi-public spaces as well as of police property.

Consultation

L.24 Involve women's organizations and women anti-violence experts in the setting of priorities for the force and in the development and implementation of training programs on women's equality and safety.

L.25 Create police-community working groups to develop ways to improve the safety of women in the community.

L.26 Encourage women's anti-violence organizations to report regularly on the local priority issues involving the police and the safety of women. Schedule these reports as part of police commission meetings. Create mechanisms to respond to those concerns, making changes where necessary. Include regular reports from the commission back to the organizations.

L.27 Create a women's safety advisory board locally and nationally in the RCMP with representation from Aboriginal and Inuit women and from women representing the diversity of women in Canada.

Co-ordination

L.28 Create protocols with community organizations to co-ordinate responses for the treatment of women and children who are victims of sexual assault and other crimes of violence. Develop crime prevention initiatives with women's organizations and other community stakeholders working against violence.

L.29 Provide or co-ordinate, with community agencies, supports for victims with disabilities. These could include TDD lines, signers, bliss board interpreters, information in braille and cultural interpreters with knowledge of issues of violence. Ensure the co-ordination and efficient dissemination of information affecting public safety through police computer networks (CPIC), timely reports to the media and other practices.

Research and Evaluation

L.30 Create mechanisms to ensure the on-going review of police service delivery involving crimes of violence from the victims' perspective. Evaluate levels of support for victims' safety and the effectiveness of the investigation processes. Use current data-tracking projects or develop new ones to review length of time and disposition for these cases. Use results as a basis for policy revisions.

Education/Promotional Activities

L.31 Work with school personnel and with women's organizations to develop violence prevention programs for schools and for the general public. Actively support crime prevention initiatives by other community organizations where priority is given to women's and children's safety.

Accountability

L.32 Publicize the complaints process by providing easy-to-understand information in a variety of languages. Ensure that the complainant is supported during the process, and do whatever else is necessary to create an accessible, fair complaints process.

L.33 Ensure the police commissions work in a transparent manner and stay accountable to women in the community on the work done to support their safety by reporting regularly on activities.

Human Resource Management

L.34 Create through the judicial councils standards of practice and behaviour that promote equality.

L.35 Develop training programs that are mandatory for judges and other adjudicators including parole board members.

Details:

The training should include:

- *recognition of gender, race and class bias;*

- *sexual abuse of power and trust;*

- *the nature of self defence for abused women;*

- *a formula for determining the risk posed by an accused;*

- *the efficacy of current treatment programs for sexual abusers and other woman abusers and realistic prospects for rehabilitation;*

- *the assessment of the expertise of experts and the value of expert testimony;*

- *the understanding of the parallels between torture and woman abuse and the understanding of the dynamics and the impact of woman abuse, including psychological and emotional abuse, and harassment.*

Legislation/Regulation/Policy

L.36 Support the safety, security and equality interests of women by enforcing legislation through the actions of the court. Ensure that sentencing reflects the severity of the crimes of woman abuse and that the harm and danger posed by sexual offenders are recognized by using the full range of sentencing allowed. Other decisions taken in the court must reflect a clear appreciation of the harms caused by the abusive behaviours perpetrated against women, especially those where there is no obvious physical injury (e.g., stalking and criminal harassment) or where there is sexual abuse by a person in a position of power or trust and the risk of harm posed by the accused. Support the security interests of children by clearly recognizing the harms of sexual and physical abuse, the psychological impact on children who witness abuse in their home and the risk of reoffending from many sexual abusers.

L.37 Ensure that policies governing conditional release practices make the safety of women and children a priority.

Programs/Services/Practices

L.38 Support the development of specialized courts or court space dedicated to the needs of children and to deal with crimes of woman abuse.

L.39 Replace preliminary hearings, wherever possible, with paper disclosure.

L.40 Make public safety interests the prime consideration in using incarceration in sentencing.

Consultation

L.41 Ensure the perspective of the victim is well represented through victim impact statements, victims' advocates, and frequent consultations on victims' issues.

L.42 Define "dangerousness" of abusers with input from women on the definition.

L.43 Develop protocols for court practices based on the *Canadian Charter of Rights and Freedoms* with input from victims.

L.44 Consult on alternatives to incarceration for crimes that do not threaten public safety.

Co-ordination

L.45 Take a leadership role in the use of the socio-legal approach to sentencing that includes treatment and post-incarceration supervision and relapse prevention treatment for abusers. Gather and integrate information and analysis from groups concerned with equality and anti-violence.

L.46 Support co-ordination between courts and victim services.

Physical Environment

L.47 Provide assistance to women to audit courthouses or locations where courts are sitting in isolated communities, and to ensure the victims do not have to have contact with those accused of crimes against them.

Accountability

L.48 Develop judicial standards of practice and behaviour for judges and justices of the peace that will promote justice and equality, and support the safety of women and of children.

L.49 Improve public access to the complaints process by publicizing the procedures and how to use them. Make proceedings of discipline committees and decisions more public. Provide detailed annual reporting of disciplinary actions. Assess need for a judicial council on Prince Edward Island.

All deans and faculty of law schools.

Human Resource Management

L.50 Recognize through promotion or other reward practices staff and faculty who work on equality-promoting initiatives.

Legislation/Regulation /Policy

L.51 Create policies to deal severely with abusive behaviour by faculty or students. Recognize the inappropriateness of such behaviour for a person who is or will be in a position of trust and power. Keep records of incidents of abuse and ensure that they are part of official records that are passed on to law societies.

Programs/Services/Practices

L.52 Integrate the issues of sexism, racism and class bias, the rights of victims and other equality issues under the *Canadian Charter of Rights and Freedoms* into all aspects of the curriculum. Introduce specific units on the experience of victims in the legal system, the nature and impact of crimes of violence including sexual abuse of persons with disabilities, ritual abuse and other crimes not yet well recognized.

L.53 Establish protocols for recording and passing on to law societies information on incidents of abuse and harassment by students who may apply in the future for admission to the society.

Consultation

L.54 Determine program priorities, and develop new curricula with women students, faculty and with women who are experts from outside the school on the nature of equality, issues of violence against women, the use of the *Canadian Charter of Rights and Freedoms* and the legal system.

L.55 Work with survivors of violence to bring needed change to legal theory and practice.

L.56 Develop partnerships with women and women's organizations and actively work toward solutions to problems women identify in the legal system.

Co-ordination

L.57 Develop co-operative, equality-promoting programs with women experts including violence survivors to support change in legal practice.

L.58 Co-ordinate curricula development with trainers of para-legals and other legal system workers with community colleges and other legal training institutes.

> **All voluntary legal associations.**

Priority Setting/Allocation of Resources

L.59 Through the Canadian Bar Association Ethics Committee, undertake initiatives to promote women's equality and support women's safety. Identify ways to reduce acquittals based on "legal" technicalities and create protocols for defence counsel to reduce victim-witness harassment in sexual assault and other woman abuse cases.

Legislation/Regulation/Policy

L.60 Develop policies to articulate the specific ways the association will support the work or actions of its members who are doing equality and safety promotion work on behalf of women and children. Create models of policies and protocols on the treatment of women clients to promote the quality and safety of women and of their children. Encourage the adoption of these policies and protocols by legal firms.

Programs/Services/Practices

L.61 Create and disseminate model human resource management policies including policies on workplace harassment and training packages to address gender inequality, racism and other discriminatory attitudes and acts.

Co-ordination

L.62 Co-ordinate initiatives designed to remedy the problems women experience in the courts.

Research and Evaluation

L.63 Gather data on the impact of the legal system on women with particular focus on the harms of gender, race and class bias.

All law societies.

Priority Setting/Allocation of Resources

L.64 Initiate, immediately, a process for more effective detection of those members who abuse, including lawyers who attempt to or waive fees for sex. Removal from practice would be obligatory until rehabilitation is assured.

Human Resource Management

L.65 Ensure comprehensive training for staff and benchers on issues of violence. Place special emphasis on sexual abuse involving breach of trust and on the impact of violence and legal system responses on women who experience compounded oppression.

Legislation/Regulation/Policy

L.66 Create specific standards of practice behaviour for lawyers that will promote equality and security for women and for children.

L.67 Create admission criteria policies that are explicit from the perspective of women's and children's safety. The policies would clearly define "good character" and the type of behaviour that would be deemed abusive and thus prohibit entry into the profession.

Consultation

L.68 Consult with women experts within and outside the profession when setting program priorities, generally, and on legal issues related to equality and safety, specifically.

Co-ordination

L.69 Ensure that the most relevant feminist analysis on issues of violence and equality, including work from outside the legal system, is made available to members.

Accountability

L.70 Increase lay membership of law society complaint and discipline committees. Appoint those with demonstrated understanding of equality issues and issues of violence, especially involving breach of trust issues, and who reflect the composition of the population.

All federal, provincial and territorial governments where relevant to their jurisdiction.

Priority Setting/Allocation of Resources

L.71 Acknowledge the present inequities in the legal system. Commit to the full realization of women's and children's rights to safety, security and equality enshrined in the *Canadian Charter of Rights and Freedoms*.

Legislation/Regulation/Policy

L.72 Review and evaluate, with women's organizations, legislative changes dealing with psychological or emotional abuse.

L.73 Amend or create new statutes where necessary to support women's equality and security interests through legislation and regulation in the following areas:

- *Criminal Code* — repeal soliciting provisions; change obscenity provisions to reflect the prohibition of sexually violent and degrading material, and add "sex" and remove "wilfully" to hate law sections.

- Recognize more clearly and explicitly in law the serious threat to security of the person and the gender-specific nature of most crimes of stalking or criminal harassment as well as the negative cumulative effects of the acts involved where the whole is much greater than the parts.

- Extend publication bans for sexual assault victims to the pretrial and other adjudicative processes.

- Recognize sexual abuse involving breach of trust as a specific crime of sexual assault.

- *Correction and Conditional Release Act* — ensure that the definition of serious harm includes emotional or psychological harm of sexual assault for women as well as for children.

- *Federal Immigration and Refugee Act* — recognize women fleeing gender persecution as refugees.

- *Provincial Crimes Compensation Acts* — extend provisions to increase the amount of compensation for victims including those of institutional abuse and to amend any time limitation in statute that would discriminate against adult survivors of incest receiving compensation.

- Civil remedies for women who are sexually exploited or abused in the consumption of pornography, by health practitioners, counsellors or therapists.

L.74 Amend human rights legislation to increase compensation for victims.

L.75 Review and amend, with consultation, the following legislation to protect children's security interests:

- child welfare legislation — to define children who witness violence as children in need of protection.

- *Divorce Act* and all legislation dealing with custody and access — violence by one spouse against another is explicitly deemed to be relevant in determining custody.

L.76 Develop clear legislation on zero tolerance requirements for self-regulating
professions concerning sexual abuse
that includes, at a minimum:

- offences and penalties for sexual
violation and abuse defined by
seriousness into several levels;

- prohibitions on practice during any
process of appeal after a finding of
guilt of sexual misconduct;

- prohibitions on any automatic reinstatement to the profession after
revocation of licence with onus on
the offender to prove there is no
longer a safety risk;

- the requirement for each self-
regulatory body to establish a
sexual abuse prevention and monitoring committee to work with
government to oversee the development and implementation of effective and accessible mechanisms for
the reporting of sexual abuse;

- the realignment of discipline hearings to ensure the fuller participation of complainants, public interest
intervenors and experts whose
interventions, will promote or
uphold the safety of the public with
testimony on issues such as the
dynamics and harms of sexual abuse
involving a breach of trust, the risk
of harm from the abuser to other
members of the public and the
statistical probability data that the
abuser will abuse again.

L.77 Enact policies to prohibit the use of
pornography and sexually degrading
material by sex offenders serving in any
correctional institution on the grounds
that it will weaken the effects of any
counselling program.

Programs/Services/Practices

L.78 Create special courts for crimes of
violence. Judges, Crown attorneys and
clerks working in these specialized
courts would be appointed for their
knowledge or aptitude to acquire
knowledge on the full range of issues of
violent crimes against women and
children.

L.79 Designate senior Crown attorneys who
have been provided with specialized
training to handle dangerous offender
applications, sexual abuse involving
breach of trust, ritual abuse and other
cases where the victims are disadvantaged because evidentiary issues are
currently not well understood.

L.80 Reinstate an expanded Court
Challenges Program.

L.81 Expand legal aid, victim support and
women's advocacy programs, including
pilot projects for women with disabilities and other victim witnesses who
have special needs in the courtroom,
until equal access for all women is
achieved.

L.82 Train legal aid lawyers to deal with
woman abuse.

L.83 Create national crime prevention initiatives that give priority to the safety of women and children. Begin with the allocation of resources for community-based violence prevention activities to shelters, rape crisis centres and other anti-violence community organizations to support a national crime prevention week/month.

L.84 Appoint a national co-ordinator for the management of sex offenders. This individual must have demonstrated understanding of the primary role that abuse of power and misogyny play in the sexual offences committed. The mandate should include the overhaul and expansion of counselling programs to recognize the element of accountability to women and to the communities served by the programs.

L.85 Create a victims' advocate office and a victims' bill of rights.

L.86 Ensure any new Aboriginal system(s) of justice are developed and administered with the full participation of Aboriginal women.

L.87 Create policies that can be used as models for hiring, performance review and promotion in legal services within the next year and generic training programs for all legal practitioners within the next two years. Give priority for hiring and promotion in government legal practice to those with specialist knowledge of equality and violence issues. Appoint those with demonstrated understanding of equality issues as judges, parole board members, human rights commissioners, other tribunal members and all other adjudicators.

Consultation

L.88 Review laws and practices to ascertain their impact on women's safety and equality and recommend appropriate changes.

Details:

• Include women's organizations, judges, Crown attorneys, police and other legal practitioners in the review process.

• Consider practices and orders that are specifically related to:

   • issues of disclosure of personal information of victim-witnesses in preliminary hearings, cross examinations and through subpoenas;

   • sexual assault by acquaintances and persons in positions of trust;

   • sentencing guidelines that reflect the severity of crimes of woman abuse;

   • evidentiary issues regarding sexual abuse of women with disabilities;

   • ritual abuse;

   • abuse of women involving pornography;

   • issues of racism;

   • abuse of domestic workers and the experience of immigrant women in the legal system;

   • practices related to circuit courts in the North and isolated communities; and

   • the review of gun control.

L.89 Develop community justice and policing initiatives with the full participation of Aboriginal and Inuit women. The women must be involved in determining appropriate sanctions for all cases of violence against women and children which may include counselling at out-post camps or community facilities administered by elders and/or counselling while incarcerated in a correctional facility.

Co-ordination

L.90 Support the co-ordination of courts and counselling programs for a more effective socio-judicial approach to sentencing by developing a framework with policies and guidelines for evaluation.

L.91 Co-ordinate a review of the status of women incarcerated for killing their abusers with the Elizabeth Fry Society and co-ordinate a review with a pardon/release process where possible.

L.92 Establish crisis response teams in all Aboriginal and Inuit communities, with membership of experts and lay persons identified by the community, to co-ordinate assessment, response, intervention and referral procedures.

Research and Evaluation

L.93 Provide funds to monitor sentencing and other judicial decision-making practices by individuals with a clear understanding of the equality issues for victims and the issues of violence from a feminist perspective.

L.94 Create equality and justice monitoring, evaluation and advocacy centres to bring Charter-based equality analysis to legal data and practices.

L.95 Monitor plea bargaining practices in crimes of violence with priority given to the murder of women, woman assault and sexual assault cases.

L.96 Initiate research projects on the costs associated with offending and re-offending.

Accountability

L.97 Amend police Acts to create civilian police complaints commissions with the specific articulated purpose of upholding the safety of women and children as well as general public safety interests.

L.98 Appoint those with specialist knowledge of sexual abuse involving breach of trust to the commissions for the adjudication of complaints of sexual offences committed by police officers. Create special sub-committees of specialists to hear those complaints or provide intensive training on the issue to the members themselves.

L.99 Increase significantly the lay membership of all judicial councils and justices of the peace review councils. Appoint those who demonstrate knowledge of legal equity issues, who bring gender equity to the council and reflect the composition of the population.

L.100 Expand powers of councils to provide a range of sanctions for behaviour violations. These could include reprimand, temporary suspensions for education, discipline and treatment or recommendations for permanent removal.

L.101 Expand powers of the councils to review judicial decisions given by other bodies, such as discipline tribunals, that overturn decisions or lighten penalties where women's safety might be affected.

L.102 Amend coroners' acts and create other legislation to compel inquests to be held after each murder of a woman to determine how the death might have been prevented and what changes might be made so other women's lives might be saved. The amendments would provide for representation by women's anti-violence or legal advocacy organizations to ensure that a victims' advocate is present and would give the coroner or designated others the responsibility for the implementation of the resulting recommendations.

L.103 Review legal system practices and legislation, regulations, policies, procedures and guidelines against the standards provided in the *Canadian Charter of Rights and Freedoms*, to find ways to remedy problem areas and ensure that victims receive the equal benefit and protection of the law and security of the person as provided in the Charter.

L.104 Report annually on progress made in implementing recommendations regarding justice initiatives made in the jurisdiction by task forces, commissions and advisors in the past five years.

WORKPLACE SECTOR

Introduction

Working for pay has become increasingly important in the lives of women in Canada. However, for many women, the workplace reinforces experiences of inequality and unequal power relations based on gender, race and class. Women are undervalued, underpaid, sexually harassed and assaulted.

Specifically, the following key participants have been identified:

- Employers (public and private sectors)

- Unions and professional associations

- Federal-provincial/territorial mechanisms (human rights commissions, ministries of labour, workers' compensation agencies, labour relations boards etc.).

Key Problems:

While socio-economic reforms, policies and practices to promote social and economic equality for women continue to be implemented, key problems do persist in terms of the safety and security of women in the workplace.

- Violence and harassment are not acknowledged as valid workplace problems nor addressed in a systematic and collaborative manner by managers and unions.

- Workplace violence and harassment are not understood as part of the wider context of violence against women, gender power relations, and race and class inequalities.

- The relationship between the ability to perform and the presence of safe working conditions is not recognized.

New Orientations for the Workplace Sector

WP.1 Eliminating violence against women in the workplace must be part of an overall strategy that addresses the economic inequality experienced by women.

WP.2 Work values must change. Such principles as co-operation, sharing and consensus building must be perceived as equal in value to control and competition.

Zero Tolerance Actions for All Organizations and Individuals in the Workplace Sector

Priority Setting/Allocation of Resources

WP.3 Subscribe to a policy of zero tolerance that supports women's safety, security and equality based on:

- **equal access to all resources and programs;**

- **equal value for women's experience in all employment policies, practices, programs and services; and**

- **an accurate reflection of women's needs in all employment and related activities.**

Accountability

WP.4 In collaboration with unions, employers must develop and implement a written code of conduct based on the Zero Tolerance Policy which promotes equality and guarantees safety and security for all workers, employees and clients.

Details:

Adherence to the code must be ensured through:

- *the adoption of a comprehensive strategy for educating workers, employees and clients about the philosophical background, the values and the principles inherent in the code;*

- *performance reviews with strong sanctions (i.e., warning, missed opportunity for a promotion, dismissal) for violating the code; and*

- *effective complaint procedures.*

Local women's organizations with expertise in this area must be involved to this undertaking.

Zero Tolerance Actions for Specific Organizations

> **All employers, unions and professional associations from both the public and private sectors working together.**

Legislation/Regulation/Policy

WP.5 Develop and implement a policy on violence in the workplace, including sexual harassment, as recommended in the Zero Tolerance Policy.

WP.6 Establish, amend or support policies for workers/employees regarding absences and poor performance caused by violence against women.

WP.7 Demonstrate a firm commitment to ending violence in the workplace in any negotiations.

Details

From a union's perspective, this could include:

- *bargaining for strong no-harassment provisions in collective agreements and contract language that deals with safe work environments and the issue of abuse;*

- *extending equal protection through anti-discrimination clauses and support to members who are lesbians, women of colour, immigrant women, women with disabilities and older women; and*

- *adopting policies that discourage/prohibit all sexist and racist practices in union functions.*

Programs/Services/Practices

WP.8 Conduct safety audits and violence prevention programs.

Education/Promotional Activities

WP.9 Educate non-traditional workplaces about the subtle forms of violence, such as the lack of integration of women workers/employees in the workplace or the isolation of women workers/employees because of their small numbers.

All federal-provincial/territorial mechanisms (human rights commissions, ministries of labour, worker's compensation agencies, labour relations boards etc.).

Legislation/Regulation/Policy

WP.10 Legally mandate policies on sexual harassment and on discrimination based on gender and race and make available resources for training and education in line with human rights codes. (Sexual harassment policies must include gender harassment. It can undermine the work atmosphere and is as harmful as the more commonly known sexual harassment).

WP.11 Ensure that labour relations laws are amended to include harassment in health and safety regulations.

WP.12 Recognize unsafe working conditions due to sexual harassment as a valid health and safety concern and compensate accordingly (including counselling costs) under workers' compensation regulations.

WP.13 Recognize post-traumatic stress disorder as a form of injury that can result from sexual harassment in the workplace.

WP.14 Ensure that winning compensation for sexual harassment under human rights acts does not prevent complainants from accessing other compensation for victims of crime as provided in federal, provincial or territorial legislation.

Research and Evaluation

WP.15 Evaluate sexual harassment policies and regulations adopted by private and public entities.

Details:

Such an evaluation must include:

•   *the handling of complaints including decisions and dispositions of cases by judicial, quasi-judicial and administrative tribunals; and*

•   *the incidence of sexual harassment of women from specific groups such as Aboriginal women, immigrant women, women of colour, women from other ethnic groups, women with disabilities, older women and lesbians.*

The Zero Tolerance Policy is to be used as a standard for evaluation.

MILITARY SECTOR

Introduction

A large public employer in Canada, the Canadian Forces has military bases throughout the country that are adjacent to or integrated into civilian communities where they have considerable impact. Many women live under the influence of military policy and procedures, specifically women members of the forces and spouses of military men.

Key Problems:

• The doctrine, culture and hierarchical structures of the Canadian Forces create an atmosphere where violence against women is fostered and tolerated.

• Spouses of military men are vulnerable physically, psychologically and financially. They are transferred frequently, often isolated and deprived of established support systems of extended family and long-time friends. The man's military career is seen as primary, and frequent changes of location make career progression very difficult for spouses. As a result, they are often dependent on husbands and on the Department of National Defence.

• The chain of command often ignores violence against women committed by military husbands. Command does not want to deal with the problems. Discipline for violence would disrupt the military career of the man and could also affect the cohesion of his unit. Women are afraid of the career consequences for their husbands if they report violence.

• Military men who resent working with women often harass women co-workers by making sexist comments and collective, sustained, serious verbal aggression designed to destroy the confidence of the women.

• Pornography is tolerated and openly displayed on bases and in training schools.

• Even though Canadian Forces policy prohibits discrimination against lesbians, the rejection of and the verbal and physical abuse of lesbians and gay men is a reality of military life.

New Orientations for the Military Sector

MI.1 The Department of National Defence must commit to equality for women and include women, both military members and spouses, in all decisions that affect their lives.

MI.2 Training of men for combat and authoritarian military structures can make men very aggressive and domineering. This must be acknowledged by the Department and the chain of command. The Department must counterbalance combat readiness with human relations training that emphasizes the inappropriateness and danger of aggression in interpersonal relationships.

MI.3 Leaders of the Canadian Forces and base commanders must question the male-dominated hierarchical culture of the forces and determine to what degree maintenance of that culture is necessary for effective operations. The system should be significantly altered to give military personnel and their spouses more control over their lives.

Zero Tolerance Actions for the Military Sector

The Department of National Defence

Priority Setting/Allocation of Resources

MI.4 Establish the zero tolerance committee called for in the policy and ensure that membership is drawn from senior ranking officers, military women and spouses of military members including representatives of the Organization of Spouses of Military Members (OSOMM).

MI.5 Strengthen the policies prohibiting sexism, racism and discrimination against lesbians and gay men and enforce policies vigorously and evenly throughout all ranks.

MI.6 Ensure that military women and the spouses of military men who live in violent situations have quick access to support services and can leave any situation of violence, regardless of where the base is located, in Canada or abroad.

MI.7 Increase resources to Family Resource Centres and clarify their mandate to include operation outside the base chain of command. Centres must maintain links with each other and work closely with zero tolerance committees.

Human Resource Management

MI.8 Increase the presence of military women throughout the administrative hierarchy of military bases at all decision-making levels.

MI.9 Adopt the objective of having 10 percent of senior officer positions filled by women, who represent the diversity of women in the Canadian population, within three years.

MI.10 Identify systemic barriers to women's participation. For example, ensure that the physical ability test does not exceed the standard required to do the job. Test women against this standard and not in competition with men.

MI.11 Make all military members and civilian staff aware of what constitutes a poisoned work environment for women and what constitutes sexual harassment. Emphasize the seriousness and consequences of breaching policies.

MI.12 Have the zero tolerance committee review every allegation of gender or sexual harassment and recommend appropriate solutions.

MI.13 Establish a telephone contact with the Department of National Defence, outside the chain of command, to facilitate reporting of harassment and assault when the woman cannot come forward for fear of repercussions.

MI.14 Keep records of all harassment cases to document the dimensions of the problem and to assist in eradicating violence against women in the ranks.

MI.15 Establish support groups to help women cope with integration into a male-dominated workplace.

MI.16 Establish a fair policy for employing civilian spouses of military members.

MI.17 Facilitate women's choice of physicians (both military members and spouses) and, where distance is a factor, provide transportation for those who would like to consult a civilian physician off the base.

Legislation/Regulation/Policy

MI.18 Have the zero tolerance committee review all policies and practices that govern the lives of military spouses and develop an action plan to implement required changes.

MI.19 Implement a protocol requiring all military personnel to:

- refrain from persuading either women spouses or military women to withdraw their complaints against male members;

- recognize that women are under pressure not to report violence;

- recognize that violence against women causes serious harm; and

- respect accommodation choices of military women and military wives, on or off base, and ensure that accommodation respects the right to privacy.

MI.20 Provide safe, accessible, affordable child care for all children of military personnel, recognizing the equal right of women spouses to use child care.

MI.21 Require strict confidentiality for all counselling and medical records with release only to authorized counselling and medical staff and not to senior ranking officers.

MI.22 Facilitate swift access for women to civilian police officers, Crown attorneys and legal services off the base, as well as to shelters and all services in the surrounding communities, even if these decisions involve air transportation.

MI.23 Prohibit the display on base premises of materials that are pornographic and degrading to women; no public funds may be used to purchase films, violent videos or any other pornographic material.

Co-ordination

MI.24 Establish links between women's services on the military base and those in neighbouring communities.

Education/Promotional Activities

MI.25 Develop an awareness program to eliminate sexism, racism and homophobia designed and delivered by feminist service providers, military women and spouses of military men, and include:

- information on all forms of violence including economic abuse;

- videos, lectures, brochures and posters addressed to military men of all ranks, presenting methods of intervention for those in positions of command and responsibility;

- knowledge of the extent and dynamics of violence;

- the repercussions of violent acts on women's health and their career development; and

- the repercussions of abusive acts on social and military life on bases.

Accountability

MI.26 Report annually to Parliament through the Minister of National Defence on progress made in the following areas:

- numbers of women members within the military including occupation, rank and self-identified race;

- cases of sexual and racial harassment dealt with and their outcome;

- cases of discrimination against lesbians and gay men and their outcome.

- policy changes made to benefit spouses of military men and an evaluation of their impact; and

- resources provided to Family Resource Centres and the programs and services offered.

Priority Setting/Allocation of Resources

MI.27 Subscribe to a client-centred model of service delivery.

MI.28 Create a community board to establish priorities and directions for activities. Membership should be democratically drawn from among military spouses and military women.

Programs/Services/Practices

MI.29 Distribute information on issues of violence, family planning and the sharing of family responsibilities.

MI.30 Arrange for training in languages generally used on the base and in the surrounding community for women who are isolated due to language barriers.

MI.31 Advocate on behalf of women who are having difficulties with the military or with service deliverers.

MI.32 Keep up-to-date information on women's resources in the civilian community and make appropriate referrals.

MI.33 Undertake a safety audit of military bases and press for the necessary modifications to ensure that each base takes action to improve women's safety. Check lighting, lanes, remote areas and recreational sites, etc.

Accountability

MI.34 Report on activities and progress annually to the general population of women on the base.

EDUCATION SECTOR

Introduction

Schools, colleges and universities significantly contribute to the social, psychological and physical development as well as to the cognitive skills of students. Students are highly influenced and shaped by the structure of the system, by curriculum content, by attitudes and behaviours of educators, by learning methods, by peer relationships and by overall institutional environments. All personnel within educational institutions must be seen and must see themselves as being in positions of trust with students.

Schools have an authoritarian structure giving educators and other staff a great deal of power relative to students. Such power dynamics undermine self-protection messages that tell students they have a right to say no on one hand, yet must bow to adult authority on the other. While it is necessary to regulate behaviour in educational institutions this must be achieved through more co-operative power sharing.

The educational system alone cannot be charged with changing society's attitudes toward women and eliminating violence. However, alongside the family and the media, educational institutions have the greatest opportunity to play a positive role in change. Working toward equality for women and zero tolerance of violence among the youth of Canada will have far-reaching effects in reducing violence against women.

The enormous demands on educational resources are recognized. However, as our consultations revealed, people in Canada clearly believe the education system has an important role to play in ending violence and promoting equality. Many feel that requisite changes could be accommodated by altering current materials and courses and by equipping educators to deliver the altered content in a manner that demonstrates equality and non-violence. This will require realignment of resources and priorities to emphasize the goals of equality and non-violence. A commitment by ministries of education, ministries of colleges and universities, boards of education, educational institutions (schools, colleges and universities), teachers' federations, voluntary bodies such as parent-teacher organizations, parent volunteers and the students themselves is essential.

Currently, the educational system is being challenged to adapt to world competitiveness standards. Any moves in that direction must incorporate the needs of women both in terms of equality and safety. Failure to do so will seriously compound existing problems and result in even greater disparities between women and men in the work force and in the sharing of Canada's prosperity.

Key Problems

- Violence among students and between students and teachers is a growing concern in schools, colleges and universities. The abuse is frequently based on sexism and/or racism. Often, there is an absence of clear, appropriate strategies to prevent or resolve violent situations.

- Some students who suffer violence either through assault or through witnessing violence in their own homes may become abusive themselves as playground bullies or in dating relationships. Others may manifest symptoms of being abused through low achievement, erratic behaviour or failure to participate. Often, despite symptoms, the abuse goes undetected.

- The physical and social environments of schools, colleges and universities frequently create inequality and danger for girls and women.

New Orientations for the Education Sector

ED.1 The entire education sector (provincial/territorial ministries of education, ministries of colleges and universities, Aboriginal/Inuit school authorities, boards of education, all educational institutions, including Aboriginal, Inuit and private schools, teachers' federations, voluntary bodies such as parent-teacher associations, parent volunteers and student governments) must create the strongest possible equality model based on gender, race and class.

Details

This includes the following specific actions:

- *altering all administrative structures and practices to better reflect equality and more equitable power sharing.*

- *requiring all faculty members and staff to be role models in encouraging others to share power and to be respectful regardless of student/faculty status, gender, race or class.*

- *making the building of student self-awareness and self-esteem a core value of all educational settings.*

- *creating a social culture that values interaction between boys and girls, women and men other than conventional dating relationships.*

- *teaching and requiring the practice of peaceful conflict resolution.*

- *emphasizing the rights of girls and women and the responsibilities of boys and men to respect these rights.*

- *ensuring that guidance counsellors have current information and have received instruction on the status of women in Canada, and are prepared to guide girls into the full range of careers.*

- *taking ameliorative measures to accelerate the attainment of equality in all aspects of education.*

Zero Tolerance Actions for All Organizations and Individuals in the Education Sector

Priority Setting/Allocation of Resources

ED.2 Implement violence prevention strategies that focus on violence against girls and women. Ensure that such programs are culturally relevant.

ED.3 Conduct safety audits of all educational facilities to identify places and situations that create danger for girls and women.

Human Resource Management

ED.4 Make the safety of girls and women a priority when selecting staff.

ED.5 Use employment equity strategies to equalize, in all occupations and at all levels, the proportion of women and men and the representation of the races within the community served.

ED.6 Train staff members to recognize the linkages between inequality and violence and to incorporate this knowledge into their work.

ED.7 Make awareness of inequality and its linkages to violence against women a formal rating factor in staff performance appraisals.

ED.8 Implement effective, accessible policies against sexual and racial violence and enforce them fairly.

Legislation/Regulation/Policy

ED.9 Develop culturally relevant protocols that outline actions to be taken when acts of violence occur. The protocols should give priority to the safety of victims and refer victims to appropriate women-centred and culturally relevant services.

ED.10 Implement sexual harassment policies with strong and effective redress mechanisms.

Consultation

ED.11 Consult widely with women's organizations, including women's teachers' federations, that have resources and knowledge in the areas of equality and ending violence.

Co-ordination

ED.12 Work closely with other education partners and women's groups to ensure a consistent message on equality and ending violence, and to share resources.

Zero Tolerance Actions for Specific Organizations or Individuals

> All student governments at elementary, secondary and post-secondary levels.

Priority Setting/Resource Allocation

ED.13 Make girls' and women's equality and safety a priority.

ED.14 Facilitate equal participation of girls and women in all structures and activities.

Programs/Services/Practices

ED.15 Monitor the institutional administration's progress on implementing zero tolerance and assist in achieving its goals.

Accountability

ED.16 Make the student body aware of all activities aimed at achieving equality and ending violence and report annually to students on progress.

> All boards of education including Aboriginal, Inuit and private schools, and all elementary and secondary schools.

Priority Setting/Allocation of Resources

ED.17 Aim at gender, race and class equality and the ending of violence as priorities. Reflect these goals in mission statements and throughout the entire strategic planning process.

ED.18 Re-align budget allocations to support implementation of the Zero Tolerance Policy.

Human Resource Management

ED.19 Recognize the positions of trust and authority held by staff in educational institutions in the selection and placement of staff.

Details

Safeguard students by:

* *evaluating sexist, racist and class attitudes at pre-employment interviews;*

* *asking at the interview and in checking references about past behaviour or complaints related to violence against girls and women; and*

* *evaluating awareness of appropriate behavioural limits with girls and women students.*

ED.20 Train staff on how to recognize symptoms of abuse and in the use of appropriate first-level intervention techniques.

ED.21 Train educators to recognize the links between gender and race inequality and violence, and to identify the full range of behaviours that constitute gender and race discrimination including the more subtle manifestations.

ED.22 Hold all educators accountable for sexist or racist behaviours they display.

ED.23 Do not hire any educator who abuses students; dismiss any educator who abuses students.

ED.24 Recognize the vulnerability of teachers to false allegations of abuse by students but avoid exaggerating the risk.

Legislation/Regulation/Policy

ED.25 Develop protocols that obligate staff members to refer student victims and student perpetrators of violence to appropriate, culturally relevant services without delay.

ED.26 Provide support, including peer support programs, for student victims and student perpetrators of violence who are undergoing counselling.

Programs/Services/Practices

ED.27 Conduct a gender-aware violence prevention program.

ED.28 Make violence prevention a part of all curricula.

ED.29 Make all programs and services (including extra-curricular and sport activities) available in an equal and appropriate fashion to all students, male and female.

ED.30 Direct particular efforts at girls in physical education and sports activities to ensure that they develop and reach their full physical potential.

ED.31 Base all educational practices and violence prevention activities on gender-aware information so girls and women derive equal benefit and protection.

ED.32 Introduce ameliorative programs, services and practices to overcome the unequal status of girls and women within society and within educational institutions.

ED.33 Implement programs that assist young mothers to stay in school.

Consultation

ED.34 Use the expertise and educational resources of women's groups in the development of policy, practices, programs and procedures and pay for these services according to scales used for other types of consultants.

Co-ordination

ED.35 Link prevention strategies and equality initiatives with wider community strategies to meet the total needs of students.

ED.36 Exchange and share knowledge and resources to ensure that all efforts within the education sector complement each other in achieving safety and equality.

Research and Evaluation

ED.37 Assess the effectiveness and success of any program, policy or practice designed to ensure girls' and women's safety and to achieve equality.

Details

The assessment should include as a minimum:

- *the differential impact on both genders;*

- *an examination of whether girls' and women's needs are being met; and*

- *an evaluation of resource use.*

Education/Promotional Activities

ED.38 Consider students' safety and equality needs in any educational activities and promotions within schools.

Accountability

ED.39 Hold all staff and students accountable for sexist and racist behaviour.

ED.40 Create clear, accessible, grievance procedures for students who are abused and ensure that students are represented on adjudicating bodies by other students or, in the case of young elementary children, by parents or children's advocates.

ED.41 Make public all policies, procedures and practices aimed at achieving equality and ending violence. This would include evaluations of progress toward those goals.

All colleges and universities.

Priority Setting/Allocation of Resources

ED.42 Make prevention of violence against women a top priority.

ED.43 Formulate and implement policies to alter the hostility toward women in the social and educational environment on campuses.

ED.44 Ensure that resource allocations equally support the activities and needs of women students.

Human Resource Management

ED.45 Accelerate employment equity programs to achieve a balance of male/female faculty more quickly.

ED.46 Train faculty on the dynamics of violence against women and its links to inequality.

ED.47 Provide support for feminist faculty members.

Legislation/Regulation/Policy

ED.48 Implement strong sexual harassment-prevention policies and protocols.

ED.49 Implement policies and protocols to deal with sexism and racism.

Programs/Services/Practices

ED.50 Make equality and the prevention of violence against women part of the course content of all faculties including professional schools such as law, medicine and social work.

ED.51 Include material on the impacts of experiencing violence on learning into the curricula of all faculties of education. It should discuss the recognition of the symptoms in a student experiencing violence, provide appropriate first-level responses to students who are suffering violence and elaborate on the links between inequality and violence.

ED.52 Ensure that diplomas and degrees granted by faculties which specialize in Aboriginal programs have equal status to the more general degrees.

ED.53 Implement an equity program that encourages girls and women to enter male-dominated fields of study. It should also support women in transforming the traditional male culture that isolates and alienates women in these fields.

ED.54 Support programs, such as women's centres, that assist women who are victims.

Co-ordination

ED.55 Link violence prevention strategies with those of the larger non-academic community.

ED.56 Use community resources and staff from shelters, rape crisis centres and women's centres to train faculty members and deliver course content on violence against women to students.

Research and Evaluation

ED.57 Work closely with service providers to decide what research is needed most urgently in the area of violence against women.

ED.58 Recognize feminist research and social action research methodology.

Accountability

ED.59 Make public all policy and program goals aimed at achieving equality and ending violence along with the annual evaluation of progress toward these goals.

> **Provincial/territorial ministries of education.**

Programs/Services/Practices

ED.60 Make the following changes to curricula.

(a) Make sex education compulsory and design courses that include material on:

- gender relationships and shared responsibility as well as biological facts;

- equality between women and men;

- relationships between lesbians and between gay men; and

- sexuality of persons with disabilities.

(b) Make life skills education compulsory and include content on positive parenting skills, such as non-violent discipline, and on prevention of violence against women and children.

(c) Make media literacy programs, that help "decode" media violence, sex-role stereotyping and the misleading portrayal of women, compulsory for schools at all levels.

(d) Alter core curricula to provide an equal portion of content about women in all their diversity.

(e) Have Canadian history curricula evaluated by Aboriginal and Inuit educators to ensure adequate and accurate content on the history of Aboriginal and Inuit peoples.

(f) Include the prevention of violence against women in the course content for all subjects.

(g) Make women's studies available as an option in high school.

ED.61 Designate a school within each province/territory as a pilot model school environment to achieve gender and race equality and the eradication of violence. Use the knowledge gained through the pilot school project to improve the environments of all schools.

All teachers' federations.

Legislation/Regulation/Policy

ED.62 Take a leadership role in reviewing professional codes of ethics for teachers. In the review, identify and remove potential or real barriers to disclosure of abuse by teachers and to holding teachers accountable for abuse inflicted by them.

Programs/Services/Practices

ED.63 Include content on equality of women and prevention of violence against women in all professional activities with teachers.

ED.64 Continue the work initiated by a number of women's federations on equality and violence issues.

ED.65 Provide in-service training to teachers on:

- recognizing their positions of trust/authority;

- recognizing that consent for sexual involvement with a student is not possible due to the power imbalance inherent in the teacher-student relationship; and

- how to maintain warm, nurturing relationships with students within safe touching boundaries.

Consultation

ED.66 Build on the working relationship currently established by women's federations with women working in the anti-violence movement.

ED.67 Continue to provide expert input into government educational policies and programs on education, children and violence.

ED.68 Take part in an open dialogue with child advocacy groups on the abuse of children by teachers.

Research and Evaluation

ED.69 Undertake research that furthers the understanding of the impact on learning when a student is experiencing violence.

Education/Promotional Activities

ED.70 Solicit and publish articles on violence against children and violence in the schools in all federation publications.

ED.71 Include information on women's equality and its links to violence in all publications.

Accountability

ED.72 Report annually on work done on the prevention of violence against women and on women's equality.

MEDIA SECTOR

Introduction

The media are an inordinately powerful source of ideas in Canadian life. Books, magazines, newspapers, television, videos, video games and radio bombard us with messages round the clock that shape our attitudes, often without our awareness.

Unfortunately, sexism, racism and violence feature prominently in media. Distorted and dangerous messages about women prevail; women are shown as subservient, in a limited range of roles that often portray them as sexual, worthy targets of male violence. Women's experiences are seldom the focus of news or current affairs, and their opinions are put forward less frequently than men's. Women are constantly used to sell products and are stalked, beaten, raped and mutilated in the name of entertainment.

There is a strong link between the portrayal of women in the media and the violence enacted against women in Canada every day. Women and children both describe how their abusers use pornography in the violent acts committed against them. The regulation of violence against women in the media is clearly a women's safety and child protection issue.

Key Problems

- For over a decade, the Canadian Radio-television Telecommunication Commission (CRTC) has encouraged broadcasters to self regulate the violence on television and the portrayal of women. Past efforts have not achieved the needed results. As long as self regulation continues to be ineffective and licences are renewed for broadcasters who deliver violent programs into Canadian homes, women doubt that the government is adequately supporting their safety and equality interests.

- The print media operate with almost no accountability to women or to the public generally, and press councils are not always receptive to the complaints filed by women. Violence against women is often sensationally reported and the incidents individualized. Less dramatic violence is ignored. There is little analysis of the systemic causes of violence. When violence is linked to equality, the media discussion is often adversarial. Important reports on violence against women are buried on inner pages and are sometimes juxtaposed with "pin-up" images of very young women. Few women are in editorial and byline positions.

- While strong, realistic images of women and of human sexuality are scarce, pornography and violent videos remain very popular and are widely available and used by young men. Canada has not yet found an effective means of stemming distribution of these harmful images.

- New technologies challenge the ability of any country to effectively regulate media. Materials often originate in foreign countries and cross borders via satellite or computer modem. Any serious attempt to eradicate violence from Canadian media will have to take these technologies into account and will require international co-operation.

- Women believe they have an essential role to play in preparing policy both for now and for the future and are currently denied this opportunity in a number ways.

New Orientations

All levels of government and all media organizations must co-operate to:

- adopt and implement zero tolerance;

- incorporate women's perspectives and experiences into all forms of media expression;

- publicly recognize the link between portrayal of violence against women and enactment of violence against women; and

- end sexual and racial stereotyping and expand the portrayal of women in their diversity.

Zero Tolerance Actions for All Organizations and Individuals in the Media Sector

Priority Setting and Allocation of Resources

M.1   Publicly recognize the significant role media play in either supporting or undermining women's equality and safety.

Human Resource Management

M.2   Ensure gender equity in hiring, in promotion, on editorial boards and in all aspects of media including technical areas and at all levels of management. Create timetables to reach gender equity in hiring within three years.

M.3   Evaluate working environments for women crew on location and provide safety supports where necessary.

M.4   Recruit women from different cultures and races and those with an understanding and sensitivity to the harms of sexism and racism and other acts and attitudes of discrimination.

M.5   Provide training on the latest research on violence and the value of its prevention as both a health promotion and crime prevention issue, and on the desensitizing impact of the media.

Legislation/Regulation/Policy

M.6   Rigorously apply sex-role stereotyping guidelines.

M.7   Create effective policies to eliminate gratuitous violence and sexist and racist portrayals that demean women, reduce sensationalism in the reporting of violence, and encourage accurate and sensitive reporting.

M.8   Develop policies that explicitly support women's and children's safety.

M.9   Realign policies throughout the organization to challenge the tolerance of violence and more explicitly support the equality of women and the prevention of violence.

Zero Tolerance Actions for Specific Organizations

All public and private broadcasters.

Programs/Services/Practices

M.10 Develop significantly more women's programming.

M.11 Create timetables to achieve gender balance in programming.

M.12 Ensure that cultural and historical representations include women in all their diversity including accurate historical representation of Aboriginal and Inuit women and their contributions to history.

M.13 Create programming on media literacy and on violence prevention.

M.14 Develop educational initiatives including distance learning packages on the less understood aspects of violence.

Consultation

M.15 Create women's programming with women's media organizations.

M.16 Include women at all stages of program development, delivery and evaluation. Conduct research with both current audiences and potential audiences.

M.17 Create program advisory boards with women experts.

M.18 Consult women's organizations on the positive uses of the new communication technologies.

Co-ordination

M.19 Develop, with women's organizations, pilot broadcasting projects that support women's safety.

M.20 Recognize the connection between depicted or described violence and its real counterpart.

M.21 Incorporate the work of anti-violence organizations into the work of the broadcaster.

M.22 Support Aboriginal and Inuit media and ethnic media in securing resources and through sharing of expertise and other resources.

Research and Evaluation

M.23 Expand data collection and analysis of programming using non-sexist, non-racist criteria of the Canadian Radio-television and Telecommunications Commission.

M.24 Regularly review research findings on violence for integration into policy development and programming.

M.25 Collect evaluations from diverse groups of women on the success of the media in reflecting their equality and safety concerns.

Educational/Promotional Activities

M.26 Initiate, with women's organizations and other community groups representing a range of cultures and races, co-operative educational activities for the public using the medium to support the message of the importance of preventing violence in terms of its human, social and financial costs.

Accountability

M.27 Create accessible processes to respond effectively to problems or complaints of sexism, racism and the treatment of issues of violence and women's safety.

M.28 Report at annual public meetings on the initiatives taken by the organization to support women's equality and the elimination of violence.

All print media organizations.

Human Resource Management

M.29 Develop proactive, culturally relevant initiatives such as hiring columnists to write on women's safety initiatives and aspects of zero tolerance.

Programs/Services/Practices

M.30 Dedicate print space as frequently as possible to the issues of violence, women's safety and equality.

Consultation

M.31 Consult with women's groups on expanding women's content in programming.

Research and Evaluation

M.32 Give resources and print space to data collection of women's perspectives on the impact of violence in their lives, the types and frequency of harassment and victimization they experience, the costs inherent in the tolerance of violence and the possible solutions. Include perspectives of women from a range of cultural backgrounds and races, all classes and ability levels.

All film and video organizations.

Human Resource Management

M.33 Promote gender equity through the allocation of resources for film and video development and production to women's production houses, women writers, producers and directors.

Legislation/Regulation/Policy

M.34 Eliminate sexist and racist practices in the development, production and distribution of films and videos including rock videos.

Programs/Services/Practices

M.35 Create opportunities in commercial enterprises to promote anti-violence initiatives and to include women at all stages of production.

M.36 Provide dedicated funding for women's production with fair portions dedicated to critically under-represented women, for example, Inuit and Aboriginal women.

Research and Evaluation

M.37 Allocate resources for data collection on less well understood aspects of women's safety and violence prevention, and equality.

M.38 Make public the figures on the support of women's production and the key messages delivered on violence and equality.

Educationa/Promotional Activities

M.39 Give priority to the use of film and video to expand understanding of the less well understood aspects of violence and the harm done by tolerating violence.

M.40 Use a portion of profits from commercial interests to develop media literacy programming.

All advertising agencies and advertisers.

Priority Setting/Allocation of Resources

M.41 Commit support to non-violent productions through advertising and sponsorship.

Programs/Services/Practices

M.42 Create anti-violence advertising for public service announcements and wherever possible in commercial work.

Research and Evaluation

M.43 Create focus groups and carry out market testing with women, taking care to represent the diversity of women in focus groups and other market research.

Education/Promotional Activities

M.44 Provide access to creative media production resources for development of public education anti-violence campaigns.

All voluntary organizations associated with media.

Legislation/Regulation/Policy

M.45 Create voluntary codes in press councils, broadcasters' associations, advertising foundations, women's media and other voluntary associations that explicitly recognize the importance of non-sexist, non-racist programming and practices as well as the value of violence prevention as a priority media activity.

Programs/Services/Practices

M.46 Develop in-service training for members and public education programming on the inter-relationship between media and violence.

M.47 Encourage members to donate air time or sponsor advertising for anti-violence against women campaigns through the Canadian Association of Broadcasters.

Consultation

M.48 Ensure participation of anti-violence organizations, women's equality seeking organizations, and member organizations in the creation of voluntary codes for broadcasting both on ending violence and on portrayal of women.

Co-ordination

M.49 Co-ordinate media partners and women's groups to create media campaigns against violence against women.

Research and Evaluation

M.50 Monitor the participation and portrayal of women in all their diversity in all aspects of media.

M.51 Fund women's organizations to do media analysis and research on women and the media.

Education/Promotional Activities

M.52 Create regular educational sessions for members and the public on the inter-relationships between women's equality, violence and the media; violence and women's health and the media's role in supporting community safety.

Accountability

M.53 Report publicly on initiatives undertaken to support equality and eliminate violence.

M.54 Create accessible complaints processes and ensure that those adjudicating complaints are appropriately trained.

All regulatory agencies and bodies.

Priority Setting/Allocation of Resources

M.55 Effectively regulate on ending violence in the media and on realistic portrayal of women in all their diversity in the media. Abandon self regulation if it cannot be made effective.

Legislation/Regulation/Policy

M.56 Build in, as a condition of licence for public broadcast, the obligation to provide programming to support women's equality, safety and the elimination of violence.

M.57 Pilot the provision of dedicated broadcast space for women through licensing.

M.58 Develop strong policy against depiction of gratuitous violence and degrading portrayals of women in all media and enforce it through licensing procedures.

Programs/Services/Practices

M.59 Create or support the creation of media literacy programming.

M.60 Recognize and give credit to non-violent programming at licence renewal.

M.61 Ensure the development of non-violent programming.

Consultation

M.62 Consult regularly with women's organizations on the impacts of media on women.

Co-ordination

M.63 Co-ordinate information from women and women's groups and studies on the links between women's safety and media violence. Share this information with regulated broadcasters.

Research and Evaluation

M.64 Monitor the portrayal of women through hearings, and other forms of data collection. Ensure monitoring takes into account sexism, racism, homophobia, age bias and prejudice against women with disabilities.

Education/Promotional Activities

M.65 Educate the public on complaints and regulatory processes to improve their access to these processes

Accountability

M.66 Report publicly on the initiatives undertaken to reduce sexism, racism and violence.

M.67 Report publicly on the use of regulation to support women's equality and safety.

M.68 Report publicly on the disposition of complaints related to women's equality and safety.

> Federal, provincial and territorial governments.

Priority Setting/Allocation of Resources

M.69 Discuss issues of women and the media in international forums and work to establish international regulation of violence against women in the media.

M.70 Recognize the responsibility governments have to use their fiscal and other powers to support public safety interests, to promote equality of all women and the enjoyment of security by all women.

M.71 Fund Aboriginal and Inuit media to the level necessary to establish a strong media communication link within and among all peoples.

Human Resource Management

M.72 Appoint individuals to regulatory, governing and advisory boards who demonstrate clear understanding of equality issues and the interrelationships between inequality and violence and violence and the media.

Legislation/Regulation/Policy

M.73 Provide regulatory agencies to cover broadcast, film and video. Set clear standards that recognize the value of preventing violence, the significant role the media can play in supporting public safety and, in particular, women's safety interests and the promotion of equality.

M.74 Develop policies that reflect the link between violence in the media and violence in society that is supported by reviews of the literature and the research done by the Canadian Radio-television and Telecommunications Commission and the National Film Board.

Programs/Services/Practices

M.75 Expand support to those with a record of producing programming that incorporates equality issues such as the women's programs of the National Film Board.

M.76 Support the implementation of an industry-wide code on television violence that specifically addresses the unacceptability of depictions of violence against women. Extend the code where possible to video and other media.

M.77 Ensure that government advertising does not support sexist, racist or violent programming in any way.

Consultation

M.78 Initiate hearings on the impacts of media on women's equality and safety.

Details

- *Involve government, the industry and women's organization in the process.*

- *The terms of reference for the hearings should include the review and assessment of the effects of sexually violent media on women's and children's safety and security; the assessment and determination of the impact of new communication technologies on women's safety and equality and the impact of related media such as video games; and recommendations on how best to utilize and limit the use of the technologies; and the development of recommendations on the nature and depth of regulation needed for the various forms of media.*

Co-ordination

M.79 Create interdisciplinary advisory panels to monitor media and make the links between media, safety and equality issues.

M.80 Co-ordinate the input of provincial, territorial or local government hearings at the federal level to promote the co-operative development of national standards.

M.81 Work with other government initiatives aimed at ending violence against women.

Research and Evaluation

M.82 Collect data to improve recognition of the links between gender-equality issues, including sexism and sex-role stereotyping, women's safety and violence prevention, and, health promotion for women.

M.83 Collect and disseminate information on the new communication technologies.

M.84 Fund research to develop the most effective and culturally relevant public education programs on the prevention of violence against girls and women and the promotion of equality.

Education/Promotional Activities

M.85 Provide educational sessions on the data and research collected.

M.86 Support women's film and other media production of educational materials on women's safety and equality. Give priority to educational productions highlighting the safety issues for specific populations of women.

M.87 Support the development of media literacy materials for parents, specifically focusing on depictions of women on television and in films.

Accountability

M.88 Report at least annually on the initiatives related to media undertaken to promote equality and women's safety.

RELIGIOUS INSTITUTIONS

Introduction

In Canada, the predominant religious ideology has been Christian. The teachings of Christianity have greatly influenced our lives, directed our sexuality and left indelible marks on all aspects of our existence, even to the point of directing legal codes and many social conventions. Today, a diversity of other religions are also practised in Canada including Judaism, Islam, Hinduism, Buddhism and Sikhism. These faiths are an omnipresent and powerful force affecting all of us whether or not we follow the religious teachings.

Religious institutions have a long history of domination, control, and exploitation of women. Through theological teachings and by example, these institutions maintain and reinforce the belief that women are inferior to men and suited primarily to a domestic role. Many religions also attempt to control women's sexuality, reproductive rights and sexual orientation. In the name of religion, women have been diminished, enslaved, reduced to silence and relegated to the sidelines of progress and development.

Patriarchal instruction within religious institutions has encouraged and excused, both actively and passively, male violence against women in the home, in society and in the religious institutions themselves. Strict rules of blind obedience to men and to religious teachings, posited as divine orders, have supported a dangerous power imbalance between women and men. Religious practices, rites, celebrations, language and symbolism all contribute to women's personal, political and social devaluation.

Very often women who have suffered male violence turn to religious advisors as their first and sometimes only confidante. They have been taught to acknowledge them as counsellors and spiritual guides who can ease pain, offer encouragement and intercede on their behalf with the Supreme Being. Women have trusted them. However, many women are now questioning the excessive influence of religious figures in matters of violence. They realize that predominantly male religious leaders do not understand the experience of violence against women nor its roots. Through lack of knowledge these leaders continue to provide women with dangerous direction that compromises their safety, leads to further revictimization and supports the tolerance of violence against them. This happens every time a woman is told to return to an abusive man.

Women have formed groups within religious structures to work toward the transformation of the institution into an egalitarian organization. Some women have become theologians, have studied the sacred books and have found alternative interpretations of words and laws that support equality of women. Increasingly, women are demanding an equal role with men, to be present on all decision-making bodies, to participate fully in the formulation of moral discourse and to be recognized as theologians in a true partnership. For some religions, women provide both the membership numbers and the support needed to sustain these institutions.

Women have a right to practice religion in an equal and safe atmosphere. Religious teachings and structures must be re-evaluated and altered to eliminate sexist and misogynist principles and practices.

Key Problems:

- In even the most progressive religions, structures remain bluntly anti-democratic. The hierarchical structure demands obedience of its members, facilitates the exercise of power and ensures the control of information. All-encompassing, unquestionable authority alienates women and makes equality a remote prospect.

- Some Christian churches still have much to answer for in their treatment of Aboriginal and Inuit peoples. The early missionaries, blind to the richness of the spiritual life of the Aboriginal and Inuit peoples, destroyed communities and brought physical, psychological, emotional and sexual violence to bear against many. Churches, along with the Canadian government, operated residential schools that separated Aboriginal and Inuit children from their parents and their communities and systematically forced these children to deny their spiritual, cultural and linguistic heritage.

- Some religious leaders have abused their positions of power and trust to sexually assault women and children. Such abuse results in profound trauma and lifelong guilt and confusion for the victim. Often abuse has been cloaked in secrecy making its continuation possible and conveying the false impression that the sexual exploitation of women and children does not exist in religious circles.

New Orientations for the Religious Sector

R.1   All religious institutions, at national, regional and community levels must acknowledge the fundamental equality of women and men, and work to revise religious teachings that promote inequality of women and support violence against women.

R.2   All religious institutions must adopt democratic structures to balance power between religious leaders and followers of the religion.

Zero Tolerance Actions for all Religious Institutions

Priority Setting/Allocation of Resources

R.3   Appoint an advisory committee of women from within the religious community to direct a comprehensive review of the teachings and structures that foster violence against women.

R.4   Direct resources to advisory committees to implement an action plan for achieving equality and ending violence.

Human Resource Management

R.5   Strengthen or adopt equity programs to achieve gender equality within all bodies. The diversity of people within the religious community served must be considered and represented.

R.6   Recruit staff who are knowledgeable about equality and about ending violence against women.

R.7 Provide training to all staff on women's inequality and its linkages to violence against women.

R.8 Remove from office or terminate the employment of any abusive spiritual leader, volunteer or staff member.

Programs/Services/Practices

R.9 Review all basic materials, training programs, videos and texts used for religious and relationship instruction to eliminate sexist, racist and homophobic images and messages.

R.10 Present discussion groups, workshops and seminars on violence against women. Include the linkages between inequality and violence.

R.11 Acknowledge and recognize the competence of feminist theologians and women members by incorporating the discourse of women into religious instruction.

R.12 In meetings with youth, emphasize equality of women and make it clear that the religious institution does not tolerate violence against women.

Co-ordination:

R.13 Appoint women's committees at all levels within the organization to co-ordinate actions on promoting equality and ending violence. Include feminist theologians, lay members of women's religious communities, volunteers from local communities and women working against violence.

R.14 Link prevention strategies with the wider secular community to remain current on resources and expertise.

Research and Evaluation

R.15 Together with the women's committees, evaluate each activity for progress toward achieving women's equality and ending violence.

R.16 Finance research activities by women who seek equality and are knowledgeable on violence against women to determine the prevalence and nature of this violence within the institution.

Accountability

R.17 Recognize that all abusers within the institution must withdraw from community service and no longer hold positions of trust and authority. Any board of inquiry on the conduct of a religious leader must include representatives of the women's committees. All decisions of such an inquiry must be made public.

R.18 Make all teaching materials used within the institution available to all community members.

R.19 Have the women's committees review all teachings to ensure the consistency of messages about women.

R.20 Recognize the injury to Aboriginal and Inuit people through the residential schools and make financial restitution to cover the costs of healing.

R.21 Recognize and respect the reclaiming of Aboriginal and Inuit spirituality by Aboriginal and Inuit peoples.

R.22   Acknowledge responsibility for any
       abuse done to victims within the
       institution and provide financial
       assistance for counselling programs and
       other forms of support for victims.

R.23   Make open decisions concerning the life
       of the religious community and include
       women and men equally in those
       decisions.

GOVERNMENT SECTOR

Introduction

The *Canadian Charter of Rights and Freedoms* guarantees equality to women, including the right to security of the person and equal benefit and protection of the law. All governments in Canada have the responsibility to assure these rights and the obligation to provide leadership to all others in Canada to uphold women's equality and safety. Throughout our consultations it was impressed upon us that governments in Canada, at all levels, are failing to live up to these responsibilities.

Key Problems:

- Government analysis does not recognize the full scope of woman abuse nor adequately link violence against women to women's unequal status in Canadian society. The absence of a strong equality framework has retarded progress towards full equality for women. Women have had too little participation in the workings of government, as elected officials, in senior policy positions and as key implementors.

- Policy consultation with women is relatively new – initiated only in the last two decades. It is often cursory in nature, is not representative of the diversity of women, and is carried out only when women's stake in the outcome is very apparent.

- There is still little understanding that all laws, policies and programs, regardless of the subject, have impacts on women as well as men.

- Government analysis is often gender neutral. Policies grounded in research that does not take into account the differential impacts of gender, race, class and abilities will persistently fail the needs of all women.

- Governments' actions on violence against women often cast anti-violence initiatives in terms of "family violence". As pointed out in Part I, defining violence against women in such terms, obscures the facts that the violence within families is overwhelmingly perpetrated by men against women, and it shares a common denominator of abuse of power with woman abuse in other settings. A "family violence" perspective ignores much violence against women outside the family, leads to gender-neutral analysis, and often places the focus on the family, rather than on the victim of violence.

- In rhetoric, governments have recognized that violence against women is a crime. However, policies and programs to deal with crime do not adequately reflect the criminal nature of woman abuse nor the size and nature of the problem. Often responses to sexual abuse including pornography are based on child protection, and ignore the harm done to women.

- Woman abuse crosses all jurisdictional boundaries, yet the division of powers within Canada makes effective response difficult. One of the largest sources of frustration reported during the Panel's consultations was the lack of clarity about jurisdictional responsibility and lack of co-ordination among jurisdictions in dealing with violence against women. Repeatedly we heard that jurisdictional disputes have blocked action that was urgently required.

- Government policies and practices are often sexist, racist and heterosexist and do not adequately take into account differences based on class, ability, age or geographic location.

- Aboriginal and Inuit peoples are particularly susceptible to deficiencies in government policy, especially at the federal level, since the lives of Aboriginal peoples are tightly regulated by government. Aboriginal and Inuit governments themselves have an impact on the lives of Aboriginal women. Policies that fail to take adequate account of culture and gender violate the rights of Aboriginal and Inuit women and have severely affected their safety and security.

- Violence against women is a violation of fundamental human rights. Globally, and in Canada, women's liberty is curtailed by violence; women's health and welfare are severely undermined by violence; and women die from violence. Canada prides itself on being a guardian and advocate of human rights at home and throughout the world. Despite public commitment, governments do not always take full account of violence against women when analysing human rights issues and designing human rights initiatives. The Government of Canada still does not adequately recognize woman abuse as a form of persecution and a genuine threat to women's life and liberty.

In other sector plans, specific actions are directed at various levels and specific departments of government, including Aboriginal and Inuit governments. The actions set out in this plan must be implemented in concert with all the others including the Equality Action Plan.

New Orientations for Governments — Federal, Provincial-Territorial, Municipal and Regional

G.1   Adopt and fully implement the Zero Tolerance Policy and the Equality Action Plan and establish the recommended accountability mechanisms.

Details:

- *Accountability mechanisms are outlined for the federal government in Section 4 of this plan. We recommend that the provincial and territorial governments adopt accountability mechanisms that parallel those proposed for the federal level. Municipalities should also develop accountability mechanisms that suit their structures and conform with the standards of accountability laid out in the Zero Tolerance Policy.*

- *Governments must require affected organizations (i.e., departments, agencies, boards, crown corporations, commissions) to develop and implement a plan for achieving the goals of zero tolerance and to report regularly to government and to women constituents on progress.*

- *Governments must provide information and support to the affected organizations for the development and implementation of the plan.*

G.2 Implement a zero tolerance contract compliance program whereby any organization which receives a government contract, grant or funding of $100,000 or more must agree to put in place zero tolerance processes and practices to support women's equality and safety within the recipient organization and through its substantive work.

Details:

- *The $100,000 criterion must be seen as a starting point with the long-term objective to have all organizations that have a fiscal relationship with government incorporate zero tolerance into their structures and work.*

- *Governments must set up the mechanisms and provide the resources to administer, provide support and monitor the compliance program.*

- *Governments must devise a means to monitor the compliance of affected organizations.*

New Orientations for Aboriginal and Inuit Governments

G.3 Adopt and fully implement the Zero Tolerance Policy and in partnership with Aboriginal and Inuit women's associations establish accountability mechanisms that will facilitate and monitor implementation of the Zero Tolerance Policy.

Zero Tolerance Actions Specifically for the Federal Government

G.4 Provide financial and other resources to Aboriginal and Inuit women's organizations to ensure the full participation of Aboriginal and Inuit women at all stages of negotiation, development and implementation of self-government.

G.5 Eliminate continuing discrimination under Bill C-31, so that Aboriginal women and their children are no longer deprived of their heritage.

G.6 Create proactive programs to increase significantly the number of adult Aboriginal and Inuit women participating in post-secondary education and vocational training programs.

G.7 Enhance educational assistance provided by Indian and Northern Affairs Canada to extend additional support to Aboriginal women, especially for single mothers.

G.8 Make educational grants available to Métis and non-status women.

G.9 Fund an Aboriginal and Inuit women's office to receive and co-ordinate the distribution of government funds provided to Aboriginal communities to deal with violence against Aboriginal and Inuit women; to act as a clearing house for information on violence against women; and to provide assistance to women working in communities in developing programs and services.

G.10 Immediately implement all housing recommendations in the Fourth Report of the Standing Committee on Aboriginal Affairs

Details:

Include the following in Aboriginal housing policy:

- *Wherever consultation with Aboriginal organizations is specified in the development of new housing policies, the full and equal participation of equivalent Aboriginal women's organizations must be ensured, whether at the national, regional or local level.*

- *All home ownership programs must ensure the full protection of women's property rights.*

- *Any and all bodies and organizations involved in the delivery of Aboriginal housing must ensure equal representation of Aboriginal women.*

- *Transfer of resources by government to any administrative body(ies) must ensure the full participation of women at all stages, with accountability to Aboriginal women's organizations.*

- *Data collection, program delivery, policy and program decisions must engage the full and equal participation of Aboriginal women.*

- *In conjunction with Ministerial Guarantees for housing, financial institutions must ensure equality of applications made by women, and women's property rights must be entrenched in all transactions.*

- *Housing needs must be determined by the community, with the full and equal participation of women from that community.*

G.11 Have women who are immigrating to Canada deal directly with immigration officers rather than communicating through their male relatives.

Details:

- *Apprise these women of their rights in Canada.*

- *Ensure that there are women immigration officials to deal with women where this is culturally dictated.*

G.12 Provide information regarding violence against women in Canada and programs, services and protections that a woman may use directly to women in their own language upon arrival in Canada.

G.13 Ensure that every woman who is new to Canada has a contact she can call upon if faced with violence.

G.14 Abolish the current Live-in Caregiver Program and replace it with changes in the immigration assessment system which place a higher value on care-giving occupations and associated qualifications.

G.15 Recognize violence against women as a human rights issue.

G.16 Include violence against women as an issue in all human rights decisions and initiatives, both nationally and internationally.

G.17 Include violence against women as an issue in all international aid and development activities.

G.18 **Create guidelines for the establishment of any future inquiries, task forces, or commissions.**

Details:

- *The proposed mandate, rules and operating procedures of any commission of inquiry or panel similar to the Canadian Panel on Violence Against Women must be outlined as clearly as possible before such a body is established.*

- *Mechanisms must be introduced to enable future members of such bodies to contact each other and exchange views on the nature of their duties and mandate before they are officially appointed.*

- *Mechanisms must be established to enable such members to assume responsibility for the refinement of their mandate and they must be given the time and opportunity to examine and negotiate its terms and conditions before they take up their duties.*

- *New mechanisms for consultations between the federal government and women's groups in Canada, based on a vision of social change, must be established as soon as possible.*

- *Mechanisms must be developed which would guarantee better representation of all population groups in Canada in projects similar to this Panel.*

Zero Tolerance Actions Specifically for Municipal and Regional Governments

G.19 **Implement an urban safety program that makes women's safety a priority at the municipal level.**

Details:

- *Design all public and semi-public spaces such as parks, streets and municipal properties to reduce opportunity for assaults on women.*

- *Use municipal by-laws to regulate display of sexually violent material.*

- *Develop community safety initiatives such as Safe City Committees which place a high priority on ending violence against women.*

Zero Tolerance Actions for Aboriginal and Inuit Governments

G.20 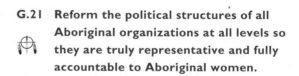 **Develop an Aboriginal Charter of Rights with the full participation of Aboriginal and Inuit women's associations. Until such time as the Charter is developed and implemented, *the Canadian Charter of Rights and Freedoms* is to apply as a minimum protection for Aboriginal and Inuit women and children.**

G.21 **Reform the political structures of all Aboriginal organizations at all levels so they are truly representative and fully accountable to Aboriginal women.**

G.22 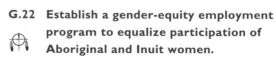 **Establish a gender-equity employment program to equalize participation of Aboriginal and Inuit women.**

SECTION 4

MONITORING AND ACCOUNTABILITY MECHANISMS

The Panel places a very high priority on measures which ensure that actions are undertaken to end violence against women and to assure their safety. Accountability – through open processes and in accordance with zero tolerance standards – is essential.

It is imperative that this National Action Plan be considered carefully, amended and expanded where appropriate, implemented, then monitored and evaluated on a regular basis.

The National Action Plan indicates that many participants must take a role in ending violence against women and promoting their equality. However, the federal government, as initiator of the Panel, has a special responsibility to respond quickly and comprehensively, by adopting the Zero Tolerance Policy, by making specific commitments to implement the National Action Plan and by helping to mobilize the support of the other partners indicated in the Plan.

To ensure that the National Action Plan receives support and that progress is both made and measured, the Panel proposes the following accountability framework.

1. Principles

- Incorporate the knowledge, experience and perspectives of individuals and groups in the non-governmental sector, i.e., service providers, front-line workers and women's organizations who have provided leadership in the provision of services for victims of violence and in violence prevention work.

- Establish a comprehensive monitoring capacity to assess, both collectively and individually, the impact of the many different departments with programs, policies and legislation pertaining to the issue of violence against women.

- Provide mechanisms at several levels to assess activities. No single mechanism can adequately monitor all activities to end violence against women in Canada.

- Strengthen the monitoring and accountability functions of existing mechanisms. Create new ones as required.

- Ensure that the composition and scope of work of these mechanisms are represenative and inclusive.

2. Objectives

- Ensure that the federal government considers the National Action Plan and responds with a clear statement of commitment in a timely fashion – no later than three months after the tabling of the Panel's final report.

• Ensure that initiatives of the federal government which have the potential to address violence against women – for example, the Canadian Strategy on Community Safety and Crime Prevention – place a high priority on violence against women and adopt a zero tolerance approach to their work and their recommendations.

• Ensure that government departments adopt a zero tolerance approach in their internal processes and their substantive work.

3. Functions

• Monitor and assess the implementation of the measures set out in the National Action Plan on a regular basis.

• Assess the scope, extent and nature of violence against women, including periodic surveys to establish whether violence is increasing or decreasing, which types of violence are increasing or decreasing and changes in the vulnerability of particular groups or populations.

• Assess the effectiveness and impact of measures taken to end violence against women by the federal government, other levels of government and non-governmental organizations.

• Assess progress on gender equality in Canada, particularly those aspects of equality which would reduce vulnerability to violence.

• Recommend additions to the National Action Plan, including pilot testing of innovative solutions.

• Report publicly on all of the above to ensure follow-up by the appropriate agencies and authorities.

4. Mechanisms

The Equality Plan includes several proposals which are vital to a comprehensive accountability framework, namely, the enactment of a status of women act to strengthen the government's commitment to gender equality and issues related to violence against women; the designation of a senior minister responsible for the status of women who would also be the lead minister for violence against women issues; a strengthened department at the federal level responsible for the status of women; the creation of a permanent advisory board to advise the government on its equality and safety plans; and the provision of sufficient resources to non-governmental women's organizations to permit their effective participation in policy development.

In addition, the Panel considers the following accountability mechanisms to be essential to ensure implementation and evaluation of the National Action Plan and the Canadian campaign to end violence against women.

• **Elevation of the Sub-committee on the Status of Women to full parliamentary committee status, with responsibility for regular review of progress toward implementation of the National Action Plan and the federal government's commitment to ending violence against women.**

Parliamentary committees can be provided with authority, responsibility and resources to undertake comprehensive reviews of government programs and legislation. (For example, the Employment Equity Act requires that reviews be conducted within five years of enactment and every three years thereafter). In response to an open call for submissions, any individual or group can provide testimony to a parliamentary committee. As the committee reports directly to Parliament, the opportunity exists for extensive political and public debate on the adequacy of measures already taken, and on proposals for new programs, policies and legislation.

When the committee undertakes this review, it should be reconstituted as a special committee with an expanded mandate and the resources necessary to fulfil that mandate, including the means to hold meetings outside Ottawa and to have experts and representatives of organizations in the non-governmental sector participate.

- **Creation by the federal government of a zero tolerance accountability board with a mandate to review and assess progress at the federal level on implementation of the National Action Plan. As the primary on-going accountability mechanism, the board would ensure that the federal government receives independent advice on a regular basis on the effectiveness of its actions to end violence against women. It would comprise members from federal government departments with responsibility for the issue of violence against women, and individuals from the non-governmental sector – with the latter being the majority. Two co-chairs would represent the government and non-governmental sectors. Secretariat services would be provided by the department within the federal government with lead and co-ordinating responsibility for violence against women issues.**

The board would meet at least three times a year, set its own agenda and process for review of progress by the federal government and would issue a report biennially to be tabled in Parliament. On request from the federal government, the board could review particular issues and provide advice to the minister and the government. It would rely on the knowledge and experience of its members, information gathered by the departmental secretariat from federal departments and/or other sources inside and outside the government – in particular the Centres of Excellence and other non-governmental organizations involved in service provision, violence prevention or research.

While the board would focus primarily on actions taken by the federal government, it would be encouraged to assess federal government action in the larger social context as well.

The board would have a fixed term of eight years to ensure implementation of the National Action Plan and the meeting of the Plan's objectives by the year 2000.

- **Creation by provincial and territorial governments of zero tolerance accountability boards modelled on the federal approach. Provincial and territorial governments have significant responsibilities in the campaign to end violence against women. Monitoring and evaluation are required to assess action taken at this level.**

Zero tolerance accountability boards at the provincial/territorial level would operate in much the same way as has been proposed for the federal level. Membership from both governmental and non-governmental sectors and public reporting on a regular basis are essential.

SECTION 5

A Call To Action For All Men and Women

Introduction

Violence against women is pervasive in Canada. We each have a story to tell: a girl molested by her uncle, a best friend whose ex-boyfriend is stalking her, an older woman who can't explain the bruises. These incidents affect us profoundly. They make us fearful for our children, wary about our own activities and often distrustful of men.

The connection between these acts of violence and the inequality of women is clear. All women in Canada are vulnerable to male violence. Race, class, age, sexual orientation, level of ability and other objective characteristics, alone or in combination, compound the risk. Until all women achieve equality they will remain vulnerable to violence, and until women are free from violence, they cannot be equal.

We have called on governments and institutions to change how they operate, to seek equality for women and to end violence against women. We now appeal to you, as an individual, to help change the status quo.

What Can I Do?

As friends, parents, children, neighbours, students, colleagues and community members we have responsibilities and opportunities to make change. The following section suggests ways you can support our National Action Plan and our goals — to achieve equality for women and to put an end to violence against women.

Many of you are already working as volunteers or staff members in women's shelters, rape crisis centres or in other services for victims and survivors. To you, we give our respect and support. Others are very committed and concerned but live busy lives leaving little time for activism and volunteer work. We offer some suggestions on how you can contribute.

We also know that some of you are active in working for equality for women and in men's groups to eliminate violence in society. You are part of the solution.

However, some men feel that the issues of equality and ending violence are not relevant to them. They may have many excuses.

- I am only concerned about violence in general; I do not feel it is right to focus on violence specifically against women.

- Violence against women is a women's issue.

- Women have achieved true equality and I don't believe this is a problem.

- I am tired of hearing about violence against women, and I think the statistics and stories are exaggerated.

- Feminists are out to destroy all men; most women don't even like feminists.

- I don't beat my wife and I don't sexually abuse my daughter so this issue is not my problem.

- I am concerned about some of these problems but there is nothing I can do.

- I am a victim too. I witnessed plenty of violence in my own life, and there's little I can do about it now.

If you agreed with any of these statements, you are not alone. You represent millions of Canadian men who do not really understand the issues involved. You may have listened to women share feelings and experiences but did not relate to the problem. Most men react with denial and defensiveness about this topic. The reality is so painful that it is easier to believe that the problem does not exist or that each case represents some isolated incident. Rationalizations are invented which allow those with power to keep things the way they are.

We need all men in Canada to make a clear commitment to women's equality and to ending all forms of violence against women. We deserve a Canadian society that will no longer tolerate the daily acts of violence against women. Is this an impossible dream or can it be a future Canadian reality? Can all men accept the challenge to examine their behaviour as individuals and as members of a community? We believe they can. Many are doing so already.

Personal Action Plan

Women or men, of any age:

You can make a positive contribution to women's equality and ending violence against women by examining your own values, the life choices you make and your behaviour, as an individual or as a member of a particular group within your workplace, your community or Canadian society at large.

We call upon you to make a personal commitment to the principles of zero tolerance — that no amount of violence is acceptable and that women's safety is a priority — and we urge you to take action now. A little action from each of us will make such a difference.

In the following paragraphs, we identify how you can turn your commitment into action.

I will:

- Acknowledge that violence is a reality for at least half the women in Canada; recognize the tolerance of violence that keeps so much of it in place.

- Create my own action plan. Decide how I can help all the organizations I am connected with become zero tolerance organizations. Choose which actions I will actively support and decide how.

Some Ways I Can Get Started

As a man, I will:

- Not be violent.

- Give up my need for power and control.

- Promote equality, not only in thought and words, but in deeds.

- Listen to the women in my life — my mother, daughters, partners, friends, neighbours and colleagues.

- Ask women about their experiences, their fears and the equality barriers they face.

- Attend community forums on violence against women and listen to the women.

- Listen. Listen some more.

- Never argue with, minimize or deny women's feelings.

- Commit to act on what I learn.

- Talk to other men to seek support.

- Never listen to men who ridicule me or make me feel like "less of a man" for working to end violence against women.

- Share responsibility for child care and home maintenance and do my part without being asked.

- Challenge any tolerance of violence or sexist behaviour.

- Give financial and political support to services for victims and survivors of violence.

- Help victims and survivors return to the state they enjoyed before the crime.

- Teach my children that violence is an abuse of power and trust and does not resolve conflicts in relationships.

- Speak out on dating violence and inequality of women.

- Never purchase nor use pornography.

- Volunteer to work in a men's support group.

- Support women who are working to end violence.

- Challenge the backlash against women who are working toward equality and toward the ending of violence.

- Ensure that no woman and no child live in silence with violence in my home or in my neighbourhood.

- Challenge other men to become part of the solution.

As a woman or man who wants to end violence against women, I will:

- Remove power and control from my list of needs.

- Practice co-operation instead of competition.

- Not laugh at women-hating jokes and racial slurs.

- Stop believing stereotypes.

- Become more knowledgeable about racism and act on that knowledge.

- Support a fully accessible culture for all women.

- Learn the true history of Aboriginal and Inuit peoples.

- Inform myself on the current realities of life for Aboriginal and Inuit peoples.

- Resist and work to eliminate heterosexism.

- Refuse to respond to aggression with aggression.

- Support equal pay for work of equal value.

- Insist that Canada builds an accessible, affordable child-care program.

- Hire a woman for the job.

- Become media literate so I can decode harmful messages about women and about violence.

- Stop denying that violence against women exists or that it's only "those women."

- Never blame women for the violence in their lives.

- Understand that the only reason I am not in an abusive relationship is by luck — not because of my race, class or ability.

- Pay attention to a child who is hurting.

- Realize that children who witness violence suffer as much as those who are actually hit.

- Believe that I don't have to go through it alone.

- Hold violent people accountable for their choice to perpetuate violence.

- Speak up!

- Take time to know what I am feeling.

- Make peace with my past.

- Talk with a woman about the reality of her life.

- Share my story.

- Believe in myself.

- Thank a woman who helped me grow.

- Resist male-defined standards of beauty.

Consumer Action

As a consumer, I will:

- Challenge the tolerance of violence and sexism in movies, rock videos, magazines, on television and radio, and all advertising.

- Boycott movies and other media that glorify violence.

- Purchase non-violent, non-sexist toys.

- Stop buying products from advertisers who exploit women in their promotions.

- Read books by women of all races.

Family Action

In my family life, I will:

- Listen to my children and try to understand their perspectives.

- Commit to non-violent problem solving and discipline and learn how to follow through on that commitment.

- Find out what my children and grandchildren are watching on television.

- Share with my partner in the management and control of all family finances.

- Encourage my daughters and granddaughters to pursue all interests, including those which are non-traditional.

Neighbourhood Action

As a neighbour, I will:

- Stop denying that violence exists in my neighbourhood.

- Reach out to a neighbour who is isolated.

Workplace Action

In my workplace, I will:

- Find out what my employer is doing concerning equality and violence against women.

- Refrain from abusing my co-workers.

- Take time to know if an employee is being abused and offer support.

- Promote awareness and awareness sessions on violence against women.

Student Action

In my school, I will:

- Urge teachers and administrators to support gender-aware violence prevention activities.

- Treat my co-students with respect.

- Promote and practice equality.

- Get involved in working out alternatives to violence.

- Not put girls down.

- Support someone who is being hurt.

Community Action

In my community, I will:

- Help my community recognize that ending violence against women is a priority.

- Find out what services exist for victims of violence.

- Work with others to fill gaps in service.

- Actively discourage violence in sports.

- Ask my family doctor to display posters and pamphlets on violence against women.

- Insist that the school make gender-aware violence prevention part of its core curriculum.

- Spend time with children who could use support and a little fun.

- Contact my local transition house, rape crisis centre, other women's groups and ask how I can learn and help.

- Get a local men's service club to sponsor a community awareness session for men on violence issues.

- Challenge local service groups to become partners in ending violence.

- Write a letter to the editor of my community newspaper in support of ending violence.

- Challenge my municipal, provincial and federal politicians to practice zero tolerance.

- Talk about equality and violence against women in my place of worship.

- Start safety audits.

For those of you who wish to take a more public and active role in ending violence against women in your community, we have developed the Community Kit. It will help you to determine the nature and extent of violence in your community and to improve the services available to women victims/survivors. It will also help you to make your community safer for women and for all those who feel vulnerable to violence.

We had the unique opportunity and privilege to meet women from coast to coast to coast in Canada who had experienced violence in their lives. What impressed us most was their courage and their strength in coming forward. They shared the most intimate and difficult details of their lives and the violence they have endured, and they urged action. We share both their pain and their hopes and we encourage you to do your part to make Canada safe and equal for all women.

APPENDICES

APPENDIX A

WOMEN'S SAFETY PROJECT

INTRODUCTION

The Women's Safety Project is an independent community-based study of women's experiences of sexual and physical assault. It is based on face-to-face interviews with 420 women living in Toronto. We initiated the study to contribute to an understanding of the prevalence, nature and impact of women's experiences of sexual violence, including sexual abuse in childhood and sexual and physical assault in intimate relationships. The analyses are based on information from these first-person accounts of a diverse and random sample of the female population in the city. The interconnections between and patterns in these forms of violence were also a major area of investigation, including the issue of repeated victimization or revictimization.

The scope of violence against women is as obvious to those who provide assistance to assaulted women or take part in other efforts to end the problem as it is to the many women who have personally experienced it.

It would hardly be an overstatement to describe the prevalence of sexual violence against women of all classes, races and ethnic backgrounds as representing a serious social epidemic. A taboo still exists on defining the issue in gender-specific terms, that is, identifying the problem as one of men's violence against women. From the way the issue is most often taken up, it seems to be more socially palatable to expose the suffering of "victims" than it is to understand and name the human agency behind the victimization. To understand the causes and the context of sexual violence in women's lives, one must look at the sexual inequality in our society, including the hierarchical relationships of race, class and gender in which sexual inequality and violence are inscribed.

Clearly not all men commit sexual violence against women. In fact, some men are now actively working to end the violence. For many other people, however, there is little awareness or understanding of the magnitude of this socially produced problem. This is not surprising given the social denial which to a large extent still surrounds sexual violence against women, and the entrenched, complex and taken-for-granted quality of the power and gender relationships which create and sustain it. Yet, it is not possible to take action to end this sexual violence without recognizing who is responsible for it and why it happens. These questions are critical if we are to create a society where children and women are not routinely subjected to sexual assault and violation, as they are today.

The findings of the Women's Safety Project confirm that sexual violence directly touches the majority of women's lives and crosses cultural and socio-economic groups. Its effects are usually long term and devastating. Our research project has taken several years and is based on many thousands of hours of labour and interviewing time. This very brief and condensed summary presents a general outline of the methodology and the preliminary statistical findings. Funding is still being sought for presentation and analysis of some of the most interesting qualitative data which includes women's accounts, in their own words, of how they make sense of their experiences and the effects these experiences have had on their lives.

HOW THE STUDY WAS CARRIED OUT

We chose to name the study the Women's Safety Project and frame the issues of sexual violence under the rubric of "women's safety" for a number of reasons. First, there has been an emerging public and media discourse about the issues of "women's fear" and "women's safety." While we were not interested in reinforcing the notion of women's fear, we did want to establish clearly the connection between violence against women and the increasing community concern for women's safety.

There is a significant degree of public acceptance of the need to improve women's safety as it applies to areas such as safer transportation and improved urban design. Yet we wanted to bring the issue closer to home, so to speak. While women's public safety is obviously very important, the almost exclusive focus of safety efforts on areas such as better street lighting obscures the fact that the greatest risk to women is from men they know, not from strangers who may be lurking in unlit streets.

In the introductory letter sent to randomly selected addresses and in the interviewers' at the door introductory explanation to women who were prospective respondents, our study emphasized that the focus was on women's safety — in both public and personal terms. We did not think it was possible to address the topic of women's safety adequately without attention to the broad range of experiences of sexual violence which violate women's safety. This includes the many experiences perpetrated within personal relationships.

At the same time, the concept of safety is so broad that it is not necessarily viewed as a personally threatening topic. We were very careful not to give the impression to prospective respondents — especially women who may have been in situations where they were currently being abused — that we had any specific information about anyone being asked to participate in the study. [1] Nor did we want to put any potential respondents at risk by raising the suspicions of abusive male partners residing at addresses receiving the letter. The social popularity and legitimacy of the concern for the greater safety of all women were therefore useful ways to pose questions on the issue in general terms. It assisted in framing the problem under investigation as a general social one — which it most certainly is — while allowing women who participated in the study to reflect on their own personal experiences as part of the larger social phenomenon of violence against women.

An interesting outcome of this strategy has been the consciousness raising effect of this use of the term safety. [2] Many women reported that being asked about experiences of violence in intimate relationships as well as experiences in public, in the context of women's safety, challenged and expanded their thinking about women's safety. Specifically, a number of women referred to how the term "safety" allowed them to recognize that it was often the men in their own lives who have undermined their personal safety. This recognition and naming subvert the socially produced split consciousness for women. This split, or denial, emphasizes that the danger to women comes from strangers and obscures the reality of women's own lived experiences, i.e., it is the men who are known to them who are more likely to pose the greatest threat to their personal safety.

THE PARAMETERS OF THE STUDY

In-depth face-to-face interviews were used to collect information. The interviews were carried out by a team of highly skilled women interviewers. Participants in the study were women between the ages of 18 and 64 years. Women needed to speak English, but were not required to read or write in English. All materials used to explain the research were translated into five different languages. [3] The interviewers also read aloud any written explanatory materials to the respondents so women who could not read could participate in the study. Interviews were carried out at a location which was convenient for the women being interviewed. This meant that women with disabilities could be included. [4]

THE INTERVIEWS

Most women chose to be interviewed in their own homes, although some interviews were completed in other places chosen by the women including offices, parks and restaurants. Interviews were conducted in private and remain confidential. [5] In addition to an introductory letter which was sent to all prospective addresses, the interviewer provided a verbal explanation about the study specifying that the project on women's safety involved asking women about experiences affecting their personal safety, including any experiences of sexual assault they may have had. This information was important to allow for women's informed consent to participate in the study.

The interviews ranged from 45 minutes to 25 hours,[6] but most interviews typically took about two hours to complete. A wide range of related topics was covered in the interview, including women's perceptions of their safety in the city, precautionary and avoidance measures women adopt to protect themselves from violence, women's attitudes about and explanations of why they think the problem of violence against women exists, attitudes about gender and some general family history.

Women were asked about abuse experiences throughout childhood and their adult years, and in-depth quantitative and qualitative information was documented about specific abuse experiences. A major part of the interviews involved women describing what happened to them in their own words, explaining the meanings they attached to these events and how they understood these experiences to have affected them at the time, as well as later on in their lives. At the end of the interview, each woman (regardless of whether or not she disclosed any abuse experiences) was left with a resource and referral kit of information about a variety of services for assaulted women.

THE SAMPLE — WHO WAS INTERVIEWED

Interviews were carried out with a random sample of 420 women living in Toronto. The sample[7] was based on a list of all the residential addresses (including houses and apartments in highrises and other buildings) throughout the city. This means that women did not need to be officially registered as voters or taxpayers to be included in the sample, nor did they have to be listed in the telephone book. Women did not have to be Canadian citizens or meet any other such criteria for participation in the study. Consequently, women in a variety of situations were eligible to be interviewed, including women with landed immigrant status or student/work visas.

Because we wanted to undertake a study which would generate information of a broadly useful and general nature, it was important that the women who were interviewed represented a random sample of the female population, i.e., a relatively diverse group of women somewhat resembling the female population in the city. In other words, we didn't simply ask women to agree to be interviewed by posting notices or by soliciting invitations through the media or word of mouth. No information about the women was known before the interview, other than that they resided at a randomly selected address. This increased the chances that the widest cross section of women would be interviewed and increased the general applicability of the findings.

Respondents included women from diverse ethnic and racial backgrounds, from diverse age and socio-economic backgrounds, immigrant women and women with disabilities. Preliminary background information about the women interviewed is provided in Appendix 3. Further analysis will extend this information.

FINDINGS ON SEXUAL ABUSE IN CHILDHOOD

One of the main aims of the study was to document women's experiences of sexual assault in childhood. For the purposes of this report, sexual abuse refers to those experiences of sexual assault which occurred before the woman reached the age of 16. In the interviews, women were asked about forced, unwanted and upsetting sexual experiences in childhood, ranging from forced or attempted forced sexual intercourse, other unwanted touching of their bodies, being forced to do sexual things to others and any other upsetting or threatening experiences they could remember and wanted to talk about.

There are two main categories of sexual abuse, depending on who the perpetrator is – incestuous and extrafamilial. Incestuous abuse includes any kind of sexual contact or attempted sexual contact that occurred between relatives, no matter how distant the relationship, before the girl turned 16 years old. Excluded from this definition are cases of consensual peer sexual contact (defined as taking place between persons of the same age or of no more than two years' difference), if these experiences are defined, by the respondent, as wanted. [8]

Extrafamilial child sexual abuse involves unwanted sexual experiences with persons unrelated by blood or marriage, ranging from sexual touching (of breasts or genitals or attempts at such touching) to forced or attempted forced sexual intercourse before the girl reached 16 years of age. In its narrow definition, it excludes some forms of actual physical touch (for example, unwanted sexual kissing, hugging or touching the body other than the breasts or genitals) as well as "non-contact" experiences such as unwanted sexual propositions, exposing of genitals and/or masturbating in front of the child, chasing, following, etc. In its broader definition, both incestuous and/or extrafamilial sexual abuse can include non-contact experiences, such as exhibitionism, sexual advances not acted upon, being followed, etc. [9]

In terms of incestuous abuse, meaning sexual contact imposed by a family member or other relative, we found that:

- 17 percent, or 71 women, reported at least one experience of incestuous abuse before reaching the age of 16 years. [10]

Generalizing from this finding suggests that approximately one in six girls has been sexually abused by a family member or other relative during childhood.

In terms of extrafamilial sexual abuse, meaning sexual contact imposed by a non-relative, we found that:

- 34 percent, or 143 women, reported at least one experience of sexual abuse by a non-relative before reaching the age of 16 years. [11]

This means that one in three girls was sexually abused by a non-relative in childhood.

When the two categories are combined, that is, sexual abuse perpetrated by someone either inside or outside the girl's family:

- 43 percent, or 178 women, reported at least one experience of incestuous and/or extrafamilial sexual abuse before reaching the age of 16 years. [12]

When additional disclosures are factored in, including less severe kinds of sexual abuse (such as unwanted sexual kisses or other non-genital sexual touching) and non-contact child sexual abuse experiences (such as having someone expose their genitals and/or masturbate in front of the child, having someone follow or verbally proposition the child), a much higher prevalence rate is obtained.

- 54 percent, or 228 women, reported an intrusive or unwanted sexual experience before reaching the age of 16 years. [13]

These findings are disturbingly high. They indicate that over half of the women interviewed in this study experienced some form of unwanted, intrusive and/or threatening sexual experience before reaching 16 years of age. [14] This points to the extreme pervasiveness and the common occurrence of sexual abuse and intrusion in most women's childhood years. The cumulative effect of these sexually abusive and intrusive experiences must be considered a major and an obviously negative factor in the psycho-social and sexual development of the majority of girls in our society.

In addition to documenting how many women reported specific types of experiences, it is also important to look at the characteristics of the assaults reported. This means analysing the characteristics of the cases of sexual abuse, [15] as opposed to reporting on how many women had specific kinds of sexual abuse experiences.

- 24 percent (114) of the cases of sexual abuse (broadly defined) were at the level of forced or attempted forced sexual intercourse.

- 58 percent (269) of the cases of sexual abuse (broadly defined) were at the level of unwanted sexual touch (or attempted touch) to the girl's chest or genitals.

The majority of the sexual abuse cases were not one-time-only events, but were perpetrated repeatedly against the girl by the same offender.

- In 58 percent (174) of the cases, sexual abuse happened more than once with the same perpetrator.

Statistics are always somewhat abstract. They remove us from the vividness and images of what is really being described. We must remember that these statistical findings describe the sexual abuse of children, often very young children, who are, by definition, vulnerable and quite powerless. In fact, just over one quarter of the sexual abuse cases were perpetrated against girls in their early childhood.

- 27 percent (47) of the 178 women who reported sexual abuse (narrowly defined) were sexually abused before reaching 8 years of age.

The great majority of sexual abuse cases were committed by known perpetrators.

- 28 percent of the cases of sexual abuse were perpetrated by family members or other relatives.

- 50 percent of the cases of sexual abuse were committed by known extrafamilial perpetrators.

- 20 percent of the cases of child sexual abuse were perpetrated by strangers.

Perpetrators in the cases of sexual abuse were overwhelmingly male.

- 96 percent (326) of the cases of child sexual abuse were perpetrated by men.

This clearly supports the necessity of a gender – based analysis of the crime of sexual abuse.

SEXUAL ASSAULT AT AGE 16 YEARS AND OVER

For the purposes of this report, sexual assault refers to those assault experiences which happened to women at or after the age of 16 years. The 1983 changes to the sexual assault law were intended to cover all kinds of unwanted sexual touching. Three types of sexual assault were identified, ranging from bottom pinching to attacks which include forced sexual intercourse (still commonly called rape) and the use of a weapon or wounding during a sexual assault. For the Women's Safety Project we documented all three types of sexual assault as defined by Canadian law.

Broadly defined, we identified sexual assault to range from any unwanted sexual touch to the body (including sexual touching of breasts or genitals, etc.) to forced sexual intercourse. [16] For the questions on sexual assault at the level of intercourse (or attempted sexual intercourse), we asked about intercourse imposed by physical force, threat of physical force or because the woman was helpless due, for example, to being asleep, unconscious or drugged. Under these circumstances, it is clear that consent to sexual intercourse is not possible.

In cases of sexual assault at the level of unwanted sexual touching/grabbing of the breasts and/or genitals:

- 44 percent, or 183 women, reported at least one experience of unwanted sexual assault at the level of unwanted sexual touching to the breasts and/or genitals at or after 16 years of age.

In cases of sexual assault at the level of forced sexual intercourse (a more restricted definition):

- 40 percent, or 168 women, reported at least one experience of forced intercourse (rape) in adulthood.

This means that more than one in three women experienced a rape in adulthood. In terms of attempted rapes:

- 31 percent, or 128 women, reported at least one experience of attempted rape in adulthood.

When these categories of rape and attempted rape are combined, as is customary in official statistics:

- 51 percent, or 212 women, reported at least one experience of sexual assault at the level of rape or attempted rape (forced or attempted forced sexual intercourse) at or after the age of 16 years.

These findings are shockingly high, especially since they exclude sexual assaults at the level of unwanted sexual touching and sexual assaults at the level of forced sexual intercourse which occurred before the woman was 16 years of age.[17]

In fact, when all cases of sexual assault are examined at the level of forced or attempted forced sexual intercourse which happened at any time in a woman's life, meaning in childhood or adulthood:

- 56 percent, or 234 women, experienced a sexual assault at the level of rape (forced sexual intercourse) or attempted rape at some point in their lives (including childhood and adulthood).

In other words, one in two women had been the victim of rape or attempted rape (sexual assault at the level of forced sexual intercourse or attempted forced intercourse) in childhood and/or adulthood.

This is twice as high as the previous and widely cited Canadian figure that one in four women has experienced a sexual assault. Furthermore, this finding refers only to a very narrow definition of sexual assault and includes only those cases at the level of forced sexual intercourse or attempted intercourse. When all kinds of sexual assault are taken into account (to include rape, attempted rape and unwanted sexual touching to the breasts or genitals), two out of three women had experienced what is legally recognized to be a sexual assault.

The implication of these findings is that public discussion about the prevalence of sexual assault in the lives of women in Canada must now acknowledge a far higher prevalence of sexual assault than was previously thought. As the results of our study show, it is more common for a woman to have had an experience of sexual assault than not.

It has often been emphasized that any and all women are at risk of being sexually assaulted. While it is important to stress that women can be and are sexually assaulted at any age, it is also critical to understand the circumstances which can make some groups of women particularly vulnerable.[18]

Our research indicates that young women are at especially high risk of being sexually assaulted.

- 51 percent of the sexual assault cases were committed against young women between 16 and 21 years of age.[19]

Clearly more needs to be done to educate young women about the risks and pervasiveness of sexual assault.

In understanding the context of sexual assault in women's lives, it is also important to analyse who the perpetrators are. Our research confirms that the overwhelming majority of sexual assaults were perpetrated against women by men who were known to them.

- 81 percent of the sexual assaults at the level of forced or attempted forced sexual intercourse were perpetrated by men who were known to the women. Nineteen percent of the sexual assaults at this level were perpetrated by strangers.

- 38 percent of the sexual assault cases at the level of rape/attempted rape (at or after the women reached 16 years of age) were perpetrated by men who were in relationships with the women they assaulted as husbands, common-law partners or boyfriends.

- 31 percent of sexual assaults at the level of rape/attempted rape were perpetrated by men who were dates and/or acquaintances of the women they sexually assaulted.

- 12 percent of the sexual assault cases at the level of rape/attempted rape were perpetrated by men known to the women in other relationships (e.g., friends, authority figures, etc.).

Clearly, this contradicts the still pervasive myth that it is dangerous, unknown men who are most likely to sexually assault women. In fact, our research confirms other studies in the area and indicates that the greatest risk of sexual assault posed to women comes from men they know, often intimately.

When rapes and attempted rapes are examined separately, we find that more than 25 percent of all rapes are committed by husbands, as opposed to the 12 percent committed by strangers. This means that husbands are responsible for more than double the number of rape cases than are strangers. However, when we examine attempted rapes only, we find that strangers are

responsible for 28 percent of all cases, whereas husbands are not reported in relation to any attempted rapes. It is evident that the more intimate the relationship, the more likely the rape attempt will actually succeed. The numbers for attempted rapes by husbands (0 percent), boyfriends/lovers (nine percent) and friends (14 percent) are low in comparison to the number of attempted rapes by non-intimates, especially dates and acquaintances (41 percent).

As is true for the majority of childhood sexual abuse cases, the overwhelming majority of the sexual assaults which occurred at or after 16 years of age were committed by men.

- 99 percent of the sexual assault cases [20] were perpetrated by men.

Again, this points to the necessity of a gender-based analysis of the crime of sexual assault.

PHYSICAL ASSAULT IN INTIMATE RELATIONSHIPS [21]

The prevalence of physical violence in women's intimate relationships was also a focus of the study. For this research we defined physical assault [22] to include any act of physical force used against a woman, ranging from slapping, hitting, shoving or being hurt in any other way, to repeated beatings and attempts on a woman's life. [23]

- 27 percent, or 115 women, reported an experience of physical abuse in an intimate relationship with a husband, live-in partner, boyfriend or date.

- 100 percent of the perpetrators of physical assault against women in the context of intimate relationships were men. [24]

An extrapolation of these findings suggests that slightly more than one in four women has experienced a physical assault (or ongoing physical assaults) in an intimate relationship with a man. This clearly represents a much higher number than the widely cited estimate that one in 10 women has been physically assaulted.

In our research we thought it important to make the links between sexual and physical assault perpetrated against women in the context of the same relationship.

- 50 percent (57) of the women reporting physical assault, also experienced sexual assault in the same relationship.

For these 57 women, there were a total of 59 cases. This represents 44 percent of the physical assault cases, which involved both physical and sexual abuse perpetrated by the same male intimate. Sexual assault is therefore an important and often present dimension of the experience of physically assaulted women.

A physical assault typically results in a woman experiencing ongoing fear. In our study, women who were physically assaulted by a male intimate usually reported high levels of fear as a result of the experience, due to the violence of the assault, as well as the possibility and unpredictability that it might happen again. This was often, but not necessarily, connected to the kinds of threats made against them, including threats on their lives.

- In 25 percent of the cases of physical assault women reported that their partners explicitly threatened to kill them.

Throughout the interview, women who reported physical abuse were also asked if they ever feared they would be killed, whether or not their partners explicitly threatened them with death.

- In 36 percent of the cases, women reporting physical assault also reported that they feared they would be killed by the man who physically assaulted them.

Typically, women reported that the fury and violence exhibited during attacks on them made them fear for their lives. Further qualitative analysis of this finding is needed to reveal women's own meanings and experiences of living with this kind of terror.

REVICTIMIZATION

Revictimization describes the finding that women who are sexually abused in childhood are several times more likely to be victimized again later in life than are women with no history of sexual abuse in childhood. Our research demonstrates that a link does exist between an experience of sexual abuse in childhood and an increased likelihood of victimization in adulthood. In other words, an experience of sexual abuse in childhood appears to render a woman more vulnerable to another experience of sexual assault later on in her life.

- 70 percent of the women who were sexually abused in childhood were also sexually assaulted after the age of 16 years. This compares with 45 percent of the women who were never sexually abused in childhood. [25]

To date, the issue of revictimization in women's lives has been relatively under-theorized. It has sometimes been a highly contentious issue for feminists, due to the potential danger of focusing on the experiences of those women who have had repeated sexual assaults in a society which is all too quick and willing to blame women for the abuse inflicted upon them by men. However, it is imperative that feminists take up the difficult and challenging issue of how some women live with the experience of repeated sexual assaults (meaning those committed by different perpetrators), as well as analyse how sexual assault in childhood might increase a woman's vulnerability to sexual assault later in her life. If we shrink from confronting the reality of this painful and complex phenomenon, we limit the ability to understand the long-term and often lifelong consequences of early experiences of sexual violation and violence in a woman's life.

A feminist analysis of revictimization has important implications for front-line work with women who are survivors of violence, for legal cases, for clinical interventions, as well as for policy, educational and political initiatives directed toward ending sexual violence in all women's lives.

Because revictimization is a highly complicated phenomenon with many contributing factors, it is an issue which has been explored in different ways. For example, in her study, Diana Russell focused on incest as a contributing cause of revictimization. According to Russell's research, "68 percent of incest victims were the victims of rape or attempted rape by a non-relative at some time in their lives compared with 38 percent of the women in [the] sample who were never incestuously abused." [26] She also found, however, that 65 percent of the women who were victims of incest at the very severe or severe levels before the age of 14 years were victimized again by rape or attempted rape by a non-relative after the age of 14. This compares with 61 percent of women who were victimized by extrafamilial child sexual abuse and 35 percent of the women who were never sexually abused before the age of 14. [27] However, the statistical difference is small enough to indicate that it may not be the particular experience of incest, but the experience of sexual abuse itself (perpetrated by a relative or a non-relative), which is linked to further sexual victimization. Russell's study was the first to provide empirical documentation that in a random sample of women, child sexual abuse is related to an increased chance of further sexual victimization later in life.[28]

Since Russell's 1986 reporting of revictimization, very little analysis has been done to understand the basis of this connection, and it has remained profoundly under-analysed. The few clinical explanatory approaches that have been offered emphasize that something about the experience of sexual abuse in childhood leaves a woman less able to protect herself than she would be had she not been sexually abused. What is consistently unexamined in these approaches is the implicit assumption that women need to develop the ability to negotiate danger, perceive cues of aggression, maintain strong boundaries and protect themselves from experiencing sexual assault. It is taken for granted that these survival strategies are a normal part of women's ability to function in society.

What remains invisible, then, is a more fundamental question. What exactly is the source of this pervasive danger from which women are expected to protect themselves? What is not explicitly integrated into these clinical explanations is the fact that revictimization could not possibly exist without a society in which large numbers of men were willing to, and actually do, sexually abuse and assault women in massive numbers.

Revictimization, therefore, cannot be explained without acknowledging the pervasive sexual and physical violence directed by many men against many women in this society. Research linking the magnitude of this violence in women's lives, and the many forms it takes, is the first step to understanding revictimization. While there is a clear and implicit victim-blaming expectation that women should know how to protect themselves, there is also a profound social denial and silence about the pervasiveness of men's violence from which protection is required. What is exceptional, then, is that so many women have learned to resist violence and negotiate safety in their lives.

Developing an understanding of revictimization requires an examination of different levels and components of the experience. We compared the numbers of women who had been raped or had experienced a rape attempt in childhood with the numbers of women who did not have this childhood experience.

- 71 percent of the women with an experience of rape or attempted rape in childhood also had an experience of rape or attempted rape in adult life. This compares with 67 percent of the women who had no childhood rape or attempted rape experiences, but who had a rape or attempted rape experience in adult life.

This comparison reveals that there is no significant difference between the women who have and have not experienced sexual assault at the level of rape or attempted rape in childhood in terms of their likelihood of experiencing a sexual assault at the same level in adulthood. In other words, a childhood experience of rape or attempted rape does not seem to be linked to increased vulnerability to an experience of rape or attempted rape after the age of 16.

This finding dispels the suggestion that women who have been sexually abused in childhood are somehow distinguishable to some perpetrators and may get more easily "picked out" or "targeted" by abusive men. It has also been inappropriately suggested that women who have been sexually abused in childhood somehow attract abusers or are drawn to men who are abusive. It is extremely important to challenge these explanations because they implicitly blame women for their victimization. Moreover, many women who have been sexually abused in childhood have reported feeling further stigmatized and blamed by the assumption that they are somehow "visible victims."

When we examine the data looking at rape and attempted rape experiences together (as reported above), there is no significant difference in terms of likelihood of revictimization. When we analyse the data by isolating only rape experiences, we see that there is a significant difference in terms of women's vulnerability to revictimization. This means that there is something specifically associated with the intrusion, trauma and violation of the experience of being raped in childhood which is one of the significant factors in revictimization, as the findings below make clear.

By analysing sexual assault only at the level of rape (in other words, by excluding all cases of attempted rape from the analysis) we find that:

- 69 percent of the women who were raped in childhood were also raped after the age of 16 years compared with 46 percent of the women in our sample who were never raped in childhood.

This suggests that women who have been raped in childhood are more likely to be raped again in their adult lives by a different perpetrator.

An important issue needs to be raised here. Many men in our society make many attempts to sexually assault women. For some women, the sexual assault attempts remain just that, attempts. But, for women already extremely victimized in childhood through rape, it appears that many of the attempted sexual assaults later in life are more likely to become another rape.

It is well documented in clinical literature that sexual abuse in childhood at the level of forced sexual intercourse is seriously traumatizing for the child. The trauma is often severe and chronic, and continues into adulthood. It is conceivable that a woman who has been rendered powerless and helpless through the experience of a rape committed against her in childhood may do what is automatic to protect herself when confronted again with a man who is sexually violating her. For example, she may "dissociate," meaning she may disconnect from her body and from feeling what is happening to her. She may go numb or deny what is going on in order to help her get through the pain of surviving it. These are some of the protective ways of coping that she may have used in childhood, and they are the same ones she may draw upon again and again throughout her life. Unfortunately, these means are not enough to stop a man intent on raping.

Our research findings indicate that multiple experiences of sexual abuse in childhood [29] are also likely to increase a woman's vulnerability to multiple sexual assaults in adulthood.

- 63 percent of women with two or more experiences of sexual abuse in childhood had two or more experiences of sexual assault after 16 years of age. This compares with 23 percent of the women who had no childhood sexual abuse and 31 percent of women who had one experience of sexual abuse in childhood. [30]

Thus, our findings suggest that two components of childhood sexual abuse are associated with revictimization, or repeated sexual assault experiences: childhood sexual abuse at the level of rape and multiple childhood sexual abuse experiences.

When these factors are examined together:

- 80 percent of women with two or more experiences of rape in childhood had two or more experiences of rape as adults. This compares with only nine percent of women who had no experiences of rape in childhood and 14 percent of the women who had one experience of rape in childhood.

This analysis on revictimization shows that there are three levels of significance for understanding the phenomenon.

- The early experience of sexual abuse in childhood creates a far greater possibility and likelihood of another experience of sexual assault later in life.

- A sexual abuse experience at the level of rape (or forced intercourse) makes it more likely that a woman will have another sexual assault at the level of rape later in life.

- Multiple experiences of sexual abuse in childhood (two or more experiences of sexual abuse committed by different perpetrators) [31] are strongly associated with multiple experiences of sexual assault after the age of 16 years.

Further analysis will extend and enrich this discussion, especially by inclusion of some of the qualitative data on this issue. Finally, in analysing revictimization in women's lives, the larger social goal of ending men's violence against women and children must always remain in view. Achieving this goal would in itself eliminate the existence of the phenomenon of revictimization.

CONCLUSION

One of the purposes of our research was to determine the connections between women's experiences of sexual abuse in childhood, sexual assault in adulthood and physical assault in intimate relationships, including revictimization. We wanted to document the number of women who had experienced multiple forms of sexual abuse and violence, as well as discover any patterns of victimization over the course of women's lives. In this way, we hoped to contribute to an analysis which puts the violence in context and "makes the links" in understanding the prevalence, impact and nature of various experiences of sexual and physical abuse.

The results of our study demonstrate the devastating "normalcy" and pervasive presence of sexual violence and intrusion in women's lives. More than one half of all the women interviewed had experienced sexual abuse in childhood and more than one half of the women interviewed had experienced a rape or attempted rape in adulthood. Often, women experience all three major forms of sexual violence under investigation – sexual abuse in childhood, sexual assault in adulthood and physical assault in an intimate relationship. In our study, nearly one in 10 of the women interviewed had experienced all three. [32]

In the interviews for the Women's Safety Project, women were also asked about a wide range of other abuses they might have experienced in a variety of contexts and relationships. These ranged from being followed or chased on the street, to receiving an obscene phone call [33] or being sexually harassed at work. When looking at this broader spectrum of traumatizing and upsetting experiences, we found that 98 percent, or 410 women, reported some kind of sexually threatening, intrusive or assault experience at some point in their lives. This finding clearly supports the assertion that sexual violence and intimidation, and the threat of this violence, affects virtually all women's lives in a very direct way.

Moreover, women's personal experiences of violence must also be analysed in the context of a society in which the reality and threat of men's sexual violence is often sensationalized in the media, and glorified and sold as entertainment in much mass culture. In other words, we are daily surrounded by reminders of its presence. As a result, the knowledge that an act of sexual violence might be directed against them exists in women's collective consciousness as a danger always to be guarded against. In this way, violence against women acts as a form of social control by creating the conditions where women often experience stress, anxiety and fear, and must (consciously or not) adopt strategies to ensure safety in their daily lives. This adds another ever-present layer to the violation of a direct experience of sexual or physical assault.

ANNEX 1
DEFINITIONS OF TERMS
DESCRIBING ABUSE
EXPERIENCES

Incestuous abuse includes any kind of exploitive sexual contact or attempted sexual contact that occurred between relatives, no matter how distant the relationship, before the girl turned 16 years old. Excluded from this definition are cases of consensual peer sexual contact (defined as taking place between persons of the same age or of no more than two years' difference), if these experiences are defined as wanted by the respondent.

Intercourse includes vaginal, anal or oral intercourse. It should also be pointed out that levels of assault are reported in terms of the highest level of sexual intrusion. This means that childhood sexual abuse experiences which are reported to involve rape (forced sexual intercourse) may, and typically do, involve all kinds of other forced sexual contact including sexual touching, etc. These additional forms of sexual intrusion are not listed for cases which exceed this level of intrusion.

Extrafamilial child sexual abuse is defined more narrowly than our definition of incestuous abuse. This definition is narrower because it excludes some forms of actual physical touching (unwanted sexual kissing, hugging or touching of the body other than the breasts or genitals) as well as verbal propositions, exposing of genitals, being chased, etc. Extrafamilial child sexual abuse, then, involves unwanted sexual experiences with persons unrelated by blood or marriage, ranging from attempted sexual touching (of breasts or genitals or attempts at such touching) to sexual assault and rape or attempted sexual assault and rape, before 16 years of age.

Physical assault/physical abuse refers to any act of physical force and/or violence used against a woman, ranging from slapping, hitting, shoving and punching to repeated beatings as well as attempts on a woman's life.

Rape refers to sexual assault at the level of forced sexual intercourse (vaginal, anal or oral). Although the term "sexual assault" is used in Canadian law, the term "rape" is perhaps more politicized for many women and more strongly captures the violation and violence of the act.

Revictimization describes the finding that women who have been abused in childhood are more likely to be victimized again later in life than are women with no history of sexual abuse in childhood. The term is also used to refer to repeated experiences of sexual victimization (at the hands of different perpetrators).

Sexual touching refers to direct touching or fondling (with a part of the body or with an object) of the genitals or breasts for sexual purposes. This also includes forcing the victim to touch the perpetrator's genitals.

Sexual intrusion refers to unwanted experiences which could include unwelcome sexual comments, being touched on the buttocks, having someone expose their genitals or masturbate in front of the respondent, being grabbed, being followed or chased, etc.

ANNEX 2
DEFINITIONS OF OTHER
RESEARCH TERMS

Methodology describes the approach, actual techniques and practices used in carrying out the research.

Interview schedule refers to the semi-structured questionnaire, or set of questions, used to interview women in the study.

Prevalence measures the number of unique cases of specific kinds of sexual violence that exist at a specific point in time. It indicates the extent of the phenomenon under investigation as reported by respondents in the survey.

Mini-questionnaire is a structured, mostly open-ended questionnaire used to gather in-depth qualitative and some quantitative data about specific experiences of sexual and physical violence.

Qualitative data refer to women's verbatim answers, information given in their own words in response to open-ended questions. These questions asked women to provide details and information about their experiences and thoughts in any way that is meaningful to them.

Quantitative data refer to summarizing in numbers the answers women provided in response to some of the questions. For example when a woman disclosed that she was sexually abused in childhood, her experience was included in a total count of the cases of sexual abuse, as well as in the count of women who reported being sexually abused.

ANNEX 3
SELECTED BACKGROUND
INFORMATION ON WOMEN
INTERVIEWED

A number of questions were asked to get some background information on the women interviewed for the project. Some descriptive information follows (Figures do not always add up to 100 percent due to rounding):

CITIZENSHIP

	# of women	% of women
Canadian Citizens	351	86.7 %
Non-Citizens		
Landed Immigrant	42	10.4 %
Student/Work Visa	9	2.2 %
Other	3	0.7 %
Missing	15	
	420	100.0 %

PLACE OF BIRTH

The table below provides information on the place of birth of women interviewed for the Women's Safety Project.

	# of women	% of women
Canada	269	
Europe		
British Isles	28	7.0 %
France	3	0.7 %
Germany	4	1.0 %
Greece	1	0.2 %
Hungary	1	0.2 %
Poland	7	1.7 %
Italy	6	1.5 %
Other Europe	8	2.0 %
Asia		
China	4	1.0 %
India/Pakistan	6	1.5 %
Other Asia	13	3.2 %
Africa	3	0.7 %
Americas		
Caribbean	2	0.5 %
Latin America	7	1.7 %
United States	22	5.5 %
Other	18	4.5 %
Missing/Refused	18	
	420	100.0 %

ETHNIC AND CULTURAL IDENTIFICATIONS

The breakdown for the cultural or ethnic groups to which women identified themselves as belonging is indicated below.

	# of women	% of women
Arab	1	0.3 %
Black	8	2.0 %
British	25	6.3 %
Caribbean	3	0.8 %
Chinese	7	1.8 %
Dutch	1	0.3 %
Filipino	7	1.8 %
Greek	5	1.3 %
Hungarian	1	0.3 %
Irish	3	0.8 %
Indo-Pakistan	6	1.5 %
Italian	13	3.3 %
Japanese	1	0.3 %
Jewish	28	6.7 %
Korean	4	1.0 %
Latin America	1	0.3 %
Latvian	3	0.8 %
Maltese	1	0.3 %
Macedonian	1	0.3 %
Native Canadian/ Aboriginal	6	1.5 %
Portuguese	12	3.0 %
Polish	8	2.0 %
Ukrainian	7	1.8 %
Yugoslavian	2	0.5 %
Other	1	0.3 %
More than two ethnic identities/cultures	47	11.9 %
No ethnic/cultural identification	199	47.4 %
	401	98.6 %

AGE DISTRIBUTION OF WOMEN IN SAMPLE

	# of women	% of women
15-19	13	3.2 %
20-24	33	8.1 %
25-29	65	16.0 %
30-34	76	18.8 %
35-39	78	19.3 %
40-44	56	13.8 %
45-49	40	9.9 %
50-54	22	5.4 %
55-59	14	3.5 %
60-64	8	2.0 %
Missing	15	
	420	100.0 %

DISABILITY

Number of women reporting a disability.

	# of women	% of women
Disability	72	17.2 %
No Disability	347	82.8 %
Missing	1	
	420	100.0 %

EDUCATIONAL BACKGROUND

	# of women	% of women
Less than Grade 9	4	1.0 %
Some high school	36	8.7 %
Completedhigh school	63	15.2 %
Completed trade school	6	1.5 %
Completed college	46	11.1 %
Some university	66	16.0 %
University degree	192	46.5 %
Missing/refused	7	
	420	100.0 %

ACKNOWLEDGMENTS

We would like to register our heartfelt appreciation to all the women who agreed to be interviewed for the Women's Safety Project (including the various pre-tests, training of the interviewers, pilot study and the random sample). Without their generosity and courage in taking the time to reveal and discuss very intimate, and often deeply painful material from their personal histories, the project would not have been possible. While we acknowledge the impossibility of ever fully doing so, we hope that the results of this project honour these women's stories.

We would like to thank the interviewers who worked on this project and acknowledge the extremely important and difficult work they carried out.

We are grateful to the following women's groups and organizations for letters of support:

Barbra Schlifer Commemorative Clinic
Brief Psychotherapy Centre for Women, Women's College Hospital
Education Wife Assault
The Elizabeth Fry Society of Toronto
Federation of Women Teachers' Association of Ontario (FWTAO)
Metro Action Committee on Public Violence Against Women and Children (METRAC)
National Action Committee on the Status of Women
Safe City Committee of Toronto
Sexual Assault Care Centre, Women's College Hospital
Special Committee on the Prevention of Child Abuse
Toronto Women Teachers' Association
Women's Legal Education and Action Fund (LEAF)

This project received financial support from the Ontario Women's Directorate, the Ministry of Community and Social Services, the Ministry of the Solicitor General (Ontario), the City of Toronto, the Ministry of Health, Ontario, Health and Welfare Canada and the Canadian Panel on Violence Against Women.

ENDNOTES

1 This was an additional precaution we took in spite of the fact that the letter was addressed not to anyone's name, but to "Dear Woman Resident." It clearly stated that the address was randomly selected by computer.

2 The qualitative data on this issue will be presented in future work, along with an expanded analysis of the methodological issues in the research.

3 Greek, Italian, Chinese, Spanish and Portuguese, representing some of the largest language groups in the city.

4 A significant exception are those women who are severely hearing impaired or deaf. In our study, some women did identify difficulty hearing as a disability, and one respondent was, in fact, profoundly deaf for much of her childhood. Given the cultural specifics of the deaf community, however, it would be most appropriate for an in-depth study on deaf and hearing impaired women's experiences of sexual and physical violence to be designed and carried out by members of that same community.

5 Each interview is identified only by an interview number. Women who agreed to be interviewed signed consent forms (which were read aloud during the first contact with the potential respondent). The consent form reiterated information about the nature of the study, including confidentiality and anonymity.

6 Longer interviews were always carried out over a series of meetings, which were scheduled and paced according to the woman's choice.

7 Designed by the Institute for Social Research, York University.

8 Our definition of incestuous abuse was essentially the same one used in Dr. Diana Russell's 1986 study, reported in *The Secret Trauma: Incest in the Lives of Girls and Women*, except that Russell included women's experiences before the age of 18 and we asked women about their experiences up to the age of 16 on our in-depth mini-questionnaires relating to childhood sexual abuse. Sexual assault experiences which occurred at the age of 16 years and over were asked about and are reported with the sexual assault data. With further analysis, we will recalculate the numbers from our study to match Russell's age cutoffs exactly, so that we can compare our findings with hers, including the prevalence rate for incestuous abuse under the age of 14.

9 Specific criteria guided our research questions and definitions of incestuous and extrafamilial abuse. However, many of the childhood experiences women reported were broader than the criteria we established. Some qualitative data were collected on these experiences.

10 Interestingly, this finding represents a slightly higher, but very similar prevalence, rate for incestuous abuse to that reported by Russell in her study of 1986, (*The Secret Trauma*, p. 60), although her findings refer to experiences before the age of 18. Russell reports that 16 percent of the women in her sample of 930 reported at least one experience of incestuous abuse before reaching 18 years.

11 In the Russell study, 31 percent of the respondents reported an experience of extrafamilial abuse before age 18.

12 This compares to the 38 percent of Russell's sample who reported at least one experience of incestuous and/or extrafamilial sexual abuse before reaching the age of 18 years.

13 The fact that 54 percent of the women in our survey reported an intrusive or unwanted sexual experience before reaching the age of 16 is consistent with the Canadian findings of the Badgely Commission, which reported that one in two girls experienced an unwanted sexual act in childhood and/or adolescence.

14 We want to caution, however, against making generalizations from this particular finding, since it includes everything from rape to an unwanted sexual kiss or "necking," to other "non-contact" but frightening experiences such as being followed or chased on the street. This finding shows the prevalent conditions of sexual intrusion and assault which many young girls must endure. Yet, we must be careful not to obscure the fact that some of these experiences might be — in relative terms at least — fairly minor in the degree of sexual intrusion and the impact of the event. An additional reason for not overgeneralizing from the finding that 54 percent of the sample experienced some form of unwanted sexual experience before the age of 16 is that some women who have been sexually abused in childhood at the more extreme levels and have suffered traumatic effects throughout their lives question why they are having such difficulties coping if the experience is so common. This points to the need for a more sustained and in-depth exploration of differences in abuse experiences and their contexts, a comparison of cognitive meanings women place on their experiences and the short- and long-term impacts these experiences have in women's lives.

On the other hand, it cannot necessarily be concluded that an experience which might appear to be more "minor" in relative terms was not a traumatic event in a woman's life. For example, a young girl may have been followed or chased on the street by a man in her childhood, and she may have escaped safely. Yet she may have feared and continued to fear that his intention was to rape and/or kill her. The meaning such an event had for a woman and whether or not she suffered any short- or long-term effects must be understood in order to comprehend the impact and level of trauma she experienced.

15   The term "cases" (referring to sexual abuse, sexual assault or physical assault cases) means a distinct experience or set of experiences committed by a perpetrator. Because some women in the study reported more than one perpetrator committing violence against them, the number of cases can exceed the number of women in the analysis. When we are analyzing the sexual abuse cases for example, we are looking at the number of reports of sexual abuse, and each case refers to a unique perpetrator.

16   The figures presented under the category "sexual assault broadly defined" all meet the criteria of sexual assault under Canadian law. These numbers give an indication of the extent of actual sexual assaults on women in this study. Of course, as with other forms of abuse asked about in our study, we would suggest that the figures are actually under-reported due to forgotten or repressed memories and/or women's choosing not to discuss specific abuse experiences due to the discomfort or pain associated with them.

For our study, we thought it to be highly important to document the entire range of sexual assault experiences in women's lives. In fact, there are a variety of other sexually intrusive, threatening and violating experiences which are excluded in the figures analysed in this section, including having genitals exposed (or being "flashed" as it is more commonly called), being followed or chased on the street and having obscene or threatening sexual comments or propositions made.

17   In assessing the implications of the finding that 51 percent of the women surveyed reported an experience of sexual assault at the level of forced intercourse or attempted intercourse, it is important to emphasize that our research was conducted before the recent (1992) changes regarding consent were made to the Canadian sexual assault laws. In our survey, we qualified the questions about sexual assault at the level of sexual intercourse or attempted sexual intercourse by asking women if they were forced, physically threatened, drugged, unconscious, asleep or otherwise helpless. Without these stringent conditions, it is possible that future research could yield even higher prevalence rates.

18   Further analysis will explore the kinds of sexual assaults perpetrated against women in this age category.

19   This number will undoubtedly be significantly higher when cases of sexual assault in the early teenage years are factored in, as will be done in future analysis.

20   Defined to include cases of forced or attempted forced sexual intercourse and unwanted sexual touching the woman's breasts and/or genitals.

21   Physical violence in relationships is described by a wide variety of terms, from the traditional and obfuscating gender-neutral labels such as "family violence," and "spouse abuse," to the more frequently used feminist term "wife assault" or "woman abuse." The term "wife assault" is clearly limiting insofar as it narrows the scope of analysis to abuse within legally sanctioned marital relationships. While the term "woman abuse" is an improvement, it has been used to refer to such a wide range of behaviours that some of the specificity which we require for the purposes of this discussion is lost. For these reasons, we use the descriptive term, "physical assault in intimate relationships" or variations on this theme. This is because we want to focus on the particularity of the experience of suffering physical assault in the context of an ongoing relationship with a dating, common-law or marital partner.

22   There has been considerable discussion in feminist literature of other significant dimensions of abuse, including verbal and psychological abuse. While these experiences were discussed in many of the cases of physical assault by an intimate, we did not include verbal or psychological abuse. Research which uses this kind of definition would no doubt lead to even greater prevalence rates than those reported here. We did, however, want to broaden the analysis of the impact and effects of physical assault in intimate relationships. Verbal abuse was explored as a component of the abuse experience, along with the many ways women's everyday lives are constricted, and their sense of self and personal safety and integrity are damaged ,as a result of the abuse. Further analysis will explore these aspects.

23   More detailed information about the kinds of force used
      and the effects of this violence was elicited on the mini-
      questionnaires relating to physical assault.

24   In fact, the question was asked in gender-neutral terms to
      allow for the possibility of disclosures of physical abuse
      by female intimates, but no cases were reported.

25   Sexual abuse and sexual assault at the level of rape or
      attempted rape and forced sexual touching of breasts or
      genitals.

26   Diana Russell, *The Secret Trauma: Incest in the Lives of
      Girls and Women* (New York: Basic Books, 1986),
      p. 158.

27   *Ibid.*, p. 159.

28   Some initial clinical and psychological explanations have
      been offered by various experts in the field, including
      Judith Herman (1992) and Jon Briere (1989).

29   Multiple experiences of sexual abuse refer here to inci-
      dents committed by multiple perpetrators, not repeated
      acts committed by the same abuser.

30   This refers to sexual abuse and sexual assault at the level
      of rape or attempted rape and forced sexual touching of
      breasts or genitals.

31   These sexual abuse experiences perpetrated by different
      offenders may each be one time only or may be repeated
      assaults. Further analysis is required to examine
      repeated assaults by the same perpetrator as a factor in
      revictimization.

32   These women had experienced each kind of sexual
      violence at least once, and a woman in this group could
      also have had more than one experience of each kind of
      violence.

33   The question about obscene phone calls explicitly asked
      if the woman had "ever been upset by receiving an
      obscene telephone call." This means that if a woman
      received an obscene phone call but did not experience it
      as threatening or upsetting, it was excluded from the
      analysis.

APPENDIX B

THE PANEL AND ITS PROCESS

The timely creation of the Canadian Panel on Violence Against Women and the impact of the documents and reports it has produced mark a turning point and new orientation in the lives of women victims of violence. With our work now completed, we feel it is appropriate to report on this experience. The comments and criticism received by the Panel and the degree of commitment on the part of those involved in its work, particularly Panel members and staff, have led us to evaluate our activities as a whole.

No attempt will be made here at a systematic review of all the matters brought to the attention of the Panel by women's groups, government authorities, the media and the public. Rather than compare the structure put at our disposal and the results of our efforts with those of similar initiatives, we believe we must conduct our evaluation on the basis of the mandate assigned to us and of what was expected of us. The results, lessons and obstacles of this extraordinary experience will become part of our collective memory. We hope that the experience will lead to better understanding of the issues raised by violence against women.

THE SOCIAL AND POLITICAL CONTEXT IN WHICH THE PANEL BEGAN ITS WORK

The underlying reasons for the Panel's creation are readily apparent. The 1989 massacre at the École Polytechnique in Montreal put governments under greater pressure to take measures against violence. A few months later, a House of Commons subcommittee published a report entitled *The War Against Women*, which contained recommendations based on consultations with organizations working against violence. Months earlier, around the time of the 20th anniversary of the Royal Commission on the Status of Women, a coalition of some 30 women's organizations had demanded a royal commission on violence against women. Although women's groups in some parts of the country did not support the royal commission approach, the federal government received letters and petitions from more than 26,000 persons, and provincial ministers and mayors in all regions of Canada supported the initiative.

The War Against Women, which also recommended a royal commission, proposed possible goals and parameters: it should promote prevention, attack the causes of inequality, rely on existing research, reflect the needs of women experiencing multiple forms of oppression and be made up of women working in front-line services. The sense of urgency was tempered by concern. Something had to be done, but not just anything; whatever it was would have to be done right. The federal government appears to have hesitated between the two possibilities of establishing a "conventional" royal commission or introducing a more flexible, less costly and, essentially, "different" mechanism.

News of the Panel's inception in August 1991 was favourably received. The media and some of the public were of course somewhat cynical about the initiative, but feminist groups, while stating that the Panel's budget could have been put to better use in basic services for women victims of violence, did not dismiss the initiative. The relatively positive reception by women's groups may perhaps be explained by the community-oriented, non-partisan and feminist backgrounds of Panel members, many of whom had considerable experience in anti-violence work. This reaction offset the cynicism expressed elsewhere at the time.

THE PANEL GETS TO WORK

The notion of "power" is at the core of all feminist demands. Feminist organizations unceasingly question this aspect of public and private life and have developed organizational practices based on independence, control, management methods and the power to determine orientations. On the other hand, Panel members and the secretariat accepted the Panel's mandate without having taken part in its development. There was nothing reprehensible in this *per se*. The Panel's mandate was not incompatible in any fundamental way with a feminist understanding of violence against women. (Had the opposite been true, members could simply have refused to sit on the Panel.) In fact, considering the progress the government had to make on the issue, the mandate even contained some progressive aspects, such as the link of violence to equality issues.

The process selected for the Panel was an interactive, community-based approach and entailed meeting women in their own surroundings. This approach coincided with the vision of Panel members. Here again, the spirit of the mandate revealed a certain sensitivity to crucially important issues regarding violence against women — a concern for more vulnerable women, in particular.

However, selecting the mechanisms for carrying out the mandate became a problem. In theory, the procedures were acceptable, but we did not try to determine, at the outset, whether they were valid or realistic. This was particularly unfortunate since the Panel had the option, if it wanted it, to initiate discussions with the Minister and her representatives, who had clearly indicated their willingness to discuss these matters. The fact that we conducted too brief an examination of our duties when we took them up has had repercussions throughout our mandate.

There was criticism of the term of the mandate. Some people told us in the early going that completing this project (a broad-based consultation in roughly 100 communities, in addition to drafting a progress report and final report) in only 15 months was an unthinkable task. A number of weeks elapsed before the Panel and secretariat were really operational. Nevertheless, we declined to make a formal request for an extension of our mandate until the last minute.

Why did we hesitate, when, in our private and professional lives, we were used to requesting, demanding and certainly never backing down, in negotiations? The most plausible explanation is that we wanted, at all costs, to avoid jeopardizing the project with missed deadlines or requests for additional funding. We did not want this Panel, which is so important for Canadian women, to be dismissed as "some women's project" that would cost a fortune and never end.

There was some criticism of the budget allocated to the Panel (approximately $10 million). And in view of the urgent need for community services for women and children who are victims of violence, it was understandable criticism. However, the budget was not disproportionate considering the scope of our mandate: to report on all forms of violence against women and to develop an action plan that would truly consider all the factors that contribute to the vulnerability of women.

As we advanced in our work, it became apparent that the obligation to carry out such a broad mandate in a relatively short time was seriously compromising our objectives. The profound commitment of members of the Panel's secretariat to the problem of violence against women and to the Panel's mission partly resolved this difficulty. Women's groups are familiar with this dynamic and live with it every day. Perhaps this strong commitment is why we did not attempt to renegotiate the scope of the mandate and the timetable of the Panel.

STRUCTURE, ALWAYS STRUCTURE

Feminists are, generally speaking, opposed to hierarchical structures. Feminist organizations have tried to develop structures that accommodate the inequalities and imbalances caused by a patriarchal society. As a result, they have experimented with management and operating methods better suited to their vision of a different society, they are more aware of the dangers of the sometimes excessive and unhealthy use of power, and they favour a redistribution of privileges.

The role and mandate of the organizational bodies created after the Panel's inception (Advisory Committee and Aboriginal Circle) were not clearly determined at the start. In addition, Panel members were not really given the opportunity to express their views on all these aspects. It should be noted that members were officially appointed to the Advisory Committee and the Aboriginal Circle only in late 1991.

The Aboriginal Circle is a noteworthy case in point. When Circle members were appointed, they were to have different status from that of Panel members: they were supposed to focus solely on those components of the process that specifically concerned Aboriginal women. Unlike the Panel and the Advisory Committee, the Aboriginal Circle consisted of representatives of some of the largest Aboriginal and Inuit women's associations in Canada.

This dichotomy quickly proved intolerable to Circle and Panel members alike. The decision was ultimately made to eliminate this "structural" distinction so that Circle members would become full-fledged members of the Panel. While this step did not resolve all difficulties, this new form of "cohabitation" was a rewarding experience. We hope this experiment, which is already under way in several feminist organizations in Canada, will constitute a definite step forward for the feminist movement and a concrete example of co-operation for political leaders.

The issue of representation on the Panel of women from cultural and racial minorities was undeniably one of the most painful and difficult questions we faced. It was debated at length by Panel members and between the Panel and several major Canadian women's organizations. Despite the spirit of the Panel's mandate, it appears that women from cultural and visible minorities, as well as women with disabilities, were inadequately represented in the Panel's makeup. It should be noted, however, that the membership of the Advisory Committee more accurately reflected the diversity of Canadian women.

For reasons of space, we cannot provide a detailed chronology of all the events and requests from women's organizations on the subject of representation. However, these requests were made to the Panel in two stages. After the initial consultations, some individuals and groups expressed a fear that the realities of racism, homophobia and class differences might only be considered secondary by the Panel. However, it was only after the community consultation tours had finished that some women's groups began to demand that three women from the cultural and visible minorities be included in the Panel's structure.

The Panel was very much aware of this issue and introduced various mechanisms to rectify the situation. We also proposed the appointment of special advisors, but this approach, unfortunately, was rejected by the women's organizations.

Including all women and their concerns is not solely a matter of numbers and structure. Our work methods and decision-making techniques, our practices and priorities, and our way of perceiving reality must also reflect their presence. It would be unrealistic to ask one individual or a small number of individuals to express such a range of views and to advance such crucially important perspectives.

The experience of Francophone women on the Panel clearly illustrates the problem. The Panel included three Francophones, a significant percentage of its total membership, and some staff members were also of Francophone origin. At first glance, then, the necessary conditions for an optimum balance between Anglophone and Francophone thinking were present. However, shaking up the established order was hard work indeed. Merely being present in large numbers is not enough to solve all problems. The experience of women in predominantly male organizations has also taught us the same lesson.

The under-representation of minority women and women experiencing multiple forms of oppression is a problem for all decision-making structures in Canada and will be an abiding concern in the future. The Panel could not resolve this complex issue alone.

However, while we believe that some progress was definitely made, political and opinion leaders will have to seek out new models applicable in all spheres of society. We hope our report contributes to those efforts.

The combination of various phenomena, such as sexism and racism, has been identified as one of the top priorities in the struggle to eliminate violence against women. The issue is clearly described in this report which sets a precedent by making a firm statement that efforts to overcome violence against women can no longer be dissociated from the struggle against sexism, racism, intolerance and inequality.

PROCESS AND RESULT: A FRAGILE BALANCE

Like community organizations, feminist organizations are questioning the traditional approaches of the institutions and systems that run our society. Feminists have reminded us that we must not make decisions or choices solely on the basis of efficiency, to the detriment of process. A healthier process which accommodates the needs of all women has a greater chance of producing satisfactory results. In some ways, democratic customs (the principle of the majority, for example) are also traps to which women have fallen victim throughout history.

The Advisory Committee has accompanied the Panel throughout its mandate and has been an important mechanism for addressing difficult issues. It has experienced some of the problems almost as intensely as the Panel itself. Its role was to provide expert advice and support to the Panel. There was confusion about the basis of membership of the committee. About half of the members were women with strong links to feminist organizations. The remainder were from various environments (institutional, judicial, police, academic), and had expertise in specific issues which we examined (e.g., elderly women). But, were the members to speak as individuals, or were they to represent their respective organizations? This was never resolved to everyone's satisfaction. A number of women's organizations wanted the Advisory Committee to consist solely of representatives of feminist organizations so it could serve as a body through which the Panel would be accountable to the feminist movement. We may suppose that the main reasons for this position were a desire to produce a report with a feminist as opposed to a more traditional perspective, a concern to solidify our credibility with women's groups and the fear that the whole project might have been concocted by the government as a stalling tactic. These concerns emerged in initial contacts with the Advisory Committee. What were the Advisory Committee's real powers? Did it have access to all the information? Did it have the power to accept or reject decisions made by the Panel? This question of accountability — i.e., to whom was the Panel accountable? — was the subject of extensive discussion.

The Panel's legal and political situation was such that it had no identity separate from government. As a result, all the Panel's actions had legal implications, not only for the members them-selves, but also for other parts of the government, for the Minister's office and for the Panel's public servants. The Panel was required, for example, to comply with several pieces of federal legislation (*Official Languages Act, Access to Information Act, Privacy Act* and the *Financial Administration Act*).

Through the process, we were aware that this initiative was introduced by the government and that we had to maintain more or less constant relations with the government authorities concerned. Given the overriding commitment of the Panel members to the issues inherent in the Panel's mandate, this was not an issue as long as the specific responsibilities of each party were clearly defined and respected. The Panel continued to conduct its proceedings as independently as possible. However, when all the "technical" information was delivered to the Panel, some members experienced "culture shock" — bureaucratic culture vs. community culture! While Panel members had some knowledge of the Canadian government system based on their experience as citizens and as leaders of organizations that had laboured in the labyrinthine workings of Canadian bureaucracy and politics, their first-hand knowledge of the workings of government was limited.

Notwithstanding these considerations, Panel members were torn between obligations to women's groups, Canadian women in general and the federal government. We were convinced that our work had to be based on the advances, knowledge, experience and analyses of women's groups. The orientation of our research activities is testimony to that fact. Nevertheless, this issue led to confusion, doubt and animosity in our relations with women's groups. Our failure to resolve it has clearly resulted in disarray and a sense of powerlessness within both the Panel and the feminist community. What mechanisms would have helped this unique project along? How could we have been accountable to both the feminist organizations and the Minister? These delicate relations between the Panel and feminist organizations are similar to those between the government and women's groups. They remind us of the shortcomings of the consultation processes often proposed by government authorities to advocacy groups and of the government's real ability to integrate and adjust to the needs of groups representing women. Perhaps the most striking lesson is that to secure the support of essential partners it is crucially important to discuss matters openly with them before the project takes final form.

It remains to be seen whether this aspect has seriously marred the quality of the report as the feminist organizations predicted it would. We sincerely believe that risks were largely offset by our unshakable conviction that all inequalities suffered by women must be eliminated if we are truly to address the deep-seated roots of violence against women.

The strategies employed for the Panel's consultations made it easier to come to these observations. They contain imperfections, but they also represent major gains and lessons learned. As explained in the Progress Report, individuals who were well established in their respective communities, and who shared the Panel's vision of the issues and of the problem of violence against women, were deliberately selected as consultation agents. Since it was impossible to reach all the individuals and organizations concerned, each consultation tour had to provide us with a representative picture of the diverse realities of women living in Canada.

At times, we were troubled about our approach. Were we right to opt for flexibility and individual expression over the traditional presentation of briefs? How could we reconcile the need for public validation of existing expertise in the community with the challenge of stimulating a dynamic that would be both interactive and engaging for the community? How could we encourage women to speak out, yet avoid the pitfalls of sensationalism? How could we create an atmosphere that was free of prejudice so that the public could discover and admit to the realities hidden in the silence and suffering of thousands of women?

This receptive and interactive community-based approach had considerable merit, but it also represented a sizable organizational challenge. Although the consultations were held in satisfactory conditions in some communities, there were problems in others. As a result, we may draw the following conclusions:

- The consultation process was relatively effective in reaching isolated or distant communities; it was more controversial in urban areas.

- The differences in the ways Aboriginal and non-aboriginal communities do and see things were clearly visible and afforded an incredible number of lessons and discoveries.

- The process revealed all the subtleties of the various types of violence against women.

- We reached a certain number of women who are more vulnerable to violence, but much remains to be done to establish true dialogue with women in the visible and cultural minorities. The Panel alone could not solve this problem — one which concerns Canadian society as a whole.

CONCLUSION

According to feminists, to lay any real claim to consensus, every group, such as the Panel, must not only examine and come to terms with various points of view, it must also involve all its members in decision making. Consensus is promoted by sharing roles, responsibilities and privileges. Unbiased communications, co-operation and the ability to question harmful behaviours and power games are also key in opening the door to consensus.

Can a feminist process be conducted within a government structure? The people who chose to sit on the Panel or the Advisory Committee were perfectly aware of the structure's benefits and constraints as were those who established the Panel itself. The question was: What could be accomplished in the conditions imposed on us?

It is important to keep in mind that the persons involved in this process revealed their personal convictions about violence against women. The intensity of their commitment, their understanding of the problem and their visions of the issues and strategies varied, but the fact that so many individuals from varied backgrounds shared such an ardent common interest is in itself extraordinary.

RECOMMENDATIONS

The Canadian Panel on Violence Against Women makes the following recommendations to the federal government specific to the structure and operations of similar bodies.

- The proposed mandate, rules and operating procedures of any commission of inquiry or panel similar to the Canadian Panel on Violence Against Women should be outlined as clearly as possible before such a body is established.

- Future members of such bodies need to be able to contact each other and exchange views on the nature of their duties and mandate before they are officially appointed.

- Mechanisms must be established to enable members to refine their mandate. They must be given the time and opportunity to examine and negotiate a panel's terms and conditions before they take up their duties.

- New mechanisms for consultations between the federal government and women's groups in Canada, based on a vision of social change, need to be established as soon as possible.

- Ways to guarantee better representation of all population groups in Canada, in projects such as this Panel, must be developed.

APPENDIX C

HOUSEHOLDER SURVEY

In the summer of 1992, the Panel co-ordinated a survey of households by means of a questionnaire distributed by members of Parliament throughout their ridings. The questionnaire asked respondents about their experience with abuse, both personally and through people they knew. It also asked whether they felt safe from violence in their own day-to-day lives and requested suggestions for priorities and solutions for all levels of government in working to end violence against women.

The Panel's householder survey was not intended to be used for definitive statistical analysis. Rather, its purpose was to allow more people in Canada to voice their experiences of and concerns about violence against women. Many people took that opportunity: 8,164 completed surveys were received from 46 ridings across Canada, 6,939 from women and 1,225 from men. By providing a forum for people in Canada to express their concerns and by opening communication between members of Parliament and constituents, the Panel's householder survey was another stepping stone on the road to ending violence against women.

Because the survey was filled out on a voluntary basis, by those who were able to obtain it from their Member of Parliament, it is in no way representative of the population of Canada. Nevertheless, it is interesting to look at the general feelings expressed by those answering the survey. Most respondents had experienced verbal harassment, with women much more likely to have been verbally harassed than men.

Further, the vast majority of survey respondents had had a personal experience of physical or sexual abuse. Older respondents were less likely to report an experience of abuse to the survey. Perhaps this reflects the role that public education has played in making younger people aware of violence against women. Almost all of those who had been assaulted in some way felt that reporting the incident to someone had been a positive action. Women's groups, transition houses and shelters were most helpful to victims of abuse. The reasons most often mentioned by victims/survivors for not reporting an incident of abuse were shame and embarrassment, fear of reprisals or of not being believed, and thinking that it was their own fault, often because the abuser had told the victim that she or he was responsible.

The survey shows that respondents feel a very different sense of personal safety at night than during the day. The majority of those surveyed feel relatively safe in their neighbourhood, on the street, in parks, at work, at home, at school and in parking lots during the daytime. At night however, many more people reported feeling unsafe. The places where the greatest threat is perceived are parks, parking lots and on the street. Women consistently felt less safe than men, even during the daytime.

Those responding to the survey felt that the most important responses to violence against women were providing safety and stable support programs for victims/survivors of abuse, safe, affordable housing for women survivors, and education from a young age onwards aimed at preventing violence against women. Survey respondents felt that programs for offenders were less effective in ending violence against women.

Giving the women and men of Canada a place to voice their experiences, frustrations, stories of survival and solutions to violence against women has been an integral part of the Panel's mandate. Getting people talking, at every level, from individuals through to the House of Commons was another important part of the Panel's purpose. Providing a forum for women and men to be heard, giving members of Parliament the opportunity to start discussion in their ridings and demonstrate their commitment to ending violence against women were some of the many things accomplished by the householder survey. Most of the members of Parliament who distributed the survey reported that the response rate was better than average. Clearly, women and men want the opportunity to talk to their representatives about violence against women, in their ridings across Canada and internationally. It is our hope that the householder survey has served as a starting point and will encourage members of Parliament to consult and begin taking action with their constituents to end violence against women. According to survey respondents, ending violence against women should be a vital priority for Canadian governments at all levels. It's up to the members to respond to that call.

HOUSEHOLDER SURVEY

RIDING	MEMBER	SURVEYS RECEIVED
Simcoe Centre, Ontario	Edna Anderson, P.C.	1563
Surrey - White Rock - South Langley, British Columbia	Benno Friesen, P.C.	542
Mississauga West, Ontario	Robert Horner, P.C.	435
London West, Ontario	Tom Hockin, P.C.	434
Témiscamingue, Quebec	Gabriel Desjardins, P.C.	378
Northumberland, Ontario	Christine Stewart, Lib.	377
Kingston and the Islands, Ontario	Peter Milliken, Lib.	377
Ottawa - Vanier, Ontario	Jean-Robert Gauthier, Lib.	359
Capilano - Howe Sound, British Columbia	Mary Collins, P.C.	331
London East, Ontario	Joe Fontana, Lib.	300
Saskatoon-Humboldt, Saskatchewan	Stanley Hovdebo, N.D.P.	291
Saint Laurent - Cartierville, Quebec	Shirley Maheu, Lib.	265
Wild Rose, Alberta	Louise Feltham, P.C.	228
Don Valley North, Ontario	Barbara Greene, P.C.	176
Winnipeg - St. James, Manitoba	John Harvard, Lib.	158
Regina - Wascana, Saskatchewan	Larry Schneider, P.C.	155
St. Boniface, Manitoba	Ronald Duhamel, Lib.	137
Churchill, Manitoba	Rod Murphy, N.D.P.	126
Windsor - Sainte Claire, Ontario	Howard McCurdy, N.D.P.	117
Carleton - Gloucester, Ontario	Eugene Bellemare, Lib.	116

HOUSEHOLDER SURVEY

RIDING	MEMBER	SURVEYS RECEIVED
Saint Hubert, Quebec	Pierette Venne, Independant	115
Cape Breton - Sydneys, Nova Scotia	Russell MacLellan, Lib.	102
Saskatoon - Dundurn, Saskatchewan	Ron Fisher, N.D.P.	94
Athabasca, Alberta	Jack Shields, P.C.	82
Acadie - Bathurst, New Brunswick	Douglas Young, Lib.	81
Wellington - Grey - Dufferin - Simcoe, Ontario	Perrin Beatty, P.C.	79
Prince George - Peace River, British Columbia	Frank Oberle, P.C.	77
Scarborough - Rouge River, Ontario	Derek Lee, Lib.	71
Edmonton - Strathcona, Alberta	Scott Thorkelson, P.C.	71
Mount Royal, Quebec	Sheila Finestone, Lib.	65
Durham, Ontario	Ross Stevenson, P.C.	59
La Prairie, Quebec	Fernand Jourdenais, P.C.	52
Terrebonne, Quebec	Jean-Marc Robitaille, P.C.	52
Prince Edward - Hastings, Ontario	Lyle Vanclief, Lib.	44
Yellowhead, Alberta	Joe Clark, P.C.	38
Victoria - Haliburton, Ontario	William Scott, P.C.	31
Charlevoix, Quebec	Brian Mulroney, P.C.	29
Red Deer, Alberta	Doug Fee, P.C.	23
Sherbrooke, Quebec	Jean Charest, P.C.	21
Beauharnois - Salaberry, Quebec	Jean-Guy Hudon, P.C.	18
Québec - Est, Quebec	Marcel Tremblay, P.C.	11
Anjou - Rivière-des-Prairies, Quebec	Jean Corbeil, P.C.	10
Elk Island, Alberta	Brian O'Kurley, P.C.	7
Beauce, Quebec	Gilles Bernier, P.C.	7
Winnipeg - South Centre, Manitoba	Lloyd Axworthy, Lib.	4
Elgin - Norfolk, Ontario	Ken Monteith, P.C.	1

The Panel gratefully acknowledges the assistance of John Brewin, N.D.P., for the permission to adapt a questionnaire designed by the Victoria Working Group on Violence and distributed by Mr. Brewin to householders in his Victoria riding.

APPENDIX D

CONSULTATION EVENTS

A. PHASE I

The Panel used an interactive and community-based approach to conduct its first round of consultations. There were seven tours: British Columbia/Alberta; Québec; Atlantic; Ontario; Saskatchewan/Manitoba; NWT/Yukon; and, Northern Quebec/Labrador. The Panel set out to visit 100 communities and ultimately held consultations in 139. The Panel met approximately 4000 individuals.

BRITISH COLUMBIA/ALBERTA

January 17, 1992

VANCOUVER, British Columbia
- Shaughnessy Hospital
- Belbrook Community Centre

RICHMOND, British Columbia
- Atira Transition House

BURNABY, British Columbia
- British Columbia Institute of Family Violence

January 18, 1992

VANCOUVER, British Columbia
- Vancouver Aboriginal Friendship Centre
- Justice Institute of British Columbia

BURNABY, British Columbia
- Multicultural Services for Battered Women

CHILLIWACK, British Columbia
- Chilliwack Community Services Centre,
- St. Thomas Anglican Church
- Upper Fraser Valley Transition Society

VICTORIA, British Columbia
- Victoria RCMP Subdivision

January 19, 1992

VANCOUVER, British Columbia
- WAVAW (Woman Against Violence Against Women)

January 20

ALKALI LAKE, British Columbia
- Alkali Lake Reserve

WILLIAMS LAKE, British Columbia
- Women's Shelter

QUESNEL, British Columbia
- Amata Transition House

VANCOUVER, British Columbia
- Crab Tree Corner Support Centre for Single Mums
- YWCA
- Office of Battered Women's Support Services
- Amata House

BURNABY, British Columbia
- Burnaby Correctional Centre for Women

COURTENAY, British Columbia
- Kinhut
- Dountenay Transition Society

KAMLOOPS, British Columbia
- Kamloops Sexual Assault Counselling Centre,
- McArthur Park Community Centre
- Kamloops Immigrant Services Society
- RCMP Detachment Offices
- University College of the Cariboo
- Coast Canadian Inn

January 21

SMITHERS, British Columbia
• Passage Transition House
• Native Friendship Centre

PRINCE GEORGE, British Columbia
• Phoenix Transition House

RICHMOND, British Columbia
• Richmond Women's Resource Centre
  (Gateway Theatre)

VANCOUVER, British Columbia
• Society of Transition Houses for British
  Columbia and the Yukon

ROUND LAKE, British Columbia
• Round Lake Native Treatment Centre

VERNON, British Columbia
• Communities Against Sexual Assault

KELOWNA, British Columbia
• Central Okanogan Elizabeth Fry Society
• Kelowna Family Centre
• Kelowna Women's Shelter

January 22

HIGH PRAIRIE, Alberta
• High Prairie Native Friendship Centre

HINTON, Alberta
• Recreation Centre

CALGARY, Alberta
• International Hotel of Calgary

ST. MARY'S, British Columbia
• St. Mary's Indian Reserve, Band Office

CRANBROOK, British Columbia
• Cranbrook Community Action Centre

January 23

GRANDE PRAIRIE, Alberta
• Northern Addiction Centre

HINTON, Alberta
• Recreation Centre

RED DEER, Alberta
• Central Alberta Women's Emergency
  Shelter
• City R.C.M.P. Detachment
• Rocky Mountain House Community Centre
• Women's Outreach Centre

MEDICINE HAT, Alberta
• Medicine Hat Provincial Building
• Medicine Hat Women's Shelter Society

TABER, B.C.
• Family and Community Social Services
  Building

January 24, 1992

FORT McMURRAY, Alberta
• Provincial Building

CAMROSE, Alberta
• St. Mary's Hospital

ST. PAUL, Alberta
• County Office

GLEICHEN, Alberta
• Gleichen Reserve

MORLEY, Alberta
• Eagle's Nest Shelter on the Morley Reserve

CALGARY, Alberta
• International Hotel of Calgary
• Old Y Centre
• Calgary Women's Emergency Shelter
  Association
• Discovery House

PINCHER CREEK, Alberta
• Labelle Mansion

BROCKETT, Alberta
• Band Council Office, Brockett-Peigan
  Reserve

LETHBRIDGE, Alberta
• Sundance Inn
• YWCA

January 25

SHERWOOD PARK, Alberta
- A. J. Ottewell Centre (The Barn)

EDMONTON, Alberta
- Edmonton Public Library
- Women's Emergency Accommodation Centre

CALGARY, Alberta
- Women's Emergency Accommodation Centre
- Old Y Centre

BLOOD, Alberta
- Standoff-Blood Reserve, Shot Boat Side Building

QUEBEC

February 9, 1992

QUEBEC CITY
- Centre communautaire services diocésains

February 10, 1992

QUEBEC CITY
- Centre Femmes d'aujourd'hui
- C.L.S.C. Basseville
- La table du roi
- Centre communautaire services diocésains

LA TUQUE
- C.L.S.C. Haut St. Maurice

STE-FOY
- Université Laval, Pavillon Jean Durand (C.E.Q.)

STE-FLAVIE (MONT JOLI), QUEBEC
- Motel La Gaspésiana

BAIE COMEAU
- C.L.S.C. D'Aquillon

February 11, 1992

SEPT-ILES
- C.L.S.C. de Sept-Iles

MISTASSINI
- Band Council Office, Mistassini Lake

CHISASIBI
- Women's Shelter

LEBEL-SUR-QUÉVILLON
- Lebel Health Centre/Centre de Santé Lebel

VAL D'OR
- Le Mi-Nordet C.L.S.C.

February 12, 1992

JONQUIÈRE
- Hôtel Roussillon

ROBERVAL
- Château Roberval

POVUNGNITUK
- Povungnituk Hospital

VILLE-MARIE
- Ville-Marie Women's Centre

February 13, 1992

ROUYN-NORANDA
- Hôtel-Motel Rouyn-Noranda

MONTREAL
- Centre St-Pierre
- YWCA
- Les ateliers d'éducation populaire de Mercier
- Centre Préfontaine
- Passages
- Simone de Beauvoir Institute
- Centre interculturel Strathearn

LAVAL
- CHOC Laval

February 14, 1992

MONTREAL
- Hôtel Delta
- Tribunal de la jeunesse
- Centre St-Pierre
- Maison Tanguay, Correctional Centre for Women
- Elizabeth Fry Society
- Catholic Community Services
- YWCA West-Island (Pointe-Claire)

SHERBROOKE
- L'Escale de L'Estrie (Sherbrooke)

February 15, 1992

HULL
- C.L.S.C de Hull

Atlantic Region

March 1, 1992

ST. JOHN'S, Newfoundland
- Radisson Hotel

March 2, 1992

ST. JOHN'S, Newfoundland
- Patrick House
- Department of Mines and Energy, Confederation Building
- Hotel Newfoundland
- Iris Kirby House

STEPHENVILLE, Newfoundland
- St. Georges Women's Centre

GANDER, Newfoundland
- Sinbad's Hotel

NAIN, Labrador
- Labrador Inuit Association
- Town Hall

SAINT JOHN, New Brunswick
- Saint John Hilton
- Hestia House

March 3, 1992

NAIN, Labrador
- Grenfell Nursing Station
- Nain Group Home

GOOSE BAY, Labrador
- Aurora Hotel
- Libra House

BATHURST, New Brunswick
- Atlantique Host

BIG COVE, New Brunswick
- Big Cove Reserve, Child and Family Services

BURNT CHURCH, New Brunswick
- Burnt Church Reserve, Burnt Church Band Council Office

NEWCASTLE, New Brunswick
- Town Hall

FREDERICTON, New Brunswick
- University of New Brunswick Campus, Ludlow Hall

March 4, 1992

MONCTON, New Brunswick
- Conseil consultatif sur la condition de la femme du Nouveau-Brunswick
- Hôtel Beauséjour Restaurant

HALIFAX, Nova Scotia
- Bryony House

FREDERICTON, New Brunswick
- University of New Brunswick Campus
- Sheraton Hotel

March 5, 1992

TRURO, Nova Scotia
- Cox Institute, Nova Scotia Agricultural College

SUMMERSIDE, Prince Edward Island
- East Prince Women's Information Centre

O'LEARY, Prince Edward Island
- Regional Services Centre, Evangeline School

NEW GLASGOW, Nova Scotia
- Trinity United Church

ANTIGONISH, Nova Scotia
- Saint Francis Xavier University

CHARLOTTETOWN, Prince Edward Island
- Rape Crisis Centre
- Charlottetown Hotel
- Richmond Hotel
- McMillan Building
- Anderson House

March 6, 1992

KENTVILLE, Nova Scotia
- Kentville Recreation Centre

BRIDGEWATER, Nova Scotia
- South Shore Regional Hospital
- Capt. Wm. Spry Community Centre

HALIFAX, Nova Scotia
- Service for Sexual Assault Victims
- Adsum House
- Veith House
- North End Library

SYDNEY, Nova Scotia
- Every Woman's Women's Centre

ONTARIO

March 22, 1992

TORONTO, Ontario
- St. Lawrence Town Hall

March 23, 1992

TORONTO, Ontario
- St. Lawrence Town Hall

WINDSOR, Ontario
- Windsor Public Library
- Sexual Assault Crisis Centre

CHATHAM, Ontario
- Family Services Kent

TIMMINS, Ontario
- Venture Inn
- Hotel Senator

NORTH BAY, Ontario
- Empire Hotel Boardroom

March 24, 1992

TORONTO, Ontario
- St. Lawrence Town Hall

GODERICH, Ontario
- Survival Through Friendship House (shelter)
- Phoenix of Huron
- Huron County Museum
- Saugeen First Nations Reserve

NORTH BAY, Ontario
- Empire Hotel

SUDBURY, Ontario
- Northbury Hotel

March 25, 1992

BARRIE, Ontario
* Barrie City Hall

GUELPH, Ontario
* Steelworkers Hall

LONDON, Ontario
* Sexual Assault Centre, Shelby Building

OWEN SOUND, Ontario
* Second Stage Housing
* Children's Aid Society

COLLINGWOOD, Ontario
* Town Hall

ORANGEVILLE, Ontario
* Orangeville and District Senior Centre

THUNDER BAY, Ontario
* Airlane Hotel

SIOUX LOOKOUT, Ontario
* Nishnawbe-Gamik Friendship Centre

March 26, 1992

LONDON, Ontario
* Intercommunity Health Centre
* Glen Cairn Public School
* Somerville House, University of Western Ontario
* Atenlos Family Violence Centre
* Battered Women's Advocacy Centre

PETERBOROUGH, Ontario
* Women's Health Care Centre

CAMPBELLFORD, Ontario
* Warkworth Penitentiary

KINGSTON, Ontario
* Community House For Self-Reliance

OTTAWA, Ontario
* Holiday Inn
* St. John The Evangelist Anglican Church
* Public Service Alliance Building

BIG TROUT LAKE, Ontario
* Infirmerie

March 27, 1992

KINGSTON, Ontario
* Prison for Women (P4W)
* Kings Community House for Self-Reliance

WOODSTOCK, Ontario
* Ingamo Family Homes

HAMILTON, Ontario
* YWCA

OTTAWA, Ontario
* Holiday Inn
* St. John The Evangelist Anglican Church

THUNDER BAY, Ontario
* Airlane Hotel

S A S K A T C H E W A N   /   M A N I T O B A

April 7, 1992

SASKATOON, Saskatchewan
* Family Support Centre
* Saskatoon Centennial Auditorium

April 8, 1992

THE PAS, Manitoba
* Town Hall

WINNIPEG, Manitoba
* Manitoba Advisory Council on the Status of Women
* Women's Employment Counselling Service
* Women's Health Clinic
* Pluri-elles
* Manitoba Federation of Labour, Union Centre
* Family Law Section of the Manitoba Bar

PRINCE ALBERT, Saskatchewan
* Marlboro Inn

SASKATOON, Saskatchewan
- National Native Alcohol & Drug Abuse Program
- Saskatoon Indian & Metis Friendship Centre
- Family Support Centre
- Saskatoon Interval House
- Centennial Auditorium

April 9, 1992

THOMPSON, Manitoba
- YM/YWCA
- Mystery Lake Hotel

DAUPHIN, Manitoba
- Dr. Vern L. Watson Art Centre
- Parkland Crisis Centre

BRANDON, Manitoba
- Royal Oak Inn, Kensington Room

LA RONGE, Saskatchewan
- La Ronge Motor Inn/Hotel

SASKATOON, Saskatchewan
- Centennial Auditorium
- Immigrant Women of Saskatchewan and Immigrant Women of Saskatoon
- Saskatoon Mental Health Clinic

April 10, 1992

CROSS LAKE, Manitoba
- Town Hall

BRANDON, Manitoba
- Royal Oak Inn, Kensington Room
- YWCA Westman Women's Shelter

MORDEN, Manitoba
- Royal Canadian Legion Hall

MELFORD, Saskatchewan
- Heritage Inn
- The North East Crisis Intervention Centre

SANDY LAKE, Saskatchewan
- Sandy Lake Indian Reserve, Sandy Lake Hall

NORTH BATTLEFORD, Saskatchewan
- North Battleford Friendship Centre
- Battleford Indian Health Centre
- Battleford and Area Sexual Assault Centre
- Battleford Interval House

April 11, 1992

CHURCHILL, Manitoba
- Community Centre

SELKIRK, Manitoba
- Women's Centre
- Friendship Centre

FORT ALEXANDER, Manitoba
- Fort Alexander Reserve, Multipurpose Building

LAC DU BONNET, Saskatchewan
- Library Community Hall

MEADOW LAKE, Saskatchewan
- Northwestern Motel

MOOSE JAW, Saskatchewan
- Moose Jaw Transition House

SWIFT CURRENT, Saskatchewan
- Southwest Safe Shelter

April 12, 1992

PORTAGE LA PRAIRIE, Manitoba
- Herman Prior Seniors' Centre

LUNDAR, Manitoba
- Lutheran Church Hall

PRINCE ALBERT, Saskatchewan
- Pinegrove Correctional Center

YORKTON, Saskatchewan
- Yorkton Friendship Centre
- Holiday Inn
- Yorkton Mental Health Centre, Yorkton Union Hospital

April 13, 1992

WINNIPEG, Manitoba
- Manitoba Advisory Council on the Status of Women
- A private home
- Osborne House
- Women's Post Treatment Centre
- Children's Home of Winnipeg
- POWER (Prostitutes and other Women for Equal Rights)
- Holiday Inn Crowne Plaza

REGINA Saskatchewan
- Circle Project
- Regina Transition Women's Society
- Senior's Education Center, University of Regina: Old College Campus
- Social Services, Family Services Bureau

FORT QU'APPELLE, Saskatchewan
- Squire Hotel

April 14, 1992

WINNIPEG, Manitoba
- Holiday Inn Crowne Plaza Winnipeg

NORTHWEST TERRITORIES/ YUKON

April 28, 1992

YELLOWKNIFE, Northwest Territories
- Northern United Place

April 29, 1992

YELLOWKNIFE, Northwest Territories
- Northern United Place
- Yellowknife Inn
- Tree of Peace Friendship Centre
- N'Dilo Community Hall

INUVIK, Northwest Territories
- Family Hall

FORT RAE, Northwest Territories
- Fort Rae-Edzo Friendship Centre
- Edzo Community Hall

WHITEHORSE, Yukon
- Whitehorse Correctional Centre
- Victoria Faulkner Women's Centre
- Yukon Inn
- Law Court Building

April 30, 1992

RANKIN INLET, Northwest Territories
- Siniktarvik Hotel

YELLOWKNIFE, Northwest Territories
- Explorer Hotel

INUVIK, Northwest Territories
- Family Hall
- Elementary and High School

FORT SMITH, Northwest Territories
- Pelican Rapids Inn
- Town Council Chambers
- McDougall Community Centre

TESLIN, Yukon
- Old Community Centre Building

WATSON LAKE, Yukon
- Help & Hope Shelter

DAWSON CITY, Yukon
- Dawson City Museum
- Band Office

May 1, 1992

IQALUIT, Northwest Territories
- Frobisher Inn
- Visitors Centre, New Library Building

FORT SMITH, Northwest Territories
- Pelican Rapids Inn

HAY RIVER, Northwest Territories
- Diamond Jenness High School
- Adult Education Centre
- Soaring Eagle Friendship Centre

WATSON LAKE, Yukon
- Help & Hope Shelter

OLD CROW, Yukon
- Yukon College

DAWSON CITY, Yukon
- Dawson City Museum

May 2, 1992

IQALUIT, Northwest Territories
- Nutaraq Place (Shelter)
- Frobisher Inn, Husky Lounge
- Anglican Parish Hall

CAMBRIDGE BAY, Northwest Territories
- Inn's North

HAY RIVER, Northwest Territories
- Ptarmigan Inn
- H.R. Dene Band Reserve, Sharing Lodge

OLD CROW, Yukon
- Yukon College

LABRADOR / NORTHERN QUEBEC

May 28, 1992

NAIN, Labrador
- Grenfell Nursing Station
- Martin Group Home
- Community Hall
- Nain Nursing Station
- Paivitsiak (Nain Day Care)

May 29, 1992

POVUNGNITUK, QUEBEC
- Invulitsivik Hospital Conference Room

May 30, 1992

POVUNGNITUK, QUEBEC
- Nain School Gymnasium

May 31, 1992

POVUNGNITUK, QUEBEC
- Invulitsivik Hospital

June 1, 1992

INUKJUAK, QUEBEC
- Mayor's Office

June 2, 1992

KUIJJUARAPIK, QUÉBEC
- Private home

B. PHASE II

1. PANEL MEETING WITH NATIONAL WOMEN'S GROUPS
Ottawa, Ontario
May 25, 1992

Following the completion of a national round of consultations, some Panel members met with national women's groups to further identify a range of solutions that would be effective in eradicating violence. The purpose of the meeting was to seek further input from national organizations in order to ensure that the expertise and analysis these groups developed over the past several decades were given full recognition.

DAWN Canada Richmond, B.C.	NAWL Ottawa, Ontario
CASAC Ottawa, Ontario Vancouver, B.C.	NOIVMWC Ottawa, Ontario
FNFCF Ottawa, Ontario	LEAF Ottawa, Ontario
NAC Toronto, Ontario	YWCA Toronto, Ontario

2. JOINT MEETING OF PANEL, ADVISORY COMMITEE AND WOMEN'S GROUPS
Ottawa, Ontario
September 19-20, 1992

A document summarizing issues to be included in the Final Report and the National Action Plan was discussed.

- Association féminine d'éducation et d'action sociale

- Cercle des fermières du Québec

- Fédération des femmes du Québec (FFQ)

- Fédération des ressources d'hébergement

- Fédération nationale des femmes canadiennes-françaises (FNFCF)

- Native Women's Association of Canada (NWAC)

- Nova Scotia Association of Women's Centre (CONNECT)

- Pauktuutit Inuit Women's Association

- Provincial Association of Transition Houses of Saskatchewan (PATHS)

- Regroupement des maisons d'hébergement

- YWCA

3. ALBERTA/NWT NETWORK OF IMMIGRANT WOMEN
Edmonton, Alberta
September 26, 1992

Panel member, Mobina Jaffer, was invited to address the group. She spoke about the Panel's work, its Final Report and the National Action Plan.

4. ROUNDTABLE ON HEALTH IN THE ABORIGINAL COMMUNITY
Ottawa, Ontario
October 5, 1992

Participants representing Aboriginal health organizations were given the opportunity to discuss the Aboriginal Foundation Document. Through small group discussions, they identified gaps, tested solutions and recommendations and accumulated further research on violence related issues.

5. NATIVE WOMEN'S ASSOCIATION OF CANADA ANNUAL MEETING
Ottawa, Ontario
October 16-18, 1992

The Aboriginal Circle was given time on the agenda to present its Foundation Document for comment and input.

6. ROUNDTABLE WITH ELDERS OF THE ABORIGINAL COMMUNITY
Kahnawake, Quebec
October 20-21, 1992

The purpose of the roundtable was to develop a national network of elders to focus on issues of healing the individual, the family and the community. The Foundation Document was used to identify gaps and test solutions and recommendations.

Theresa Augustine
Big Cove,
New Brunswick

Shirley Bear
Perth-Andover,
New Brunswick

Ernie Benedict
Cornwall,
Ontario

Johnson Blacksmith
Cross Lake,
Manitoba

Winnie Cockney
Inuvik,
NWT

Elizabeth Colin
Fort McPherson,
Yukon

William Commanda
Maniwaki,
Quebec

Diane Kay*
Inuvik,
NWT

Peal Keenan
Whitehorse,
Yukon

Ernie Knockwood
Cape Breton,
Nova Scotia

Harold Laporte
Fredericton,
New Brunswick

Ed Louie
Keremeos,
British Columbia

Mary Louie
Keremeos,
British Columbia

Liza Mosher
Sudbury,
Ontario

Lena Nottaway
Rapid Lake,
Quebec

Peter O'Chiese
Whitehorse,
Yukon

Maggie Paul
Fredericton,
New Brunswick

Alan Paupanekis*
Cross Lake,
Manitoba

Marie Ross
Ottawa,
Ontario

Herman Saulis
Fredericton,
New Brunswick

Geraldine Stand-up
Kahnawake,
Quebec

Flora Tabagon
Parry Sound,
Ontario

Leslie Tabagon*
Toronto,
Ontario

Gordon Wasteste
Regina,
Saskatchewan

Vicki Wilson
Prince Albert,
Sask.

Attendant

7. WOMEN WITH DISABILITIES THINKTANK
Ottawa, Ontario
October 28, 1992

The purpose of the thinktank was to discuss violence issues relative to women with disabilities. A document summarizing relevant issues was reviewed. Comments were recorded and used in the development of the Final Report and the National Action Plan. Representatives of the following organizations and a number of individual experts attended.

- Canadian Association of Independent Living Centre

- CHANNAL

- CHEZ DORIS

- Council of the Disabled

- Deaf Children Society

- NWT Council for the Disabled

- Saskatchewan Voice of the Handicapped

8. MÉTIS WOMEN CONFERENCE EDMONTON, ALBERTA
November 27-29, 1992

Aboriginal Circle member, Winnifred Giesbrecht, addressed the participants of the Métis Women's Conference. The Aboriginal Foundation Document was presented. Feedback received was used in the development of the Final Report and the National Action Plan.

9. CHURCHES ROUNDTABLE
Ottawa, Ontario
December 1, 1992

The Aboriginal Circle, Panel members and church representatives met to discuss the issue of residential schools and the role of churches in the aboriginal community. Feedback and input was provided for use in the development of the National Action Plan.

- Aboriginal Rights Coalition (ARC)
- Anglican Church of Canada
- CCCB - Catholic Bishops
- Church Council on Justice and Corrections
- Presbyterian Church of Canada
- United Church of Canada

10. YOUTH ROUNDTABLE
Toronto, Ontario
January 9, 1993

A document highlighting relevant issues on young women, date rape and education was discussed. Feedback and input was provided for use in the development of the National Action Plan. Representatives from the following organizations and independent youths participated.

- Toronto Board of Education
  Toronto
- Canadian Teachers' Federation
  Ottawa

- Covenant House
  Toronto, Ontario
- Girl Guides of Canada
  Markham, Ontario
- YWCA
  Toronto, Ontario

11. YOUTH ROUNDTABLE
Ottawa, Ontario
January 15, 1993

A document highlighting relevant issues on Young women, date rape and education was discussed. Feedback and input was provided for use in the development of the National Action Plan. Individuals and representatives from the following organizations participated.

- Aboriginal Youth Council of Canada
  Ottawa, Ontario
- Big Sisters Association
  Ottawa, Ontario
- Canadian Advisory Council on the Status of Women (CACSW)
  Edmonton, Alberta
- Canadian Advisory Council on the Status of Women (CACSW)
  Ottawa, Ontario
- Canadian Ethnocultural Council
  Ottawa, Ontario
- Canadian Youth Foundation
  Longueuil, Quebec
- Direction Jeunesse
  Ottawa, Ontario
- Environmental Youth Alliance
  Ottawa, Ontario
- Federation of Women's Teachers' Association of Ontario and Canadian Teachers' Federation
  Mississauga, Ontario

- Girl Guides of Canada
  Kanata, Ontario

- Girl Guides of Canada
  Nepean, Ontario

- Girl Guides of Canada
  Pointe-Claire, Québec

- Glebe Women's Issues Group
  Ottawa, Ontario

- Guides Francophones du Canada
  Montreal, Quebec

- Inuit Tapirisat of Canada
  Ottawa, Ontario

- Leaders/YWCA
  Ottawa, Ontario

- National Round Table on the Environment
  and Economy
  Ottawa, Ontario

- Organisation des femmes dans l'Association
  nationale des étudiants et étudiantes du
  Québec
  Montreal, Quebec

- Ottawa University
  Ottawa, Ontario

- Status of Women Office
  Carleton University
  Ottawa, Ontario

- St. Patrick's High School
  Ottawa, Ontario

- Student Action for Viable Earth (S.A.V.E.)
  Tour
  Ottawa, Ontario

- Women's Centre
  Carleton University
  Ottawa, Ontario

- Youth NWT
  Calgary, Alberta

- Youth representatives for the Native
  Women's Association of Canada (NWAC)
  Edmonton, Alberta

12. **PAUKTUUTIT ANNUAL GENERAL MEETING AND INUIT TAPIRISAT OF CANADA — HEALTH, HOUSING AND JUSTICE ROUNDTABLE**
Happy Valley, Goosebay, Labrador
February 23-28, 1993

Aboriginal Circle member, Martha Flaherty, addressed the delegates and spoke of the development of the Inuit content of the Final Report and the Panel's goals. Through informal consultation, the delegates provided input and feedback on The Community Kit.

APPENDIX E

A. SUBMISSIONS

The Panel received 105 written submissions by mail from various organizations. Included were discussion papers/reports on the causes of violence against women, descriptions or critiques of community programs, and policy recommendations for the Panel's consideration. The Panel also received correspondence from 118 individuals. For confidentiality and safety reasons, this list cannot be published.

Action Group Against Harassment and Discrimination in the Workplace

Alberta Council of Womens Shelters

Association des enseignantes et des enseignants francophones du Nouveau-Brunswick

Barrie & District Rape Crisis Line

Battered Women's Support Services

Birdsong Communications Ltd.

Bridges Employment Training Project

British Columbia Women's Institute

Canadian Advisory Council on the Status of Women

Canadian Association for the Advancement of Women and Sport and Physical Activity (CAAWS)

Canadian Association of Women Executives and Entrepreneurs

Canadian Federation of University Women, B.C. Council

Canadian Federation of University Women, Saskatoon Club

Canadian Medical Association

Canadian Nurses Association

Canadian Organisation for the Rights of Prostitutes (C.O.R.P.)

Chivers Greckol and Kanee Barristers and Solicitors, Department of Public Health City of Toronto

City Police, City of London

Coalition Against Sexual Abuse of Children

Committee Against Pornography

Hollow Water First Nations Community Holistic Healing Circle

Concerned Nurses for Patients Rights - Informed Consent - Ethics (P.R.I.C.E.)

Corporation of the City of North Vancouver

Corrections Research and Policy Development Branch, Ministry of the Solicitor General of Canada

Crabtree Corner YWCA

Crime Prevention Society, Nova Scotia Department of Solicitor General

Davidson Enterprises Inc.

Department of Psychiatry St. Boniface Hospital

Dundurn Community Legal Services

Family Service Association of Metropolitan Toronto

Family Services of Greater Vancouver,

Family Support Co-ordinator, Simcoe County Regional Council of the Ontario Association for Community Living

Burnt Church Family Violence Project

Family Violence Subcommittee, North York Inter-Agency and Community Council

Fédération des femmes du Québec

Federation of Medical Women of Canada

Federation of Women Teachers' Association of Ontario

Golden Women's Resource Centre

Grande Cache Transition House Society

Grey Bruce Family Violence Prevention Committee

Group Against Pornography (GAP), Manitoba

Hey - way' - noqu', Healing Circle for Addictions Society

Immigrant and Visible Minority Women Against Abuse

Ingamo Family Homes Inc.

Ingamo Pre-Employment Training Program

Jewish Family & Child Service

Joint Committee RE Sexual Abuse of Patients by Physicians

Justice Electronics

Le conseil du civisme de Montréal

L'Intersyndicale des femmes

London Caucus of the Men's Network for Change

London Coordinating Committee to End Woman Abuse

MA MAWI WI CHI I'I'ATA Centre

Manitoba Advisory Council on the Status of Women

Manitoba Council on Aging

Manitoba Teachers' Society, McMaster House

Mediawatch - National Watch on Images of Women in the Media Inc.

MicMac Family & Children's Services of Nova Scotia

NA'AMAT Inc.

National Association of Canadians of Origins in India

Nechi Institute

New Brunswick Advisory Council on the Status of Women

North Shore Community Services

Ontario Association of Interval & Transition Houses

Open Living Unit, Burnaby Correction Centre for Women

Patricia Centre for Children and Youths

Popular Theatre Alliance of Manitoba

Prince Edward Island Advisory Council on the Status of Women

Project Safe Run Foundation, Property Underwriter, Special Lines Division

Race Relations & Multiculturalism, Toronto Board of Education

Regroupement des CLSC du Montréal Métropolitain

Research and Communications Associate Committee for Contact with the Government, Council of Christian Reformed Churches in Canada

Saskatchewan Justice - Pine Grove Correctional
    Centre

S.A.V.E.

Shelter & Outreach - YWCA, Peterborough,
    Victoria & Halburton

Sistering

Southwest Safe Shelter

Status of Women Council of NWT

Sûreté du Québec

Surrey Women for Action

The Association of Junior Leagues, Inc.

The Children's Aid Society, Treatment Group
    for Men

The Concept Group

The Council on Aging Ottawa-Carleton

University of Windsor

Urgence-Femmes

Vancouver Rape Relief & Women's Shelter

Vancouver Young Women's Christian
    Association

West Area Family Counselling, Social Services

Western Manitoba Coalition for Equality Rights
    in the Canadian Constitution

White Ribbon Foundation

Woman Source Consultants

Women's Employment Counselling Service of
    Winnipeg Inc.

Women's Health Office - McMaster University

Women's Issues Group of the University
    Women's Club of North York

Women's Policy Office, Government of
    Newfoundland & Labrador

Woodlawn Medical Consultants

Working Against Violence Everywhere

Yorkdale Secondary School and Adult Learning
    Centre

Yukon Association for Community Living

B. CONSULTATION SUBMISSIONS

Many written submissions were received in support of testimony heard by the Panel during consultation events. The following 245 submissions were received from organizations. We also received 164 submissions from individuals, however, for confidentiality and safety reasons, this list cannot be published.

BRITISH COLUMBIA/ALBERTA (TOUR 1)

British Columbia

ALBERTA FAMILY AND SOCIAL SERVICES
Taber Child Abuse Committee
Taber

ATIRA TRANSITION HOUSE
Richmond

BRITISH COLUMBIA NURSES UNION
Vancouver

CONGRESS OF BLACK WOMEN OF CANADA
Vancouver Chapter
Vancouver

CRABTREE CORNER, YWCA
Vancouver

CRANBROOK WOMEN'S CENTRE
Cranbrook

DISTRICT OF NORTH VANCOUVEr
Vancouver

FAMILY SCHOOL LIAISON
Taber

IMMIGRANT AND VISIBLE MINORITY WOMEN OF B.C.
Kelowna

JUSTICE INSTITUTE FOR BRITISH COLUMBIA
THE UNIT AGAINST PORNOGRAPHY
Vancouver

KAMLOOPS WOMEN'S RESOURCE GROUP SOCIETY
Kamloops

KELOWNA FAMILY CENTRE
Kelowna

KELOWNA WOMEN'S RESOURCE CENTRE
Kelowna

KOOTENAY EAST YOUTH PROGRAM
Cranbrook

KTUNAXA/KINBASKET TRIBAL COUNCIL
St. Mary's Reserve

NORTH SHORE WOMEN'S CENTRE
Vancouver

NORTHERN COUNSELLING AND CONSULTING SERVICES
Smithers

PRINCE GEORGE AND DISTRICT ELIZABETH FRY SOCIETY
Prince George

SIMON FRASER UNIVERSITY
Vancouver

TABER DISTRICT OFFICE FAMILY AND SOCIAL SERVICES
Taber

THOMPSON VALLEY FAMILY SERVICES ASSOCIATION
Kamloops

UNIVERSITY OF B.C.
Campus Safety for Women
Vancouver

VI LUCAN - ALDERMAN (DISTRICT OF ELKFORD)
Cranbrook

WOMEN'S COMMITTEE, S.U.C.C.E.S.S.
Vancouver

WOMEN'S EMERGENCY SHELTER
Kamloops

Alberta

SETTLER SCHOOL DISTRICT
Camrose

SUPERINTENDENT OF SCHOOLS
Camrose

WOMEN'S EMERGENCY ACCOMMODATION
CENTRE
Edmonton

QUEBEC
(TOUR 2)

A.Q.D.R.
Jonquière

ASSISTANCE AUX FEMMES DE MONTRÉAL
Montreal

ASSOCIATION DES RESSOURCES INTERVENANT
AUPRES DES HOMMES VIOLENTS (ARIHV)
Montreal

ASSOCIATION DE MONTRÉAL POUR LA
DÉFICIENCE INTELLECTUELLE
Montreal

BUSINESS AND PROFESSIONAL WOMEN'S CLUB
OF MONTRÉAL
Montreal

C.A.V.A.C. - CENTRE D'AIDE AUX VICTIMES
D'ACTES CRIMINELS
Jonquière

CONSEIL CONSULTATIF CANADIEN SUR LE STATUT
DE LA FEMME
Quebec

CENTRE DE FEMMES LA SOURCE INC.
Roberval

CLSC DE LA JONQUIÈRE
Jonquière

ÉCOLE DE PSYCHOLOGIE, UNIVERSITÉ LAVAL
Quebec

LE REGROUPEMENT PROVINCIAL DES MAISONS
D'HEBERGEMENT ET DE TRANSITION POUR FEMMES
VICTIMES DE VIOLENCE CONJUGALE
Montreal

LES CERCLES DE FERMIÈRES DU QUÉBEC
Quebec

RÉCIF - 02
Roberval

SECOURS AUX FEMMES
Montreal

UNIVERSITÉ CONCORDIA - WOMEN'S CENTRE
Montreal

VICTIMES DE POLYTECHNIQUE
Montreal

ATLANTIC REGION
(TOUR 3)

New Brunswick

BIG COVE FIRST NATION
Big Cove

FACULTY OF LAW, UNIVERSITY OF NEW
BRUNSWICK AD HOC COMMITTEE ON GENDER
RELATED POLICY
Fredericton

FAMILY VIOLENCE TREATMENT NETWORK
Fredericton, New Brunswick

FREDERICTON RAPE CRISIS CENTRE
Fredericton

LA COALITION
Bathurst

MURIEL MCQUEEN FERGUSSON FOUNDATION
Fredericton

NEW BRUNSWICK ADVISORY COUNCIL ON THE
STATUS OF WOMEN
Moncton

NEW BRUNSWICK NURSES UNION
Fredericton

SAINT JOHN POLICE FORCE
FAMILY PROTECTION UNIT
Saint John

WOMEN IN TRANSITION HOUSE INC.
Fredericton

WOMEN WORKING WITH IMMIGRANT WOMEN
Fredericton

Nova Scotia

ACADIA UNIVERSITY
Kentville

AD SUM HOUSE
Halifax

ANTIGONISH WOMEN'S RESOURCE
Antigonish

BYRONY HOUSE
Halifax

DALHOUSIE LEGAL SERVICES
Halifax

ELIZABETH FRY SOCIETY, CAPE BRETON
Sydney

FAMILY SERVICES ASSOCIATION
Halifax

GUYSBOROUGH LEARNING OPPORTUNITIES FOR
WOMEN
New Glasgow/ Antigonish

HEATHER HENDERSON
(REGIONAL REPRESENTATIVE AND STAFF NURSE
AT THE GRACE HOSPITAL)
Halifax

HORIZON HOUSE
Kentville

INSTITUTE FOR THE STUDY OF WOMEN
MOUNT SAINT VINCENT UNIVERSITY
Halifax

KENTVILLE POLICE SERVICE
Kentville

L'ASSOCIATION DES ACADIENNES DE LA
NOUVELLE-ÉCOSSE
Halifax

NAOMI SOCIETY FOR VICTIMS OF
FAMILY VIOLENCE
Antigonish

NOVA SCOTIA ADVISORY COUNCIL ON THE
STATUS OF WOMEN
Halifax

PRESIDENT'S ADVISORY COMMITTEE ON SEXUAL
HARASSMENT
Kentville

PROJECT NEW START
Halifax

PUBLIC SERVICE ALLIANCE OF CAPE BRETON
REGIONAL WOMEN'S COMMITTEE
Sydney

SECOND STORY WOMEN'S CENTRE
Bridgewater

SINGLE PARENT CENTRE
Halifax

SOUTH SHORE SURVIVORS OF CHILD
SEXUAL ABUSE
Bridgewater

SOUTH WEST NOVA TRANSITION HOUSE
ASSOCIATION, JUNIPER HOUSE
Bridgewater

TEARMANN SOCIETY FOR BATTERED WOMEN
New Glasgow

THE FAMILY VIOLENCE COMMITTEE OF
COMMUNITY AGENCIES
New Glasgow

THE HALIFAX TRANSITION HOUSE ASSOCIATION
FOR ABUSED WOMEN AND THEIR CHILDREN
Halifax

THE RED DOOR
Kentville

TRANSITION HOUSE ASSOCIATION OF
NOVA SCOTIA
Halifax

TRANSITION HOUSE ASSOCIATION OF
NOVA SCOTIA
New Glasgow

TRINITY UNITED CHURCH
New Glasgow

WOMEN'S INSTITUTES OF NOVA SCOTIA
Truro

Newfoundland

BAY ST. GEORGE WOMEN'S COUNCIL
(COMMITTEE ON ISSUES OF VIOLENCE)
Stephenville

CENTRAL NEWFOUNDLAND REGIONAL
COMMITTEE ON FAMILY VIOLENCE
St.John's

COALITION OF CITIZENS AGAINST PORNOGRAPHY
St. John's

INTERAGENCY COMMITTEE ON VIOLENCE
AGAINST WOMEN AND PROVINCIAL ASSOCIATION
AGAINST FAMILY VIOLENCE
St.John's

IRIS KIRBY HOUSE
St. John's

RCMP
Stephenville

MENTAL HEALTH SERVICES
Gander

WOMEN'S POLICY OFFICE
St.John's

Prince Edward Island

LENNOX ISLAND MICMAC RESERVE
O'Leary

THE EDITOR
O'Leary

ONTARIO
(TOUR 4)

ANNEX WOMEN'S ACTION COMMITTEE
Toronto

APPLE HOUSE
Oshawa

ASSOCIATION FÉMININE D'ÉDUCATION ET
D'ACTION SOCIALE
Ottawa

ATENLOS FAMILY VIOLENCE CENTRE
London

B'NAI BRITH WOMEN OF CANADA
Toronto

CANADIAN ASSOCIATION FOR THE ADVANCEMENT
OF WOMEN IN SPORT AND PHYSICAL ACTIVITY
Ottawa

CANADIAN RESEARCH INSTITUTE FOR THE
ADVANCEMENT OF WOMEN
Ottawa

CANADIAN ABORTION RIGHTS ACTION LEAGUE
(CARAL)
Ottawa

CASANDRA (COALITION AGAINST SEXIST AND
RACIST ADVERTISING)
Toronto

CATHOLIC FAMILY SERVICES
Downsview

DENISE HOUSE
Oshawa

DEPARTMENT OF SOCIAL SERVICES
REGION OF DURHAM
Toronto

DEVELOPMENT INITIATIVES INC.
    Guelph

DUNDURN COMMUNITY LEGAL SERVICES
    Hamilton

ELGIN COUNTY DELEGATION FORUM
    London

FAMILY TRANSITION PLACE
    Orangeville

FAMILY SERVICES CENTRE
    Ottawa

FAMILY VIOLENCE MANAGEMENT SERVICE
OF CATULPA TAMARAC CHILD & FAMILY
SERVICE AGENCY
    Simcoe County

FÉDÉRATION DES FEMMES CANADIENNES -
FRANÇAISES
    Ottawa

FRESH START MEN'S GOUP - HIATUS HOUSE
    Windsor\Chatham, Ontario

GLOUCESTER POLICE SERVICE
    Ottawa

HELEN KELLY COMMUNITY HEALTH UNIT
    Orangeville

HIGH SCHOOL STUDENTS
THE ONTARIO SECONDARY SCHOOL STUDENTS'
ASSOCIATION'S PROJECT B.A.S.E.
    Orangeville

IMMIGRANT WOMEN AND REFUGEE WOMEN
    Toronto

IMMIGRANT WOMEN AND WOMEN OF COLOR
    Toronto

LABOUR COUNCIL OF METROPOLITAN TORONTO
& YORK REGION
    Toronto

L'ACCUEIL FRANCOPHONE DE THUNDER BAY
    Thunder Bay

MATCH INTERNATIONAL CENTRE
    Ottawa

METRAC (METRO ACTION COMMITTEE ON
PUBLIC VIOLENCE AGAINST WOMEN
AND CHILDREN)
    Toronto

MOTHERS ON TRIAL
    Toronto

MY SISTER'S PLACE TRANSITION HOUSE
    Alliston

MY FRIEND'S HOUSE
    Collingwood

NATIONAL COUNCIL OF WOMEN
    Ottawa

NATIVE WOMEN'S ASSOCIATION OF CANADA
    Ottawa

NORTH YORK WOMEN'S CENTRE
    Toronto

OJIBWAY FAMILY RESOURCE CENTRE
    North Bay

OTTAWA RAPE CRISIS CENTRE
    Ottawa

OTTAWA REGIONAL WOMEN'S COMMITTEE
PUBLIC SERVICE ALLIANCE OF CANADA
    Ottawa

OTTAWA MULTICULTURAL HOMEMAKERS
ASSOCIATION
    Ottawa

PAUKTUUTIT (INUIT WOMEN'S ASSOCIATION
OF CANADA)
    Ottawa

PERTH COUNTY SHELTER
    Perth

RESOURCES AGAINST PORNOGRAPHY
    Toronto

RIVERDALE IMMIGRANT WOMEN'S CENTRE
  Toronto

SCARBOROUGH CULTURAL INTERPRETER SERVICE
  Scarborough

SEXUAL ABUSE SURVIVORS OF HALDIMAND-
NORFOLK
  Perth

Sexual Assault Centre of Guelph-Wellington
Women In Crisis
  Guelph

SEXUAL ASSAULT CRISIS CENTRE
  Windsor

SOUTH ASIA FAMILY SUPPORT SERVICES
  Scarborough

SUBCOMMITTEE ON THE NEEDS OF ADULT
SURVIVORS OF CHILD SEXUAL ABUSE
  Guelph

SWAN (STOP WOMAN ABUSE NOW)
  Goderich

THE CANADIAN HOME ECONOMICS ASSOCIATION
  Ottawa

"THE CHURCH LEADERS'" - CONFERENCE OF
CATHOLIC BISHOPS
  Ottawa

THE DECEMBER 6TH COALITION REGION
OF WATERLOO
  Toronto

THE GUELPH CHAPTER OF THE CANADIAN
FEDERATION OF UNIVERSITY WOMEN
  Guelph

THE HEALING CENTRE FOR WOMEN
  Ottawa

THE KINGSTON PORNOGRAPHY ACTION
COMMITTEE
  Kingston

THE ONTARIO NATIVE WOMEN`S ASSOCIATION
  Thunder Bay

THE SEXUAL ASSAULT SUPPORT CENTRE
  Ottawa

THE WOMEN'S PROJECT
THE AIDS COMMITTEE OF OTTAWA
  Ottawa

TORONTO SAFE CITY COMMITTEE
  Toronto

TORONTO WOMEN IN FILM & TELEVISION
  Toronto

VICTIMS ADVOCATE
  Ottawa

VICTIM\WITNESS ASSISTANCE PROGRAM
  Windsor

VICTIM WITNESS ASSISTANCE PROGRAM, CROWN
ATTORNEY'S OFFICE, VICTIM SERVICES, WINDSOR
POLICE SERVICES

SEXUAL ASSAULT TREATMENT CENTRE,
GRACE HOSPITAL
SEXUAL ASSAULT CRISIS CENTRE
  Windsor

VIVA ASSOCIATES
  Toronto

WARKWORTH INSTITUTION - THE LIVING GROUP
  Campbellford

W.A.V.E.
  Toronto

WINDSOR WOMEN'S INCENTIVE CENTRE
  Windsor\Chatham

WOMEN'S EMERGENCY CENTRE
  Woodstock

WORK & FAMILY LIFE COMMITTEE ADVISORY
COMMITTEE FOR EQUITY
  Toronto

YWCA
  Hamilton

YWCA OF TORONTO
  Toronto

ZONTA CENTRE
Ottawa

SASKATCHEWAN/MANITOBA
(TOUR 5)

Saskatchewan

ANGLICAN PARISH OF INDIAN HEAD
Fort Qu'Appelle

CHILDREN'S HAVEN, CHILD CRISIS CENTRE
Prince Albert

CONGRESS OF BLACK WOMEN (REGINA CHAPTER)
Regina

DISABLED WOMEN'S NETWORK (DAWN)
Regina

FACULTY OF SOCIAL WORK
UNIVERSITY OF REGINA
Regina

FRESH START SEX OFFENDER PROGRAM
Saskatoon

IMMIGRANT WOMEN OF SASKATCHEWAN
Prince Albert

IMMIGRANT WOMEN OF SASKATCHEWAN
Saskatoon

INDIAN HEALTH CENTRE INC.
North Battleford

LA RONGE NATIVE WOMEN'S COUNCIL
La Ronge

LLOYDMINSTER COMMITTEE FOR THE TREATMENT
AND PREVENTION OF FAMILY VIOLENCE NEEDS
ASSESSMENT
North Battleford

LLOYDMINSTER INTERVAL HOME SOCIETY
North Battleford

LUTHER COLLEGE
Moose Jaw/Swift Current

MAYOR'S TASK FORCE ON FAMILY VIOLENCE
Prince Albert

MEADOW LAKE TRIBAL COUNCIL, MEADOW
LAKE DISTRICT TREATY INDIAN WOMEN'S GROUP
Meadow Lake

NORTH EAST CRISIS INTERVENTION CENTRE
Melfort

NORTHERN MEDICAL SERVICES
Meadow Lake

NORTHERN WOMEN'S RESOURCE SERVICE INC.
Prince Albert

ROMAN CATHOLIC ARCHDIOCESE OF REGINA
SOCIAL JUSTICE DEPT.
Regina

SASKATCHEWAN HUMAN RIGHTS COMMISSION
Saskatoon

SASKATCHEWAN WOMEN'S INSTITUTES
Saskatoon

SASKATCHEWAN VOICE OF THE HANDICAPPED
Saskatoon

SASKATOON COUNCIL OF WOMEN
Saskatoon

SASKATOON SEXUAL ASSAULT AND
INFORMATION CENTRE
Saskatoon

SEXUAL ASSAULT SERVICES OF SASKATCHEWAN
Saskatoon

SOPHIA HOUSE
Regina

SWIFT CURRENT SHELTER
Moose Jaw\Swift Current

THE EMERGENCY SHELTER FOR WOMEN
Prince Albert

THE SOUTHWEST SAFE SHELTER
Moose Jaw\Swift Current

YWCA OF SASKATOON
Saskatoon

Manitoba

AGE AND OPPORTUNITY (E.A.R.C.)
Winnipeg

CANADIAN MENTAL HEALTH ASSOCIATION -
WOMEN AND MENTAL HEALTH WORK GROUP
Winnipeg

BRANDON SHELTER
Brandon

BRANDON TEACHERS' ASSOCIATION - EQUALITY
IN EDUCATION COMMITTEE
Brandon

BRANDON UNIVERSITY STUDENT'S UNION
Brandon

BRANDON MENTAL HEALTH SERVICE
Brandon

CONGRESS OF BLACK WOMEN OF MANITOBA
Winnipeg

CROSS LAKE BAND OF INDIANS
Cross Lake

CROSS LAKE EDUCATION AUTHORITY
Cross Lake

CHURCHILL HEALTH CENTRE
Churchill

FAMILY VIOLENCE - LAKESHORE WIFE ABUSE
COMMITTEE
Lundar

FEDERATION OF JUNIOR LEAGUES OF CANADA
Winnipeg

GAP (GROUP AGAINST PORNOGRAPHY)
Winnipeg

INDIGENOUS WOMEN'S COLLECTIVE
Winnipeg

KEEWATIN TRIBAL COUNCIL
Thompson

MANITOBA ACTION COMMITTEE ON THE STATUS
OF WOMEN
Brandon

MANITOBA ACTION COMMITTEE ON THE STATUS
OF WOMEN
Winnipeg

MANITOBA ADVISORY COUNCIL ON THE STATUS
OF WOMEN
Winnipeg

MANITOBA ASSOCIATION OF WOMEN
AND THE LAW
Winnipeg

MANITOBA INTERFAITH IMMIGRATION COUNCIL
Winnipeg

MANITOBA TEACHER'S SOCIETY
Winnipeg

MIAMI COLLEGIATE
Morden

NATIVE WOMEN'S TRANSITION CENTRE
Winnipeg

NONGAM/IKWE
Winnipeg

NORTHERN WOMEN'S RESOURCE SERVICE INC
The Pas

PARKLAND CRISIS CENTRE
Dauphin

PARKLAND STATUS OF WOMEN
Dauphin

POWER - PROSTITUTES AND OTHER WOMEN FOR
EQUAL RIGHTS
Winnipeg

RÉSEAU
Winnipeg

SOUTHWEST CRISIS SERVICES INC.
Winnipeg

THOMPSON CRISIS CENTRE
   Garden Hill

YOUNG WOMEN'S CHRISTIAN ASSOCIATION
(YWCA) OF BRANDON
   Brandon

NORTHWEST TERRITORIES
(TOUR 6)

Northwest Territories

ANNETTE DOWLING & ASSOCIATES
SOCIAL WORK CONSULTANTS
   Fort Smith

ARVIAT FAMILY VIOLENCE COMMITTEE
   Rankin Inlet

CANADIAN MENTAL HEALTH ASSOCIATION/
NWT DIVISION
   Yellowknife

KATAUJAQ SOCIETY
   Rankin Inlet

NORTHERN ADDICTION SERVICES -
TREATMENT CENTRE
   Yellowknife

ROMAN CATHOLIC DIOCESE OF MACKENZIE
   Yellowknife

STATUS OF WOMEN COUNCIL OF THE NWT
   Yellowknife

Yukon

CANADIAN RESEARCH INSTITUTE FOR THE
ADVANCEMENT OF WOMEN
   Whitehorse

EARLY CHILDHOOD DEVELOPMENT PROGRAM
YUKON COLLEGE
   Whitehorse

KAUSHEE'S WOMEN'S SHELTER PLACE
   Whitehorse

LESBIAN ISSUE COMMITTEE
   Whitehorse

MINISTER RESPONSIBLE FOR THE STATUS
OF WOMEN, YUKON MINISTER OF JUSTICE
   Whitehorse

VIOLENCE AGAINST WOMEN COLLECTIVE OF
YUKON STATUS OF WOMEN'S COUNCIL
   Whitehorse

WOLVERINE CONSULTING CO. LTD.
   Whitehorse

YUKON ADVISORY COUNCIL ON WOMEN'S ISSUES
   Whitehorse

YUKON COLLEGE, TESLIN CAMPUS
   Teslin

APPENDIX F

PANEL DOCUMENTS AND PRODUCTS*

**Ending Violence Against Women...
Your Chance To Do Something About It !**
Consultations by the Canadian Panel on Violence Against Women

A Progress Report

The Road to Healing (Map)
(Cree, Oji-Cree, Inuktituk, English and French)

A Landscape of Violence (Map)

Collecting the Voices: A Scrapbook

Changing the Landscape: Ending Violence — Achieving Equality
Final Report of the Canadian Panel on Violence Against Women

Changing the Landscape: Ending Violence — Achieving Equality
Executive Summary\National Action Plan

Changing the Landscape — Inuit Chapter
(Inuktituk - Syllabic and Orthography, English)

Changing the Landscape — Aboriginal Chapter
(Cree, English and French)

Without Fear
(video)

Without Fear - Video Facilitator's Guide

The Community Kit

RESEARCH PAPERS CONTRACTED BY THE CANADIAN PANEL ON VIOLENCE AGAINST WOMEN

Adult Survivors of Child Sexual Abuse/Incest
Linda McLeod and Associates

Aspects of Canadian Popular Culture: Messages About Violence and Gender Behaviour
Sandra Campbell

Elder Abuse
Linda McLeod and Asssociates

Inuit Women: The Realities and Issues Surrounding Violence Against Women
Sophie Tom

Pornography
Jillian Ridington

Ritual Abuse
Daniela Coates

Sexual Assault
Linda McLeod and Associates

Violence Against Foreign Domestic Workers in Canada
Judith Nicholson

Violence Against Immigrant Women of Colour
Fauzia Rafiq

Violence Against Lesbians: Issues and Solutions
Adonica Huggins

Violence Against Native Women
Teressa Nahanee

Violence Against Women and Sexual Harassment
Anne Robinson and Monique Gauvin

Violence Against Women in Rural Settings
Wendy Milne

Violence Against Women of Colour
Rozena Maart

* *All materials produced in English and French unless otherwise indicated.*

Wife Assault
Linda McLeod and Associates

**Women's Safety Project : A Community-Based
Study of Sexual Violence in Women's Lives -
Summary of Key Statistical Findings**
Melanie Randall and Lori Haskell

**Young Women and Violence:
A Collective Response**
Francine Lavoie

**Report on Findings From the Householder
Survey produced by:**
The Coopers & Lybrand Consulting Group in
conjunction with The Canadian Panel on
Violence Against Women